THE COMPLETE POETRY
OF JOHN DONNE

The Anchor Seventeenth-Century Series presents the major—and significant minor—texts in English of the seventeenth century in authoritative and inexpensive editions. Prepared especially for Anchor Books by a distinguished group of American and Canadian scholars, these newly edited texts meet the highest standards of scholarship and readability. Each volume incorporates the latest textual and critical discoveries, and the series as a whole is designed to provide a reliable access to the literature of the seventeenth century.

JOHN T. SHAWCROSS, Professor of English at Douglass College, Rutgers University, received his Ph.D. degree from New York University. A member of the editorial board of *Seventeenth-Century News,* he is also treasurer of the Milton Society of America. His publications include THE COMPLETE ENGLISH POETRY OF JOHN MILTON, in the Anchor Seventeenth-Century Series, and a volume of studies of Milton's language, to which he is a contributor and co-editor, which was published as a commemorative on the tercentenary of the first edition of *Paradise Lost.* Professor Shawcross is also a contributor to THE PROSE WORKS OF JOHN MILTON, which will be published soon in the Anchor Seventeenth-Century Series.

JOHN DONNE
By kind permission of the Marquis of Lothian

THE COMPLETE POETRY OF
JOHN DONNE

WITH AN INTRODUCTION

NOTES AND VARIANTS

BY

JOHN T. SHAWCROSS

ANCHOR BOOKS

DOUBLEDAY & COMPANY, INC.

GARDEN CITY, NEW YORK

The Anchor Seventeenth-Century Series
is published by Doubleday Anchor Books
under the General Editorship of
Professor J. Max Patrick, New York University

This edition has been especially prepared for
Anchor Books and has never before appeared in book form.

Anchor Books edition: 1967

CONTENTS

Contents

Contents vii

Contents ix

LIST OF ABBREVIATIONS

EA = *Études Anglaises*
ELH = *ELH; A Journal of English Literary History*
ES = *English Studies*
HLQ = *Huntington Library Quarterly*
JEGP = *Journal of English and Germanic Philology*
KR = *Kenyon Review*
MLN = *Modern Language Notes*
MLQ = *Modern Language Quarterly*
MP = *Modern Philology*
NQ = *Notes and Queries*
PBSA = *Papers of the Bibliographical Society of America*
PQ = *Philological Quarterly*
QJS = *Quarterly Journal of Speech*
RES = *Review of English Studies*
RN = *Renaissance News*
SB = *Studies in Bibliography*
SCN = *Seventeenth-Century News*
SEL = *Studies in English Literature*
SP = *Studies in Philology*
TLS = *The Times Literary Supplement*
TSE = *Tulane Studies in English*
UTQ = *University of Toronto Quarterly*

CHRONOLOGY OF DONNE'S LIFE

1572(?). Born in London between January 24 and June 19 to Roman Catholic parents.

1576. Father, John, warden of Ironmongers' Company, died, January 16; will proved February 8. Mother married Dr. John Symmings, President of Royal College of Physicians, between May 18 and July 17. Family moved to Little Trinity Lane.

1583. Family moved to parish of St. Bartholomew the Less (late in year).

1584–87. At Oxford; matriculated at Hart Hall (latter absorbed into Hertford College) on October 23, 1584.

1587–90. According to Walton, at Trinity College, Cambridge, but unlikely; perhaps abroad with army in Lowlands. Death of stepfather, July 7, 1588; mother moved to St. Saviour's parish in Southwark.

1591. Mother married Richard Rainsford (before February 7). Portrait in soldier's garb with Spanish quotation made by William Marshall. At Thavies Inn.

1592–95. At Lincoln's Inn: entered May 6, 1592; may have left during late 1595 or early 1596. Master of the Revels in 1593; elected Christmas Steward in 1594 but did not serve. Brother, Henry, after arrest (May 1593) for harboring a seminary priest (William Harrington), died of a fever in Newgate (Clink Prison). Admitted to share in father's estate (June 23, 1593). Admitted to share in brother's estate (April 1594). Apparently instructing Thomas, fifteen-year-old son of Christopher Danby of Yorkshire after July 20, 1595 (action for payment brought in 1598; PRO, C.3, 266/93).

1596. Took part in Essex's expedition against Cadiz (June–August).

1597. Took part in Azores Islands expedition (July–October).

1597–1602. Secretary to Sir Thomas Egerton at York House in the Strand, London. *Metempsychosis* composed (c. August 1601). Member of Parliament from Brackley, Northampton, October 27–December 19, 1601. Married Anne More (December 1601), Egerton's niece; dismissed soon afterward. Moved near the Savoy. Imprisoned in the Fleet (February 1602) by Sir George More; marriage ratified (April 27, 1602) by Archbishop of Canterbury.

1602–04. Living at Pyrford with Sir Francis Wolley, wife's cousin. Daughter Constance born (1603); son John born (1604).

1605–09. Travel in France and Italy (?) with Sir Walter Chute (1605–April 1606). Living at Mitcham; also had lodgings in the Strand. Son George born (May 1605). Worked with Thomas Morton (1606–1610), whose offer of a benefice if Donne took Anglican orders was refused. Son Francis born (January 1607); daughter Lucy born (August 1608); daughter Bridget born (December 1609). Prefatory verses in Jonson's *Volpone* (1607). Engaged on composition of *Biathanatos* (published c. 1646) in 1608 after being seriously ill, perhaps as recurrent effect of typhoid fever in youth. Frequently at Twickenham, residence of Countess of Bedford (1608–10).

1610–11. Residence at Drury House. Honorary M.A. from Oxford (April 17, 1610) and incorporated at Cambridge the next day. Daughter Mary born (1611). Publications: *Pseudo-Martyr* (1610), *Ignatius his Conclave* (two Latin, one English eds., 1611), *The Anatomie of the World* (1611).

1611–12. With Sir Robert Drury in France and Low Countries (November 1611–September 1612). Eighth child probably born dead (January 1612). Living in Drury Lane (September 1612). Publication: *The First and Second Anniversaries* (1612).

1613. Son Nicholas born (August 1613); died within year. Publications: "Elegy on Prince Henry."

1614.   Member of Parliament from Taunton, Somerset (April 5 to
        June 7). Daughter Mary died (May); son Francis died
        (November).

1615.   Took Anglican orders (January 23). Received through King
        Honorary D.D. from Cambridge (March). Daughter Mar-
        garet born (April). First surviving sermon preached before
        Queen at Greenwich (April 30). *Essays in Divinity* prob-
        ably composed during 1615–19.

1616.   Vicar of Keyston and Sevenoaks, Kent. Reader in Divinity
        to the Benchers of Lincoln's Inn (October–February 1622).
        Daughter Elizabeth born (June). Publication: thirteen
        problems in Latin translation by Ludovicus Ronzaeus,
        *Problematum Miscellaneorum, Antaristotelicorum, centuria
        dimidiata.*

1617.   First sermon at Paul's Cross (March 24); preached to Earl
        of Dorset at Knole (July 27). Death of wife (August 15),
        seventh day after birth of twelfth child (seven surviving);
        buried in churchyard of St. Clement Danes.

1619–20. Attached to Viscount Doncaster's mission to Germany (May
        1619–December 1620).

1621.   Appointed Dean of St. Paul's (November 19). Publication:
        Anniversaries (Ed. 2).

1622.   Publications: *A Sermon Upon The xv. Verse Of The xx.
        Chapter Of The Booke of Judges* (three issues; should be
        Judges v 20); *A Sermon Upon The viii. Verse Of The i.
        Chapter Of The Acts of The Apostles.*

1623.   Seriously ill (winter); composed *Devotions* (published
        1624). Publications: *Encaenia* (on John x 22); *Three Ser-
        mons Upon Speciall Occasions.*

1624.   Appointed vicar of St. Dunstan's in the West (March).
        Publications: *Devotions upon Emergent Occasions* (Ed. 1,
        two issues; Ed. 2); *A Sermon Upon . . . The Acts of the
        Apostles* (reprint); *Three Sermons Upon Speciall Occasions*
        (reprint).

1625. Retires to Magdalen Danvers' house at Chelsea (autumn) because of plague. Publications: *The First Sermon Preached To King Charles, At Saint James* (on Psalms xi 3); *Foure Sermons Upon Speciall Occasions; Anniversaries* (Ed. 3).

1626. Publications: *Ignatius his Conclave* (Ed. 2); *A Sermon, Preached To The Kings M^{tie.} at Whitehall* (on Isaiah i 1); *Five Sermons Upon Speciall Occasions.*

1627. Daughter Lucy died (January). Publications: *Devotions upon Emergent Occasions* (Ed. 3, two issues); *A Sermon Of Commemoration Of The Lady Danvers* (on 2 Peter iii 13).

1628. Sat on commission of Prerogative Court of Canterbury (appointed June 13).

1629. Sat on commission at Lambeth Palace (June).

1630. Drew up will (December 13).

1631. Preached "Deaths Duell" sermon before King (February 25). Died in London, March 31; survived by six children.

Posthumous Publications: *Deaths Duell,* 1632, 1633 (three issues). *Poems,* 1633; succeeding editions (augmented) or issues of *Poems* in 1635, 1639, 1649, 1650, 1654, 1669. *Juvenilia: Or Certaine Paradoxes and Problemes,* 1633 (two eds.); *Paradoxes, Problems, Essays, Characters* (with Epigrams), 1652; additional "Probleme" from Bodleian MS Tanner 299, published in *Paradoxes and Problemes,* 1923. *Ignatius his Conclave,* 1634, 1635, 1653. *Devotions Upon Emergent Occasions,* 1634, 1638. *Biathanatos,* c. 1646, 1648. *Essays In Divinity,* 1651. *Six Sermons Upon Severall Occasions,* 1634; *Sapientia Clamitans, Wisdome crying out to Sinners: Of Mans timely Remembring of his Creator* (sermon three in collection, on Eccles. xii 1), 1638, 1639; *LXXX Sermons,* 1640; *Fifty Sermons,* 1649; *XXVI Sermons,* 1660 (actually twenty-three); additional sermon on Psalms xxxviii 9 from MS in Potter and Simpson, II.6, pp. 144 ff. Some letters published with *Poems,* in *Letters to Severall Persons of Honour,* 1651 (reissue 1654), in Walton's *Life of George Herbert,* 1670, in other seventeenth-century collections, in nineteenth-century printings of MSS, in Gosse's *Life,* and in twentieth-century studies or editions of Donne; no complete edition exists.

INTRODUCTION

Literary popularity depends upon the mood of the age, and the poetry of John Donne has seesawed critically as public mood has changed since it first circulated in manuscript at the end of the sixteenth century. What the twentieth century has found to its liking other ages have also approved: "wittiness," frankness in handling sexual themes, the paradox of appearance and reality, unusual rhythms and versification, odd images, and intellectualism. Perhaps more than any other author Donne became a symbol of what poets and critics found desirable or undesirable in poetry.

In his own lifetime his poetry was imitated, copied out into miscellanies, and honored by almost complete collections more frequently than that of any other author. He was erroneously assigned poems in the miscellanies either because they were imitative of authentic ones or because his name lent prestige. Yet in the midst of such praise Ben Jonson raised a probably too frequent and too cursory criticism, that for not keeping accent (that is, metric patterns), Donne should be hanged. There are in fact few poems of Donne that do not "keep accent," the notable ones being the satires, which purposely wrench the meter to achieve sarcasm and humor. William Drummond's lament in the 1620s of metaphysical ideas and scholastic quiddities, though he did not cite Donne, reproved the paradoxes of his poetry rather than the so-called "metaphysical" conceits and tortuous syntax in which they were expressed. But these conceits were the bane of Thomas Hobbes, Dryden, Pope, and of course Samuel Johnson, who pilloried Abraham Cowley for "a kind of *discordia concors*, a combination of dissimilar images, or discovery of occult resemblances in things apparently unlike." The problem for Johnson was that "most heterogeneous ideas are yoked by violence together."

In Donne's age, as generally in the twentieth century, readers' interest in Donne's poetry lay in the wittiness of Jack Donne's love themes: the ugly mistress, jealousy, his mistress's preparations before going to bed with him, the anatomical progress of lovemaking, the fickleness of woman and man's indifference to it, the usury extorted by Love, Donne's curse or legacy to those who follow him into his former world of love—plus sincere love, and love's awakening, and love's continuance even after death. This was the poetry of the roué, the man-about-town, the returned soldier, the antisentimentalist. He saw the "marrow" in the bone, as Eliot put it.

The poetry of Dr. Donne, Dean of St. Paul's, was not so well read, or even known, either in his day or during the first half of our own century. Although most of his "divine" poems were written before Donne took orders, they have been assigned by tradition to the foremost preacher of England in the later 1610s and '20s—someone quite distinct from Jack the Libertine. This notion of a "split personality" has reappeared during the nineteenth- and twentieth-century revivals of Donne, partly because such a view was fostered by the author himself. Jonson reported that he repented having written certain poems and sought to destroy all of them after he had taken orders. In a letter to his friend Sir Robert Carr, to whom he sent a manuscript copy of *Biathanatos* in 1619, Donne wrote, "It was written by me many years since . . . let any that your discretion admits to the sight of it, know the date of it; and that it is a Book written by *Jack Donne*, and not by D. *Donne . . . .*"

Where many readers of Donne in the Elizabethan and Jacobean ages praised subject matter and treatment, some found difficulty in poetic expression and too much intellectualization. During the seventeenth and eighteenth centuries the former minority became the majority (witness Pope's "improvement" of the satires), and it took such poets as Coleridge and Browning to discern the worth that a former age had recognized. As the reappraisal continued, it brought forth new texts, like A. B. Grosart's, Charles Norton's, and E. K. Chambers', and finally culminated in 1899 with the still standard biography of Edmund Gosse. At least here was all Donne's poetry generally available for a reading public that was expanding greatly with the spread of education and increase of leisure. But despite the excellent and still significant edition of Sir Herbert J. C. Grierson in 1912, insufficient attention was paid to the "divine" poems, the epicedes, or the verse letters; interest was still fixed on the wittiness of Jack Donne's love themes.

A main contribution to this revival was the publication of a selection of such poems by Grierson in his 1921 collection of *The Metaphysical Poets*. And the fervid reaction of T. S. Eliot to this collection popularized a poet who was cast as a reactionary against divisive elements in life— for in the sociological and ideological upheavals of Elizabeth's age was seen the strife of the modern world, rent by war and economic collapse. Besides, Donne's work offered the means to pull poetry out of the morass of "romanticism." How was poetry to be written, Eliot asked, "in an age lacking a traditional framework of ideas, without succumbing to the 'heresy' of the personal philosophy . . . or . . . without dissolving into emotionalism or sensationalism?" The answer was to re-create the thought or the emotion—in the words of Ezra Pound to "make it new." Donne had been kidnapped, as Merritt Y. Hughes so aptly expressed it.

What arose, then, during the 1920s and '30s was a voice of "neo-orthodoxy," one that offered a solution to the problem of a lack of faith caused by the idolatry of reason, one that returned spirituality to its proper sphere above materialism, one that helped explain man's alienation as documented by the theories of Freud. But valid as this voice is, we are finally coming to realize it is not the full voice of Donne—not even of Jack Donne.

Too often critical writing—and the way in which critical problems are posed—reflect the narrowness and prejudgment of the critic. Faced with the stereotype of a two-personality Donne, his champions have stressed the love elegies and songs and sonnets without recognizing their thematic relationship to other poems. Or without full recognition, one suspects, of their message. Like Eliot, many have thus myopically viewed Donne as Milton's antithesis, although only his style and approach ultimately differ. Some, such as E. M. W. Tillyard, have found in Donne only that which they anathematize in poetic technique, and so he falls into disrepute; again Milton is ranged beside him, but as infinite superior. Not long after World War II, frequent eulogies placed Donne in a poetic grave, as if for another century's sleep. True, the mood of the early 1950s was such that Donne, who supposedly spoke only to a conservative strain in the 1920s, a nonconservative era, was thought to have little to say to a "silent" generation. But the reports of his demise as an exciting poet and poetic force have been proved premature. Today we see not a split personality, but one always intense, concerned with the need for love and faith, one hoping for spiritual transcendence rather than scholastic unity, one whose broad view of life embraced his own inheritance, his era, and the mundane and spiritual worlds beyond him.

This latest approach to Donne's poetry—and it has not come suddenly but has been growing steadily for the last twenty years—reflects the accelerated growth of historical, mythic, metaphoric, rhetorical, and psychological criticism. It forces us to reread all the poetry, to analyze the love poems for philosophic and religious precepts, as well as the verse letters for their historical and rhetorical contexts, and to see in Donne's concerns and imagery the same preoccupations as those of the author of *On the Morning of Christ's Nativity* and *Paradise Lost*. The mood of the '60s seems to be one dominated by a kind of fusion of beliefs and causes, but instead of one belief canceling another, each approach to literature has intensified examination of the works.

Donne's total poetic output is not really large: there are five satires, perhaps seventeen love elegies, fifty-eight poems called songs and sonnets (although not a single sonnet of the usual definition), twenty-three epigrams, thirty-seven verse letters, three epithalamions, six or so poems inspired by acquaintances' deaths, the incomplete *Metempsychosis,* and divine poems (including twenty-one sonnets, a sonnet sequence, six occasional poems, three hymns, and a few others), plus incidental items. The patterns of metrical structure generally vary from iambic pentameter couplets for elegiac, occasional, and satiric verse; sonnet form for serious personal verse; and stanzaic form for songlike treatment or material and for epic matter. The songs and sonnets exhibit the most variety, perhaps because of the rivalry of versification during Donne's age. They are all stanzaic with varying patterns of length, line length, and rhyme scheme. Only *A Feaver, A Valediction forbidding mourning,* and *The Extasie* repeat a pattern, tetrameter quatrains, rhyming *abab.* However, their lengths are different. All this, though, allows one to observe the poem as poem, not simply as versified philosophy. The creative process that Donne experienced becomes a creative process that the reader shares and cannot avoid.

The reading of Donne's poetry demands close attention to the exactness of the word he has employed, to the rhythm of a kind of speech that belies cute poeticism, to the rapid association of thoughts or images, to the extended comparisons and elaboration of the trope through a number of lines (if not the whole poem), and to the thought or emotion that is being created as we read. Basically, all Donne's poems are dramatic, not only the songs and sonnets. They are immediate and involving. Just as in a situation in life, so in a Donne poem the participant's understanding is developed and changed as the situation itself moves through time. It is often difficult to know where the poem is going to end, therefore, and this feeling persists even after we have read the poem several times. For the situation that is depicted becomes so real to us as we read that we lose ourselves all over again in the verse. The technique is enhanced by the layers of meaning that Donne can load into a phrase, by the oddity of his metaphor, by the relatively simple device of punning, or by ambiguity in syntax. It is for this reason that editors pay so much attention to the text and to the punctuation especially. The aim of a Donne poem, however, is to create a vision—both for the author and the reader; for this to occur, all parts must work together to one end. It is obvious therefore that Donne's poetry, as it rushes to its conclusion, must be aided in its course by every element it touches. Each successive element—word, image, form of expression—comments upon each past one, making it more important or less, adding or subtracting meaning. Such poetry is not easy reading, but it is such gratifying reading, so enjoyable and enlightening both in the process and at the conclusion, that one can prophesy only that the popularity of Donne will continue in our age. Our mood may be different from that of the 1920s, but so is our understanding and appreciation of Donne.

Despite that popularity and attendant scholarly activity, no complete annotated edition of Donne's poetry exists. The present edition attempts to provide notes that illuminate for the reader Donne's frequently involved syntax, his alchemical, scientific, sexual, and religious imagery, and his archaic language or allusive material. Since he often used specifically connotative words, to pun or to produce an additional level of meaning, annotations will often point out double (or triple) meanings. But—and this is most important—the reader must recognize that annotations are never conclusive: beyond supplying information, the notes try to hint at additional meanings and levels of interpretation which the reader should explore for himself. Footnotes or brief glosses to difficult or obscure words will be found at the foot of the text page. The NOTES referred to in the footnotes are the Explanatory Notes, a more extended commentary which will be found at the back of the book.

For a fuller understanding of Donne and his poetry, I have included an up-to-date biographical table, a chronology of the poems as well as it can currently be established, and textual notes. The texts have been newly studied through all known versions to try to achieve a form that comes close to what Donne (rather than his copyists or editors) intended.

Text

The sources of text for most of the poems are numerous. I have attempted to examine and collate all known printed and manuscript sources. These are listed in the Textual Notes, which are to be found in the back of the book. The posthumous printing of most of the poems seems to have been based on a manuscript or manuscripts that were not superior to some of the extant manuscripts and only somewhat superior to others. Indeed, some manuscripts seem closer to Donne than the probably editorialized printings. Thus it is difficult to establish a definitive text, even in verbal variants. Selected verbal variants are recorded in the notes for selected texts, the appearance of each poem in each source examined being noted. (Some manuscripts seem to postdate printing, but were obviously derived from manuscript sources. I include only apparent seventeenth-century manuscripts.) For the most part the earliest printing is used unless a later version or the reading of a consensus of manuscripts seems to be closer to Donne's "original." The text is therefore, like others before it, eclectic and somewhat subjectively based. Variants from the copy text in punctuation, spelling, capitalization, italicization, indentation, and stanzaic form are also given; no record of these very important matters for a Donne poem in either printed or manuscript versions is included, since such items are frequently haphazard and often indefensible. Since standards of punctuation, spelling, etc., were not established at this time and since changes inevitably crept in as a text went through various hands, the numbers of variations even in a single word on a single page may be high. Variants also exist among extant copies of single editions, notably those of 1633 and 1635. Emendations are kept to a minimum and made in the direction of some significant edition(s) or manuscript(s), as indicated. A special index records variations from Miss Gardner's text, with brief statements where necessary of my reasons for these differences. (There are numerous differences from Grierson's texts for a multitude of reasons, such as different copy text, lack of editorial emendation, different manuscript readings, etc., but only slight differences from Manley's edition of the *Anniversaries*.) Of course, the danger of a plethora of so-called scholarly texts is present, but a revision of Grierson's, eschewing certain misreadings which often seem to have arisen from delicacy and certain modernizations which obscure subtleties, has long been needed. Where textual conclusions are in variance with those of others, the evidence will have to be weighed by time to end with, hopefully, a definitive text.

The practice of inserting an apostrophe to indicate elision has generally been followed. It is consistently followed in preterites and participles where "e" would create another syllable (e.g. "deliver'd," No. 121, line 10), in combinations of "the" and "to" where the vowel is not pronounced (e.g. "the'seaven," No. 32, line 4, and "to'advance," No. 33, line 9), and in the coalescing of two contiguous vowels from two different words (e.g. "Vertue'attir'd," No. 63, line 18, which is given three metrical beats). In the latter case the vowels are really pronounced but within one beat, as in Italian. Where syncope is necessary for meter (e.g. in "discoverers," No. 32, line 12), no elision is indicated unless an apostrophe appears in the copy text.

All translations are new attempts at literalness by the editor. Donne's ideas, it is felt, can be approximated only by such a literal approach.

Canon

Groundwork in establishing the authentic canon of Donne's poetical work was undertaken by Professor H. J. C. Grierson in his two-volume edition of 1912. In that edition will be found those poems rejected by Grierson which had been attributed to Donne in print or manuscript, either through imitation of an authentic poem or through his popularity with compilers of commonplace books. Slight textual revisions were made in a new edition by Grierson in 1929, including the addition, from those rejected poems, of *To the Countesse of Huntingdon* (No. 131, "That unripe side of earth"), and the rejection of "Ode: Of our Sense of Sinne," printed among the Divine Poems. The former poem seems to be fragmentary and possibly composite; yet it may be entirely Donne's. *Elegies XIII* and *XIV* ("Hark, news, O Envy" and "I sing no harm, good sooth") have generally been rejected (see the argument of George Williamson in *TLS*, August 18, 1932, 581) but consistently printed in editions of the poems. These I do not print in conviction of their spuriousness and in hope of helping rid Donne of their inferiority. Despite the publication of the elegy called "The Expostulation" (No. 22) in Jonson's *Underwood* (1640), and the ensuing controversy, it is usually accepted today as Donne's, although Miss Gardner has recently argued against attribution. (William B. Hunter, Jr., prints the elegy in the Anchor edition of Jonson's poems for completeness, while indicating that it is Donne's.) The verse letter in alternating stanzas written by Henry Goodyere and Donne was published in Grierson's apocrypha, but Roger Bennett replaced it to full status, noting that "no one has challenged Donne's authorship of the alternate stanzas" (p. xxvi). Printed as "Dubia" by Miss Gardner are two additional elegies (Nos. 21, 23), *Sapho to Philænis* (No. 24), *Sonnet. The Token* (No. 78), and *Selfe Love* (No. 80).

The epigram *The Jughler* (No. 101), found in the Westmoreland and Hawthornden MSS, was first given by Bennett, who knew only the former version as Grierson did not list its appearance in either manuscript. The epigram to Scaliger was reproduced by Keynes in the *Bibliography*, and this is the first edition of the poems to include it; and the one-line epigraph (not, of course, really a poem) printed with the frontispiece of *Deaths Duell* (No. 194) was included in Helen Gardner's edition of *The Divine Poems*. The poem beginning "When my harte was mine owne" (No. 81) was attributed to Donne by Sir Edmund Chambers in *RES*, VII (1931), 69–71, and printed by Bennett, but Miss Gardner rejects it categorically. If Donne's, it was apparently unperfected and may have served, as Chambers suggested, as material for elegies here numbered 12 and 13. One new poem is added to the canon with this edition: No. 102, *Faustus*. Found in only the Hawthornden MS, it was not mentioned by Grierson in his remarks on that collection.

The verses headed "Incipit Joannes Dones" in *Coryat's Crudities* (London, 1611), the first line of which is "Lo her's a man, worthy indeed to trauell," were noted by Grierson in 1912, but they have not generally been accepted into the canon. A poem entitled "To his friend Captaine *Iohn Smith*, and his Worke" ("I know not how Desert more great can rise"), published in Smith's *The Generall Historie of Virginia, New-England and the Summer Isles* (London, 1624), p. A$_{1v}$, has been argued as Donne's (by Robert L. Hickey, in *PQ*, XXVI [1947], 181–192) because of his interest in the Virginia colony, but I reject it (as does Stanley Johnson in *ELH*, XIV [1947], 138, n. 37) on the basis of syntax, vocabulary, and meter. I omit the epigrams translated by J[asper] Main and published in *Paradoxes, Problemes, Essays, Characters* (London, 1652), pp. 88–103, as spurious.

The attribution of the third stanza of *The Prohibition* (No. 47) to

Donne has been questioned, with the suggestion that it may be Thomas
Roe's. Such question arises from a lack of understanding of the poem's
point and its organization; see the explanatory note to that poem. The
distich beginning "Transiit in Sequanam Mœnus," and titled *Epigramma*,
is printed here as lines 3–4 of *De Libro cum mutuaretur, Impresso* (No.
144), as given in 1635 and as argued by H. W. Garrod in *RES*, XXI
(1945), 38–42. Those who have questioned the authorship of the distich
have not been aware of its relation with that poem and may have been
misled by the inaccurate (but ubiquitous) translation of Alexander
Grosart. One recent attribution, not otherwise available in collections of
Donne's works, is also appended.

Included are representative poems on Donne or in praise of his work
which appeared in the early editions. A number of musical renditions
are reproduced from a variety of composers.

Arrangement and Chronology

The conventional arrangement of Donne's poems has been by type:
songs and sonnets, love elegies, epigrams, etc. Such categorization can be
seen in the first collected edition of 1633 and continued more rigidly in
the ensuing early editions, probably because the manuscript(s) which
furnished material employed that kind of arrangement. However, the
categories are not distinct or without error: for example, some of the
divine poems were printed in 1633 preceding the songs and sonnets,
which in turn are interrupted by the anniversaries; and the funeral
elegy on the L. C. (No. 146) is given amidst the love elegies. The specific
order within a category likewise varies among the manuscripts; some
revisions within each category are made on the basis of consensus of the
collections and apparent date (e.g., of the Verse Letters). I note Grierson's numbering of the love elegies and of the holy sonnets and Miss
Gardner's rearrangement of the latter for the reader's convenience. For
ease of reference, I have assigned a number to each poem. A list is also
provided for use with Combs and Sullens' *Concordance;* and two indexes
record all titles (including Latin and translations) and all first lines (including Latin and translations).

The chronology of Donne's poems is uncertain, particularly that of the
epigrams, the love elegies, and most of the songs and sonnets. Yet some
semblance of order can be made, and this I present here in an index to
afford an examination of the development of Donne's themes, images,
and prosody. This chronological schedule cites briefly what has previously
been adduced to date the poems and what may be suggested from a
fresh perusal. Dating is and must be very tentative; perhaps, however, it
will elicit new discussion which will lead to more positive dating. All
year dates throughout this edition are New Style.

Acknowledgments

The present work would not have been possible without the aid of a number of friends, collectors, librarians, and libraries. I wish to thank Professor J. Max Patrick, general editor of this series, who read the manuscript and improved the annotations markedly; Professor Arthur Axelrad, who checked many details for me in the Huntington Library holdings; Sir Geoffrey Keynes, who made available materials in his own library; Professor James H. Osborn, who allowed me to collate Donne manuscripts in his collection; the Society of Antiquaries of Scotland; the Delegates of the Clarendon Press; and the staffs of the Folger Shakespeare Library, the Huntington Library, the Yale University Library, the Harvard University Libraries, the Cambridge University Library, the Bodleian Library, and the Rare Book Room of the New York Public Library. To the trustees, administrators, and librarians of the following libraries I owe great thanks for their aid in helping me amass the numerous texts involved: Yale University Library, New York Public Library, Rutgers University Library, the Huntington Library, the Folger Shakespeare Library, the Harvard University Libraries, the Berg Collection in the New York Public Library, the Arents Collection in the New York Public Library, the Morgan Library of New York, the British Museum, the Bodleian Library, Cambridge University Library, the Library of Christ Church College (Oxford University), Emmanuel College Library (Cambridge University), Chetham's Library, the Victoria and Albert Museum, the National Library of Scotland, Edinburgh University Library, the Library of Queen's College (Oxford University), the Rosenbach Foundation of Philadelphia, St. Paul's Cathedral Library, the Library of the University of London, Sterling Library (University of London), the Library of Trinity College (Cambridge University), Trinity College Library (Dublin), the Library of St. Michael's College (Tenbury Wells), the Library of St. John's College (Cambridge), the National Library of Wales (Aberystwyth), the South African Public Library (Cape Town, Republic of South Africa), and the Duke of Portland Library of the University of Nottingham. For permission to quote variants from these various manuscripts I sincerely thank all persons and organizations as here noted.

This edition has been completed through the aid of a grant from the Research Council of Rutgers—the State University of New Jersey.

John T. Shawcross

Bloomfield, N.J.
January 1967

ELEGIES TO DONNE

An Elegie upon the death of the Deane of Pauls, Dr. Iohn Donne.

Can we not force from widdowed Poetry,
Now thou art dead (Great DONNE) one Elegie
To crowne thy Hearse? Why yet dare we not trust
Though with unkneaded dowe-bak't prose thy dust,
Such as the uncisor'd Churchman from the flower   5
Of fading Rhetorique, short liv'd as his houre,
Dry as the sand that measures it, should lay
Upon thy Ashes, on the funerall day?
Have we no voice, no tune? Did'st thou dispense
Through all our language, both the words and sense?   10
'Tis a sad truth; The Pulpit may her plaine,
And sober Christian precepts still retaine,
Doctrines it may, and wholesome Uses frame,
Grave Homilies, and Lectures, But the flame
Of thy brave Soule, that shot such heat and light,   15
As burnt our earth, and made our darknesse bright,
Committed holy Rapes upon our Will,
Did through the eye the melting heart distill;
And the deepe knowledge of darke truths so teach,
As sense might judge, what phansie could not reach;   20
Must be desir'd for ever. So the fire,
That fills with spirit and heat the Delphique quire,
Which kindled first by thy Promethean breath,
Glow'd here a while, lies quench't now in thy death;
The Muses garden with Pedantique weedes   25
O'rspred, was purg'd by thee; The lazie seeds
Of servile imitation throwne away;
And fresh invention planted, Thou didst pay
The debts of our penurious bankrupt age;
Licentious thefts, that make poëtique rage   30
A Mimique fury, when our soules must bee
Possest, or with Anacreons Extasie,
Or Pindars, not their owne; The subtle cheat
Of slie Exchanges, and the jugling feat
Of two-edg'd words, or whatsoever wrong   35
By ours was done the Greeke, or Latine tongue,
Thou hast redeem'd, and open'd Us a Mine
Of rich and pregnant phansie, drawne a line

Of masculine expression, which had good
Old Orpheus seene, Or all the ancient Brood   40
Our superstitious fooles admire, and hold
Their lead more precious, then thy burnish't Gold,
Thou hadst beene their Exchequer, and no more
They each in others dust, had rak'd for Ore.
Thou shalt yield no precedence, but of time,   45
And the blinde fate of language, whose tun'd chime
More charmes the outward sense; Yet thou maist claime
From so great disadvantage greater fame,
Since to the awe of thy imperious wit
Our stubborne language bends, made only fit   50
With her tough-thick-rib'd hoopes to gird about
Thy Giant phansie, which had prov'd too stout
For their soft melting Phrases. As in time
They had the start, so did they cull the prime
Buds of invention many a hundred yeare,   55
And left the rifled fields, besides the feare
To touch their Harvest, yet from those bare lands
Of what is purely thine, thy only hands
(And that thy smallest worke) have gleaned more
Then all those times, and tongues could reape before;   60
But thou art gone, and thy strict lawes will be
Too hard for Libertines in Poetrie.
They will repeale the goodly exil'd traine
Of gods and goddesses, which in thy just raigne
Were banish'd nobler Poems, now, with these   65
The silenc'd tales o'th'Metamorphoses
Shall stuffe their lines, and swell the windy Page,
Till Verse refin'd by thee, in this last Age,
Turne ballad rime, Or those old Idolls bee
Ador'd againe, with new apostasie;   70
Oh, pardon mee, that breake with untun'd verse
The reverend silence that attends thy herse,
Whose awfull solemne murmures were to thee
More then these faint lines, A loud Elegie,
That did proclaime in a dumbe eloquence   75
The death of all the Arts, whose influence
Growne feeble, in these panting numbers lies
Gasping short winded Accents, and so dies:
So doth the swiftly turning wheele not stand
In th'instant we withdraw the moving hand,   80

But some small time maintaine a faint weake course
By vertue of the first impulsive force:
And so whil'st I cast on thy funerall pile
Thy crowne of Bayes, Oh, let it crack a while,
And spit disdaine, till the devouring flashes   85
Suck all the moysture up, then turne to ashes.
I will not draw the envy to engrosse
All thy perfections, or weepe all our losse;
Those are too numerous for an Elegie,
And this too great, to be express'd by mee.   90
Though every pen should share a distinct part,
Yet art thou Theme enough to tyre all Art;
Let others carve the rest, it shall suffice
I on thy Tombe this Epitaph incise.
   Here lies a King, that rul'd as hee thought fit   95
   The universall Monarchy of wit;
   Here lie two Flamens, and both those, the best,
   Apollo's first, at last, the true Gods Priest.

Tho[mas] Carie
[ed. 1633]

To the Memorie of My Ever Desired Friend
Dr. Donne.

To have liv'd eminent, in a degree
Beyond our lofty'st flights, that is, like Thee,
Or t'have had too much merit, is not safe;
For, such excesses finde no Epitaph.
At common graves we have Poetique eyes   5
Can melt themselves in easie Elegies,
Each quill can drop his tributary verse,
And pin it, like the Hatchments, to the Hearse:
But at Thine, Poeme, or Inscription
(Rich soule of wit, and language) we have none.   10
Indeed a silence does that tombe befit,
Where is no Herald left to blazon it.
Widow'd invention justly doth forbeare
To come abroad, knowing Thou art not here,

Late her great Patron; Whose Prerogative   15
Maintain'd, and cloth'd her so, as none alive
Must now presume, to keepe her at thy rate,
Though he the Indies for her dowre estate.
Or else that awfull fire, which once did burne
In thy cleare Braine, now falne into thy Urne   20
Lives there, to fright rude Empiricks from thence,
Which might prophane thee by their Ignorance.
Who ever writes of Thee, and in a stile
Unworthy such a Theme, does but revile
Thy precious Dust, and wake a learned Spirit   25
Which may revenge his Rapes upon thy Merit.
For, all a low pitch't phansie can devise,
Will prove, at best, but Hallow'd Injuries.
    Thou, like the dying Swanne, didst lately sing
Thy Mournfull Dirge, in audience of the King;   30
When pale lookes, and faint accents of thy breath,
Presented so, to life, that peece of death,
That it was fear'd, and prophesi'd by all,
Thou thither cam'st to preach thy Funerall.
O! had'st Thou in an Elegiacke Knell   35
Rung out unto the world thine owne farewell,
And in thy High Victorious Numbers beate
And solemne measure of thy griev'd Retreat;
Thou might'st the Poets service now have mist
As well, as then thou did'st prevent the Priest;   40
And never to the world beholding bee
So much, as for an Epitaph for thee.
    I doe not like the office. Nor is 't fit
Thou, who did'st lend our Age such summes of wit,
Should'st now re-borrow from her bankrupt Mine,   45
That Ore to Bury Thee, which once was Thine,
Rather still leave us in thy debt; And know
(Exalted Soule) more glory 't is to owe
Unto thy Hearse, what we can never pay,
Then, with embased Coine those Rites defray.   50
    Commit we then Thee to Thy selfe: Nor blame
Our drooping loves, which thus to thy owne Fame
Leave Thee Executour. Since, but thine owne,
No pen could doe Thee Justice, nor Bayes Crowne
Thy vast desert; Save that, wee nothing can   55
Depute, to be thy Ashes Guardian.

So Jewellers no Art, or Metall trust
To forme the Diamond, but the Diamonds dust.

H[enry] K[ing]
[ed. 1633]

To the deceased Author,
Upon the *Promiscuous* printing of his Poems,
the *Looser sort,* with the *Religious.*

When thy *Loose* raptures, *Donne,* shall meet with Those
    That doe confine
  Tuning, unto the Duller line,
And sing not, but in *Sanctified Prose;*
    How will they, with sharper eyes,   5
The *Fore-skinne* of thy phansie circumcise?
And feare, thy *wantonnesse* should now, begin
Example, that hath ceased to be *Sin?*

And that *Feare* fannes their *Heat;* whilst knowing eyes
    Will not admire   10
  At this *Strange Fire,*
That here is *mingled with thy Sacrifice:*
    But dare reade even thy *Wanton Story,*
  As thy *Confession,* not thy *Glory.*
And will so envie *Both* to future times,   15
That they would buy thy *Goodnesse,* with thy *Crimes.*

[Sir] Tho[mas] Browne
[ed. 1633]

An Elegie upon Dr. Donne.

Is *Donne,* great *Donne* deceas'd? then England say
Thou'hast lost a man where language chose to stay
And shew it's gracefull power. I would not praise
That and his vast wit (which in these vaine dayes

Make many proud) but as they serv'd to unlock   5
That Cabinet, his minde: where such a stock
Of knowledge was repos'd, as all lament
(Or should) this generall cause of discontent.
    And I rejoyce I am not so severe,
But (as I write a line) to weepe a teare   10
For his decease; Such sad extremities
May make such men as I write *Elegies.*
    And wonder not; for, when a generall losse
Falls on a nation, and they slight the crosse,
God hath rais'd *Prophets* to awaken them   15
From stupifaction; witnesse my milde pen,
Not us'd to upbraid the world, though now it must
Freely and boldly, for, the cause is just.
    Dull age, Oh I would spare thee, but th'art worse,
Thou art not onely dull, but hast a curse   20
Of black ingratitude; if not, couldst thou
Part with *miraculous Donne,* and make no vow
For thee and thine, successively to pay
A sad remembrance to his dying day?
    Did his youth scatter *Poetrie,* wherein   25
Was all Philosophie? Was every sinne,
Character'd in his *Satyres?* made so foule
That some have fear'd their shapes, & kept their soule
Freer by reading verse? Did he give *dayes*
Past marble monuments, to those, whose praise   30
He would perpetuate? Did hee (I feare
The dull will doubt:) these at his twentieth yeare?
    But, more matur'd: Did his full soule conceive,
And in harmonious-holy-numbers weave
A *Crowne of sacred sonets,* fit to adorne   *La Corona.*   35
A dying Martyrs brow: or, to be worne
On that blest head of *Mary Magdalen:*
After she wip'd Christs feet, but not till then?
Did hee (fit for such penitents as shee
And hee to use) leave us a *Litany?*   40
Which all devout men love, and sure, it shall,
As times grow better, grow more classicall.
Did he write *Hymnes,* for piety and wit
Equall to those great grave *Prudentius* writ?
Spake he all *Languages?* knew he all *Lawes?*   45
The grounds and use of *Physicke;* but because
'Twas mercenary wav'd it? Went to see

That blessed place of *Christs nativity?*
Did he returne and preach him? preach him so
As none but hee did, or could do? They know   50
(Such as were blest to heare him know) 'tis truth.
Did he confirme thy age? convert thy youth?
Did he these wonders? And is this deare losse
Mourn'd by so few? (few for so great a crosse.)
But sure the silent are ambitious all   55
To be *Close Mourners* at his Funerall;
If not; In common pitty they forbare
By repetitions to renew our care;
Or, knowing, griefe conceiv'd, conceal'd, consumes
Man irreparably, (as poyson'd fumes   60
Do waste the braine) make silence a safe way
To'inlarge the Soule from these walls, mud and clay,
(Materialls of this body) to remaine
With *Donne* in heaven, where no promiscuous paine
Lessens the joy wee have, for, with *him,* all   65
Are satisfyed with *joyes essentiall.*
My thoughts, Dwell on this *Joy,* and do not call
Griefe backe, by thinking of his Funerall;
Forget he lov'd mee; Waste not my sad yeares;
(Which haste to *Davids* seventy, fill'd with feares 70
And sorrow for his death;) Forget his parts,
Which finde a living grave in good mens hearts;
And, (for, my first is daily paid for sinne)
Forget to pay my second sigh for him:
Forget his powerfull preaching; and forget   75
I am his *Convert.* Oh my frailtie! let
My flesh be no more heard, it will obtrude
This lethargie: so should my gratitude,
My vowes of gratitude should so be broke;
Which can no more be, then *Donnes* vertues spoke   80
By any but himselfe; for which cause, I
Write no *Encomium,* but an *Elegie.*

Iz[aak] Wa[lton]
[ed. 1633]

AN ELEGIE UPON DR. DONNE.
70. seventy, *Ed.* / ~)

To John Donne.

Donne, the delight of Phœbus, and each Muse,
    Who, to thy one, all other braines refuse;
Whose every work, of thy most early wit,
    Came forth example, and remaines so, yet:
Longer a knowing, than most wits doe live;   5
    And which no'n affection praise enough can give!
To it, thy language, letters, arts, best life,
    Which might with halfe mankind maintain a strife;
All which I mean to praise, and, yet, I would;
    But leave, because I cannot as I should!   10

B[en] Jons[on]
[ed. 1650]

To John Donne.

Who shall doubt, *Donne,* where I a *Poet* bee,
When I dare send my *Epigrammes* to thee?
That so alone canst judge, so'alone do'st make:
And, in thy censures, evenly, dost take
As free simplicity, to dis-avow,   5
As thou hast best authority, t'allow.
Read all I send: and, if I finde but one
Mark'd by thy hand, and with the better stone,
My title's seal'd. Those that for claps doe write,
Let punees, porters, players praise delight,   10
And, till they burst, their backs, like asses load:
A man should seek great glory, and not broad.

B[en] Jon[son]
[ed. 1650]

THE COMPLETE POETRY OF JOHN DONNE

Satires

1 *Satyre* I.

A way thou fondling motley humorist,
Leave mee, and in this standing woodden chest,
Consorted with these few bookes, let me lye
In prison, 'and here be coffin'd, when I dye;
Here are Gods conduits, grave Divines; and here   5
Natures Secretary, the Philosopher;
And jolly Statesmen, which teach how to tie
The sinewes of a cities mistique bodie;
Here gathering Chroniclers, and by them stand
Giddie fantastique Poëts of each land.   10
Shall I leave all this constant company,
And follow headlong, wild uncertaine thee?
First sweare by thy best love in earnest
(If thou which lov'st all, canst love any best)
Thou wilt not leave mee in the middle street,   15
Though some more spruce companion thou dost meet,
Not though a Captaine do come in thy way
Bright parcell gilt, with forty dead mens pay,
Not though a briske perfum'd piert Courtier
Deigne with a nod, thy courtesie to answer.   20
Nor come a velvet Justice with a long
Great traine of blew coats, twelve, or fourteen strong,
Wilt thou grin or fawne on him, or prepare
A speech to Court his beautious sonne and heire!
For better or worse take mee, or leave mee: 25
To take, and leave mee is adultery.
Oh monstrous, superstitious puritan,
Of refin'd manners, yet ceremoniall man,
That when thou meet'st one, with enquiring eyes
Dost search, and like a needy broker prize   30
The silke, and gold he weares, and to that rate
So high or low, dost raise thy formall hat:

SATYRE I.
1. *fondling motley humorist:* the foolishly pampered body, subject at various times to the four humours (blood, phlegm, yellow bile, black bile—happiness, indifference, anger, melancholy). See further, NOTES.
2. *chest:* room, library, compared here to the coffin of the body.
6. *Philosopher:* probably the generic meaning is intended, although Aristotle is often cited.
22. *blew coats:* liveried servants.
30. *prize:* appraise.

That wilt consort none, untill thou have knowne
What lands hee hath in hope, or of his owne,
As though all thy companions should make thee   35
Jointures, and marry thy deare company.
Why should'st thou that dost not onely approve,
But in ranke itchie lust, desire, and love
The nakednesse and barenesse to enjoy,
Of thy plumpe muddy whore, or prostitute boy   40
Hate vertue, though shee be naked, and bare:
At birth, and death, our bodies naked are;
And till our Soules be unapparrelled
Of bodies, they from blisse are banished.
Mans first blest state was naked, when by sinne   45
Hee lost that, yet hee was cloath'd but in beasts skin,
And in this course attire, which I now weare,
With God, and with the Muses I conferre.
But since thou like a contrite penitent,
Charitably warn'd of thy sinnes, dost repent   50
These vanities, and giddinesses, loe
I shut my chamber doore, and come, lets goe.
But sooner may a cheape whore, who hath beene
Worne by as many severall men in sinne,
As are black feathers, or musk-colour hose,   55
Name her childs right true father, 'mongst all those:
Sooner may one guesse, who shall beare away
The'Infanta'of London, Heire to'an India,
And sooner may a gulling weather-Spie
By drawing forth heavens Scheme tell certainly   60
What fashion'd hats, or ruffes, or suits next yeare
Our subtile-witted antique youths will weare;
Then thou, when thou depart'st from mee, canst show
Wither, why, when, or with whom thou wouldst go.
But how shall I be pardon'd my offence   65
That thus have sinn'd against my conscience?
Now we are in the street; He first of all
Improvidently proud, creepes to the wall,

36. *Jointures:* deeds of co-ownership of an estate, as that given by a wife as dowry.
    43–44, 58: See NOTES.
    59. *gulling weather-Spie:* a deceitful weather forecaster, a fraudulent astrologer.
    68. See NOTES.

And so imprison'd, and hem'd in by mee
Sells for a little state his libertie, 70
Yet though he cannot skip forth now to greet
Every fine silken painted foole we meet,
He them to him with amorous smiles allures,
And grins, smacks, shrugs, and such an itch endures,
As prentises, or schoole-boyes which doe know 75
Of some gay sport abroad, yet dare not goe.
And as fidlers stop lowest, at highest sound,
So to the most brave, stoops hee nigh'st the ground.
But to a grave man, he doth move no more
Then the wise politique horse would heretofore, 80
Or thou O Elephant or Ape wilt doe,
When any names the King of Spaine to you.
Now leaps he upright, Joggs me'and cryes, Do'you see
Yonder well favour'd youth? Which? Oh, 'tis hee
That dances so divinely; Oh, said I, 85
Stand still, must you dance here for company?
Hee droopt, wee went, till one (which did excell
Th'Indians, in drinking his Tobacco well)
Met us; they talk'd; I whisper'd, let us goe,
'T may be you smell him not, truely I doe; 90
He heares not mee, but, on the other side
A many-colour'd Peacock having spide,
Leaves him and mee; I for my lost sheep stay;
He followes, overtakes, goes on the way,
Saying, him whom I last left, all repute 95
For his device, in hansoming a sute,
To judge of lace, pinke, panes, print, cut, and plight,
Of all the Court, to have the best conceit;
Our dull Comedians want him, let him goe;
But Oh, God strengthen thee, why stoop'st thou so? 100

77, 78. See NOTES.
79. *grave:* soberly dressed.
80. *horse:* a performing horse (called Morocco, from its supposed origin) exhibited by a showman named Banks during the 1590s; the elephant and ape were added to the act from 1594.
95. *repute:* esteem.
96. *hansoming:* making attractive or pleasing.
97. *pinke:* an ornamental, somewhat scalloped pattern. *panes:* cloth strips. *plight:* condition (of the clothes); pleat.
98. *best conceit:* the most favorable opinion.
99. *Comedians:* those interested only in the amusing, unserious, make-believe side of life.

Why, he hath travayld. Long? no, but to me
Which understand none, he doth seeme to be
Perfect French, and Italian; I replyed,
So is the Poxe; He answered not, but spy'd
More men of sort, of parts, and qualities;   105
At last his Love he in a windowe spies,
And like light dew exhal'd, he flings from mee
Violently ravish'd to his lechery.
Many were there, he could command no more;
Hee quarrell'd, fought, bled; and turn'd out of dore   110
  Directly came to mee hanging the head,
  And constantly a while must keepe his bed.

2   *Satyre* II.

Sir; though (I thanke God for it) I do hate
Perfectly all this towne, yet there's one state
In all ill things so excellently best,
That hate, toward them, breeds pitty towards the rest;
Though Poëtry indeed be such a sinne   5
As I thinke that brings dearths, and Spaniards in,
Though like the Pestilence and old fashion'd love,
Ridlingly it catch men; and doth remove
Never, till it be sterv'd out; yet their state
Is poore, disarm'd, like Papists, not worth hate: 10
One, (like a wretch, which at Barre judg'd as dead,
Yet prompts him which stands next, and cannot reade,

104. *Poxe:* syphilis.
107. *light dew:* erotic perspiration.
109. *Many:* others awaiting their turn with the whore.   *command no more:*
both further intercourse and further sexual vigor.
111–112. See NOTES.
SATYRE II.
2. *one state:* the court of law, particularly the lawyer's part in its operation.
6. *dearths:* costliness (and famine).   *Spaniards:* passionate avowers of their
love.
7. *Pestilence:* the plague.   *old fashion'd love:* true and sincere love.
8. *catch:* entangle, charm.
9. *sterv'd out:* destroyed (particularly by famine or cold).
11. *One:* a playwright.   *wretch:* a person under trial and so guilty as to make
death mandatory. But he successfully prompts another defendant, who was not
given benefit of clergy because illiterate.

And saves his life) gives ideot actors meanes
(Starving himselfe) to live by'his labor'd sceanes.
As in some Organ, Puppits dance above 15
And bellows pant below, which them do move.
One would move Love by rithmes; but witchcrafts charms
Bring not now their old feares, nor their old harmes.
Rammes, and slings now are seely battery,
Pistolets are the best Artillerie. 20
And they who write to Lords, rewards to get,
Are they not like singers at doores for meat?
And they who write, because all write, have still
That excuse for writing, and for writing ill;
But hee is worst, who (beggarly) doth chaw 25
Others wits fruits, and in his ravenous maw
Rankly digested, doth those things out-spue,
As his owne things; and they'are his owne, 'tis true,
For if one eate my meate, though it be knowne
The meate was mine, th'excrement is his owne: 30
But these do mee no harme, nor they which use
To out-doe Dildoes, and out-usure Jewes;
To'out-drinke the sea, to'out-sweare the Letanie;
Who with sinnes all kindes as familiar bee
As Confessors; and for whose sinfull sake 35
Schoolemen new tenements in hell must make:
Whose strange sinnes, Canonists could hardly tell
In which Commandements large receit they dwell.
But these punish themselves; the insolence
Of Coscus onely breeds my just offence, 40

14. *Starving himselfe:* although killing himself by deprivation for his art.
15. *Puppits:* the hands and feet of the organist.
19. *seely:* feeble.
20. *Pistolets:* refers also to Spanish coins.
25. *chaw:* chew.
27. *Rankly:* coarsely, inadequately.
32. *Dildoes:* objects used as phalluses.
35. *Confessors:* priests who hear others' confessions.
36. *Schoolemen:* the Scholastics who classified and disputed philosophic arguments on the basis of fine distinctions. Each sin was assigned its own section of Hell.
37. *Canonists:* experts in canon law.
38. *Commandements:* of the area controlled by one of the Ten Commandments. *large receit:* broadly inclusive domain; place to receive the sinners.
40. *Coscus:* a name perhaps chosen because it was used by the anonymous author of the vapid sonnet sequence *Zepheria* (1594); often used in contemporary poetry for a court pleader.

Whom time (which rots all, and makes botches poxe,
And plodding on, must make a calfe an oxe)
Hath made a Lawyer; which was alas of late
But a scarse Poët, jollier of this state,
Then are new benefic'd ministers, he throwes   45
Like nets, or lime-twigs, wheresoever he goes,
His title'of Barrister, on every wench,
And wooes in language of the Pleas, and Bench:
A motion, Lady. Speake Coscus; I'have beene
In love, ever since *tricesimo* of'the Queene,   50
Continuall claimes I'have made, injunctions got
To stay my rivals suit, that hee should not
Proceed; spare mee; In Hillary terme I went,
You said, If I return'd next size in Lent,
I should be in remitter of your grace;   55
In th'interim my letters should take place
Of affidavits: words, words, which would teare
The tender labyrinth of a soft maids eare,
More, more, then ten Sclavonians scolding, more
Then when winds in our ruin'd Abbeyes rore;   60
Which sicke with Poëtrie, and possest with muse
Thou wast, and mad, I hop'd; but men which chuse
Law practise for meere gaine, bold soule, repute
Worse then imbrothel'd strumpets prostitute.

41. *makes botches poxe:* makes syphilis from pustules.
45. *ministers:* those receiving church preference in the form of a rectory or perpetual curacy.
46. *lime-twigs:* snares.
47. *wench:* usually signifying a whore.
48. *Pleas, and Bench:* Court of Common Pleas, and the Queen's Bench, highest court of common law, attended by the Queen.
49. *A motion:* an application for a ruling.
50. *tricesimo:* the thirtieth year of the Queen's reign (1588). One manuscript gives "37°," that is, 1595.
52. *rivals suit:* see NOTES.
53. *Hillary terme:* January session of the Westminster Courts.
54. *size:* assize, the session of the judges of a superior court. Coscus has left his Lady to attend court from January to around March.
55. *remitter:* that is, I should regain possession of you by dint of having had first possession, antedating my rival's claim.
59. *Sclavonians:* referring to the rapid, harsh sound of Slavic speech.
61. *muse:* both contemplation and poetic inspiration.
62. *mad:* carried away with desire.
63. *repute:* are esteemed.
64. *strumpets:* strumpets who.

Now like an owlelike watchman, hee must walke   65
His hand still at a bill, now he must talke
Idly, like prisoners, which whole months will sweare
That onely suretiship hath brought them there,
And to'every suitor lye in every thing,
Like a Kings favourite, yea like a King;   70
Like a wedge in a blocke, wring to the barre,
Bearing like Asses, and more shamelesse farre
Then carted whores, lye, to the grave Judge; for
Bastardy'abounds not in Kings titles, nor
Symonie'and Sodomy in Churchmens lives,   75
As these things do in him; by these he thrives.
Shortly'(as the sea) hee'will compasse all our land;
From Scots, to Wight; from Mount, to Dover strand.
And spying heires melting with luxurie,
Satan will not joy at their sinnes, as hee.   80
For as a thrifty wench scrapes kitching-stuffe,
And barrelling the droppings, and the snuffe,
Of wasting candles, which in thirty yeare
(Relique-like kept) perchance buyes wedding geare;
Peecemeale he gets lands, and spends as much time   85
Wringing each Acre, as men pulling prime.
In parchments then, large as his fields, hee drawes
Assurances, bigge, as gloss'd civill lawes,
So huge, that men (in our times forwardnesse)
Are Fathers of the Church for writing lesse.   90
These hee writes not; nor for these written payes,
Therefore spares no length; as in those first dayes

66. *still at a bill:* still looking out for money.
68. *suretiship:* having become liable for payment of the debt of another, who has defaulted.
71. *wedge:* the lower die of an anvil used in Roman coinage. *barre:* the upper die against which the wedge presses. "Wring" is an infinitive following "he must," l. 66.
72. *Asses:* Roman coins, the obverse of which usually pictured Janus, the two-faced god. See further, Notes.
73. *carted whores:* those rounded up and brought before a judge (one who is severe in his punishment).
74–76, 78. See Notes.
82. *snuffe:* the charred material of a candlewick.
84. *Relique-like kept:* kept as if an object of religious veneration.
86. *pulling prime:* acquiring the best in quality, the larger part; from pulling the winning card in a popular card game.
88. *Assurances:* pledges (of land).

When Luther was profest, He did desire
Short *Pater nosters*, saying as a Fryer
Each day his beads, but having left those lawes,   95
Addes to Christs prayer, the Power and glory clause.
But when he sells or changes land, he'impaires
His writings, and (unwatch'd) leaves out, *ses heires*
As slily'as any Commenter goes by,
Hard words, or sense; or in Divinity   100
As controverters, in vouch'd Texts, leave out
Shrewd words, which might against them cleare the doubt:
Where are those spred woods which cloth'd hertofore
Those bought lands? not built, nor burnt within dore.
Where's th'old landlords troops, and almes? In great hals   105
Carthusian fasts, and fulsome Bachanalls
Equally'I hate, meanes blesse; in rich mens homes
I bid kill some beasts, but no Hecatombs;
None starve, none surfet so; But (Oh) we'allow,
Good workes as good, but out of fashion now,   110
Like old rich wardrops; but my words none drawes
Within the vast reach of th'huge statute lawes.

3 *Satyre* III.

Kinde pitty chokes my spleene; brave scorn forbids
Those teares to issue which swell my eye-lids,
I must not laugh, nor weepe sinnes, and be wise,
Can railing then cure these worne maladies?

94. *Pater nosters:* the prayer "Our Father which art in heaven" (Luke xi
2–4), repeated often in the rosary.
96. *the Power and glory clause:* the phrase added to the "Our Father" by
Protestants: "For thine is the Kingdom and the Power and the Glory, Forever
and ever."
98. *ses heires:* "his heirs"; that is, the land will not devolve upon the heirs of
the purchaser but will default to the lawyer.
99. *goes by:* avoids, passes over.
104. *not . . . dore:* the woods have not been used for building or for warmth,
but let rot. See further, NOTES.
105. *almes:* charities (from the landlord).
106. *Carthusian:* pertaining to an austere and abstemious religious order.
108. *Hecatombs:* great slaughters.
SATYRE III.
1. *spleene:* the seat of anger and ridicule. *brave:* superior.

Is not our Mistresse faire Religion,   5
As worthy'of all our Soules devotion,
As vertue was to the first blinded age?
Are not heavens joyes as valiant to asswage
Lusts, as earths honour was to them? Alas,
As wee do them in meanes, shall they surpasse   10
Us in the end, and shall thy fathers spirit
Meete blinde Philosophers in heaven, whose merit
Of strict life may be'imputed faith, and heare
Thee, whom hee taught so easie wayes and neare
To follow, damn'd? O if thou dar'st, feare this,   15
This feare great courage, and high valour is;
Dar'st thou ayd mutinous Dutch, and dar'st thou lay
Thee in ships woodden Sepulchers, a prey
To leaders rage, to stormes, to shot, to dearth?
Dar'st thou dive seas, and dungeons of the earth?   20
Hast thou couragious fire to thaw the ice
Of frozen North discoveries? and thrise
Colder then Salamanders, like divine
Children in th'oven, fires of Spaine, and the'line,
Whose countries limbecks to our bodies bee,   25
Canst thou for gaine beare? and must every hee
Which cryes not, Goddesse, to thy Mistresse, draw,
Or eate thy poysonous words? courage of straw!
O desperate coward, wilt thou seeme bold, and
To thy foes and his (who made thee to stand   30
Sentinell in his worlds garrison) thus yeeld,
And for forbidden warres, leave th'appointed field?
Know thy foes, the foule Devill h'is, whom thou
Strivest to please: for hate, not love, would allow
Thee faine, his whole Realme to be quit; and as   35
The worlds all parts wither away and passe,

7. *first blinded:* before the light of God's revelation.
8. *valiant:* strong.
9. *as . . . them?:* rather than salvation is for us. The "them" of the "first blinded age" are the worthies of pagan antiquity (the "blinde Philosophers" of l. 12).
17. *mutinous Dutch:* see NOTES.
23. Salamanders were supposed to be able to withstand fire.
24. *Children:* Shadrach, Meshach, and Abednego (Dan. iii 20–30). *fires of Spaine:* the autos-da-fé of the Inquisition. *the line:* the equator.
25. *limbecks:* alembics.
30. *his:* God's.
33. *foes:* as follows, the devil, the world, and the flesh.
35. *his:* God's.

So the worlds selfe, thy other lov'd foe, is
In her decrepit wayne, and thou loving this,
Dost love a wither'd and worne strumpet; last,
Flesh (it selfes death) and joyes which flesh can taste,   40
Thou lovest; and thy faire goodly soule, which doth
Give this flesh power to taste joy, thou dost loath;
Seeke true religion. O where? Mirreus
Thinking her unhous'd here, and fled from us,
Seekes her at Rome, there, because hee doth know   45
That shee was there a thousand yeares agoe,
He loves her ragges so, as wee here obey
The statecloth where the Prince sate yesterday.
Crants to such brave Loves will not be inthrall'd,
But loves her onely, who'at Geneva'is call'd   50
Religion, plaine, simple, sullen, yong,
Contemptuous, yet unhansome. As among
Lecherous humors, there is one that judges
No wenches wholsome, but course country drudges.
Graius stayes still at home here, and because   55
Some Preachers, vile ambitious bauds, and lawes
Still new like fashions, bid him thinke that shee
Which dwels with us, is onely perfect, hee
Imbraceth her, whom his Godfathers will
Tender to him, being tender, as Wards still   60
Take such wives as their Guardians offer, or
Pay valewes. Carelesse Phrygius doth abhorre
All, because all cannot be good, as one
Knowing some women whores, dares marry none.
Graccus loves all as one, and thinkes that so   65
As women do in divers countries goe
In divers habits, yet are still one kinde;
So doth, so is Religion; and this blind-
nesse too much light breeds; but unmoved thou
Of force must one, and forc'd but one allow;   70
And the right; aske thy father which is shee,
Let him aske his; though truth and falshood bee

43 ff. *Mirreus etc.*: the various religious groups are represented by Mirreus,
Roman Catholic; Crants, l. 49, Calvinist; Graius, l. 55, adherent of the English
or Anglican church; Phrygius, l. 62, rejector of all creeds; Graccus, l. 65, eclectic
who considers all basically alike.
44. *here*: England.
62. *Pay valewes:* see NOTES.

Neare twins, yet truth a little elder is;
Be busie to seeke her, beleeve mee this,
Hee's not of none, nor worst, that seekes the best.   75
To'adore, or scorne an image, or protest,
May all be bad; doubt wisely, in strange way
To stand inquiring right, is not to stray;
To sleepe, or runne wrong, is: on a huge hill,
Cragged, and steep, Truth stands, and hee that will   80
Reach her, about must, and about must goe;
And what the'hills suddennes resists, winne so;
Yet strive so, that before age, deaths twilight,
Thy Soule rest, for none can worke in that night.
To will, implyes delay, therefore now doe.   85
Hard deeds, the bodies paines; hard knowledge too
The mindes indeavours reach, and mysteries
Are like the Sunne, dazling, yet plaine to'all eyes;
Keepe the'truth which thou hast found; men do not stand
In so ill case, that God hath with his hand   90
Sign'd Kings blanck-charters to kill whom they hate,
Nor are they Vicars, but hangmen to Fate.
Foole and wretch, wilt thou let thy Soule be tyed
To mans lawes, by which she shall not be tryed
At the last day? Oh, will it then boot thee   95
To say a Philip, or a Gregory,
A Harry, or a Martin taught thee this?
Is not this excuse for mere contraries,
Equally strong? cannot both sides say so?
That thou mayest rightly'obey power, her bounds know;   100
Those past, her nature,'and name is chang'd; to be
Then humble to her is idolatrie;
As streames are, Power is; those blest flowers that dwell
At the rough streames calme head, thrive and do well,
But having left their roots, and themselves given   105
To the streames tyrannous rage, alas are driven

---

79. *huge hill:* see NOTES.
81. Must wind his way up around the hill, reaching the summit of truth indirectly.
84. "I must work the works of him that sent me, while it is day: the night
cometh, when no man can work" (John ix 4).
96–97. *Philip . . . Martin:* see NOTES.
101. *Those past:* once her bounds are passed.

Through mills, and rockes, and woods, and at last, almost
Consum'd in going, in the sea are lost:
So perish Soules, which more chuse mens unjust
Power from God claym'd, then God himselfe to trust.   110

4   *Satyre* IV.

Well; I may now receive, and die; My sinne
Indeed is great, but I have beene in
A Purgatorie, such as fear'd hell is
A recreation and scant map of this.
My minde, neither with prides itch, nor yet hath been   5
Poyson'd with love to see, or to bee seene,
I had no suit there, nor new suite to shew,
Yet went to Court; But as Glaze which did goe
To'a Masse in jest, catch'd, was faine to disburse
The hundred markes, which is the Statutes curse;   10
Before he scapt, So'it pleas'd my destinie
(Guilty'of my sin of going,) to thinke me
As prone to'all ill, and of good as forget-
full, as proud, as lustfull,'and as much in debt,
As vaine, as witlesse, and as false as they   15
Which dwell at Court, for once going that way.
Therefore I suffered this; Towards me did runne
A thing more strange, then on Niles slime, the Sunne
E'r bred, or all which into Noahs Arke came:
A thing, which would have pos'd Adam to name,   20
Stranger then seaven Antiquaries studies,
Then Africks Monsters, Guianaes rarities,

SATYRE IV. See NOTES.
    1. *receive:* the sacrament of Extreme Unction.
    3. *Purgatorie:* that is, the royal Court.
    4. *scant:* only approximate.
    7. Neither a plea to make at Court to satisfy my pride nor a suit of clothes to show off.
    8. *Glaze:* an invented character whose name indicates his transparent superficiality.
    10. A fine of a hundred marks (silver coins worth 13/4d.) was imposed on those who attended a Roman Catholic mass.
    20. *pos'd:* puzzled.
    22. *Guianaes rarities:* see NOTES.

Stranger then strangers; One, who for a Dane,
In the Danes Massacre had sure beene slaine,
If he had liv'd then; And without helpe dies,   25
When next the Prentises 'gainst strangers rise.
One, whom the watch at noone lets scarce goe by,
One, to'whom, the'examining Justice sure would cry,
Sir, by your priesthood tell me what you are.
His cloths were strange, though coarse; and black, though bare;   30
Sleevelesse his jerkin was, and it had beene
Velvet, but 'twas now (so much ground was seene)
Become Tufftaffatie; and'our children shall
See it plaine Rashe awhile, then nought at all.
This thing hath travail'd, and saith, speakes all tongues   35
And only knoweth what to all States belongs.
Made of th'Accents, and best phrase of all these,
He speakes no language; If strange meats displease,
Art can deceive, or hunger force my tast,
But Pedants motley tongue, souldiers bumbast,   40
Mountebankes drugtongue, nor the termes of law
Are strong enough preparatives, to draw
Me to beare this, yet I must be content
With his tongue: in his tongue, call'd complement:
In which he can win widdowes, and pay scores,   45
Make men speake treason, cosen subtlest whores,
Out-flatter favorites, or outlie either
Jovius, or Surius, or both together.

23. *strangers:* foreigners.
24. *Danes Massacre:* see NOTES.
25–26. That is, one who would be killed, if he had no help to block such action, whenever native would-be politicians began to move into influential court positions held by foreigners.
27. That is, one who would scarcely be admitted by sentinels even at noon (when his actions could be easily observed and, if suspicious, easily thwarted).
29. *priesthood:* proclamations making Jesuits liable to arrest were passed in 1581 and 1585.
33. *Tufftaffatie:* a thin glossy silk.
34. *Rashe:* a smooth silk fabric; that is, it will continue to be worn down, and later generations will see it as rash and then not at all.
40. *motley:* confusing because of a pedant's diverse and complex knowledge. *bumbast:* soldiers' boasts of military and personal exploits.
41. *drugtongue:* jargon of sellers of quack medicines.
42. *preparatives:* medicinals used to make him taut enough to endure this experience.
45. *scores:* accounts, monetary reckonings.
48. *Jovius:* Paolo Giovio (1483–1553), who wrote *Historia sui temporis.* *Surius:* Laurentius Surius (1522–78), a Carthusian monk who wrote an ecclesiastical history.

He names mee,'and comes to mee; I whisper, God!
How have I sinn'd, that thy wraths furious rod,   50
This fellow chuseth me? He saith, Sir,
I love your judgement; Whom doe you prefer,
For the best linguist? And I seelily
Said, that I thought Calepines Dictionarie;
Nay, but of men, most sweet Sir. Beza then,   55
Some Jesuites, and two reverend men
Of our two Academies, I nam'd; There
He stopt mee,'and said; Nay, your Apostles were
Good pretty linguists, and so Panurge was;
Yet a poore gentleman; All these may passe   60
By travaile. Then, as if he would have sold
His tongue, he prais'd it, and such words told
That I was faine to say, If you'had liv'd, Sir,
Time enough to have beene Interpreter
To Babells bricklayers, sure the Tower had stood.   65
He adds, If of court life you knew the good,
You would leave lonenesse; I said, not alone
My lonenesse is, but Spartanes fashion,
To teach by painting drunkards, doth not last
Now; Aretines pictures have made few chast;   70
No more can Princes courts, though there be few
Better pictures of vice, teach me vertue;
He, like to'a high stretcht lute string squeakt, O Sir,
'Tis sweet to talke of Kings. At Westminster,
Said I, The man that keepes the Abbey tombes,   75
And for his price doth with who ever comes,

50. *rod:* see Notes.
53. *seelily:* weakly.
54. *Calepines Dictionarie:* a polyglot dictionary edited by Ambrose Calepine (1455–1511) in 1502.
55. *Beza:* Theodore Beza (1519–1605), a French Calvinist who wrote annotations on the New Testament, noted for his casuistry (popularly identified with Jesuits).
57. *two Academies:* Cambridge and Oxford. See further, Notes.
59. *linguists:* referring to the gift of tongues given to the Apostles by the Holy Ghost at Pentecost. *Panurge:* the roguish, cowardly, and libertine favorite of Pantagruel in Rabelais' novel *Gargantua.*
61. *travaile:* punning on "travel" and "work."
67–68. His aloneness is not unique; it is rigorously followed by others.
69. That is, what is learned from observing vice does not maintain moral fiber.
70. *Aretines:* Pietro Aretino (1492–1556), whose sonnets satirized the lascivious paintings of Giulio Romano (1499–1546).

Of all our Harries, and our Edwards talke,
From King to King and all their kin can walke:
Your eares shall heare nought, but Kings; your eyes meet
Kings only; The way to it, is Kingstreet.   80
He smack'd, and cry'd, He's base, Mechanique, coarse,
So'are all your Englishmen in their discourse.
Are not your Frenchmen neate? Mine? as you see,
I'have but one frenchman, looke, hee followes mee.
Certes they'are neatly cloth'd. I, of this minde am,   85
Your only wearing is your Grogaram.
Not so Sir, I have more. Under this pitch
He would not flie; I chaff'd him; But as Itch
Scratch'd into smart, and as blunt iron ground
Into an edge, hurts worse: So, I (foole) found,   90
Crossing hurt mee; To fit my sullennesse,
He to'another key, his stile doth addresse,
And askes, what newes? I tell him of new playes.
He takes my hand, and as a Still, which staies
A Sembriefe, 'twixt each drop, he nigardly,   95
As loth to'enrich mee, so tells many'a lie.
More then ten Hollensheads, or Halls, or Stowes,
Of triviall houshold trash he knowes; He knowes
When the Queene frown'd, or smil'd, and he knowes what
A subtle States-man may gather of that;   100
He knowes who loves; whom; and who by poyson
Hasts to an Offices reversion;
He knowes who'hath sold his land, and now doth beg
A licence, old iron, bootes, shooes, and egge-
shels to transport; Shortly boyes shall not play   105
At span-counter, or blow-point, but they pay

80. *Kingstreet:* running from Charing Cross to Westminster Palace.
81. *smack'd:* made a sharp, loud noise with his mouth. *Mechanique:* vulgar, common.
84. *one frenchman:* apparently a French servant.
85. *Certes:* certainly.
86. *Grogaram:* a coarse fabric of silk, mohair, and wool.
87. *pitch:* height to which a falcon soars before swooping down.
94. *Still:* a device for distilling liquids by drops.
95. *Sembriefe:* an interval of time (half a breve) equal to a musical measure.
97. *Hollensheads, Halls, Stowes:* Ralph Holinshed, John Hall, and John Stow, authors of long chronicles of England, that frequently report unhistorical anecdotes.
106. *span-counter:* a game in which counters were thrown near those of an opponent to capture them when the opposing counters could be spanned by the

Toll to some Courtier;'And wiser then all us,
He knowes what Ladie is not painted; Thus
He with home-meats tries me; I belch, spue, spit,
Looke pale, and sickly, like a Patient; Yet   110
He thrusts on more; And as if he'undertooke
To say Gallo-Belgicus without booke
Speakes of all States, and deeds, that have been since
The Spaniards came, to the losse of Amyens.
Like a bigge wife, at sight of loathed meat,   115
Readie to travaile: So I sigh, and sweat
To heare this Makeron talke in vaine: For yet,
Either my humour, or his owne to fit,
He like a priviledg'd spie, whom nothing can
Discredit, Libells now 'gainst each great man.   120
He names a price for every office paid;
He saith, our warres thrive ill, because delai'd;
That offices are entail'd, and that there are
Perpetuities of them, lasting as farre
As the last day; And that great officers,   125
Doe with the Pirates share, and Dunkirkers.
Who wasts in meat, in clothes, in horse, he notes;
Who loves Whores, who boyes, and who goats.
I more amas'd then Circes prisoners, when
They felt themselves turne beasts, felt my selfe then   130
Becomming Traytor, and mee thought I saw
One of our Giant Statutes ope his jaw

---

hand.   *blow-point:* a game in which arrows were blown through a pipe at numbers, the highest sum winning.

108. Suggesting that the lady's red complexion comes from disease rather than cosmetics.

109. *home-meats:* homely titbits.

112. *Gallo-Belgicus: Mercurius Gallo-Belgicus,* a Latin compilation begun in 1594 of events of the continental wars; it frequently reported hearsay.

113–114. Events between 1588 and March 1597, when Amiens was captured by the Spaniards.

115–116. Even the sight of food nauseates a pregnant woman ready to give birth, and she is repelled when her husband approaches for intercourse; the point is the speaker must accept the inevitable.

117. *Makeron:* one who affects foreign ways; a fop; one who talks in confused foreign tongues.

123. *entail'd:* aside from the obscene pun, inalienable settling of such offices on a specific family.

125. *last day:* Judgment Day.

126. *Dunkirkers:* referring to a haven for privateers in French Flanders.

129. *Circes prisoners:* Ulysses' men who were turned into swine.

132. *One of our Giant Statutes:* one delivering an authoritative decree (as if from God). See further, NOTES.

To sucke me in; for hearing him, I found
That as burnt venome Leachers do grow sound
By giving others their soares, I might growe   135
Guilty, and he free: Therefore I did shew
All signes of loathing; But since I am in,
I must pay mine, and my forefathers sinne
To the last farthing; Therefore to my power
Toughly and stubbornly I beare this crosse; But the'houre   140
Of mercy now was come; He tries to bring
Me to pay a fine to scape his torturing,
And saies, Sir, can you spare me; I said, willingly;
Nay, Sir, can you spare me'a crowne? Thankfully'I
Gave it, as Ransome; But as fidlers, still,   145
Though they be paid to be gone, yet needs will
Thrust one more jigge upon you: so did hee
With his long complementall thankes vexe me.
But he is gone, thankes to his needy want,
And the prerogative of my Crowne: Scant   150
His thankes were ended, when I, (which did see
All the court fill'd with more strange things then hee)
Ran from thence with such or more hast, then one
Who feares more actions, doth make from prison;
At home in wholesome solitarinesse   155
My precious soule began, the wretchednesse
Of suiters at court to mourne, and a trance
Like his, who dreamt he saw hell, did advance
It selfe on mee, Such men as he saw there,
I saw at court, and worse, and more; Low feare   160
Becomes the guiltie, not the'accuser; Then,
Shall I, nones slave, of high borne, or rais'd men
Feare frownes? And, my Mistresse Truth, betray thee
To th'huffing braggart, puft Nobility?
No, no, Thou which since yesterday hast beene   165
Almost about the whole world, hast thou seene,
O Sunne, in all thy journey, Vanitie,
Such as swells the bladder of our court? I

134. *Leachers:* lewd persons who burn as a result of their disease.
139. *to my power:* to the extent of my ability.
148. *complementall:* ceremonious and insincere.
150. *Scant:* scarcely.
158. *his:* Dante's.
164. *huffing:* arrogantly blustering.
168. *bladder:* indicating its emptiness and lack of usefulness.

Thinke he which made your waxen garden, and
Transported it from Italy to stand   170
With us, at London, flouts our Presence, for
Just such gay painted things, which no sappe, nor
Tast have in them, ours are, And naturall
Some of the stocks are, their fruits, bastard all.
'Tis ten a clock and past; All whom the Mues,   175
Baloune, Tennis, Dyet, or the stewes,
Had all the morning held, now the second
Time made ready, that day, in flocks, are found
In the Presence, and I, (God pardon mee.)
As fresh, and sweet their'Apparrells be, as bee   180
The fields they sold to buy them; For a King
Those hose are, cry the flatterers; And bring
Them next weeke to the Theatre to sell;
Wants reach all states; Me seemes they doe as well
At stage, as court; All are players, who e'r lookes   185
(For themselves dare not goe) o'r Cheapside books,
Shall finde their wardrops Inventory; Now,
The Ladies come; As Pirats, which doe know
That there came weak ships fraught with Cutchannel,
The men board them; and praise, as they thinke, well, 190
Their beauties; they the mens wits; Both are bought.
Why good wits ne'r weare scarlet gownes, I thought
This cause, These men, mens wits for speeches buy,
And women buy all reds which scarlets die.
He call'd her beauty limetwigs, her haire net.   195
She feares her drugs ill laid, her haire loose set;

169. *waxen garden:* an artificial garden exhibited by Italian puppeteers.
173. *ours:* our persons of rank.
174. *stocks:* main stems of a plant; "naturall" was a synonym for "bastard."
175. *Mues:* stables.
176. *Baloune:* a game like football played with a large inflated ball.   *Dyet:*
eating.   *stewes:* brothels.
179. *In the Presence:* in the assembly of the court, in the presence of the nobility.
184. *Wants reach all states:* the need for such things is found in all ranks.
186. *Cheapside books:* account books of secondhand clothing shops in Cheapside.
188. *Pirats:* pirate ships (a common image for a prostitute).
189. *Cutchannel:* cochineal, a red or purple coloring agent from Central
America.
191. *bought:* bribed, hoodwinked.
194. Referring to the woman arrayed in purple and scarlet color known as
the whore of Babylon (Rev. xvii 4). "Scarlet gownes" (l. 192) were the usual
dress of lawyers.
195. *lime-twigs:* snares.

Would not Heraclitus laugh to see Macrine,
From hat, to shooe, himselfe at doore refine,
As if the Presence were a Moschite, and lift
His skirts and hose, and call his clothes to shrift,   200
Making them confesse not only mortall
Great staines and holes in them; but veniall
Feathers and dust, wherewith they fornicate:
And then by *Durers* rules survay the state
Of his each limbe, and with strings the odds trye   205
Of his neck to his legge, and wast to thighe.
So in immaculate clothes, and Symetrie
Perfect as circles, with such nicetie
As a young Preacher at his first time goes
To preach, he enters, and a Lady'which owes   210
Him not so much as good will, he arrests,
And unto her protests protests protests
So much as at Rome would serve to have throwne
Ten Cardinalls into the'Inquisition;
And whisperd by Jesu, so often, that A   215
Pursevant would have ravish'd him away
For saying of our Ladies psalter; But 'tis fit
That they each other plague, they merit it.
But here comes Glorius that will plague them both,
Who, in the other extreme, only doth   220
Call a rough carelessenesse, good fashion;
Whose cloak his spurres teare; whom he spits on

197. *Heraclitus:* the weeping philosopher, who laughed because he believed that all things carried in themselves their opposites, and thus that nothing was permanent.   *Macrine:* a made-up name, as is "Glorius," l. 219.

199. *Moschite:* mosque. Donne compares Macrine's entering court to a Mohammedan's entering a mosque.

200. *shrift:* confession.

201–203. Mortal sins which stain or damage the soul are contrasted with venial sins like vanity and turmoil; also referring to sexual implements and snuff.

204. *Durers rules:* referring to the artist Albrecht Dürer's concepts of the human body's proportions.

205. *the odds trye:* measure the proportions.

208. *such nicetie:* excessive elegance.

212. In answer to her protests he protests that there should be no protests against his action. He is, of course, a Prqtestant.

214. *Inquisition:* the inquiry into heresy.

216. *Pursevant:* frequently "Topcliffe" is found here in the manuscripts, referring to Richard Topcliffe (1532–1609), well known for his cruelty in discovering and examining Roman Catholics.

217. *saying:* reciting (the psalms of the Virgin Mary).

He cares not, His ill words doe no harme
To him; he rusheth in, as if arme, arme,
He meant to crie; And though his face be'as ill   225
As theirs which in old hangings whip Christ, still
He strives to looke worse, he keepes all in awe;
Jeasts like a licenc'd foole, commands like law.
Tyr'd, now I leave this place, and but pleas'd so
As men which from gaoles to'execution goe,   230
Goe through the great chamber (why is it hung
With the seaven deadly sinnes?) being among
Those Askaparts, men big enough to throw
Charing Crosse for a barre, men that doe know
No token of worth, but Queenes man, and fine   235
Living, barrells of beefe, flaggons of wine.
I shooke like a spyed Spie; Preachers which are
Seas of Wits and Arts, you can, then dare,
Drowne the sinnes of this place, for, for mee
Which am but a scarce brooke, it enough shall bee   240
To wash the staines away; though I yet
With *Macchabees* modestie, the knowne merit
Of my worke lessen: yet some wise man shall,
I hope, esteeme my writs Canonicall.

5   *Satyre* V.

Thou shalt not laugh in this leafe, Muse, nor they
Whom any pitty warmes; He which did lay
Rules to make Courtiers, (hee being understood
May make good Courtiers, but who Courtiers good?)

226. *hangings:* tapestries depicting the scourging of Christ.

231. *the great chamber:* where public audiences were held.

232. *seaven deadly sinnes:* a tapestry picturing pride, covetousness, lust, anger, gluttony, envy, and sloth.

233. *Askaparts:* in "St. Bevis of Southampton" (a fourteenth-century medieval lay), a giant thirty feet tall, here connoting the Beefeaters.

233–234. *men . . . barre:* thus showing their strength.

240. *scarce:* meager.

242. *Macchabees modestie:* "I too will here conclude my account. If it has been well and pointedly written, that is what I wanted; but if it is poor, mediocre work, that was all I could do" (2 Macc. xv 37–38).

244. *writs Canonicall:* vestment, doctrine.

Frees from the sting of jests all who'in extreme   5
Are wreched or wicked: of these two a theame
Charity and liberty give me. What is hee
Who Officers rage, and Suiters misery
Can write, and jest? If all things be in all,
As I thinke, since all, which were, are, and shall   10
Bee, be made of the same elements:
Each thing, each thing implyes or represents.
Then man is a world; in which, Officers
Are the vast ravishing seas; and Suiters,
Springs; now full, now shallow, now drye; which, to   15
That which drownes them, run: These selfe reasons do
Prove the world a man, in which, officers
Are the devouring stomacke, and Suiters
The excrements, which they voyd. All men are dust;
How much worse are Suiters, who to mens lust   20
Are made preyes. O worse then dust, or wormes meat,
For they do eate you now, whose selves wormes shall eate.
They are the mills which grinde you, yet you are
The winde which drives them; and a wastfull warre
Is fought against you, and you fight it; they   25
Adulterate lawe, and you prepare their way
Like wittals, th'issue your owne ruine is;
Greatest and fairest Empresse, know you this?
Alas, no more then Thames calme head doth know
Whose meades her armes drowne, or whose corne o'rflow: 30
You Sir, whose righteousnes she loves, whom I
By having leave to serve, am most richly
For service paid, authoriz'd, now beginne
To know and weed out this enormous sinne.
O Age of rusty iron! Some better wit   35
Call it some worse name, if ought equall it;
The iron Age *that* was, when justice was sold, now
Injustice is sold deerer farre; allow

SATYRE V.
    6. *theame:* object of "give," whose subject is "Charity" and "liberty."
    8. See NOTES.
    24. *warre:* see NOTES.
    27. *wittals:* men who know of their wives' infidelity and accept it as inevitable.
    28. *Empresse:* Elizabeth I.
    31. *You Sir:* Sir Thomas Egerton, Lord Keeper after 1596, who had conducted various prosecutions between 1581 and 1592.
    37. *iron Age:* ironically, the forsaken world at the opening of the bronze age by Astraea, goddess of justice, because of human corruption.

All demands, fees, and duties; gamsters, anon
The mony which you sweat, and sweare for, is gon   40
Into other hands: So controverted lands
Scape, like Angelica, the strivers hands.
If Law be in the Judges heart, and hee
Have no heart to resist letter, or fee,
Where wilt thou'appeale? powre of the Courts below   45
Flow from the first maine head, and these can throw
Thee, if they sucke thee in, to misery,
To fetters, halters; But if the'injury
Steele thee to dare complaine, Alas, thou goest
Against the stream, when upwards: when thou'art most   50
Heavy'and most faint; and in these labours they,
'Gainst whom thou should'st complaine, will in the way
Become great seas, o'r which, when thou shalt bee
Forc'd to make golden bridges, thou shalt see
That all thy gold was drown'd in them before;   55
All things follow their like, only who have may have more.
Judges are Gods; he who made and said them so,
Meant not that men should be'forc'd to them to goe,
By meanes of Angels; When supplications
We send to God, to Dominations,   60
Powers, Cherubins, and all heavens Courts, if wee
Should pay fees as here, Daily bread would be
Scarce to Kings; so 'tis. Would it not anger
A Stoicke, a coward, yea a Martyr,
To see a Pursivant come in, and call   65
All his cloathes, Copes; Bookes, Primers; and all
His Plate, Challices; and mistake them away,
And aske a fee for comming? Oh, ne'r may
Faire lawes white reverend name be strumpeted,
To warrant thefts: she is established   70
Recorder to Destiny, on earth, and shee
Speakes Fates words, and but tells us who must bee

41. *controverted:* disputed.
42. *Angelica:* daughter of Gallaphrone, king of Cathay, whose fortress Albracca was besieged by Agrican, king of Tartary, among others seeking Angelica's hand (Boiardo, *Orlando Innamorato,* I, x, 26).
53. *Become great seas:* that is, become important officers of the state.
59. *Angels:* punning on the gold coins.
60–61. *Dominations, Powers, Cherubins:* three orders of angels.
66. *Copes:* capelike vestments of ecclesiastical officers. *Primers:* prayer books.

Rich, who poore, who in chaires, who in jayles:
Shee is all faire, but yet hath foule long nailes,
With which she scracheth Suiters; In bodies 75
Of men, so in law, nailes are th'extremities,
So'Officers stretch to more then Law can doe,
As our nailes reach what no else part comes to.
Why barest thou to yon Officer? Foole, Hath hee
Got those goods, for which erst men bar'd to thee? 80
Foole, twice, thrice, thou hast bought wrong, and now hungerly
Beg'st right; But that dole comes not till these dye.
Thou had'st much, and lawes Urim and Thummim trie
Thou wouldst for more; and for all hast paper
Enough to cloath all the great Carricks Pepper. 85
Sell that, and by that thou much more shalt leese,
Then Haman, when he sold his Antiquities.
O wretch that thy fortunes should moralize
Esops fables, and make tales, prophesies.
Thou'art the swimming dog whom shadows cosened, 90
And div'st, neare drowning, for what vanished.

6 Upon Mr. Thomas Coryats Crudities.

Oh to what heigth will love of greatnesse drive
Thy leaven'd spirit, *Sesqui-superlative?*
Venice vast lake thou'hadst seen, and wouldst seeke than
Some vaster thing, and foundst a Curtizan.

73. *chaires:* official seats of authority.
78. Our nails can reach to scratch our posteriors. The next line (besides meaning doffing one's hat) makes obscene reference to officers.
83. *Urim and Thummim:* jewels in Aaron's breastplate (Exod. xxviii 30), which were considered mediums for the revelation of God's will.
84. *Thou wouldst for more:* Thou wouldst put the Urim and Thummim of the law to proof for more.
85. *Carricks:* see NOTES.
86. *leese:* lose, be ruined.
87. *Haman:* see NOTES.
90. *swimming dog:* Aesop's tale of "The Dog and The Shadow" ("The Dog Carrying Meat"), which moralizes on greediness.
UPON MR. THOMAS CORYATS CRUDITIES.
Thomas Coryats Crudities: a collection of tales and adventures from many countries was published in 1611 by eccentric traveler and wit Thomas Coryate, who died in 1617.
2. *leaven'd:* raised, inflated. *Sesqui-superlative:* one and a half times greatest (most exaggerated).

That inland Sea having discover'd well   5
A Cellar-gulfe, where one might sayle to hell
From Heydelberg, thou longdst to see: and thou
This Booke greater then all producest now.
Infinit worke, which doth so farre extend,
That none can study it to any end.   10
T'is no one thing; it is not fruite nor roote,
Nor poorely limited with head or foote.
If man be therefore man, because he can
Reason, and laugh, thy booke doth halfe make man.
One halfe beeing made, thy modesty was such,   15
That thou on th'other halfe wouldst never touch.
When wilt thou be at full, great Lunatique?
Not till thou'exceed the world? canst thou be like
A prosperous nose-borne wenne, which sometimes growes
To be farre greater then the mother-nose?   20
Go then, and as to thee, when thou didst go,
Munster did Townes, and *Gesner* Authors show,
Mount now to *Gallo-belgicus:* appeare
As deepe a States-man, as a Gazettier.
Homely'and familiarly, when thou com'st backe,   25
Talke of *Will* Conquerour, and *Prester Jacke.*
Go bashfull man, lest here thou blush to looke
Upon the progresse of thy glorious booke,
To which both Indies sacrifices send;
The west sent gold, which thou didst freely spend,   30

5. *inland Sea:* apparently the Mediterranean, but also the courtesan's genital parts. See further, NOTES.

7. *Heydelberg:* the German university town, known for homosexuality among students.

12. *head or foote:* beginning or end.

14. *halfe make man:* that is, it makes him laugh. Man is a full man because he already has reason to realize the book's idiocy.

17. *Lunatique:* punning on the fullness of the moon, which is a bit more than a fourth of the size of earth.

19. *prosperous:* well filled, big.

22. *Munster:* Sebastian Münster (1489–1552), who wrote the *Cosmography of the Universe* (1541). *Gesner:* Konrad von Gesner (1516–65), who compiled the *Bibliotheca Universalis, sive Catalogus Omnium Scriptorum in Linguis Latina, Græca, et Hebraica* (1545).

23. *Gallo-belgicus:* see Donne's epigram on *Mercurius Gallo-Belgicus* (No. 96).

26. *Prester Jacke:* a legendary medieval priest of fabulous wealth and power.

28. *progresse:* see NOTES.

30. See NOTES.

(Meaning to see't no more) upon the presse.
The East sends hither her deliciousnesse;
And thy leaves must imbrace what comes from thence,
The Myrrhe, the Pepper, and the Frankincense.
This magnifies thy leav's; but if they stoope   35
To neighbour wares, when Merchants do unhoope
Voluminous barrels; if thy leaves do then
Convey these wares in parcels unto men;
If for vast Tomes of Currans, and of Figs,
Of medcinall, and Aromatique twigs,   40
Thy leaves a better method do provide,
Divide to pounds, and ounces subdivide;
If they stoope lower yet, and vent our wares,
Home-*manufactures*, to thicke popular Faires,
If *omni-prægnant* ther, upon warme stals   45
They hatch all wares for which the buyer cals,
Then thus thy leaves we justly may commend,
That they all kind of matter comprehend.
Thus thou, by meanes which th'Ancients never tooke,
A Pandect makst, and Universall booke.   50
The bravest Heroes, for publike good
Scatter'd in divers lands, their lims and bloud.
Worst malefactors, to whom men are prize,
Do publike good cut in Anatomies,
So will thy booke in peeces: For a Lord   55
Which casts at Portescues, and all the board,
Provide whole bookes; each leafe enough will be
For friends to passe time, and keepe companie.
Can all carouse up thee? No, thou must fit
Measures; and fill out for the half-pint wit.   60
Some shall wrap pils, and save a friends life so,
Some shall stop muskets, and so kill a fo.

31–34. See NOTES.
36. *wares:* referring to the use of the paper in the book as wrapping for various objects. Since the book is so "traveled" and so "learned," Donne uses an image showing its possible ubiquity and vast knowledge.
50. *Pandect:* a complete digest.
54. *cut in Anatomies:* that is, when their corpses are dissected for scientific research.
56. *Portescues:* Portuguese coins, the great crusadoes. *board:* ship.
57. *Provide whole bookes:* that is, provide whole books (rather than just leaves) only for a lord who will throw money away gambling, or for a shipload of sailors.
59. *carouse up:* drink deeply of.
62. *stop:* fill up, be placed inside the barrel of.

Thou shalt not ease the Critiques of next age
So much, at once their hunger to asswage.
Nor shall wit-pyrates hope to finde thee lye   65
All in one bottome, in one Librarie.
Some leaves may paste strings there in other bookes,
And so one may, which on another lookes,
Pilfer, alas, a little wit from you,
But hardly [a] much; and yet I thinke this true;   70
As *Sybils* was, your booke is mysticall,
For every peece is as much worth as all.
Therefore mine impotency I confesse;
The healths which my braine beares must be farre lesse;
Thy Gyant-wit o'rethrowes me, I am gone,   75
And rather then reade all, I would reade none.

[a] I meane from one page which shall paste strings in a booke.

7   *In eundem Macaronicon.*

Quot, dos *hæc*, LINGUISTS perfetti, *Disticha* fairont,
  Tot cuerdos STATES-MEN, *hic* livre fara *tuus*.
Es *sat* a MY l'honneur estre *hic* inteso; Car I LEAVE
  L'honra, de personne nestre creduto, *tibi*.

7A   *On the same macaronic composition.*

As these two double verses, perfect linguists, create
so many prudent statesmen, this book will fashion your book.
It is enough to my credit to be understood herein; for I leave
the reverence of anyone not to be believed to you.

  63–64. That is, even if future critics don't want to read any more of your
book, they shall not be satisfied by reading any of it.
  67. *may . . . bookes:* may be used as a backing in the spine of a book.
  71. *Sybils:* the book of a prophetess who attended the oracle at Delphi.
IN EUNDEM MACARONICON.
  Macaronicon: a gibe at *Coryats Crudities;* see first note to previous poem.
Macaronic verse is a burlesque compounded of vernacular words from modern languages, Latin, and hybrids. Here the Latin is given in italics, English
in small capitals, and romance languages in roman type.
  2. That is, if you can understand Coryate, you'll be in a good position to
write a learned treatise.

Elegies

8 Elegie: The Bracelet.
Upon the losse of his Mistresses Chaine,
for which he made satisfaction.

Not that in colour it was like thy haire,
For Armelets of that thou maist let me weare:
Nor that thy hand it oft embrac'd and kist,
For so it had that good, which oft I mist:
Nor for that silly old moralitie,   5
That as these linkes are tyed, our love should bee:
Mourne I that I thy seavenfold chaine have lost;
Nor for the luck sake; but the bitter cost.
O, shall twelve righteous Angels, which as yet
No leaven of vile soder did admit;   10
Nor yet by any fault have straid or gone
From the first state of their Creation;
Angels, which heaven commanded to provide
All things to me, and be my faithfull guide;
To gaine new friends, t'appease great enemies;   15
To comfort my soule, when I lie or rise.
Shall these twelve innocents, by thy severe
Sentence (dread judge) my sins great burden beare?
Shall they be damn'd, and in the furnace throwne,
And punisht for offences not their owne?   20
They save not me, they doe not ease my paines,
When in that hell they'are burnt and tyed in chains:
Were they but Crownes of France, I cared not,
For, most of them, their naturall Countreys rot
I think possesseth, they come here to us,   25
So leane, so pale, so lame, so ruinous.
And howsoe'r French Kings most Christian be,
Their Crownes are circumcis'd most Jewishly;

ELEGIE: THE BRACELET. See NOTES.
   1–2. See NOTES.
   7. *seavenfold:* see NOTES.
   24. *naturall Countreys rot:* syphilis, ascribed to France. "Natural" suggests it is appropriate to France and develops from a lack of constraint. A result was baldness; compare "Crownes," l. 23.
   26. *ruinous:* refers to the debasement of French currency; compare the "purity" of English angels, ll. 9–10.
   28. Refers to the control of monetary affairs by Jewish moneylenders and thus to the control of royal prerogative. Coins are "circumcised" by having their edges trimmed, reducing their value.

Or were they Spanish Stamps, still travelling,
That are become as Catholique as their King,   30
Those unlickt beare-whelps, unfil'd pistolets
That (more than Canon shot) availes or lets;
Which negligently left unrounded, looke
Like many angled figures, in the booke
Of some great Conjurer which would enforce   35
Nature, as these doe justice, from her course;
Which, as the soule quickens head, feet and heart,
As streames, like veines, run through th'earth's every part,
Visit all Countries, and have slily made
Gorgeous *France*, ruin'd, ragged and decay'd;   40
Scotland, which knew no State, proud in one day:
And mangled seventeen-headed *Belgia:*
Or were it such gold as that wherewithall
Almighty *Chymiques* from each minerall,
Having by subtle fire a soule out-pull'd;   45
Are dirtely and desperately gull'd:
I would not spit to quench the fire they'are in,
For, they are guilty of much hainous Sin.
But, shall my harmlesse angels perish? Shall
I lose my guard, my ease, my food, my all?   50
Much hope which they should nourish will be dead.
Much of my able youth, and lustyhead
Will vanish; if thou love let them alone,
For thou wilt love me lesse when they are gone,

29 ff. *Stamps:* agents (both men and coins) stamped with the authority of
the king. Donne alludes to the prevalence of Spanish bribery of other Western Europeans, who thus became Spanish agents.
30. *Catholique:* universal, ubiquitous (plus the religious sense). Philip II,
who had been married to Queen Mary of England and who sought to wed
Elizabeth, was the leading Catholic monarch of the day. He died in 1598.
31. *unfil'd pistolets:* disorganized users of little guns (doing service in the
Spanish Netherlands); rough-edged and "unrounded" (l. 33) Spanish gold
coins.
32. *lets:* impedes, hinders.
34. *angled:* with a pun on "angel" and "English."
42. *seventeen-headed Belgia:* the seventeen provinces of the lowlands
(Netherlands and Belgium) at war for independence from Spain (see further, NOTES); alludes also to the fabulous Hydra, which grew two heads each
time one of its nine original heads was cut off.
43–48. See NOTES.
44. *Chymiques:* alchemists.
52. *lustyhead:* vitality, gaiety.

Oh be content that some lowd squeaking Cryer   55
Well-pleas'd with one leane thred-bare groat, for hire,
May like a devill roare through every street;
And gall the finders conscience, if they meet.
Or let mee creepe to some dread Conjurer,
Which with phantastique scheames fils full much paper;   60
Which hath divided heaven in tenements,
And with whores, theeves, and murderers stuft his rents
So full, that though hee passe them all in sinne,
He leaves himselfe no roome to enter in.
And if, when all his art and time is spent,   65
Hee say 'twill ne'r be found; Oh be content;
Receive from him that doome ungrudgingly,
Because he is the mouth of destiny.
    Thou say'st (alas) the gold doth still remaine,
Though it be chang'd, and put into a chaine,   70
So in the first falne angels, resteth still
Wisdome and knowledge; but, 'tis turn'd to ill:
As these should doe good works; and should provide
Necessities; but now must nurse thy pride,
And they are still bad angels; Mine are none;   75
For, forme gives being, and their forme is gone:
Pitty these Angels yet; their dignities
Passe Vertues, Powers, and Principalities.
    But, thou art resolute; Thy will be done;
Yet with such anguish, as her onely sonne   80
The Mother in the hungry grave doth lay,
Unto the fire these Martyrs I betray.
Good soules, (for you give life to every thing)
Good Angels, (for good messages you bring)
Destin'd you might have beene to such a one,   85
As would have lov'd and worship'd you alone:
One which would suffer hunger, nakednesse,
Yea death, ere he would make your number lesse.

55. *Cryer:* town crier.
56. *groat:* an old silver coin, now less valuable.
62. *stuft his rents:* (1) paid his rent for property (carrying through the image of "tenements"), (2) increased his income, (3) stuffed his mouth and anus. The conjurer's false gods have taken over heaven's residence.
78. *Vertues, Powers, and Principalities:* three orders of angels. See further, NOTES.
87–88. *hunger, nakednesse, Yea death:* alluding to Jesus' temptation, ascent to Golgotha, and crucifixion.

But, I am guilty of your sad decay;
May your few fellowes longer with me stay.   90
    But ô thou wretched finder whom I hate
So, that I almost pitty thy estate:
Gold being the heaviest metal amongst all,
May my most heavy curse upon thee fall:
Here fetter'd, manacled, and hang'd in chains,   95
First mayst thou bee; then chaind to hellish paines;
Or be with forraine gold brib'd to betray
Thy Countrey,'and faile both of that and thy pay.
May the next thing thou stoop'st to reach, containe
Poyson, whose nimble fume rot thy moist braine;   100
Or libels, or some interdicted thing,
Which negligently kept, thy ruine bring.
Lust-bred diseases rot thee;'and dwell with thee
Itching desire, and no abilitie.
May all the hurt which ever Gold wrought;   105
All mischiefes which all devils ever thought;
Want after plenty; poore and gouty age;
The plagues of travellers; love; marriage
Afflict thee, and at thy lives last moment,
May thy swolne sinnes themselves to thee present.   110
    But, I forgive; repent thee honest man:
Gold is Restorative, restore it then:
Or if with it thou beest loath to'depart,
Because 'tis cordiall, would twere at thy heart.

101. *libels:* with added meaning of "little books."
104. *no abilitie:* (to engage in intercourse).
112. *Gold is Restorative:* an alchemical belief that the elixir of gold would heal disease and prolong life indefinitely.
114. *cordiall:* (1) restorative, (2) a red liquid to be drunk (the elixir), (3) belonging to the heart.

9 *Elegie: The Comparison.*

As the sweet sweat of Roses in a Still,
As that which from chaf'd muskats pores doth trill,
As the Almighty Balme of th'early East,
Such are the sweat drops of my Mistris breast,
And on her necke her skin such lustre sets,   5
They seeme no sweat drops, but pearle carcanetts.
Ranke sweaty froth thy Mistresse's brow defiles,
Like spermatique issue'of ripe menstruous boiles,
Or like the skumme, which, by needs lawlesse law
Enforc'd, Sanserra's starved men did draw   10
From parboild shooes, and bootes, and all the rest
Which were with any soveraigne fatnes blest,
And like vile lying stones in saffrond tinne,
Or warts, or wheales, they hang upon her skinne.
Round as the world's her head, on every side,   15
Like to the fatall Ball which fell on Ide,
Or that whereof God had such jealousie,
As, for the ravishing thereof we die.
Thy *head* is like a rough-hewne statue'of jeat,
Where marks for eyes, nose, mouth, are yet scarce set;   20
Like the first Chaos, or flat seeming face
Of Cynthia, when th'earths shadowes her embrace.

ELEGIE: THE COMPARISON. See NOTES.
   1. *Still:* distillery (for making perfume).
   2. *chaf'd muskats:* heated grapes (with the smell of musk).   *trill:* trickle.
   3. *Balme:* the balm of Gilead, a fragrant balsam (Jer. xlvi 11–12).
   6. *carcanetts:* ornamental necklaces.
   8. Like germ-filled pus which issues from ripe boils (of venereal disease)
around a woman's genitals.
   9. *by needs lawlesse law:* by the uncustomary and profane law of necessity.
   10. *Sanserra's starved men:* Catholics besieged the Protestants of Sancerre on
the Loire for nine months in 1573.
   12. *soveraigne:* effectual (of furnishing nourishment).
   13. *saffrond tinne:* tin dyed yellow-orange (in imitation of gold) and em-
bedded with false jewels.
   14. *wheales:* pustules.
   16. *fatall Ball:* the golden apple which Eris, the goddess of discord, threw
among Juno, Minerva, and Venus, which started an argument resulting in the
Trojan War.   *Ide:* Mount Ida in Greece.
   17. *that:* the apple of the tree of good and evil in Paradise.
   22. *Cynthia:* the moon.

Like Proserpines white beauty-keeping chest,
Or Joves best fortunes urne, is her faire brest.
Thine's like worme eaten trunkes, cloth'd in seals skin,   25
Or grave, that's dust without, and stinke within.
And like that slender stalke, at whose end stands
The wood-bine quivering, are her armes and hands.
Like rough bark'd elmboughes, or the russet skin
Of men late scurg'd for madnes, or for sinne,   30
Like Sun-parch'd quarters on the citie gate,
Such is thy tann'd skins lamentable state.
And like a bunch of ragged carrets stand
The short swolne fingers of thy gouty hand.
Then like the Chymicks masculine equall fire,   35
Which in the Lymbecks warme wombe doth inspire
Into th'earths worthlesse durt a soule of gold,
Such cherishing heat her best lov'd part doth hold.
Thine's like the dread mouth of a fired gunne,
Or like hot liquid metalls newly runne   40
Into clay moulds, or like to that Ætna
Where round about the grasse is burnt away.
Are not your kisses then as filthy,'and more,
As a worme sucking an invenom'd sore?
Doth not thy fearefull hand in feeling quake,   45
As one which gath'ring flowers, still feares a snake?
Is not your last act harsh, and violent,
As when a Plough a stony ground doth rent?
So kisse good Turtles, so devoutly nice
Are Priests in handling reverent sacrifice,   50
And such in searching wounds the Surgeon is
As wee, when wee embrace, or touch, or kisse.
Leave her, and I will leave comparing thus,
She, and comparisons are odious.

23. *Proserpines:* the Queen of Hades', whose symbol was the horn of plenty.
30. *scurg'd:* flogged; a common method of attempting to drive out madness by beating devils from the body.
31. The approaches to the city gate were lined by dilapidated houses unshaded by nearby trees or shrubbery.
35. *Chymicks:* alchemist's. *equall fire:* equal to her fire.
36. *Lymbecks:* of the alembic, used in the transmutation of baser metal to gold.
38. *her best lov'd part:* her genital organ, which is filled with his, turning baseness into splendor.
41. *Ætna:* an active volcano in Sicily.
47. *act:* intercourse.
49. *Turtles:* turtledoves.

10 *Elegie: The Perfume.*

Once, and but once found in thy company,
All thy suppos'd escapes are laid on mee;
And as a thiefe at barre, is question'd there
By all the men, that have beene rob'd that yeare,
So am I, (by this traiterous meanes surpriz'd)   5
By thy Hydroptique father catechiz'd.
Though he had wont to search with glazed eyes,
As though he came to kill a Cockatrice,
Though hee hath oft sworne, that hee would remove
Thy beauties beautie, and food of our love,   10
Hope of his goods, if I with thee were seene,
Yet close and secret, as our soules, we'have beene.
Though thy immortall mother which doth lye
Still buried in her bed, yet will not dye,
Takes this advantage to sleepe out day-light,   15
And watch thy entries, and returnes all night,
And, when she takes thy hand, and would seeme kind,
Doth search what rings, and armelets she can finde,
And kissing notes the colour of thy face,
And fearing least thou'art swolne, doth thee embrace;   20
To trie if thou long, doth name strange meates,
And notes thy palenesse, blushing, sighs, and sweats;
And politiquely will to thee confesse
The sinnes of her owne youths ranke lustinesse;
Yet love these Sorceries did remove, and move   25
Thee to gull thine owne mother for my love.
Thy little brethren, which like Faiery Sprights
Oft skipt into our chamber, those sweet nights,
And kist, and ingled on thy fathers knee,
Were brib'd next day, to tell what they did see.   30

ELEGIE: THE PERFUME. See NOTES.
  2. *escapes:* sins of the flesh which have escaped consummation.
  3. *at barre:* in court.
  5. *traiterous:* faithless.
  6. *Hydroptique:* unsatisfied.
  8. *Cockatrice:* a fabulous serpent with a deadly look.
  10. *beautie:* her inheritance, her chief attractiveness.
  20. *swolne:* with child.
  21. *To trie if thou long:* to test whether you crave something (because of pregnancy). *strange meates:* odd things to eat.
  26. *gull:* dupe.
  29. *ingled:* fondled.

The grim eight-foot-high iron-bound serving-man,
That oft names God in oathes, and onely than,
He that to barre the first gate, doth as wide
As the great Rhodian Colossus stride,
Which, if in hell no other paines there were,   35
Makes mee feare hell, because he must be there:
Though by thy father he were hir'd to this,
Could never witnesse any touch or kisse;
But Oh, too common ill, I brought with mee
That, which betray'd mee to my enemie: 40
A loud perfume, which at my entrance cryed
Even at thy fathers nose, so were wee spied.
When, like a tyran King, that in his bed
Smelt gunpowder, the pale wretch shivered;
Had it beene some bad smell, he would have thought   45
That his owne feet, or breath, that smell had wrought.
But as wee in our Ile emprisoned,
Where cattell onely,'and diverse dogs are bred,
The pretious Unicornes, strange monsters, call,
So thought he good, strange, that had none at all.   50
I taught my silkes, their whistling to forbeare,
Even my opprest shoes, dumbe and speechlesse were,
Onely, thou bitter sweet, whom I had laid
Next mee, mee traiterously hast betraid,
And unsuspected hast invisibly   55
At once fled unto him, and staid with mee.
Base excrement of earth, which dost confound
Sense, from distinguishing the sicke from sound;
By thee the seely Amorous sucks his death
By drawing in a leprous harlots breath;   60
By thee, the greatest staine to mans estate
Falls on us, to be call'd effeminate;

34. *Colossus:* a statue of Apollo, about 120 feet high, astride the harbor of Rhodes.
41. *loud:* strong.
47. *our Ile:* England, but also man's private, unworldly self.
49–50. Just as unknowingly we call precious unicorns strange monsters, so her father thought what was good (the perfume) was strange, since he had none.
57. *excrement:* growth (the perfume derived from such as flowers).
59. *By thee:* through perfume or because of perfume. *seely Amorous:* simple lover.
60. *leprous:* diseased.

Though you be much lov'd in the Princes hall,
There, things that seeme, exceed substantiall.
Gods, when yee fum'd on altars, were pleas'd well,　　　　65
Because you'were burnt, not that they lik'd your smell;
You'are loathsome all, being taken simply'alone,
Shall wee love ill things joyn'd, and hate each one?
If you were good, your good doth soone decay;
And you are rare, that takes the good away.　　　　70
All my perfumes, I give most willingly
To'embalme thy fathers corse; What? will hee die?

11　*Elegie: Jealosie.*

Fond woman which would'st have thy husband die,
And yet complain'st of his great jealousie;
If swolne with poyson, hee lay in'his last bed,
His body with a sere-barke covered,
Drawing his breath, as thick and short, as can　　　　5
The nimblest crocheting Musitian,
Ready with loathsome vomiting to spue
His Soule out of one hell, into a new,
Made deafe with his poore kindreds howling cries,
Begging with few feign'd teares, great legacies,　　　　10
Thou would'st not weepe, but jolly,'and frolicke bee,
As a slave, which to morrow should be free,
Yet weep'st thou, when thou seest him hungerly
Swallow his owne death, hearts-bane jealousie.

64. The sense is: Those things (like loving perfume) that seem sincere are more commonplace than those that are (like loving effeminacy).
67. *simply'alone:* not compounded with something; not on a person.
69. *decay:* evaporate.
70. *rare:* insufficient.
72. *will hee die?:* because he likes this perfume which is a rarity to him.
ELEGIE: JEALOSIE. See NOTES.
1. *Fond:* affectionate, foolish. *die:* pun on the meaning "to have sexual intercourse."
4. *sere-barke:* a cloth saturated with wax to act medicinally; a waterproof shroud.
6. *crocheting:* breaking a long note into crotchets (quarter notes) or embellishing with crotchets.
10. *few:* a few.
13. *hungerly:* hungrily, hungry-looking.
14. *hearts-bane jealousie:* jealousy which poisons and destroys the heart.

O give him many thanks, he'is courteous,   15
That in suspecting kindly warneth us.
Wee must not, as wee us'd, flout openly,
In scoffing ridles, his deformitie;
Nor at his boord together being satt,
With words, nor touch, scarce lookes adulterate.   20
Nor when he swolne, and pamper'd with great fare
Sits downe, and snorts, cag'd in his basket chaire,
Must wee usurpe his owne bed any more,
Nor kisse and play in his house, as before.
Now I see many dangers; for that is   25
His realme, his castle, and his diocesse.
But if, as envious men, which would revile
Their Prince, or coyne his gold, themselves exile
Into another countrie,'and doe it there,
Wee play'in another house, what should we feare?   30
There we will scorne his houshold policies,
His seely plots, and pensionary spies,
As the inhabitants of Thames right side
Do Londons Mayor, or Germans, the'Popes pride.

12 *Elegie.*

Oh, let mee not serve so, as those men serve
Whom honours smoakes at once fatten and sterve;
Poorely enrich't with great mens words or lookes;
Nor so write my name in thy loving bookes

18. *deformitie:* moral flaw (jealousy); disfigurement (obesity): his great eating is a symbol of reduced sexual appetite.
19. *boord:* table.
20. "Do not debase our few brief looks with word or touch," with emphasis on the adulterous nature of the looks.
22. *basket chaire:* a deep wicker armchair; it holds the corpulent husband as a basket holds bread.
25. *dangers:* both "perils" and "ranges of authority."
26. The image is continued in the "Prince," the Lord-Mayor of London, and the Pope.
32. *seely:* feeble.   *pensionary spies:* servants who spy on us.
33. The district south of the Thames was the haunt of cutthroats, thieves, etc.
ELEGIE [NO. 12]. See NOTES.
2. *honours smoakes:* "smoakes of honour" suggests visible but empty results of honorable action and the repute from good name which once was but is no longer intact.   *at once:* at the same time.   *sterve:* starve; also die by freezing.

As those Idolatrous flatterers, which still 5
Their Princes stiles, with many Realmes fulfill
Whence they no tribute have, and where no sway.
Such services I offer as shall pay
Themselves, I hate dead names: Oh then let mee
Favorite in Ordinary, or no favorite bee. 10
When my Soule was in her owne body sheath'd,
Nor yet by oathes betroth'd, nor kisses breath'd
Into my Purgatory, faithlesse thee,
Thy heart seem'd waxe, and steele thy constancie.
So, carelesse flowers strow'd on the waters face, 15
The curled whirlepooles suck, smack, and embrace,
Yet drowne them; so, the tapers beamie eye
Amorously twinkling, beckens the'giddie flie,
Yet burnes his wings; and such the devill is,
Scarce visiting them, who'are intirely his. 20
When I behold a streame, which, from the spring,
Doth with doubtfull melodious murmuring,
Or in a speechlesse slumber, calmely ride
Her wedded channels bosome, and then chide
And bend her browes, and swell if any bough 25
Do but stoop downe, to kisse her upmost brow:
Yet, if her often gnawing kisses winne
The traiterous banks to gape, and let her in,
She rusheth violently, and doth divorce
Her from her native, and her long-kept course, 30
And rores, and braves it, and in gallant scorne,
In flattering eddies promising retorne,
She flouts the channell, who thenceforth is drie;
Then say I; that is shee, and this am I.
Yet let not thy deepe bitternesse beget 35
Carlesse despaire in mee, for that will whet
My minde to scorne; and Oh, love dull'd with paine
Was ne'r so wise, nor well arm'd as disdaine.
Then with new eyes I shall survay thee,'and spie
Death in thy cheekes, and darknesse in thine eye; 40

6. *stiles:* steles, cemetery monuments. *fulfill:* fill up.
   10. *Favorite in Ordinary:* one who is actually and regularly preferred or endowed.
   13. *Purgatory:* "faithlesse thee," where the soul must stay until purged of sin.
   17. *tapers:* candle's.
   24. *channels bosome:* the riverbed.
   25. *browes:* symbolizing a kind of rapid.
   28. *traiterous:* since he betrays the confidence of his kinsman, the riverbed.

Though hope bred faith and love; thus taught, I shall
As nations do from Rome, from thy love fall.
My hate shall outgrow thine, and utterly
I will renounce thy dalliance: and when I
Am the Recusant, in that resolute state,   45
What hurts it mee to be'excommunicate?

13 *Elegie.*

Natures lay Ideot, I taught thee to love,
And in that sophistrie, Oh, thou dost prove
Too subtile: Foole, thou didst not understand
The mystique language of the eye nor hand:
Nor couldst thou judge the difference of the aire   5
Of sighes, and say, this lies, this sounds despaire:
Nor by the'eyes water call a maladie
Desperately hot, or changing feaverously.
I had not taught thee then, the Alphabet
Of flowers, how they devisefully being set   10
And bound up, might with speechlesse secrecie
Deliver arrands mutely,'and mutually.
Remember since all thy words us'd to bee
To every suitor; *I, 'if my friends agree.*
Since, houshold charmes, thy husbands name to teach,   15
Were all the love trickes, that thy wit could reach;
And since, an houres discourse could scarce have made
One answer in thee, and that ill arraid
In broken proverbs, and torne sentences.
Thou art not by so many duties his,   20
That from the'worlds Common having sever'd thee,
Inlaid thee, neither to be seene, nor see,

45. *Recusant:* one who refuses to conform to a specific religion.
46. *excommunicate:* cut off from partaking of love's communion.
ELEGIE [NO. 13]. See NOTES.
    1. *lay:* ignorant. The poem is addressed to his mistress.
    2. *sophistrie:* deceptively subtle argument.
    7. *water:* tears.
    10. *devisefully:* schemingly.
    15. *thy husbands name to teach:* to reveal to you your husband's name.
    17–18. *could . . . thee:* could scarce have evoked one reply from you.
    20–23. The sense is: You cannot become someone else's through the many
services to love (taught by me) that have severed you from the outside world

As mine: who have with amorous delicacies
Refin'd thee'into a blis-full paradise.
Thy graces and good words my creatures bee,   25
I planted knowledge and lifes tree in thee,
Which Oh, shall strangers taste? Must I alas
Frame and enamell Plate, and drinke in glasse?
Chafe waxe for others seales? breake a colts force
And leave him then, beeing made a ready horse?   30

14 *Elegie: Loves Warre.*

Till I have peace with thee, warr other men,
And when I have peace, can I leave thee then?
All other Warrs are scrupulous; Only thou
O fayr free Citty, maist thy selfe allow
To any one: In Flanders, who can tell   5
Whether the Maister presse or men rebell?
Only we know, that which all Ideots say,
They beare most blows which come to part the fray.
France in her lunatique giddines did hate
Ever our men, yea and our God of late.   10
Yet she relyes upon our Angels well
Which nere returne; no more then they which fell.

---

and hidden you as my own, neither to be seen nor to see others. The image is
agricultural, the common being the land held in common with others and the
"laying in" referring to enclosing for private use.

26. *lifes tree:* referring to the tree of good and evil in paradise (l. 24); and
with phallic meaning.

28. Contrasting hidden and uncommon love with public and ordinary love.

29. *Chafe . . . seales:* heat wax to put seals on others' letters. His desire was
to seal her off from others.

30. *horse:* with sexual connotation, as in "chafe," "seales," "colts force."

ELEGIE: LOVES WARRE. See NOTES.

1. *warr:* wage war with.

3. *scrupulous:* honest, honorable.

8. The English sustained the most defeats in attempting to settle the uprisings
of the people of the Lowlands against their rulers.

10. *our God of late:* the English had recently become Protestants; the French
were Roman Catholic.

11. *Angels:* the coins, and a pun on the similarity with "Angles" or Englishmen. Those who fell in the French wars became angels; those who return are
no longer innocent and angelic.

Sick Ireland is with a strange warr possest
Like to'an Ague; now raging, now at rest;
Which time will cure: yet it must doe her good   15
If she were purg'd, and her head vayne let blood.
And Midas joyes our Spanish journeys give,
We touch all gold, but find no food to live.
And I should be in that hott parching clime
To dust and ashes turnd before my time.   20
To mew me in a Ship, is to enthrall
Me in a prison, that weare like to fall;
Or in a Cloyster; save that ther men dwell
In a calme heaven, here in a swaggering hell.
Long voyages are long consumptions   25
And ships are carts for executions.
Yea they are Deaths; ist not all one to fly
Into an other World, as t'is to dy?
Here let mee warr; in these armes let me ly;
Here let me parle, batter, bleede, and dy.   30
Thy armes imprison me, and myne armes thee,
Thy hart thy ransome is, take myne for mee.
Other men war that they their rest may gayne;
But we will rest that we may fight agayne.
Those warrs the'ignorant, these th'experienc'd love,   35
There wee are allwayes under, here above.
There Engins farr off breed a just trew feare,
Neere thrusts, pikes, stabs, yea bullets hurt not here.
There lyes are wrongs; here safe uprightly ly;
There men kill men, we'will make one by and by.   40

16. *Let blood:* see Notes.
17. *joyes:* desire for more wealth. But all they get are luxuries, not the necessities of life which were meager in England at this time.
21. *mew:* enclose.
22. *that weare like:* that might be about.
24. *swaggering:* both "boasting and strutting" undeservedly and "quarrel-
some."
25. *long consumptions:* see Notes.
26. *carts for executions:* see Notes.
30. *parle, batter, bleede, and dy:* with double meaning of winning her over
by talk, by wearing down resistance, by show of anguish, and by sexual intercourse. Physical connotations also adhere to the last three verbs.
36. *above:* both as superior beings and physically.
38. *pikes:* long wooden weapons with pointed steel heads. *hurt not here:*
again with additional connotations for the four nouns.
39. *uprightly:* supinely stretched out. *ly:* there falsehoods (and men lying
dead) are sins (and injustices); here you may openly prevaricate without fear
of harm (and may recline without fear of dying).
40. *will make one:* will become a single being; will create a new being.

Thou nothing; I not halfe so much shall do
In these warrs, as they may which from us two
Shall spring. Thousands we see which travaile not
To warrs; but stay swords, armes, and shott
To make at home; And shall not I do then 45
More glorious service staying to make men?

15 *Elegie: Going to Bed.*

Come, Madam, come, all rest my powers defie,
Until I labour, I in labour lie.
The foe oft-times having the foe in sight,
Is tir'd with standing though he never fight.
Off with that girdle, like heavens Zone glittering, 5
But a far fairer world incompassing.
Unpin that spangled breastplate which you wear,
That th'eyes of busie fooles may be stopt there.
Unlace your self, for that harmonious chyme,
Tells me from you, that now it is bed time. 10
Off with that happy busk, which I envie,
That still can be, and still can stand so nigh.
Your gown going off, such beautious state reveals,
As when from flowry meads th'hills shadowe steales.
Off with that wyerie Coronet and shew 15
The haiery Diadem which on you doth grow:
Now off with those shooes, and then softly tread
In this loves hallow'd temple, this soft bed.
In such white robes, heaven's Angels us'd to be
Receavd by men: thou Angel bringst with thee 20
A heaven like Mahomets Paradice, and though
Ill spirits walk in white, we easly know,
By this these Angels from an evil sprite,
Those set our hairs, but these our flesh upright.

ELEGIE: GOING TO BED. See NOTES.
  2. Until I work up a sweat by intercourse, I lie in bed in agony waiting.
  4. *standing* and *fight:* there are double meanings here.
  7. *breastplate:* bodice.
  9. *chyme:* sound (made by the lacets and stays of her corset).
  11. *busk:* corset.
  14. *steales:* moves slowly away.
  21. *Mahomets Paradice:* Islam was supposed to teach that heaven is full of fleshly delights.
  24. *upright:* referring to stiffening before intercourse.

Licence my roaving hands, and let them go,   25
Behind, before, above, between, below.
O my America! my new-found-land,
My kingdome, safeliest when with one man man'd,
My Myne of precious stones: My Emperie,
How blest am I in this discovering thee!   30
To enter in these bonds, is to be free;
Then where my hand is set, my seal shall be.
    Full nakedness! All joyes are due to thee,
As souls unbodied, bodies uncloth'd must be,
To taste whole joyes. Jems which you women use   35
Are like Atlanta's balls, cast in mens views,
That when a fools eye lighteth on a Jem,
His earthly soul may covet theirs, not them:
Like pictures or like books gay coverings made
For lay-men, are all women thus array'd.   40
Themselves are mystick books, which only wee
(Whom their imputed grace will dignifie)
Must see reveal'd. Then since that I may know;
As liberally, as to a Midwife shew
Thy self: cast all, yea, this white lynnen hence,   45
There is no pennance due to innocence:
    To teach thee I am naked first; why than
What needst thou have more covering then a man?

27. *America:* not only because it is newly discovered and to be inhabited, but my hope because it is unknown. "Discovering" (l. 30) also suggests "uncovering."
   32. *seal:* both "impression" and "sign of ownership."
   36. *Atlanta's balls:* Atalanta, a swift runner, was defeated by Hippomenes in a race (the result to be her hand in marriage or death) by three golden apples given him by Venus, which he threw in her path. Donne's use of the legend reverses the sexual situation, but Atalanta's stooping to pick up the apples had become proverbial for man's attachment to glittering, material things.
   40. *lay-men:* here, the general reader rather than the professional who would seek out a book.
   43. *know:* with a second sexual meaning.
   44. *liberally:* both "freely" and "lewdly."
   46. You will not receive penance for remaining innocent of sin or me, or for remaining in your virginal white; you should not wear penitential vestment (as white clothing was considered), for innocence does not require penance.

16 *Elegie: Change.*

Although thy hand and faith, and good workes too,
Have seal'd thy love which nothing should undoe,
Yea though thou fall backe, that apostasie
Confirme thy love; yet much, much I feare thee.
Women are like the Arts, forc'd unto none,   5
Open to'all searchers, unpriz'd, if unknowne.
If I have caught a bird, and let him flie,
Another fouler using these meanes, as I,
May catch the same bird; and, as these things bee,
Women are made for men, not him, nor mee.   10
Foxes and goats; all beasts change when they please,
Shall women, more hot, wily, wild then these,
Be bound to one man, and did Nature then
Idly make them apter to'endure then men?
They'are our clogges, not their owne; if a man bee   15
Chain'd to a galley, yet the galley'is free;
Who hath a plow-land, casts all his seed corne there,
And yet allowes his ground more corne should beare;
Though Danuby into the sea must flow,
The sea receives the Rhene, Volga, and Po.   20
By nature, which gave it, this liberty
Thou lov'st, but Oh! canst thou love it and mee?
Likenesse glues love: Then if soe thou doe,
To make us like and love, must I change too?
More then thy hate, I hate'it, rather let mee   25
Allow her change, then change as oft as shee,
And soe not teach, but force my'opinion
To love not any one, nor every one.

ELEGIE: CHANGE. See NOTES.
   3. *fall backe:* both "relapse" and literally "fall back" upon our bed. By abandoning her seal of love to one man and bedding with me she confirms her love for me.
   4. *feare:* am uncertain of.
   6. *unknowne:* pun on the meaning "to know sexually."
   11. *Foxes and goats:* proverbial symbols of cunning and lechery.
   15. *clogges:* weights which hinder motion.
   18. *allowes:* concedes.
   23. *Likenesse:* besides meaning "similarity" of interest, belief, etc., the poet satirically puns that when two people really *like* each other, their *love* (sexual relation) is steadfast. See further, NOTES.
   26. *her:* see NOTES.

To live in one land, is captivitie,
To runne all countries, a wild roguery;   30
Waters stincke soone, if in one place they bide,
And in the vast sea are worse putrifi'd:
But when they kisse one banke, and leaving this
Never looke backe, but the next banke doe kisse,
Then are they purest; Change'is the nursery   35
Of musicke, joy, life, and eternity.

17 *Elegie: The Anagram.*

Marry, and love thy *Flavia*, for, shee
Hath all things, whereby others beautious bee,
For, though her eyes be small, her mouth is great,
Though they be Ivory, yet her teeth be jeat,
Though they be dimme, yet she is light enough,   5
And though her harsh haire fall, her skinne is rough;
What though her cheeks be yellow, her haire's red,
Give her thine, and she hath a maydenhead.
These things are beauties elements, where these
Meet in one, that one must, as perfect, please.   10
If red and white and each good quality
Be in thy wench ne'r aske where it doth lye.
In buying things perfum'd, we aske; if there
Be muske and amber in it, but not where.
Though all her parts be not in th'usuall place,   15
She'hath yet an Anagram of a good face.
If we might put the letters but one way,
In the leane dearth of words, what could wee say?
When by the Gamut some Musitions make
A perfect song, others will undertake,   20

ELEGIE: THE ANAGRAM. See NOTES.
  4. *they:* her teeth.
  5. *they:* her eyes.
  8. *thine:* hair (thus she has a head of hair like a maiden's) and head (sexual organ; thus she has intercourse for the first time).
  14. *amber:* ambergris.
  16. That is, the parts of her face can be rearranged to create a good face, and what can be said of her face can be revised into different meanings.
  19. *Gamut:* the range of recognized musical notes.

By the same Gamut chang'd, to equall it.
Things simply good, can never be unfit;
She's faire as any, if all be like her,
And if none bee, then she is singular.
All love is wonder; if wee justly doe   25
Account her wonderfull, why'not lovely too?
Love built on beauty, soone as beauty, dies,
Chuse this face, chang'd by no deformities;
Women are all like Angels; the faire be
Like those which fell to worse; but such as shee,   30
Like to good Angels, nothing can impaire:
'Tis lesse griefe to be foule, then to'have beene faire.
For one nights revels, silke and gold we chuse,
But, in long journeyes, cloth, and leather use.
Beauty is barren oft; best husbands say   35
There is best land, where there is foulest way.
Oh what a soveraigne Plaister will shee bee
If thy past sinnes have taught thee jealousie!
Here needs no spies, nor eunuches; her commit
Safe to thy foes; yea, to a Marmosit.   40
When Belgiaes citties, the round countries drowne,
That durty foulenesse guards, and armes the towne:
So doth her face guard her; and so, for thee,
Which, forc'd by businesse, absent oft must bee,
Shee, whose face, like clouds, turnes the day to night,   45
Who, mightier then the sea, makes Moores seem white,
Who, though seaven yeares, she in the Stews had laid,
A Nunnery durst receive, and thinke a maid,
And though in childbeds labour she did lie,
Midwifes would sweare, 'twere but a tympanie,   50
Whom, if shee'accuse her selfe, I credit lesse
Then witches, which impossibles confesse,

---

22. *simply:* by being simple. *unfit:* both "inappropriate" and "made different, taken apart."
   35. *husbands:* tillers, cultivators.
   35–36. See Notes.
   37. *soveraigne Plaister:* supreme application for wounds (a court plaster).
   40. *Marmosit:* an ugly little fellow.
   41. *When:* until. *round:* not flat (as are the Lowlands, i.e. the Netherlands); those surrounding (Spain and France). Refers to the War of Independence against Spain, particularly during the 1580s and '90s.
   42. *foulenesse:* because waterways filled with sewage "disfigured" the land.
   47. *Stews:* brothels.
   50. *tympanie:* distention (of the belly).

Whom Dildoes, Bedstaves, and her Velvet Glasse
Would be as loath to touch as Joseph was:
One like none, and lik'd of none, fittest were,   55
For, things in fashion every man will weare.

18   *Elegie: On his Mistris.*

By our first strange and fatall interview,
By all desires which thereof did ensue,
By our long starving hopes, by that remorse
Which my words masculine perswasive force
Begot in thee, and by the memory   5
Of hurts, which spies and rivals threatned me,
I calmely beg. But by thy fathers wrath,
By all paines, which want and divorcement hath,
I conjure thee, and all the oathes which I
And thou have sworne to seale joynt constancy,   10
Here I unsweare, and overswear them thus,
Thou shalt not love by wayes so dangerous.
Temper, ô faire Love, loves impetuous rage,
Be my true Mistris still, not my faign'd Page;
I'll goe, and, by thy kinde leave, leave behinde   15
Thee, onely worthy to nurse in my minde,
Thirst to come backe; ô if thou die before,
My soule from other lands to thee shall soare.
Thy (else Almighty) beautie cannot move
Rage from the Seas, nor thy love teach them love,   20
Nor tame wilde Boreas harshnesse; Thou hast reade
How roughly hee in peeces shivered
Faire Orithea, whom he swore he lov'd.

53. *Dildoes, Bedstaves, and her Velvet Glasse:* phalluses, bedboards, and her velvet-backed mirror.

54. *Joseph:* he repeatedly refused to lie with the wife of his master Potiphar, the Egyptian. She avenged herself by having him jailed on a false charge of attempted seduction (Gen. xxxix 7–20).

ELEGIE: ON HIS MISTRIS. See NOTES.

3. *remorse:* pity.

9. *conjure:* solemnly beseech.

14. *faign'd Page:* his mistress has thought to accompany him on his military travels, disguised as his page.

21. *Boreas:* the north wind, who loved the Athenian princess Orithyia; but here the poet has his wintry qualities bring about her death.

Fall ill or good, 'tis madnesse to have prov'd
Dangers unurg'd; Feed on this flattery, 25
That absent Lovers one in th'other be.
Dissemble nothing, not a boy, nor change
Thy bodies habite, nor mindes; bee not strange
To thy selfe onely.'All will spie in thy face
A blushing womanly discovering grace; 30
Richly cloath'd Apes, are call'd Apes, and as soone
Ecclips'd as bright we call the Moone the Moone.
Men of France, changeable Camelions,
Spittles'of diseases, shops of fashions,
Loves fuellers, and the rightest company 35
Of Players, which upon the worlds stage be,
Will quickly know thee, and no lesse, alas!
Th'indifferent Italian, as we passe
His warme land, well content to thinke thee Page,
Will hunt thee with such lust, and hideous rage, 40
As *Lots* faire guests were vext. But none of these
Nor spungy'hydroptique Dutch shall thee displease,
If thou stay here. O stay here, for, for thee
England is onely'a worthy Gallerie,
To walke in expectation, till from thence 45
Our greatest King call thee to his presence.
When I am gone, dreame me some happinesse,
Nor let thy lookes our long hid love confesse,
Nor praise, nor dispraise me, nor blesse nor curse
Openly loves force, nor in bed fright thy Nurse 50
With midnights startings, crying out, oh, oh
Nurse, ô my love is slaine, I saw him goe

33. *Men of France:* known for their amorousness.
34. *Spittles' of diseases:* brothels.
35. *Loves fuellers:* those that increase passionate love or sell aphrodisiacs.
rightest: that is, actors who disguise themselves not to deceive.
37. *know:* with added sexual meaning. "Quickly" thus connotes "animatedly, passionately." *alas:* possible pun on "a lass."
38. *indifferent:* because he pursued homosexual as well as heterosexual affairs.
41. *Lots faire guests:* in perverted Sodom (Gen. xviii–xix).
42. *hydroptique:* thirsty (because of the watery lowlands in which they lived) and thus of insatiable appetites.
44. *Gallerie:* a place where she may be viewed but not touched.
46. *King:* God.
50–52. Perhaps with conscious allusion to Juliet.

O'r the white Alpes alone; I saw him I,
Assail'd, fight, taken, stabb'd, bleed, fall, and die.
Augure me better chance, except dread *Jove*   55
Thinke it enough for me to'have had thy love.

19   *Elegie: His Picture.*

Here take my Picture, though I bid farewell;
Thine, in my heart, where my soule dwels, shall dwell.
'Tis like me now, but I dead, 'twill be more
When wee are shadowes both, then 'twas before.
When weather-beaten I come backe; my hand,   5
Perhaps with rude oares torne, or Sun beams tann'd,
My face and brest of hairecloth, and my head
With cares rash sodaine stormes, being o'rspread,
My body'a sack of bones, broken within,
And powders blew staines scatter'd on my skinne;   10
If rivall fooles taxe thee to'have lov'd a man,
So foule, and course, as, Oh, I may seeme than,
This shall say what I was: and thou shalt say,
Doe his hurts reach mee? doth my worth decay?
Or doe they reach his judging minde, that hee   15
Should now love lesse, what hee did love to see?
That which in him was faire and delicate,
Was but the milke, which in loves childish state
Did nurse it: who now is growne strong enough
To feed on that, which to'disus'd tasts seemes tough.   20

55. *Augure me better chance:* foresee a better fate for me.   *except:* unless.
ELEGIE: HIS PICTURE. See NOTES.
5. *When . . . backe:* perhaps a reference to one of Donne's early trips to the
Continent.
10. *powders:* gunpowder's.
15. *they:* his hurts.
17–20. "For every one that useth milk is unskilful in the word of righteousness: for he is a babe. But strong meat belongeth to them that are of full age,
even those who by reason of use have their senses exercised to discern both
good and evil" (Heb. v 13–14).
19. *it:* love.
20. *disus'd:* unaccustomed.

20 *Elegie: Loves Progress.*

Who ever loves, if he do not propose
The right true end of love, he's one that goes
To sea for nothing but to make him sick:
Love is a bear-whelp born, if we o're lick
Our love, and force it new strange shapes to take,   5
We erre, and of a lump a monster make.
Were not a Calf a monster that were grown
Face'd like a man, though better then his own?
Perfection is in unitie: preferr
One woman first, and then one thing in her.   10
I, when I value gold, may think upon
The ductilness, the application,
The wholsomness, the ingenuitie,
From rust, from soil, from fire ever free:
But if I love it, 'tis because 'tis made   15
By our new nature (Use) the soul of trade.
    All these in women we might think upon
(If women had them) and yet love but one.
Can men more injure women then to say
They love them for that, by which they're not they?   20
Makes virtue woman? must I cool my bloud
Till I both be, and find one wise and good?
May barren Angels love so. But if we
Make love to woman; virtue is not she:
As beauty'is not nor wealth: He that strayes thus   25
From her to hers, is more adulterous,
Then if he took her maid. Search every sphear
And firmament, our *Cupid* is not there:
He's an infernal god and under ground,
With *Pluto* dwells, where gold and fire abound;   30
Men to such Gods, their sacrificing Coles
Did not in Altars lay, but pits and holes:

ELEGIE: LOVES PROGRESS. See NOTES.
    2. *true end of love:* to have intercourse. As the rest of the poem indicates, there is a graphic pun on "end" (see ll. 92, 96).
    6. *lump:* the two during intercourse. Lines 4–6 refer to an unnatural inverted sexual position.
    14. *soil:* both "stain" since gold is untarnishable and "earth" since they can easily be separated. *from fire ever free:* the alchemical belief that gold alone is not affected by fire (see Aristotle, *Meteorologica,* III, vi, 378c).

Although we see Celestial bodies move
Above the earth, the earth we Till and love:
So we her ayres contemplate, words and heart,   35
And virtues; but we love the Centrique part.
  Nor is the soul more worthy, or more fit
For love, then this, as infinit as it.
But in attaining this desired place
How much they erre; that set out at the face!   40
The hair a Forest is of Ambushes,
Of springes, snares, fetters and manacles:
The brow becalms us when 'tis smooth and plain,
And when 'tis wrinckled, shipwracks us again.
Smooth, 'tis a Paradice, where we would have   45
Immortal stay, and wrinckled 'tis our grave.
The Nose (like to the first Meridian) runs
Not 'twixt an East and West, but 'twixt two suns;
It leaves a Cheek, a rosie Hemisphere
On either side, and then directs us where   50
Upon the Islands fortunate we fall,
Not faint *Canaries*, but *Ambrosiall*,
Her swelling lips; To which when we are come,
We anchor there, and think our selves at home,
For they seem all: there Syrens songs, and there   55
Wise Delphick Oracles do fill the ear;
There in a Creek where chosen pearls do swell
The Rhemora her cleaving tongue doth dwell.
These, and (the glorious Promontory)'her Chin
Ore past; and the streight *Hellespont* between   60
The *Sestos* and *Abydos* of her breasts,
(Not of two Lovers, but two loves the neasts)
Succeeds a boundless sea, but yet thine eye
Some Island moles may scatter'd there descry;

36. *Centrique part:* her genitals.
52. Playing upon the Canary Islands and the faintly odorous wine made there, and the nectar of the gods.
55. *Syrens:* maidens who tried to lure Ulysses and his men to their death.
56. *Delphick Oracles:* the ancient oracle at Delphi, sacred to Apollo, foretold the future.
58. *Rhemora:* a fish with a suction disk on its head by which it clings to other fish or ships. *cleaving:* with both meanings ("separating" and "clinging").
61. *Sestos and Abydos:* ancient towns in Turkey, one in Europe (the scene of the legend of Hero and Leander) and one in Asia Minor.
62. *two loves the neasts:* that is, her breasts are the snug retreat of two kinds of love (sexual and mammary).
64. *moles:* spots on the skin lying like islands on her ocean-skin.

And Sailing towards her *India,* in that way   65
Shall at her fair Atlantick Naval stay;
Though thence the Current be thy Pilot made,
Yet ere thou be where thou wouldst be embay'd,
Thou shalt upon another Forest set,
Where many Shipwrack, and no further get.   70
When thou art there, consider what this chace
Mispent by thy beginning at the face.
   Rather set out below; practice my Art,
Some Symetry the foot hath with that part
Which thou dost seek, and is thy Map for that   75
Lovely enough to stop, but not stay at:
Least subject to disguise and change it is:
Men say the Devil never can change his.
It is the Emblem that hath figured
Firmness; 'tis the first part that comes to bed.   80
Civilitie we see refin'd: the kiss
Which at the face began, transplanted is,
Since to the hand, since to the'imperial knee,
Now at the Papal foot delights to be:
If Kings think that the nearer way, and do   85
Rise from the foot, Lovers may do so too.
For as free Spheres move faster far then can
Birds, whom the air resists, so may that man
Which goes this empty and Ætherial way,
Then if at beauties elements he stay.   90
Rich Nature hath in women wisely made
Two purses, and their mouths aversely laid:

   65. *India:* since it was unexplored and mysterious; since it was the source of precious things and spices.
   66. *Naval:* both anatomical navel and middle point.
   67. The sense is: though you let your excitement freely pilot you onward.
   74. *Symetry:* likeness.
   78. Through an identification with Pan (represented as half goat), the devil had a cleft foot.
   79. *Emblem:* a picture portraying (figuring) the moral of the verse accompanying it. Just as the foot here symbolizes constancy, so the well-known compass emblem of the Belgian printer Christopher Plantin showed a fixed foot, labeled "Constantia" and signifying dependability.
   83–84. Refers to kissing a woman's hand, a king's knee (as one bows before him), and the Pope's foot (as at ordination).
   85. *nearer:* more intimate, closer in affection.
   89. *empty:* unoccupied (by material elements of beauty).
   92. *Two purses:* implying physical likeness to a pouch and use as receptacle. *aversely:* both "in unfavorable position" and "in opposite direction" (to the other).

They then, which to the lower tribute owe,
That way which that Exchequer looks, must go:
He which doth not, his error is as great,   95
As who by Clyster gave the Stomack meat.

21   Elegie: His parting from her.

Since she must go, and I must mourn, come night,
Environ me with darkness, whilst I write:
Shadow that hell unto me, which alone
I am to suffer when my Love is gone.
Alas the darkest Magick cannot do'it,   5
Thou and great Hell to boot are shadows to'it.
Should *Cinthia* quit thee, *Venus*, and each starre,
It would not forme one thought dark as mine are.
I could lend thee obscureness now, and say,
Out of my self, There should be no more Day,   10
Such is already my felt want of sight,
Did not the fires within me force a light.
Oh Love, that fire and darkness should be mixt,
Or to thy Triumphs soe strange torments fixt?
Is't because thou thy self art blind, that wee   15
Thy Martyrs must no more each other see?
Or tak'st thou pride to break us on the wheel,
And view old Chaos in the Pains we feel?
Or have we left undone some mutual Right,
Through holy fear, that merits thy despight?   20
No, no. The falt was mine, impute'it to me,
Or rather to conspiring destinie,
Which (since I lov'd for forme before) decreed,
That I should suffer when I lov'd indeed:
And therefore now, sooner then I can say,   25
I saw the golden fruit, 'tis rapt away.

   94. *Exchequer:* the lower "purse" in which is to be deposited the "tribute"
owed.
   96. *Clyster:* an enema.   *meat:* food.
ELEGIE: HIS PARTING FROM HER. See NOTES.
   7. *Cinthia:* the moon.   *Venus:* the evening star.
   17. *the wheel:* an old form of torture in which the victim's legs were broken.
   23. *for forme:* for fashion's sake.
   26. *golden fruit:* an allusion to the golden apples of the Hesperides.   *rapt:*
transported, with a side glance at its being hidden by covering.

Or as I'had watcht one drop in a vast stream,
And I left wealthy only in a dream.
Yet Love, thou'rt blinder then thy self in this,
To vex my Dove-like friend for my amiss: 30
And, where my own glad truth may expiate
Thy wrath, to make her fortune run my fate.
So blinded Justice doth, when Favorites fall,
Strike them, their house, their friends, their followers all.
Was't not enough that thou didst dart thy fires 35
Into our blouds, inflaming our desires,
And made'st us sigh and glow, and pant, and burn,
And then thy self into our flame did'st turn?
Was't not enough, that thou didst hazard us
To paths in love so dark, so dangerous: 40
And those so ambush'd round with houshold spies,
And over all thy husbands towring eyes
That flam'd with oylie sweat of jealousie,
Yet went we not still on with Constancie?
Have we not kept our guards, like spie on spie? 45
Had correspondence whilst the foe stood by?
Stoln (more to sweeten them) our many blisses
Of meetings, conference, embracements, kisses?
Shadow'd with negligence our most respects?
Varied our language through all dialects, 50
Of becks, winks, looks, and often under-boards
Spoak dialogues with our feet far from our words?
Have we prov'd all these secrets of our Art,
Yea, thy pale inwards, and thy panting heart?
And, after all this passed Purgatory, 55
Must sad divorce make us the vulgar story?
First let our eyes be rivited quite through
Our turning brains, and both our lips grow to:
Let our armes clasp like Ivy, and our fear
Freese us together, that we may stick here, 60
Till fortune, that would rive us with the deed
Strain her eyes open, and yet make them bleed.
For Love it cannot be, whom hitherto
I have accus'd, should such a mischief doe.
Oh fortune, thou'rt not worth my least exclame, 65
And plague enough thou hast in thy own shame.
Do thy great worst, my friend and I have armes,
Though not against thy strokes, against thy harmes.

51. *under-boards:* under the table.
58. *grow to:* grow together.

Rend us in sunder, thou canst not divide
Our bodies so, but that our souls are ty'd,   70
And we can love by letters still and gifts,
And thoughts and dreams; Love never wanteth shifts.
I will not look upon the quickning Sun,
But straight her beauty to my sense shall run;
The ayre shall note her soft, the fire most pure;   75
Water suggest her clear, and the earth sure;
Time shall not lose our passages; the Spring
How fresh our love was in the beginning;
The Summer how it ripen'd in the eare;
And Autumn, what our golden harvests were.   80
The Winter I'll not think on to spite thee,
But count it a lost season, so shall shee.
And dearest Friend, since we must part, drown night
With hope of Day, burthens well born are light.
Though cold and darkness longer hang somewhere,   85
Yet *Phœbus* equally lights all the Sphere.
And what he cannot in like Portion pay,
The world enjoyes in Mass, and so we may.
Be then ever your self, and let no woe
Win on your health, your youth, your beauty: so   90
Declare your self base fortunes Enemy,
No less be your contempt then constancy:
That I may grow enamour'd on your mind,
When my own thoughts I there reflected find.
For this to th'comfort of my Dear I vow,   95
My Deeds shall still be what my words are now;
The Poles shall move to teach me ere I start;
And when I change my Love, I'll change my heart;
Nay, if I wax but cold in my desire,
Think, heaven hath motion lost, and the world, fire: 100
Much more I could, but many words have made
That, oft, suspected which men would perswade;
Take therefore all in this: I love so true,
As I will never look for less in you.

70. *that:* because.
75–76. Air, fire, water, and earth were historically considered the four elements of matter.
77. *passages:* acts; that is, shall not lack examples of our intercourse.
97. That is, the earth's poles shall change their movement (thus showing
me how to change) before I become inconstant.

22 *Elegie: The Expostulation.*

To make the doubt cleare, that no woman's true,
    Was it my fate to prove it strong in you?
Thought I, but one had breathed purest aire,
    And must she needs be false because she's faire?
Is it your beauties marke, or of your youth,   5
    Or your perfection, not to study truth?
Or thinke you heaven is deafe, or hath no eyes?
    Or those it hath, smile at your perjuries?
Are vowes so cheape with women, or the matter
    Whereof they'are made, that they are writ in water,   10
And blowne away with winde? Or doth their breath
    (Both hot and cold) at once make life and death?
Who could have thought so many accents sweet
    Form'd into words, so many sighs should meete
As from our hearts, so many oathes, and teares   15
    Sprinkled among, (all sweeter by our feares
And the divine impression of stolne kisses,
    That seal'd the rest) should now prove empty blisses?
Did you draw bonds to forfet? signe to breake?
    Or must we reade you quite from what you speake,   20
And finde the truth out the wrong way? or must
    Hee first desire you false, would wish you just?
O I prophane, though most of women be
    This kinde of beast, my thought shall except thee;
My dearest love, though froward jealousie,   25
    With circumstance might urge thy'inconstancie,
Sooner I'll thinke the Sunne will cease to cheare
    The teeming earth, and *that* forget to beare,
Sooner that rivers will runne back, or Thames
    With ribs of Ice in June would bind his streames;   30
Or Nature, by whose strength the world endures,
    Would change her course, before you alter yours;
But O that treacherous breast to whom weake you
    Did trust our Counsells, and wee both may rue,

ELEGIE: THE EXPOSTULATION. See NOTES.
  19. *to forfet . . . breake:* only in order to forfeit them; sign them only to break them.
  21. *the wrong way:* by reversal of what you say.
  22. *would:* who would.
  28. *that:* not only the natural growth of vegetation, but the minerals, etc., believed to be engendered by the sun's action.

Having his falshood found too late, 'twas hee   35
    That made me *cast* you guilty, and you me,
Whilst he, black wretch, betray'd each simple word
    Wee spake, unto the cunning of a third;
Curst may hee be, that so our love hath slaine,
    And wander on the earth, wretched as *Cain*,   40
Wretched as hee, and not deserve least pitty;
    In plaguing him, let misery be witty;
Let all eyes shunne him, and hee shunne each eye,
    Till hee be noysome as his infamie;
May he without remorse deny God thrice,   45
    And not be trusted more on his Soules price;
And after all selfe torment, when hee dyes,
    May Wolves teare out his heart, Vultures his eyes,
Swine eate his bowels, and his falser tongue
    That utter'd all, be to some Raven flung,   50
And let his carrion coarse be'a longer feast
    To the Kings dogges, then any other beast;
Now have I curst, let us our love revive;
    In mee the flame was never more alive;
I could beginne againe to court and praise,   55
    And in that pleasure lengthen the short dayes
Of my lifes lease; like Painters that do take
    Delight, not in made worke, but whiles they make;
I could renew those times, when first I saw
    Love in your eyes, that gave my tongue the law   60
To like what you lik'd; and at maskes and playes
    Commend the selfe same Actors, the same wayes;
Aske how you did, and often with intent
    Of being officious, be impertinent;
All which were such soft pastimes, as in these   65
    Love was as subtilly catch'd, as a disease;
But being got it is a treasure sweet,
    Which to defend is harder then to get:
And ought not be prophan'd on either part,
    For though 'tis got by *chance*, 'tis kept by *art*.   70

38. *third:* the two lovers are considered one.
45. As Simon Peter had denied Jesus in the court of the high priest.
64. *officious:* obliging, kind.

23 *Elegie: Variety.*

The heavens rejoyce in motion, why should I
Abjure my so much lov'd variety,
And not with many youth and love divide?
Pleasure is none, if not diversifi'd:
The sun that sitting in the chaire of light   5
Sheds flame into what else so ever doth seem bright,
Is not contented at one Signe to Inne,
But ends his year and with a new beginnes.
All things doe willingly in change delight,
The fruitfull mother of our appetite: 10
Rivers the clearer and more pleasing are,
Where their fair spreading streames run wide and farr;
And a dead lake that no strange bark doth greet,
Corrupts it self and what doth live in it.
Let no man tell me such a one is faire,   15
And worthy all alone my love to share.
Nature in her hath done the liberall part
Of a kinde Mistresse, and imploy'd her art
To make her loveable, and I aver
Him not humane that would turn back from her: 20
I love her well, and would, if need were, dye
To doe her service. But followes it that I
Must serve her onely, when I may have choice?
The law is hard, and shall not have my voice.
The last I saw in all extreames is faire,   25
And holds me in the Sun-beames of her haire;
Her nymph-like features such agreements have
That I could venture with her to the grave:
Another's brown, I like her not the worse,
Her tongue is soft and takes me with discourse.   30
Others, for that they well descended are,
Do in my love obtain as large a share;
And though they be not fair, tis much with mee
To win their love onely for their degree.

ELEGIE: VARIETY. See NOTES.
    7. *Signe:* referring to zodiacal signs. Sagittarius sees the ending of the sun's year (December 21) and Capricorn opens the new year (December 22). *to Inne:* to lodge, as at an inn.
    13. And a stagnant lake that a foreign ship cannot visit.
    25. *in all extreames:* that is, in all extremities of the body.
    34. *degree:* position in the range of variety.

And though I faile of my required ends,   35
The'attempt is glorious and it self commends.
How happy were our Syres in ancient times,
Who held plurality of loves no crime!
With them it was accounted charity
To stirre up race of all indifferently;   40
Kindreds were not exempted from the bands:
Which with the Persian still in usage stands.
Women were then no sooner ask'd then won,
And what they did was honest and well done.
But since this title honour hath been us'd,   45
Our weake credulity hath been abus'd;
The golden laws of nature are repeald,
Which our first Fathers in such reverence held;
Our liberty revers'd and Charter's gone,
And we made servants to opinion,   50
A monster in no certain shape attir'd,
And whose originall is much desir'd,
Formlesse at first, but growing on it fashions,
And doth prescribe manners and laws to nations.
Here love receiv'd immedicable harmes,   55
And was dispoiled of his daring armes.
A greater want then is his daring eyes,
He lost those awfull wings with which he flies;
His sinewy bow, and those immortall darts
Wherewith he'is wont to bruise resisting hearts;   60
Onely some few strong in themselves and free
Retain the seeds of antient liberty,
Following that part of love although deprest,
And make a throne for him within their brest,
In spight of modern censures him avowing   65
Their Soveraigne, all service him allowing.
Amongst which troop although I am the least,
Yet equall in perfection with the best,
I glory in subjection of his hand,
Nor ever did decline his least command: 70
For in whatever forme the message came
My heart did open and receive the same:
But time will in his course a point discry
When I this loved service must deny.

55. *love:* Cupid.
63. *deprest:* suppressed.

For our allegiance temporary is, 75
With firmer age returnes our liberties.
What time in years and judgement we repos'd,
Shall not so easily be to change dispos'd
Nor to the art of severall eyes obeying,
But beauty with true worth securely weighing, 80
Which being found assembled in some one,
Wee'l leave her ever, and love her alone.

24 *Sapho to Philænis.*

Where is that holy fire, which *Verse* is said
  To have? is that inchanting force decai'd?
Verse that drawes *Natures* workes, from *Natures* law,
  Thee, her best worke, to her worke cannot draw.
Have my teares quench'd my old *Poetique* fire; 5
  Why quench'd they not as well, that of *desire?*
Thoughts, my mindes creatures, often are with thee,
  But I, their maker, want their libertie.
Onely thine image, in my heart, doth sit,
  But that is waxe, and fires environ it. 10
My fires have driven, thine have drawne it hence;
  And I am rob'd of *Picture, Heart,* and *Sense.*
Dwells with me still mine irksome *Memory,*
  Which, both to keepe, and lose, grieves equally.
That tells me'how faire thou art: Thou art so faire, 15
  As, *gods,* when *gods* to thee I doe compare,
Are grac'd thereby; And to make blinde men see,
  What things *gods* are, I say they'are like to thee.

SAPHO TO PHILÆNIS.
  Sappho: Greek poetess (fl. 600 B.C.) who wrote love lyrics to young girls (such as Philænis, whose name means "a female friend") of whom she was enamored.
  1–2. See NOTES.
  2. *inchanting:* not only "charming" and "deluding," but also the force which moves one to put one's reaction into song.
  3–4. See NOTES.
  11. *drawne it:* "it" is ambivalently both the image of Philænis and the heart of Sappho (as the next line shows); thus "drawne" means both "painted" and "pulled."

For, if we justly call each silly *man*
 A *litle world,* What shall we call thee than?   20
Thou art not soft, and cleare, and strait, and faire,
 As *Down,* as *Stars, Cedars,* and *Lillies* are,
But thy right hand, and cheek, and eye, only
 Are like thy other hand, and cheek, and eye.
Such was my *Phao*'awhile, but shall be never,   25
 As thou, wast, art, and, oh, maist be ever.
Here lovers sweare in their *Idolatrie,*
 That I am such; but *Griefe* discolors me.
And yet I grieve the lesse, least *Griefe* remove
 My beauty,'and make me'unworthy of thy love.   30
Plaies some soft boy with thee, oh there wants yet
 A mutuall feeling which should sweeten it.
His chinne, a thorny hairy'unevennesse
 Doth threaten, and some daily change possesse.
Thy body is a naturall *Paradise,*   35
 In whose selfe, unmanur'd, all pleasure lies,
Nor needs *perfection;* why shouldst thou than
 Admit the tillage of a harsh rough man?
Men leave behinde them that which their sin showes,
 And are as theeves trac'd, which rob when it snows.   40
But of our dallyance no more signes there are,
 Then *fishes* leave in streames, or *Birds* in aire.
And betweene us all sweetnesse may be had;
 All, all that *Nature* yields, or *Art* can adde.
My two lips, eyes, thighs, differ from thy two,   45
 But so, as thine from one another doe;
And, oh, no more; the likenesse being such,
 Why should they not alike in all parts touch?
Hand to strange hand, lippe to lippe none denies;
 Why should they brest to brest, or thighs to thighs?   50

19. *silly:* frail.
20. *litle world:* man's head, thus brain, was frequently likened to the spherical world.
25. *Phao:* Phaon was a handsome legendary ferryman of Lesbos, whom Sappho loved unrequitedly; she was supposed to have cast herself from the Leucadian rock into the sea through despair of him.
31. *wants:* is lacking.
32. *it:* the playing of Philænis and the boy.
36. *unmanur'd:* not cultivated, not fondled.
39. *that which their sin showes:* children begotten in "sinful" intercourse. As footsteps identify the thief, so children point out their fathers.

Likenesse begets such strange selfe flatterie,
    That touching my selfe, all seemes done to thee.
My selfe I'embrace, and mine owne hands I kisse,
    And amorously thanke my selfe for this.
Me, in my glasse, I call thee; But alas,   55
    When I would kisse, teares dimme mine *eyes*, and *glasse*.
O cure this loving madnesse, and restore
    Me to mee; thee, my *halfe*, my *all*, my *more*.
So may thy cheekes red outweare scarlet dye,
    And their white, whitenesse of the *Galaxy*,   60
So may thy mighty,'amazing beauty move
    Envy'in all *women*, and in all *men*, *love*,
And so be *change*, and *sicknesse*, farre from thee,
    As thou by comming neere, keep'st them from me.

55. *glasse:* mirror.
59. *outweare:* outlive, devalue.
63. *change, and sicknesse:* that is, female ills.

Songs and Sonets

25 *The Message.*

Send home my long strayd eyes to mee,
Which (Oh) too long have dwelt on thee,
Yet since there they have learn'd such ill,
   Such forc'd fashions,
   And false passions,   5
     That they be
     Made by thee
Fit for no good sight, keep them still.

Send home my harmlesse heart againe,
Which no unworthy thought could staine,   10
Which if'it be taught by thine
   To make jestings
   Of protestings,
     And crosse both
     Word and oath,   15
Keepe it, for then 'tis none of mine.

Yet send me back my heart and eyes,
That I may know, and see thy lyes,
And may laugh and joy, when thou
   Art in anguish   20
   And dost languish
     For some one
     That will none,
Or prove as false as thou art now.

THE MESSAGE.
   8. *good:* honest, virtuous.
   14. *crosse:* cancel.
   23. That will have none of you.

JOHN COPRARIO

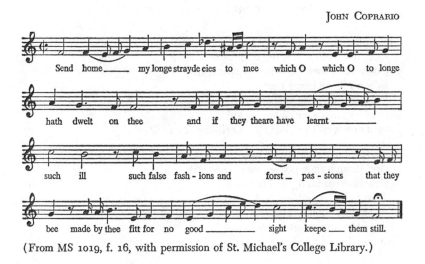

(From MS 1019, f. 16, with permission of St. Michael's College Library.)

26 *Witchcraft by a picture.*

I fixe mine eye on thine, and there
   Pitty my picture burning in thine eye,
My picture drown'd in a transparent teare,
   When I looke lower I espie;
     Hadst thou the wicked skill   5
By pictures made and mard, to kill,
How many wayes mightst thou performe thy will?

But now I'have drunke thy sweet salt teares,
   And though thou poure more I'll depart;
My picture vanish'd, vanish feares,   10
   That I can be endamag'd by that art;
     Though thou retaine of mee
One picture more, yet that will bee,
Being in thine owne heart, from all malice free.

27 *The Baite.*

Come live with mee, and bee my love,
And wee will some new pleasures prove
Of golden sands, and christall brookes:
With silken lines, and silver hookes.

There will the river whispering runne   5
Warm'd by thy eyes, more then the Sunne.
And there the'inamor'd fish will stay,
Begging themselves they may betray.

WITCHCRAFT BY A PICTURE.
    4. *lower:* more deeply.
    6. In witchcraft one method of killing was to make a picture of someone and then destroy it.
THE BAITE.
    Written as a sequel to Christopher Marlowe's "Come live with me, and be my love."
    8. Begging for your bait out of their love, which will lead to their being caught.

When thou wilt swimme in that live bath,
Each fish, which every channell hath,
Will amorously to thee swimme,
Gladder to catch thee, then thou him.

If thou, to be so seene, beest loath,
By Sunne, or Moone, thou darknest both,
And if my selfe have leave to see,
I need not their light, having thee.

Let others freeze with angling reeds,
And cut their legges, with shells and weeds,
Or treacherously poore fish beset,
With strangling snare, or windowie net:

Let coarse bold hands, from slimy nest
The bedded fish in banks out-wrest,
Or curious traitors, sleavesilke flies
Bewitch poore fishes wandring eyes.

For thee, thou needst no such deceit,
For thou thy selfe art thine owne bait;
That fish, that is not catch'd thereby,
Alas, is wiser farre then I.

10

15

20

25

28   *The Apparition.*

When by thy scorne, O murdresse, I am dead,
     And that thou thinkst thee free
From all solicitation from mee,
Then shall my ghost come to thy bed,
And thee, fain'd vestall, in worse armes shall see;
Then thy sicke taper will begin to winke,
And he, whose thou art then, being tyr'd before,
Will, if thou stirre, or pinch to wake him, thinke
     Thou call'st for more,
And in false sleepe will from thee shrinke,

5

10

17. *reeds:* rods made from reeds.
23. *sleavesilke:* floss, untwisted silk that tangles easily.
THE APPARITION.
6. *sicke:* pale and dying.   *to winke:* to flicker (from a ghost's being near).

And then poore Aspen wretch, neglected thou
Bath'd in a cold quicksilver sweat wilt lye
    A veryer ghost then I;
What I will say, I will not tell thee now,
Lest that preserve thee; and since my love is spent,   15
I'had rather thou shouldst painfully repent,
Then by my threatnings rest still innocent.

    11. *Aspen:* quivering.
    12. *quicksilver:* mercury or liquid silver of the alchemists, who combined it with ore to obtain gold or silver; the quicksilver could easily be removed, leaving the precious metal. In a reversal the poet says that the woman will be left with quicksilver sweat when her lover, who is like a precious metal, turns away, not to couple her. Quicksilver was also used to treat syphilis.
    13. *veryer:* truer.
    15. *Lest that preserve thee:* "Lest that keep thee safe from harm" and "Lest that keep thee protected like game for sport" by having you circumvent my curse or my calamitous information.

WILLIAM LAWES

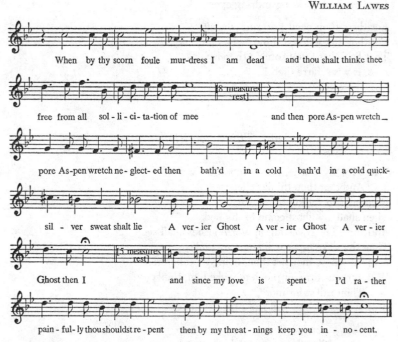

(From MS D.C.I. 69, pp. 13–14, reverse, with permission of Edinburgh University Library.)

29 *The broken heart.*

He is starke mad, who ever sayes,
　　That he hath beene in love an houre,
Yet not that love so soone decayes,
　　But that it can tenne in lesse space devour;
Who will beleeve mee, if I sweare　　　　　　　　　　　5
That I have had the plague a yeare?
　　Who would not laugh at mee, if I should say,
　　I saw a flaske of *powder burne a day?*

Ah, what a trifle is a heart,
　　If once into loves hands it come!　　　　　　　　　10
All other griefes allow a part
　　To other griefes, and aske themselves but some;
They come to us, but us Love draws,
Hee swallows us, and never chawes:
　　By him, as by chain'd shot, whole rankes doe dye,　　15
　　He is the tyran Pike, our hearts the Frye.

If 'twere not so, what did become
　　Of my heart, when I first saw thee?
I brought a heart into the roome,
　　But from the roome, I carried none with mee;　　　20
If it had gone to thee, I know
Mine would have taught thine heart to show
　　More pitty unto mee: but Love, alas,
　　At one first blow did shiver it as glasse.

Yet nothing can to nothing fall,　　　　　　　　　　25
　　Nor any place be empty quite,
Therefore I thinke my breast hath all
　　Those peeces still, though they be not unite;

THE BROKEN HEART.
　　14. *chawes:* chews.
　　15. *chain'd shot:* shot consisting of two balls or half balls united by a short chain; it, of course, struck down "whole rankes" with one firing.
　　16. *Frye:* small fish, prey of the voracious pike.
　　25. Refers to the idea that no matter is indestructible.
　　26. Refers to the idea that an absolute vacuum is impossible.

And now as broken glasses show
A hundred lesser faces, so   30
   My ragges of heart can like, wish, and adore,
   But after one such love, can love no more.

30   *Lecture upon the Shadow.*

Stand still, and I will read to thee
A Lecture, Love, in loves philosophy.
   These three houres that we have spent,
   Walking here, Two shadowes went
Along with us, which we our selves produc'd;   5
But, now the Sunne is just above our head,
   We doe those shadowes tread;
   And to brave clearnesse all things are reduc'd.
   So whilst our infant loves did grow,
   Disguises did, and shadowes, flow,   10
   From us, and our care; but, now 'tis not so.

That love hath not attain'd the high'st degree,
Which is still diligent lest others see.

Except our loves at this noone stay,
We shall new shadowes make the other way.   15
   As the first were made to blinde
   Others; these which come behinde
Will worke upon our selves, and blind our eyes.

   29. *glasses:* mirrors.
   30. *A hundred:* implying unity (see l. 28).
LECTURE UPON THE SHADOW.
   2. *Love:* his loved one.
   3–17. See NOTES.
   7. Since the shadows disappear, the shadows seem underfoot.
   8. *brave:* courageous, superior; "clear" because there is no shadowy darkness.
   9. *infant:* immature and early. See further, NOTES.
   14. *Except:* unless.
   15. See NOTES.
   16–18. Others are blinded by the disguising of their love; that is, others do
not see their love. The lovers, however, are blinded in a different sense: the sun
shines directly into their eyes and they do not recognize their love's decline.

If our loves faint, and westwardly decline;
  To me thou, falsly, thine,   20
    And I to thee mine actions shall disguise.
  The morning shadowes weare away,
  But these grow longer all the day,
  But oh, loves day is short, if love decay.

Love is a growing, or full constant light;   25
And his first minute, after noone, is night.

31 *A Valediction forbidding mourning.*

As virtuous men passe mildly'away,
  And whisper to their soules, to goe,
Whilst some of their sad friends doe say,
  The breath goes now, and some say, no.

So let us melt, and make no noise,   5
  No teare-floods, nor sigh-tempests move,
T'were prophanation of our joyes
  To tell the layetie our love.

Moving of th'earth brings harmes and feares,
  Men reckon what it did and meant,   10
But trepidation of the spheares,
  Though greater farre, is innocent.

20–21. Thou shall disguise thine actions falsely to me, and I shall disguise mine actions falsely to thee.
24. *loves day:* that is, the period when the sun is very bright.
26. Once love starts to wane even slightly, it is as if it had completely died.
A VALEDICTION FORBIDDING MOURNING.
According to Walton, written to Donne's wife when Donne went to the Continent with Sir Robert Drury in 1611.
2. See NOTES.
5. *melt:* part, dissolve our being together; perhaps release the soul through a kiss.
6. *move:* stir up.
7. *prophanation:* desecration (of the sacred—note "layetie") and vulgarization (a pun on "layetie").
9. Referring to the belief that earthquakes and similar natural phenomena were signs of God's wrath and of further disasters.
11. *trepidation:* both (1) the supposed tremulous movement of the *primum mobile,* the outermost sphere of the Ptolemaic universe, which imparted this movement to each succeeding sphere and (2) fear of heavenly occurrences; though more frequent and more important, since heavenly, they are nonetheless harmless.

Dull sublunary lovers love
  (Whose soule is sense) cannot admit
Absence, because it doth remove   15
  Those things which elemented it.

But we by'a love, so much refin'd,
  That our selves know not what it is,
Inter-assured of the mind,
  Care lesse, eyes, lips, and hands to misse.   20

Our two soules therefore, which are one,
  Though I must goe, endure not yet
A breach, but an expansion,
  Like gold to ayery thinnesse beate.

If they be two, they are two so   25
  As stiffe twin compasses are two,
Thy soule the fixt foot, makes no show
  To move, but doth, if the'other doe.

And though it in the center sit,
  Yet when the other far doth rome,   30
It leanes, and hearkens after it,
  And growes erect, as that comes home.

Such wilt thou be to mee, who must
  Like th'other foot, obliquely runne.
Thy firmnes makes my circle just,   35
  And makes me end, where I begunne.

13. *sublunary:* earthly and, since influenced by the moon, given to ebb and flow of love.
14. *sense:* dependent on sensual gratification.
16. *elemented:* created, composed.
22. *endure not yet:* do not nevertheless allow.
26. *twin compasses:* the two legs of a compass. See further, Notes.
31. *hearkens:* perhaps implying that she awaits news of and from him.
32. *as that comes home:* the circumscribing foot returns to the center as the compass is closed.
34. *obliquely:* not moving in a straight line. See further, Notes.
35–36. See Notes.

32 *The good-morrow.*

I wonder by my troth, what thou, and I
Did, till we lov'd? were we not wean'd till then?
But suck'd on countrey pleasures, childishly?
Or snorted we in the'seaven sleepers den?
T'was so; But this, all pleasures fancies bee.   5
If ever any beauty I did see,
Which I desir'd, and got, t'was but a dreame of thee.

And now good morrow to our waking soules,
Which watch not one another out of feare;
For love, all love of other sights controules,   10
And makes one little roome, an every where.
Let sea-discoverers to new worlds have gone,
Let Maps to others, worlds on worlds have showne,
Let us possesse one world, each hath one, and is one.

My face in thine eye, thine in mine appeares,   15
And true plaine hearts doe in the faces rest,
Where can we finde two better hemispheares
Without sharpe North, without declining West?
What ever dyes, was not mixt equally;
If our two loves be one, or, thou and I   20
Love so alike, that none doe slacken, none can die.

THE GOOD-MORROW.
   3. *countrey:* rustic, unsophisticated; but neither has been without sexual activity.
   4. Seven Christian youths of Ephesus, according to legend, took refuge in a cave during the persecution of Emperor Decius and awakened about two centuries later. Their prolonged sleep is contrasted with the poet's former nightly affairs (ll. 6–7) and the couple's present awakening.
   5. *But this:* except for our love.
   11. *roome:* their bedroom, in which they bid good-morrow.
   13. *others:* other people.
   14. *each . . . is one:* each hath the world of the other, and each is a world to the other.
   17. See NOTES.
   18. *sharpe:* bitterly cold. *declining:* where the sun descends; that is, their love admits neither coldness to the other nor abatement.
   19. *equally:* uniformly; with unified result. The belief was alchemically commonplace.

33 *Song.*

Goe, and catche a falling starre,
   Get with child a mandrake roote,
Tell me, where all past yeares are,
   Or who cleft the Divels foot,
Teach me to heare Mermaides singing,   5
Or to keep off envies stinging,
          And finde
          What winde
Serves to'advance an honest minde.

If thou beest borne to strange sights,   10
   Things invisible to see,
Ride ten thousand daies and nights,
   Till age snow white haires on thee,
Thou, when thou retorn'st, wilt tell mee
All strange wonders that befell thee,   15
          And sweare
          No where
Lives a woman true, and faire.

If thou findst one, let mee know,
   Such a Pilgrimage were sweet,   20
Yet doe not, I would not goe,
   Though at next doore wee might meet,
Though shee were true, when you met her,
And last, till you write your letter,
          Yet shee   25
          Will bee
False, ere I come, to two, or three.

song: "Goe, and catche a falling starre."
   2. The forked root of the mandragora resembled the human form.
   4. The devil's foot was considered cleft because of identification with goats
and Pan.

ANONYMOUS

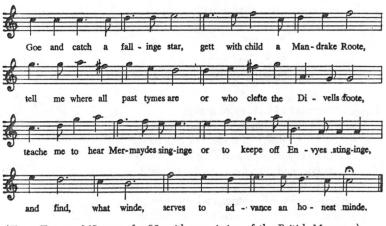

Goe and catch a fall - inge star, gett with child a Man-drake Roote,

tell me where all past tymes are or who clefte the Di - vells foote,

teache me to hear Mer-maydes sing-inge or to keepe off En - vyes .sting-inge,

and find, what winde, serves to ad -·vance an ho - nest minde.

(From Egerton MS 2013, f. 586, with permission of the British Museum.)

34 *Womans constancy.*

Now thou hast lov'd me one whole day,
To morrow when thou leav'st, what wilt thou say?
Wilt thou then Antedate some new made vow?
  Or say that now
We are not just those persons, which we were?   5
Or, that oathes made in reverentiall feare
Of Love, and his wrath, any may forsweare?
Or, as true deaths, true maryages untie,
So lovers contracts, images of those,
Binde but till sleep, deaths image, them unloose?   10

WOMANS CONSTANCY.
 8. *true:* real.
 9. *images of those:* "types" of marriages.

Or, your owne end to Justifie,
For having purpos'd change, and falsehood; you
Can have no way but falsehood to be true?
Vaine lunatique, against these scapes I could
    Dispute, and conquer, if I would,   15
    Which I abstaine to doe,
For by to morrow, I may thinke so too.

35   "Image of her whom I love."

Image of her whom I love, more then she,
  Whose faire impression in my faithfull heart,
Makes mee her *Medall,* and makes her love mee,
  As Kings do coynes, to which their stamps impart
The value: goe, and take my heart from hence,   5
  Which now is growne too great and good for me:
Honours oppresse weake spirits, and our sense
  Strong objects dull; the more, the lesse wee see.

When you are gone, and *Reason* gone with you,
  Then *Fantasie* is Queene and Soule, and all;   10
She can present joyes meaner then you do;
  Convenient, and more proportionall.
So, if I dreame I have you, I have you,
  For, all our joyes are but fantasticall.
And so I scape the paine, for paine is true;   15
  And sleepe which locks up sense, doth lock out all.

After a such fruition I shall wake,
  And, but the waking, nothing shall repent;
And shall to love more thankfull Sonnets make,
  Then if more *honour, teares,* and *paines* were spent.   20

    14. *lunatique:* an erratic person (like the inconstant moon); the word puns on the influence of the moon (Luna) over the man's mistress, and his infatuated "insanity." It suggests that the speaker is the woman. *scapes:* escapes, deceptions.
"IMAGE OF HER WHOM I LOVE." See NOTES.
    8. *the more:* the stronger the image (intellectual concept of her).
    11. *meaner:* more common, ones that are appropriate to a dream and more harmonious.
    17. *After a such fruition:* after such pleasure from attainment.

But dearest heart, and dearer image stay;
    Alas, true joyes at best are *dreame* enough;
Though you stay here you passe too fast away:
    For even at first lifes *Taper* is a snuffe.

Fill'd with her love, may I be rather grown   25
Mad with much *heart,* then *ideott* with none.

36   *The Sunne Rising.*

      Busie old foole, unruly Sunne,
        Why dost thou thus,
Through windowes, and through curtaines call on us?
Must to thy motions lovers seasons run?
      Sawcy pedantique wretch, goe chide   5
       Late schoole boyes, and sowre prentices,
  Goe tell Court-huntsmen, that the King will ride,
    Call countrey ants to harvest offices;
Love, all alike, no season knowes, nor clyme,
Nor houres, dayes, moneths, which are the rags of time.   10

      Thy beames, so reverend, and strong
        Why shouldst thou thinke?
I could eclipse and cloud them with a winke,
But that I would not lose her sight so long:
      If her eyes have not blinded thine,   15
       Looke, and to morrow late, tell mee,
  Whether both the'India's of spice and Myne
    Be where thou leftst them, or lie here with mee.
Aske for those Kings whom thou saw'st yesterday,
And thou shalt heare, All here in one bed lay.   20

24. For even in the beginning the candle signifying lifetime is a burned wick (is being put out).
26. *ideott:* one without sense (see l. 16).
THE SUNNE RISING.
  8. *offices:* duties.
  9. *all alike:* when the partners love in complete unity.
  17. *India's:* the East Indies (spices) and the West Indies (gold mines).

   She'is all States, and all Princes, I,
   Nothing else is.
Princes doe but play us; compar'd to this,
All honor's mimique; All wealth alchimie;
   Thou sunne art halfe as happy'as wee,   25
   In that the world's contracted thus.
 Thine age askes ease, and since thy duties bee
 To warme the world, that's done in warming us.
Shine here to us, and thou art every where;
This bed thy center is, these walls, thy spheare.   30

37 *The Indifferent.*

I can love both faire and browne,
Her whom abundance melts, and her whom want betraies,
Her who loves lonenesse best, and her who maskes and plaies,
Her whom the country form'd, and whom the town,
Her who beleeves, and her who tries,   5
Her who still weepes with spungie eyes,
And her who is dry corke, and never cries;
I can love her, and her, and you and you,
I can love any, so she be not true.

Will no other vice content you?   10
Wil it not serve your turn to do, as did your mothers?
Or have you all old vices spent, and now would finde out others?
Or doth a feare, that men are true, torment you?

 21. I am all Princes that rule over all the States (governments) which she is.
 24. *alchimie:* counterfeit.
 26. *thus:* into the narrow space of our bed.
 30. *spheare:* the sun's orbit around the earth (center) in the Ptolemaic system.
THE INDIFFERENT.
 1. *both . . . browne:* both those with blonde hair (considered beautiful) and brunettes.
 2. *her whom want betraies:* her who sells herself for money.
 5. Her who trusts her lover, and her who tests him.
 10. *no other vice:* than being true.

Oh we are not, be not you so,
Let mee, and doe you, twenty know.   15
Rob mee, but binde me not, and let me goe.
Must I, who came to travaile thorow you,
Grow your fixt subject, because you are true?

Venus heard me sigh this song,
And by Loves sweetest Part, Variety, she swore,   20
She heard not this till now; and that it should be so no more.
She went, examin'd, and return'd ere long,
And said, alas, Some two or three
Poore Heretiques in love there bee,
Which thinke to stablish dangerous constancie.   25
But I have told them, since you will be true,
You shall be true to them, who'are false to you.

38   *Loves Usury.*

For every houre that thou wilt spare mee now,
        I will allow,
Usurious God of Love, twenty to thee,
When with my browne, my gray haires equall bee;
Till then, Love, let my body raigne, and let   5
Mee travell, sojourne, snatch, plot, have, forget,
Resume my last yeares relict: thinke that yet
        We'had never met.

15. *know:* with sexual meaning (like "turn" and "do" in l. 11).
16. *Rob mee:* refers to the belief that sexual intercourse shortened the length of life.
17. *who . . . you:* (1) who was cursed to work through Eve's fall, (2) who was born through woman's labor pains, (3) who has passed from one affair to another, (4) who has been a tourist through your country (body). The last meaning is continued contrastingly in the next line when he protests becoming woman's "fixt subject."
LOVES USURY. See NOTES.
4. *haires:* see NOTES.
6. *snatch:* seize opportunities. The verbs carry sexual connotations: labor in sexual ecstasy, linger in intercourse, engage in a hasty sexual act, plot to seduce, possess carnally, and forget when intercourse is over.
7. *relict:* loved one, now discarded.

Let mee thinke any rivalls letter mine,
    And at next nine   10
Keepe midnights promise; mistake by the way
The maid, and tell the Lady'of that delay;
Onely let mee love none, no, not the sport;
From country grasse, to comfitures of Court,
Or cities quelque choses, let report   15
    My minde transport.

This bargaine's good; if when I'am old, I bee
    Inflam'd by thee,
If thine owne honour, or my shame, or paine,
Thou covet, most at that age thou shalt gaine.   20
Doe thy will then, then subject and degree,
And fruit of love, Love I submit to thee,
Spare mee till then, I'll beare it, though she bee
    One that loves mee.

39 *The Canonization.*

For Godsake hold your tongue, and let me love,
    Or chide my palsie, or my gout,
My five gray haires, or ruin'd fortune flout,
    With wealth your state, your minde with Arts improve,

9. *letter:* besides the note of assignation, Donne refers to a letter patent, which allowed a moneylender to engage in normally illegal activities.

10–11. *And . . . promise:* and at nine o'clock in the evening keep the rival's expected midnight visit. In addition, nine signifies the genitals; thus in stanzas one and two where promiscuity is emphasized there are nine requests each.

13. *not the sport:* neither the game of love nor lovemaking itself.

15. *report:* stories concerning simple country girls, confections from the Court, and dainty trifles from the city. Each noun refers to a different love-bed: grass, comfortable lounges, whatever is available.

21–22. *subject . . . love:* the person to be loved, the depth of that love, and the result of that love.

THE CANONIZATION. See NOTES.

3–4. Line 3 contrasts with l. 4: flout my hair, or improve your mind; flout my ruined fortune, or increase your wealth.

Take you a course, get you a place, 5
Observe his honour, or his grace,
Or the Kings reall, or his stamped face
Contemplate, what you will, approve,
So you will let me love.

Alas, alas, who's injur'd by my love? 10
What merchants ships have my sighs drown'd?
Who saies my teares have overflow'd his ground?
When did my colds a forward spring remove?
When did the heats which my veines fill
Adde one more, to the plaguie Bill? 15
Soldiers finde warres, and Lawyers finde out still
Litigious men, which quarrels move,
Though she and I do love.

Call us what you will, wee'are made such by love;
Call her one, mee another flye, 20
We'are Tapers too, and at our owne cost die,
And wee in us finde the'Eagle and the dove.
The Phœnix ridle hath more wit
By us, we two being one, are it.
So, to one neutrall thing both sexes fit. 25
Wee dye and rise the same, and prove
Mysterious by this love.

5. *a course:* a line of action leading to worldly achievement. *a place:* a job, a position; particularly, l. 6 indicates, a subservient one under a legal, political, or noble master.

6. Look either upon a judge or a cleric or a nobleman; treat (your master) with ceremonious honor or grace.

8. *Contemplate:* look upon and think about the king or his likeness on a coin; that is, be a courtier or a businessman who handles money. "Reall" also means "royal," a Spanish coin. *approve:* try out.

15. *the plaguie Bill:* the published list of deaths from the plague.

17. *which quarrels move:* who start quarrels.

20. *flye:* the taper-fly which burns itself to death by approaching a flame. It was considered hermaphroditic and resurrectable as A. B. Chambers relates in *JEGP,* LXV (1966).

21. *Tapers:* candles which diminish by burning, as the lovers shorten their lives by lovemaking (a popular belief).

22. *the'Eagle and the dove:* the powerful and the meek; righteousness and mercy. See NOTES.

23. *The Phœnix:* a fabulous, unique bird which contained both sexes and which was perpetuated from its own ashes.

25–27. "We, in coitus, become sexless ('neutrall'), for one sex cancels the other; our sexual drive dies and, like the Phoenix, we rise mysteriously two different sexes as we were before." See further, NOTES.

Wee can dye by it, if not live by love,
   And if unfit for tombes and hearse
Our legend bee, it will be fit for verse;   30
   And if no peece of Chronicle wee prove,
      We'll build in sonnets pretty roomes;
      As well a well wrought urne becomes
The greatest ashes, as halfe-acre tombes,
   And by these hymnes, all shall approve   35
   Us *Canoniz'd* for Love.

And thus invoke us; You whom reverend love
   Made one anothers hermitage;
You, to whom love was peace, that now is rage,
   Who did the whole worlds soule extract, and drove   40
      Into the glasses of your eyes
      So made such mirrors, and such spies,
That they did all to you epitomize,
   Countries, Townes, Courts: Beg from above
   A patterne of your love!   45

40   *The triple Foole.*

   I am two fooles, I know,
For loving, and for saying so
   In whining Poëtry;
But where's that wiseman, that would not be I,
   If she would not deny?   5

29. *hearse:* poetic tributes to the dead were pinned on the bier or hearse.
31. And if we are not recorded in history books because of our love; and if we do not beget such progeny as that recorded in 1 Chronicles i–ix.
32. *sonnets:* little songs.   *roomes:* places to hold our ashes and also stanzas (in Italian).
33. *becomes:* befits.
35. *approve:* confirm.
40. *drove:* that is, forced penetratingly into each other's eyes by their gazing at each other. The whole world was to be seen in the eyes of the lovers, for to them their love was the whole world.
44–45. As saints in the religion of love, ask the God of Love for a pattern of your love for us to follow.
THE TRIPLE FOOLE.
   triple: three implies completeness, thus he is the supreme or ultimate fool.

Then as th'earths inward narrow crooked lanes
Do purge sea waters fretfull salt away,
   I thought, if I could draw my paines,
Through Rimes vexation, I should them allay,
Griefe brought to numbers cannot be so fierce, 10
For, he tames it, that fetters it in verse.

   But when I have done so,
Some man, his art and voice to show,
   Doth Set and sing my paine,
And, by delighting many, frees againe 15
   Griefe, which verse did restraine.
To Love, and Griefe tribute of Verse belongs,
But not of such as pleases when 'tis read,
   Both are increased by such songs:
For both their triumphs so are published, 20
And I, which was two fooles, do so grow three;
Who are a little wise, the best fooles bee.

41 *Loves infinitenesse.*

If yet I have not all thy love,
Deare, I shall never have it all,
I cannot breath one other sigh, to move;
Nor can intreat one other teare to fall.
And all my treasure, which should purchase thee, 5
Sighs, teares, and oathes, and letters I have spent,
Yet no more can be due to mee,
Then at the bargaine made was ment,
If then thy gift of love were partiall,
That some to mee, some should to others fall, 10
   Deare, I shall never have Thee All.

10. *numbers:* verses.
   14. *Set:* set to music. Among the settings of his poems which have come down are those included in this edition.
LOVES INFINITENESSE. See NOTES.
   5. *purchase thee:* win thee over.

Or if then thou gavest mee all,
All was but All, which thou hadst then,
But if in thy heart, since, there be or shall,
New love created bee, by other men,   15
Which have their stocks intire, and can in teares,
In sighs, in oathes, and letters outbid mee,
This new love may beget new feares,
For, this love was not vowed by thee,
And yet it was, thy gift being generall,   20
The ground, thy heart is mine, what ever shall
    Grow there, deare, I should have it all.

Yet I would not have all yet,
Hee that hath all can have no more,
And since my love doth every day admit   25
New growth, thou shouldst have new rewards in store;
Thou canst not every day give me thy heart,
If thou canst give it, then thou never gavest it:
Loves riddles are, that though thy heart depart,
It stayes at home, and thou with losing savest it: 30
But wee will have a way more liberall,
Then changing hearts, to joyne them, so wee shall
    Be one, and one anothers All.

ANONYMOUS

Deer - est Love I doo not ___ goe, for wea - ri - ness of thee

or that ___ all the ___ world can shewe a ___ fit - ter love for me

But since that ___ I must _____ dye att last tis best to use my - - -

selfe in Jeast, thus ___ by fain - ed ___ Death _____ to Die.

(From MS 1018, f. 44b, with permission of St. Michael's College.)

    14. *since:* since that time.
    29. *riddles:* paradoxes.
    30. "For whosoever will save his life shall lose it; but whosoever shall lose his life for my sake and the gospel's, the same shall save it" (Mark viii 35).

42 *Song.*

Sweetest love, I do not goe,
   For wearinesse of thee,
Nor in hope the world can show
   A fitter Love for mee,
     But since that I   5
Must dye at last, 'tis best,
To use my selfe in jest
   Thus by fain'd deaths to dye;

Yesternight the Sunne went hence,
   And yet is here to day,   10
He hath no desire nor sense,
   Nor halfe so short a way:
     Then feare not mee,
But beleeve that I shall make
Speedier journeyes, since I take   15
   More wings and spurres then hee.

O how feeble is mans power,
   That if good fortune fall,
Cannot adde another houre,
   Nor a lost houre recall!   20
     But come bad chance,
And wee joyne to'it our strength,
And wee teach it art and length,
   It selfe o'r us to'advance.

SONG: "Sweetest love, I do not goe."
   Perhaps written when Donne went to the Continent with Sir Robert Drury
(July 1611).
   7. To become used to death by feigning to die in jest.
   23. *length:* longer life.
   26. Since a sigh was supposed to use up a drop of blood.
   27. *unkindly kinde:* kind one who by weeping is unkind to me.

When thou sigh'st, thou sigh'st not winde,   25
    But sigh'st my soule away,
When thou weep'st, unkindly kinde,
    My lifes blood doth decay.
      It cannot bee
That thou lov'st mee, as thou say'st,   30
If in thine my life thou waste,
    Thou art the best of mee.

Let not thy divining heart
    Forethinke me any ill,
Destiny may take thy part,   35
    And may thy feares fulfill,
      But thinke that wee
Are but turn'd aside to sleepe;
They who one another keepe
    Alive, ne'r parted bee.   40

43   *The Legacie.*

When I dyed last, and, Deare, I dye
    As often as from thee I goe,
    Though it be but an houre agoe,
And Lovers houres be full eternity,
I can remember yet, that I   5
    Something did say, and something did bestow;
Though I be dead, which sent mee, I should be
Mine owne executor and Legacie.

THE LEGACIE.

    1–6. The sense is: I die every time I leave you, though I am gone only an hour; even though a lover's hour is a full eternity, I can remember still that when I died last, I said and bestowed something.

    7–8. Though he is dead, he himself is what he would bestow, and he will act as the administrator of this legacy. He has died from his own decision to leave.

I heard mee say, Tell her anon,
   That my selfe, that is you, not I,   10
   Did kill me,'and when I felt mee dye,
I bid mee send my heart, when I was gone,
But I alas could there finde none,
   When I had ripp'd me,'and search'd where hearts should lye;
It kill'd mee'againe, that I who still was true,   15
In life, in my last Will should cozen you.

Yet I found something like a heart,
   But colours it, and corners had,
   It was not good, it was not bad,
It was intire to none, and few had part.   20
As good as could be made by art
   It seem'd, and therefore for our losses sad,
I meant to send this heart in stead of mine,
But oh, no man could hold it, for twas thine.

44 *A Feaver.*

Oh doe not die, for I shall hate
   All women so, when thou art gone,
That thee I shall not celebrate,
   When I remember, thou wast one.

But yet thou canst not die, I know;   5
   To leave this world behinde, is death,
But when thou from this world wilt goe,
   The whole world vapors with thy breath.

11. *Did kill me:* the poet dies because he leaves his loved one, but his self (his heart) is possessed by his loved one, and thus he kills himself by leaving her.

15–16. The poet dies again when he can not find his heart to bequeath to his loved one, for he would deceive her if he had no heart to give.

17–18. The vital organ which has kept him alive is something like a heart, but it is changeable (fickle) like color and imperfect (since only the circle and the sphere were perfect forms). Although no one else has possessed his heart, some few had received some of its affection in the past (l. 20).

22. *our losses sad:* their mutual loss of each other.

24. Even this seeming heart cannot be given, for it is his beloved's already.

A FEAVER.

5. Because you do not leave the world behind but rather remain as vapors (the soul of the world).

Or if, when thou, the worlds soule, goest,
　　It stay, tis but thy carkasse then,　　　　　　　　　10
The fairest woman, but thy ghost,
　　But corrupt wormes, the worthyest men.

O wrangling schooles, that search what fire
　　Shall burne this world, had none the wit
Unto this knowledge to aspire,　　　　　　　　　　15
　　That this her feaver might be it?

And yet she cannot wast by this,
　　Nor long beare this torturing wrong,
For much corruption needfull is
　　To fuell such a feaver long.　　　　　　　　　　20

These burning fits but meteors bee,
　　Whose matter in thee is soone spent.
Thy beauty,'and all parts, which are thee,
　　Are unchangeable firmament.

Yet t'was of my minde, seising thee,　　　　　　　25
　　Though it in thee cannot persever.
For I had rather owner bee
　　Of thee one houre, then all else ever.

9–12. The world will be the body that holds your soul; the fairest of women will be only a shadow of you, and the worthiest men only corrupt worms (inhabiting the dead carcass of the world).

13. *wrangling schooles:* the various philosophic groups (e.g. the Stoics, the Gnostics, the Patristic Fathers) believed the world would be destroyed by a great fire, but differed on its source and nature. However, they mainly disagreed not over means, but over date, tokens, and extent. They did not have the intelligence to realize that his loved one's fever might be that fire. Usually it was thought the final conflagration might occur from the sun's being too close to the earth, here implying the begetting of her fever by his love.

20. *to fuell:* to keep such a fever burning.

21. *meteors:* astronomical bodies whose heat is soon dissipated.

25. The world had the same idea as I, in trying to gain possession of you, even if for a short while.

45 *Aire and Angels.*

Twice or thrice had I loved thee,
Before I knew thy face or name;
So in a voice, so in a shapelesse flame,
Angells affect us oft, and worship'd bee;
   Still when, to where thou wert, I came,   5
Some lovely glorious nothing I did see,
    But since, my soule, whose child love is,
Takes limmes of flesh, and else could nothing doe,
    More subtile then the parent is,
Love must not be, but take a body too,   10
    And therefore what thou wert, and who
        I bid Love aske, and now
That it assume thy body, I allow,
And fixe it selfe in thy lip, eye, and brow.

Whilst thus to ballast love, I thought,   15
And so more steddily to have gone,
With wares which would sinke admiration,
I saw, I had loves pinnace overfraught,
    Ev'ry thy haire for love to worke upon
Is much too much, some fitter must be sought;   20
    For, nor in nothing, nor in things
Extreme, and scattring bright, can love inhere;

AIRE AND ANGELS.
    1. *thee:* an image which turned out to be you.
    6. *nothing:* that is, she is made of air, ethereal. Though like an angel, she has only the bodily form of one; see note, l. 24.
    8. *limmes of flesh:* his own body, but he emphasizes carnality.
    9. *subtile:* tenuous, airy.
    15. *to ballast:* to stabilize, but also to weigh down.
    16. *steddily:* that is, to avoid fickleness and inconstancy.
    18. *I saw:* this contrasts with "I thought" just as the actual woman contrasts with his image of her in l. 1.   *pinnace:* a light sailing vessel used as a tender to provision other ships, etc.
    22. *scattring bright:* nor in things which are radiantly bright (such as angels, which are shapeless flames). Love cannot become a fixed element in her body if it is nothing (only air) or too corporal (only human) or angelic. To work out of this difficulty, she is conceived in ll. 23–24 as being not an angel, but like an angel in taking its airy form, and as being more than nothing in taking on angelic form.

Then as an Angell, face, and wings
Of aire, not pure as it, yet pure doth weare,
  So thy love may be my loves spheare;   25
      Just such disparitie
As is twixt Aire and Angells puritie,
'Twixt womens love, and mens will ever bee.

46   *Breake of day.*

'Tis true, 'tis day, what though it be?
O wilt thou therefore rise from me?
Why should we rise, because 'tis light?
Did we lie downe, because 'twas night?
Love which in spight of darkness brought us hether,   5
Should in despight of light keepe us together.

Light hath no tongue, but is all eye;
If it could speake as well as spie,
This were the worst, that it could say,
That being well, I faine would stay,   10
And that I lov'd my heart and honor so,
That I would not from him, that had them, goe.

Must businesse thee from hence remove?
Oh, that's the worst disease of love,
The poore, the foule, the false, love can   15
Admit, but not the busied man.
He which hath businesse, and makes love, doth doe
Such wrong, as when a maryed man doth wooe.

---

24. *it:* the angel. Lines 23–24 read: Then as an angel doth wear face and
wings of air—face and wings not so pure as the angel itself is, but nevertheless
pure—so etc. As incorporeal beings, angels were purer than the air which they
took for body.
25. So thy love, which is pure air, may be the province (body, heaven) of my
love, which is as pure as an angel.
BREAKE OF DAY.
    The poem is spoken by a woman.
    18. That is, a married man makes love hurriedly with his wife because he
is supposed to (it is his business), not because he wants to. The couple are
obviously not married.

BREAKE OF DAY

WILLIAM CORKINE

T'is true,   t'is day,   what though it   be?   and will you there-fore rise _____ from me?   What will you rise,   what will you rise   be - cause tis   light?   Did we lye downe _____   be - cause twas _____   Night?   Love that in spight   of   dark - nesse brought us he - ther,   In spight of   Light should keepe us still   to - ge   -   ther,   In   spight of   Light should keepe   us   still _   to -   ge - ther.   In   spight   of   Light   should keepe   us   still   to - ge   -   -   ther.

(From Second Book of Ayres, f. B$_1$b, with permission of the Huntington Library.)

47   *The Prohibition.*

> Take heed of loving mee,
> At least remember, I forbade it thee;
> Not that I shall repaire my'unthrifty wast
> Of Breath and Blood, upon thy sighes, and teares,
> By being to thee then what to me thou wast;   5

THE PROHIBITION. See NOTES.
   1. *Take heed:* beware.
   4. *upon:* with.
   5. That is, cold.

But, so great Joy, our life at once outweares,
Then, least thy love, by my death, frustrate bee,
If thou love mee, take heed of loving mee.

      Take heed of hating mee,
Or too much triumph in the Victorie.   10
Not that I shall be mine owne officer,
And hate with hate againe retaliate;
But thou wilt lose the stile of conquerour,
If I, thy conquest, perish by thy hate.
Then, least my being nothing lessen thee,   15
If thou hate mee, take heed of hating mee.

      Yet, love and hate mee too,
So, these extreames shall neythers office doe;
Love mee, that I may die the gentler way;
Hate mee, because thy love'is too great for mee;   20
Or let these two, themselves, not me decay;
So shall I live thy Stage, not triumph bee;
Lest thou thy love and hate and mee undoe,
To let mee live, Oh love and hate mee too.

48   *The Anniversarie.*

   All Kings, and all their favorites,
   All glory'of honors, beauties, wits,
The Sun it selfe, which makes times, as they passe,
Is elder by a yeare, now, then it was
When thou and I first one another saw: 5

6. *so great Joy:* such great joy from mutual love.
10. That is, beware of exulting in your victory over me.
11. *officer:* officer of law (who might ask the penalty of an eye for an eye).
15. *lessen thee:* diminish your glory.
18. Shall not do their respective functions, since one cancels the other.
19. *gentler way:* both more gently than that described in stanza two, and through intercourse.
22. Thus alive I shall be the stage for your constant victorie, not, dead, your single triumph.
THE ANNIVERSARIE.
1-3. That is, hours, days, years are reckoned by the movement of the sun as the kings, favorites, glory grow older or expire.

All other things, to their destruction draw,
    Only our love hath no decay;
This, no to morrow hath, nor yesterday,
Running it never runs from us away,
But truly keepes his first, last, everlasting day.   10

    Two graves must hide thine and my coarse,
      If one might, death were no divorce.
Alas, as well as other Princes, wee,
(Who Prince enough in one another bee,)
Must leave at last in death, these eyes, and eares,   15
Oft fed with true oathes, and with sweet salt teares;
    But soules where nothing dwells but love
(All other thoughts being inmates) then shall prove
This, or a love increased there above,
When bodies to their graves, soules from their graves remove.   20

    And then wee shall be throughly blest,
      But wee no more, then all the rest.
Here upon earth, we'are Kings, and none but wee
Can be such Kings, nor of such subjects bee;
Who is so safe as wee? where none can doe   25
Treason to us, except one of us two.
    True and false feares let us refraine,
Let us love nobly,'and live, and adde againe
Yeares and yeares unto yeares, till we attaine
To write threescore, this is the second of our raigne.   30

18. *inmates:* temporary lodgers (as at an inn).
19. *This:* that death is no divorce. *there above:* in heaven.
22. *all the rest:* of those in heaven.
24. *such Kings:* in contrast with the temporal kings of l. 1, who with their favorites and glories pass on, and who are not safe from treason.
29–30. *till . . . threescore:* until we attain full (Biblical) life.
30. *this . . . raigne:* on earth, we have attained the second year of our reign as such kings (l. 24); in heaven, we shall begin our second lifetime as kings.

49 A *Valediction of my name, in the window.*

I.

My name engrav'd herein,
Doth contribute my firmnesse to this glasse,
  Which, ever since that charme, hath beene
  As hard, as that which grav'd it, was;
Thine eye will give it price enough, to mock   5
    The diamonds of either rock.

II.

  'Tis much that Glasse should bee
As all confessing, and through-shine as I,
  'Tis more, that it shewes thee to thee,
  And cleare reflects thee to thine eye.   10
But all such rules, loves magique can undoe,
    Here you see mee, and I am you.

III.

  As no one point, nor dash,
Which are but accessaries to this name,
  The showers and tempests can outwash,   15
  So shall all times finde mee the same;
You this intirenesse better may fulfill,
    Who have the patterne with you still.

A VALEDICTION OF MY NAME, IN THE WINDOW.
    3. *charme:* magical happening, magical decoration. See further, NOTES.
    4. *it:* a diamond.
    6. All the diamonds known to man (those from old rock and those from new rock) as D. C. Allen shows in *MLN*, LX (1945), 54–55.
    8. *through-shine:* transparent.
    12. Because she sees his name and because she sees herself reflected where his name is.
    17–18. You may better achieve this completeness by always having the pattern with you (see ll. 31–32 and n.).
    18. *patterne:* the original from which the name was engraved (both the signature and the man himself—image or his picture).

IV.

Or if too hard and deepe
This learning be, for a scratch'd name to teach,   20
   It, as a given deaths head keepe,
   Lovers mortalitie to preach,
Or thinke this ragged bony name to bee
    My ruinous Anatomie.

V.

Then, as all my soules bee,   25
Emparadis'd in you, (in whom alone
   I understand, and grow and see,)
   The rafters of my body, bone
Being still with you, the Muscle, Sinew,'and Veine,
    Which tile this house, will come againe.   30

VI.

Till my returne, repaire
And recompact my scatter'd body so.
   As all the vertuous powers which are
   Fix'd in the starres, are said to flow
Into such characters, as graved bee   35
    When these starres have supremacie:

21. *deaths head:* a *memento mori* which he has given her.
23. *ragged bony:* "ragged" because the name is composed of a number of rounded letters, difficult to engrave in glass; "bony" because his usual signature was "Jo: Donne" with an underscoring (note the "point" and "dash" of l. 13) and a capital "D" about the same size as the last four letters and looking something like a T-bone.
24. *My ruinous Anatomie:* my body which shows the ravages of time (being ill-clothed and thin). He seems at this time to be lacking in mental and physical strength and vitality (ll. 28–30).
25. *my soules:* my rational, vegetative, sensitive souls (corresponding to rafters, muscle and sinew, vein of ll. 28–29).
28. *rafters:* the outward supports (the senses) of the roof (the head). Four was the number of the body, three of the soul; together (ll. 31–32) they will create eternity for the lovers (compare *Legacie,* l. 4).
30. *tile:* the muscle, sinew, and vein furnish the building material of the body.
32. *so:* by keeping the pattern with you always (see notes to ll. 17–18).
36. *have supremacie:* are shining forth.

VII.

So since this name was cut
When love and griefe their exaltation had,
   No doore 'gainst this names influence shut,
    As much more loving, as more sad,   40
'Twill make thee; and thou shouldst, till I returne,
      Since I die daily, daily mourne.

VIII.

When thy'inconsiderate hand
Flings ope this casement, with my trembling name,
   To looke on one, whose wit or land,   45
    New battry to thy heart may frame,
Then thinke this name alive, and that thou thus
      In it offendst my Genius.

IX.

And when thy melted maid,
Corrupted by thy Lover's gold, and page,   50
   His letter at thy pillow'hath laid,
    Disputed it, and tam'd thy rage,
And thou begin'st to thaw towards him, for this,
      May my name step in, and hide his.

38. His leaving was a time of grief at separation and a time of manifest love.
Thus the engraved name holds both emotions.
    39. Compare with the opening of the casement (l. 44).
    42. Thus she is asked to show only the greater sadness, not the greater lov-
ingness; that is, to remain faithful (compare stanza eight). *die:* from grief at
being parted from her.
    46. *battry:* amorous assault.
    48. *Genius:* protecting spirit.
    49. *melted:* softened up.
    50. *page:* male servant, who joins her maid in doing the lover's bidding.
    52. *Disputed it:* debated whether to resist or succumb. It is the maid and page
who dispute it to the woman and then tame her rage at the suggestion.

X.

And if this treason goe   55
To'an overt act, and that thou write againe;
   In superscribing, this name flow
   Into thy fancy, from the pane.
So, in forgetting thou remembrest right,
     And unaware to mee shalt write.   60

XI.

But glasse, and lines must bee,
No meanes our firme substantiall love to keepe;
   Neere death inflicts this lethargie,
   And this I murmure in my sleepe;
Impute this idle talke, to that I goe,   65
     For dying men talke often so.

50   *The Autumnall.*

No *Spring*, nor *Summer* Beauty hath such grace,
   As I have seen in one *Autumnall* face,
Yong *Beauties* force our love, and that's a *Rape*,
   This doth but *counsaile*, yet you cannot scape.

If t'were a *shame* to love, here t'were no *shame*,   5
   Affection here takes *Reverences* name.
Were her first yeares the *Golden Age;* That's true,
   But now shee's *gold* oft tried, and ever new.

56. *overt act:* in distinction from her treason of intent in l. 53.   *write againe:* write back to him.

57. *this name flow:* may this name flow.

63. *lethargie:* forgetfulness.

65. *to that I goe:* to that I am going away.

66. Donne plays upon the symbolic death which absence causes and on the apparent fact that he is very ill and near death.

THE AUTUMNALL. See NOTES.

4. *counsaile:* recommend.   *scape:* escape.

7. *the Golden Age:* like the earliest age of the world when all was happiness and peace.

8. *tried:* tested.

That was her torrid and inflaming time,
    This is her tolerable *Tropique clyme*.   10
Faire eyes, who askes more heate then comes from hence,
    He in a fever wishes pestilence.

Call not these wrinkles, *graves;* If *graves* they were,
    They were *Loves graves;* for else he is no where.
Yet lies not Love *dead* here, but here doth sit   15
    Vow'd to this trench, like an *Anachorit*.

And here, till hers, which must be his *death*, come,
    He doth not digge a *Grave*, but build a *Tombe*.
Here dwells he, though he sojourne ev'ry where,
    In *Progresse*, yet his standing house is here.   20

Here, where still *Evening* is; not *noone*, nor *night;*
    Where no *voluptuousnesse*, yet all delight.
In all her words, unto all hearers fit,
    You may at *Revels*, you at *counsaile*, sit.

This is loves timber, youth his under-wood;   25
    There he, as wine in *June*, enrages blood,
Which then comes seasonabliest, when our tast
    And appetite to other things, is past.

Xerxes strange *Lydian* love, the *Platane* tree,
    Was lov'd for age, none being so large as shee,   30
Or else because, being yong, nature did blesse
    Her youth with ages glory, *Barrennesse*.

If we love things long sought, *Age* is a thing
    Which we are fifty yeares in compassing.
If transitory things, which soone decay,   35
    Age must be lovelyest at the latest day.

10. *tolerable Tropique clyme:* temperate zone (Tropic of Cancer).
12. He, mad, wishes death.
13. *graves:* deep engravings. As "Love's graves," they became the resting places of the God of Love.
16. *Anachorit:* one who is a recluse to devote himself to his god.
20. *Progresse:* with added meaning of an official journey as of a king.
24. *sit:* by her talking about you.
25. *under-wood:* small, young trees or brush in contrast to seasoned wood.
29. Xerxes, King of Persia, had a plane tree in Lydia ornamented with gold, guarded from theft. It bore no fruit; thus it was "barren."

But name not *Winter-faces,* whose skin's slacke;
   Lanke, as an unthrifts purse; but a soules sacke;
Whose *Eyes* seeke light within, for all here's shade;
   Whose *mouthes* are holes, rather worne out, then made;   40
Whose every tooth to'a severall place is gone,
   To vexe their soules at *Resurrection;*

Name not these living *Deaths-heads* unto mee,
   For these, not *Ancient,* but *Antique* be;
I hate extreames; yet I had rather stay   45
   With *Tombs,* then *Cradles,* to weare out a day.

Since such loves naturall lation is, may still
   My love descend, and journey downe the hill,
Not panting after growing beauties, so,
   I shall ebbe out with them, who home-ward goe.   50

51   *Twicknam garden.*

Blasted with sighs, and surrounded with teares,
   Hither I come to seeke the spring,
   And at mine eyes, and at mine eares,
Receive such balmes, as else cure every thing,
   But O, selfe traytor, I do bring   5
The spider love, which transubstantiates all,
   And can convert Manna to gall,
And that this place may thoroughly be thought
   True Paradise, I have the serpent brought.

41. *severall:* different.
43. *Deaths-heads: mementi mori,* reminders of death.
47. *lation:* motion. "Such" is subject of "is."
48. *hill:* of life.
TWICKNAM GARDEN. See NOTES.
  1. *surrounded:* overflowing.
  6. *spider:* poisonous. *transubstantiates:* changes the substance of.
  7. *Manna to gall:* that which is sweet to that which is bitter; that which nourishes to that which vexes. Thus he betrays himself, for his love of the Countess will change her affection for him to dislike.
  9. *serpent:* Satan, evil, temptation, envy.

'Twere wholsomer for mee, that winter did   10
  Benight the glory of this place,
  And that a grave frost did forbid
These trees to laugh and mocke mee to my face;
  But that I may not this disgrace
Indure, nor leave this garden, Love let mee   15
  Some senslesse peece of this place bee;
Make me a mandrake, so I may groane here,
  Or a stone fountaine weeping out my yeare.

Hither with christall vyals, lovers come,
  And take my teares, which are loves wine,   20
  And try your mistresse Teares at home,
For all are false, that tast not just like mine;
  Alas, hearts do not in eyes shine,
Nor can you more judge womans thoughts by teares,
  Then by her shadow, what she weares.   25
O perverse sexe, where none is true but shee,
  Who's therefore true, because her truth kills mee.

52 *Valediction of the booke.*

I'll tell thee now (deare Love) what thou shalt doe
  To anger destiny, as she doth us,
  How I shall stay, though she Esloygne me thus
And how posterity shall know it too;

10. *wholsomer:* more spiritually and mentally healthful. The paradox rests on spring's being the period of inspiration and verdure and winter's being the period of ill health and barrenness. *that:* if.

12. *grave:* heavy, deathly.

16. *senslesse:* insensible.

18. *weeping:* again referring to his tears (l. 1). The mandrake was supposed to groan when uprooted, paralleling the sighs of l. 1.

21. *try:* test (by comparison with his from the fountain).

26–27. O perverse sex, where none is faithful and honest except her who is faithful by being perverse toward me; she is perverse because her faithfulness to her husband kills me.

VALEDICTION OF THE BOOKE.

3. *Esloygne me:* take me away.

How thine may out-endure   5
Sybills glory, and obscure
Her who from Pindar could allure,
And her, through whose helpe *Lucan* is not lame,
And her, whose booke (they say) *Homer* did finde, and name.

Study our manuscripts, those Myriades   10
Of letters, which have past twixt thee and mee,
Thence write our Annals, and in them will bee
To all whom loves subliming fire invades,
Rule and example found;
There, the faith of any ground   15
No schismatique will dare to wound,
That sees, how Love this grace to us affords,
To make, to keep, to use, to be these his Records.

This Booke, as long-liv'd as the elements,
Or as the worlds forme, this all-graved tome   20
In cypher writ, or new made Idiome;
Wee for loves clergie only'are instruments,
When this booke is made thus,
Should againe the ravenous
Vandals and Goths inundate us,   25
Learning were safe; in this our Universe
Schooles might learne Sciences, Spheares Musick, Angels Verse.

6. *Sybills:* probably the Cumaean Sibyl, who aided Aeneas in his descent to Hell.

7. *Her:* Corinna the Boetian, who taught Pindar to write but who defeated him five times in poetic contests. *who . . . allure:* who could allure (draw away) glory from Pindar.

8. *her:* Polla Argentaria, who helped her husband revise the first three books of *Pharsalia*. Perhaps the lameness refers to the weak, plodding quality of some of the writing; there is a noticeable change in tone in the later books.

9. *her:* probably Phantasia of Memphis, who composed an epic poem on the siege of Troy; the name assigned by Homer, of course, was *The Iliad*. Just as the four references had been inspirational, so the woman has also inspired the poet to write "those Myriades of letters."

13. *subliming:* purifying; sublimation converted a solid (man) into a vapor (ethereal being) by heat (passion), and then reconverted that into a purer solid than the original by cooling (abatement of passion).

15. *ground:* fundamental rule or example.

20. *tome:* punning on the word "tomb" which is "all-graved" and "long-lived."

21. Written in code or newly devised expression (since they themselves are Love's Records, l. 18).

22. We are documents to be understood only by those who are ministers of love.

25. *Vandals and Goths:* barbarian invaders of Rome. *inundate:* overwhelm and annihilate us through putting out "loves subliming fire."

Here Loves Divines, (since all Divinity
  Is love or wonder) may finde all they seeke,
  Whether abstract spirituall love they like,   30
Their Soules exhal'd with what they do not see,
     Or loth so to amuze
     Faiths infirmitie, they chuse
     Something which they may see and use;
  For, though minde be the heaven, where love doth sit,   35
Beauty'a convenient type may be to figure it.

Here more then in their bookes may Lawyers finde,
  Both by what titles Mistresses are ours,
  And how prerogative these states devours,
Transferr'd from Love himselfe, to womankinde.   40
     Who though from heart, and eyes,
     They exact great subsidies,
     Forsake him who on them relies
  And for the cause, honour, or conscience give,
Chimeraes, vaine as they, or their prerogative.   45

Here Statesmen, (or of them, they which can reade,)
  May of their occupation finde the grounds,
  Love and their art alike it deadly wounds,
If to consider what 'tis, one proceed,
     In both they doe excell   50
     Who the present governe well,
     Whose weaknesse none doth, or dares tell;
  In this thy booke, such will their nothing see,
As in the Bible some can finde out Alchimy.

31. *exhal'd with:* filled out with the spirit of.
32. *amuze:* beguile.
36. Beauty may be a convenient symbol to represent it.
38. *titles:* legal claims for ownership.
39. And how the right of lordship to collect rents eats up these estates.
44–45. And as their reason, they cite honor or conscience, which are imaginary fancies, as empty as they or their prerogative.
47. *grounds:* principles.
48. *art:* politics. *it:* examination (l. 49).
50. *both:* love and politics.
51. As opposed to preparing for the future. Opportunists in love and politics are intended.
53. *such . . . see:* such people will see their hollowness.
54. *finde out:* show the falsity of.

Thus vent thy thoughts; abroad I'll studie thee,   55
   As he removes farre off, that great heights takes;
   How great love is, presence best tryall makes,
But absence tryes how long this love will bee;
      To take a latitude
      Sun, or starres, are fitliest view'd   60
      At their brightest, but to conclude
Of longitudes, what other way have wee,
But to marke when, and where the darke eclipses bee?

53 *Communitie.*

Good wee must love, and must hate ill,
For ill is ill, and good good still,
   But there are things indifferent,
Which wee may neither hate, nor love,
But one, and then another prove,   5
   As wee shall finde our fancy bent.

If then at first wise Nature had
Made women either good or bad,
   Then some wee might hate, and some chuse,
But since shee did them so create,   10
That we may neither love, nor hate,
   Onely this rests, All, all may use.

56. Like one who moves away from his object of study in order to determine its height.
58. *tryes:* tests.
59–63. The images of latitude and longitude are employed because the lovers will be at different geographic places. They can symbolically graph each other's love by determining latitude, which depends on their love (the brightness of the heavenly bodies) and by determining longitude, which depends on their grief (the dark eclipses). (Compare *Valediction of my name, in the window,* No. 49, stanzas 6 and 7.)
COMMUNITIE.
  Communitie: referring to the similar or common character of all women, who are neither bad nor good.
  2. *still:* always.
  5. *prove:* test.
  12. Only this is left to decide the question: all men may test all women sexually to determine whether they are good or bad.

If they were good it would be seene,
Good is as visible as greene,
    And to all eyes it selfe betrayes: 15
If they were bad, they could not last,
Bad doth it selfe, and others wast,
    So, they deserve nor blame, nor praise.

But they are ours as fruits are ours,
He that but tasts, he that devours,   20
    And he that leaves all, doth as well:
Chang'd loves are but chang'd sorts of meat,
And when hee hath the kernell eate,
    Who doth not fling away the shell?

54 *Loves growth.*

I scarce beleeve my love to be so pure
    As I had thought it was,
    Because it doth endure
Vicissitude, and season, as the grasse;
Me thinkes I lyed all winter, when I swore,   5
My love was infinite, if spring make'it more.
But if this medicine, love, which cures all sorrow
With more, not onely bee no quintessence,
But mixt of all stuffes, paining soule, or sense,
And of the Sunne his working vigour borrow,   10

14. *as greene:* as the greenness of living things of nature. If women are good, they are naturally good; they would have been imbued with good by God, who has imbued vegetation with green.
21. *doth as well:* each doth equally well. Some women should be "tasted," some should be fully loved, some should be shunned.
22–24. Women are like the fruits of nature (nutmeats): when man changes his mistress, it is like eating a different nutmeat for variety, and when he has savored what she has to offer, he casts her body aside.
LOVES GROWTH.
8. *quintessence:* the fifth element of life (ether), pure and separate from the other elements. Love is not only not pure, distinct and ethereal; it is a mixture of all things ("elemented," l. 13) that cause pain.
10. Thus stronger in spring than in winter.

Love's not so pure, and abstract, as they use
To say, which have no Mistresse but their Muse,
But as all else, being elemented too,
Love sometimes would contemplate, sometimes do.

And yet no greater, but more eminent,   15
   Love by the spring is growne;
     As, in the firmament,
Starres by the Sunne are not inlarg'd, but showne,
Gentle love deeds, as blossomes on a bough,
From loves awaken'd root do bud out now.   20
If, as in water stir'd more circles bee
Produc'd by one, love such additions take,
Those like to many spheares, but one heaven make,
For, they are all concentrique unto thee,
And though each spring doe adde to love new heate,   25
As princes doe in times of action get
New taxes, and remit them not in peace,
No winter shall abate the springs encrease.

55   *Loves exchange.*

Love, any devill else but you,
Would for a given Soule give something too.
At Court your fellowes every day,
Give th'art of Riming, Huntsmanship, and play,
For them who were their owne before;   5
Onely'I have nothing which gave more,
But am, alas, by being lowly, lower.

14. Love sometimes would contemplate how it would use its working vigor; sometimes it would actually employ it. Complex things both think and do; love is both platonic and physical.
15. *eminent:* conspicuous.
18. *showne:* made to seem larger.
24. You are the center around which the spheres of "gentle love deeds" circumfuse, like the sun around which the heavenly spheres revolve. Each group constitutes but one heaven.
26. *times of action:* war or similar financial emergencies.
LOVES EXCHANGE.
2. *given:* both "particular" and "given over" to love.
3. *your fellowes:* fellow devils.
6. Only I, who gave more than the followers of your fellow devils, have received nothing.

I aske no dispensation now
To falsifie a teare, or sigh, or vow,
I do not sue from thee to draw   10
A *non obstante* on natures law,
These are prerogatives, they inhere
In thee and thine; none should forsweare
Except that hee *Loves* minion were.

Give mee thy weaknesse, make mee blinde,   15
Both wayes, as thou and thine, in eies and minde;
Love, let me never know that this
Is love, or, that love childish is.
Let me not know that others know
That she knowes my paine, least that so   20
A tender shame make me mine owne new woe.

If thou give nothing, yet thou'art just,
Because I would not thy first motions trust;
Small townes which stand stiffe, till great shot
Enforce them, by warres law *condition* not.   25
Such in loves warfare is my case,
I may not article for grace,
Having put love at last to shew this face.

This face, by which he could command
And change the'Idolatrie of any land,   30
This face, which wheresoe'r it comes,
Can call vow'd men from cloisters, dead from tombes,
And melt both Poles at once, and store
Deserts with cities, and make more
Mynes in the earth, then Quarries were before.   35

8. *now:* now that my soul has been given to you. He asks no dispensation
because now, truly in love, he does not wish to falsify.
    11. *non obstante:* an edict whereby a law was abrogated and its violation
authorized.
    14. *minion:* agent.
    24–25. By the law of war, small towns which hold out against siege until
heavy attack subdues them cannot set conditions of surrender.
    28. *put:* forced.   *this face:* both "this attitude of love" and "the face of my
love" (as in the next stanza).
    32. *vow'd men:* refers to the religious vow of celibacy.

For this, love is enrag'd with mee,
Yet kills not; if I must example bee
To future Rebells; If th'unborne
Must learne, by my being cut up, and torne:
Kill, and dissect me, Love; for this   40
Torture against thine owne end is,
Rack't carcasses make ill Anatomies.

56 *Confined Love.*

Some man unworthy to'be possessor
Of old or new love, himselfe being false or weake,
  Thought his paine and shame would be lesser,
If on womankind he might his anger wreake,
      And thence a law did grow,   5
      One should but one man know;
      But are other creatures so?

Are Sunne, Moone, or Starres by law forbidden,
To'smile where they list, or lend away their light?
  Are birds divorc'd, or are they chidden   10
If they leave their mate, or lie abroad a night?
      Beasts doe no joyntures lose
      Though they new lovers choose,
      But we'are made worse then those.

Who'e'r rigg'd faire ship to lie in harbors,   15
And not to seeke new lands, or not to deale withall?
  Or built faire houses, set trees, and arbors,
Only to'lock up, or else to let them fall?

36. *For this:* For having held out against love.
39. Refers to Orpheus, who was torn to pieces by sexually frenzied Thracian
women, devotees of Dionysius, because he resisted their advances; his dismem-
bered head floated down the Hebrus to the island of Lesbos.
42. Bodies tortured by the rack make poor objects for dissection. Also, referring to the visual effects on man of the torments of love.
CONFINED LOVE.
6. One man is allowed to know only one love. The line indicates that the
speaker is a woman.
11. *a night:* perhaps "at night," perhaps "for a night."
16. *deale:* trade. The ship was a commonplace image for prostitution.

Good is not good, unlesse
A thousand it possesse,   20
But doth wast with greedinesse.

57   *The Dreame.*

Deare love, for nothing lesse then thee
Would I have broke this happy dreame,
        It was a theame
For reason, much too strong for phantasie,
Therefore thou wakd'st me wisely; yet   5
My Dreame thou brok'st not, but continued'st it,
Thou art so truth, that thoughts of thee suffice,
To make dreames truths; and fables histories;
Enter these armes, for since thou thoughtst it best,
Not to dreame all my dreame, let's act the rest.   10

As lightning, or a Tapers light,
Thine eyes, and not thy noise wak'd mee;
        Yet I thought thee
(For thou lovest truth) an Angell, at first sight,
But when I saw thou sawest my heart,   15
And knew'st my thoughts, beyond an Angels art,
When thou knew'st what I dreamt, when thou knew'st when
Excesse of joy would wake me, and cam'st then,
I doe confesse, it could not chuse but bee
Prophane, to thinke thee any thing but thee.   20

21. *wast:* waste away.
THE DREAME.
  4. *reason:* thought when awake.
  7. *so:* such. "Truth" here probably includes "fidelity" and "constancy," though even this is part of the dream.
  10. *act:* pointing to the fact that it is nevertheless part of a dream. Some MSS less effectively give "do."
  16. According to Aquinas angels could not read one's thoughts.
  19–20. Paradoxically, though it is profane to call a human a celestial being, here it is profane to call his loved one anything but herself.

Comming and staying show'd thee, thee,
But rising makes me doubt, that now,
    Thou art not thou.
That love is weake, where feare's as strong as hee;
'Tis not all spirit, pure, and brave,   25
If mixture it of *Feare, Shame, Honor,* have;
Perchance as torches which must ready bee,
Men light and put out, so thou deal'st with mee,
Thou cam'st to kindle, goest to come; Then I
Will dreame that hope againe, but else would die.   30

58 *A Valediction of weeping.*

    Let me powre forth
My teares before thy face, whil'st I stay here,
For thy face coines them, and thy stampe they beare,
And by this Mintage they are something worth,
    For thus they bee   5
    Pregnant of thee;
Fruits of much griefe they are, emblemes of more,
When a teare falls, that thou falls which it bore,
So thou and I are nothing then, when on a divers shore.

    On a round ball   10
A workeman that hath copies by, can lay
An Europe, Afrique, and an Asia,
And quickly make that, which was nothing, *All,*

  21. *show'd thee, thee:* showed you to be yourself.
  22. *doubt:* fear.
  27–28. You light me and put me out as men do torches, but I must be ready when you do kindle me (make me impassioned).
  29. You came and kindled me; then you leave to come again to rekindle me. The rekindling is necessary because the dream has been broken. However, there is a sexual pun on the word "come," as in "comming," l. 21, and "rising," l. 22.
  30. *else would die:* both "if I were not able to dream of you, I would die" and "although I would rather have intercourse."
A VALEDICTION OF WEEPING.
  3. *coines:* causes them to be.
  8. *that thou:* "that" is a demonstrative adjective modifying "thou"; his tear which was pregnant with "thee" has given birth by letting "that thou" fall.
  9. *So:* he because his tears can no longer be coined and only they are valuable, and she because without his tears she cannot be born.
  11. *lay:* perhaps "paste" or "draw."
  13. *nothing:* because of the resemblance of the shape of a tear to a zero.

So doth each teare,
Which thee doth weare,   15
A globe, yea world by that impression grow,
Till thy teares mixt with mine doe overflow
This world, by waters sent from thee, my heaven dissolved so.

O more then Moone,
Draw not up seas to drowne me in thy spheare,   20
Weepe me not dead, in thine armes, but forbeare
To teach the sea, what it may doe too soone;
Let not the winde
Example finde,
To doe me more harme, then it purposeth;   25
Since thou and I sigh one anothers breath,
Who e'r sighes most, is cruellest, and hasts the others death.

59 *Loves Alchymie.*

Some that have deeper digg'd loves Myne then I,
Say, where his centrique happinesse doth lie:
I'have lov'd, and got, and told,
But should I love, get, tell, till I were old,
I should not finde that hidden mysterie;   5
Oh, 'tis imposture all:
And as no chymique yet th'Elixar got,
But glorifies his pregnant pot,

16. *yea world:* more than just a blank globe, a world, because it bears her impression (like a country).
16–17. My tears continue creating worlds with your impressions on them until you begin to cry with me here ("This world," l. 18) where we are parting.
18. *by waters . . . so:* as a result of your tears, my happiness melted into tears.
19. *more then Moone:* not just a satellite of the world, but the world itself.
20. *spheare:* presence.
LOVES ALCHYMIE.
2. *centrique happinesse:* the center of love's happiness; for man, woman's genitals. Indirectly, Donne contrasts ethereal and intellectual love with earthly and sexual love, with graphic reference to coitus.
7. *chymique:* alchemist. *Elixar:* a substance which transmutes base metals to gold. The import is: the love that "I" have dug from the mine of l. 1 is base,

    If by the way to him befall
Some odoriferous thing, or medicinall,   10
    So, lovers dreame a rich and long delight,
    But get a winter-seeming summers night.

Our ease, our thrift, our honor, and our day,
Shall we, for this vaine Bubles shadow pay?
    Ends love in this, that my man,   15
Can be as happy'as I can; If he can
Endure the short scorne of a Bridegroomes play?
    That loving wretch that sweares,
'Tis not the bodies marry, but the mindes,
    Which he in her Angelique findes,   20
    Would sweare as justly, that he heares,
In that dayes rude hoarse minstralsey, the spheares.
    Hope not for minde in women; at their best,
    Sweetnesse, and wit they'are, but, *Mummy,* possest.

60   *The Flea.*

Marke but this flea, and marke in this,
How little that which thou deny'st me is;
It suck'd me first, and now sucks thee,
And in this flea, our two bloods mingled bee;
Thou know'st that this cannot be said   5
A sinne, nor shame, nor losse of maidenhead,
    Yet this enjoyes before it wooe,
    And pamper'd swells with one blood made of two,
    And this, alas, is more then wee would doe.

---

not "gold," and no elixir to transmute it has been found. The elixir of life was to be a panacea for all ills of the flesh.
    12. *winter-seeming summers night:* cold, short night.
    17. "Endure the brief mockery of a wedding ceremony" and "Endure the short-lived disdain accompanying intercourse."
    22. *dayes:* wedding day's. *the spheares:* the music of the spheres.
    24. *Mummy:* body without mind; and a drug prepared from a mummified body, supposedly healing and life-giving. See further, NOTES.
THE FLEA.
    2. *deny'st me:* she has not yielded to his advances.
    4. Thus there is a trinity within the flea; three works throughout the poem as a symbol of "all in one." The three anatomical sections of the flea—abdomen, thorax, and legs—should perhaps be recalled also.

Oh stay, three lives in one flea spare,   10
Where wee almost, yea more then maryed are.
This flea is you and I, and this
Our mariage bed, and mariage temple is;
Though parents grudge, and you, w'are met,
And cloysterd in these living walls of Jet.   15
   Though use make you apt to kill mee,
   Let not to that, selfe murder added bee,
   And sacrilege, three sinnes in killing three.

Cruell and sodaine, hast thou since
Purpled thy naile, in blood of innocence?   20
Wherein could this flea guilty bee,
Except in that drop which it suckt from thee?
Yet thou triumph'st, and saist that thou
Find'st not thy selfe, nor mee the weaker now;
   'Tis true, then learne how false, feares bee;   25
   Just so much honor, when thou yeeld'st to mee,
   Will wast, as this flea's death tooke life from thee.

61   *The Curse.*

Who ever guesses, thinks, or dreames he knowes
Who is my mistris, wither by this curse;
   His only,'and only'his purse
   May some dull heart to love dispose,

16. *kill me:* referring perhaps to her coldness, perhaps to the sexual meaning of "die."
18. *sacrilege:* since the flea is a temple. *sinnes:* that is, should she kill the flea.
THE CURSE.
   Triads are used throughout because three was the number of superstition. Likewise there are five curses each in stanzas one and two, and seven curses each in stanzas three and four because of the magic charms and conjuring of devils which cluster around those numbers.
   4. "May some listless woman incline (be disposed) to love only his money and no one else's money"; that is, let the one who tries to identify the poet's mistress have an unexciting mistress who gives herself to him to acquire his money but who gives herself freely to others. There is also a sexual pun on the word "wither."

And shee yeeld then to all that are his foes;   5
   May he be scorn'd by one, whom all else scorne,
   Forsweare to others, what to her he'hath sworne,
   With feare of missing, shame of getting torne:

Madnesse his sorrow, gout his cramp, may hee
Make, by but thinking, who hath made him such: 10
     And may he feele no touch
     Of conscience, but of fame, and bee
Anguish'd, not that 'twas sinne, but that 'twas shee:
   In early and long scarcenesse may he rot,
   For land which had been his, if he had not   15
   Himselfe incestuously an heire begot:

May he dreame Treason, and beleeve, that hee
Meant to performe it, and confesse, and die,
     And no record tell why:
     His sonnes, which none of his may bee,   20
Inherite nothing but his infamie:
   Or may he so long Parasites have fed,
   That he would faine be theirs, whom he hath bred,
   And at the last be circumcis'd for bread:

The venom of all stepdames, gamsters gall,   25
What Tyrans, and their subjects interwish,
     What Plants, Mynes, Beasts, Foule, Fish,
     Can contribute, all ill which all
Prophets, or Poets spake; And all which shall
   Be'annex'd in schedules unto this by mee,   30
   Fall on that man; For if it be a shee
   Nature before hand hath out-cursed mee.

6. By a woman, whom all other women scorn.
8. Torn between fear of not winning her and shame of winning her.
9. *gout his cramp:* with sexual implication.
12. *fame:* notoriousness.
14. *scarcenesse:* poverty.
15–16. Done himself out of his inheritance by begetting a child incestuously who through the woman would have prior claim.
19. No record restore his reputation, erroneously damaged.
23. *whom he hath bred:* both his sons, who in later life might take care of him, and something like maggots breeding from a decaying carcass (because of disease or reduction of wealth).
24. Become a Jew in order to obtain sustenance, since proverbially Jews, the moneylenders of London, were miserly.
25. *gamsters:* both "gamblers'" and "lewd persons'."
30. *schedules:* documents, codicils.
31. *a shee:* that is, who tries to guess the identity of the poet's mistress.

62 *The Extasie.*

Where, like a pillow on a bed,
    A Pregnant banke swel'd up, to rest
The violets reclining head,
    Sat we two, one anothers best;

Our hands were firmely cimented   5
    With a fast balme, which thence did spring,
Our eye-beames twisted, and did thred
    Our eyes, upon one double string,

So to'entergraft our hands, as yet
    Was all the meanes to make us one,   10
And pictures in our eyes to get
    Was all our propagation.

As 'twixt two equall Armies, Fate
    Suspends uncertaine victorie,
Our soules, (which to advance their state,   15
    Were gone out,) hung 'twixt her, and mee.

And whil'st our soules negotiate there,
    Wee like sepulchrall statues lay;
All day, the same our postures were,
    And wee said nothing, all the day.   20

If any, so by love refin'd,
    That he soules language understood,
And by good love were growen all minde,
    Within convenient distance stood,

THE EXTASIE.

    Extasie: Christian mystics used this term for a state of extreme and abnormal awareness. See further, NOTES.
    4. *one anothers best:* each was the other's best pillow.
    6. *fast:* firmly stuck. *which thence did spring:* which balm (perspiration) sprang from our hands.
    9. *entergraft:* unite by mutual grafting, a horticultural method of propagation of a species by inserting a shoot of a plant into a stem or root.
    9–10. *as . . . one:* at this time this was the only way by which to couple ourselves.
    16. *out:* of our bodies.

He (though he knew not which soule spake,   25
   Because both meant, both spake the same)
Might thence a new concoction take,
   And part farre purer then he came.

This Extasie doth unperplex
   (We said) and tell us what we love,   30
Wee see by this, it was not sexe,
   Wee see, we saw not what did move:

But as all severall soules containe
   Mixture of things, they know not what,
Love, these mixt soules, doth mixe againe,   35
   And makes both one, each this and that.

A single violet transplant,
   The strength, the colour, and the size,
(All which before was poore, and scant,)
   Redoubles still, and multiplies.   40

When love, with one another so
   Interinanimates two soules,
That abler soule, which thence doth flow,
   Defects of lonelinesse controules.

Wee then, who are this new soule, know,   45
   Of what we are compos'd, and made,
For, th'Atomies of which we grow,
   Are soules, whom no change can invade.

But O alas, so long, so farre
   Our bodies why doe wee forbeare?   50
They'are ours, though they'are not wee, Wee are
   The'intelligences, they the spheares.

27. *concoction:* a new kind of purification by heat (an alchemical process for refining crude matter).

32. We now see that we did not see before what aroused our emotions.

36. *each this and that:* each of the two becomes partly this which he was and partly that which was the other.

37. Transplant a single violet and the strength, etc. The violet would be transplanted to a pregnant bank (the parallel female soul).

42. *Interinanimates:* both "mutually breathes life into" and "mutually removes the consciousness of." The latter stresses the oneness of the abler soul which results when the individual souls are "inanimated."

44. *lonelinesse:* aloneness, separation.

47. *th'Atomies of:* the atoms from.

51–52. *Wee . . . spheares:* we (the minds) are the directors; our bodies are their provinces. "Intelligences" are also angels; each of the nine orders of angels commanded one of the nine spheres of Ptolemaic astronomy.

We owe them thankes, because they thus,
    Did us, to us, at first convay,
Yeelded their forces, sense, to us,   55
    Nor are drosse to us, but allay.

On man heavens influence workes not so,
    But that it first imprints the ayre,
Soe soule into the soule may flow,
    Though it to body first repaire.   60

As our blood labours to beget
    Spirits, as like soules as it can,
Because such fingers need to knit
    That subtile knot, which makes us man:

So must pure lovers soules descend   65
    T'affections, and to faculties,
Which sense may reach and apprehend,
    Else a great Prince in prison lies.

To'our bodies turne wee then, that so
    Weake men on love reveal'd may looke;   70
Loves mysteries in soules doe grow,
    But yet the body is his booke.

And if some lover, such as wee,
    Have heard this dialogue of one,
Let him still marke us, he shall see   75
    Small change, when we'are to bodies gone.

55. *sense:* feeling, sensibility.
56. *drosse:* worthless scum of molten metals. *allay:* alloy, a substance composed of two or more metals by their being fused and dissolving in each other when molten.
57–58. Any influences from the heavenly bodies on man work first through the air in which the heavenly bodies revolve.
62. *Spirits:* spirits were vapors or rarefied liquids extracted from the blood; they mediated between body and soul.
63. *need:* are needed.
66. To passions and to powers of action.
68. *a great Prince:* "the abler soul" of l. 43.
70. *Weake men:* those who need visual proof of love's mysteries.
74. *of one:* spoken by but one soul (but resultant from two).
76. *when . . . gone:* when our souls have left; when we are dead.

I have done one braver thing
    Then all the *Worthies* did,
And yet a braver thence doth spring,
    Which is, to keepe that hid.

It were but madnes now t'impart   5
    The skill of specular stone,
When he which can have learn'd the art
    To cut it can finde none.

So, if I now should utter this,
    Others (because no more   10
Such stuffe to worke upon, there is,)
    Would love but as before.

But he who lovelinesse within
    Hath found, all outward loathes,
For he who colour loves, and skinne,   15
    Loves but their oldest clothes.

If, as I have, you also doe
    Vertue'attir'd in woman see,
And dare love that, and say so too,
    And forget the Hee and Shee;   20

And if this love, though placed so,
    From prophane men you hide,
Which will no faith on this bestow,
    Or, if they doe, deride:

THE UNDERTAKING.
    1. *braver thing:* the superior (bold) thing done is (ll. 17–19) to see virtue in women and to love that virtue. The poem is entitled "Platonic Love" in several MSS.
    2. *Worthies:* the nine Worthies were Joshua, David, Judas Maccabaeus, Hector, Alexander, Julius Caesar, Arthur, Charlemagne, and Godfrey of Bouillon. They were not notable for spiritual love.
    6. *skill:* art needed to cut and to use; also, ability or magic. *specular stone:* selenite (supposedly then scarce), whose crystalline structure reflected and dilated light; cut into sheets, it was used alchemically in making glass and was called *lapis specularis.* It was also used in conjuration.
    16. *oldest clothes:* the external physical attributes of the women loved.
    20. Forget the difference between male and female sex.

Then you have done a braver thing   25
  Then all the *Worthies* did.
And a braver thence will spring
  Which is, to keepe that hid.

64   *Loves Deitie.*

I long to talke with some old lovers ghost,
  Who dyed before the god of Love was borne:
I cannot thinke that hee, who then lov'd most,
  Sunke so low, as to love one which did scorne.
But since this god produc'd a destinie,   5
And that vice-nature, custome, lets it be;
  I must love her, that loves not mee.

Sure, they which made him god, meant not so much:
  Nor he, in his young godhead practis'd it.
But when an even flame two hearts did touch,   10
  His office was indulgently to fit
Actives to passives. Correspondencie
Only his subject was; It cannot bee
  Love, till I love her, that loves mee.

But every moderne god will now extend   15
  His vast prerogative, as far as Jove.
To rage, to lust, to write to, to commend,
  All is the purlewe of the God of Love.
Oh were wee wak'ned by this Tyrannie
To'ungod this child againe, it could not bee   20
  That I should love, who loves not mee.

LOVES DEITIE.
    3. *lov'd most:* "primarily loved" and "loved most women."
    5. *destinie:* lovers' fate of unhappiness.
    6. *vice-nature:* that which takes the place of nature; but Donne implies that
it is vicious.
    8. *so much:* (power).
    10. *even:* of equal intensity.
    11. *indulgently:* compliantly.
    12. *Actives to passives:* men to women.
    14. *till . . . mee:* till it is mutual.
    15. *moderne:* new-fashioned.
    18. *purlewe:* domain.

Rebell and Atheist too, why murmure I,
   As though I felt the worst that love could doe?
Love might make me leave loving, or might trie
   A deeper plague, to make her love mee too,   25
Which since she loves before, I'am loth to see;
Falshood is worse then hate; and that must bee,
   If shee whom I love, should love mee.

65 *Loves diet.*

To what a combersome unwieldinesse
And burdenous corpulence my love had growne,
   But that I did, to make it lesse,
   And keepe it in proportion,
Give it a diet, made it feed upon   5
That which love worst endures, *discretion.*

Above one sigh a day I'allow'd him not,
Of which my fortune, and my faults had part;
   And if sometimes by stealth he got
   A she sigh from my mistresse heart,   10
And thought to feast on that, I let him see
'Twas neither very sound, nor meant to mee;

If he wroung from mee'a teare, I brin'd it so
With scorne or shame, that him it nourish'd not;
   If he suck'd hers, I let him know   15
   'Twas not a teare, which hee had got,
His drinke was counterfeit, as was his meat;
For, eyes which rowle towards all, weepe not, but sweat.

22. *Rebell and Atheist:* because he rebels against Love's destiny and because he disbelieves in the god of love.
26. *loves before:* already has a lover.
27. Her love for me would of necessity be false because of her previous love.
LOVES DIET.
6. That is, he has reduced his love by being discreet.
7. *him:* love.
8. Of the sighs, some were for my poor fortune and my faults.
12. The line is a crux. "To" may mean "for" although no such use is otherwise recorded and why it should have been used in place of "for" is unexplained. Perhaps we should read: "'Twas to mee neither very sound, nor meant." That is, it seems to him that it was neither sincere nor intended, having been got by stealth. *very sound:* "true sound" or "truly sincere."
13. *brin'd:* salted.
17. *meat:* that which nourished him, her sighs in stanza two.

What ever he would dictate, I writ that,
But burnt my letters; When she writ to me,   20
   And that that favour made him fat,
   I said, if any title bee
Convey'd by this, Ah, what doth it availe,
To be the fortieth name in an entaile?

Thus I reclaim'd my buzard love, to flye   25
At what, and when, and how, and where I chuse;
   Now negligent of sport I lye,
   And now as other Fawkners use,
I spring a mistresse, sweare, write, sigh and weepe:
And the game kill'd, or lost, goe talke, and sleepe.   30

66   *The Will.*

   Before I sigh my last gaspe, let me breath,
   Great love, some Legacies; Here I bequeath
   Mine eyes to *Argus*, if mine eyes can see,
   If they be blinde, then Love, I give them thee;
   My tongue to Fame; to'Embassadours mine eares;   5
      To women or the sea, my teares.
    Thou, Love, hast taught mee heretofore
  By making mee serve her who'had twenty more,
That I should give to none, but such, as had too much before.

21. *And:* omit for meaning.
24. *an entaile:* a document indicating line of descent of ownership or in-heritance. As the fortieth name on her list, he can expect not to gain title to her. Forty implies trial and privation from its Biblical use, as in the Temptation in the Wilderness; he must fast in *Loves diet* through forty suitors.
25. *buzard:* rapacious but slow.
28. *Fawkners:* falconers.
29. *spring:* rouse (as from a covert). *sweare . . . weepe:* methods of killing his game.
THE WILL.
3. *Argus:* a hundred-eyed monster whom Hera commanded to guard Io after she had been changed to a heifer. The succeeding bequests in ll. 3–6 likewise duplicate attributes of the heirs. Those in ll. 10–15, 19–24 snidely criticize the absence of such attributes in these heirs; his point is that like these heirs he does not possess these attributes either. In stanza four he gives back what he has received; in stanza five he gives that which is useless to those heirs.
8. *twenty:* used crassly because of its monetary relationship.

My constancie I to the planets give,   10
My truth to them, who at the Court doe live;
Mine ingenuity and opennesse,
To Jesuites; to'Buffones my pensivenesse;
My silence to'any, who abroad hath beene;
    My mony to a Capuchin.   15
My Love taught'st me, by'appointing mee
 To love there, where no love receiv'd can be,
Onely to give to such as have an incapacitie.

My faith I give to Roman Catholiques;
All my good works unto the Schismaticks   20
Of Amsterdam; my best civility
And Courtship, to an Universitie;
My modesty I give to souldiers bare;
    My patience let gamesters share.
Thou Love taughtst mee, by making mee   25
 Love her that holds my love disparity,
Onely to give to those that count my gifts indignity.

I give my reputation to those
Which were my friends; Mine industrie to foes;
To Schoolemen I bequeath my doubtfulnesse;   30
My sicknesse to Physitians, or excesse;
To Nature, all that I in Ryme have writ;
    And to my company my wit.
Thou Love, by making mee adore
Her, who begot this love in mee before,   35
Taughtst me to make, as though I gave, when I did but restore.

To him for whom the passing bell next tolls,
I give my physick bookes; my writen rowles
Of Morall counsels, I to Bedlam give;
My brazen medals, unto them which live   40

15. *a Capuchin:* a monk who took a vow of poverty.
18. *incapacitie:* (to use such bequests).
20–21. *Schismaticks Of Amsterdam:* those Calvinists whose salvation would be effected through justification by faith only and not through justification by good works.
22. *Courtship:* courtliness, highbred and stately politeness.
23. *bare:* naked; he refers to soldiers' immodesty about keeping themselves fully clothed and to their sexual indulgence.
26. *disparity:* that is, beneath her, an indignity.
29. *foes:* since foes had made him work harder to defend or prove himself.
30. *Schoolemen:* medieval divines (e.g. Saint Thomas Aquinas) who disputed philosophical and theological problems on empirical bases.
39. *Bedlam:* an insane asylum in London.
40. *medals:* antiquarian coins.

In want of bread; To them which passe among
    All forrainers, mine English tongue.
Thou, Love, by making mee love one
Who thinkes her friendship a fit portion
For yonger lovers, dost my gifts thus disproportion.   45

Therefore I'll give no more; But I'll undoe
The world by dying; because love dies too.
Then all your beauties will bee no more worth
Then gold in Mines, where none doth draw it forth;
And all your graces no more use shall have   50
    Then a Sun dyall in a grave.
Thou Love taughtst mee, by making mee
Love her, who doth neglect both mee and thee,
To'invent, and practise this one way, to'annihilate all three.

67   *The Funerall.*

Who ever comes to shroud me, do not harme
    Nor question much
That subtile wreath of haire, which crowns my arme;
The mystery, the signe you must not touch,
    For 'tis my outward Soule,   5
Viceroy to that, which then to heaven being gone,
    Will leave this to controule,
And keepe these limbes, her Provinces, from dissolution.

For if the sinewie thread my braine lets fall
    Through every part,   10
Can tye those parts, and make mee one of all;
These haires which upward grew, and strength and art
    Have from a better braine,
Can better do'it; Except she meant that I
    By this should know my pain,   15
As prisoners then are manacled, when they'are condemn'd to die.

45. *disproportion:* mismatch.
54. *To'invent, and practise:* to think up and accomplish.
THE FUNERALL.
    3. See *The Relique* (No. 70), l. 6.
    9. *sinewie thread:* the sinews of his nervous system which unite him into one being.
    14. *do'it:* tie the body's parts together. *Except:* unless.

What ere shee meant by'it, bury it with me,
　　For since I am
Loves martyr, it might breed idolatrie,
If into others hands these Reliques came;　　　　　　20
　　As 'twas humility
To'afford to it all that a Soule can doe,
　　So, 'tis some bravery,
That since you would save none of mee, I bury some of you.

68　*The Blossome.*

Little think'st thou, poore flower,
　Whom I have watch'd sixe or seaven dayes,
And seene thy birth, and seene what every houre
Gave to thy growth, thee to this height to raise,
And now dost laugh and triumph on this bough,　　　5
　　　Little think'st thou
That it will freeze anon, and that I shall
To morrow finde thee falne, or not at all.

Little think'st thou poore heart
　That labour'st yet to nestle thee,　　　　　　10
And think'st by hovering here to get a part
In a forbidden or forbidding tree,
And hop'st her stiffenesse by long siege to bow:
　　　Little think'st thou,
That thou to morrow, ere that Sunne doth wake,　　　15
Must with this Sunne, and mee a journey take.

But thou which lov'st to bee
　Subtile to plague thy selfe, wilt say,
Alas, if you must goe, what's that to mee?
Here lyes my businesse, and here I will stay:　　　20

　20. An allusion to Roman Catholic idolatry of martyrs and reverence for their relics.
　21–22. As it would be submission to give to it all that a soul can do; this soul is, of course, only a viceroy.
　23. *bravery:* show of boldness.
THE BLOSSOME.
　12. *tree:* the woman with whom he wishes to have an affair, but she is forbidden him and is cold to his advances.
　15. *Sunne:* his beloved.
　17. *thou:* his heart, considered both the physical heart and the mind as the seat of affection throughout the poem (see ll. 27 and 32).

You goe to friends, whose love and meanes present
        Various content
To your eyes, eares, and tongue, and every part.
If then your body goe, what need you'a heart?

  Well then, stay here; but know,   25
    When thou hast stayd and done thy most;
A naked thinking heart, that makes no show,
Is to a woman, but a kinde of Ghost;
How shall shee know my heart; or having none,
      Know thee for one?   30
Practise may make her know some other part,
But take my word, shee doth not know a Heart.

  Meet mee at London, then,
    Twenty dayes hence, and thou shalt see
Mee fresher, and more fat, by being with men,   35
Then if I had staid still with her and thee.
For Gods sake, if you can, be you so too:
      I would give you
There, to another friend, whom wee shall finde
As glad to have my body, as my minde.   40

69   *The Primrose.*

    Upon this Primrose hill,
      Where, if Heav'n would distill
A shoure of raine, each severall drop might goe
To his owne primrose, and grow Manna so;
And where their forme, and their infinitie   5
      Make a terrestriall Galaxie,
      As the small starres doe in the skie:
I walke to finde a true Love; and I see
That 'tis not a mere woman, that is shee,
But must, or more, or lesse then woman bee.   10

  22. *content:* satisfaction.
  26. *most:* (to win her).
THE PRIMROSE. See NOTES.
  4. *Manna:* spiritual nourishment.
  6. *Galaxie:* the Milky Way.
  8. *true Love:* both "my beloved" and "a primrose as a symbol of true love."
The usual primrose has five petals (l. 22); those with four (l. 12 and the "lesse"
of ll. 10 and 13) and those with six (l. 12 and the "more" of ll. 10 and 15)
were such symbols.

      Yet know I not, which flower
      I wish; a sixe, or foure;
For should my true-Love lesse then woman bee,
She were scarce any thing; and then, should she
Be more then woman, shee would get above   15
      All thought of sexe, and thinke to move
      My heart to study'her, and not to love;
Both these were monsters; Since there must reside
Falshood in woman, I could more abide,
She were by art, then Nature falsify'd.   20

      Live Primrose then, and thrive
      With thy true number five;
And women, whom this flower doth represent,
With this mysterious number be content;
Ten is the farthest number; if halfe ten   25
      Belonge unto each woman, then
      Each woman may take halfe us men,
Or if this will not serve their turne, Since all
Numbers are odde, or even, and they fall
First into this five, women may take us all.   30

    18. *monsters:* things which depart from the normal form of the species. Four indicated body, earthiness; thus a four-petaled primrose symbolized only bodily woman. Six indicated human perfection; thus a six-petaled primrose symbolized one above womanliness.

    20. Besides the obvious meaning of being artificially beautiful rather than naturally not what she is supposed to be, the poet implies that since she must be false, being woman, he prefers that she become his love through seduction than through her own emotive response.

    25. *ten:* signifies the end of computation and is thus perfect; it is the whole and perfect number in Pythagorean thought. See further, NOTES.

    27. That is, to achieve completeness and perfection. The line may be interpreted as (1) take half a man, his other half coupling with some other woman, and (2) take many men sexually.

    28. *turne:* with obvious sexual connotation.

    30. *five:* two and three (the first even and first odd numbers, omitting unity) total five, which is woman; in medieval thought two was feminine and three masculine, and their combination a symbol of marriage. See further, NOTES.

When my grave is broke up againe
Some second ghest to entertaine,
(For graves have learn'd that woman-head
To be to more then one a Bed)
            And he that digs it, spies   5
A bracelet of bright haire about the bone,
        Will he not let'us alone,
And thinke that there a loving couple lies,
Who thought that this device might be some way
To make their soules, at the last busie day,   10
Meet at this grave, and make a little stay?

If this fall in a time, or land,
Where mis-devotion doth command,
Then, he that digges us up, will bring
Us, to the Bishop, and the King,   15
        To make us Reliques; then
Thou shalt be'a Mary Magdalen, and I
        A something else thereby;
All women shall adore us, and some men;
And since at such time, miracles are sought,   20
I would have that age by this paper taught
What miracles wee harmelesse lovers wrought.

First, we lov'd well and faithfully,
Yet knew not what wee lov'd, nor why,
Difference of sex no more wee knew,   25
Then our Guardian Angells doe;

THE RELIQUE.

1–2. Multiple burials in one grave were commonplace.

3. *woman-head:* womanhood; characteristic of a woman.

6. *a bracelet:* see NOTES.

10. *last busie day:* Judgment Day.

13. *mis-devotion:* both "idolatry" and "devotion to the wrong things" (such as sexual appetite).

17. *Mary Magdalen:* a reformed sinner and later canonized saint; Jesus cast seven devils out of her (Mark xvi 9). She was one who accompanied Jesus' body to its sepulchre, discovering later that the body was gone. Perhaps Donne refers to Magdalen Herbert.

18. *A something else:* perhaps a David (see No. 154, l. 42, and n.); perhaps a Christ. Thus the miracles of the lovers have added meaning.

20. Aquinas stated that God honors relics by working miracles in their presence.

25. Meaning that their love was not sexual but spiritual.

26. Angels, of course, were neuters.

Comming and going, wee
Perchance might kisse, but not between those meales;
　　Our hands ne'r toucht the seales,
Which nature, injur'd by late law, sets free:　　　　30
These miracles wee did; but now alas,
All measure, and all language, I should passe,
Should I tell what a miracle shee was.

71　*The Dampe.*

When I am dead, and Doctors know not why,
　　And my friends curiositie
Will have me cut up to survay each part,
When they shall finde your Picture in my heart,
　　You thinke a sodaine dampe of love　　　　5
　　Will through all their senses move,
And worke on them as mee, and so preferre
Your murder, to the name of Massacre.

Poore victories; But if you dare be brave,
　　And pleasure in your conquest have,　　　　10
First kill th'enormous Gyant, your *Disdaine,*
And let th'enchantresse *Honor,* next be slaine,
　　And like a Goth and Vandall rize,
　　Deface Records, and Histories
Of your owne arts and triumphs over men,　　　　15
And without such advantage kill me then.

For I could muster up as well as you
　　My Gyants, and my Witches too,
Which are vast *Constancy,* and *Secretnesse,*
But these I neyther looke for, nor professe;　　　　20

27–28. *Comming . . . kisse:* kissing in salutation and in leave-taking.
28. *meales:* a kiss is the food of the soul.
29–30. The meaning is: We never engaged in that relationship which nature allows but which man's law has curbed. "Seales" also carries the connotation of hymen, particularly in view of the injury mentioned.
32. I should transcend all poetry and all language.
33. See NOTES.
THE DAMPE.
5. *dampe:* depression; noxious exhalation.
7. *preferre:* raise (your murder of me to massacre by killing all who see your picture).
13. *Goth and Vandall:* barbarian groups that sacked the Roman Empire.

Kill mee as Woman, let mee die
    As a meere man; doe you but try
Your passive valor, and you shall finde than,
In that you'have odds enough of any man.

72   The Dissolution.

Shee'is dead; And all which die
    To their first Elements resolve;
And wee were mutuall Elements to us,
        And made of one another.
My body then doth hers involve,   5
And those things whereof I consist, hereby
In me abundant grow, and burdenous,
        And nourish not, but smother.
My fire of Passion, sighes of ayre,
Water of teares, and earthly sad despaire,   10
        Which my materialls bee,
But ne'r worne out by loves securitie,
Shee, to my losse, doth by her death repaire,
        And I might live long wretched so
But that my fire doth with my fuell grow.   15

21. *die:* have sexual intercourse and experience diminishing vigor; thus, "kill me as a woman generally makes a man die."

22. *meere man:* (1) not as a giant or great person, and (2) not as a partner exceptionally endowed, but (3) as nothing less than a man. *try:* test.

24. With such passivity you have the advantage over any man.
THE DISSOLUTION.

Dissolution: the word has four meanings which operate throughout the poem: (1) the disintegration of the body at death, (2) a stage in the alchemical process, (3) the annulment of a marriage, (4) sexual completion. See further, NOTES.

5. *involve:* the sexual connotation is underscored by the Hippocratic theory that the primary elements are contained in male and female semen in separation until recombined.

6. *hereby:* by her death. The "things" gain meaning from each of the concepts of dissolution above.

10. *earthly:* earthy.

11. Which are my four elements: fire, air, water, and earth.

12. *ne'r:* nearly.

15. *my fire:* his passion for his loved one now that she is dead. Fire (the male element) may ruin an alchemical experiment if there is excessive heat, as may flooding (water being the female element).

Now as those Active Kings
Whose foraine conquest treasure brings,
Receive more, and spend more, and soonest breake:
This (which I am amaz'd that I can speake)
This death, hath with my store   20
My use encreas'd.
And so my soule more earnestly releas'd,
Will outstrip hers; As bullets flowen before
A latter bullet may o'rtake, the pouder being more.

73   *A Jeat Ring sent.*

Thou art not so black, as my heart,
Nor halfe so brittle, as her heart, thou art;
What would'st thou say? shall both our properties by thee bee
    spoke,
Nothing more endlesse, nothing sooner broke?

Marriage rings are not of this stuffe;   5
Oh, why should ought lesse precious, or lesse tough
Figure our loves? Except in thy name thou have bid it say,
    I'am cheap, and nought but fashion, fling me'away.

Yet stay with mee since thou art come,
Circle this fingers top, which did'st her thombe.   10
Be justly proud, and gladly safe, that thou dost dwell with me,
    She that, Oh, broke her faith, would soon breake thee.

18. *breake:* become bankrupt.
21. *use:* expenditure; sexual activity (his "store" being increased by heightened passion).
23. *outstrip hers:* because the rapid growth of his passion will dissolve his soul faster than hers dissolves through death. *flowen:* shot.
A JEAT RING SENT.
1. *black:* constant.
4. Endless as his love and as the circle of the ring itself; brittle as her heart and as the jet from which the ring is made.
6. That is, than the gold of marriage rings.
7. *Figure:* represent.
8. *fling:* perhaps a pun on the French *jette* is intended.

74 *Negative love.*

I never stoop'd so low, as they
Which on an eye, cheeke, lip, can prey,
   Seldome to them, which soare no higher
   Then vertue or the minde to'admire,
For sense, and understanding may   5
   Know, what gives fuell to their fire:
My love, though silly, is more brave,
For may I misse, when ere I crave,
If I know yet, what I would have.

If that be simply perfectest   10
Which can by no way be exprest
   But *Negatives,* my love is so.
   To All, which all love, I say no.
If any who deciphers best,
   What we know not, our selves, can know,   15
Let him teach mee that nothing; This
As yet my ease, and comfort is,
Though I speed not, I cannot misse.

NEGATIVE LOVE.

    1. *they:* physical lovers.
    3. *Seldome to:* I seldom stoop to. *them:* platonic lovers.
    7. *silly:* humble, plain. *is more brave:* is superior and requires more courage (not to succumb to cravings, l. 8).
    8. *misse:* fail to acquire. *crave:* (a woman).
    13. I decline all the attributes of woman which everyone else loves.
    14–15. If any who knows how to decipher things can know what we ourselves do not know. The one who "deciphers" removes the cipher (the nothing).
    16. The paradox is built on the absence of any physical, mental, or moral attribute of the woman; that is, he loves no single thing. But, of course, he therefore loves the woman as a unified being. The circle which is a zero (a nothing) was considered the perfect figure. Throughout the poem are both negatives and nothings: "never," "no" (3), "know" (4), "not" (3), "negatives," "nothing."
    17. *As yet:* until then.
    18. *misse:* (since I want nothing).

75   *The Expiration.*

So, so, breake off this last lamenting kisse,
   Which sucks two soules, and vapors Both away,
Turne thou ghost that way, and let mee turne this,
   And let our selves benight our happiest day,
We ask'd none leave to love; nor will we owe   5
   Any, so cheape a death, as saying, Goe;

Goe; and if that word have not quite kil'd thee,
   Ease mee with death, by bidding mee goe too.
Oh, if it have, let my word worke on mee,
   And a just office on a murderer doe.   10
Except it be too late, to kill me so,
   Being double dead, going, and bidding, goe.

2. *vapors:* reduces both to vaporous forms.
4. *benight:* bring to an end. A pun on "beknight," confer dignity upon.
upon.
5–6. Nor will we be indebted to anyone for so cheap a death as that if they
told us to part.
10. *doe:* cause me to die also, for a murderer should lose his life in retribu-
tion.
11. *Except:* unless.
12. As I may be dead in two ways: by leaving you and by telling you to leave
me.

ALFONSO FERRABOSCO

(From Ayres, 1609, f. C₂b, with permission of the Huntington Library)

76   *The Computation.*

For the first twenty yeares, since yesterday,
  I scarce beleev'd, thou could'st be gone away,
For forty more, I fed on favours past,
  And forty'on hopes, that thou would'st, they might last.
Teares drown'd one hundred, and sighes blew out two,   5
  A thousand, I did neither thinke, nor doe,
  Or not divide, all being one thought of you;
  Or in a thousand more, forgot that too.
Yet call not this long life; But thinke that I
Am, by being dead, Immortall; Can ghosts die?   10

THE COMPUTATION.
  Computation: since there are a total of 2400 years recorded in the poem, it would seem that each hour away from one's beloved is like a hundred years.
  4. *would'st . . . last:* wished the favors might continue.
  7. *Or not divide:* or else I did not divide them between thinking or doing something.
  8. *that:* apparently the "one thought of you."
  10. *dead:* the sexual sense of the word indicates the meaning.   *die:* expire.

77 *The Paradox.*

No lover saith, I love, nor any other
    Can judge a perfect Lover;
Hee thinkes that else none can, nor will agree,
    That any loves but hee:
I cannot say I lov'd, for who can say   5
    Hee was kill'd yesterday?
Love with excesse of heat, more yong then old,
    Death kills with too much cold;
Wee dye but once, and who lov'd last did die,
    Hee that saith twice, doth lye: 10
For though hee seeme to move, and stirre a while,
    It doth the sense beguile.
Such life is like the light which bideth yet
    When the lights life is set,
Or like the heat, which fire in solid matter   15
    Leaves behinde, two houres after.
Once I lov'd and dy'd; and am now become
    Mine Epitaph and Tombe.
Here dead men speake their last, and so do I;
    Love-slaine, loe, here I lye.   20

THE PARADOX.

    1. To engage in sexual intercourse was "to die." Thus no lover will live to say that he loves or (l. 6) that he was killed yesterday.

    7. Love kills with excess of heat (passion), and more of the young than the old. Paradoxically Death (the second dying of l. 10) kills with too much cold, but more of the old than the young.

    9. *last:* lately.

    12. *the sense beguile:* deceive one's senses.

    14. *lights life:* the sun.

    19. *Here:* in their epitaphs on their tombs.

78   *Sonnet. The Token.*

Send me some token, that my hope may live,
    Or that my easelesse thoughts may sleep and rest;
Send me some honey to make sweet my hive,
    That in my passion I may hope the best.
I beg noe ribbond wrought with thine owne hands,   5
    To knit our loves in the fantastick straine
Of new-toucht youth; nor Ring to shew the stands
    Of our affection, that as that's round and plaine,
So should our loves meet in simplicity.
    No, nor the Coralls which thy wrist infold,   10
Lac'd up together in congruity,
    To shew our thoughts should rest in the same hold;
No, nor thy picture, though most gracious,
    And most desir'd, because best like the best;
Nor witty Lines, which are most copious,   15
    Within the Writings which thou hast addrest.

    Send me nor this, nor that, t'increase my store,
    But swear thou thinkst I love thee, and no more.

79   *Farewell to love.*

        Whilst yet to prove,
I thought there was some Deitie in love
    So did I reverence, and gave
Worship, as Atheists at their dying houre
Call, what they cannot name, an unknowne power,   5
    As ignorantly did I crave:

SONNET. THE TOKEN.
    7. *new-toucht:* (by love).   *the stands:* extent, level.
    11. Strung together in similar, harmonious shapes and sizes.
    12. *should . . . hold:* should be as similar and harmonious.
    16. *addrest:* written.
FAREWELL TO LOVE.
    1. While still unknowing.

Thus when
Things not yet knowne are coveted by men,
    Our desires give them fashion, and so
As they waxe lesser, fall, as they sise, grow.   10

But, from late faire
His highnesse sitting in a golden Chaire,
    Is not lesse cared for after three dayes
By children, then the thing which lovers so
Blindly admire, and with such worship wooe;   15
    Being had, enjoying it decayes:
            And thence,
What before pleas'd them all, takes but one sense,
    And that so lamely, as it leaves behinde
A kinde of sorrowing dulnesse to the minde.   20

Ah cannot wee,
As well as Cocks and Lyons jocund be,
    After such pleasures, unlesse wise
Nature decreed (since each such Act, they say,
Diminisheth the length of life a day)   25
    This; as shee would man should despise
            The sport,
Because that other curse of being short,
    And onely for a minute made to be
Eager, desires to raise posterity.   30

9. *fashion:* form.
10. As these unknown things grow smaller, our desires abate; as they swell,
our desires grow. Since Donne is talking of the sexual act in this poem, these
words seem to have a physical double meaning.
12. A gingerbread figure made to look like a king on a throne, desired by
children at a recent fair.
14. *the thing:* intercourse.
18. *them all:* all the senses. *takes:* lays hold of.
19. *as:* that.
23–23. According to Galen, cocks and lions are vivacious after intercourse.
25. A popular belief.
26. *as shee would:* because she wished that.
26–27. *despise The sport:* that is, not despise sexual union, but despise the
wanton sport which some make of it.
28. Referring to the briefness of the complete sexual act.
29–30. Here referring specifically to the momentary time of seminal emission.
30. Creates desires to procreate. That is, the shortness of the act was decreed
by nature to increase desire in order to raise posterity. The "sorrowing dulnesse" accompanying sexual union is necessary to counteract this increased
desire due to brevity. This is perhaps the "one sense" of l. 18: reason. There is
probably a pun on "posterity" meaning one's anatomical posterior.

Since so, my minde
Shall not desire what no man else can finde,
   I'll no more dote and runne
To pursue things which had indammag'd me.
And when I come where moving beauties be,   35
   As men doe when the summers Sunne
        Growes great,
Though I admire their greatnesse, shun their heat;
   Each place can afford shadowes. If all faile,
'Tis but applying worme-seed to the Taile.   40

80   *Selfe Love.*

He that cannot chuse but love,
And strives against it still,
Never shall my fancy move;
For he loves 'gaynst his will;

Nor he which is all his own,   5
And cannot pleasure chuse,
When I am caught he can be gone,
And when he list refuse.

Nor he that loves none but faire,
For such by all are sought;   10
Nor he that can for foul ones care,
For his Judgement then is nought:

Nor he that hath wit, for he
Will make me his jest or slave;
Nor a fool, for when others, . . .   15
He can neither want nor crave.

35. *moving beauties:* women whose beauty stirs one.
39. *If all faile:* If all the beauties fail to move me.
40. The poet says (1) that shunning these beauties is like applying an anaphrodisiac to his sexual organ, and ironically (2) that if he does nonetheless succumb to woman's "heat," it is only applying his generative seed to her (to beget children).
SELFE LOVE.
   The speaker is a woman, who rejects various types of lovers.
5. *all his own:* egoistic.
8. *list:* please.
9. *faire:* beautiful women.

Nor he that still his Mistresse payes,
For she is thrall'd therefore:
Nor he that payes not, for he sayes
Within shee's worth no more.   20

Is there then no kinde of men
Whom I may freely prove?
I will vent that humour then
In mine own selfe love.

17. *still:* always.
18. *is thrall'd therefore:* is made a slave thereby.
20. *Within:* "to himself," with a probable obscene pun.
22. *prove:* approve.
23. *humour:* fancy, whim; disposition.

81 "When my harte was mine owne."

When my harte was mine owne and not by vowes
Betrothd, nor by my sighes breathd into thee,
What looks, teares, passions and yet all but showes
Did mutely begg and steale my harte from me.
Through thine eyes mee thought I could behold   5
Thy hart as pictures through a Christall glasse.
Thy hart seemd soft and pure as liquid gold;
Thy faith seemd bright and durable as brasse.
But as all princes ere they have obtaind
Free soveraignty doe guild their words and deeds   10
With piety and right when they have gaind
Full sway dare boldly then sow vicious seedes,
Soe after conquest thou doost me neglect.
Could not thy once pure heart else now forbeare,
Nay more abhorr an amorous respect   15
To any other? Oh towards me I feare
Thy harte to steele, that faith to waxe doth turne,
Which takinge heate from every amorous Eye
Melts with their flames as I consume and burne
With shame t'have hopd for womans constancy.   20
Yet I had thy first oaths and it was I
That taught thee first loves language t'understand
And did reveale pure loves high mistery
And had thy harte deliver'd by thy hand;

And in exchange I gave thee such a harte   25
As had it bene example unto thine,
None could have challenged the smallest parte
Of it or thy love. They had all bene mine;
They had bene pure; they had bene innocent
As Angells are. How often to that end   30
To cleare my selfe of any foule intent
Did both in precepts and examples bend!
And must it now be an Injurious lott
To chafe and heate waxe for an others seale,
To'enamell and to guild a precious pott   35
And drinck in earth my selfe? O I appeale
Unto thy soule whether I have not cause
To change my happiest wishes to this curse,
That thou from changinge still mayst never pause
And every change may be from worse to worse.   40
Yet my hart can not wish nor thought conceave
Of ill to thine, nor can falshood whett
My dull minde to revenge. That I will leave
To thee, for thine owne guilt will that begett.
Falshood in others will noe more appeare   45
Then inck dropt on mudd or raine on grasse,
But in thy harte framd soe white and cleere
Twill show like blotts in paper, scratches'in glasse.
Then for thine owne respect and not for mine,
Pitty thy selfe in yet beinge true, and free   50
Thy minde from wandring. Doe but yet decline
All other loves and I will pardon thee,
But looke that I have all, for, deare, let me
Eyther thine only love or noe love be.

"WHEN MY HARTE WAS MINE OWNE." See NOTES.
    34. *chafe:* heat; the redundancy is not typical of Donne.   *an others seale:*
with double meaning.

82 A *nocturnall upon* S. Lucies *day,*
Being the shortest day.

Tis the yeares midnight, and it is the dayes,
Lucies, who scarce seaven houres herself unmaskes,
 The Sunne is spent, and now his flasks
 Send forth light squibs, no constant rayes;
  The worlds whole sap is sunke: 5
The generall balme th'hydroptique earth hath drunk,
Whither, as to the beds-feet, life is shrunke,
Dead and enterr'd; yet all these seeme to laugh,
Compar'd with mee, who am their Epitaph.

Study me then, you who shall lovers bee   10
At the next world, that is, at the next Spring:
 For I am every dead thing,
 In whom love wrought new Alchimie.
  For his art did expresse
A quintessence even from nothingnesse,   15
From dull privations, and leane emptinesse:
He ruin'd mee, and I am re-begot
Of absence, darknesse, death; things which are not.

A NOCTURNALL UPON S. LUCIES DAY.
 S. *Lucies day:* St. Lucy's Day is December 13; the poem was ostensibly written during the evening ("a nocturnall," "the dayes midnight") preceding it
("her Eve," l. 44). See further, NOTES.
 1. *midnight:* the time of longest darkness and, for nature, the period of sleep
(from which it would awaken in spring, l. 11).
 3. *flasks:* little containers of gunpowder; that is, the stars.
 4. *squibs:* balls of powder which burn and explode with a crack; that is, the
stars shine only in flashes.
 5. Since it is winter, the sap in plants has not risen and they languish.
 6. *balme:* life-giving rain. *hydroptique:* thirsty.
 7. *beds-feet:* seemingly opposite to "bedhead." The image is that of a dying
man whose life as he lies in bed seems to ebb from his head downward.
 7–8. *life . . . enterr'd:* vegetal life has withered ("shrunk" because of the
absence of water), died, and retired into the earth.
 14. *expresse:* squeeze out.
 15. *quintessence:* the highest, most concentrated essence of any substance,
ether.
 16. *dull privations:* melancholy absences or denials of emotions or necessities;
the loss of his wife. *leane emptinesse:* lack of emotional drive experienced
after great shock. Perhaps too there is a pictorial connotation.
 17. *ruin'd:* made (of me) the ruin of a man (mentally, emotionally, and
physically).

All others, from all things, draw all that's good,
Life, soule, forme, spirit, whence they beeing have;   20
   I, by loves limbecke, am the grave
   Of all, that's nothing. Oft a flood
      Have wee two wept, and so
Drownd the whole world, us two; oft did we grow
To be two Chaosses, when we did show   25
Care to ought else; and often absences
Withdrew our soules, and made us carcasses.

But I am by her death, (which word wrongs her)
Of the first nothing, the Elixer grown;
   Were I a man, that I were one,   30
   I needs must know; I should preferre,
      If I were any beast,
Some ends, some means; Yea plants, yea stones detest,
And love; all, all some properties invest;
If I an ordinary nothing were,   35
As shadow,'a light, and body must be here.

But I am None; nor will my Sunne renew.
You lovers, for whose sake, the lesser Sunne
   At this time to the Goat is runne
   To fetch new lust, and give it you,   40
      Enjoy your summer all;
Since shee enjoyes her long nights festivall,

19–27. The stanza works through the creation of the seas, chaos, and man.
21. *limbecke:* alembic, the apparatus used in the "new Alchimie."
24. *us two:* in apposition with "the whole world."
26. *Care to ought else:* grief to anything or anyone other than ourselves; "chaos" was a void lying outside earth and the heavens.
29. *first nothing:* the primordial nothing (ether or quintessence or elixir) which existed before the Creation. See further, NOTES.
33. *Some ends, some means:* some objectives, hopes, and the ways to attain them.
34. *invest:* put on.
36. *As:* such as.
37. *my Sunne:* his wife.
39–40. The goat was proverbially lecherous; those who were not to be resurrected at Judgment Day were also known as goats.
41. *your summer:* perhaps "your" should be stressed, not only because he has no hope for the coming summer, but because of the loss of the past summer.
42. *festivall:* signifying (1) her sleep of death, (2) her resurrection, and (3) this particular long night.

Let mee prepare towards her, and let mee call
This houre her Vigill, and her Eve, since this
Both the yeares, and the dayes deep midnight is.   45

43. *prepare towards:* "prepare to go to" through devotion. Basically the poem
is concerned with his rebirth (or resurrection) after the death of his wife. This
must be accompanied by his sun—continuing the vegetation image—through
devotion to her.

44. *Vigill:* the watch kept on the night before a feast with prayer and devotion.

Epigrams

83   *Hero* and *Leander*.

Both rob'd of aire, we both lye in one ground,
Both whom one fire had burnt, one water drownd.

84   *Pyramus* and *Thisbe*.

Two, by themselves, each other, love and feare
Slaine, cruell friends, by parting have joyn'd here.

85   *Niobe*.

By childrens birth, and death, I am become
So dry, that I am now mine owne sad tombe.

86   *A burnt ship.*

Out of a fired ship, which, by no way
But drowning, could be rescu'd from the flame,
Some men leap'd forth, and ever as they came
Neere the foes ships, did by their shot decay;
So all were lost, which in the ship were found,   5
  They in the sea being burnt, they in the burnt ship drown'd.

Hero and Leander: the lovers who drowned in the Hellespont.
  2. Note the inclusion of the four elements: air, earth, fire and water.
  Pyramus and Thisbe: legendary lovers who made love through a chink in a
wall. Keeping a tryst, Thisbe lost her cloak which a lioness smeared with blood;
Pyramus, thinking her dead, killed himself, and Thisbe, returning, killed herself.
  2. Apparently "friends" is subject of "have joyn'd."
  Niobe: proud of her many children, Niobe compared herself to Leto, mother
of Diana and Apollo, who for punishment slew her children. Weeping profusely,
she was changed into a stone by Jove.

87 *Fall of a wall.*

Under an undermin'd, and shot-bruis'd wall
A too-bold Captaine perish'd by the fall,
Whose brave misfortune, happiest men envi'd,
That had a towne for tombe, his bones to hide.

88 *A lame begger.*

I am unable, yonder begger cries,
To stand, or move; if he say true, hee *lies.*

89 *A selfe accuser.*

Your mistris, that you follow whores, still taxeth you:
'Tis strange that she should thus confess it, though'it be true.

90 *A licentious person.*

Thy sinnes and haires may no man equall call,
For, as thy sinnes increase, thy haires doe fall.

91 *Cales and Guyana.*

If you from spoyle of th'old worlds fardest end
To the new world your kindled valors bend
What brave examples then do prove it trew
That one things end doth still begine a new.

Cales and Guyana: Cádiz and Guiana.
1. *you:* probably Sir Walter Ralegh, who claimed to have urged interception
of the Spanish fleet in the West after the fall of Cádiz (1596). He was a com-
mander in the expedition and wrote *Discoverie of Guiana* (1596) to prove his
exploration of that area in 1595.

92 *Sir John Wingefield.*

Beyond th'old Pillers many'have travailed
Towards the Suns cradle, and his throne, and bed.
A fitter Piller our Earle did bestow
In that late Iland; for he well did know
Farther then Wingefield no man dares to go.   5

93 *Antiquary.*

If in his Studie he hath so much care
To'hang all old strange things, let his wife beware.

94 *Disinherited.*

Thy father all from thee, by his last Will
Gave to the poore; Thou hast good title still.

95 *The Lier.*

Thou in the fields walkst out thy supping howres
And yet thou swearst thou hast supd like a king;
Like Nabuchadnezar perchance with grass and flowres,
A sallet worse then Spanish dyeting.

Sir John Wingefield: quartermaster-general of the army, who was killed at
Cádiz in 1596; he is the "fitter Piller" of l. 3.
   1. *Pillers:* the Pillars of Hercules, two promontories at the east end of the
Strait of Gibraltar.
   3. *our Earle:* Robert Devereux, Earl of Essex (1566–1601).
   4. *late Iland:* Cádiz lies further west and thus the sun sets there later. It is not
an island, but is built on a narrow spit projecting five miles into the sea and
lying northwest of the Isla de León.
   Antiquary: see NOTES.
THE LIER
   3. *Nabuchadnezar:* king of Babylon, who went mad and ate grass as did oxen
(Dan. iv 33).
   4. *Spanish dyeting:* refers to the preponderance of vegetables of the leek
family in the Spanish diet.

Like *Esops* fellow-slaves, O *Mercury,*
Which could do all things, thy faith is; and I
Like *Esops* selfe, which nothing; I confesse
I should have had more faith, if thou hadst lesse;
Thy credit lost thy credit: 'Tis sinne to doe,   5
In this case, as thou wouldst be done unto,
To beleeve all: Change thy name: thou art like
Mercury in stealing, but lyest like a *Greeke.*

97 *Phryne.*

Thy flattering picture, *Phryne,* is like thee,
Onely in this, that you both painted be.

98 *An obscure writer.*

Philo, with twelve yeares study, hath beene griev'd,
To'be understood, when will hee be beleev'd?

Mercurius Gallo-Belgicus: an annual (first published in 1594) which chronicled foreign news, not only of France and Belgium; its Latin and its reports were often faulty.

1. *Esops fellow-slaves:* In the *Life* of Aesop (see Lloyd W. Daly, tr., *Aesop Without Morals* [New York, 1961], pp. 41–42) is related the following story: Xanthus the Philosopher was purchasing slaves, of whom he asked, "What do you know how to do?" Two answered, "Everything," whereupon Aesop laughed. When next Xanthus asked the same thing of Aesop, his answer was, "Nothing. The others know everything."

8. The name is, of course, in Latin. Mercury was the patron of thieves, and Sinon, who told the Trojans lies about the wooden horse, was proverbial.

Phryne: any courtesan.

AN OBSCURE WRITER

1. *Philo:* although a specific person may have been in Donne's mind, he seems to use this name for its pedantic connotation: it means "love of" something.

99 *Klockius.*

Klockius so deeply'hath sworne, ne'r more to come
In bawdie house, that hee dares not goe home.

100 *Ralphius.*

Compassion in the world againe is bred:
Ralphius is sick, the broker keeps his bed.

101 *The Jughler.*

Thou call'st me'effeminat, for I love womens joyes;
I call not thee manly, though thou follow boyes.

102 *Faustus.*

Faustus keepes his sister and a whore,
Faustus keepes his sister and no more.

Klockius: probably a "sly person" from the Dutch *kloek*. One MS reads "Rawlings" in l. 1; perhaps intended was John Rawlins of the Inner Temple, who, during the trial of 1615, had accused the Earl of Somerset of aiding his wife (Lady Frances Howard) in murdering Sir Thomas Overbury. Donne celebrated the Earl's marriage in December 1613 with an epithalamion (No. 108).

1. *come:* both "enter" and "have seminal emission."
Ralphius: a member of the lower class was often given the name Ralph.
2. *broker:* pawnbroker.

THE JUGHLER

1. *womens joyes:* both things enjoyed by women and the joys which women yield.
2. *follow boyes:* both do as youngsters do and pursue boys for sexual purposes.
Faustus: the name is common in epigrams of the period (see those written by Sir John Harington) and seems here not to refer to the necromancer of Wittenberg.

103　*Raderus.*

Why this man gelded *Martiall* I muse,
Except himselfe alone his tricks would use,
As *Katherine,* for the Courts sake, put downe Stewes.

104　*Ad Autorem.*

Emendare cupis Joseph qui tempora; Leges
　Præmia, supplicium, Religiosa cohors
Quod iam conātr frustra, Conabere frustra;
　Si per te non sunt deteriora sat est.

104A　*To the author.*

You Joseph wish to improve chronology somehow; laws,
rewards, punishment the pious throng
undertake now in vain since you will in error presume;
it is enough if on account of you the times are not worse.

105　*Ad Autorem.*

Non eget Hookerus tanto tutamine; Tanto
　Tutus qui impugnat sed foret Auxilio.

Raderus: Matthew Rader (1561–1634), a German Jesuit editor of Martial
(1602).
　3. *Katherine:* a frequent name for cooks and servants, but perhaps punning
on Catherine Parr, who managed the royal household both before and after
Henry VIII's death, and who was married five times. *Stewes:* punning on
the meaning "brothels."
　Ad Autorem: Joseph Scaliger, who, after surveying methods of measuring
time in *A New Work Concerning the Correction of Chronology* (1583), tried
to revise ancient calendars and dates on a scientific basis.

105A *To the author.*

Hooker is not in need of so much defence;
but he who attacks may be supported by so much assistance.

Ad Autorem: William Covell, author of *Defence of the five books of Ecclesi-astical Policie: written by Mr Richard Hooker* (1603).

1–2. that is, the arguments of Hooker's antagonist (author of *A Christian Letter of certain English Protestants to Master R. Hooker*, 1599, sometimes ascribed to Thomas Cartwright) are given support by Covell's thinking them worthy of answer. Hooker's work had been published in 1593 (Books I–IV) and 1597 (Book V); *A Christian Letter* contended that Hooker undermined the XXXIX Articles of Faith of the Church of England.

Epithalamions

The Sun-beames in the East are spred,
Leave, leave, faire Bride, your solitary bed,
   No more shall you returne to it alone,
It nourseth sadnesse, and your bodies print,
Like to a grave, the yielding downe doth dint;   5
   You and your other you meet there anon;
   Put forth, put forth that warme balme-breathing thigh,
Which when next time you in these sheets wil smother
   There it must meet another,
      Which never was, but must be, oft, more nigh;   10
Come glad from thence, goe gladder then you came,
To day put on perfection, and a womans name.

Daughters of London, you which bee
Our Golden Mines, and furnish'd Treasurie,
   You which are Angels, yet still bring with you   15
Thousands of Angels on your mariage daies,
Help with your presence, and devise to praise
   These rites, which also unto you grow due;
   Conceitedly dresse her, and be assign'd,
By you, fit place for every flower and jewell,   20
   Make her for love fit fewell
      As gay as Flora, and as rich as Inde;
So may shee faire and rich, in nothing lame,
To day put on perfection, and a womans name.

And you frolique Patricians,   25
Sonnes of these Senators wealths deep oceans,
   Ye painted courtiers, barrels of others wits,
Yee country men, who but your beasts love none,
Yee of those fellowships whereof hee's one,
   Of study'and play made strange Hermaphrodits,   30

EPITHALAMION MADE AT LINCOLNES INNE. See NOTES.
   4. *nourseth:* fosters.
   5. *dint:* dent, imprint.
   12. *put on perfection:* since woman without man is not complete. Compare
also *The Primrose,* n. to l. 25.
   16. *Angels:* gold coins; that is, their dowries.
   22. *Flora:* goddess of flowers.
   23. *lame:* physically disabled, halting; perhaps with a sexual pun concerning
her husband.
   29. *fellowships:* here, groups within Lincoln's Inn concerned with study or
with frolicsome recreation; since study (community with men) and play (com-

Here shine; This Bridegroom to the Temple bring.
Loe, in yon path which store of straw'd flowers graceth,
  The sober virgin paceth;
    Except my sight faile, 'tis no other thing;
Weep not nor blush, here is no griefe nor shame,   35
To day put on perfection, and a womans name.

Thy two-leav'd gates faire Temple'unfold,
And these two in thy sacred bosome hold,
  Till, mystically joyn'd, but one they bee;
Then may thy leane and hunger-starved wombe   40
Long time expect their bodies and their tombe,
  Long after their owne parents fatten thee;
  All elder claimes, and all cold barrennesse,
All yeelding to new loves bee far for ever,
  Which might these two dissever,   45
    Alwaies, all th'other may each one possesse;
For, the best Bride, best worthy'of praise and fame,
To day puts on perfection, and a womans name.

Oh winter dayes bring much delight,
Not for themselves, but for they soon bring night;   50
  Other sweets wait thee then these diverse meats,
Other disports then dancing jollities,
Other love tricks then glancing with the eyes;
  But that the Sun still in our halfe Spheare sweates;
  Hee flies in winter, but he now stands still,   55
Yet shadowes turne; Noone point he hath attain'd,
  His steeds will bee restrain'd,
    But gallop lively downe the Westerne hill;
Thou shalt, when he hath runne the worlds half frame,
To night put on perfection, and a womans name.   60

The amorous evening starre is rose,
Why should not then our amorous starre inclose
  Her selfe in her wish'd bed? Release your strings
Musicians, and dancers take some truce
With these your pleasing labours, for great use   65
  As much wearinesse as perfection brings;

---

munity with women) are opposites, these fellows may be considered hermaphroditic.
  56. *Yet shadowes turne:* past noon, shadows lie in an opposite direction.
  58. *But:* otherwise they will.

    You, and not only you, but all toyl'd beasts
Rest duly;'at night all their toyles are dispensed;
But in their beds commenced
    Are other labours, and more dainty feasts;   70
She goes a maid, who, least she turne the same,
To night puts on perfection, and a womans name.

Thy virgins girdle now untie,
And in thy nuptiall bed (loves alter) lye
    A pleasing sacrifice; now dispossesse   75
Thee of these chaines and robes which were put on
T'adorne the day, not thee; for thou, alone,
    Like vertue'and truth, art best in nakednesse;
        This bed is onely to virginitie
A grave, but, to a better state, a cradle;   80
Till now thou wast but able
    To be what now thou art; then that by thee
No more be said, *I may bee,* but, *I am,*
To night put on perfection, and a womans name.

Even like a faithfull man content,   85
That this life for a better should be spent;
    So, shee a mothers rich stile doth preferre,
And at the Bridegroomes wish'd approach doth lye,
Like an appointed lambe, when tenderly
    The priest comes on his knees t'embowell her;   90
        Now sleep or watch with more joy; and O light
Of heaven, to morrow rise thou hot, and early;
This Sun will love so dearely
    Her rest, that long, long we shall want her sight;
Wonders are wrought, for shee which had no maime,   95
To night puts on perfection, and a womans name.

    70. *labours:* punning also on child-bearing. *dainty feasts:* e.g., kisses, the food of the soul.
    71. *turne:* return, and with sexual meaning.
    86. Referring to the belief that sexual intercourse reduced one's life-span.
    87. *stile:* the primary meaning is "title," "designation."
    90. *t'embowell:* punningly, "to hide in the inward parts."
    94. *want:* lack.
    95. *maime:* see l. 23; the word had the additional significance of "privation of the use of a part of the body."

107 An Epithalamion, Or mariage Song
on the Lady Elizabeth, and Count Palatine
being married on St. Valentines day.

I.

Haile Bishop Valentine, whose day this is,
    All the Aire is thy Diocis,
    And all the chirping Choristers
And other birds are thy Parishioners,
    Thou marryest every yeare   5
The Lirique Larke, and the grave whispering Dove,
The Sparrow that neglects his life for love,
The household Bird, with the red stomacher,
    Thou mak'st the black bird speed as soone,
As doth the Goldfinch, or the Halcyon;   10
The husband cocke lookes out, and straight is sped,
And meets his wife, which brings her feather-bed.
This day more cheerfully then ever shine,
This day, which might enflame thy self, Old Valentine.

II.

Till now, Thou warmd'st with multiplying loves   15
    Two larkes, two sparrowes, or two Doves,
    All that is nothing unto this,
For thou this day couplest two Phœnixes;
    Thou mak'st a Taper see
What the sunne never saw, and what the Arke   20
(Which was of foules, and beasts, the cage, and park,)
Did not containe, one bed containes, through Thee,

AN EPITHALAMION, OR MARIAGE SONG ON THE LADY ELIZABETH.
    Mariage Song . . .: Elizabeth, daughter of James I, and Frederick, Elector of
the Palatine, later King of Bohemia, were married on February 14, 1613. The
marriage settlement had been made by Sir Robert Drury, with Donne accompanying him as secretary, the year before.
    3. *Choristers:* birds were supposed to choose their mates on St. Valentine's
Day.
    8. *red stomacher:* the robin; a stomacher was an ornamental covering worn
by both men and women.
    10. *Halcyon:* a kingfisher, supposedly bringing calm.
    14. *enflame:* with the passion of these two. A bright red heart is an emblem
of St. Valentine.
    18. *Phœnixes:* referring to the fabulous, unique bird containing both sexes;
it was immortal, reviving from its own ashes after its death-fire. Since there was
only one phoenix, it could not have been on Noah's ark.

Two Phœnixes, whose joyned breasts
Are unto one another mutuall nests,
Where motion kindles such fires, as shall give   25
Yong Phœnixes, and yet the old shall live.
Whose love and courage never shall decline,
But make the whole year through, thy day, O Valentine.

III.

Up then faire Phœnix Bride, frustrate the Sunne,
   Thy selfe from thine affection   30
   Takest warmth enough, and from thine eye
All lesser birds will take their Jollitie.
    Up, up, faire Bride, and call,
Thy starres, from out their severall boxes, take
Thy Rubies, Pearles, and Diamonds forth, and make   35
Thy selfe a constellation, of them All,
   And by their blazing, signifie,
That a Great Princess falls, but doth not die;
Bee thou a new starre, that to us portends
Ends of much wonder; And be Thou those ends.   40
Since thou dost this day in new glory shine,
May all men date Records, from this thy Valentine.

IV.

Come forth, come forth, and as one glorious flame
   Meeting Another, growes the same,
   So meet thy Fredericke, and so   45
To an unseparable union growe,
   Since separation
Falls not on such things as are infinite,
Nor things which are but one, can disunite.
You'are twice inseparable, great, and one;   50
   Goe then to where the Bishop staies,
To make you one, his way, which divers waies
Must be effected; and when all is past,
And that you'are one, by hearts and hands made fast,
You two have one way left, your selves to'entwine,   55
Besides this Bishops knot, or Bishop Valentine.

27. *courage:* sexual desire.
40. *Ends:* both "conclusions" and "purposes."
52. *his way:* through the marriage ceremony as contrasted with the way by which they themselves will make them one (sexually, emotionally).

V.

But oh, what ailes the Sunne, that here he staies,
   Longer to day, then other daies?
   Staies he new light from these to get?
And finding here such store, is loth to set?   60
   And why doe you two walke,
So slowly pac'd in this procession?
Is all your care but to be look'd upon,
And be to others spectacle, and talke?
   The feast, with gluttonous delaies,   65
Is eaten, and too long their meat they praise,
The masquers come too late, and'I thinke, will stay,
Like Fairies, till the Cock crow them away.
Alas, did not Antiquity assigne
A night, as well as day, to thee, O Valentine?   70

VI.

They did, and night is come; and yet wee see
   Formalities retarding thee.
   What meane these Ladies, which (as though
They were to take a clock in peeces,) goe
   So nicely'about the Bride;   75
A Bride, before a good night could be said,
Should vanish from her cloathes, into her bed,
As Soules from bodies steale, and are not spy'd.
   But now she'is laid; What though shee bee?
Yet there are more delayes, For, where is he?   80
He comes, and passes through Spheare after Spheare.
First her sheetes, then her Armes, then any where.
Let not this day, then, but this night be thine,
Thy day was but the eve to this, O Valentine.

VII.

Here lyes a shee Sunne, and a hee Moone here,   85
   She gives the best light to his Spheare,
   Or each is both, and all, and so
They unto one another nothing owe,

67. *masquers:* those who attend the festivities wearing masks; here, entertainers presenting a kind of play with dancing and music.
74. *to take a clock in peeces:* each talking to the bride a minute or two, followed by another lady, and so forth.
75. *nicely:* foolishly.
85. Usually the sun was considered masculine; the moon, feminine.

And yet they doe, but are
So just and rich in that coyne which they pay,   90
That neither would, nor needs forbeare, nor stay,
Neither desires to be spar'd, nor to spare,
    They quickly pay their debt, and then
Take no acquittances, but pay again;
They pay, they give, they lend, and so let fall   95
No such occasion to be liberall.
More truth, more courage in these two do shine,
Then all thy turtles have, and sparrows, Valentine.

VIII.

And by this act of these two Phenixes
    Nature againe restored is,   100
    For since these two are two no more,
Ther's but one Phenix still, as was before.
    Rest now at last, and wee
As Satyres watch the Sunnes uprise, will stay
Waiting, when your eyes open'd, let out day,   105
Onely desir'd, because your face wee see;
    Others neare you shall whispering speake,
And wagers lay, at which side day will breake,
And win by'observing, then, whose hand it is
That opens first a curtaine, hers or his;   110
This will be tryed to morrow after nine,
Till which houre, wee thy day enlarge, O Valentine.

    94. *acquittances:* receipts for debts paid.
    98. *turtles:* turtledoves, symbols of love.
    104. *Satyres:* lecherous demigods, who would not be glad to see the sunrise and thus end their pleasure-filled night.
    104–106. The sense is: "We will stay until your eyes are finally opened, letting day shine forth from them, for we wish the sun to rise only so that we may see your face."
    110. *curtaine:* that around the bed.
    112. *enlarge:* make longer than the normal twenty-four hours, the new day beginning only when a curtain is drawn.

1613. *December* 26.

Allophanes *finding* Idios *in the country in Christmas time, repre-*
hends his absence from court, at the mariage Of the Earle of
Sommerset, Idios *gives an account of his purpose therein, and*
of his absence thence.

Allophanes.

Unseasonable man, statue of ice,
    What could to countries solitude entice
Thee, in this yeares cold and decrepit time?
    Natures instinct drawes to the warmer clime
Even small birds, who by that courage dare,   5
    In numerous fleets, saile through their Sea, the aire.
What delicacie can in fields appeare,
    Whil'st Flora'herselfe doth a freeze jerkin weare?
Whil'st windes do all the trees and hedges strip
    Of leafes, to furnish roddes enough to whip   10
Thy madnesse from thee; and all springs by frost
    Have taken cold, and their sweet murmure lost;
If thou thy faults or fortunes would'st lament
    With just solemnity, do it in Lent;
At Court the spring already'advanced is,   15
    The Sunne stayes longer up; and yet not his
The glory is, farre other, other fires.
    First, zeale to Prince and State; then loves desires
Burne in one brest, and like heavens two great lights,
    The first doth governe dayes, the other nights.   20
And then that early light, which did appeare
    Before the Sunne and Moone created were;

ECCLOGUE.
    at the mariage Of the Earle of Sommerset: Robert Carr, created Viscount
Rochester in 1611 and Earl of Somerset in 1613, a favorite of James I, was married on December 26, 1613, to Frances Howard, who was divorced from the
Earl of Essex shortly before her remarriage. *Allophanes,* meaning "with another sound" and thus "one sounding like another," was Sir Robert Carr (or
Ker), later Earl of Ancrum, a friend of Donne's and protégé of Somerset. *Idios,*
meaning "proper" or "peculiar" and thus "a private or ignorant person" (see l.
91), was Donne, who held no place at court.
    5. *courage:* sexual desire (also l. 122).
    8. *Flora:* goddess of flowers.

The Princes favour is defus'd o'r all,
    From which all Fortunes, Names, and Natures fall;
Then from those wombes of starres, the Brides bright eyes,   25
    At every glance, a constellation flyes,
And sowes the Court with starres, and doth prevent
    In light and power, the all-ey'd firmament;
First her eyes kindle other Ladies eyes,
    Then from their beames their jewels lusters rise,   30
And from their jewels torches do take fire,
    And all is warmth, and light, and good desire;
Most other Courts, alas, are like to hell,
    Where in darke plotts, fire without light doth dwell:
Or but like Stoves, for lust and envy get   35
    Continuall, but artificiall heat;
Here zeale and love growne one, all clouds disgest,
    And make our Court an everlasting East.
And can'st thou be from thence?

Idios.   No, I am there.
    As heaven, to men dispos'd, is every where,   40
So are those Courts, whose Princes animate,
    Not onely all their house, but all their State.
Let no man thinke, because he is full, he hath all,
    Kings (as their patterne, God) are liberall
Not onely'in fulnesse, but capacitie,   45
    Enlarging narrow men, to feele and see,
And comprehend the blessings they bestow.
    So, reclus'd hermits often times do know
More of heavens glory, then a worldling can.
    As man is of the world, the heart of man,   50
Is an epitome of Gods great booke
    Of creatures, and man need no farther looke;
So is the Country'of Courts, where sweet peace doth,
    As their one common soule, give life to both,
I am not then from Court.

Allophanes.   Dreamer, thou art.   55
    Think'st thou fantastique that thou hast a part
In the East-Indian fleet, because thou hast
    A little spice, or Amber in thy taste?

27. *prevent:* precede.
37. *disgest:* discharge, send forth.
58. *Amber:* ambergris, often used in cooking.

Because thou art not frozen, art thou warme?
   Seest thou all good because thou seest no harme?   60
The earth doth in her inward bowels hold
   Stuffe well dispos'd, and which would faine be gold,
But never shall, except it chance to lye,
   So upward, that heaven gild it with his eye;
As, for divine things, faith comes from above,   65
   So, for best civill use, all tinctures move
From higher powers; From God religion springs,
   Wisdome, and honour from the use of Kings.
Then unbeguile thy selfe, and know with mee,
   That Angels, though on earth employd they bee,   70
Are still in heav'n, so is hee still at home
   That doth, abroad, to honest actions come.
Chide thy selfe then, O foole, which yesterday
   Might'st have read more then all thy books bewray;
Hast thou a history, which doth present   75
   A Court, where all affections do assent
Unto the Kings, and that, that Kings are just?
   And where it is no levity to trust?
Where there is no ambition, but to'obey,
   Where men need whisper nothing, and yet may;   80
Where the Kings favours are so plac'd, that all
   Finde that the King therein is liberall
To them, in him, because his favours bend
   To vertue, to the which they all pretend?
Thou hast no such; yet here was this, and more,   85
   An earnest lover, wise then, and before.
Our little Cupid hath sued Livery,
   And is no more in his minority,
Hee is admitted now into that brest
   Where the Kings Counsells and his secrets rest.   90
What hast thou lost, O ignorant man?

    64. Alchemy believed that the sun's rays changed elements in the earth to precious metals or jewels.
    66. *tinctures:* active principles of any substance; roseate hues which alchemically symbolized resurrection or immortality.
    74. *bewray:* reveal.
    77. *that:* a Court.
    87. *sued:* pleaded for. Cupid, as a small boy, was usually depicted naked; livery indicates that he now is in the service of another (Somerset).
    90. *rest:* that is, into the breast of Somerset, the king's confidant.

Idios.   I knew
  All this, and onely therefore I withdrew.
To know and feele all this, and not to have
  Words to expresse it, makes a man a grave
Of his owne thoughts; I would not therefore stay   95
  At a great feast, having no Grace to say.
And yet I scap'd not here; for being come
  Full of the common joy, I utter'd some;
Reade then this nuptiall song, which was not made
  Either the Court or mens hearts to invade,   100
But since I'am dead, and buried, I could frame
  No Epitaph, which might advance my fame
So much as this poor song, which testifies
  I did unto that day some sacrifice.

Epithalamion.

I.

The time of the Mariage.

Thou art repriv'd old yeare, thou shalt not die,   105
  Though thou upon thy death bed lye,
  And should'st within five dayes expire,
Yet thou art rescu'd by a mightier fire,
  Then thy old Soule, the Sunne,
When he doth in his largest circle runne.   110
The passage of the West or East would thaw,
And open wide their easie liquid jawe
To all our ships, could a Promethean art
Either unto the Northerne Pole impart
The fire of these inflaming eyes, or of this loving heart.   115

II.

Equality of persons.

But undiscerning Muse, which heart, which eyes,
  In this new couple, dost thou prize,

  101. *since:* until.
  113. *Promethean:* referring to Prometheus, who stole fire from heaven and
gave it to man.

When his eye as inflaming is
As hers, and her heart loves as well as his?
    Be tryed by beauty,'and than   120
The bridegroome is a maid, and not a man.
If by that manly courage they be tryed,
Which scornes unjust opinion; then the bride
Becomes a man. Should chance or envies Art
Divide these two, whom nature scarce did part?   125
Since both have both th'enflaming eyes, and both the loving heart.

III.

Raysing of the Bridegroome.

Though it be some divorce to thinke of you
    Singly, so much one are you two,
    Yet let me here contemplate thee,
First, cheerfull Bridegroome, and first let mee see,   130
    How thou prevent'st the Sunne,
And his red foming horses dost outrunne,
How, having laid downe in thy Soveraignes brest
All businesses, from thence to reinvest
Them, when these triumphs cease, thou forward art   135
To shew to her, who doth the like impart,
The fire of thy inflaming eyes, and of thy loving heart.

IV.

Raising of the Bride.

But now, to Thee, faire Bride, it is some wrong,
    To thinke thou wert in Bed so long,
    Since Soone thou lyest downe first, tis fit   140
Thou in first rising should'st allow for it.
    Pouder thy Radiant haire,
Which if without such ashes thou would'st weare,
Thou, which, to all which come to looke upon,
Art meant for Phœbus, would'st be Phaëton.   145

120. *Be tryed:* if these hearts or eyes are tested (or compared).
120–124. The lines denote that Somerset is handsome and Frances courageous.
131. *prevent'st:* surpass.
145. *Phœbus:* the son (Somerset). Phaëthon, the son of Helios (Phœbus),
was permitted to drive the chariot of the sun for one day, but he drove so reck-
lessly that he almost set the world on fire.

For our ease, give thine eyes, th'unusuall part
Of joy, a Teare; so quencht, thou maist impart,
To us that come, thy'inflaming eyes, to him, thy loving heart.

V.

Her Apparrelling.

Thus thou descend'st to our infirmitie.
  Who can the Sun in water see.   150
   Soe dost thou, when in silke and gold,
Thou cloudst thy selfe; since wee which doe behold,
  Are dust, and wormes, 'tis just
Our objects be the fruits of wormes and dust;
Let every Jewell be a glorious starre,   155
Yet starres are not so pure, as their spheares are.
And though thou stoope, to'appeare to us, in part,
Still in that Picture thou intirely art,
Which thy inflaming eyes have made within his loving heart.

VI.

Going to the Chappell.

Now from your Easts you issue forth, and wee,   160
  As men which through a Cipres see
   The rising sun, doe thinke it two,
Soe, as you goe to Church, doe thinke of you,
  But that vaile being gone,
By the Church rites you are from thenceforth one.   165
The Church Triumphant made this match before,
And now the Militant doth strive no more.
Then, reverend Priest, who Gods Recorder art,
Doe, from his Dictates, to these two impart
All blessings, which are seene, or thought, by Angels eye or heart.   170

VII.

The Benediction.

Blest payre of Swans, Oh may you interbring
  Daily new joyes, and never sing,

150. *see:* reflected, for we cannot look directly without being blinded.
154. *the fruits of wormes and dust:* silk and gold.
169. *Dictates:* authoritative powers as clergyman.
172. *never sing:* the swan is supposed to sing only just before its death.

Live, till all grounds of wishes faile,
Till honor, yea till wisedome grow so stale,
    That, new great heights to trie,   175
It must serve your ambition, to die;
Raise heires, and may here, to the worlds end, live
Heires from this King, to take thankes, you, to give,
Nature and grace doe all, and nothing Art.
May never age, or error overthwart   180
With any West, these radiant eyes, with any North, this heart.

VIII.

Feasts and Revells.

But you are over-blest. Plenty this day
    Injures; it causeth time to stay;
    The tables groane, as though this feast
Would, as the flood, destroy all fowle and beast.   185
    And were the doctrine new
That the earth mov'd, this day would make it true;
For every part to dance and revell goes.
They tread the ayre, and fal not where they rose.
Though six houres since, the Sunne to bed did part,   190
The masks and banquets will not yet impart
A sunset to these weary eyes, A Center to this heart.

IX.

The Brides going to bed.

What mean'st thou Bride, this companie to keep?
    To sit up, till thou faine wouldst sleep?
    Thou maist not, when thou'art laid, doe so.   195
Thy selfe must to him a new banquet grow,
    And you must entertaine
And doe all this daies dances o'r againe.
Know that if Sun and Moone together doe
Rise in one point, they doe not set so too.   200

    173. *grounds:* foundations, bases (for).
    178. *to take thankes, you, to give:* to take the thanks which you will give.
    179. Nature (the raising of children) and grace (virtues such as of a king) accomplish all things; art (artifice and craft) achieves nothing.
    181. The West symbolized decline; the North, coldness.
    191. *masks:* both masks for the eyes and entertainments.
    200. If you both rise to leave, you will not leave the banquet hall together; you, the moon, must precede him, the sun.

Therefore thou maist, faire Bride, to bed depart,
Thou art not gone, being gone, where e'r thou art,
Thou leav'st in him thy watchfull eyes, in him thy loving heart.

X.

The Bridegroomes comming.

As he that sees a starre fall, runs apace,
 And findes a gellie in the place,   205
 So doth the Bridegroome hast as much,
Being told this starre is falne, and findes her such,
 And as friends may looke strange,
 By a new fashion, or apparrells change,
Their soules, though long acquainted they had beene,   210
These clothes, their bodies, never yet had seene.
Therefore at first shee modestly might start,
But must forthwith surrender every part,
As freely, as each to'each before, gave either eye or heart.

XI.

The good-night.

Now, as in Tullias tombe, one lampe burnt cleare,   215
 Unchang'd for fifteene hundred yeare,
 May these love-lamps we here enshrine,
In warmth, light, lasting, equall the divine;
 Fire ever doth aspire,
And makes all like it selfe, turnes all to fire,   220
But ends in ashes, which these cannot doe,
For none of these is fuell, but fire too.
This is joyes bonfire, then, where loves strong Arts
Make of so noble individuall parts
One fire of foure inflaming eyes, and of two loving hearts.   225

Idios.

As I have brought this song, that I may doe
 A perfect sacrifice, I'll burne it too.

207. *such:* that is, gone from the room.
215. *Tullias:* Cicero's daughter, whose body was reported to have been found near an unearthed tomb on the Appian Way, wherein a lamp was burning.

Allophanes.

No Sr. This paper I have justly got,
   For, in burnt incense, the perfume is not
His only that presents it, but of all;   230
   What ever celebrates this Festivall
Is common, since the joy thereof is so.
   Nor may your selfe be Priest: But let me goe,
Backe to the Court, and I will lay'it upon
   Such Altars, as prize your devotion.   235

Verse Letters

109   *The Storme.*   To Mr. *Christopher Brooke.*

Thou which art I, ('tis nothing to be soe)
Thou which art still thy selfe, by these shalt know
Part of our passage; And, a hand, or eye
By *Hilliard* drawne, is worth an history,
By a worse painter made; and (without pride)   5
When by thy judgment they are dignifi'd,
My lines are such. 'Tis the preheminence
Of friendship onely to'impute excellence.
England to whom we'owe, what we be, and have,
Sad that her sonnes did seeke a forraine grave   10
(For, Fates, or Fortunes drifts none can soothsay,
Honour and misery have one face and way.)
From out her pregnant intrailes sigh'd a winde
Which at th'ayres middle marble roome did finde
Such strong resistance, that it selfe it threw   15
Downeward againe; and so when it did view
How in the port, our fleet deare time did leese,
Withering like prisoners, which lye but for fees,
Mildly it kist our sailes, and, fresh, and sweet,
As, to a stomack sterv'd, whose insides meete,   20
Meate comes, it came; and swole our sailes, when wee
So joyd, as *Sara*'her swelling joy'd to see.
But 'twas but so kinde, as our countrimen,
Which bring friends one dayes way, and leave them then.
Then like two mighty Kings, which dwelling farre   25
Asunder, meet against a third to warre,

THE STORME.
   The Storme: see "Thy friend, whom thy deserts" (No. 120). The storm took
place during the Island Expedition in 1597; see also *The Calme.*
   4. *Hilliard:* Nicholas Hilliard (1537–1619), first English miniature painter.
   14. *marble roome:* the middle air where were generated storms, hail, wind,
etc.
   17. *leese:* lose.
   18. *which lye but for fees:* which stay imprisoned because they do not have
money to bribe the gaolers.
   21. *Meate:* food.
   22. *her swelling:* Sarah, the wife of Abraham, after many years of barrenness
bore Isaac (Gen. xvii 15–21, xxi 1–3).
   23–24. Perhaps referring to the division of the fleet as a result of disagree-
ments between Essex and Ralegh.

The South and West winds joyn'd, and, as they blew,
Waves like a rowling trench before them threw.
Sooner then you read this line, did the gale,
Like shot, not fear'd, till felt, our sailes assaile;   30
And what at first was call'd a gust, the same
Hath now a stormes, anon a tempests name.
Ionas, I pitty thee, and curse those men,
Who when the storm rag'd most, did wake thee then;
Sleepe is paines easiest salve, and doth fullfill   35
All offices of death, except to kill.
But when I wakt, I saw, that I saw not.
I, and the Sunne, which should teach mee'had forgot
East, West, day, night, and I could onely say,
If'the world had lasted, now it had beene day.   40
Thousands our noyses were, yet wee 'mongst all
Could none by his right name, but thunder call:
Lightning was all our light, and it rain'd more
Then if the Sunne had drunke the sea before;
Some coffin'd in their cabbins lye,'equally   45
Griev'd that they are not dead, and yet must dye.
And as sin-burd'ned soules from graves will creepe,
At the last day, some forth their cabbins peepe:
And tremblingly'aske what newes, and doe heare so,
Like jealous husbands, what they would not know.   50
Some sitting on the hatches, would seeme there,
With hideous gazing to feare away feare.
Then note they the ships sicknesses, the Mast
Shak'd with this ague, and the Hold and Wast
With a salt dropsie clog'd, and all our tacklings   55
Snapping, like too-high-stretched treble strings.
And from our totterd sailes, ragges drop downe so,
As from one hang'd in chaines, a yeare agoe.

27. *winds joyn'd:* placing the storm around August since the west wind blows
during late spring and early summer, the south wind during late summer and
autumn.

32. *anon:* then immediately.

33. *Ionas:* Jonah (as given in the Douai Bible), who was cast overboard
during a tempest by his shipmates for disobedience to God. When the tempest
struck, Jonah went below to sleep but was wakened by the shipmaster who
wanted to know the cause of the evil that had befallen them (Jonah i 5–16).

44. *drunke:* swallowed up; the sun, though standing for the heavens, is used
as image both because of its evaporative qualities and because of the lack of
precipitation during the summer months.

54. *Wast:* unused section below deck.

55. *dropsie:* accumulation of water.

Even our Ordinance plac'd for our defence,
Strive to breake loose, and scape away from thence.   60
Pumping hath tir'd our men, and what's the gaine?
Seas into seas throwne, we suck in againe;
Hearing hath deaf'd our saylers; and if they
Knew how to heare, there's none knowes what to say.
Compar'd to these stormes, death is but a qualme,   65
Hell somewhat lightsome, and the'Bermuda calme.
Darknesse, lights elder brother, his birth-right
Claims o'r this world, and to heaven hath chas'd light.
All things are one, and that one none can be,
Since all formes, uniforme deformity   70
Doth cover, so that wee, except God say
Another *Fiat*, shall have no more day.
So violent, yet long these furies bee,
That though thine absence sterve me,'I wish not thee.

110   *The Calme.*

Our storme is past, and that storms tyrannous rage,
A stupid calme, but nothing it, doth swage.
The fable is inverted, and farre more
A blocke afflicts, now, then a storke before.

63. *Hearing:* of the noises of the storms.
66. *Bermuda:* an area noted for hurricane weather.
67. *lights elder brother:* Chaos begot Erebus (primeval darkness), and in one version of the myth he and Night begot Day. See also Gen. i 2–4: "and darkness was upon the face of the deep. . . . And God said, Let there be light: and there was light. And God saw the light, that it was good: and God divided the light from the darkness."
70. *formes:* things of beauty.
72. *Fiat:* "Let it be done," referring to the creation of light in Gen. i 3.
74. *sterve:* cause me to die. *wish not thee:* (here).
THE CALME.
Written during the Islands Voyage (1597), which was undertaken to capture the Spanish fleet and cargo off the Azores. Perhaps the poem was sent to Christopher Brooke; compare *The Storme* (No. 109).
2. The calm relieves the storm, but nothing lessens the calm, which is "stupid" because the ship is unmoving, languishing.
3. *fable:* Aesop's fable of the frogs whose request for a king was granted by Jove. However, he gave them a Log, but its immobility brought forth a new request, answered now by a snake which afflicted them. The snake became a stork in medieval versions.

Stormes chafe, and soone weare out themselves, or us;   5
In calmes, Heaven laughs to see us languish thus.
As steady'as I can wish, that my thoughts were,
Smooth as thy mistresse glasse, or what shines there,
The sea is now. And, as the Iles which wee
Seeke, when wee can move, our ships rooted bee.   10
As water did in stormes, now pitch runs out
As lead, when a fir'd Church becomes one spout.
And all our beauty, and our trimme, decayes,
Like courts removing, or like ended playes.
The fighting place now seamens ragges supply;   15
And all the tackling is a frippery.
No use of lanthornes; and in one place lay
Feathers and dust, to day and yesterday.
Earths hollownesses, which the worlds lungs are,
Have no more winde then the'upper valt of aire.   20
We can nor lost friends, nor sought foes recover,
But meteorlike, save that wee move not, hover.
Onely the Calenture together drawes
Deare friends, which meet dead in great fishes jawes:
And on the hatches as on Altars lyes   25
Each one, his owne Priest, and owne Sacrifice.

6. Compare Psalms ii 2–4: "The kings of the earth set themselves . . . against the Lord, and against his anointed, saying, Let us break their bands asunder, and cast away their cords from us. He that sitteth in the heavens shall laugh: the Lord shall have them in derision."
8. *glasse:* looking glass.
11. *runs out:* apparently from the melting of the pitch by the intense and steady heat.
12. *lead:* used in glazing and framing of windowpanes.
15. *fighting place:* the platform near the lower mast where the topmast rigging was spread.
16. *frippery:* second-hand clothing store.
17. *lanthornes:* a lantern was hung in the high stem for ships following to steer by.
18. *Feathers and dust:* that is, even these lighter-than-air substances are stationary because of the lack of wind.
19. *Earths hollownesses:* cognate with Aeolus' cave of winds.
20. *upper valt of aire:* considered a kind of vacuum; winds, etc., were generated in the middle air.
21. *lost friends:* Ralegh's ships were separated from the main fleet, not joining them until they reached the Azores.
22. *meteorlike:* referring to such as whirlwinds, hail, halos, rainbows, etc.
23. *Calenture:* a delirium reported from the tropics, in which the sea appears a green field; sailors would attempt to leap into it.
26. *Sacrifice:* referring to burnt offerings (because of the intense heat).

Who live, that miracle do multiply
Where walkers in hot Ovens, doe not dye.
If in despite of these, wee swimme, that hath
No more refreshing, then our brimstone Bath,   30
But from the sea, into the ship we turne,
Like parboyl'd wretches, on the coales to burne.
Like *Bajazet* encag'd, the sheepheards scoffe,
Or like slacke sinew'd *Sampson*, his haire off,
Languish our ships. Now, as a Miriade   35
Of Ants, durst th'Emperours lov'd snake invade,
The crawling Gallies, Sea-gaoles, finny chips,
Might brave our Pinnaces, now bed-ridde ships.
Whether a rotten state, and hope of gaine,
Or, to disuse mee from the queasie paine   40
Of being belov'd, and loving, or the thirst
Of honour, or faire death, out pusht mee first,
I lose my end: for here as well as I
A desperate may live, and a coward die.
Stagge, dogge, and all which from, or towards flies,   45
Is paid with life, or pray, or doing dyes.
Fate grudges us all, and doth subtly lay
A scourge, 'gainst which wee all forget to pray,
He that at sea prayes for more winde, as well
Under the poles may begge cold, heat in hell.   50
What are wee then? How little more alas
Is man now, then before he was? he was
Nothing; for us, wee are for nothing fit;
Chance, or our selves still disproportion it.
Wee have no power, no will, no sense; I lye,   55
I should not then thus feele this miserie.

28. *walkers in hot Ovens:* Shadrach, Meshach, and Abednego (Dan. iii 13–30).

33. *Bajazet:* emperor of the Turks who was imprisoned in a cage by Tamburlaine, formerly a Scythian shepherd (see Marlowe's *Tamburlaine*, Part I).

36. *Emperours:* Tiberius'; the story of his snake's being eaten by ants (a warning of the force in numbers) is told by Suetonius.

37. The multitudinous insects which inhabit kitchens, brigs, or discarded pieces of fish aboard ship.

38. *Pinnaces:* light, maneuverable vessels used as scouters.

40. *disuse mee:* separate myself.

44. A *desperate:* one without hope.

45–46. A deer or all which flies from death is paid with life; a dog or all which flies toward death is paid with reward (its prey) or dies in the process.

48. *forget:* neglect.

54. *it:* the scourge.

111 To Sr. *Henry Wootton.*

Here's no more newes, then vertue,'I may as well
Tell you *Calis,* or St *Michaels* tale for newes, as tell
That vice doth here habitually dwell.

Yet, as to'get stomachs, we walke up and downe,
And toyle to sweeten rest, so, may God frowne,   5
If, but to loth both, I haunt Court, or Towne.

For here no one is from the'extremitie
Of vice, by any other reason free,
But that the next to'him, still, is worse then hee.

In this worlds warfare, they whom rugged Fate,   10
(Gods Commissary,) doth so throughly hate,
As in'the Courts Squadron to marshall their state:

If they stand arm'd with seely honesty,
With wishing prayers, and neat integritie,
Like Indians 'gainst Spanish hosts they bee.   15

Suspitious boldnesse to this place belongs,
And to'have as many eares as all have tongues;
Tender to know, tough to acknowledge wrongs.

Beleeve mee Sir, in my youths giddiest dayes,
When to be like the Court, was a playes praise,   20
Playes were not so like Courts, as Courts'are like playes.

Then let us at these mimicke antiques jeast,
Whose deepest projects, and egregious gests
Are but dull Moralls of a game at Chests.

But now 'tis incongruity to smile,   25
Therefore I end; and bid farewell a while,
At Court; though *From Court,* were the better stile.

TO SR. HENRY WOOTTON [NO. 111].
    See "Sir, more then kisses . . ." (No. 112).
    2. *Calis:* Cádiz, referring to the expedition of 1596. *St Michaels:* the isles
of St. Michael are the Azores, referring to the expedition of 1597.
    3. *here:* in the court.
    11. *Commissary:* deputy; officially one who represents a bishop.
    12. As to place them in the body of men of the Court.
    13. *seely:* feeble.
    22. *antiques:* buffoons.
    24. *Chests:* chess; morals such as "pawns are expendable" or "never leave the
queen unguarded."

112 To Sr. *Henry Wotton.*

Sir, more then kisses, letters mingle Soules;
For, thus friends absent speake. This ease controules
The tediousnesse of my life: But for these
I could ideate nothing, which could please,
But I should wither in one day, and passe   5
To'a bottle'of Hay, that am a locke of Grasse.
Life is a voyage, and in our lifes wayes
Countries, Courts, Towns are Rockes, or Remoraes;
They breake or stop all ships, yet our state's such,
That though then pitch they staine worse, wee must touch.   10
If in the furnace of the even line,
Or under th'adverse icy poles thou pine,
Thou know'st two temperate Regions girded in,
Dwell there: But Oh, what refuge canst thou winne
Parch'd in the Court, and in the country frozen?   15
Shall cities built of both extremes be chosen?
Can dung, and garlike be'a perfume? or can
A Scorpion, and Torpedo cure a man?
Cities are worst of all three; of all three
(O knottie riddle)'each is worst equally.   20
Cities are Sepulchers; they who dwell there
Are carcases, as if no such there were.
And Courts are Theaters, where some men play
Princes, some slaves, all to one end, and of one clay.
The Country is a desert, where no good,   25
Gain'd, as habits, not borne is understood.

TO SR. HENRY WOTTON [NO. 112].
Henry Wotton: adherent of the Earl of Essex and later Ambassador to Venice
under James I (1604–24), Wotton (1568–1639) attended New College, Oxford, from 1584 to 1588, toured the continent from 1588 to 1594, was in the
services of Essex from 1595 to 1600. He was again abroad after Essex's fall
through 1603 when Elizabeth died. See also "Here's no more newes" (No.
111), "Went you to conquer?" (No. 128), and "After those reverend papers"
(No. 129).
6. *bottle:* bundle. *locke:* tuft. Compare Psalms xxxvii 1–2: "Fret not thyself
because of evil-doers, neither be thou envious against the workers of iniquity.
For they shall soon be cut down like the grass, and wither as the green herb."
10. *though . . . worse:* though they (the country, court, and town) stain
worse than pitch.
11. *even line:* the equator.
18. *Torpedo:* a fish, the electric ray.
20. That is, when one lives in any one of the three, it seems worst.
24. *one end:* death.

There men become beasts, and prone to more evils;
In cities blockes, and in a lewd court, devills.
As in the first Chaos confusedly
Each elements qualities were in th'other three;   30
So pride, lust, covetize, being severall
To these three places, yet all are in all,
And mingled thus, their issue'incestuous.
Falshood is denizon'd. Virtue'is barbarous.
Let no man say there, Virtues flintie wall   35
Shall locke vice in mee, I'll do none, but know'all.
Men are spunges, which to poure out, receive,
Who know false play, rather then lose, deceive.
For in best understandings, sinne beganne,
Angels sinn'd first, then Devills, and then man.   40
Onely perchance beasts sinne not; wretched wee
Are beasts in all, but white integritie.
I thinke if men, which in these places live
Durst looke for themselves, and themselves retrive,
They would like strangers greet themselves, seeing then   45
Utopian youth, growne old Italian.
    Be thou thine owne home, and in thy selfe dwell;
Inne any where, continuance maketh hell.
And seeing the snaile, which every where doth rome,
Carrying his owne house still, still is at home.   50
Follow (for he is easie pac'd) this snaile,
Bee thine owne Palace, or the world's thy gaile.
And in the worlds sea, do not like corke sleepe
Upon the waters face; nor in the deepe
Sinke like a lead without a line: but as   55
Fishes glide, leaving no print where they passe,
Nor making sound; so, closely thy course goe,
Let men dispute, whether thou breathe, or no:
Onely'in this one thing, be no Galenist. To make
Courts hot ambitions wholesome, do not take   60
A dramme of Countries dulnesse; do not adde
Correctives, but as chymiques, purge the bad.

28. *blockes:* blockheads.
30. The elements are earth, air, fire, and water.
31. *covetize:* inordinate desire.
46. Ideal youth grown into lecherous old men.
53. *sleepe:* remain unmovingly.
59. *Galenist:* one who, following Galen, considered illness the result of humour imbalance.
62. *chymiques:* chemists, who followed Paracelsus' ideas of purgation by means of an antagonistic substance.

But, Sir, I'advise not you, I rather doe
Say o'er those lessons, which I learn'd of you:
Whom, free from German schismes, and lightnesse   65
Of France, and faire Italies faithlesnesse,
Having from these suck'd all they had of worth,
And brought home that faith, which you carried forth,
I throughly love. But if my selfe, I'have wonne
To know my rules, I have, and you have

DONNE: 70

113   To Mr. *Rowland Woodward.*

Like one who'in her third widdowhood doth professe
Her selfe a Nunne, tyed to retirednesse,
So'affects my muse now, a chast fallownesse.

Since shee to few, yet to too many'hath showne
How love-song weeds, and Satyrique thornes are growne   5
Where seeds of better Arts, were early sown.

Though to use, and love Poëtrie, to mee,
Betroth'd to no'one Art, be no'adulterie;
Omissions of good, ill, as ill deeds bee.

For though to us it seeme,'and be light and thinne,   10
Yet in those faithfull scales, where God throwes in
Mens workes, vanity weighs as much as sinne.

If our Soules have stain'd their first white, yet wee
May cloth them with faith, and deare honestie,
Which God imputes, as native puritie.   15

64. *say o'er:* repeat.
65–66. See Notes.
TO MR. ROWLAND WOODWARD.
See "Zealously my Muse" (No. 118).
  1. *third widdowhood:* Donne refers to three groups of previous verse: probably the songs and sonnets ("love-song weeds," l. 5), the satires and elegies
("Satyrique thornes," l. 5), and the verse letters ("seeds of better Arts," l. 6);
not all poems now placed in these categories were written by this time. His
statement of fallowness in his muse may be an allusion to the unfinished
Metempsychosis of c. August 1601.
  9. Omissions of doing good are as evil as doing wrong.
  11. *scales:* God's scales of justice. See further, Notes.
  14. *honestie:* glorious chastity; that is, right thinking.

There is no Vertue, but Religion:
Wise, valiant, sober, just, are names, which none
Want, which want not Vice-covering discretion.

Seeke wee then our selves in our selves; for as
Men force the Sunne with much more force to passe,   20
By gathering his beames with a christall glasse;

So wee, If wee into our selves will turne,
Blowing our sparkes of vertue, may outburne
The straw, which doth about our hearts sojourne.

You know, Physitians, when they would infuse   25
Into any'oyle, the Soule of Simples, use
Places, where they may lie still warme, to chuse.

So workes retirednesse in us; to rome
Giddily and bee every where, but at home,
Such freedome doth a banishment become.   30

Wee are but farmers of our selves, yet may,
If we can stocke our selves, and thrive, uplay
Much, much deare treasure for the great rent day.

Manure thy selfe then, to thy selfe be'approv'd,
And with vaine outward things be no more mov'd,   35
But to know, that I love thee'and would be lov'd.

17. *Wise, valiant, sober, just:* the cardinal virtues prudence, fortitude, temperance, justice.
18. *Vice-covering discretion:* names which those who cover up their vices by discretion have given to them; names which those who do not need such discretion, since they are not given to vice, do not lack.
21. *christall glasse:* magnifying glass.
23. *outburne:* burn away.
26. *Soule of Simples:* virtue (essence, ability) of medicinal herbs. The idea is present in Paracelsus' *On the Separations of the Elements from Metals.*
27. *to chuse:* that is, used to choose places where these "simples" may remain constantly heated.
28. *retirednesse:* Donne was in a kind of retirement in 1602–4 when living at Pyrford with his wife's cousin.
30. *doth a banishment become:* doth become a banishment.
31. *farmers:* tenant farmers (since God, not we, owns our selves).
33. *great rent day:* Judgment Day when one will offer up to God his payment of his soul's "rent" of his fleshly tabernacle. See further, NOTES.

114 To Mr. *T. W.*

All haile sweet Poët, more full of more strong fire,
　Then hath or shall enkindle any spirit,
　I lov'd what nature gave thee, but this merit
Of wit and Art I love not but admire;
Who have before or shall write after thee,　　　　　　　5
Their workes, though toughly laboured, will bee
　Like infancie or age to mans firme stay,
　Or earely and late twilights to mid-day.

Men say, and truly, that they better be
　Which be envyed then pittied: therefore I,　　　　　　10
　Because I wish thee best, doe thee envie:
O wouldst thou, by like reason, pitty mee,
But care not for mee: I, that ever was
In Natures, and in fortunes gifts, alas,
　(Before thy grace got in the Muses Schoole　　　　　　15
　A monster and a begger,) am a foole.

Oh how I grieve, that late borne modesty
　Hath got such root in easie waxen hearts,
　That men may not themselves, their owne good parts
Extoll, without suspect of surquedrie,　　　　　　　　20
For, but thy selfe, no subject can be found
Worthy thy quill, nor any quill resound
　Thy worth but thine: how good it were to see
　A Poëm in thy praise, and writ by thee.

Now if this song be too'harsh for rime, yet, as　　　　　25
　The Painters bad god made a good devill,
　'Twill be good prose, although the verse be evill,
If thou forget the rime as thou dost passe.
Then write, that I may follow, and so bee
Thy debter, thy'eccho, thy foyle, thy zanee.　　　　　　30
　I shall be thought, if mine like thine I shape,
　All the worlds Lyon, though I be thy Ape.

TO MR. T. W. [NO. 114].
　　T. W.: Thomas Woodward; see "Hast thee harsh verse" (No. 115).
　　7. *stay*: stand.
　　15–16. *Before . . . begger*: that is, before you wrote, making that which I
had written monstrous and beggarly.
　　20. *surquedrie*: arrogance, presumption.
　　26. Referring to incompetent painters whose poor depiction of a godly figure
looks like a well-drawn devil.
　　30. *zanee*: imitator.

115   To Mr. *T. W.*

Hast thee harsh verse as fast as thy lame measure
   Will give thee leave, to him; My pain, and pleasure.
I have given thee, and yet thou art too weake,
   Feete, and a reasoning soule and tongue to speake.
Plead for me, and so by thine and my labour   5
   I am thy Creator, thou my Saviour.
Tell him, all questions, which men have defended
   Both of the place and paines of hell, are ended;
And 'tis decreed our hell is but privation
   Of him, at least in this earths habitation: 10
And 'tis where I am, where in every street
   Infections follow, overtake, and meete:
Live I or die, by you my love is sent,
   And you'are my pawnes, or else my Testament.

116   To Mr. *T. W.*

Pregnant again with th'old twins Hope, and Feare,
Oft have I askt for thee, both how and where
Thou wert, and what my hopes of letters were;

As in our streets sly beggers narrowly
Watch motions of the givers hand and eye,   5
And evermore conceive some hope thereby.

TO MR. T. W. [NO. 115].
   T. W.: Thomas Woodward, brother of Rowland (see note to No. 118). He
was baptized July 16, 1576, at St. Mary le Bow's, London. (He seems not to
be the Thomas Woodward who entered Lincoln's Inn on October 8, 1597, and
who apparently was called to the bar on November 26, 1605, and to the bench
on May 22, 1620.) See also "Pregnant again with th'old twins Hope, and
Feare" (No. 116), "At once, from hence, my lines and I depart" (No. 117),
and "All haile sweet Poët" (No. 114).
   7. *defended:* debated.
   12. *Infections:* the plague which was virulent in London during 1592–93.
   14. *pawnes:* pledges (of love). *Testament:* solemn covenant (if I live); last
will (if I die).
TO MR. T. W. [NO. 116].
   T. W.: Thomas Woodward; see "Hast thee harsh verse" (No. 115).
   6. *conceive:* picking up the imagery of "pregnant."

And now thy Almes is given, thy letter'is read,
And body risen againe, the which was dead,
And thy poore starveling bountifully fed.

After this banquet my Soule doth say grace,   10
And praise thee for'it, and zealously imbrace
Thy love, though I thinke thy love in this case
   To be as gluttons, which say 'midst their meat,
   They love that best of which they most do eat.

117   To Mr. *T. W.*

At once, from hence, my lines and I depart,
I to my soft still walks, they to my Heart;
I to the Nurse, they to the child of Art;

Yet as a firme house, though the Carpenter
Perish, doth stand: as an Embassadour   5
Lyes safe, how e'r his king be in danger:

So, though I languish, prest with Melancholy,
My verse, the strict Map of my misery,
Shall live to see that, for whose want I dye.

Therefore I envie them, and doe repent,   10
That from unhappy mee, things happy'are sent;
Yet as a Picture, or bare Sacrament,
   Accept these lines, and if in them there be
   Merit of love, bestow that love on mee.

   13. *meat:* food, meal.
TO MR. T. W. [NO. 117].
   T. W.: Thomas Woodward; see "Hast thee harsh verse" (No. 115).
   3. *Nurse:* the nurse of art; that is, leisure.
   9. *want:* lack.
   10. *them:* my lines.
   12. *bare Sacrament:* unconcealed pledge; also, a pun on baptism offered to
this "child of Art."

118   To Mr. *R. W.*

Zealously my Muse doth salute all thee,
Enquiring of that mistique trinitee
Wherof thou'and all to whom heavens do infuse
Like fyer, are made; thy body, mind, and Muse.
Dost thou recover sicknes, or prevent?   5
Or is thy Mind travaild with discontent?
Or art thou parted from the world and mee
In a good skorn of the worlds vanitee?
Or is thy devout Muse retyr'd to sing
Upon her tender Elegiaque string?   10
Our Minds part not, joyne then thy Muse with myne,
For myne is barren thus devorc'd from thyne.

119   To Mr. *R. W.*

Muse not that by thy mind thy body'is led:
For by thy mind, my mind's distempered.
So thy Care lives long, for I bearing part
It eates not only thyne, but my swolne hart.
And when it gives us intermission   5
We take new harts for it to feede upon.
But as a lay mans genius doth controule
Body and mind; the Muse beeing the Soules Soule

TO MR. R. W. [NO. 118].
    R. W.: Rowland Woodward, brother of Thomas, baptized August 23, 1573,
at St. Mary le Bow's, London. He entered Lincoln's Inn on January 21, 1591;
went to Venice with Sir Henry Wotton in July 1604; was imprisoned by the
Inquisition as a spy, and was attacked by robbers in France in 1607; entered
the service of the Bishop of London; and died in 1636/7. (See M. C. Deas,
RES, VII [1931], 454–57, for most of the preceding.) See further, NOTES.
    4. *Muse:* heart or soul; the Spirit of God.
    8. *good:* proper, valid.
TO MR. R. W. [NO. 119].
    R. W.: Rowland Woodward, who apparently had not written to Donne re-
cently. Compare the trinity of "body, mind, and Muse" in "Zealously my
Muse" (No. 118).
    2. *distempered:* both "unsettled" and "dissolved in due proportion."
    4. *swolne:* proud.
    7. *genius:* guardian angel.

Of Poets, that methinks should ease our anguish,
Allthough our bodyes wither and minds languish.   10
Wright then, that my griefes which thyne got may bee
Cur'd by thy charming soveraigne melodee.

120   To Mr. *C. B.*

Thy friend, whom thy deserts to thee enchaine,
  Urg'd by this unexcusable'occasion,
  Thee and the Saint of his affection
Leaving behinde, doth of both wants complaine;
And let the love I beare to both sustaine   5
  No blott nor maime by this division,
  Strong is this love which ties our hearts in one,
And strong that love pursu'd with amorous paine;
But though besides thy selfe I leave behind
  Heavens liberall and earths thrice-fairer Sunne,   10
  Going to where sterne winter aye doth wonne,
Yet, loves hot fires, which martyr my sad minde,
  Doe send forth scalding sighes, which have the Art
  To melt all Ice, but that which walls her heart.

11. *got:* created.
TO MR. C. B.
   C. B.: Christopher Brooke, brother of Samuel, had been a friend and chamber-fellow of Donne's at Lincoln's Inn; he helped effect Donne's elopment. *The Storme* (No. 109) was also addressed to him, and perhaps *The Calme* (No. 110) should be.
   3. *his affection:* a loved one, who is also "earths thrice-fairer Sunne" (l. 10); see also the next note.
   11. *wonne:* dwell. Perhaps this is an allusion to Donne's imprisonment in the Fleet in February 1602, where no sun would shine. Thus it is an "unexcusable'occasion" (l. 2). He has been "martyred" for his love; yet in order to live with Donne at this time (l. 14), Anne would not oppose her father's wishes.

121 To Mr. *E. G.*

Even as lame things thirst their perfection, so
The slimy rimes bred in our vale below,
Bearing with them much of my love and hart,
Fly unto that Parnassus, wher thou art.
There thou oreseest London: Here I have beene   5
By staying in London too much overseene.
Now pleasures dirth our City doth posses,
Our Theaters are filld with emptines.
As lancke and thin is every street and way
As a woman deliver'd yesterday.   10
Nothing whereat to laugh my spleene espyes
But bearbaitings or Law exercise.
Therfore Ile leave'it, and in the Cuntry strive
Pleasure, now fled from London, to retrive.
Do thou so too: and fill not like a Bee   15
Thy thighs with hony, but as plenteously
As Russian Marchants, thy selfes whole vessell load,
And then at Winter retaile it here abroad.
Blesse us with Suffolks sweets; and as it is
Thy garden, make thy hive and warehouse this.   20

TO MR. E. G.
   E. G.: usually identified as Everard Guilpin, author of *Skialetheia* (1598);
Donne's verse letter is similar in idea and tone to Guilpin's *Satyra quinta,* which
owes much to Donne's first satire.
   1. *thirst:* long for.
   4. *Parnassus:* mountain haunt of the Muses, signifying poetic creativity. Guilpin resided at Highgate, a hill near London.
   8. The theaters were closed during 1592–93 because of the plague.
   11. *spleene:* melancholy.
   12. *Law exercise:* the practicing of law in the courts; compare *Satyre IV*
(No. 4).
   20. *this:* London. Guilpin was from Suffolk, his mother again residing there
sometime after 1591.

122 To Mr. *R. W.*

If, as mine is, thy life a slumber be,
  Seeme, when thou read'st these lines, to dreame of me,
Never did Morpheus nor his brother weare
  Shapes soe like those Shapes, whom they would appeare,
As this my letter is like me, for it   5
  Hath my name, words, hand, feet, heart, minde and wit;
It is my deed of gift of mee to thee,
  It is my Will, my selfe the Legacie.
So thy retyrings I love, yea envie,
  Bred in thee by a wise melancholy,   10
That I rejoyce, that unto where thou art,
  Though I stay here, I can thus send my heart,
As kindly'as any'enamor'd Patient
  His Picture to his absent Love hath sent.

All newes I thinke sooner reach thee then mee;   15
  Havens are Heavens, and Ships wing'd Angels be,
The which both Gospell, and sterne threatnings bring;
  Guyanaes harvest is nip'd in the spring,
I feare; And with us (me thinkes) Fate deales so
  As with the Jewes guide God did; he did show   20
Him the rich land, but bar'd his entry in,
  Oh, slownes is our punishment and sinne;
Perchance, these Spanish businesse being done,
  Which as the Earth betweene the Moone and Sun
Eclipse the light which Guyana would give,   25
  Our discontinued hopes we shall retrive:
But if (as all th'All must) hopes smoake away,
  Is not Almightie Vertue'an India?

TO MR. R. W. [NO. 122].
  R. W.: Rowland Woodward; see "Zealously my Muse" (No. 118).
  3. *Morpheus:* god of dreams, whose name means the fashioner of shapes. The brother intended was probably Phantasus, god of dreams of inanimate objects.
  13. *enamor'd Patient:* one who is patient and enduring.
  18. *Guyanaes:* Guiana's; c. July 1597 the English fleet was thwarted from establishing its flag at the mouth of the Amazon.
  20. *Jewes guide:* Moses, who asked to "see the good land that is beyond Jordan, that goodly mountain, and Lebanon," was told by the Lord, "Get thee up into the top of Pisgah, and lift up thine eyes westward, and northward, and southward, and eastward, and behold it with thine eyes: for thou shalt not go over this Jordan" (Deut. iii 25, 27).
  23. *these Spanish businesse:* the expedition to the Azores, July–October 1597.
  28. *an India:* a mine whose wealth may be brought forth.

If men be worlds, there is in every one
  Some thing to answere in some proportion   30
All the worlds riches: And in good men, this
  Vertue, our formes forme and our soules soule is.

123   To Mr. *R. W.*

Kindly'I envy thy songs perfection
  Built of all th'elements as our bodyes are:
  That litle'of earth that'is in it, is a faire
Delicious garden where all sweetes are sowne.
In it is cherishing fyer which dryes in mee   5
  Griefe which did drowne me: and halfe quench'd by it
  Are satirique fyres which urg'd me to have writt
In skorne of all: for now I admyre thee.
  And as Ayre doth fullfill the hollownes
  Of rotten walls; so it myne emptines,   10
Where tost and movd it did begett this sound
Which as a lame Eccho'of thyne doth rebound.
  Oh I was dead: but since thy song new life did give,
  I recreated even by thy creature live.

124   To Mr. *S. B.*

O thou which to search out the secret parts
  Of the'India, or rather Paradise
  Of knowledge, hast with courage and advise
Lately launch'd into the vast Sea of Arts,

32. *formes forme:* bodies' body.
To Mr. R. W. [No. 123].
  R. W.: Rowland Woodward; see "Zealously my Muse" (No. 118).
  1. *Kindly:* with a pun on the meaning of the song as a child of Woodward's mind.
  2. *all th'elements:* earth, fire, water, air; proper combination yields perfection.
  10. *it:* your poem (filled).
  14. *recreated:* both "given pleasure" and "re-created."
To Mr. S. B. [No. 124].
  S. B.: Samuel Brooke, brother of Christopher, officiated at Donne's marriage. He became chaplain to Prince Henry, James I, and Charles I.
  4. Perhaps a reference to Brooke's matriculation at Trinity College, Cambridge, in early 1593.

Disdaine not in thy constant travailing 5
   To doe as other Voyagers, and make
   Some turnes into lesse Creekes, and wisely take
Fresh water at the Heliconian spring;
I sing not, Siren like, to tempt; for I
   Am harsh; nor as those Scismatiques with you, 10
   Which draw all wits of good hope to their crew;
But seeing in you bright sparkes of Poetry,
   I, though I brought no fuell, had desire
   With these Articulate blasts to blow the fire.

125 To Mr. *I. L.*

Of that short Roll of friends writ in my heart
   Which with thy name begins, since their depart,
Whether in the'English Provinces they be,
   Or drinke of Po, Sequan, or Danubie,
There's none that sometimes greets us not, and yet 5
   Your Trent is Lethe'; that past, us you forget.
You doe not duties of Societies,
   If from the'embrace of a lov'd wife you rise,
View your fat Beasts, stretch'd Barnes, and labour'd fields,
   Eate, play, ryde, take all joyes which all day yeelds, 10
And then againe to your embracements goe:
   Some houres on us your frends, and some bestow
Upon your Muse, else both wee shall repent,
   I that my love, she that her guifts on you are spent.

8. *Heliconian spring:* Castalia at the base of Mount Helicon, a haunt of the Muses; it symbolizes poetic achievement.
10. *Scismatiques:* alluding to the schismatic controversy waged by Richard and Gabriel Harvey and Thomas Nashe over the character and works of Robert Greene; the vituperative publications reached their height in 1592–93.
TO MR. I. L.
   I. L.: that is, "J. L.," who is unidentified; see also "Blest are your North parts" (No. 127).
3. *English Provinces:* counties lying outside the metropolitan area of London.
4. Usually considered a reference to Sir Henry Wotton, who was abroad in 1589–94. *Sequan:* the river Seine.
6. *Trent:* a river of north central England flowing to the northeast. *Lethe:* river of forgetfulness. *that past:* once having gone into the country past the Trent.
9. *stretch'd:* extensive, filled.
14. Donne is both chiding that he should have expended his love on J. L. and lamenting that the influence of his love has been exhausted.

126   To Mr. *B. B.*

Is not thy sacred hunger of science
    Yet satisfy'd? Is not thy braines rich hive
    Fulfil'd with hony which thou dost derive
From the Arts spirits and their Quintessence?
Then weane thy selfe at last, and thee withdraw   5
    From Cambridge thy old nurse, and, as the rest,
    Here toughly chew, and sturdily digest
Th'immense vast volumes of our common law;
And begin soone, lest my griefe grieve thee too,
    Which is, that that which I should have begun   10
    In my youthes morning, now late must be done;
And I, as Giddy Travellers, must doe,
    Which stray or sleepe all day, and having lost
    Light and strength, darke and tir'd must then ride post.

If thou unto thy Muse be marryed,   15
    Embrace her ever, ever multiply,
    Be far from me that strange Adulterie
To tempt thee and procure her widowhed.
My Muse, (for I had one,) because I'am cold,
    Divorc'd her selfe, the cause being in me,   20
    That I can take no new in Bigamye,
Not my will only but power doth withhold.
Hence comes it, that these Rymes which never had
    Mother, want matter, and they only have
    A little forme, the which their Father gave;   25
They are prophane, imperfect, oh, too bad
    To be counted Children of Poetry
    Except confirm'd and Bishoped by thee.

TO MR. B. B.
    B. B.: Beaupré Bell received degrees from Emmanuel College, Cambridge (1591), and Queen's (1594); he was admitted to Lincoln's Inn on May 5, 1594 (ll. 7–9).
    28. Confirmation, administered by a bishop, is the rite conferred upon those entering maturity.

127 To Mr. *I. L.*

Blest are your North parts, for all this long time
    My Sun is with you, cold and darke'is our Clime;
Heavens Sun, which staid so long from us this yeare,
    Staid in your North (I thinke) for she was there,
And hether by kinde nature drawne from thence,   5
    Here rages, chafes and threatens pestilence;
Yet I, as long as shee from hence doth staie,
    Thinke this no South, no Sommer, nor no day.
With thee my kinde and unkinde heart is run,
    There sacrifice it to that beauteous Sun: 10
And since thou'art in Paradise and need'st crave
    No joyes addition, helpe thy friend to save.
So may thy pastures with their flowery feasts,
    As suddenly as Lard, fat thy leane beasts;
So may thy woods oft poll'd, yet ever weare   15
    A greene, and when thee list, a golden haire;
So may all thy sheepe bring forth Twins; and so
    In chace and race may thy horse all out goe;
So may thy love and courage ne'r be cold;
    Thy Sonne ne'r Ward; Thy lov'd wife ne'r seem old;   20
But maist thou wish great things, and them attaine,
    As thou telst her and none but her my paine.

TO MR. I. L. [NO. 127].
    I. L.: see "Of that short Roll of friends writ in my heart" (No. 125).
    2. *My Sun:* some loved one; Donne uses the same image in "Thy friend,
whom thy deserts to thee enchaine" (No. 120) and *A nocturnall* (No. 82).
    3. May–July 1594; see John Stow, *Annales* (1631), p. 769: "many great
showres of raine: but in the moneths of June and July much more; for it com-
monly rained euery day or night, till Saint Iames day [July 25], and two dayes
after together mist extreamely: all which, not withstanding in the moneth of August, there followed a faire haruest."
    6. *pestilence:* the plague, which had raged during 1593.
    12. Help to save thy friend.
    15. *poll'd:* having had their tops cut off.
    19. *courage:* sexual desire.
    22. *her:* "My Sun" (l. 2).

128   *H. W. in Hiber. belligeranti.*

Went you to conquer? and have so much lost
Your self, that what in you was best and most,
Respective frendship, should so quickly dye?
In publique gaine my share'is not such that I
Would loose your love for Ireland: better cheap   5
I pardon death (who though he do not reap
Yet gleanes hee many of our frends away)
Then that your waking mind should bee a pray
To lethargies. Lett shotts, and boggs, and skeines
With bodies deale, as fate bidds or restreynes;   10
Ere sicknesses attack, yong death is best,
Who payes before his death doth scape arrest.
Lett not your soule (at first with graces filld
And since and thorough crooked lymbecks, stild
In many schooles and courts, which quicken it,)   15
It self unto the Irish negligence submit.
I aske not labor'd letters which should weare
Long papers out: nor letters which should feare
Dishonest cariage: or a seers art:
Nor such as from the brayne come, but the hart.   20

H. W. IN HIBER. BELLIGERANTI.
   H. W. in Hiber. belligeranti: "To Henry Wotton fighting in Ireland." He
apparently fought under the Earl of Essex in 1599. See also "Sir, more then
kisses" (No. 112).
   5–6. *better . . . death:* It is better that I pardon death while it has conquered few.
   6–7. *who . . . away:* Many of the more illustrious were lost in the hostilities.
   9. *skeines:* Irish daggers.
   14. *crooked lymbecks, stild:* curved (and deceitful) alembics distilled.
   15. *quicken it:* make it lively.
   19. *cariage:* stealing (because of their secret contents).   *seers art:* because in
code.

129   To Sir *H. W.* at his
going Ambassador to *Venice.*

After those reverend papers, whose soule is
    Our good and great Kings lov'd hand and fear'd name,
By which to you he derives much of his,
    And (how he may) makes you almost the same,

A Taper of his Torch, a copie writ   5
    From his Originall, and a faire beame
Of the same warme, and dazeling Sun, though it
    Must in another Sphere his vertue streame:

After those learned papers which your hand
    Hath stor'd with notes of use and pleasures too,   10
From which rich treasury you may command
    Fit matter whether you will write or doe:

After those loving papers, where friends send
    With glad griefe, to your Sea-ward steps, farewel,
Which thicken on you now, as prayers ascend   15
    To heaven in troupes at'a good mans passing bell:

Admit this honest paper, and allow
    It such an audience as your selfe would aske;
What you must say at Venice this meanes now,
    And hath for nature, what you have for taske.   20

To sweare much love, not to be chang'd before
    Honour alone will to your fortune fit;
Nor shall I then honour your fortune, more
    Then I have done your honour wanting it.

But 'tis an easier load (though both oppresse)   25
    To want, then governe greatnesse, for wee are
In that, our owne and onely businesse,
    In this, wee must for others vices care;

'Tis therefore well your spirits now are plac'd
    In their last Furnace, in activity;   30
Which fits them (Schooles and Courts and warres o'rpast)
    To touch and test in any best degree.

TO SIR H. W. [NO. 129].
    H. W.: Henry Wotton; see "Sir, more then kisses" (No. 112). He was
knighted by King James on July 8, 1604, and sailed for Venice on July 13.
    30. *last Furnace:* for their final forging.

For mee, (if there be such a thing as I)
    Fortune (if there be such a thing as shee)
Spies that I beare so well her tyranny,   35
    That she thinks nothing else so fit for mee;

But though she part us, to heare my oft prayers
    For your increase, God is as neere mee here;
And to send you what I shall begge, his staires
    In length and ease are alike every where.   40

130   To Sr. *Henry Goodyere.*

Who makes the Past, a patterne for next yeare,
    Turnes no new leafe, but still the same things reads,
Seene things, he sees againe, heard things doth heare,
    And makes his life, but like a paire of beads.

A Palace, when 'tis that, which it should be,   5
    Leaves growing, and stands such, or else decayes,
But hee which dwels there, is not so; for hee
    Strives to urge upward, and his fortune raise;

So had your body'her morning, hath her noone,
    And shall not better; her next change is night: 10
But her faire larger guest, to'whom Sun and Moone
    Are sparkes, and short liv'd, claimes another right.

The noble Soule by age growes lustier,
    Her appetite, and her digestion mend,
Wee must not sterve, nor hope to pamper her   15
    With womens milke, and pappe unto the end.

Provide you manlyer dyet; you have seene
    All libraries, which are Schools, Camps, and Courts;
But aske your Garners if you have not beene
    In harvests, too indulgent to your sports.   20

39. *staires:* Jacob's ladder to heaven (Gen. xxviii 12).
TO SR. HENRY GOODYERE.
    Henry Goodyere: (1571–1628), member of the privy council under James,
lived at Polesworth in Warwickshire. He was fond of falconry as ll. 34–36
show. See also "Since ev'ry Tree begins to blossome now" (No. 135).
    20. *sports:* diversions, pleasures.

Would you redeeme it? then your selfe transplant
　A while from hence. Perchance outlandish ground
Beares no more wit, then ours, but yet more scant
　Are those diversions there, which here abound.

To be a stranger hath that benefit,　　　　　　　　　　25
　Wee can beginnings, but not habits choke.
Goe; whither? hence; you get, if you forget;
　New faults, till they prescribe in us, are smoake.

Our soule, whose country'is heaven, and God her father,
　Into this world, corruptions sinke, is sent,　　　　30
Yet, so much in her travaile she doth gather,
　That she returnes home, wiser then she went;

It payes you well, if it teach you to spare,
　And make you'asham'd, to make your hawks praise, yours,
Which when herselfe she lessens in the aire,　　　　35
　You then first say, that high enough she toures.

However, keepe the lively tast you hold
　Of God, love him as now, but feare him more,
And in your afternoones thinke what you told
　And promis'd him, at morning prayer before.　　　　40

Let falshood like a discord anger you,
　Else be not froward; But why doe I touch
Things, of which none is in your practise new,
　And Tables, or fruit-trenchers teach as much;

But thus I make you keepe your promise Sir,　　　　45
　Riding I had you, though you still staid there,
And in these thoughts, although you never stirre,
　You came with mee to Micham, and are here.

22. *outlandish:* foreign.
28. *prescribe:* claim title.
30. *corruptions sinke:* that is, the world is the sink (collection sewer) of corruptions.
33. *to spare:* to be temperate.
36. *toures:* towers, turns round and round in expanding circles.
44. *trenchers:* overeaters.

131 *To the Countesse of Huntingdon.*

That unripe side of earth, that heavy clime
That gives us man up now, like *Adams* time
Before he ate; mans shape, that would yet bee
(Knew they not it, and fear'd beasts companie)
So naked at this day, as though man there   5
From Paradise so great a distance were,
As yet the newes could not arrived bee
Of *Adams* tasting the forbidden tree;
Depriv'd of that free state which they were in,
And wanting the reward, yet beare the sinne.   10
　　But, as from extreme hights who downward looks,
Sees men at childrens shapes, Rivers at brookes,
And loseth younger formes; so, to your eye,
These (Madame) that without your distance lie,
Must either mist, or nothing seeme to be,   15
Who are at home but wits mere *Atomi*.
But, I who can behold them move, and stay,
Have found my selfe to you, just their midway;
And now must pitty them; for, as they doe
Seeme sick to me, just so must I to you,   20
Yet neither will I vexe your eyes to see
A sighing Ode, nor crosse-arm'd Elegie.
I come not to call pitty from your heart,
Like some white-liver'd dotard that would part
Else from his slipperie soule with a faint groane,   25
And faithfully, (without you smil'd) were gone.
I cannot feele the tempest of a frowne,
I may be rais'd by love, but not throwne down.

TO THE COUNTESSE OF HUNTINGDON.
　　The Countesse of Huntingdon: Elizabeth Stanley, daughter of the fifth Earl
of Derby, married Henry Hastings, fifth Earl of Huntingdon, in 1603. Her
mother married Sir Thomas Egerton in 1600. See also "Man to Gods image"
(No. 141), and further, NOTES.
　　9. *free state:* having free will to choose good (obedience) or evil (disobedience).
　　10. *wanting the reward:* lacking the punishment.
　　14. *that without your distance lie:* that lie outside your purview.
　　16. *wits mere Atomi:* those of whom he speaks are considered the basic con-
stituents of wit in their own sphere.
　　18. Have placed myself in relationship to you, right between them and you.
　　26. *without:* unless.

Though I can pittie those sigh twice a day,
I hate that thing whispers it selfe away.   30
Yet since all love is fever, who to trees
Doth talke, doth yet in loves cold ague freeze.
'Tis love, but, with such fatall weaknesse made,
That it destroyes it selfe with its owne shade.
Who first look'd sad, griev'd, pin'd, and shew'd his paine,   35
Was he that first taught women, to disdaine.
   As all things were one nothing, dull and weake,
Untill this raw disorder'd heape did breake,
And severall desires led parts away,
Water declin'd with earth, the ayre did stay,   40
Fire rose, and each from other but unty'd,
Themselves unprison'd were and purify'd:
So was love, first in vast confusion hid,
An unripe willingnesse which nothing did,
A thirst, an Appetite which had no ease,   45
That found a want, but knew not what would please.
What pretty innocence in those dayes mov'd?
Man ignorantly walk'd by her he lov'd;
Both sigh'd and enterchang'd a speaking eye,
Both trembled and were sick, both knew not why.   50
That naturall fearefulnesse that struck man dumbe,
Might well (those times consider'd) man become.
As all discoverers whose first assay
Findes but the place, after, the nearest way:
So passion is to womans love, about,   55
Nay, farther off, than when we first set out.
It is not love that sueth, or doth contend;
Love either conquers, or but meets a friend.
Man's better part consists of purer fire,
And findes it selfe allow'd, ere it desire.   60
Love is wise here, keepes home, gives reason sway,
And journeys not till it finde summer-way.
A weather-beaten Lover but once knowne,
Is sport for every girle to practise on.
Who strives through womans scornes, women to know,   65
Is lost, and seekes his shadow to outgoe;
It must bee sicknesse after one disdaine,
Though he be call'd aloud, to looke againe.

42. *unprison'd were and purify'd:* the creation of the elements out of chaos.

Let others sigh, and grieve; one cunning sleight
Shall freeze my Love to Christall in a night.   70
I can love first, and (if I winne) love still;
And cannot be remov'd, unlesse she will.
It is her fault if I unsure remaine,
Shee onely can untie, and binde againe.
The honesties of love with ease I doe,   75
But am no porter for a tedious woe.
    But (madame) I now thinke on you; and here
Where we are at our hights, you but appeare,
We are but clouds, you rise from our noone-ray,
But a foule shadow, not your breake of day.   80
You are at first hand all that's faire and right,
And others good reflects but backe your light.
You are a perfectnesse, so curious hit,
That youngest flatteries doe scandall it.
For, what is more doth what you are restraine,   85
And though beyond, is downe the hill againe.
We'have no next way to you, we crosse to it:
You are the straight line, thing prais'd, attribute,
Each good in you's a light; so many'a shade
You make, and in them are your motions made.   90
These are your pictures to the life. From farre
We see you move, and here your *Zani's* are:
So that no fountaine good there is, doth grow
In you, but our dimme actions faintly shew.
    Then finde I, if mans noblest part be love,   95
Your purest luster must that shadow move.
The soule with body, is a heaven combin'd
With earth, and for mans ease, but nearer joyn'd.
Where thoughts the starres of soule we understand,
We guesse not their large natures, but command.   100

79. The punctuation is that of the poem's first edition, 1635. Lines 78–80, thus different from Grierson's revision, say that man ("we") at his height of greatness still reflects only a foul shadow because he is, as it were, a cloud; she (the Countess) appears only at man's height of greatness, rising (like the sun) from his noon, but this, of course, is not her dawn, for she has been "faire and right" since her birth. (Donne had known the Countess when she was a child.)

84. *youngest:* immaturest, weakest.
85. For what is more perfect (God) doth limit what you are.
92. *Zani's:* imitators.

And love in you, that bountie is of light,
That gives to all, and yet hath infinite.
Whose heat doth force us thither to intend,
But soule we finde too earthly to ascend,
'Till slow accesse hath made it wholy pure,   105
Able immortall clearnesse to endure.
Who dares aspire this journey with a staine,
Hath waight will force him headlong backe againe.
No more can impure man retaine and move
In that pure region of a worthy love: 110
Then earthly substance can unforc'd aspire,
And leave his nature to converse with fire:
Such may have eye, and hand; may sigh, may speak;
But like swoln bubles, when they'are high'st they break.
    Though far removed Northerne fleets scarce finde   115
The Sunnes comfort; others thinke him too kinde.
There is an equall distance from her eye,
Men perish too farre off, and burne too nigh.
But as ayre takes the Sunne-beames equall bright
From the first Rayes, to his last opposite: 120
So able men, blest with a vertuous Love,
Remote or neare, or howsoe'r they move;
Their vertue breakes all clouds that might annoy,
There is no Emptinesse, but all is Joy.
He much profanes whom violent heats do move   125
To stile his wandring rage of passion, *Love*.
Love that imparts in everything delight,
Is fain'd, which only tempts mans appetite.
Why love among the vertues is not knowne
Is, that love is them all contract in one.   130

132   Amicissimo, et meritissimo BEN. JONSON.
In Vulponem.

Quod arte ausus es hic tuâ, POETA,
Si auderent hominum Deique juris
Consulti, veteres sequi æmularierque,
O omnes saperemus ad salutem.

> 102. *hath infinite:* is infinite, hath infinite light to give.
> 130. *contract:* contracted.

His sed sunt veteres araneosi;   5
Tam nemo veterum est sequutor, ut tu
Illos quòd sequeris novator audis.
Fac tamen quod agis; tuíque primâ
Libri canitie induantur horâ:
Nam cartis pueritia est neganda,   10
Nascantúrque senes, oportet, illi
Libri, queis dare vis perennitatem.
Priscis, ingenium facit, labórque
Te parem; hos superes, ut et futuros,
Ex nostrâ vitiositate sumas,   15
Quâ priscos superamus, et futuros.

132A   To the most friendly and deserving
Ben Jonson. On his "Volpone."

If, what here you have dared with your skill, O Poet,
the deliberators of the law of men and God
had dared to follow and to emulate the ancients,
O might we all taste of salvation.
But to these men the ancients are full of cobwebs;   5
no one is such a follower of the ancients as you
because you, restorer of the old, follow those you approve.
Follow still what you pursue; and may your books
be adorned with old age from their first hour:
for assuredly youth is to be denied to literary works,   10
and it is necessary that these books are born aged things,
by which let your power be given immortality.
Genius and toil render you equal
to the ancients; outlive them so that
you may ransom future men from our corruption,   15
in which we surpass the past and future ages.

TO . . . BEN. JONSON.
   3. (Tr. 2) *Consulti* (*deliberators*): referring to those who argue the "true"
religion, those who follow their own interpretations rather than the words of the
Great Fathers (like Augustine). Donne emphasizes Jonson's adherence to classical form and classical comic aims of satire and reform.

133 To Mrs. *M. H.*

Mad paper stay, and grudge not here to burne
 With all those sonnes whom my braine did create,
At lest lye hid with mee, till thou returne
 To rags againe, which is thy native state.

What though thou have enough unworthinesse   5
 To come unto great place as others doe,
That's much; emboldens, pulls, thrusts I confesse,
 But 'tis not all; Thou should'st be wicked too.

And, that thou canst not learne, or not of mee;
 Yet thou wilt goe? Goe, since thou goest to her   10
Who lacks but faults to be a Prince, for shee,
 Truth, whom they dare not pardon, dares preferre.

But when thou com'st to that perplexing eye
 Which equally claimes *love* and *reverence*,
Thou wilt not long dispute it, thou wilt die;   15
 And, having little now, have then no sense.

Yet when her warme redeeming hand, which is
 A miracle; and made such to worke more,
Doth touch thee (saples leafe) thou grow'st by this
 Her creature; glorify'd more then before.   20

Then as a mother which delights to heare
 Her early child mis-speake halfe utter'd words,
Or, because majesty doth never feare
 Ill or bold speech, she Audience affords.

And then, cold speechlesse wretch, thou diest againe, 25
 And wisely; what discourse is left for thee?
For, speech of ill, and her, thou must abstaine,
 And is there any good which is not shee?

Yet maist thou praise her servants, though not her,
 And wit, and vertue,'and honour her attend,   30
And since they'are but her cloathes, thou shalt not erre,
 If thou her shape and beauty'and grace commend.

TO MRS. M. H.
 M. H.: Magdalen Herbert; see "Her of your name, whose fair inheritance"
(No. 159).
 1. *Mad:* senseless.
 19. *saples:* because it is made from rags and because it lacks vitality.
 22. *early:* young.

Who knowes thy destiny? when thou hast done,
  Perchance her Cabinet may harbour thee,
Whither all noble'ambitious wits doe runne,   35
  A nest almost as full of Good as shee.

When thou art there, if any, whom wee know,
  Were sav'd before, and did that heaven partake,
When she revolves his papers, marke what show
  Of favour, she alone, to them doth make.   40

Marke, if to get them, she o'r skip the rest,
  Marke, if shee read them twice, or kisse the name;
Marke, if she doe the same that they protest,
  Marke, if she marke whether her woman came.

Marke, if slight things be'objected, and o'r blowne,   45
  Marke, if her oathes against him be not still
Reserv'd, and that shee grieves she's not her owne,
  And chides the doctrine that denies Freewill.

I bid thee not doe this to be my spie;
  Nor to make my selfe her familiar;   50
But so much I doe love her choyce, that I
  Would faine love him that shall be lov'd of her.

134 *To the Countesse of* Bedford.

Madame,
Reason is our Soules left hand, Faith her right,
By these wee reach divinity, that's you;
Their loves, who have the blessings of your light,
Grew from their reason, mine from faire faith grew.

38. *sav'd:* retained, given salvation.
39. *his:* referring apparently to Sir John Danvers, whom she married in 1608.
43. *if . . . protest:* if she does what they affirm their writer does (such as, "press your letter to my heart").
44. Or is she oblivious to interruption.
TO THE COUNTESSE OF BEDFORD.
Countesse of Bedford: Lucy Harington Russell (who died in 1627) was married to Edward, third Earl of Bedford, in 1594. She was lady-in-waiting to Queen Elizabeth. She resided at Twickenham Park and was patron of several scholars and poets. Her patronage of Donne seems to have ended in 1614. See further, NOTES.
1. The right hand was the stronger, the more divine.

But as, although a squint lefthandednesse   5
Be'ungracious, yet we cannot want that hand,
So would I, not to encrease, but to'expresse
My faith, as I beleeve, so understand.

Therefore I study you first in your Saints,
Those friends, whom your election glorifies,   10
Then in your deeds, accesses, and restraints,
And what you reade, and what your selfe devize.

But soone, the reasons why you'are lov'd by all,
Grow infinite, and so passe reasons reach,
Then backe againe to'implicite faith I fall,   15
And rest on what the Catholique voice doth teach;

That you are good: and not one Heretique
Denies it: if he did, yet you are so.
For, rockes, which high top'd and deep rooted sticke,
Waves wash, not undermine, nor overthrow.   20

In every thing there naturally growes
A *Balsamum* to keepe it fresh, and new,
If 'twere not injur'd by extrinsique blowes;
Your birth and beauty are this Balme in you.

But, you of learning and religion,   25
And vertue,'and such ingredients, have made
A methridate, whose operation
Keepes off, or cures what can be done or said.

Yet, this is not your physicke, but your food,
A dyet fit for you; for you are here   30
The first good Angell, since the worlds frame stood,
That ever did in womans shape appeare.

6. *want:* lack.
10. *election:* referring to the Calvinistic doctrine of the elite.
16. *Catholique:* universal; but signifying also the Roman Catholic doctrine of salvation through goodness.
22. *Balsamum:* balm, considered a preserver and panacea for the body; with it one is in a state of grace.
27. *methridate:* an antidote against poison.

Since you are then Gods masterpeece, and so
His Factor for our loves; do as you doe,
Make your returne home gracious; and bestow   35
This life on that; so make one life of two.
  For so God helpe mee,'I would not misse you there
  For all the good which you can do me here.

135 *A Letter written by Sr. H. G. and J. D.*
alternis vicibus.

Since ev'ry Tree beginns to blossome now
Perfuminge and enamelinge each bow,
Hartes should as well as they, some fruits allow.

For since one old poore sunn serves all the rest,
You sev'rall sunns that warme, and light each brest   5
Doe by that influence all your thoughts digest.

And that you two may soe your vertues move,
On better matter then beames from above,
Thus our twin'd soules send forth these buds of love.

As in devotions men Joyne both there hands,
Wee make our's doe one Act, to seale the bands,   10
By which w'enthrall our selves to your Commaunds.

And each for others faith and zeale stand bound,
As safe as spirits are from any wound,
Soe free from impure thoughts they shalbe found.   15

Admit our magique then by which wee doe
Make you appeere to us, and us to you,
Supplying all the Muses in you twoe.

33. *Gods masterpeece:* since she is an angel in woman's form.
34. *Factor:* causative agent, creator.
35. *home:* Twickenham.
A LETTER WRITTEN BY SR. H. G. AND J. D.
 A Letter . . . : The italicized stanzas ("in alternating turns") were written by Sir Henry Goodyere; see "Who makes the Past, a patterne for next yeare" (No. 130).
 5. *sunns:* their loved ones, the "you two" of l. 7.

Wee doe consider noe flower that is sweet,
But wee your breath in that exhaling meet,   20
And as true Types of you, them humbly greet.

Heere in our Nightingales, we heere you singe
Who soe doe make the whole yeare through a springe,
And save us from the feare of Autumns stinge.

In Anchors calme face wee your smoothnes see,   25
Your mindes unmingled, and as cleare as shee
That keepes untoucht her first virginitie.

Did all St. Edith nunns descend againe
To honor Polesworth with their cloystre'd traine,
Compar'd with you each would confesse some stayne.   30

Or should wee more bleed out our thoughts in Inke
Noe paper (though it would bee glad to drinke
Those drops) could comprehend what wee doe thinke.

For t'were in us ambition to write
Soe, that because wee two, you two unite,   35
Our letter should as you, bee infinite.

136   *To the Countesse of* Bedford.

Honour is so sublime perfection,
And so refinde; that when God was alone
And creaturelesse at first, himselfe had none;

But as of the'elements, these which wee tread,
Produce all things with which wee'are joy'd or fed,   5
And, those are barren both above our head:

22. *Nightingales:* heard in spring, the nightingale portended success in love.
25. *Anchors:* anchorites'.
27. *first:* native, bodily.
28. *St. Edith nunns:* St. Edith, daughter of King Egbert, and other nuns had been expelled from their Benedictine nunnery at Polesworth by Sir Robert Marmion. After a costly entertainment at Tamworth Castle, Marmion had a vision of her in his sleep; she bid him restore the abbey to her successors or he would suffer an evil death and be damned to hell. He repented and restored the nunnery, which was dissolved in 1539.
TO THE COUNTESSE OF BEDFORD [NO. 136].
See "Reason is our Soules left hand" (No. 134).
4. *these:* earth and water.
6. *those:* air and fire (light).

So from low persons doth all honour flow;
Kings, whom they would have honour'd, to us show,
And but *direct* our honour, not *bestow*.

For when from herbs the pure part must be wonne   10
From grosse, by Stilling, this is better done
By despis'd dung, then by the fire of Sunne.

Care not then, Madame,'how low your praysers lye;
In labourers balads oft more piety
God findes, then in *Te Deums* melodie.   15

And, ordinance rais'd on Towers so many mile
Send not their voice, nor last so long a while
As fires from th'earths low vaults in *Sicil* Isle.

Should I say I liv'd darker then were true,
Your radiation can all clouds subdue,   20
But one, 'tis best light to contemplate you.

You, for whose body God made better clay,
Or tooke Soules stuffe such as shall late decay,
Or such as needs small change at the last day.

This, as an Amber drop enwraps a Bee,   25
Covering discovers your quicke Soule; that we
May in your through-shine front your hearts thoughts see.

You teach (though wee learne not) a thing unknowne
To our late times, the use of specular stone,
Through which all things within without were shown.   30

Of such were Temples; so'and of such you are;
Beeing and *seeming* is your equall care,
And *vertues* whole *summe* is but *know* and *dare*.

But as our Soules of growth and Soules of sense
Have birthright of our reasons Soule, yet hence   35
They fly not from that, nor seeke presidence.

11. *Stilling:* distilling.
12. *dung:* horse dung, alchemically considered a source of heat.
15. *Te Deums:* hymns of praise to God ("We praise thee, O God").
18. Referring to Mount Etna.
21. *one:* the divine light of God.
26. *quicke:* living.
27. *through-shine:* translucent.
29. *specular stone:* see *The undertaking:* (No. 63), n. to l. 6.
34–35. The body and the heart controlled by the mind; the natural spirits (of the liver), vital spirits (of the heart), and animal spirits (of the brain); the

Natures first lesson, so, discretion,
Must not grudge zeale a place, nor yet keepe none,
Not banish it selfe, nor religion.

Discretion is a wisemans Soule, and so   40
Religion is a Christians, and you know
How these are one; her yea, is not her no.

Nor may we hope to sodder still and knit
These two, and dare to breake them; nor must wit
Be colleague to religion, but be it.   45

In those poor types of God (round circles) so
Religions tipes, the peeclesse centers flow,
And are in all the lines which all wayes goe.

If either ever wrought in you alone
Or principally, then religion   50
Wrought your ends, and your wayes discretion.

Goe thither stil, goe the same way you went,
Who so would change, do covet or repent;
Neither can reach you, great and innocent.

137 *To the Countesse of* Bedford.

Madame,
You have refin'd mee, and to worthyest things
Vertue, Art, Beauty, Fortune, now I see
Rarenesse, or use, not nature value brings;
And such, as they are circumstanc'd, they bee.
    Two ills can nere perplexe us, sinne to'excuse;   5
    But of two good things, we may leave and chuse.

---

vegetable soul (that defining generation or augmentation, and corruption or
decay) and the sensitive soul (that defining motion and perception) are sub-
sumed by the rational soul.
    42. *her yea, is not her no:* What prudence allows, so does religion.
    46. *round circles:* perfections, infinities.
TO THE COUNTESSE OF BEDFORD [NO. 137].
    See "Reason is our Soules left hand" (No. 134).
    4. *circumstanc'd:* governed by circumstances.

Therefore at Court, which is not vertues clime,
Where a transcendent height, (as, lownesse mee)
Makes her not be, or not show: all my rime
Your vertues challenge, which there rarest bee;   10
  For, as darke texts need notes: there some must bee
  To usher vertue, and say, *This is shee.*

So in the country'is beauty; to this place
You are the season (Madame) you the day,
'Tis but a grave of spices, till your face   15
Exhale them, and a thick close bud display.
  Widow'd and reclus'd else, her sweets she'enshrines
  As China, when the Sunne at Brasill dines.

Out from your chariot, morning breaks at night,
And falsifies both computations so;   20
Since a new world doth rise here from your light,
We your new creatures, by new recknings goe.
  This showes that you from nature lothly stray,
  That suffer not an artificiall day.

In this you'have made the Court the'Antipodes,   25
And will'd your Delegate, the vulgar Sunne,
To doe profane autumnall offices,
Whilst here to you, wee sacrificers runne;
  And whether Priests, or Organs, you wee'obey,
  We sound your influence, and your Dictates say.   30

Yet to that Deity which dwels in you,
Your vertuous Soule, I now not sacrifice;
These are *Petitions,* and not *Hymnes;* they sue
But that I may survay the edifice.
  In all Religions as much care hath bin   35
  Of Temples frames, and beauty,'as Rites within.

11. *darke:* obscure, ambiguous.
13. *this place:* Twickenham.
18. *dines:* is at high noon.
24. *artificiall day:* since a natural day is twenty-four hours, the shorter period when light shines known as day is artificial.
25. *Antipodes:* the direct opposite (night, the absence of light).
27. *autumnall:* referring to the equal durations of light and night (as at the autumnal equinox). The natural sun can produce light for only part of the natural day.
30. *Dictates:* thus implying that she is a deity (l. 31).

As all which goe to Rome, doe not thereby
Esteeme religions, and hold fast the best,
But serve discourse, and curiosity,
With that which doth religion but invest,   40
    And shunne th'entangling laborinths of Schooles,
    And make it wit, to thinke the wiser fooles:

So in this pilgrimage I would behold
You as you'are vertues temple, not as shee,
What walls of tender christall her enfold,   45
What eyes, hands, bosome, her pure Altars bee;
    And after this survay, oppose to all
    Bablers of Chappels, you th'Escuriall.

Yet not as consecrate, but merely'as faire;
On these I cast a lay and country eye.   50
Of past and future stories, which are rare,
I finde you all record, and prophecie.
    Purge but the booke of Fate, that it admit
    No sad nor guilty legends, you are it.

If good and lovely were not one, of both   55
You were the transcript, and originall,
The Elements, the Parent, and the Growth,
And every peece of you, is both their All,
    So'intire are all your deeds, and you, that you
    Must do the same thinge still; you cannot two.   60

But these (as nice thinne Schoole divinity
Serves heresie to furder or represse)
Tast of Poëtique rage, or flattery,
And need not, where all hearts one truth professe;
    Oft from new proofes, and new phrase, new doubts grow,   65
    As strange attire aliens the men wee know.

    41. *Schooles:* the schismatic theologians who dispute doctrine.
    45. *tender:* emphasizing the crystal's clarity and brilliance rather than coldness and hardness.
    48. *Escuriall:* El Escorial, a magnificent and vast structure north of Madrid, built by Philip II.
    53. *booke of Fate:* Book of Life in which are recorded man's deeds and his reward.
    60. *you cannot two:* you can not do two different things or two different kinds of deeds.
    61. *nice:* foolish.

Leaving then busie praise, and all appeale,
To higher Courts, sense decree is true,
The Mine, the Magazine, the Commonweale,
The story'of beauty,'in Twicknam is, and you.   70
    Who hath seene one, would both; As, who had bin
    In Paradise, would seeke the Cherubin.

138   *To the Countesse of* Bedford.

T'have written then, when you writ, seem'd to mee
    Worst of spirituall vices, Simony,
And not t'have written then, seemes little lesse
    Then worst of civill vices, thanklessenesse.
In this, my debt I seem'd loath to confesse,   5
    In that, I seem'd to shunne beholdingnesse.
But 'tis not soe, *nothings,* as I am, may
    Pay all they have, and yet have all to pay.
Such borrow in their payments, and owe more
    By having leave to write so, then before.   10
Yet since rich mines in barren grounds are showne,
    May not I yeeld (not gold) but coale or stone?
Temples were not demolish'd, though prophane:
    Here *Peter Joves,* there *Paul* hath Dian's Fane.
So whether my hymnes you admit or chuse,   15
    In me you'have hallowed a Pagan Muse,
And denizend a stranger, who mistaught
    By blamers of the times they mard, hath sought
Vertues in corners, which now bravely doe
    Shine in the worlds best part, or all it, you.   20

67. *busie:* officious.
69. *Magazine:* the storehouse.
72. Thus Twickenham becomes Paradise, and Lucy an angel who inhabits it.
TO THE COUNTESSE OF BEDFORD [NO. 138].
    See "Reason is our Soules left hand" (No. 134).
2. *Simony:* in that such writing seems insincere, a bid for preferment by
Lady Bedford.
14. *Fane:* temple, church. Peter founded the Church of Rome (paganly
Jove's), and Paul expounded purity and faith to the Romans, the Corinthians,
the Galatians, and other former devotees of Diana, in the Pauline Epistles.
19. *bravely:* excellently.

I have beene told, that vertue'in Courtiers hearts
    Suffers an Ostracisme, and departs.
Profit, ease, fitnesse, plenty, bid it goe,
    But whither, only knowing you, I know;
Your (or you) vertue two vast uses serves,   25
    It ransomes one sex, and one Court preserves;
There's nothing but your worth, which being true,
    Is knowne to any other, not to you.
And you can never know it; To admit
    No knowledge of your worth, is some of it.   30
But since to you, your praises discords bee,
    Stoop, others ills to meditate with mee.
Oh! to confesse wee know not what we should,
    Is halfe excuse, wee know not what we would.
Lightnesse depresseth us, emptinesse fills,   35
    We sweat and faint, yet still goe downe the hills;
As new Philosophy arrests the Sunne,
    And bids the passive earth about it runne,
So wee have dull'd our minde, it hath no ends;
    Onely the bodie's busie, and pretends;   40
As dead low earth ecclipses and controules
    The quick high Moone: so doth the body, Soules.
In none but us, are such mixt engines found,
    As hands of double office: For, the ground
We till with them; and them to heav'n wee raise;   45
    Who prayer-lesse labours, or, without this, prayes,
Doth but one halfe, that's none; He which said, *Plough*
    And looke not back, to looke up doth allow.
Good seed degenerates, and oft obeyes
    The soyles disease, and into cockle strayes.   50
Let the minds thoughts be but transplanted so,
    Into the body,'and bastardly they grow.
What hate could hurt our bodies like our love?
    Wee but no forraigne tyrans could remove,
These not ingrav'd, but inborne dignities,   55
    Caskets of soules; Temples, and Palaces:

26. *one sex:* see NOTES.
35–36. See NOTES.
37. *new Philosophy:* the new science of Kepler and Galileo, which replaced
the geocentric theory of the universe with the solar.
43. *mixt engines:* mingled and twofold (as in gender) agents.
47–48. *Plough . . . back:* see NOTES.
50. *cockle:* weedy plants (such as darnel).
54–56. See NOTES.

For, bodies shall from death redeemed bee,
   Soules but preserv'd, not naturally free;
As men to'our prisons, new soules to'us are sent,
   Which learne vice there, and come in innocent.   60
First seeds of every creature are in us,
   What ere the world hath bad, or pretious,
Mans body can produce, hence hath it beene
   That stones, wormes, frogges, and snakes in man are seene:
But who ere saw, though nature can worke soe,   65
   That pearle, or gold, or corne in man did grow?
We'have added to the world Virginia,'and sent
   Two new starres lately to the firmament;
Why grudge wee us (not heaven) the dignity
   T'increase with ours, those faire soules company!   70
But I must end this letter, though it doe
   Stand on two truths, neither is true to you.
Vertue hath some perversenesse; For she will
   Neither beleeve her good, nor others ill.
Even in you, vertues best paradise,   75
   Vertue hath some, but wise degrees of vice.
Too many vertues, or too much of one
   Begets in you unjust suspition.
And ignorance of vice, makes vertue lesse,
   Quenching compassion of our wrechednesse.   80
But these are riddles; Some aspersion
   Of vice becomes well some complexion.
Statesmen purge vice with vice, and may corrode
   The bad with bad, a spider with a toad:
For so, ill thralls not them, but they tame ill   85
   And make her do much good against her will,
But in your Commonwealth or world in you
   Vice hath no office, or good worke to doe.
Take then no vitious purge, but be content
   With cordiall vertue, your knowne nourishment.   90

57–58. See Notes.
68. *Two new starres:* the new stars in Cygnus (the Swan; 1600) and Sepentarius (1604) discovered by Kepler and described by him in *De Stella Nova* (1606). Perhaps also there is an allusion to the deaths of Lady Markham, May 4, 1609, and Mrs. Boulstred, August 4, 1609. Interest in Virginia was notably high in 1609.
72. *two truths:* the wickedness of the world and your goodness (l. 74).

139 *To the Countesse of* Bedford.
On New-yeares day.

This twilight of two yeares, not past nor next,
   Some embleme is of mee, or I of this,
Who Meteor-like, of stuffe and forme perplext,
    Whose *what,* and *where,* in disputation is,
     If I should call mee *any thing,* should misse.   5

I summe the yeares, and mee, and finde mee not
   Debtor to th'old, nor Creditor to th'new,
That cannot say, My thankes I have forgot,
    Nor trust I this with hopes, and yet scarce true,
     This bravery is since these times shew'd mee you.   10

In recompence I would show future times
   What you were, and teach them to'urge towards such.
Verse embalmes vertue;'and Tombs, or Thrones of rimes,
    Preserve fraile transitory fame, as much
     As spice doth bodies from corrupt aires touch.   15

Mine are short-liv'd; the tincture of your name
   Creates in them, but dissipates as fast,
New spirits: for, strong agents with the same
    Force that doth warme and cherish, us doe wast;
     Kept hot with strong extracts, no bodies last: 20

So, my verse built of your just praise, might want
   Reason and likelihood, the firmest Base,
And made of miracle, now faith is scant,
    Will vanish soone, and so possesse no place,
     And you, and it, too much grace might disgrace.   25

When all (as truth commands assent) confesse
   All truth of you, yet they will doubt how I,
One corne of one low anthills dust, and lesse,
    Should name, know, or expresse a thing so high,
     And not an inch, measure infinity.   30

TO THE COUNTESSE OF BEDFORD [NO. 139].
   See "Reason is our Soules left hand" (No. 134).
   1. *two yeares:* that ending and that beginning.
   3. *perplext:* made of matter and form in a chaotic state.
   16. *Mine:* my verses.
   28. *corne:* particle.

I cannot tell them, nor my selfe, nor you,
    But leave, lest truth b'endanger'd by my praise,
And turne to God, who knowes I thinke this true,
    And useth oft, when such a heart mis-sayes,
    To make it good, for, such a praiser prayes.   35

Hee will best teach you, how you should lay out
    His stock of *beauty, learning, favour, blood;*
He will perplex security with doubt,
    And cleare those doubts; hide from you,'and shew you good,
    And so increase your appetite and food;   40

Hee will teach you, that good and bad have not
    One latitude in cloysters, and in Court;
Indifferent there the greatest space hath got;
    Some pitty'is not good there, some vaine disport,
    On this side, sinne with that place may comport.   45

Yet he, as hee bounds seas, will fixe your houres,
    Which pleasure, and delight may not ingresse,
And though what none else lost, be truliest yours,
    Hee will make you, what you did not, possesse,
    By using others, not vice, but weakenesse.   50

He will make you speake truths, and credibly,
    And make you doubt, that others doe not so:
Hee will provide you keyes, and locks, to spie,
    And scape spies, to good ends, and hee will show
    What you may not acknowledge, what not know.   55

For your owne conscience, he gives innocence,
    But for your fame, a discreet warinesse,
And though to scape, then to revenge offence
    Be better, he showes both, and to represse
    Joy, when your state swells, *sadnesse* when 'tis lesse.   60

From need of teares he will defend your soule,
    Or make a rebaptizing of one teare;
Hee cannot, (that's, he will not) dis-inroule
    Your name; and when with active joy we heare
    This private Ghospell, then 'tis our New Yeare.   65

38. *perplex:* confound.
47. *ingresse:* enter.
48. *what none else lost:* innocence.
61. *defend:* prohibit.
65. *Ghospell:* statement of that which is true, with overtones of salvation.
New Year's Day is the feast of the circumcision of Jesus, the affirmation of the
Great Covenant of Faith and Obedience to God made by Abraham.

140 To Sr. *Edward Herbert.* At *Julyers.*

Man is a lumpe, where all beasts kneaded bee,
    Wisdome makes him an Arke where all agree;
The foole, in whom these beasts do live at jarre,
    Is sport to others, and a Theater,
Nor scapes hee so, but is himselfe their prey;   5
    All which was man in him, is eate away,
And now his beasts on one another feed,
    Yet couple'in anger, and new monsters breed;
How happy'is hee, which hath due place assign'd
    To'his beasts, and disaforested his minde!   10
Empail'd himselfe to keepe them out, not in;
    Can sow, and dares trust corne, where they have bin;
Can use his horse, goate, wolfe, and every beast,
    And is not Asse himselfe to all the rest.
Else, man not onely is the heard of swine,   15
    But he's those devills too, which did incline
Them to a headlong rage, and made them worse:
    For man can adde weight to heavens heaviest curse.
As Soules (they say) by our first touch, take in
    The poysonous tincture of Originall sinne,   20
So, to the punishments which God doth fling,
    Our apprehension contributes the sting.
To us, as to his chickins, he doth cast
    Hemlocke, and wee as men, his hemlocke taste.
We do infuse to what he meant for meat,   25
    Corrosivenesse, or intense cold or heat.
For, God no such specifique poyson hath
    As kills we know not how; his fiercest wrath
Hath no antipathy, but may be good
    At lest for physicke, if not for our food.   30
Thus man, that might be'his pleasure, is his rod,
    And is his devill, that might be his God.

TO SR. EDWARD HERBERT. AT JULYERS.
    Sr. Edward Herbert: son of Magdalen Herbert, he was first Baron of Cherbury (1563–1648). See further, NOTES.
    1. *beasts:* see NOTES.
    6. *eate:* the archaic past participle, pronounced "et."
    10. *disaforested:* taken away privileges (judgment, etc.) and reduced to ordinary standards.
    15–17. See NOTES.
    24. *hemlocke:* a poisonous herb.

Since then our businesse is, to rectifie
   Nature, to what she was, wee'are led awry
By them, who man to us in little show;   35
   Greater then due, no forme we can bestow
On him; for Man into himselfe can draw
   All, All his faith can swallow,'or reason chaw.
All that is fill'd, and all that which doth fill,
   All the round world, to man is but a pill,   40
In all it workes not, but it is in all
   Poysonous, or purgative, or cordiall,
For, knowledge kindles Calentures in some,
   And is to others icy *Opium*.
As brave as true, is that profession than   45
   Which you doe use to make; that you know man.
This makes it credible, you have dwelt upon
   All worthy bookes; and now are such an one.
Actions are authors, and of those in you
   Your friends finde every day a mart of new.   50

141 *To the Countesse of Huntingdon.*

Madame,
Man to Gods image, *Eve*, to mans was made,
   Nor finde wee that God breath'd a soule in her,
Canons will not Church functions you invade,
   Nor lawes to civill office you preferre.

Who vagrant transitory Comets sees,   5
   Wonders, because they'are rare; But a new starre
Whose motion with the firmament agrees,
   Is miracle; for, there no new things are;

42. *cordiall:* stimulating, invigorating (especially to the heart).
43. *Calentures:* tropical fevers accompanied by delusions.
44. *Opium:* the narcotic which induces hallucinations accompanied by chills.
45. *brave:* excellent.
TO THE COUNTESSE OF HUNTINGDON: [NO. 141].
  See "That unripe side of earth, that heavy clime" (No. 131).
  1. That is, woman was not made to God's image.
  3–4. The sense seems to be: Canon laws will not infringe upon church functions for you, nor do you prefer canon laws to civil activity.

In woman so perchance milde innocence
    A seldome comet is, but active good   10
A miracle, which reason scapes, and sense;
    For, Art and Nature this in them withstood.

As such a starre, the *Magi* led to view
    The manger-cradled infant, God below.
By vertues beames by fame deriv'd from you,   15
    May apt soules, and the worst may, vertue know.

If the worlds age, and death be argu'd well
    By the Sunnes fall, which now towards earth doth bend,
Then we might feare that vertue, since she fell
    So low as woman, should be neare her end.   20

But she's not stoop'd, but rais'd; exil'd by men
    She fled to heaven, that's heavenly things, that's you;
She was in all men, thinly scatter'd then,
    But now amass'd, contracted in a few.

She guilded us: But you are gold, and Shee;   25
    Us she inform'd, but transubstantiates you;
Soft dispositions which ductile bee,
    Elixarlike, she makes not cleane, but new.

Though you a wifes and mothers name retaine,
    'Tis not as woman, for all are not soe,   30
But vertue having made you vertue,'is faine
    T'adhere in these names, her and you to show,

Else, being alike pure, wee should neither see,
    As, water being into ayre rarify'd,
Neither appeare, till in one cloud they bee,   35
    So, for our sakes you do low names abide;

Taught by great constellations, which being fram'd,
    Of the most starres, take low names, *Crab*, and *Bull*,
When single planets by the *Gods* are nam'd,
    You covet not great names, of great things full.   40

    12. For Art and Nature resisted good's existence in women.
    22. *fled to heaven:* although he speaks of virtue in general (the "active good" of l. 10), there seems to be an allusion to Astraea, the goddess of justice, who fled from the world at the beginning of the Bronze Age because of man's sinfulness.
    26. She gives herself existence within us, but she actually changes you to herself.
    38. *Crab, and Bull:* Cancer and Taurus.
    39. *Gods:* such as Venus, Jupiter.

So you, as woman, one doth comprehend,
    And in the vaile of kindred others see;
To some ye are reveal'd, as in a friend,
    And as a vertuous Prince farre off, to mee.

To whom, because from you all vertues flow,   45
    And 'tis not none, to dare contemplate you,
I, which doe so, as your true subject owe
    Some tribute for that, so these lines are due.

If you can thinke these flatteries, they are,
    For then your judgement is below my praise,   50
If they were so, oft, flatteries worke as farre,
    As Counsels, and as farre th'endeavour raise.

So my ill reaching you might there grow good,
    But I remaine a poyson'd fountaine still;
But not your beauty, vertue, knowledge, blood   55
    Are more above all flattery, then my will.

And if I flatter any, 'tis not you
    But my owne judgement, who did long agoe
Pronounce, that all these praises should be true,
    And vertue should your beauty,'and birth outgrow.   60

Now that my prophesies are all fulfill'd,
    Rather then God should not be honour'd too,
And all these gifts confess'd, which hee instill'd,
    Your selfe were bound to say that which I doe.

So I, but your Recorder am in this,   65
    Or mouth, or Speaker of the universe,
A ministeriall notary, for 'tis
    Not I, but you and fame, that make this verse;

I was your Prophet in your yonger dayes,
And now your Chaplaine, God in you to praise.   70

42. *vaile:* covering, disguise.
58. *long agoe:* see Notes.

142 A *Letter to the Lady* Carey, *and Mrs.* Essex Riche, *From* Amyens.

Madame,
Here where by All All Saints invoked are,
'Twere too much schisme to be singular,
And 'gainst a practise generall to warre.

Yet turning to Saincts, should my'humility
To other Sainct then you directed bee,   5
That were to make my schisme, heresie.

Nor would I be a Convertite so cold,
As not to tell it; If this be too bold,
Pardons are in this market cheaply sold.

Where, because Faith is in too low degree,   10
I thought it some Apostleship in mee
To speake things which by faith alone I see.

That is, of you, who are a firmament
Of virtues, where no one is growne, or spent,
They'are your materials, not your ornament.   15

Others whom wee call vertuous, are not so
In their whole substance, but, their vertues grow
But in their humours, and at seasons show.

For when through tastlesse flat humilitie
In dow bak'd men some harmelessenes we see,   20
'Tis but his *flegme* that's *Vertuous,* and not Hee:

Soe is the Blood sometimes; who ever ran
To danger unimportun'd, he was than
No better then a *sanguine* Vertuous man.

A LETTER TO THE LADY CAREY, AND MRS. ESSEX RICHE. See NOTES.
   7. *Convertite:* convert.
   9. *Pardons:* the selling of indulgences had long been a major contention against the Church.
   10. At issue was the debate between justification by faith and justification by good works.
   20. *In dow bak'd men:* compare "Man is a lumpe, where all beasts kneaded bee" (No. 140).
   21. *flegme:* equanimity. The other three humours are reviewed in the succeeding lines: blood, black bile (melancholy), yellow bile (choler).

So cloysterall men, who, in pretence of feare   25
All contributions to this life forbeare,
Have Vertue'in *Melancholy,* and'only there.

Spirituall *Cholerique* Crytiques, which in all
Religions find faults, and forgive no fall,
Have, through this zeale, Vertue but in their Gall.   30

We'are thus but parcel guilt; to Gold we'are growne
When Vertue is our Soules complexion;
Who knowes his Vertues name or place, hath none.

Vertue'is but aguish, when 'tis severall,
By'occasion wak'd, and circumstantiall.   35
True vertue'is *Soule,* Alwaies in all deeds *All.*

This Vertue thinking to give dignitie
To your soule, found there no infirmitie,
For, your soule was as good Vertue, as shee;

Shee therefore wrought upon that part of you   40
Which is scarce lesse then soule, as she could do,
And so hath made your beauty, Vertue too.

Hence comes it, that your Beauty wounds not hearts,
As Others, with prophane and sensuall Darts,
But as an influence, vertuous thoughts imparts.   45

But if such friends by the'honor of your sight
Grow capable of this so great a light,
As to partake your vertues, and their might,

What must I thinke that influence must doe,
Where it findes sympathie and matter too,   50
Vertue, and beauty'of the same stuffe, as you?

Which is, your noble worthie sister, shee
Of whom, if what in this my Extasie
And revelation of you both I see,

I should write here, as in short Galleries   55
The Master at the end large glasses ties,
So to present the roome twice to our eyes,

  56. *glasses:* mirrors.

So I should give this letter length, and say
That which I said of you; there is no way
From either, but by the'other not to stray.   60

May therefore this be'enough to testifie
My true devotion, free from flattery;
He that beleeves himselfe, doth never lie.

143 *To the Countesse of* Bedford.
Begun in France but never perfected.

Though I be *dead,* and buried, yet I have
    (Living in you,) Court enough in my grave,
As oft as there I thinke my selfe to bee,
    So many resurrections waken mee.
That thankfullnesse your favours have begot   5
    In mee, embalmes mee, that I doe not rot;
This season as 'tis Easter, as 'tis spring,
    Must both to growth and to confession bring
My thoughts dispos'd unto your influence, so,
    These verses bud, so these confessions grow;   10
First I confesse I have to others lent
    Your stock, and over prodigally spent
Your treasure, for since I had never knowne
    Vertue or beautie, but as they are growne
In you, I should not thinke or say they shine,   15
    (So as I have) in any other Mine;
Next I confesse this my confession,
    For, 'tis some fault thus much to touch upon
Your praise to you, where half rights seeme too much,
    And make your minds sincere complexion blush.   20

TO THE COUNTESSE OF BEDFORD [NO. 143].
    See "Reason is our Soules left hand" (No. 134). The poem was written
while Donne was in France with the Drurys in 1611–12, but apparently was
left unfinished, as noted.
    7. *Easter:* dating the poem c. April 22, 1612 (N.S.).
    12. *stock:* the main stem of a plant, from which his verses bud (l. 10).

Next I confesse my'impenitence, for I
   Can scarce repent my first fault, since thereby
Remote low Spirits, which shall ne'r read you,
   May in lesse lessons finde enough to doe,
By studying copies, not Originals,   25
   Desunt cætera.

144   De Libro cum mutuaretur, Impresso, Domi à pueris frustatim lacerato, et post reddito Manuscripto.

Doctissimo Amicissimoque v. D.D. Andrews.

Parturiunt madido quæ nixu præla, recepta;
   Sed quæ scripta manu sunt, veneranda magis.
Transiit in Sequanam Mœnus; Victoris in ædes,
   Et Francofurtum, te revehente meat.
Qui liber in pluteos, blattis, cinerique relictos,   5
   Si modo sit præli sanguine tinctus, abit;
Accedat calamo scriptus, reverenter habetur,
   Involat et veterum scrinia summa Patrum.
Dicat Apollo modum; Pueros infundere libro
   Nempe vetustatem canitiemque novo.   10
Nil mirum, medico pueros de semine natos,
   Hæc nova fata libro posse dedisse novo.
Si veterem faciunt pueri, qui nuperus, Annon
   Ipse Pater, Iuvenem, me dabit arte, senem?
Hei miseris senibus; nos vertit dura senectus   15
   Omnes in pueros, neminem at in Iuvenem.
Hoc tibi servasti præstandum, Antique Dierum,
   Quo viso, et vivit, et juvenescit Adam.
Interea, Infirmæ fallamus tædia vitæ,
   Libris, et Cœlorum æmulâ amicitiâ.   20
Hos inter, qui à te mihi redditus, iste libellus,
   Non mihi tam charus, tam meus, ante fuit.

24. *lesse:* inferior.
16. *Desunt cætera:* the remaining verses are lacking.

144A   Concerning a printed book which,
when it was borrowed, was torn to pieces
by the children in the house,
and was later returned in manuscript.

To a most learned and most friendly man of God, Dr. Andrews.

What presses bring forth may be recovered with moist pains;
but those written by hand are more venerable.
The river Main passed into the Seine, into the sanctuary of the
    victor,
and Frankfort, having conveyed you back, departs.
Any book abandoned on bookshelves to moths and dust,   5
if it be dyed only with blood of the press, dies;
should it resemble that written with pen, it is cherished re-
    spectfully,
and it takes possession of the topmost bookcases of the ancient
    fathers.
Apollo may relate the way that boys assuredly pour
over a new book old age and hoariness.   10
It is not astonishing that children sprung from doctor's seed
are able to deliver this late fortune to a new-born book.
If youths make old what is recent, will not
their sire himself by his art confer youth in me, an old man?
Ah, unfortunate old men; harsh age transforms us   15
all into children, but not one to youth.
This you have reserved for yourself as your responsibility, ancient
    of days,
in whose sight man lives and grows young again.

DE LIBRO . . . : See NOTES.
    3–4. The German river Main becomes a tributary of the Seine, and Frank-
fort on the Main was an important center of the book trade. It would seem that
Andrews resided in Germany and Donne in Paris (as he did in 1612, having
visited Germany with the Drurys). Garrod interprets "the sanctuary of the
victor" as Andrews' home, but the book's fate there hardly makes that likely.
Rather, Donne is the "victor" since this manuscript version is superior, he
writes, to the printed version which was destroyed. The sanctuary is thus
Donne's topmost bookshelves.
    6. Lat. *sanguine* / Eng. *blood:* ink.
    9. *Apollo:* god of poetry and learning; appropriately he was also god of
healing.
    14. Donne was probably about forty-one when this was written.

Meanwhile, we cheat the weariness of feeble life
with books and the emulous friendship of heaven.   20
Amid these volumes, that little book, which was returned by you
    to me,
was not so dear to me before as this my very own.

145 *To the Countesse of Salisbury.* August. 1614.

Faire, great, and good, since seeing you, wee see
What Heaven can doe, and what any'Earth can be:
Since now your beauty shines, now when the Sunne
Growne stale, is to so low a value runne,
That his disshevel'd beames and scatter'd fires   5
Serve but for Ladies Periwigs and Tyres
In lovers Sonnets: you come to repaire
Gods booke of creatures, teaching what is faire.
Since now, when all is wither'd, shrunke, and dri'd,
All Vertues ebb'd out to a dead low tyde,   10
All the worlds frame being crumbled into sand,
Where every man thinks by himselfe to stand,
Integritie, friendship, and confidence,
(Ciments of greatnes) being vapor'd hence,
And narrow man being fill'd with little shares,   15
Court, Citie, Church, are all shops of small-wares,
All having blowne to sparkes their noble fire,
And drawne their sound gold-ingot into wyre;
All trying by a love of littlenesse
To make abridgments, and to draw to lesse,   20
Even that nothing, which at first we were;
Since in these times, your greatnesse doth appeare,
And that we learne by it, that man to get
Towards him, thats infinite, must first be great.

22. The same printed volume is owned by many people; only Donne owns
such a manuscript version.
TO THE COUNTESSE OF SALISBURY.
   The Countesse of Salisbury: Catharine Howard, daughter of Thomas, first
Earl of Suffolk, married William Cecil, second Earl of Salisbury, in 1608.
   6. *Periwigs and Tyres:* the likening of ladies' wigs and headdresses to the
rays of the sun.
   9. That is, in August, and referring to religious and political difficulties such
as those of James' second parliament (the "Addled" Parliament), called in
April 1614 and dissolved in June. Donne was a member from Taunton.
   24. *him:* God.

Since in an age so ill, as none is fit 25
So much as to accuse, much lesse mend it,
(For who can judge, or witnesse of those times
Where all alike are guiltie of the crimes?)
Where he that would be good, is thought by all
A monster, or at best fantasticall: 30
Since now you durst be good, and that I doe
Discerne, by daring to contemplate you,
That there may be degrees of faire, great, good,
Through your light, largenesse, vertue understood:
If in this sacrifice of mine, be showne 35
Any small sparke of these, call it your owne.
And if things like these, have been said by mee
Of others; call not that Idolatrie.
For had God made man first, and man had seene
The third daies fruits, and flowers, and various greene, 40
He might have said the best that he could say
Of those faire creatures, which were made that day;
And when next day he had admir'd the birth
Of Sun, Moone, Stars, fairer then late-prais'd earth,
Hee might have said the best that he could say, 45
And not be chid for praising yesterday:
So though some things are not together true,
As, that another is worthiest, and, that you:
Yet, to say so, doth not condemne a man,
If when he spoke them, they were both true than. 50
How faire a proofe of this, in our soule growes?
Wee first have soules of growth, and sense, and those,
When our last soule, our soule immortall came,
Were swallow'd into it, and have no name.
Nor doth he injure those soules, which doth cast 55
The power and praise of both them, on the last;
No more doe I wrong any; I adore
The same things now, which I ador'd before,
The subject chang'd, and measure; the same thing
In a low constable, and in the King 60
I reverence; His power to worke on mee;
So did I humbly reverence each degree

40–44. "And the earth brought forth grass, and herb yielding seed after his kind, and the tree yielding fruit, whose seed was in itself, after his kind: and God saw that it was good. And the evening and the morning were the third day" (Gen. i 12–13). On the fourth day "lights" were created in the firmament of heaven. Man was created on the sixth day.

Of faire, great, good, but more, now I am come
From having found their *walkes,* to find their *home.*
And as I owe my first soules thankes, that they   65
For my last soule did fit and mould my clay,
So am I debtor unto them, whose worth,
Enabled me to profit, and take forth
This new great lesson, thus to study you;
Which none, not reading others, first, could doe.   70
Nor lacke I light to read this booke, though I
In a darke Cave, yea in a Grave doe lie;
For as your fellow Angells, so you doe
Illustrate them who come to study you.
The first whom we in Histories doe finde   75
To have profest all Arts, was one borne blind:
He lackt those eyes beasts have as well as wee,
Not those, by which Angels are seene and see;
So, though I'am borne without those eyes to live,
Which fortune, who hath none her selfe, doth give,   80
Which are, fit meanes to see bright courts and you,
Yet may I see you thus, as now I doe;
I shall by that, all goodnesse have discern'd,
And though I burne my librarie, be learn'd.

72. Apparently he was living at Taunton; his daughter Mary had died in
May.
76. *one borne blind:* Tiresias.

Epicedes and Obsequies

Sorrow, who to this house scarce knew the way:
Is, Oh, heire of it, our All is his prey.
This strange chance claimes strange wonder, and to us
Nothing can be so strange, as to weepe thus;
'Tis well his lifes loud speaking workes deserve,   5
And give praise too, our cold tongues could not serve:
'Tis well, hee kept teares from our eyes before,
That to fit this deepe ill, we might have store.
Oh, if a sweet briar, climbe up by'a tree,
If to'a paradise that transplanted bee,   10
Or fell'd, and burnt for holy sacrifice,
Yet, that must wither, which by it did rise,
As we for him dead: though no familie
Ere rigg'd a soule for heavens discoverie
With whom more Venturers more boldly dare   15
Venture their states, with him in joy to share.
Wee lose what all friends lov'd, him; he gaines now
But life by death, which worst foes would allow,
If hee could have foes, in whose practise grew
All vertues, whose names subtile Schoolmen knew;   20
What ease, can hope that wee shall see'him, beget,
When wee must die first, and cannot dye yet?
His children are his pictures, Oh they bee
Pictures of him dead, senselesse, cold as he.
Here needs no marble Tombe, since hee is gone,   25
He, and about him, his, are turn'd to stone.

ELEGIE ON THE L. C.
    L. C.: perhaps the Lord Chamberlain, Henry Carey (1524?–July 23, 1596), first Lord Hunsdon, and important adviser to the Queen. See NOTES.
    9. The old fable of the oak and the briar was amplified most notably by Spenser in the February eclogue of *The Shepheardes Calender.*
    19–20. The sense is: The actions of any such foes merely make his virtues more evident.

147   *Epitaph on Himselfe.* To the Countesse
of Bedford.

MADAME,
That I might make your Cabinet my tombe,
   And for my fame which I love next my soule,
Next to my soule provide the happiest roome,
   Admit to that place this last funerall Scrowle.
     Others by Wills give Legacies, but I   5
     Dying, of you doe beg a Legacie.

My Fortune and my choice this custome break,
When we are speechlesse grown, to make stones speak,
Though no stone tel thee what I was, yet thou
In my graves inside seest what thou art now: 10
Yet thou'art not yet so good, till death us lay
To ripe and mellow here, we'are stubborne Clay.
Parents make us earth, and soules dignifie
Us to be glasse; here to grow gold we lie;
Whilst in our soules sinne bred and pamper'd is,   15
Our soules become wormeaten carkases;
So we our selves miraculously destroy.
Here bodies with less miracle enjoy
Such priviledges, enabled here to scale
Heaven, when the Trumpets ayre shall them exhale.   20

EPITAPH ON HIMSELFE.
   See "Reason is our Soules left hand" (No. 134). Perhaps the poem was
written in 1608 when Donne was seriously ill.
   1. *Cabinet:* a small private room used for consultation; here a kind of library.
   2. *fame:* reputation.
   7. *My Fortune and my choice:* what has befallen me in life and my exercise
of decision in life.   *custome:* object of "break"; of giving rather than receiving
a legacy.
   13. *earth:* man is made from dust and to dust returns, since he is mortal.
   14. *glasse:* which reflects God's blessings; alchemically ruby glass was a kind
of elixir, red symbolizing immortality.   *to grow gold:* gold was alchemically
considered indestructible; it was thought a product only of proper dissolution.
   16. *wormeaten carkases:* contrasting with worm-eaten bodies in the grave;
this paradox is the miracle achieved (l. 17).
   20. *Trumpets ayre:* the sound of the Trumpet of Judgment Day when man's
breath (of life) will entirely be exhaled.

Heare this, and mend thy selfe, and thou mendst me,
By making me being dead, doe good to thee,
 And thinke me well compos'd, that I could now
 A last-sicke houre to syllables allow.

148 *Elegie to the Lady Bedford.*

You that are she and you, that's double shee,
 In her dead face, halfe of your selfe shall see;
Shee was the other part, for so they doe
 Which build them friendships, become one of two;
So two, that but themselves no third can fit,   5
 Which were to be so, when they were not yet
Twinnes, though their birth *Cusco*, and *Musco* take,
 As divers starres one Constellation make,
Pair'd like two eyes, have equall motion, so
 Both but one meanes to see, one way to goe;   10
Had you dy'd first, a carcasse shee had beene;
 And wee your rich Tombe in her face had seene;
She like the Soule is gone, and you here stay
 Not a live friend; but th'other halfe of clay;
And since you act that part, As men say, here   15
 Lies such a Prince, when but one part is there;
And do all honour and devotion due
 Unto the whole, so wee all reverence you;
For, such a friendship who would not adore
 In you, who are all what both were before,   20
Not all, as if some perished by this,
 But so, as all in you contracted is;
As of this all, though many parts decay,
 The pure which elemented them shall stay;

23. *well compos'd:* being prepared for death; composing in his last moments
a well-wrought poem of faith.
ELEGIE TO THE LADY BEDFORD.
 See "Reason is our Soules left hand" (No. 134).
 1. *she:* perhaps Lady Markham, who died on May 4, 1609, at Twickenham,
the home of Lady Bedford, her cousin.
 7. *Cusco, and Musco:* Cuzco, Inca capital of Peru, and Moscow. The images
of the poem seem to indicate that Lady Bedford and the dead lady were basically opposite (and complementary) personalities.

And though diffus'd, and spread in infinite,   25
    Shall recollect, and in one All unite:
So madame, as her Soule to heaven is fled,
    Her flesh rests in the earth, as in the bed;
Her vertues do, as to their proper spheare,
    Returne to dwell with you, of whom they were;   30
As perfect motions are all circular,
    So they to you, their sea, whence lesse streames are;
Shee was all spices, you all metalls; so
    In you two wee did both rich Indies know;
And as no fire, nor rust can spend or waste   35
    One dramme of gold, but what was first shall last,
Though it bee forc'd in water, earth, salt, aire,
    Expans'd in infinite, none will impaire;
So, to your selfe you may additions take,
    But nothing can you lesse, or changed make,   40
Seeke not in seeking new, to seeme to doubt,
    That you can match her, or not be without;
But let some faithfull booke in her roome be,
    Yet but of *Judith* no such booke as shee.

149   *Elegie on the Lady* Marckham.

Man is the World, and death the Ocean,
    To which God gives the lower parts of man.
This Sea invirons all, and though as yet
    God hath set markes, and bounds, twixt us and it,

33–34. Spices came from the East Indies, gold and silver supposedly from the West Indies.

36. *gold:* the only metal considered not subject to disintegration. Compare Matt. xx 16: "So the last shall be first, and the first last: for many be called, but few chosen."

43. *faithfull booke:* the Bible which Lady Bedford should read to fill the void which death has created.

44. *Judith:* the book of the Apocrypha which tells of Judith's slaying of Nebuchadnezzar's general, Holofernes. Perhaps the likeness for Donne lay in both Lady Markham's and Judith's being widows who remained faithful to their husbands.

ELEGIE ON THE LADY MARCKHAM.

Lady Marckham: Lady Bridget Markham died on May 4, 1609, at Twickenham Park, the residence of her cousin, Lucy, Countess of Bedford. She was the widow of Sir Anthony Markham and a patroness of poets.

Yet doth it rore, and gnaw, and still pretend,   5
    And breaks our bankes, when ere it takes a friend.
Then our land waters (teares of passion) vent;
    Our waters, then, above our firmament,
(Teares which our Soule doth for her sins let fall)
    Take all a brackish tast, and Funerall,   10
And even these teares, which should wash sin, are sin.
    We, after Gods *Noe*, drowne our world againe.
Nothing but man of all invenom'd things
    Doth worke upon itselfe, with inborne stings.
Teares are false Spectacles, we cannot see   15
    Through passions mist, what wee are, or what shee.
In her this sea of death hath made no breach,
    But as the tide doth wash the slimie beach,
And leaves embroder'd workes upon the sand,
    So is her flesh refin'd by deaths cold hand.   20
As men of China,'after an ages stay,
    Do take up Porcelane, where they buried Clay;
So at this grave, her limbecke, which refines
    The Diamonds, Rubies, Saphires, Pearles, and Mines,
Of which this flesh was, her soule shall inspire   25
    Flesh of such stuffe, as God, when his last fire
Annuls this world, to recompence it, shall,
    Make and name then, th'Elixar of this All.
They say, the sea, when it gaines, loseth too;
    If carnall Death (the yonger brother) doe   30
Usurpe the body,'our soule, which subject is
    To th'elder death, by sinne, is freed by this;
They perish both, when they attempt the just;
    For, graves our trophies are, and both deaths dust.
So, unobnoxious now, she'hath buried both;   35
    For, none to death sinnes, that to sinne is loth.
Nor doe they die, which are not loth to die,
    So hath she this, and that virginity.
Grace was in her extremely diligent,
    That kept her from sinne, yet made her repent.   40

23. *limbecke:* alembic.
24. *Mines:* precious metals.
28. *Elixar:* the substance which will create all these transmutations.
33. *attempt:* tempt, try to subdue.
35. *unobnoxious:* both deaths are now incapable of dealing death.
38. *virginity:* virgin in not having sinned and not having died as here defined.

Of what small spots pure white complaines! Alas,
    How little poyson breakes a christall glasse!
She sinn'd, but just enough to let us see
    That God's word must be true, All, sinners be.
Soe much did zeale her conscience rarefie,   45
    That, extreme truth lack'd little of a lye,
Making omissions, acts; laying the touch
    Of sinne, on things that sometimes may be such.
As *Moses* Cherubines, whose natures doe
    Surpasse all speed, by him are winged too: 50
So would her soule, already'in heaven, seeme then,
    To clyme by teares, the common staires of men.
How fit she was for God, I am content
    To speake, that death his vaine hast may repent.
How fit for us, how even and how sweet,   55
    How good in all her titles, and how meet,
To have reform'd this forward heresie,
    That women can no parts of friendship bee;
How Morall, how Divine shall not be told,
    Lest they that heare her vertues, thinke her old: 60
And lest we take Deaths part, and make him glad
    Of such a prey, and to his tryumph adde.

150   *Elegie on Mris*. Boulstred.

Death I recant, and say, unsaid by mee
    What ere hath slip'd, that might diminish thee.
Spirituall treason, atheisme 'tis, to say,
    That any can thy Summons disobey.
Th'earths face is but thy Table; there are set   5
    Plants, cattell, men, dishes for Death to eate.
In a rude hunger now hee millions drawes
    Into his bloody,'or plaguy, or sterv'd jawes.

49. *As Moses Cherubines:* in Exodus xxv Moses was instructed to make a
tabernacle and a mercy seat with two golden cherubs on either end. See further,
NOTES.
ELEGIE ON MRIS. BOULSTRED.
    Mris. Boulstred: Cecilia, daughter of Edward Bulstrode, was baptized on
February 12, 1584, and died at Twickenham on August 4, 1609. She was re-
lated to Lucy, Countess of Bedford.

Now hee will seeme to spare, and doth more wast,
   Eating the best first, well preserv'd to last.   10
Now wantonly he spoiles, and eates us not,
   But breakes off friends, and lets us peecemeale rot.
Nor will this earth serve him; he sinkes the deepe
   Where harmelesse fish monastique silence keepe,
Who (were Death dead) by Roes of living sand,   15
   Might spunge that element, and make it land.
He rounds the aire, and breakes the hymnique notes
   In birds, Heavens choristers, organique throats,
Which (if they did not dye) might seeme to bee
   A tenth ranke in the heavenly hierarchie.   20
O strong and long-liv'd death, how cam'st thou in?
   And how without Creation didst begin?
Thou hast, and shalt see dead, before thou dyest,
   All the foure Monarchies, and Antichrist.
How could I thinke thee nothing, that see now   25
   In all this All, nothing else is, but thou.
Our births and lives, vices, and vertues, bee
   Wastfull consumptions, and degrees of thee.
For, wee to live, our bellowes weare, and breath,
   Nor are wee mortall, dying, dead, but death,   30
And though thou beest, O mighty bird of prey,
   So much reclaim'd by God, that thou must lay
All that thou kill'st at his feet, yet doth hee
   Reserve but few, and leaves the most to thee.
And of those few, now thou hast overthrowne   35
   One whom thy blow makes, not ours, nor thine own.
She was more stories high: hopelesse to come
   To'her Soule, thou'hast offer'd at her lower roome.
Her Soule and body was a King and Court:
   But thou hast both of Captaine mist and fort.   40
As houses fall not, though the King remove,
   Bodies of Saints rest for their soules above.
Death gets 'twixt soules and bodies such a place
   As sinne insinuates 'twixt just men and grace,
Both worke a separation, no divorce.   45
   Her Soule is gone to usher up her corse,

16. *spunge that element:* soak up that water.
20. There were nine orders of angels.
24. *foure Monarchies:* Babylon, Persia, Greece, and Rome. The Fifth Monarchy is the millennium when Christ will rule.
38. *offer'd:* made an attempt.   *lower roome:* body.

Which shall be'almost another soule, for there
    Bodies are purer, then best Soules are here.
Because in her, her virtues did outgoe
    Her yeares, would'st thou, O emulous death, do so?   50
And kill her young to thy losse? must the cost
    Of beauty,'and wit, apt to doe harme, be lost?
What though thou found'st her proofe 'gainst sins of youth?
    Oh, every age a diverse sinne pursueth.
Thou should'st have stay'd, and taken better hold,   55
    Shortly ambitious; covetous, when old,
She might have prov'd: and such devotion
    Might once have stray'd to superstition.
If all her vertues must have growne, yet might
    Abundant virtue'have bred a proud delight.   60
Had she persever'd just, there would have bin
    Some that would sinne, mis-thinking she did sinne.
Such as would call her friendship, love, and faine
    To sociablenesse, a name profane,
Or sinne, by tempting, or, not daring that,   65
    By wishing, though they never told her what.
Thus might'st thou'have slain more soules, had'st thou not crost
    Thy selfe, and to triumph, thine army lost.
Yet though these wayes be lost, thou hast left one,
    Which is, immoderate griefe that she is gone.   70
But we may scape that sinne, yet weepe as much,
    Our teares are due, because we are not such.
Some teares, that knot of friends, her death must cost,
    Because the chaine is broke, though no linke lost.

151   *Elegie: Death.*

Language thou art too narrow, and too weake
    To ease us now; great sorrow cannot speake;
If we could sigh out accents, and weepe words,
    Griefe weares, and lessens, that tears breath affords.
Sad hearts, the lesse they seeme the more they are,   5
    (So guiltiest men stand mutest at the barre)

    64. *a name profane:* hypocrite.

Not that they know not, feele not their estate,
　　But extreme sense hath made them desperate;
Sorrow, to whom we owe all that we bee;
　　Tyrant, in the'fift and greatest Monarchy,　　　　　　　10
Was't, that she did possesse all hearts before,
　　Thou hast kil'd her, to make thy Empire more?
Knew'st thou some would, that knew her not, lament,
　　As in a deluge perish th'innocent?
Was't not enough to have that palace wonne,　　　　　　15
　　But thou must raze it too, that was undone?
Had'st thou staid there, and look'd out at her eyes,
　　All had ador'd thee that now from thee flies,
For they let out more light, then they tooke in,
　　They told not when, but did the day beginne;　　　　　20
She was too Saphirine, and cleare for thee;
　　Clay, flint, and jeat now thy fit dwellings be;
Alas, shee was too pure, but not too weake;
　　Who e'r saw Christall Ordinance but would break?
And if wee be thy conquest, by her fall　　　　　　　　25
　　Th'hast lost thy end, for in her perish all;
Or if we live, we live but to rebell,
　　They know her better now, that knew her well;
If we should vapour out, and pine, and die;
　　Since, shee first went, that were not miserie;　　　　30
Shee chang'd our world with hers; now she is gone,
　　Mirth and prosperity is oppression;
For of all morall vertues she was all,
　　The Ethicks speake of vertues Cardinall;
Her soule was Paradise; the Cherubin　　　　　　　　35
　　Set to keepe it was grace, that kept out sinne;
Shee had no more then let in death, for wee
　　All reape consumption from one fruitfull tree;

ELEGIE: DEATH.
　　7. *estate:* situation, condition.
　　10. *greatest Monarchy:* England; the other monarchies were Babylon, Persia, Greece, and Rome. But see also No. 150, n. to l. 24.
　　15–16. The woman whose death is mourned had previously been sorrowed. The O'Flaherty MS cites Mrs. Boulstred, who died at Twickenham on August 4, 1609, three months after her kinswoman Lady Markham. See also *Elegie on Mris. Boulstred* (No. 150).
　　21. *Saphirine:* transparent like a sapphire.
　　24. Who ever saw anything decreed to be crystal which would not break?
　　26. *end:* both "aim" and "cessation" of sorrow.
　　38. *fruitfull tree:* the Tree of Knowledge, the eating of whose fruit by Adam and Eve brought mortality into the world.

God tooke her hence, lest some of us should love
 Her, like that plant, him and his lawes above,   40
And when wee teares, hee mercy shed in this,
 To raise our mindes to heaven where now she is;
Who if her vertues would have let her stay
 Wee'had had a Saint, have now a holiday;
Her heart was that strange bush, where, sacred fire,   45
 Religion, did not consume, but inspire
Such piety, so chast use of Gods day,
 That what we turne to feast, she turn'd to pray,
And did prefigure here, in devout tast,
 The rest of her high Sabaoth, which shall last;   50
Angels did hand her up, who next God dwell,
 (For she was of that order whence most fell)
Her body left with us, lest some had said,
 Shee could not die, except they saw her dead;
For from lesse vertue, and lesse beautiousnesse,   55
 The Gentiles fram'd them Gods and Goddesses.
The ravenous earth that now wooes her to be
 Earth too, will be a *Lemnia;* and the tree
That wraps that christall in a wooden Tombe,
 Shall be tooke up spruce, fill'd with diamond;   60
And we her sad glad friends all beare a part
 Of griefe, for all would waste a Stoicks heart.

44. *holiday:* a holy day, a saint's festival.

45. *strange bush:* the burning bush of Exodus iii 2, which inspired faith in
Moses: "And the angel of the Lord appeared unto him in a flame of fire out of
the midst of a bush: and he looked, and, behold, the bush burned with fire, and
the bush was not consumed."

52. *order:* the seraphim, the highest order of angels, from whose ranks came
most of the fallen angels.

58. *Lemnia:* terra Lemnia, a red clay found on Lemnos. It was an antidote
to poison and was used by alchemists to transmute crystal into diamond.

60. *spruce:* meaning that a spruce tree will grow where she is buried and,
apparently, that her coffin itself will be transformed to spruce. (The earliest
example of the latter usage in the NED is 1670.) Perhaps there is also a pun
on the meaning "quickly."

152   *Elegie* On the untimely Death of the *incomparable Prince,* Henry.

Look to Me, *Faith;* and look to my *Faith,* GOD:
For, both my *Centres* feel This *Period.*
Of *Waight,* one *Centre;* one, of *Greatness* is:
And REASON is That *Centre;* FAITH is This.
For into'our *Reason* flowe, and there doe end,   5
All that this naturall World doth comprehend;
Quotidian things, and Equi-distant hence,
Shut-in for Men in one *Circumference:*
But, for th'enormous *Greatnesses,* which are
So disproportion'd and so angulare,   10
As is GOD's *Essence, Place,* and *Providence,*
Where, How, When, What, Soules do departed hence:
These *Things (Eccentrique* else) on *Faith* do strike;
Yet neither All, nor upon all alike:
For, *Reason,* put t'her best *Extension,*   15
Almost meetes *Faith,* and makes both *Centres* one:
And nothing ever came so neer to This,
As *Contemplation* of that PRINCE wee misse.
For, All that *Faith* could credit Mankinde *could,*
Reason still seconded that This PRINCE *would.*   20
If then, least Movings of the *Centre* make
(More then if whole Hell belcht) the World to shake,
What must This doo, *Centres* distracted so,
That Wee see not what to beleeve or knowe?

ELEGIE ON . . . PRINCE HENRY.
   Prince Henry: The Prince of Wales (James I's elder son) died of typhoid
fever on November 6, 1612, at the age of eighteen. See further, NOTES.
   2. *Centres:* refers to Kepler's first law of planetary motion that planets revolve around the sun in elliptical orbits, each orbit having two foci. One center
is reason (of importance); the other is faith (of eminence).   *Period:* end of
life, but punning on a period as a dot and a center as a dot; also equating the
period and thus Prince Henry with the sun.
   7. *Quotidian:* short-lived, since reason is limited and imperfect compared
with faith.
   9–11. But these greatnesses are not (or should not be) disproportioned or
angular because God's omniscience, His omnipresence, and His omnipotence
are perfect. Circles were considered perfect; angular things, imperfect.
   13. *Eccentrique else:* rather than moving in a perfect circle.
   16. Thus describing a circle rather than an ellipse. The point is, the mourner
must have faith in God's ways (as in this death), making his understanding or
justification thereof coincide with his faith.
   23. *distracted:* drawn in different directions.

Was it not well believ'd, till now; that *Hee,*   25
Whose *Reputation* was an *Extasie*
On Neighbour States; which knew not Why to wake
Till *Hee* discoverd what wayes *Hee* would take:
From *Whom* what *Princes* angled (when they tryed)
Mett a *Torpedo,* and were stupified: 30
And Others studies, how *Hee* would be bent,
Was His great *Father's* greatest Instrument,
And activ'st spirit to convey and tye
This soule of *Peace* through *Christianitie?*
Was it not well believ'd, that *Hee* would make   35
This *general Peace* th'eternall overtake?
And that *His* Times might have stretcht out so far
As to touch Those of which they *Emblems* are?
For to confirm this just Belief, that Now
The *last Dayes* came; wee saw Heaven did allow   40
That but from *His* aspect and Excercise,
In *Peace*-full times, Rumors of *Warrs* should rise.
But *now* This *Faith* is *Heresie:* wee must
Still stay, and vexe our *Great-Grand-Mother,* Dust.
Oh! Is God prodigall? Hath He spent his store   45
Of Plagues on us? and only now, when more
Would ease us much, doth he grudge Miserie,
And will not lett's enjoy our *Curse,* to *Dye?*
As, for the Earth throw'n lowest downe of all,
'Twere an *Ambition* to desire to fall: 50
So God, in our *desire* to *dye,* dooth know
Our Plot for *Ease,* in beeing *Wretched* so.
Therfore *Wee live:* though such a Life wee have
As but so manie *Mandrakes* on his Grave.
    What had *His growth* and *generation* donne?   55
When what wee are, his *putrefaction*
Sustains in us, Earth; which *Griefs* animate:
Nor hath our World now other *soule* then That.
And could *Grief* gett so high as Heav'n, that *Quire*
Forgetting This, their new joy would desire   60

30. *Torpedo:* a fish, the electric ray.
38. *Those:* those times of eternal peace in Heaven.
44. *Dust:* the earth from which man was created and the world potentially at
war in 1612. (The Thirty Years' War was to begin in 1618.)
54. *Mandrakes:* refers to the mandrake's manlike form, its supernatural abilities to promote conception, and its groan on being uprooted.

(With grief to see him) *Hee* had staid belowe,
To rectifie Our *Errors* They foreknowe.
   Is th'other *Centre*, REASON, faster, then?
Where should wee look for That, now w'are not Men?
For, if our *Reason* be our *Connexion*   65
With *Causes*, now to us there can be none.
For, as, if all the *Substances* were spent,
'Twere Madnes to enquire of *Accident:*
So is't to looke for *Reason*, HEE being gone,
The only *Subject* REASON wrought upon.   70
   If *Faith* have such a *chaine*, whose divers Links
Industrious Man discerneth, as he thinks,
When Miracle dooth ioine; and to steal-in
A new link Man knowes not where to begin:
At a much deader Fault must *Reason* bee,   75
Death having broke-off such a Link as *Hee*.
But, now, for us with busie *Proofs* to come
That w'have no *Reason*, would prove we had some:
So would just *Lamentations*. Therfore Wee
May safelier say, that Wee are dead, then *Hee*.   80
So, if our *Griefs* wee doo not well declare,
W'have double Excuse; *Hee* is not *dead*, Wee are.
Yet I would not dye yet; for though I bee
Too-narrow, to think HIM, as *Hee* is HEE
(Our *Soule's* best Bayting and Mid-*period*   85
In her long *Journey* of *Considering* GOD)
Yet (no Dishonor) I can reach Him *thus;*
As *Hee* embrac't the *Fires* of *Love* with us.
Oh! May I (*since* I live) but see or hear
That *Shee-Intelligence* which mov'd This *Sphear*,   90
I pardon Fate my Life. Who-e'r thou bee
Which hast the noble *Conscience*, Thou art *Shee*.

63. *faster:* more steadfast.

68. *Accident:* in Aristotelian logic the accidents were the ten categories into which all knowledge can be reduced; though substance connects all other accidents, it cannot be perceived except through those other accidents. Since substance is spent (through the Prince's death), it is futile to look to Quantity, Quality, Relation, Place, Time, Posture, Possession, Action, or Passion for comprehension of substance.

85. *Bayting:* halting.

90. *Shee-Intelligence:* the nine Muses (or Sirens) were said to travel about the earth each on one of the spheres of the Ptolemaic universe (*Republic*, X, 616–17). Each uttered one harmonious tone, creating the music of the spheres. In Christian thought the intelligences governing the spheres were angels.

I conjure Thee by all the *Charmes Hee* spoke,
By th'Oathes which only you *Two* never broke,
By all the *Soules* yee sigh't; that if you see   95
These Lines, you wish I knew *Your Historie:*
So, much as *You Two mutual Heavens* were *here,*
I were an *Angel singing* what *You* were.

      To the Countesse of Bedford.
Madame,
I Have learn'd by those lawes wherein I am a little conversant,
that hee which bestowes any cost upon the dead, obliges him
which is dead, but not the heire; I do not therefore send this pa-
per to your Ladyship, that you should thanke mee for it, or
thinke that I thanke you in it; your favours and benefits to mee
are so much above my merits, that they are even above my
gratitude, if that were to be judged by words which must expresse
it: But, Madame, since your noble brothers fortune being yours,
the evidences also concerning it are yours, so his vertue being
yours, the evidence concerning it, belong also to you, of which by
your acceptance this may be one peece, in which quality I humbly
present it, and as a testimony how intirely your familie pos-
sesseth

                Your Ladiships most humble
                  and thankfull servant
                John Donne.

    153   *Obsequies to the Lord Harrington,*
  brother to the Lady Lucy, Countesse of Bedford.

Faire soule, which wast, not onely,'as all soules bee,
Then when thou wast infused, harmony,
But did'st continue so; and now dost beare
A part in Gods great organ, this whole Spheare:

   94. *you Two:* reason and faith.
OBSEQUIES TO THE LORD HARRINGTON.
   Lord Harrington: John Harington, second Baron of Exton, died at his sister's
house on February 27, 1614. While traveling in France and Italy in 1613, he
was poisoned, probably by design.

If looking up to God; or downe to us,   5
Thou finde that any way is pervious,
Twixt heav'n and earth, and that mans actions doe
Come to your knowledge, and affections too,
See, and with joy, mee to that good degree
Of goodnesse growne, that I can studie thee,   10
And, by these meditations refin'd,
Can unapparell and enlarge my minde,
And so can make by this soft extasie,
This place a map of heav'n, my selfe of thee.
Thou seest mee here at midnight, now all rest;   15
Times dead-low water; when all mindes devest
To morrows businesse, when the labourers have
Such rest in bed, that their last Church-yard grave,
Subject to change, will scarce be'a type of this,
Now when the clyent, whose last hearing is   20
To morrow, sleeps, when the condemned man,
(Who when hee opes his eyes, must shut them than
Againe by death,) although sad watch hee keepe,
Doth practice dying by a little sleepe,
Thou at this midnight seest mee, and as soone   25
As that Sunne rises to mee, midnight's noone,
All the world growes transparent, and I see
Through all, both Church and State, in seeing thee;
And I discerne by favour of this light,
My selfe, the hardest object of the sight.   30
God is the glasse; as thou when thou dost see
Him who sees all, seest all concerning thee,
So, yet unglorified, I comprehend
All, in these mirrors of thy wayes, and end;
Though God be our true glass, through which we see   35
All, since the beeing of all things is hee,
Yet are the trunkes which doe to us derive
Things, in proportion fit by perspective,
Deeds of good men, for by their living here,
Vertues, indeed remote, seeme to be nere;   40
But where can I affirme, or where arrest
My thoughts on his deeds? which shall I call best?
For fluid vertue cannot be look'd on,
Nor can endure a contemplation;

31. *glasse:* mirror.
37. *trunkes:* as trunks of a tree which produce (derive) branches.

As bodies change, and as I do not weare   45
Those Spirits, humors, blood I did last yeare,
And, as if on a streame I fixe mine eye,
That drop, which I looked on, is presently
Pusht with more waters from my sight, and gone,
So in this sea of vertues, can no one   50
Bee'insisted on; vertues, as rivers, passe,
Yet still remaines that vertuous man there was;
And as if man feed on mans flesh, and so
Part of his body to another owe,
Yet at the last two perfect bodies rise,   55
Because God knowes where every Atome lyes;
So, if one knowledge were made of all those,
Who knew his minutes well, hee might dispose
His vertues into names, and ranks; but I
Should injure Nature, Vertue,'and Destinie,   60
Should I divide and discontinue so,
Vertue, which did in one intirenesse grow.
For as, hee that would say, spirits are fram'd
Of all the purest parts that can be nam'd,
Honours not spirits halfe so much, as hee   65
Which sayes, they have no parts, but simple bee;
So is't of vertue; for a point and one
Are much entirer then a million.
And had Fate meant to have his vertues told,
It would have let him live to have beene old,   70
So then, that vertue'in season, and then this,
We might have seene, and said, that now he is
Witty, now wise, now temperate, now just:
In good short lives, vertues are faine to thrust,
And to be sure betimes to get a place,   75
When they would exercise, lacke time, and space.
So was it in this person, forc'd to bee
For lack of time, his owne epitome.
So to exhibit in few yeares as much,
As all the long breath'd Chronicles can touch;   80
As when an Angell down from heav'n doth flye,
Our quick thought cannot keepe him company,

55. *at the last:* at Judgment Day.
68. *entirer:* more complete.

Wee cannot thinke, now hee is at the Sunne,
Now through the Moon, now he through th'aire doth run,
Yet when he's come, we know he did repaire   85
To all twixt Heav'n and Earth, Sunne, Moon, and Aire.
And as this Angell in an instant knowes,
And yet wee know, this sodaine knowledge growes
By quick amassing severall formes of things,
Which he successively to order brings;   90
When they, whose slow-pac'd lame thoughts cannot goe
So fast as hee, thinke that he doth not so;
Just as a perfect reader doth not dwell,
On every syllable, nor stay to spell,
Yet without doubt, hee doth distinctly see   95
And lay together every A, and B;
So, in short liv'd good men, is'not understood
Each severall vertue, but the compound good.
For, they all vertues paths in that pace tread,
As Angells goe, and know, and as men read.   100
O why should then these men, these lumps of Balme
Sent hither, this worlds tempests to becalme,
Before by deeds they are diffus'd and spred,
And so make us alive, themselves be dead?
O Soule, O circle, why so quickly bee   105
Thy ends, thy birth and death, clos'd up in thee?
Since one foot of thy compasse still was plac'd
In heav'n, the other might securely'have pac'd
In the most large extent, through every path,
Which the whole world, or man, the'abridgment hath.   110
Thou knowst, that though the tropique circles have
(Yea and those small ones which the Poles engrave,)
All the same roundnesse, evennesse, and all
The endlesnesse of the'equinoctiall;
Yet, when we come to measure distances,   115
How here, how there, the Sunne affected is,
When he doth faintly worke, and when prevaile,
Onely great circles, then, can be our scale:

83–84. *at . . . Moon:* the spheres of the sun and the moon, in the Ptolemaic
system.
93. *perfect:* accomplished.
101. *Balme:* alchemically considered a panacea.
107. *still:* for ever.
110. *man, the'abridgment:* compare "I am a little world" (*Holy Sonnet,* No.
175, l. 1) and "Man is the World" (*Elegie on the Lady Marckham,* No. 149,
l. 1).

So, though thy circle to thy selfe expresse
All, tending to thy endlesse happinesse,   120
And wee, by our good use of it may trye,
Both how to live well young, and how to die,
Yet, since we must be old, and age endures
His Torrid Zone at Court, and calentures
Of hot ambitions, irrelegions ice,   125
Zeales agues, and hydroptique avarice,
Infirmities which need the scale of truth,
As well as lust and ignorance of youth;
Why did'st thou not for these give medicines too,
And by thy doing tell us what to doe?   130
Though as small pocket-clocks, whose every wheele
Doth each mismotion and distemper feele,
Whose *hand* gets shaking palsies, and whose *string*
(His sinewes) slackens, and whose *Soule*, the spring,
Expires, or languishes, whose pulse, the *flye*,   135
Either beates not, or beates unevenly,
Whose voice, the *Bell*, doth rattle, or grow dumbe,
Or idle,'as men, which to their last houres come,
If these clockes be not wound, or be wound still,
Or be not set, or set at every will;   140
So, youth is easiest to destruction,
If then wee follow all, or follow none;
Yet, as in great clocks, which in steeples chime,
Plac'd to informe whole towns, to'imploy their time,
An error doth more harme, being generall,   145
When, small clocks faults, only'on the wearer fall.
So worke the faults of age, on which the eye
Of children, servants, or the State relie.
Why wouldst not thou then, which hadst such a soule,
A clock so true, as might the Sunne controule,   150
And daily hadst from him, who gave it thee,
Instructions, such as it could never be
Disordered, stay here, as a generall
And great Sun-dyall, to have set us All?
O why wouldst thou be any instrument   155
To this unnaturall course, or why consent

126. *hydroptique:* thirsty, greedy.
128. *lust:* strong eagerness.
133. *string:* nerve or tendon.
135. *flye:* a governor consisting of rotating vanes.
139. *still:* continually.

To this, not miracle, but Prodigie,
That when the ebbs, longer then flowings be,
Vertue, whose flood did with thy youth begin,
Should so much faster ebb out, then flow in?   160
Though her flood was blowne in, by thy first breath,
All is at once sunke in the whirle-poole death.
Which word I would not name, but that I see
Death, else a desert, growne a Court by thee.
Now I grow sure, that if a man would have   165
Good companie, his entry is a grave.
Mee thinkes all Cities, now, but Anthills bee,
Where, when the severall labourers I see,
For children, house, Provision, taking paine,
They'are all but Ants, carrying eggs, straw, and grain;   170
And Church-yards are our cities, unto which
The most repaire, that are in goodnesse rich.
There is the best concourse, and confluence,
There are the holy suburbs, and from thence
Begins Gods City, New Jerusalem,   175
Which doth extend her utmost gates to them;
At that gate then Triumphant soule, dost thou
Begin thy Triumph; But since lawes allow
That at the Triumph day, the people may,
All that they will, 'gainst the Triumpher say,   180
Let me here use that freedome, and expresse
My griefe, though not to make thy Triumph lesse.
By law, to Triumphs none admitted bee,
Till they as Magistrates get victorie,
Though then to thy force, all youthes foes did yield,   185
Yet till fit time had brought thee to that field,
To which thy ranke in this state destin'd thee,
That there thy counsailes might get victorie,
And so in that capacitie remove
All jealousies 'twixt Prince and subjects love,   190
Thou could'st no title, to this triumph have,
Thou didst intrude on death, usurp'dst a grave.
Then (though victoriously) thou'hadst fought as yet
But with thine owne affections, with the heate
Of youths desires, and colds of ignorance,   195
But till thou should'st successefully advance

157. *Prodigie:* "unnaturall course," extraordinary sign.
164. *Court:* administrator of justice.
178. *Triumph:* triumphal procession.

Thine armes 'gainst forraine enemies, which are
Both Envy,'and acclamations popular,
(For, both these engines equally defeate,
Though by a divers Mine, those which are great,)   200
Till then thy War was but a civill War,
For which to Triumph, none admitted are;
No more are they, who though with good successe,
In a defensive war, their power expresse.
Before men triumph, the dominion   205
Must be *enlarg'd,* and not *preserv'd* alone;
Why should'st thou then, whose battailes were to win
Thy selfe, from those straits nature put thee in,
And to deliver up to God that state,
Of which he gave thee the vicariate,   210
(Which is thy soule and body) as intire
As he, who takes endeavours, doth require,
But didst not stay, t'enlarge his kingdome too,
By making others, what thou didst, to doe;
Why shouldst thou Triumph now, when Heav'n no more   215
Hath got, by getting thee, then't had before?
For, Heav'n and thou, even when thou livedst here,
Of one another in possession were;
But this from Triumph most disables thee.
That, that place which is conquered, must bee   220
Left safe from present warre, and likely doubt
Of imminent commotions to breake out.
And hath he left us so? or can it bee
His territory was no more then Hee?
No, we were all his charge, the Diocis   225
Of ev'ry'exemplar man, the whole world is,
And he was joyned in commission
With Tutelar Angels, sent to every one.
But though this freedome to upbraid, and chide
Him who Triumph'd, were lawfull, it was ty'd   230
With this, that it might never reference have
Unto the Senate, who this triumph gave;
Men might at Pompey jeast, but they might not
At that authoritie, by which he got

200. *Though by a divers Mine:* though they arise from different sources.
233. *Pompey:* Pompey the Great (148–106 B.C.), who at the age of twenty-two defeated Marius' factions in Italy, Africa, and Sicily, for which he was honored with the title Magnus.

Leave to Triumph, before, by age, he might;   235
So, though triumphant soule, I dare to write,
Mov'd with a reverentiall anger, thus,
That thou so earely wouldst abandon us;
Yet I am farre from daring to dispute
With that great soveraigntie, whose absolute   240
Prerogative hath thus dispens'd with thee,
'Gainst natures lawes, which just impugners bee
Of early triumphs; And I (though with paine)
Lessen our losse, to magnifie thy gaine
Of triumph, when I say, It was more fit,   245
That all men should lacke thee, then thou lack it.
Though then in our time, be not suffered
That testimonie of love, unto the dead,
To die with them, and in their graves be hid,
As Saxon wives, and French soldarii did;   250
And though in no degree I can expresse
Griefe in great Alexanders great excesse,
Who at his friends death, made whole townes devest
Their walls and bullwarks which became them best:
Doe not, faire soule, this sacrifice refuse,   255
That in thy grave I doe interre my Muse,
Who, by my griefe, great as thy worth, being cast
Behind hand, yet hath spoke, and spoke her last.

To Sir Robert Carr.
   SIR,
*I presume you rather try what you can doe in me, then what I can
doe in verse; you know my uttermost when it was best, and even
then I did best when I had least truth for my subjects. In this
present case there is so much truth as it defeats all Poetry. Call
therefore this paper by what name you will, and, if it bee not
worthy of you nor of him, we will smother it, and be it your sacrifice. If you had commanded mee to have waited on his body to
Scotland and preached there, I would have embraced your obliga-*

250. *soldarii:* retainers or vassals of a chieftain. Tacitus tells of such wifely
action in Chapter 8 and of such retainers in Chapter 14 of *On the Situation,
Manners, and People of Germany.*
   253. *friends:* Hephæstion's, who died of an ague. See further, Notes.
   258. *her last:* perhaps, in contemplation of his clerical life which was to begin within a few months, Donne refers to a renunciation of poetry.

tion with much alacrity; But, I thanke you that you would com-
mand me that which I was loather to doe, for, even that hath given
a tincture of merit to the obedience of

> Your poore friend and
> servant in Christ Jesus
> I. D.

154   An hymne to the Saints,
and to Marquesse Hamylton.

Whether that soule which now comes up to you
Fill any former ranke or make a new,
Whether it take a name nam'd there before,
Or be a name it selfe, and *order* more
Then was in heaven till now; (for may not hee   5
Bee so, if every severall Angell bee
A *kind* alone?) What ever order grow
Greater by him in heaven, wee doe not so;
One of your orders growes by his accesse;
But, by his losse grow all our *orders* lesse;   10
The name of *Father, Master, Friend,* the name
Of *Subject* and of *Prince,* in one are lame;
Faire mirth is dampt, and conversation black,
The *household* widdow'd, and the *garter* slack;
The *Chappell* wants an eare, *Councell* a tongue;   15
Story, a theame; and *Musicke* lacks a song;
Blest *order* that hath him, the losse of him
Gangreend all *Orders* here; all lost a limbe.
Never made body such hast to confesse
What a soule was; All former comelinesse   20
Fled, in a minute, when the soule was gone,
And, having lost that beauty, would have none,
So fell our *Monasteries,* in an instant growne
Not to lesse houses, but, to heapes of stone;

AN HYMNE TO THE SAINTS, AND TO MARQUESSE HAMYLTON.
   Marquesse Hamylton: James Hamilton, born in 1584, died on March 2, 1625.
See further, Notes.
   2. *ranke:* of angels.
   14. *garter:* referring to the Order of the Garter; knighthood has been weak-
ened and made imperfect by Hamilton's death.

So sent this body that faire forme it wore,   25
Unto the spheare of formes, and doth (before
His soule shall fill up his sepulchrall stone,)
Anticipate a Resurrection;
For, as in his fame, now, his soule is here,
So, in the forme thereof his bodie's there;   30
And if, faire soule, not with first *Innocents*
Thy station be, but with the *Pænitents*,
(And, who shall dare to aske then when I am
Dy'd scarlet in the blood of that pure Lambe,
Whether that colour, which is scarlet then,   35
Were black or white before in eyes of men?)
When thou rememb'rest what sins thou didst finde
Amongst those many friends now left behinde,
And seest such sinners as they are, with thee
Got thither by repentance, Let it bee   40
Thy wish to wish all there, to wish them cleane;
Wish *him* a *David*, *her* a *Magdalen*.

42. *David . . . Magdalen:* David, king of Israel for forty years and ancestor
of Jesus, repented his sins and begged the Lord not to punish his people because
of him (2 Sam. xxiv 17), with his dying breath even forgiving Shimei, who
had cursed him (1 Kings ii 8–9); Mary Magdalen, who wept upon discovering
that the sepulcher of Jesus was empty, had been cured of evil demons by him.

An Anatomy of the World.
Wherein, By occasion of the untimely death of Mistris Elizabeth
Drury the frailty and the decay of this whole World is represented.

To The Praise of the Dead, and the Anatomy.

Wel dy'de the world, that we might live to see
This world of wit, in his Anatomee:
No evill wants his good: so wilder heyres
Bedew their fathers Toombs with forced teares,
Whose state requites their los: whils thus we gain   5
Well may wee walk in blacks, but not complaine.
Yet, how can I consent the world is dead
While this Muse lives? which in his spirits stead
Seemes to informe a world: and bids it bee,
In spight of losse, or fraile mortalitee?   10
And thou the subject of this wel-borne thought,
Thrise noble maid, couldst not have found nor sought
A fitter time to yeeld to thy sad Fate,
Then whiles this spirit lives; that can relate
Thy worth so well to our last nephews eyne,   15
That they shall wonder both at his, and thine:
Admired match! where strives in mutuall grace
The cunning Pencill, and the comely face:
A taske, which thy faire goodnes made too much
For the bold pride of vulgar pens to touch;   20
Enough is us to praise them that praise thee,
And say that but enough those praises bee,
Which had'st thou liv'd, had hid their fearefull head
From th'angry checkings of thy modest red:
Death bars reward and shame: when envy's gone,   25
And gaine; 'tis safe to give the dead their owne.

THE FIRST ANNIVERSARIE.
   First Anniversarie: Written a few months after the death of Elizabeth Drury,
who was buried on December 17, 1610, the poem offers elegiac lament, praise,
and consolation to Sir Robert Drury, Elizabeth's father and Donne's patron.
See further, NOTES. The term "anniversarie" was attached to the poem in letters written in 1611 and 1612; it signifies a yearly celebration of a saint's death
date, prayers being offered up for the souls of the dead. Donne's later anniversaries would include praise and consolation, but would not stress lament.

As then the wise Egyptians wont to lay
More on their Tombes, then houses: these of clay,
But those of brasse, or marble were; so wee
Give more unto thy Ghost, then unto thee.   30
Yet what we give to thee, thou gav'st to us,
And may'st but thanke thy selfe, for being thus:
Yet what thou gav'st, and wert, O happy maid,
Thy grace profest all due, where 'tis repayd.
So these high songs that to thee suited bine,   35
Serve but to sound thy makers praise, in thine,
Which thy deare soule as sweetly sings to him
Amid the Quire of Saints and Seraphim,
As any Angels tongue can sing of thee;
The subjects differ, tho the skill agree: 40
For as by infant-yeares men judge of age,
Thy early love, thy vertues, did presage
What an hie part thou bear'st in those best songs
Whereto no burden, nor no end belongs.
Sing on, thou Virgin soule, whose lossefull gaine   45
Thy love-sicke Parents have bewayl'd in vaine;
Never may thy name be in our songs forgot
Till we shall sing thy ditty, and thy note.

[Joseph Hall?]

The First Anniversary.
An Anatomy of the World.

When that rich soule which to her Heaven is gone,   *The entrie*
Whom all do celebrate, who know they'have one,   *into the*
(For who is sure he hath a soule, unlesse   *worke.*
It see, and Judge, and follow worthinesse,
And by Deedes praise it? He who doth not this,   5
May lodge an In-mate soule, but tis not his.)
When that Queene ended here her progresse time,
And, as t'her standing house, to heaven did clymbe,

Anatomy: analysis, dissection into constituent elements.
    4. *see, and Judge, and follow:* resulting from reason, a faculty of the rational soul.
    6. *lodge:* give lodging space to. *In-mate:* confinement against the soul's wishes is suggested.
    7. *progresse:* a monarch's passage through some area.
    8. *standing house:* permanent dwelling.

Where, loth to make the Saints attend her long,
Shee's now a part both of the Quire, and Song,   10
This world, in that great earth-quake languished;
For in a common Bath of teares it bled,
Which drew the strongest vitall spirits out:
But succour'd then with a perplexed doubt,
Whether the world did loose or gaine in this,   15
(Because since now no other way there is
But goodnes, to see her, whom all would see,
All must endevour to be good as shee,)
This great consumption to a fever turn'd,
And so the world had fits; it joy'd, it mourn'd.   20
And, as men thinke, that Agues physicke are,
And th'Ague being spent, give over care,
So thou, sicke world, mistak'st thy selfe to bee
Well, when alas, thou'rt in a Letargee.
Her death did wound, and tame thee than, and than   25
Thou mightst have better spar'd the Sunne, or Man;
That wound was deepe, but 'tis more misery,
That thou hast lost thy sense and memory.
T'was heavy then to heare thy voyce of mone,
But this is worse, that thou art speechlesse growne.   30
Thou hast forgot thy name, thou hadst; thou wast
Nothing but she, and her thou hast o'rpast.
For as a child kept from the Font, untill
A Prince, expected long, come to fulfill
The Ceremonies, thou unnam'd hadst laid,   35
Had not her comming, thee her Palace made:
Her name defin'd thee, gave thee forme and frame,
And thou forgetst to celebrate thy name.
Some moneths she hath beene dead (but being dead,
Measures of times are all determined)   40
But long shee'ath beene away, long, long, yet none
Offers to tell us who it is that's gone.
But as in states doubtfull of future heyres,
When sicknes without remedy, empayres
The present Prince, they're loth it should be said,   45
The Prince doth languish, or the Prince is dead:
So mankind feeling now a generall thaw,
A strong example gone equall to law,

13. *vitall spirits:* those of the heart, which work through the blood.
32. *o'rpast:* forgotten.
33. *the Font:* (of baptism).
40. Time is measured in terms of her life-span. *determined:* terminated.

The Cyment which did faithfully compact
And glue all vertues, now resolv'd, and slack'd,   50
Thought it some blasphemy to say sh'was dead;
Or that our weakenes was discovered
In that confession; therefore spoke no more
Then tongues, the soule being gone, the losse deplore.
But though it be too late to succour thee,   55
Sicke world, yea dead, yea putrified, since shee
Thy'intrinsique Balme, and thy preservative,
Can never be renew'd, thou never live,
I (since no man can make thee live) will trie,
What we may gaine by thy Anatomy.   60
Her death hath taught us dearely, that thou art
Corrupt and mortall in thy purest part.
Let no man say, the world it selfe being dead,
'Tis labour lost to have discovered
The worlds infirmities, since there is none   65
Alive to study this dissectione;
For there's a kind of world remaining still,   *What life*
Though shee which did inanimate and fill   *the world*
The world, be gone, yet in this last long night,   *hath still.*
Her Ghost doth walke; that is, a glimmering light,   70
A faint weake love of vertue and of good
Reflects from her, on them which understood
Her worth; And though she have shut in all day,
The twi-light of her memory doth stay;
Which, from the carcasse of the old world, free,   75
Creates a new world; and new creatures be
Produc'd: The matter and the stuffe of this,
Her vertue, and the forme our practice is.
And though to be thus Elemented, arme
These Creatures, from hom-borne intrinsique harme,   80
(For all assum'd unto this Dignitee,
So many weedlesse Paradises bee,

50. *resolv'd:* dissolved.
57. *intrinsique:* necessary to being, elemental. *Balme:* a panacea and life-giving substance. With balm one was in a state of grace; without it, in a state of original sin.
59. *trie:* test, assay.
61. *dearely:* lovingly; with great loss.
73. *shut in all day:* hidden all light (her radiance).
78. *forme:* in the form of matter, according to Aristotle, lies the individuating element. *our practice:* that which we usually do. This new world is made of virtue, but its nature depends on man's acts.
81. *assum'd unto:* received and took upon themselves.

Which of themselves produce no venemous sinne,
Except some forraine Serpent bring it in)
Yet, because outward stormes the strongest breake,   85
And strength it selfe by confidence growes weake,
This new world may be safer, being told
The dangers and diseases of the old: *The sicknesses*
For with due temper men do then forgoe,   *of the world.*
Or covet things, when they their true worth know.   90
There is no health; Physitians say that we   *Impossibility*
At best, enjoy, but a neutralitee.   *of health.*
And can there be worse sicknesse, then to know
That we are never well, nor can be so?
We are borne ruinous: poore mothers crie,   95
That children come not right, nor orderly,
Except they headlong come, and fall upon
An ominous precipitation.
How witty's ruine? how importunate
Upon mankinde? It labour'd to frustrate   100
Even Gods purpose; and made woman, sent
For mans reliefe, cause of his languishment.
They were to good ends, and they are so still,
But accessory, and principall in ill.
For that first mariage was our funerall: 105
One woman at one blow, then kill'd us all,
And singly, one by one, they kill us now.
We doe delightfully our selves allow
To that consumption; and profusely blinde,
We kill our selves, to propagate our kinde.   110

84. Alluding to the former Eden before Satan entered in the guise of a snake.
95. *ruinous:* both ruined by original sin and corruptible.
96. That children do not emerge from the womb in a preferable position or without difficulty, at the expected time.
98. *precipitation:* punning upon the rapid, headfirst emergence of the child and the expelled fluid.
99. *How witty's ruine?:* how ingenious is ruin?, how imaginative is ruin?
102. *For mans reliefe:* as the creation of Eve was intended for Adam. *languishment:* both his "mooning" over love and his exhaustion after intercourse.
105. *funerall:* because of the sin and death which Eve's tasting of the apple of the Tree of Knowledge brought. There is a glance at the word "die" as suggestive of intercourse, continued in ll. 106–10.
109. *consumption:* wasting away.
110. Intercourse was believed to reduce one's life-span.

And yet we doe not that; we are not men:
There is not now that mankinde, which was then
When as the Sunne, and man, did seeme to strive,
(Joynt tenants of the world) who should survive.   *Shortnesse*
When Stag, and Raven, and the long-liv'd tree,   *of life.*   115
Compar'd with man, dy'de in minoritee.
When, if a slow-pac'd starre had stolne away
From the observers marking, he might stay
Two or three hundred yeares to see't againe,
And then make up his observation plaine;   120
When, as the age was long, the sise was great:
Mans growth confess'd, and recompenc'd the meat:
So spacious and large, that every soule
Did a faire Kingdome, and large Realme controule:
And when the very stature thus erect,   125
Did that soule a good way towards Heaven direct.
Where is this mankind now? who lives to age,
Fit to be made *Methusalem* his page?
Alas, we scarse live long enough to trie
Whether a new made clocke runne right, or lie.   130
Old Grandsires talke of yesterday with sorrow,
And for our children we reserve to morrow.
So short is life, that every peasant strives,
In a torne house, or field, to have three lives.
And as in lasting, so in length is man   135
Contracted to an inch, who was a span.   *Smalenesse*
For had a man at first, in Forrests stray'd,   *of stature.*
Or shipwrack'd in the Sea, one would have laid
A wager that an Elephant, or Whale
That met him, would not hastily assaile   140
A thing so equall to him: now alas,
The Fayries, and the Pigmies well may passe

111. *yet:* if.
115. *long-liv'd tree:* probably the oak.
116. *in minoritee:* while still young, while still minors.
122. *confess'd . . . meat:* gave evidence of the food and equaled it.
128. *Methusalem:* the Biblical patriarch who lived 969 years (Gen. v 27).
his: Methusalem's.
129. *trie:* find out.
134. *torne:* dilapidated. *three lives:* past, present, future.
136. *span:* nine inches; the measurement suggests man's former ability to
encompass the world, as it were, in his hand. See further, NOTES.

As credible; mankind decayes so soone,
We're scarse our Fathers shadowes cast at noone.
Onely death addes t'our length: nor are we growne   145
In stature to be men, till we are none.
But this were light, did our lesse volume hold
All the old Text; or had we chang'd to gold
Their silver; or dispos'd into lesse glas,
Spirits of vertue, which then scattred was.   150
But 'tis not so: w'are not retir'd, but dampt;
And as our bodies, so our mindes are cramp't:
'Tis shrinking, not close-weaving, that hath thus,
In minde and body both bedwarfed us.
We seeme ambitious, Gods whole worke t'undoe;   155
Of nothing he made us, and we strive too,
To bring our selves to nothing backe; and we
Do what we can, to do't so soone as hee.
With new diseases on our selves we warre,
And with new phisicke, a worse Engin farre.   160
Thus man, this worlds Vice-Emperor, in whom
All faculties, all graces are at home;
And if in other Creatures they appeare,
They're but mans ministers, and Legats there,
To worke on their rebellions, and reduce   165
Them to Civility, and to mans use.
This man, whom God did wooe, and loth t'attend
Till man came up, did downe to man descend,
This man, so great, that all that is, is his,
Oh what a trifle, and poore thing he is!   170
If man were any thing, he's nothing now:
Helpe, or at least some time to wast, allow

144. Referring to the lack of shadows at noon.
145–46. Since in death man is stretched out.
147. *light:* of little importance. *our lesse volume:* our smaller size.
148. *old Text:* the word of God in the Bible. There is also a pun on "volume."
See further, NOTES.
148–49. *gold . . . silver:* the ages of man. The alchemist constantly sought
the philosopher's stone to transform other metals into gold.
149. *lesse glas:* that is, man's body, which would be transparent for the world
to see its contents (virtue); perhaps also implying less brittle by acquiring po-
tency and strength (virtue).
151. *dampt:* stifled, restrained.
160. *new phisicke:* new mineral drugs of the Paracelsians.
161. *Vice-Emperor:* see NOTES.
167. *attend:* wait.
169. *This man:* Christ.

T'his other wants, yet when he did depart
With her, whom we lament, he lost his hart.
She, of whom th'Auncients seem'd to prophesie,   175
When they call'd vertues by the name of shee;
She in whom vertue was so much refin'd,
That for Allay unto so pure a minde
Shee tooke the weaker Sex, she that could drive
The poysonous tincture, and the stayne of *Eve*,   180
Out of her thoughts, and deeds; and purifie
All, by a true religious Alchimy;
Shee, shee is dead; shee's dead: when thou knowest this,
Thou knowest how poore a trifling thing man is.
And learn'st thus much by our Anatomee,   185
The heart being perish'd, no part can be free.
And that except thou feed (not banquet) on
The supernaturall food, Religion,
Thy better Grouth growes withered, and scant;
Be more then man, or thou'rt lesse then an Ant.   190
Then, as mankinde, so is the worlds whole frame
Quite out of joynt, almost created lame:
For, before God had made up all the rest,
Corruption entred, and deprav'd the best:
It seis'd the Angels, and then first of all   195
The world did in her Cradle take a fall,
And turn'd her braines, and tooke a generall maime
Wronging each joynt of th'universall frame.
The noblest part, man, felt it first; and than
Both beasts and plants, curst in the curse of man.   200
So did the world from the first houre decay,   *Decay of nature*
The evening was beginning of the day,   *in other parts.*
And now the Springs and Sommers which we see,
Like sonnes of women after fifty bee.
And new Philosophy cals all in doubt,   205
The Element of fire is quite put out;

180. *tincture:* active quality or substance which stains; in alchemical thought,
blood was a virtuous tincture which would create penitential purification.

187. *banquet:* eat more sparingly and delicately, not specifically for sustenance.

204. *sonnes of women after fifty:* see NOTES.

205. *new Philosophy:* science, particularly astronomy; that of Galileo, Kepler,
etc.

206. The new philosophy has shown that the sun and stars are other than
only fire. Fire was considered purest of the elements and the generator of life;
purity as a concept is now impossible, fire as resurrection (in the symbol of the

The Sun is lost, and th'earth, and no mans wit
Can well direct him, where to looke for it.
And freely men confesse, that this world's spent,
When in the Planets, and the Firmament   210
They seeke so many new; they see that this
Is crumbled out againe to'his Atomis.
'Tis all in pieces, all cohærence gone;
All just supply, and all Relation:
Prince, Subject, Father, Sonne, are things forgot,   215
For every man alone thinkes he hath got
To be a Phœnix, and that there can bee
None of that kinde, of which he is, but hee.
This is the worlds condition now, and now
She that should all parts to reunion bow,   220
She that had all Magnetique force alone,
To draw, and fasten sundred parts in one;
She whom wise nature had invented then
When she observ'd that every sort of men
Did in their voyage in this worlds Sea stray,   225
And needed a new compasse for their way;
Shee that was best, and first originall
Of all faire copies; and the generall
Steward to Fate; shee whose rich eyes, and brest,
Guilt the West Indies, and perfum'd the East;   230
Whose having breath'd in this world, did bestow
Spice on those Isles, and bad them still smell so,
And that rich Indie which doth gold interre,
Is but as single money, coyn'd from her:
She to whom this world must it selfe refer,   235
As Suburbs, or the Microcosme of her,

---

phoenix and of the conflagration which will lead to the New Heavens and New
Earth) is extinguished; zeal and faith have disappeared.
  207–8. Other theories of the order of the universe than the geocentric (Ptolemaic) had been proposed.
  207. *wit:* imagination.
  210–11. That is, through using the telescope.
  212. *crumbled:* indicating both the disorder of the world through the dis-
crediting of Scholastic thought and the resulting decay and diminution of man's
view of the world. *his Atomis:* the world's small constituent particles.
  213. *cohærence:* (1) cohesiveness, (2) interrelationship, (3) meaning.
  214. *just:* proper, rightful.
  217. *Phœnix:* the unique bird who was reborn from its own ashes.
  220. *bow:* incline.
  230. The West Indies were renowned for precious ores, and the East Indies,
for aromatic herbs and spices.

Shee, shee is dead; shee's dead: when thou knowst this,
Thou knowst how lame a cripple this world is.
And learnst thus much by our Anatomy,
That this worlds generall sickenesse doth not lie   240
In any humour, or one certaine part;
But, as thou sawest it rotten at the hart,
Thou seest a Hectique fever hath got hold
Of the whole substance, not to be contrould,
And that thou hast but one way, not t'admit   245
The worlds infection, to be none of it.
For the worlds subtilst immateriall parts
Feele this consuming wound, and ages darts.
For the worlds beauty is decayd, or gone,
Beauty, that's colour, and proportion.   *Disformity*   250
We thinke the heavens enjoy their Sphericall   *of parts.*
Their round proportion embracing all.
But yet their various and perplexed course,
Observ'd in divers ages doth enforce
Men to finde out so many'Eccentrique parts,   255
Such divers downe-right lines, such overthwarts,
As disproportion that pure forme. It teares
The Firmament in eight and fortie sheeres,
And in those constellations there arise
New starres, and old do vanish from our eyes: 260
As though heav'n suffred earth-quakes, peace or war,
When new Townes rise, and olde demolish'd are.
They have empayld within a Zodiake
The free-borne Sunne, and keepe twelve signes awake

243. *Hectique:* slowly wasting, consumptive.
247. *subtilst:* thinnest.
253. *perplexed:* complicated, involved.
256. *downe-right:* vertical. *overthwarts:* transverse lines.
258. *sheeres:* parts. The catalogue of Hipparchus in Ptolemy's *Almagest* divides the stars into forty-eight constellations.
260. *New starres:* those discovered in Cassiopeia by Brahe in 1572, in Cygnus by Kepler in 1600, in Ophiuchus by Kepler in 1604, and the Galaxy by Galileo in 1610.
263–64. *empayld . . . Sunne:* because it is now the center around which the other planetary bodies revolve.
264. *twelve signes:* the divisions of the zodiac, among which are (l. 265) the Goat (Capricorn, the winter solstice) and the Crab (Cancer, the summer solstice). As Tropics (l. 267) these two signs also control the approach of the sun toward the poles. The Tropic of Capricorn lies in the southern hemisphere; that of Cancer, in the northern.

To watch his steps; the Goat and Crabbe controule,   265
And fright him backe, who els to eyther Pole,
(Did not these Tropiques fetter him) might runne:
For his course is not round; nor can the Sunne
Perfit a Circle, or maintaine his way
One inche direct; but where he rose to day   270
He comes no more, but with a cousening line,
Steales by that point, and so is Serpentine:
And seeming weary with his reeling thus,
He meanes to sleepe, being now falne nearer us.
So, of the Starres which boast that they do runne   275
In Circle still, none ends where he begunne.
All their proportion's lame, it sinks, it swels.
For of Meridians, and Parallels,
Man hath weav'd out a net, and this net throwne
Upon the Heavens, and now they are his owne.   280
Loth to goe up the hill, or labor thus
To goe to heaven, we make heaven come to us.
We spur, we raine the stars, and in their race
They're diversly content t'obey our pace.
But keepes the earth her round proportion still?   285
Doth not a Tenarif, or higher Hill
Rise so high like a Rocke, that one might thinke
The floating Moone would shipwracke there, and sink?
Seas are so deepe, that Whales being strooke to day,
Perchance to morrow, scarse at middle way   290
Of their wish'd journeys end, the bottom, dye.
And men, to sound depths, so much line untie,
As one might justly thinke, that there would rise
At end thereof, one of th'Antipodies:
If under all, a Vault infernall be,   295
(Which sure is spacious, except that we

271. *cousening:* deceitful through gradual change.
281. *hill:* the mythic symbol of the difficult path to heaven; compare Hesiod's
Hill of Virtue and the "holy hill of Zion" (Psalms ii 6).
283. *raine:* put reins upon, as on a horse.
284. That is, the stars go fast or slow according to our astronomical view of
them.
286. *Tenarif:* the highest peak in the Canary Islands.
289. *strooke:* fatally harpooned.
294. *Antipodies:* those living on the opposite side of the earth.
295. *a Vault infernall:* Hell, thought of as in the center of the earth.
296. *except that:* unless.

Invent another torment, that there must
Millions into a strait hote roome be thrust)
Then solidnes, and roundnes have no place.
Are these but warts, and pock-holes in the face   300
Of th'earth? Thinke so: But yet confesse, in this
The worlds proportion disfigur'd is,
That those two legges whereon it doth relie,   *Disorder in*
Reward and punishment are bent awrie.   *the world.*
And, Oh, it can no more be questioned,   305
That beauties best, proportion, is dead,
Since even griefe it selfe, which now alone
Is left us, is without proportion.
Shee by whose lines proportion should bee
Examin'd, measure of all Symmetree,   310
Whom had that Ancient seen, who thought soules made
Of Harmony, he would at next have said
That Harmony was shee, and thence infer,
That soules were but Resultances from her,
And did from her into our bodies go,   315
As to our eyes, the formes from objects flow:
Shee, who if those great Doctors truely said
That th'Arke to mans proportions was made,
Had beene a type for that, as that might be
A type of her in this, that contrary   320
Both Elements, and Passions liv'd at peace
In her, who caus'd all Civill warre to cease.
Shee, after whom, what forme soe're we see,
Is discord, and rude incongruitee,
Shee, shee is dead, she's dead; when thou knowst this, 325
Thou knowst how ugly'a monster this world is:
And learnst thus much by our Anatomee,
That here is nothing to enamor thee:
And that, not onely faults in inward parts,
Corruptions in our braines, or in our harts,   330
Poysoning the fountaines, whence our actions spring,
Endanger us: but that if every thing
Be not done fitly'and in proportion,
To satisfie wise, and good lookers on,

300. As they would appear to an inhabitant of a distant planet.
311. *that Ancient:* probably Pythagoras, who also believed in transmigration of souls.
312. *at next:* in her next (transmigrated) life.
314. *Resultances:* emanations.

(Since most men be such as most thinke they bee)   335
They're lothsome too, by this Deformitee.
For good, and well, must in our actions meete:
Wicked is not much worse than indiscreet.
But beauties other second Element,
Colour, and lustre now, is as neere spent.   340
And had the world his just proportion,
Were it a ring still, yet the stone is gone.
As a compassionate Turcoyse which doth tell
By looking pale, the wearer is not well,
As gold fals sicke being stung with Mercury,   345
All the worlds parts of such complexion bee.
When nature was most busie, the first weeke,
Swadling the new-borne earth, God seemd to like,
That she should sport herselfe sometimes, and play,
To mingle,'and vary colours every day: 350
And then, as though she could not make inow,
Himselfe his various Rainbow did allow.
Sight is the noblest sense of any one,
Yet sight hath onely color to feed on,
And color is decayd: summers robe growes   355
Duskie, and like an oft dyed garment showes.
Our blushing redde, which us'd in cheekes to spred,
Is inward sunke, and onely'our soules are redde.
Perchance the world might have recovered,
If she whom we lament had not beene dead: 360
But shee, in whom all white, and redde, and blue
(Beauties ingredients) voluntary grew,
As in an unvext Paradise; from whom
Did all things verdure, and their lustre come,
Whose composition was miraculous,   365
Being all color, all Diaphanous,
(For Ayre, and Fire but thicke grosse bodies were,
And liveliest stones but drowsie,'and pale to her,)
Shee, shee is dead; shee's dead: when thou knowst this,
Thou knowst how wan a Ghost this our world is: 370

343. *Turcoyse:* turquoise.
352. *Rainbow:* symbol of God's covenant with Noah that "the waters shall no more become a flood to destroy all flesh" (Gen. ix 15).
358. *redde:* color of penitence and resurrection.
363. *unvext:* without discord, without affliction.
368. *liveliest:* most gleaming and radiant.

And learnst thus much by our Anatomee,
That it should more affright, then pleasure thee.
And that, since all faire color then did sinke,
Tis now but wicked vanity to thinke,
To color vitious deeds with good pretence, 375
Or with bought colors to illude mens sense.
Nor in ought more this worlds decay appeares,
Then that her influence the heav'n forbeares,
Or that the Elements doe not feele this,
The father, or the mother barren is. 380
The clouds conceive not raine, or doe not powre
In the due birth-time, downe the balmy showre.
Th'Ayre doth not motherly sit on the earth,
To hatch her seasons, and give all things birth.
Spring-times were common cradles, but are toombes; 385
And false-conceptions fill the generall wombes.
Th'Ayre showes such Meteors, as none can see,
Not onely what they meane, but what they bee.
Earth such new wormes, as would have troubled much,
Th'Egyptian Mages to have made more such. 390
What Artist now dares boast that he can bring
Heaven hither, or constellate any thing,
So as the influence of those starres may bee
Imprisond in an Herbe, or Charme, or Tree,
And doe by touch, all which those starres could do? 395
The art is lost, and correspondence too.
For heaven gives little, and the earth takes lesse,
And man least knowes their trade, and purposes.
If this commerce twixt heaven and earth were not
Embarr'd, and all this trafique quite forgot, 400
Shee, for whose losse we have lamented thus,
Would worke more fully'and pow'rfully on us.

Weaknesse in the want of correspondence of heaven and earth.

376. *illude:* deceive.
378–80. The stars were supposed to influence growth on earth; the heavens are the father, and earth, the mother.
387. *Meteors:* formerly considered portents of disaster.
389. *wormes:* symbolic of procreative elements and of sinfulness.
390. *Mages:* magicians.
391. *Artist:* astrologer, occultist.
392. *constellate:* create something with the magical power of a constellation.
396. *correspondence:* a major approach to learning and understanding in medieval and Renaissance thought; without it the ordered relationships among things would seem to have disappeared.

Since herbes, and roots, by dying, lose not all,
But they, yea Ashes too, are medicinall,
Death could not quench her vertue so, but that   405
It would be (if not follow'd) wondred at:
And all the world would be one dying Swan,
To sing her funerall prayse, and vanish than.
But as some Serpents poyson hurteth not,
Except it be from the live Serpent shot,   410
So doth her vertue need her here, to fit
That unto us; she working more then it.
But she, in whom, to such maturity,
Vertue was growne, past growth, that it must die,
She from whose influence all Impressions came,   415
But, by Receivers impotencies, lame,
Who, though she could not transubstantiate
All states to gold, yet guilded every state,
So that some Princes have some temperance;
Some Counsaylors some purpose to advance   420
The common profite; and some people have
Some stay, no more then Kings should give, to crave;
Some women have some taciturnity;
Some Nunneries, some graines of chastity.
She that did thus much, and much more could doe,   425
But that our age was Iron, and rusty too,
Shee, shee is dead; shee's dead; when thou knowst this,
Thou knowst how drie a Cinder this world is.
And learnst thus much by our Anatomy,
That 'tis in vaine to dew, or mollifie   430
It with thy Teares, or Sweat, or Blood: no thing
Is worth our travaile, griefe, or perishing,
But those rich joyes, which did possesse her hart,
Of which shee's now partaker, and a part.
But as in cutting up a man that's dead,   *Conclusion.*   435
The body will not last out to have read

404. *Ashes:* for example, potash.
405. *vertue:* the meaning "power" is also intended.
407–8. The swan is supposed to sing only before its death, and then most beautifully.
420. *Counsaylors:* lawyers.
422. *stay:* self-restraint.
424. *Nunneries:* houses of prostitution.
426. *Iron:* that age to which the world had declined from the Gold, Silver, and Bronze Ages. It suggests corruption and sinfulness.
436. *read:* lectured, given instruction.

On every part, and therefore men direct
Their speech to parts, that are of most effect;
So the worlds carcasse would not last, if I
Were punctuall in this Anatomy. 440
Nor smels it well to hearers, if one tell
Them their disease, who faine would think they're wel.
Here therefore be the end: And, blessed maid,
Of whom is meant what ever hath beene said,
Or shall be spoken well by any tongue, 445
Whose name refines course lines, and makes prose song,
Accept this tribute, and his first yeares rent,
Who till his darke short tapers end be spent,
As oft as thy feast sees this widow'd earth,
Will yearely celebrate thy second birth, 450
That is, thy death. For though the soule of man
Be got when man is made, 'tis borne but than
When man doth die. Our body's as the wombe,
And as a mid-wife death directs it home.
And you her creatures, whom she workes upon 455
And have your last, and best concoction
From her example,'and her vertue, if you
In reverence to her, doe thinke it due,
That no one should her prayses thus reherse,
As matter fit for Chronicle, not verse, 460
Vouchsafe to call to minde, that God did make
A last, and lastingst peece, a song. He spake
To *Moses* to deliver unto all,
That song: because hee knew they would let fall
The Law, the Prophets, and the History, 465
But keepe the song still in their memory.

440. *were punctuall:* paid attention to small points.
447. *first yeares rent:* payment for Drury's patronage (paid in advance), as one offers up to God his soul's "rent" for its fleshly tabernacle. Compare No. 113, n. to l. 33.
449. *feast:* day of celebration for a saint. *widow'd:* (by the death of virtue, by the removal of the father Heaven).
450. *second birth:* resurrection to everlasting day in heaven. See further, NOTES.
460. *Chronicle:* religious history; 1 Chron. i–viii relate the descendants of Adam to David (ancestor of Jesus) through the sons of Benjamin (whose name means "son of my right hand").
462–64. See NOTES.
465. The Law is given in Leviticus and Deuteronomy (cf. Deut. xxxiii 2, 4); the Prophets came later with Isaiah *et al.* (cf. Deut. xxxiv 10); the History is given in Genesis, Exodus, and Numbers.

Such an opinion (in due measure) made
Me this great Office boldly to invade.
Nor could incomprehensiblenesse deterre
Me, from thus trying to emprison her.   470
Which when I saw that a strict grave could do,
I saw not why verse might not doe so too.
Verse hath a middle nature: heaven keepes soules,
The grave keeps bodies, verse the fame enroules.

156 *A Funerall Elegie.*

Tis lost, to trust a Tombe with such a ghest,
    Or to confine her in a Marble chest.
Alas, what's Marble, Jeat, or Porphiry,
    Priz'd with the Chrysolite of eyther eye,
Or with those Pearles, and Rubies which shee was?   5
    Joyne the two Indies in one Tombe, 'tis glas;
And so is all to her materials,
    Though every inche were ten escurials.
Yet shee's demolish'd: Can we keepe her then
    In workes of hands, or of the wits of men?   10
Can these memorials, ragges of paper, give
    Life to that name, by which name they must live?
Sickly, alas, short-liv'd, aborted bee
    Those Carkas verses, whose soule is not shee.
And can shee, who no longer would be shee,   15
    Being such a Tabernacle, stoope to bee
In paper wrap't; Or, when she would not lie
    In such a house, dwell in an Elegie?

467. *in due measure:* in iambic pentameter couplets, considered the verse
form most appropriate to render heroic song. It is "strict" (l. 471) in not allowing for variation, in being drawn tightly together, in rigor and exactness.
A FUNERALL ELEGIE.
    Written shortly after the death of Elizabeth, the fifteen-year-old daughter
of Sir Robert Drury, who was buried on December 17, 1610.
    2–5. The marble is parallel with pearls, the jet with the pupils of her eyes, and
porphyry with rubies. Elizabeth was buried in a very elaborate marble tomb.
    6. *two Indies:* noted for jewels, but all such materials compared with Eliza-
beth are glass.
    8. *escurials:* the Escorial was a vast structure north of Madrid built by
Philip II.

But 'tis no matter; we may well allow
    Verse to live so long as the world will now.   20
For her death wounded it. The world containes
    Princes for armes, and Counsailors for braines,
Lawyers for tongues, Divines for hearts, and more,
    The Rich for stomachs, and for backes the Pore;
The Officers for hands, Merchants for feet   25
    By which remote and distant Countries meet.
But those fine spirits, which doe tune and set
    This Organ, are those peeces which beget
Wonder and love; And these were shee; and shee
    Being spent, the world must needes decrepit bee.   30
For since death will proceed to triumph still,
    He can finde nothing, after her, to kill,
Except the world it selfe, so great as shee.
    Thus brave and confident may Nature bee,
Death cannot give her such another blow,   35
    Because shee cannot such another show.
But must we say shee's dead? May't not be said
    That as a sundred Clocke is peece-meale laid,
Not to be lost, but by the makers hand
    Repolish'd, without error then to stand,   40
Or as the Affrique Niger streame enwombs
    It selfe into the earth, and after comes,
(Having first made a naturall bridge, to passe
    For many leagues,) farre greater then it was,
May't not be said, that her grave shall restore   45
    Her, greater, purer, firmer, then before?
Heaven may say this, and joy in't; but can wee
    Who live, and lacke her, here this vantage see?
What is't to us, alas, if there have beene
    An Angell made a Throne, or Cherubin?   50
We lose by't: And as aged men are glad
    Being tastlesse growne, to joy in joyes they had,
So now the sicke starv'd world must feed upone
    This joy, that we had her, who now is gone.
Rejoyce then nature, and this world, that you   55
    Fearing the last fires hastning to subdue

28. *This Organ:* the funeral elegy which Donne is writing.
50. *Throne:* a higher angel, third in rank.   *Cherubin:* second only to a seraph.
56. *last fires:* a reference to the supposed conflagration which will bring about the end of the world.

Your force and vigor, ere it were neere gone,
  Wisely bestow'd, and layd it all on one.
One, whose cleare body was so pure, and thin,
  Because it neede disguise no thought within.   60
T'was but a through-light scarfe, her minde t'enroule,
  Or exhalation breath'd out from her soule.
One, whom all men who durst no more, admir'd;
  And whom, who ere had worth enough, desir'd;
As when a Temple's built, Saints emulate   65
  To which of them, it shall be consecrate.
But as when Heav'n lookes on us with new eyes,
  Those new starres ev'ry Artist exercise,
What place they should assigne to them they doubt,
  Argue,'and agree not, till those starres go out: 70
So the world studied whose this peece should be,
  Till she can be no bodies else, nor shee:
But like a Lampe of Balsamum, desir'd
  Rather t'adorne, then last, shee soone expir'd;
Cloath'd in her Virgin white integrity;   75
  For mariage, though it doe not staine, doth dye.
To scape th'infirmities which waite upone
  Woman, shee went away, before sh'was one.
And the worlds busie noyse to overcome,
  Tooke so much death, as serv'd for *opium*.   80
For though she could not, nor could chuse to die,
  Shee'ath yeelded to too long an Extasie.
He which not knowing her sad History,
  Should come to read the booke of destiny,
How faire, and chast, humble, and high shee'ad beene,   85
  Much promis'd, much perform'd, at not fifteene,
And measuring future things, by things before,
  Should turne the leafe to reade, and reade no more,
Would thinke that eyther destiny mistooke,
  Or that some leafes were torne out of the booke.   90

61. *through-light:* transparent. *t'enroule:* to enwrap.
65. *emulate:* vie to excel each other (to determine).
68. Those new stars set every necromancer to thinking.
73. *Balsamum:* balm, used both as perfume and for its curative properties.
The more usual oil would be burned for continuous illumination. The lines al-
lude to the wise virgins who filled their lamps with oil to await the Bridegroom
(Matt. xxv 1–13); Elizabeth has filled hers, but with balm.
76. That is, marriage removes virgin whiteness, but does not corrupt. "Dye"
also implies intercourse, untainted in marriage.
82. *Extasie:* mystic trance.

But 'tis not so: Fate did but usher her
  To yeares of Reasons use, and then infer
Her destiny to her selfe; which liberty
  She tooke but for thus much, thus much to die.
Her modesty not suffering her to bee   95
  Fellow-Commissioner with destinee,
Shee did no more but die; if after her
  Any shall live, which dare true good prefer,
Every such person is her delegate,
  T'accomplish that which should have beene her fate.   100
They shall make up that booke, and shall have thankes
  Of fate and her, for filling up their blanks.
For future vertuous deeds are Legacies,
  Which from the gift of her example rise.
And 'tis in heav'n part of spirituall mirth,   105
  To see how well, the good play her, on earth.

FINIS.

157   *Of the Progres of the Soule.*

Wherein: By occasion of the Religious death of Mistris Elizabeth
Drury the incommodities of the Soule in this life and her exaltation in the next, are contemplated.

The second Anniversary

The Harbinger to the Progres.

Two soules move here, and mine (a third) must move
Paces of admiration, and of love;
Thy soule (Deare Virgin) whose this tribute is,
Mov'd from this mortall sphere to lively blisse;
And yet moves still, and still aspires to see   5
The worlds last day, thy glories full degree:

92–93. *and . . . selfe:* and then Fate did leave her destiny to herself to de-
termine.
OF THE PROGRES OF THE SOULE . . . THE SECOND ANNIVERSARY.
    Written a year after Elizabeth Drury's death while Donne was in France with
Sir Robert Drury, the poem offers a second year's rent (l. 520) in advance.
It appeals to man's refinding of understanding; it is a vision of the release of
the soul from its bodily prison and its return to heaven. See further, NOTES.

Like as those starres which thou ore-lookest farre,
Are in their place, and yet still moved are:
No soule (whiles with the luggage of this clay
It clogged is) can follow thee halfe way;   10
Or see thy flight; which doth our thoughts outgoe
So fast, that now the lightning moves but slow:
But now thou art as high in heaven flowne
As heav'ns from us; what soule besides thine owne
Can tell thy joyes, or say he can relate   15
Thy glorious Journals in that blessed state?
I envie thee (Rich soule) I envy thee,
Although I cannot yet thy glory see:
And thou (Great spirit) which her's follow'd hast
So fast, as none can follow thine so fast;   20
So far, as none can follow thine so farre
(And if this flesh did not the passage barre
Had'st raught her) let me wonder at thy flight
Which long agone had'st lost the vulgar sight
And now mak'st proud the better eyes, that thay   25
Can see thee less'ned in thine aery way;
So while thou mak'st her soules Hy progresse knowne
Thou mak'st a noble progresse of thine owne,
From this worlds carcasse having mounted hie
To that pure life of Immortalitie;   30
Since thine aspiring thoughts themselves so raise
That more may not beseeme a creatures praise,
Yet still thou vow'st her more; and every yeare
Mak'st a new progresse, while thou wandrest here;
Still upwards mount; and let thy makers praise   35
Honor thy Laura, and adorne thy laies.
And since thy Muse her head in heaven shrouds
Oh let her never stoope below the clouds:
And if those glorious sainted soules may know
Or what we doe, or what we sing below,   40
Those acts, those songs shall still content them best
Which praise those awfull powers that make them blest.

                              [Joseph Hall]

The Second Anniversary.

Of The Progres of the Soule.

Nothing could make mee sooner to confesse   *The entrance.*
That this world had an everlastingnesse,
Then to consider, that a yeare is runne,
Since both this lower worlds, and the Sunnes Sunne,
The Lustre, and the vigor of this All,   5
Did set; t'were Blasphemy, to say, did fall.
But as a ship which hath strooke saile, doth runne,
By force of that force which before, it wonne,
Or as sometimes in a beheaded man,
Though at those two Red seas, which freely ran,   10
One from the Trunke, another from the Head,
His soule be saild, to her eternall bed,
His eies will twinckle, and his tongue will roll,
As though he beckned, and cal'd backe his Soul,
He graspes his hands, and he puls up his feet,   15
And seemes to reach, and to step forth to meet
His soule; when all these motions which we saw,
Are but as Ice, which crackles at a thaw:
Or as a Lute, which in moist weather, rings
Her knell alone, by cracking of her strings.   20
So strugles this dead world, now shee is gone;
For there is motion in corruption.
As some Daies are, at the Creation nam'd,
Before the sunne, the which fram'd Daies, was fram'd,
So after this sunnes set, some show appeares,   25
And orderly vicisitude of yeares.
Yet a new Deluge, and of Lethe flood,
Hath drown'd us all, All have forgot all good,

Progres: journey as of a king through his lands.
    4. *lower worlds, and the Sunnes Sunne:* Elizabeth, who is symbolized as the center and source of light and energy for the earth (lower world) and the earth's sun (in the middle world).
    7. *strooke:* lowered.
    8. *wonne:* acquired, gathered.
    10. *Red seas:* there is a glance at the Exodus of the children of Israel from bondage to Mount Sinai.
    23–24. See NOTES.
    26. *vicisitude:* alternation as of night and day.
    27. *Deluge:* referring to Noah's flood, sent by God to drown the wickedness of man (Gen. vi ff.). *Lethe:* the river of forgetfulness.

Forgetting her, the maine Reserve of all;
Yet in this Deluge, grosse and generall,   30
Thou seest mee strive for life; my life shalbe,
To bee hereafter prais'd, for praysing thee,
Immortal Mayd, who though thou wouldst refuse
The name of Mother, be unto my Muse,
A Father since her chast Ambition is,   35
Yearely to bring forth such a child as this.
These Hymes may worke on future wits, and so
May great Grand-children of thy praises grow.
And so, though not Revive, embalme, and spice
The world, which else would putrify with vice.   40
For thus, Man may extend thy progeny,
Untill man doe but vanish, and not die.
These Hymns thy issue, may encrease so long,
As till Gods great Venite change the song.
Thirst for that time, O my insatiate soule,   *A just*   45
And serve thy thirst, with Gods safe-sealing Bowle.   *disestimation*
Be thirsty still, and drinke still till thou goe;   *of this world.*
'Tis th'onely Health, to be Hydropique so.
Forget this rotten world; And unto thee,
Let thine owne times as an old story be,   50
Be not concern'd: study not why, nor whan;
Doe not so much, as not beleeve a man.
For though to erre, be worst, to try truths forth,
Is far more busines, then this world is worth.
The World is but a Carkas; thou art fed   55
By it, but as a worme, that carcas bred;

33–44. See Notes.
35. *Father:* that is, procreative force.
37. *Hymes:* perhaps punning on "hims." *wits:* those with creative abilities, imagination.
44. *Gods great Venite:* Judgment Day when God calls man to him. On earth, the song is Psalm xcv, the first word of which is *Venite,* "O come." See further, Notes.
45. margin *disestimation:* despising.
45–48. For the emphasis on thirst, see Notes.
46. *safe-sealing:* the servants of God are sealed of the living God in their foreheads by angels (Rev. vii 2–3). *Bowle:* chalice containing the Eucharist.
48. *Hydropique:* insatiably thirsty.
50. *story:* history.
53. *try:* put (truths) to the test.
56. *worme:* maggot (bred by the carcass).

And why shouldst thou, poore worme, consider more,
When this world will grow better then before,
Then those thy fellow-wormes doe thinke upone
That carkasses last resurrectione.   60
Forget this world, and scarse thinke of it so,
As of old cloaths, cast off a yeare agoe.
To be thus stupid is Alacrity;
Men thus lethargique have best Memory.
Looke upward; that's towards her, whose happy state   65
We now lament not, but congratulate.
Shee, to whom all this world was but a stage,
Where all sat harkning how her youthfull age
Should be emploid, because in all, shee did,
Some Figure of the Golden times, was hid.   70
Who could not lacke, what ere this world could give,
Because shee was the forme, that made it live;
Nor could complaine, that this world was unfit,
To be staid in, then when shee was in it;
Shee that first tried indifferent desires   75
By vertue,'and vertue by religious fires,
Shee to whose person Paradise adhear'd,
As Courts to Princes; shee whose eies enspheard
Star-light inough, t'have made the South controll,
(Had shee beene there) the Star-full Northern Pole,   80
Shee, shee is gone; she'is gone; when thou knowest this,
What fragmentary rubbidge this world is
Thou knowest, and that it is not worth a thought;
He honors it too much that thinks it nought.
Thinke then, My soule, that death is but a Groome,   *Contemplation*   85
Which brings a Taper to the outward roome,   *of our state in*
Whence thou spiest first a little glimmering light, *our death-bed.*
And after brings it nearer to thy sight:
For such approches doth Heaven make in death.
Thinke thy selfe laboring now with broken breath,   90

63. *stupid:* stupefied.
66. *congratulate:* salute; take pleasure in.
70. *Golden times:* the earliest classical age, when there was no corruption
and all was blissful.
72. *forme:* the essential principle; the creative soul.
75. *tried:* tested. *indifferent:* neither bad nor good.
82. *rubbidge:* rubbish.
85. *Groome:* manservant.
88. Heaven is pictured as being pervaded by endless morning light.

And thinke those broken and soft Notes to bee
Division, and thy happiest Harmonee.
Thinke thee laid on thy death bed, loose and slacke;
And thinke that but unbinding of a packe,
To take one precious thing, thy soule, from thence.   95
Thinke thy selfe parch'd with fevers violence,
Anger thine Ague more, by calling it
Thy Physicke; chide the slacknesse of the fit.
Thinke that thou hearst thy knell, and think no more,
But that, as Bels cal'd thee to Church before,   100
So this, to the Triumphant Church, cals thee.
Thinke Satans Sergeants round about thee bee,
And thinke that but for Legacies they thrust;
Give one thy Pride, to'another give thy Lust:
Given them those sinnes which they gave thee before,   105
And trust th'immaculate blood to wash thy score.
Thinke thy frinds weeping round, and thinke that thay
Weepe but because they goe not yet thy way.
Thinke that they close thine eyes, and thinke in this,
That they confesse much in the world, amisse,   110
Who dare not trust a dead mans eye with that,
Which they from God, and Angels cover not.
Thinke that they shroud thee up, and thinke from thence
They reinvest thee in white innocence.
Thinke that thy body rots, and (if so lowe,   115
Thy soule exalted so, thy thoughts can goe,)
Think thee a Prince, who of themselves create
Wormes which insensibly devoure their state.
Thinke that they bury thee, and thinke that rite
Laies thee to sleepe but a saint Lucies night.   120
Thinke these things cheerefully: and if thou bee
Drowsie or slacke, remember then that shee,
Shee whose Complexion was so even made,
That which of her Ingredients should invade
The other three, no Feare, no Art could guesse: 125
So far were all remov'd from more or lesse.

92. *Division:* a melodic run.
99. *knell:* tolling of the passing (or death) bell.
102. *Sergeants:* bailiffs who apprehend debtors.
106. *score:* wound; twentyfold sins. Twenty connotes venality.
114. *reinvest:* reclothe.
120. *saint Lucies night:* December 13, the date of the winter solstice in the
seventeenth century, and thus the longest night of the year.
123. *Complexion:* resulting from the four humours: blood, phlegm, black bile,
and yellow bile.

But as in Mithridate, or just perfumes,
Where all good things being met, no one presumes
To governe, or to triumph on the rest,
Onely because all were, no part was best.   130
And as, though all doe know, that quantities
Are made of lines, and lines from Points arise,
None can these lines or quantities unjoynt,
And say this is a line, or this a point,
So though the Elements and Humors were   135
In her, one could not say, this governes there.
Whose even constitution might have wonne
Any disease to venter on the Sunne,
Rather then her: and make a spirit feare
That he to disuniting subject were.   140
To whose proportions if we would compare
Cubes, th'are unstable; Circles, Angulare;
Shee who was such a Chaine, as Fate emploies
To bring mankind, all Fortunes it enjoies,
So fast, so even wrought, as one would thinke,   145
No Accident could threaten any linke;
Shee, shee embrac'd a sicknesse, gave it meat,
The purest Blood, and Breath, that ere it eat.
And hath taught us that though a good man hath
Title to Heaven, and plead it by his Faith,   150
And though he may pretend a conquest, since
Heaven was content to suffer violence,
Yea though he plead a long possession too,
(For they'are in Heaven on Earth, who Heavens workes do,)
Though he had right, and power, and Place before,   155
Yet Death must usher, and unlocke the doore.
Thinke further on thy selfe, my soule, and thinke   *Incommodities*
How thou at first wast made but in a sinke;   *of the Soule*
Thinke that it argued some infermitee,   *in the Body.*
That those two soules, which then thou foundst in mee,   160

127. *Mithridate:* an antidote compounded of various ingredients.
138. *venter:* venture.
140. That he were subject to disuniting.
146. *Accident:* chance occurrence.
147. *meat:* food.
152. "And from the days of John the Baptist until now the kingdom of heaven suffereth violence, and the violent take it by force" (Matt. xi 12).
158. *sinke:* sewer.
160. *two soules:* vegetable soul, possessed by plants, governing growth and corruption; the sensitive soul, possessed by man and animals, governing motion and perception. The third soul was the rational, unique in man and subsuming the other two.

Thou fedst upon, and drewst into thee, both
My second soule of sence, and first of growth.
Thinke but how poore thou wast, how obnoxious,
Whom a small lump of flesh could poison thus.
This curded milke, this poore unlittered whelpe   165
My body, could, beyond escape, or helpe,
Infect thee with originall sinne, and thou
Couldst neither then refuse, nor leave it now.
Thinke that no stubborne sullen Anchorit,
Which fixt to'a Pillar, or a Grave doth sit   170
Bedded and Bath'd in all his Ordures, dwels
So fowly'as our soules, in their first-built Cels.
Thinke in how poore a prison thou didst lie
After, enabled but to sucke, and crie.
Thinke, when t'was growne to most, t'was a poore Inne,   175
A Province Pack'd up in two yards of skinne,
And that usurp'd, or threatned with the rage
Of sicknesses, or their true mother, Age.
But thinke that Death hath now enfranchis'd thee,   *Her liberty*
Thou hast thy'expansion now and libertee;   *by death.*   180
Thinke that a rusty Peece, discharg'd, is flowen
In peeces, and the bullet is his owne,
And freely flies: This to thy soule allow,
Thinke thy sheell broke, thinke thy Soule hatch'd but now.
And thinke this slow-pac'd soule, which late did cleave,   185
To'a body,'and went but by the bodies leave,
Twenty, perchance, or thirty mile a day,
Dispatches in a minute all the way,
Twixt Heaven, and Earth: shee staies not in the Ayre,
To looke what Meteors there themselves prepare;   190
Shee carries no desire to know, nor sense,
Whether th'Ayrs middle Region be intense,
For th'Element of fire, shee doth not know,
Whether shee past by such a place or no;

163. *obnoxious:* subject to harm.
164. Compare "Man is a lumpe where all beasts kneaded bee" (No. 140).
165. *unlittered:* unborn.
175. *growne to most:* fully grown.   *Inne:* emphasizing its transiency.
179. *enfranchis'd:* liberated.
189–206. She moves through the regions of earth, water, air, and fire, and the spheres of the Moon, Venus, Mercury, Sun, Mars, Jupiter (Jove), Saturn ("his father"), and the Fixed Stars (the Firmament). The order given for Venus and Mercury is that of Tycho Brahe rather than Ptolemy.
192. *intense:* turbulent.

She baits not at the Moone, nor cares to trie, 195
Whether in that new world, men live, and die.
Venus retards her not, to'enquire, how shee
Can, (being one Star) Hesper, and Vesper bee;
Hee that charm'd Argus eies, sweet Mercury,
Workes not on her, who now is growen all Ey; 200
Who, if shee meete the body of the Sunne,
Goes through, not staying till his course be runne;
Who finds in Mars his Campe, no corps of Guard;
Nor is by Jove, nor by his father barrd;
But ere shee can consider how shee went, 205
At once is at, and through the Firmament.
And as these stars were but so many beades
Strunge on one string, speed undistinguish'd leades
Her through those spheares, as through the beades, a string,
Whose quicke succession makes it still one thing: 210
As doth the Pith, which least our Bodies slacke,
Strings fast the little bones of necke, and backe;
So by the soule doth death string Heaven and Earth,
For when our soule enjoyes this her third birth,
(Creation gave her one, a second, grace,) 215
Heaven is as neare, and present to her face,
As colours are, and objects, in a roome
Where darknesse was before, when Tapers come.
This must, my soule, thy long-short Progresse bee;
To'advance these thoughts, remember then, that shee, 220
Shee, whose faire body no such prison was,
But that a soule might well be pleas'd to passe
An Age in her; shee whose rich beauty lent
Mintage to others beauties, for they went
But for so much, as they were like to her; 225
Shee, in whose body (if wee dare prefer
This low world, to so high a mark, as shee,)
The Westerne treasure, Esterne spiceree,

195. *baits:* pauses. *trie:* determine.
198. Venus was called Hesperus (or Vesper) as the evening star.
199. *Argus:* a hundred-eyed herdsman whom Juno set to guard Io, who had been changed into a heifer by Jove; he was killed by Mercury, and Juno placed his eyes in the peacock's tail.
208. *undistinguish'd:* without stops or separate stations.
218. *Tapers:* candles.
228. The West Indies were known for gold and jewels; the East Indies, for spices.

Europe, and Afrique, and the unknowen rest
Were easily found, or what in them was best;   230
And when w'have made this large Discoveree,
Of all in her some one part there will bee
Twenty such parts, whose plenty'and riches is
Inough to make twenty such worlds as this;
Shee, whom had they knowne, who did first betroth   235
The Tutelar Angels, and assign'd one, both
To Nations, Cities, and to Companies,
To Functions, Offices, and Dignities,
And to each severall man, to him, and him,
They would have given her one for every limme;   240
Shee, of whose soule, if we may say, t'was Gold,
Her body was th'Electrum, and did hold
Many degrees of that; we understood
Her by her sight, her pure and eloquent blood
Spoke in her cheekes, and so distinckly wrought,   245
That one might almost say, her bodie thought,
Shee, shee, thus richly,'and largely hous'd, is gone:
And chides us slow-pac'd snailes, who crawle upon
Our prisons prison, earth, nor thinkes us well
Longer, then whil'st we beare our brittle shell.   250
But 'twere but little to have chang'd our roome,   *Her ignorance in*
If, as we were in this our living Tombe   *this life and*
Oppress'd with ignorance, we still were so.   *knowledge in*
Poore soule in this thy flesh what do'st thou know.   *the next.*
Thou know'st thy selfe so little,'as thou know'st not,   255
How thou did'st die, nor how thou wast begot.
Thou neither knowst, how thou at first camest in,
Nor how thou took'st the poyson of mans sin.
Nor dost thou, (though thou knowst, that thou art so)
By what way thou art made immortall, know.   260
Thou art too narrow, wretch, to comprehend
Even thy selfe: yea though thou wouldst but bend
To know thy body. Have not all soules thought
For many ages, that our body'is wrought
Of Ayre, and Fire, and other Elements?   265
And now they thinke of new ingredients,

242. *Electrum:* according to Paracelsus, the middle substance between ore and metal, being thus neither perfect nor imperfect; it is also an alloy of four-fifths gold to one-fifth silver.
    249. *prisons:* body's.
    266. *new ingredients:* salt, sulphur, mercury, as used by Paracelsus to counter bodily disorders.

And one soule thinkes one, and another way
Another thinkes, and 'tis an even lay.
Knowst thou but how the stone doth enter in
The bladders Cave, and never breake the skin?   270
Knowst thou how blood, which to the hart doth flow,
Doth from one ventricle to th'other go?
And for the putrid stuffe, which thou dost spit,
Knowst thou how thy lungs have attracted it?
There are no passages so that there is   275
(For ought thou knowst) piercing of substances.
And of those many'opinions which men raise
Of Nailes and Haires, dost thou know which to praise?
What hope have we to know our selves, when wee
Know not the least things, which for our use bee?   280
We see in Authors, too stiffe to recant,
A hundred controversies of an Ant.
And yet one watches, starves, freeses, and sweats,
To know but Catechismes and Alphabets
Of unconcerning things, matters of fact;   285
How others on our stage their parts did Act;
What Caesar did, yea, and what Cicero said.
Why grasse is greene, or why our blood is red,
Are mysteries which none have reach'd unto.
In this low forme, poore soule what wilt thou doe?   290
When wilt thou shake off this Pedantery,
Of being taught by sense, and Fantasy?
Thou look'st through spectacles; small things seeme great,
Below; But up unto the watch-towre get,

268. *lay:* wager.
275–76. That is, since there are no passages into the body for the stone, the blood, or the expectoration, the parts of the body concerned must be pierced with holes for entry. Penetration of one substance by another opposes the Aristotelian concept of the impossibility of mixing substances.
277–80. That is, many opinions are offered to explain how nails and hair grow and what their usefulness is.
281. *stiffe:* intractable.
282. Ironically, since the ant is small, a creature of habit, and ubiquitous, and should therefore supply uniform evidence.
283. *watches:* stays awake.
284. *Catechismes:* sets of stock questions and answers. *Alphabets:* rudiments, ABCs.
285. *unconcerning:* indifferent, unimportant.
286. *on our stage:* in life, on earth.
292. *Fantasy:* creative imagination.
294. *the watch-towre:* symbolizing the mind.

And see all things despoyld of fallacies: 295
Thou shalt not peepe through lattices of eies,
Nor heare through Laberinths of eares, nor learne
By circuit, or collections to discerne.
In Heaven thou straight know'st all, concerning it,
And what concernes it not, shall straight forget.   300
There thou (but in no other schoole) maist bee
Perchance, as learned, and as full, as shee,
Shee who all Libraries had throughly red
At home, in her owne thoughts, and practised
So much good as would make as many more: 305
Shee whose example they must all implore,
Who would or doe, or thinke well, and confesse
That aie the vertuous Actions they expresse,
Are but a new, and worse edition,
Of her some one thought, or one action: 310
Shee, who in th'Art of knowing Heaven, was growen
Here upon Earth, to such perfection,
That shee hath, ever since to Heaven shee came,
(In a far fairer print,) but read the same:
Shee, shee, not satisfied with all this waite,   315
(For so much knowledge, as would over-fraite
Another, did but Ballast her) is gone,
As well t'enjoy, as get perfectione.
And cals us after her, in that shee tooke,
(Taking herselfe) our best, and worthiest booke.   320
Returne not, my soule, from this extasee,   *Of our company in this*
And meditation of what thou shalt bee,   *life and in the next.*
To earthly thoughts, till it to thee appeare,
With whom thy conversation must be there.
With whom wilt thou Converse? what station   325
Canst thou choose out, free from infection,
That wil nor give thee theirs, nor drinke in thine?
Shalt thou not finde a spungy slack Divine
Drinke and sucke in th'Instructions of Great men,
And for the word of God, vent them agen?   330

292. *collections:* accumulations (of your learning); inferences.
308. *aie:* always.
315. *waite:* weight.
324. *conversation:* association.
325. *Converse:* associate, live.
330. *vent:* discharge, but windily.

Epicedes and Obsequies

301

Are there not some Courts, (And then, no things bee
So like as Courts) which, in this let us see,
That wits and tongues of Libellars are weake,
Because they doe more ill, then these can speake?
The poyson'is gone through all, poysons affect   335
Chiefly the cheefest parts, but some effect
In Nailes, and Haires, yea excrements, will show;
So will the poyson of sinne, in the most low.
Up, up, my drowsie soule, where thy new eare
Shall in the Angels songs no discord heare;   340
Where thou shalt see the blessed Mother-maid
Joy in not being that, which men have said.
Where shee'is exalted more for being good,
Then for her interest, of mother-hood.
Up to those Patriarckes, which did longer sit   345
Expecting Christ, then they'have enjoy'd him yet.
Up to those Prophets, which now gladly see
Their Prophecies growen to be Historee.
Up to th'Apostles, who did bravely runne
All the Sunnes course, with more light then the Sunne. 350
Up to those Martyrs, who did calmely bleed
Oyle to th'Apostles Lamps, dew to their seed.
Up to those Virgins, who thought that almost
They made joyntenants with the Holy Ghost,
If they to any should his Temple give.   355
Up, up, for in that squadron there doth live
Shee, who hath carried thether new degrees
(As to their number) to their dignitees.
Shee, who beeing to herselfe a state, enjoyd
All royalties which any state emploid,   360

342. *that . . . said:* Virgin, but stressing the fact of conception of Jesus rather than denying her sinlessness. Some have seen a repudiation of the Immaculate Conception in these lines.

343–44. Compare Luke xi 27–28: "a certain woman . . . said unto him, Blessed is the womb that bare thee, and the paps which thou hast sucked. But he said, Yea rather, blessed are they that hear the word of God, and keep it."

345. *Patriarckes:* those of the Old Testament.

352. *dew to their seed:* "Blood of martyrs is the seed of the Church" (Tertullian, *Apologeticus,* 50).

354. *joyntenants:* jointures, unions, joint tenancies.

355. *Temple:* "Know ye not that ye are the temple of God, and that the Spirit of God dwelleth in you? If any man defile the temple of God, him shall God destroy; for the temple of God is holy, which temple ye are" (1 Cor. iii 16–17).

360. *royalties:* prerogatives of a sovereign.

For shee made wars, and triumph'd; reson still
Did not o'rthrow, but rectifie her will:
And shee made peace, for no peace is like this,
That beauty'and chastity together kisse:
Shee did high justice; for shee crucified   365
Every first motion of rebellious pride:
And shee gave pardons, and was liberall,
For, onely'herselfe except, shee pardond all:
Shee coynd, in this, that her impressions gave
To all our actions all the worth they have: 370
Shee gave protections; the thoughts of her brest
Satans rude Officers could nere arrest.
As these prerogatives being met in one,
Made her a soveraigne state, religion
Made her a Church; and these two made her all.   375
Shee who was all this All, and could not fall
To worse, by company; (for shee was still
More Antidote, then all the world was ill,)
Shee, shee doth leave it, and by Death, survive
All this, in Heaven; whither who doth not strive   380
The more, because shee'is there, he doth not know
That accidentall joyes in Heaven doe grow.
But pause, My soule, and study ere thou fall
On accidentall joyes, th'essentiall.   *Of essentiall joy in*
Still before Accessories doe abide   *this life and in the next.*   385
A triall, must the principall be tride.
And what essentiall joy can'st thou expect
Here upon earth? what permanent effect
Of transitory causes? Dost thou love
Beauty? (And beauty worthyest is to move)   390
Poore couse'ned cose'nor, that she, and that thou,
Which did begin to love, are neither now.
You are both fluid, chang'd since yesterday;
Next day repaires, (but ill) last daies decay.
Nor are, (Although the river keep the name)   395
Yesterdaies waters, and to daies the same.

363–64. "Mercy and truth are met together; righteousness and peace have kissed each other" (Psalms lxxxv 10).

376. *all this All:* Compare "And when all things shall be subdued unto him, then shall the Son also himself be subject unto him that put all things under him, that God may be all in all" (1 Cor. xv 28).

382. *accidentall:* nonessential, not deriving from the essence of something.

So flowes her face, and thine eies, neither now
That saint, nor Pilgrime, which your loving vow
Concernd, remaines; but whil'st you thinke you bee
Constant, you'are howrely in inconstancee.   400
Honour may have pretence unto our love,
Because that God did live so long above
Without this Honour, and then lov'd it so,
That he at last made Creatures to bestow
Honour on him; not that he needed it,   405
But that, to his hands, man might grow more fit.
But since all honors from inferiors flow,
(For they doe give it; Princes doe but show
Whom they would have so honord) and that this
On such opinions, and capacities   410
Is built, as rise, and fall, to more and lesse,
Alas, tis but a casuall happinesse.
Hath ever any man to'himselfe assign'd
This or that happinesse, to'arrest his minde,
But that another man, which takes a worse,   415
Thinks him a foole for having tane that course?
They who did labour Babels tower t'erect,
Might have considerd, that for that effect,
All this whole solid Earth could not allow
Nor furnish forth Materials enow;   420
And that this Center, to raise such a place
Was far too little, to have beene the Base;
No more affoords this world, foundatione
To'erect true joye, were all the meanes in one.
But as the Heathen made them severall gods,   425
Of all Gods Benefits, and all his Rods,
(For as the Wine, and Corne, and Onions are
Gods unto them, so Agues bee, and war)
And as by changing that whole precious Gold
To such small Copper coynes, they lost the old,   430
And lost their onely God, who ever must
Be sought alone, and not in such a thrust,

401. *pretence:* claim.
417. *Babels tower:* Made of brick and slime, the Tower of Babel was to reach
to heaven, but the Lord, recognizing that "now nothing will be restrained from
them, which they have imagined to do," confounded the people's language and
scattered them over the earth (Gen. xi 1–9).
426. *Rods:* punishments.
427. *Corne:* grain.
432. *thrust:* crowd.

So much mankind true happinesse mistakes;
No Joye enjoyes that man, that many makes.
Then, soule, to thy first pitch worke up againe;   435
Know that all lines which circles doe containe,
For once that they the center touch, do touch
Twice the circumference; and be thou such.
Double on Heaven, thy thoughts on Earth emploid;
All will not serve; Onely who have enjoyd   440
The sight of God, in fulnesse, can thinke it;
For it is both the object, and the wit.
This is essentiall joy, where neither hee
Can suffer Diminution, nor wee;
Tis such a full, and such a filling good;   445
Had th'Angels once look'd on him, they had stood.
To fill the place of one of them, or more,
Shee whom we celebrate, is gone before.
Shee, who had Here so much essentiall joye,
As no chance could distract, much lesse destroy;   450
Who with Gods presence was acquainted so,
(Hearing, and speaking to him) as to know
His face, in any naturall Stone, or Tree,
Better then when in Images they bee:
Who kept, by diligent devotion,   455
Gods Image, in such reparation,
Within her heart, that what decay was growen,
Was her first Parents fault, and not her own:
Who being solicited to any Act,
Still heard God pleading his safe precontract;   460
Who by a faithfull confidence, was here
Betroth'd to God, and now is married there,
Whose twilights were more cleare, then our mid day,
Who dreamt devoutlier, then most use to pray;
Who being heare fild with grace, yet strove to bee,   465
Both where more grace, and more capacitee
At once is given: shee to Heaven is gone,
Who made this world in some proportion
A heaven, and here, became unto us all,
Joye, (as our joyes admit) essentiall.   470
But could this low world joyes essentiall touch,   *Of accidentall joyes*
Heavens accidentall joyes would passe them much.   *in both places.*

446. *they had stood:* they would have remained in heaven rather than have
fallen.

How poore and lame, must then our casuall bee?
If thy Prince will his subjects to call thee
My Lord, and this doe swell thee, thou art than,   475
By being a greater, growen to be lesse Man.
When no Physician of Redresse can speake,
A joyfull casuall violence may breake
A dangerous Apostem in thy brest;
And whilst thou joyest in this, the dangerous rest,   480
The bag may rise up, and so strangle thee.
What eie was casuall, may ever bee.
What should the Nature change? Or make the same
Certaine, which was but casuall, when it came?
All casuall joye doth loud and plainly say,   485
Onely by comming, that it can away.
Onely in Heaven joies strength is never spent;
And accidentall things are permanent.
Joy of a soules arrivall neere decaies;
For that soule ever joyes, and ever staies.   490
Joy that their last great Consummation
Approches in the resurrection;
When earthly bodies more celestiall
Shalbe, then Angels were, for they could fall;
This kind of joy doth every day admit   495
Degrees of grouth, but none of loosing it.
In this fresh joy, tis no small part, that shee,
Shee, in whose goodnesse, he that names degree,
Doth injure her; (Tis losse to be cald best,
There where the stuffe is not such as the rest)   500
Shee, who left such a body, as even shee
Onely in Heaven could learne, how it can bee
Made better; for shee rather was two soules,
Or like to full, on both sides written Rols,
Where eies might read upon the outward skin,   505
As strong Records for God, as mindes within.
Shee, who by making full perfection grow,
Peeces a Circle, and still keepes it so,
Long'd for, and longing for'it, to heaven is gone,
Where shee receives, and gives addition.   510

479. *Apostem:* abscess.
482. *eie:* always.
491. *last great Consummation:* in the background are Jesus' last words on the cross, "Consummatus est" ("It is finished," John xix 30).
508. *Circle:* a symbol of perfection.

Here in a place, where mis-devotion frames   *Conclusion.*
A thousand praiers to saints, whose very names
The ancient Church knew not, Heaven knowes not yet,
And where, what lawes of poetry admit,
Lawes of religion have at least the same,   515
Immortall Maid, I might invoque thy name.
Could any Saint provoke that appetite,
Thou here shouldst make mee a french convertite.
But thou wouldst not; nor wouldst thou be content,
To take this, for my second yeeres true Rent,   520
Did this Coine beare any'other stampe, then his,
That gave thee power to doe, me, to say this.
Since his will is, that to posteritee,
Thou shouldest for life, and death a patterne bee,
And that the world should notice have of this,   525
The purpose, and th'Autority is his;
Thou art the Proclamation; and I ame
The Trumpet, at whose voice the people came.

FINIS.

511. *Here in a place:* that is, in Roman Catholic France.

517. *appetite:* desire.

518. *convertite:* convert.

520. *second yeeres true Rent:* see n. to *First Anniversarie,* l. 447.

521. *stampe:* impression, image.

527–28. "Behold, the Lord hath proclaimed unto the end of the world, Say ye to the daughter of Zion, Behold, thy Salvation cometh" (Isa. lxii 11); "for the trumpet shall sound, and the dead shall be raised incorruptible, and we shall be changed. . . . O death, where is thy sting? O grave, where is thy victory?" (1 Cor. xv 52, 55).

---◦◄{ *Metempsychosis* }►◦---

Metempsychosis.

Poêma Satyricon.

Epistle.

Others at the Porches and entries of their Buildings set their
Armes; I, my picture; if any colours can deliver a minde so plaine,
and flat, and through light as mine. Naturally at a new Author, I
doubt, and sticke, and doe not say quickly, good. I censure much
and taxe; And this liberty costs mee more then others, by how   5
much my owne things are worse then others. Yet I would not be
so rebellious against my selfe, as not to doe it, since I love it; nor
so unjust to others, to do it *sine talione.* As long as I give them as
good hold upon mee, they must pardon mee my bitings. I forbid
no reprehender, but him that like the Trent Councell forbids not   10
bookes, but Authors, damning what ever such a name hath or
shall write. None writes so ill, that he gives not some thing exem-
plary, to follow, or flie. Now when I beginne this booke, I have
no purpose to come into any mans debt; how my stocke will hold
out I know not; perchance waste, perchance increase in use; if I   15
doe borrow any thing of Antiquitie, besides that I make account
that I pay it to posterity, with as much and as good: You shall still
finde mee to acknowledge it, and thanke not him onely that hath
digg'd out treasure for mee, but that hath lighted mee a candle
to the place. All which I will bid you remember, (for I will have   20
no such Readers as I can teach) is, that the Pithagorian doctrine

METEMPSYCHOSIS.
   This history of the passing of the soul at death into another body, from the
Creation to Donne's day (had it been completed), is dated August 16, 1601.
See further, Notes. The soul lives in the apple of the forbidden tree, in a plant,
in a bird, in a fish, in a whale, in a mouse, in a wolf, in a dog-wolf, in an ape,
and finally in Themach, sister and wife to Cain.
   5. *taxe:* accuse.
   8. *sine talione:* without retaliation.
   10. *Trent Councell:* in its last meeting (held at the end of 1563), this
ecumenical council authorized the pope to catalogue forbidden books; ten rules
governing the Index were published in March 1564.
   21. *Pithagorian doctrine:* the transmigration of the soul enunciated in the
poem; Pythagoras was supposed to believe also that a pure life released the soul
from any kind of body, which was otherwise its tomb or prison. See further,
Notes.

doth not onely carry one soule from man to man, nor man
to beast, but indifferently to plants also: and therefore you must
not grudge to finde the same soule in an Emperour, in a Post-
horse, and in a Mucheron, since no unreadinesse in the soule, but   25
an indisposition in the organs workes this. And therefore though
this soule could not move when it was a Melon, yet it may remember, and now tell mee, at what lascivious banquet it was serv'd.
And though it could not speake, when it was a spider, yet it can
remember, and now tell me, who used it for poyson to attaine   30
dignitie. How ever the bodies have dull'd her other faculties,
her memory hath ever been her owne, which makes me so seriously deliver you by her relation all her passages from her first
making when shee was that apple which Eve eate, to this time
when shee is hee, whose life you shall finde in the end of this   35
booke.

The Progresse of the Soule.

First Song.

I.

I sing the progresse of a deathlesse soule,
Whom Fate, which God made, but doth not controule,
Plac'd in most shapes; all times before the law
Yoak'd us, and when, and since, in this I sing.
And the great world to his aged evening;   5
From infant morne, through manly noone I draw.
What the gold Chaldee,'or silver Persian saw,
Greeke brasse, or Roman iron, is in this one;
A worke t'outweare *Seths* pillars, bricke and stone,
    And (holy writt excepted) made to yeeld to none.   10

25. *Mucheron:* mushroom.
30–31. *used . . . dignitie:* used the spider's venom to kill someone from
whom the murderer inherited a title or position.
35. *hee:* according to Jonson, Calvin, but the contemporary context shows
that this is not correct. Lines 57–60 place the ending in England, and thus
Donne seems to refer to contemporary man (as he is observed in England).
The Progresse of the Soule, *First Song.*
2. *doth not controule:* that is, the soul has free will; God foresees but does
not decree.
3–4. *before . . . us:* before conduct or custom bound us.
7–8. Referring to the four ages of man: gold, silver, brass (bronze), and iron.
9. *Seths pillars:* two pillars (one brick, one stone) were inscribed with Seth's
children's discoveries concerning heavenly bodies and their order; thus if one
were destroyed, the other would remain.

II.

Thee, eye of heaven, this great Soule envies not,
By thy male force, is all wee have, begot.
In the first East, thou now beginst to shine,
Suck'st early balme, and Iland spices there,
And wilt anon in thy loose-rein'd careere   15
At Tagus, Po, Sene, Thames, and Danow dine,
And see at night thy Westerne land of Myne,
Yet hast thou not more nations seene then shee,
That before thee, one day beganne to bee,
    And thy fraile light being quench'd, shall long, long out live   20
    thee.

III.

Nor holy *Janus* in whose soveraigne boate
The Church, and all the Monarchies did floate;
That swimming Colledge, and free Hospitall
Of all mankinde, that cage and vivarie
Of fowles, and beasts, in whose wombe, Destinie   25
Us, and our latest nephewes did install
(From thence are all deriv'd, that fill this All)
Did'st thou in that great stewardship embarke
So diverse shapes into that floating parke,
    As have beene mov'd, and inform'd by this heavenly sparke.   30

11–12. Alchemists believed the sun generated both animate and inanimate matter.

15. *careere:* swift course, and referring to Apollo's chariot racing across the sky.

16. *Tagus . . . Danow:* rivers of Spain, Italy, France (the Seine), England, and Central Europe (the Danube).

17. *Westerne land of Myne:* the West Indies were supposed to have deposits of silver, gold, and other precious metals.

19. Since this soul existed before the creation of the earth, it existed before God created light out of chaos. It existed in Satan and the other fallen angels.

21. *Janus:* the two-faced God who controlled doors and thus the beginnings of things. The creations listed are thus ambivalent of good and evil; compare stanza LII. Janus was equated with Noah by Annius of Viterbo.

23. *Colledge:* both institution incorporating all knowledge and a prison. *Hospitall:* both institution of refuge from ills and house of prostitution.

24. *vivarie:* place of birth.

26. *latest nephewes:* most recent descendants.

27. *this All:* earth.

29. *parke:* an enclosed area stocked with game.

30. *inform'd:* given form and reason.

IV.

Great Destiny the Commissary'of God,
That hath mark'd out a path and period
For every thing, who, where wee of-spring tooke,
Our wayes and ends seest at one instant; Thou
Knot of all causes, thou whose changelesse brow   35
Ne'r smiles nor frownes, O vouch thou safe to looke
And shew my story,'in thy eternall booke.
That (if my prayer be fit) I may'understand
So much my selfe, as to know with what hand,
    How scant, or liberall this my lifes race is spand.   40

V.

To my sixe lustres almost now outwore,
Except thy booke owe mee so many more,
Except my legend be free from the letts
Of steepe ambition, sleepie povertie,
Spirit-quenching sicknesse, dull captivitie,   45
Distracting businesse, and from beauties nets,
And all that calls from this, and to'others whets,
O let me not launch out, but let mee save
Th'expense of braine and spirit; that my grave
    His right and due, a whole unwasted man may have.   50

VI.

But if my dayes be long, and good enough,
In vaine this sea shall enlarge, or enrough
It selfe; for I will through the wave, and fome,
And shall in sad lone wayes, a lively spright
Make my darke heavy Poëm light, and light.   55
For though through many streights, and lands I roame,
I launch at paradise, and I saile towards home;

35. *Knot:* intricately intertwined cord. A cause, according to Peter Ramus, was that by which a thing (object or idea or occurrence) existed.
40. *spand:* limited. The distance that the hand could stretch was considered nine inches, called a span.
41. *sixe lustres:* thirty years, a lustrum being a period of five years.
43. *letts:* hindrances.
46. *nets:* entrapments.
55. *light, and light:* "light" as opposed to "darke" (thus, illuminating), and as opposed to "heavy" (thus, humorous as a "poêma satyricon" was supposed to be).

The course I there began, shall here be staid,
Sailes hoised there, stroke here, and anchors laid
   In Thames, which were at Tigrys, and Euphrates waide.   60

VII.

For the great soule which here amongst us now
Doth dwell, and moves that hand, and tongue, and brow,
Which as the Moone the sea, moves us, to heare
Whose story, with long patience you will long;
(For 'tis the crowne, and last straine of my song)   65
This soule to'whom *Luther,* and *Mahomet* were
Prisons of flesh; this soule which oft did teare,
And mend the wracks of th'Empire, and late Rome,
And liv'd when every great change did come,
   Had first in paradise, a low, but fatall roome.   70

VIII.

Yet no low roome, nor then the greatest, lesse,
If (as devout and sharpe men fitly guesse)
That Crosse, our joy, and griefe, where nailes did tye
That All, which alwayes was all, every where,
Which could not sinne, and yet all sinnes did beare;   75
Which could not die, yet could not chuse but die;
Stood in the selfe same roome in Calvarie,
Where first grew the forbidden learned tree,
For on that tree hung in security
   This Soule, made by the Makers will from pulling free.   80

IX.

Prince of the orchard, faire as dawning morne,
Fenc'd with the law, and ripe as soone as borne
That apple grew, which this Soule did enlive,

60. *waide:* weighed; that is, the anchor of his ship of life was raised in the cradle of civilization to sail the sea of life.

65. *crowne:* high point.

72. *sharpe:* sagacious.

74. See Notes.

78. *the forbidden learned tree:* the Tree of Knowledge of Good and Evil in Eden, which reputedly stood on the same spot as the Crucifixion. The following stanzas on the fall of Adam and Eve recall the introduction of Sin, Death, and Labor into the world.

80. *pulling free:* modifying "will" and meaning the free will of God (without exertion or coercion).

Till the then climing serpent, that now creeps
For that offence, for which all mankinde weepes,   85
Tooke it, and t'her whom the first man did wive
(Whom and her race, only forbiddings drive)
He gave it, shee, t'her husband, both did eate;
So perished the eaters, and the meate:
    And wee (for treason taints the blood) thence die and sweat.   90

X.

Man all at once was there by woman slaine,
And one by one we'are here slaine o'er againe
By them. The mother poison'd the well-head,
The daughters here corrupt us, Rivolets;
No smalnesse scapes, no greatnesse breaks their nets;   95
She thrust us out, and by them we are led
Astray, from turning, to whence we are fled.
Were prisoners Judges, 'twould seeme rigorous,
Shee sinn'd, we beare; part of our paine is, thus
    To love them, whose fault to this painfull love yoak'd us.   100

XI.

So fast in us doth this corruption grow,
That now wee dare aske why wee should be so.
Would God (disputes the curious Rebell) make
A law, and would not have it kept? Or can
His creatures will, crosse his? Of every man   105
For one, will God (and be just) vengeance take?
Who sinn'd? t'was not forbidden to the snake
Nor her, who was not then made; nor is't writ
That Adam cropt, or knew the apple; yet
    The worme and she, and he, and wee endure for it.   110

    84–85. Refers to Gen. iii 14: "And the Lord God said unto the serpent, Because thou hast done this . . . upon thy belly shalt thou go, and dust shalt thou eat all the days of thy life."

    89. *meate:* both the apple containing this soul and flesh itself.

    91–94. Aside from its appearance in a number of the Songs and Sonnets, this idea was common in religion and supplied men with reasons for their failures in life.

    97. *turning:* a satiric double pun: though women have led men into sin, they do not allow them to detour from the path of life, which is their means for salvation, and by sexual intercourse ("turning" in bed), which is man's solace.

    103. *curious Rebell:* he who questions whether God allows salvation to man; apparently a Calvinist, who believed in the doctrine of the elect and the reality of man's depravity.

XII.

But snatch mee heavenly Spirit from this vaine
Reckoning their vanities, lesse is their gaine
Then hazard still, to meditate on ill,
Though with good minde, their reasons like those toyes
Of glassie bubbles, which the gamesome boyes   115
Stretch to so nice a thinnes through a quill
That they themselves breake, doe themselves spill:
Arguing is heretiques game, and Exercise
As wrastlers, perfects them; Not liberties
   Of speech, but silence; hands, not tongues, end heresies.   120

XIII.

Just in that instant when the serpents gripe,
Broke the slight veines, and tender conduit-pipe,
Through which this soule from the trees root did draw
Life, and growth to this apple, fled away
This loose soule, old, one and another day.   125
As lightning, which one scarce dares say, he saw,
'Tis so soone gone, (and better proofe the law
Of sense, then faith requires) swiftly she flew
To'a darke and foggie Plot; Her, her fates threw
   There through th'earths pores, and in a Plant hous'd her anew. 130

XIV.

The plant thus abled, to it selfe did force
A place, where no place was; by natures course
As aire from water, water fleets away
From thicker bodies, by this root throng'd so
His spungie confines gave him place to grow,   135

114. *toyes:* small, showy objects designed for diversion rather than utility.
119–20. That is, heresies are bred by talk; they are ended by silence and works.
129. *foggie:* marshy, "spungie" (l. 135).
130. *a Plant:* a mandrake (l. 160), which resembled man's form and was thus, for Donne's purpose, an appropriate plant for this soul, escaping from the miraculous plant, to reside in. Man's vegetative soul (that defining generation and decay) required the soul first inhabit a plant.
134. *thicker:* denser, having a higher density. *throng'd:* compressed, squeezed in.

Just as in our streets, when the people stay
To see the Prince, and have so fill'd the way
That weesels scarce could passe, when she comes nere
They throng and cleave up, and a passage cleare,
    As if, for that time, their round bodies flatned were.   140

XV.

His right arme he thrust out towards the East,
West-ward his left; th'ends did themselves digest
Into ten lesser strings, these fingers were:
And as a slumberer stretching on his bed,
This way he this, and that way scattered   145
His other legge, which feet with toes upbeare;
Grew on his middle parts, the first day, haire,
To show, that in loves businesse hee should still
A dealer bee, and be us'd well, or ill:
    His apples kindle,'his leaves, force of conception kill.   150

XVI.

A mouth, but dumbe, he hath; blinde eyes, deafe eares,
And to his shoulders dangle subtile haires;
A young *Colossus* there hee stands upright,
And as that ground by him were conquered
A leafie garland weares he on his head   155
Enchas'd with little fruits, so red and bright
That for them you would call your Loves lips white;
So, of a lone unhaunted place possest,
Did this soules second Inne, built by the guest,
    This living buried man, this quiet mandrake, rest.   160

XVII.

No lustfull woman came this plant to grieve,
But t'was because there was none yet but Eve:

142. *digest:* divide.
149. A *dealer:* an agent, referring to the belief that mandrakes could help in the begetting of children. Hair, of course, shows virility.
150. The round fruits of the mandrake were used as an aphrodisiac and the leaves as a narcotic and soporific.
152. *subtile:* fine.
153. *Colossus:* referring to the huge statue of Apollo that dominated the harbor at Rhodes.
156. *Enchas'd:* ornamented.

And she (with other purpose) kill'd it quite;
Her sinne had now brought in infirmities,
And so her cradled child, the moist red eyes   165
Had never shut, nor sleept since it saw light;
Poppie she knew, she knew the mandrakes might,
And tore up both, and so coold her childs blood;
Unvirtuous weeds might long unvex'd have stood;
    But hee's short liv'd, that with his death can doe most good.   170

XVIII.

To an unfetterd soules quick nimble hast
Are falling stars, and hearts thoughts, but slow pac'd:
Thinner then burnt aire flies this soule, and she
Whom foure new comming, and foure parting Suns
Had found, and left the Mandrakes tenant, runnes   175
Thoughtlesse of change, when her firme destiny
Confin'd, and enjayld her, that seem'd so free,
Into a small blew shell, the which a poore
Warme bird orespread, and sat still evermore,
    Till her inclos'd child kickt, and pick'd it selfe a dore.   180

XIX.

Outcrept a sparrow, this soules moving Inne,
On whose raw armes stiffe feathers now begin,
As childrens teeth through gummes, to breake with paine,
His flesh is jelly yet, and his bones threds,
All a new downy mantle overspreads,   185
A mouth he opes, which would as much containe
As his late house, and the first howre speaks plaine,
And chirps alowd for meat. Meat fit for men
His father steales for him, and so feeds then
    One, that within a moneth, will beate him from his hen.   190

XX.

In this worlds youth wise nature did make hast,
Things ripen'd sooner, and did longer last;

163. *other purpose:* to use as an opiate, as explained in the following lines.
169. *Unvirtuous:* lacking in extraordinary abilities. *unvex'd:* uninjured, un-
touched.
173. *Thinner:* more transparent, more rarefied. *burnt aire:* smoke.
175. *tenant:* tenancy, abode.
184. *threds:* thin and weak like threads.

Already this hot cocke in bush and tree,
In field and tent oreflutters his next hen;
He asks her not, who did so tast, nor when,   195
Nor if his sister, or his neece shee be,
Nor doth she pule for his inconstancie
If in her sight he change, nor doth refuse
The next that calls, both liberty doe use;
    Where store is of both kindes, both kindes may freely chuse.   200

XXI.

Men, till they tooke laws which made freedome lesse,
Their daughters, and their sisters did ingresse,
Till now unlawfull, therefore ill, t'was not.
So jolly, that it can move this soule is,
The body so free of his kindnesses,   205
That selfe-preserving it hath now forgot,
And slackneth so the soules, and bodies knot,
Which temperance streightens; freely'on his she friends
He blood, and spirit, pith, and marrow spends,
    Ill steward of himself, himselfe in three yeares ends.   210

XXII.

Else might he long have liv'd; man did not know
Of gummie blood, which doth in holly grow,
How to make bird-lime, nor how to deceive
With faind calls, hid nets, or enwrapping snare
The free inhabitants of the Plyant aire.   215
Man to beget, and woman to conceive
Askt not of rootes, nor of cock-sparrowes, leave:
Yet chuseth hee, though none of these he feares,
Pleasantly three, then streightned twenty yeares
    To live, and to encrease his race, himselfe outweares.   220

197. *pule:* moan.
204. *jolly:* joyous.
207. *knot:* interrelationship.
208. *streightens:* corrects (punningly, to its knotted form again); reforms (by setting it on its proper course); confines and restricts ("straitens").
212. *gummie blood:* viscous sap.
213. *bird-lime:* a substance made from the bark of the holly, used to ensnare small birds.
219. *streightned:* punning on the meanings lying prone and stiff, being reformed, and being restricted.
220. Popular was the belief that sexual intercourse shortened one's life.

XXIII.

This cole with overblowing quench'd and dead,
The Soule from her too active organs fled
T'a brooke; a female fishes sandie Roe
With the males jelly, newly lev'ned was,
For they had intertouch'd as they did passe, 225
And one of those small bodies, fitted so,
This soule inform'd, and abled it to row
It selfe with finnie oares, which she did fit,
Her scales seem'd yet of parchment, and as yet
    Perchance a fish, but by no name you could call it. 230

XXIV.

When goodly, like a ship in her full trim,
A swan, so white that you may unto him
Compare all whitenesse, but himselfe to none,
Glided along, and as he glided watch'd,
And with his arched necke this poore fish catch'd. 235
It mov'd with state, as if to looke upon
Low things it scorn'd, and yet before that one
Could thinke he sought it, he had swallow'd cleare
This, and much such, and unblam'd devour'd there
    All, but who too swift, too great, or well armed were. 240

XXV.

Now swome a prison in a prison put,
And now this Soule in double walls was shut,
Till melted with the Swans digestive fire,
She left her house the fish, and vapour'd forth;
Fate not affording bodies of more worth 245
For her as yet, bids her againe retire
T'another fish, to any new desire
Made a new prey; For, he that can to none
Resistance make, nor complaint, sure is gone.
    Weaknesse invites, but silence feasts oppression. 250

221. *This cole:* the sparrow, fierily passionate.
224. *lev'ned:* impregnated.
227. *inform'd:* gave form to.
229. *of parchment:* imaginary; of living matter but not vibrant.
239. *much such:* many similar fishes. *unblam'd:* unsinning, blameless.

XXVI.

Pace with her native streame, this fish doth keepe,
And journeyes with her, towards the glassie deepe,
But oft retarded, once with a hidden net
Though with greate windowes, for when need first taught
These tricks to catch food, then they were not wrought   255
As now, with curious greedinesse to let
None scape, but few, and fit for use, to get,
As, in this trap a ravenous pike was tane,
Who, though himselfe distrest, would faine have slain
   This wretch, so hardly are ill habits left againe.   260

XXVII.

Here by her smallnesse shee two deaths orepast,
Once innocence scap'd, and left the'oppressor fast;
The net through-swome, she keepes the liquid path,
And whether she leape up sometimes to breath
And suck in aire, or finde it underneath,   265
Or working parts like mills, or limbecks hath
To make the water thinne, and airelike faith
Cares not, but safe the Place she's come unto
Where fresh, with salt waves meet, and what to doe
   She knowes not, but betweene both makes a boord or two.   270

XXVIII.

So farre from hiding her guests, water is
That she showes them in bigger quantities
Then they are. Thus doubtfull of her way,
For game and not for hunger a sea Pie
Spied through this traiterous spectacle, from high,   275
The seely fish where it disputing lay,
And t'end her doubts and her, beares her away:

254. *windowes:* openings (of the net).
258. *tane:* taken.
266. *working parts like mills, or limbecks:* fins, such as on water wheels, or a
system of retorts (like gills) for moving and distilling liquid.
267. *thinne:* less dense and resistant.
270. *makes a boord or two:* tacks one way, then another.
274. *sea Pie:* common name for the oyster catcher (*Haematopus ostralegus*).
276. *seely:* foolish.

Exalted she'is, but to the'exalters good,
As are by great ones, men which lowly stood.
    It's rais'd, to be the Raisers instrument and food.   280

XXIX.

Is any kinde subject to rape like fish?
Ill unto man, they neither doe, nor wish:
Fishers they kill not, nor with noise awake,
They doe not hunt, nor strive to make a prey
Of beasts, nor their yong sonnes to beare away;   285
Foules they pursue not, nor do undertake
To spoile the nests industrious birds do make;
Yet them all these unkinde kinds feed upon,
To kill them is an occupation,
    And lawes make fasts, and lents for their destruction.   290

XXX.

A sudden stiffe land-winde in that selfe houre
To sea-ward forc'd this bird, that did devour
The fish; he cares not, for with ease he flies,
Fat gluttonies best orator: at last
So long hee hath flowen, and hath flowen so fast   295
That many leagues at sea, now tir'd hee lyes,
And with his prey, that till then languisht, dies:
The soules no longer foes, two wayes did erre,
The fish I follow,'and keepe no calender
    Of the'other; he lives yet in some great officer.   300

XXXI.

Into an embrion fish, our Soule is throwne
And in due time throwne out againe, and growne
To such vastnesse as, if unmanacled
From Greece, Morea were, and that by some
Earthquake unrooted, loose Morea swome,   305

    280. *instrument:* helper.
    281. *kinde:* species.   *rape:* seizure and plunder.
    290. *fasts:* Fridays and similar Ember days when Roman Catholics abstain
from eating meat and particularly eat fish.   *lents:* referring to the period of
forty fast days before Easter.
    298. *two wayes did erre:* by gluttony and by sloth.
    300. *officer:* governmental official.
    304. *Morea:* Peloponnesus, connected to Greece by an isthmus.

Or seas from Africks body'had severed
And torne the hopefull Promontories head,
This fish would seeme these, and, when all hopes faile,
A great ship overset, or without saile
   Hulling, might (when this was a whelp) be like this whale.   310

XXXII.

At every stroake his brazen finnes do take,
More circles in the broken sea they make
Then cannons voices, when the aire they teare:
His ribs are pillars, and his high arch'd roofe
Of barke that blunts best steele, is thunder-proofe,   315
Swimme in him swallow'd Dolphins, without feare,
And feele no sides, as if his vast wombe were
Some Inland sea, and ever as hee went
Hee spouted rivers up, as if he ment
   To joyne our seas, with seas above the firmament.   320

XXXIII.

He hunts not fish, but as an officer,
Stayes in his court, at his owne net, and there
All suitors of all sorts themselves enthrall;
So on his backe lyes this whale wantoning,
And in his gulfe-like throat, sucks every thing   325
That passeth neare. Fish chaseth fish, and all,
Flyer and follower, in this whirlepoole fall;
O might not states of more equality
Consist? and is it of necessity
   That thousand guiltlesse smals, to make one great, must die?   330

XXXIV.

Now drinkes he up seas, and he eates up flocks,
He justles Ilands, and he shakes firme rockes.
Now in a roomefull house this Soule doth float,
And like a Prince she sends her faculties
To all her limbes, distant as Provinces.   335

    307. *the hopefull Promontories head:* the Cape of Good Hope.
    310. *Hulling:* striking the side of the ship.
    315. *barke:* tough outer skin.

The Sunne hath twenty times both crab and goate
Parched, since first lanch'd forth this living boate.
'Tis greatest now, and to destruction
Nearest; There's no pause at perfection.
    Greatnesse a period hath, but hath no station.   340

XXXV.

Two little fishes whom hee never harm'd,
Nor fed on their kinde, two not throughly arm'd
With hope that they could kill him, nor could doe
Good to themselves by'his death: they did not eate
His flesh, nor suck those oyles, which thence outstreat,   345
Conspir'd against him, and it might undoe
The plot of all, that the plotters were two,
But that they fishes were, and could not speake.
How shall a Tyran wise strong projects breake,
    If wreches can on them the common anger wreake?   350

XXXVI.

The flaile-finnd Thresher, and steel-beak'd Sword-fish
Onely attempt to doe, what all doe wish.
The Thresher backs him, and to beate begins;
The sluggard Whale yeelds to oppression,
And t'hide himselfe from shame and danger, downe   355
Begins to sinke; the Swordfish upward spins,
And gores him with his beake; his staffe-like finnes,
So well the one, his sword the other plyes,
That now a scoffe, and prey, this tyran dyes,
    And (his owne dole) feeds with himselfe all companies.   360

XXXVII.

Who will revenge his death? or who will call
Those to account, that thought, and wrought his fall?
The'heires of slaine kings, wee see are often so
Transported with the joy of what they get,
That they, revenge, and obsequies forget,   365

336. *crab and goate:* the zodiacal signs of the summer and winter solstices.
That is, twenty years have passed.
    345. *outstreat:* exude.
    351. *Thresher:* a shark which rounds up fish by flailing its great tail.

Nor will against such men the people goe,
Because h'is now dead, to whom they should show
Love in that act. Some kings by vice being growne
So needy'of subjects love, that of their own
    They thinke they lose, if love be to the dead Prince shown.   370

XXXVIII.

This Soule, now free from prison, and passion,
Hath yet a little indignation
That so small hammers should so soone downe beat
So great a castle.'And having for her house
Got the streight cloyster of a wreched mouse   375
(As basest men that have not what to eate,
Nor enjoy ought, doe farre more hate the great
Then they, who good repos'd estates possesse)
This Soule, late taught that great things might by lesse
    Be slain, to gallant mischiefe doth herselfe addresse.   380

XXXIX.

Natures great master-peece, an Elephant,
The onely harmlesse great thing; the giant
Of beasts; who thought, no more had gone, to make one wise
But to be just, and thankfull, loth to'offend,
(Yet nature hath given him no knees to bend)   385
Himselfe he up-props, on himselfe relies
And foe to none, suspects no enemies,
Still sleeping stood; vex't not his fantasie
Blacke dreames; like an unbent bow, carelesly
    His sinewy Proboscis did remisly lie.   390

XL.

In which as in a gallery this mouse
Walk'd, and surveid the roomes of this vast house,
And to the braine, the soules bedchamber, went,
And gnaw'd the life cords there; Like a whole towne
Cleane undermin'd, the slaine beast tumbled downe;   395
With him the murtherer dies whom envy sent
To kill, not scape, for, only hee that ment
To die, did ever kill a man of better roome,
And thus he made his foe, his prey, and tombe:
    Who cares not to turn back, may any whither come.   400

400. *any whither:* to any place.

XLI.

Next, hous'd this Soule a Wolves yet unborne whelp,
Till the best midwife, Nature, gave it helpe,
To issue. It could kill, as soone as goe:
Abel, as white, and milde as his sheepe were,
(Who in that trade of Church, and kingdomes, there   405
Was the first type) was still infested soe,
With this wolfe, that it bred his losse and woe;
And yet his bitch, his sentinell attends
The flocke so neere, so well warnes and defends,
  That the wolfe, (hopelesse else) to corrupt her, intends.   410

XLII.

Hee tooke a course, which since, succesfully,
Great men have often taken, to espie
The counsels, or to breake the plots of foes.
To Abels tent he stealeth in the darke,
On whose skirts the bitch slept; ere she could barke,   415
Attach'd her with streight gripes, yet hee call'd those,
Embracements of love; to loves worke he goes,
Where deeds move more then words; nor doth she show,
Nor much resist, nor needs hee streighten so
  His prey, for, were shee loose, she would nor barke, nor goe.   420

XLIII.

Hee hath engag'd her; his, she wholy bides;
Who not her owne, none others secrets hides.
If to the flocke he come, and Abell there,
She faines hoarse barkings, but she biteth not,
Her faith is quite, but not her love forgot.   425

404. *Abel:* the second son of Adam and Eve, "a keeper of sheep," who was slain by his older brother Cain, "a tiller of the ground," because the Lord respected Abel and his offering.

405. *that trade:* of pastor (shepherd). He is "the first type" because he was martyred for his proper tending of his flock, as Jesus was.

407. *wolfe:* the context suggests the wolf that does not enter by the door to catch and scatter the sheep (John x 1–18).

416. *Attach'd:* also implying "attacked." *gripes:* grips, clasps.

418. *show:* (resistance).

At last a trap, of which some every where
Abell had plac'd ends all his losse, and feare,
By the Wolves death; and now just time it was
That a quicke soule should give life to that masse
    Of blood in Abels bitch, and thither this did passe.   430

XLIV.

Some have their wives, their sisters some begot,
But in the lives of Emperours you shall not
Reade of a lust the which may equall this;
This wolfe begot himselfe, and finished
What he began alive, when hee was dead;   435
Sonne to himselfe, and father too, hee is
A ridling lust, for which Schoolemen would misse
A proper name. The whelpe of both these lay
In Abels tent, and with soft Moaba,
    His sister, being yong, it us'd to sport and play.   440

XLV.

Hee soone for her too harsh, and churlish grew,
And Abell (the dam dead) would use this new
For the field. Being of two kindes thus made,
He, as his dam, from sheepe drove wolves away,
And as his Sire, he made them his owne prey.   445
Five yeares he liv'd, and cosen'd with his trade,
Then hopelesse that his faults were hid, betraid
Himselfe by flight, and by all followed,
From dogges, a wolfe; from wolves, a dogge he fled;
    And, like a spie to both sides false, he perished.   450

XLVI.

It quickned next a toyfull Ape, and so
Gamesome it was, that it might freely goe
From tent to tent, and with the children play.

429. *quicke:* living.
434–35. That is, since the soul within the wolf passes into the offspring of
the wolf and Abel's dog, it is as if the wolf has begotten himself, is his own father and his own son, begins to live at the moment he dies.
437. *Schoolemen:* those medieval academicians who disputed minor differences among things, attempting to classify them into specific categories.
439. *Moaba:* Moab was the son of Lot and his eldest daughter. Donne uses
a feminine form of the name to indicate Moab's incestuous birth.
446. *cosen'd with his trade:* deceived Abel by protecting the sheep.
451. *quickned:* enlivened, gave life to. *toyfull:* amorous and sportive.

His organs now so like theirs hee doth finde,
That why he cannot laugh, and speake his minde,   455
He wonders. Much with all, most he doth stay
With Adams fift daughter *Siphatecia,*
Doth gaze on her, and, where she passeth, passe,
Gathers her fruits, and tumbles on the grasse,
    And wisest of that kinde, the first true lover was.   460

XLVII.

He was the first that more desir'd to have
One then another; first that ere did crave
Love by mute signes, and had no power to speake;
First that could make love faces, or could doe
The valters sombersalts, or us'd to wooe   465
With hoiting gambolls, his owne bones to breake
To make his mistresse merry; or to wreake
Her anger on himselfe. Sinnes against kinde
They easily doe, that can let feed their minde
    With outward beauty; beauty they in boyes and beasts do find.   470

XLVIII.

By this misled, too low things men have prov'd,
And too high; beasts and angels have beene lov'd;
This Ape, though else through-vaine, in this was wise,
He reach'd at things too high, but open way
There was, and he knew not she would say nay;   475
His toyes prevaile not, likelier meanes he tries,
He gazeth on her face with teare-shot eyes,
And up lifts subtly with his russet pawe
Her kidskinne apron without feare or awe
    Of nature; nature hath no gaole, though shee hath law.   480

XLIX.

First she was silly'and knew not what he ment.
That vertue, by his touches, chaft and spent,

454. *organs:* bodily parts.
457. *Siphatecia:* non-Biblical daughters and sons of Adam (see ll. 487, 509)
are named in apocryphal literature.
466. *hoiting:* noisily mirthful, but also clumsy.
473. *else through-vaine:* otherwise totally foolish.
476. *toyes:* amorous antics.
481. *silly:* lacking in understanding.
482. *That vertue:* temperance, which would have created cold resistance;
"chaft" implies excitation and warmth due to rubbing.

Succeeds an itchie warmth, that melts her quite;
She knew not first, now cares not what he doth,
And willing halfe and more, more then halfe loth,   485
She neither puls nor pushes, but outright
Now cries, and now repents; when *Tethlemite*
Her brother, entred, and a great stone threw
After the Ape, who, thus prevented, flew.
   This house thus batter'd downe, the Soule possest a new.   490

L.

And whether by this change she lose or win,
She comes out next, where the'Ape would have gone in.
Adam and *Eve* had mingled bloods, and now
Like Chimiques equall fires, her temperate wombe
Had stew'd and form'd it: and part did become   495
A spungie liver, that did richly'allow,
Like a free conduit, on a high hils brow,
Life-keeping moisture unto every part,
Part hardned it selfe to a thicker heart,
   Whose busie furnaces lifes spirits do impart.   500

LI.

Another part became the well of sense,
The tender well arm'd feeling braine, from whence,
Those sinowie strings which do our bodies tie,
Are raveld out, and fast there by one end,
Did this Soule limbes, these limbes a soule attend,   505
And now they joyn'd: keeping some quality
Of every past shape, she knew treachery,
Rapine, deceit, and lust, and ills enow
To be a woman. *Themech* she is now,
   Sister and wife to *Caine, Caine* that first did plow.   510

   486. *puls nor pushes:* that is, toward nor away from her.
   489. *prevented:* frustrated, forestalled.
   492. That is, the soul is given birth by Siphatecia, becoming Themach (l. 509).
   494. *Chimiques equall fires:* uniform and unvarying fires by which the al-chemist hoped to produce an elixir. The mixture of materials, properly com-bined, was discussed in male and female terms; the alembic was often identified with the womb.

LII.

Who ere thou beest that read'st this sullen Writ,
Which just so much courts thee, as thou dost it,
Let me arrest thy thoughts, wonder with mee,
Why plowing, building, ruling and the rest,
Or most of those arts, whence our lies are blest,   515
By cursed *Cains* race invented be,
And blest *Seth* vext us with Astronomie.
Ther's nothing simply good, nor ill alone,
Of every quality comparison,
    The onely measure is, and judge, opinion.   520

516. *cursed Cains race:* the Lord cursed Cain from the earth so that when
he tilled the ground, it would not yield its strength, but his descendants built
cities, became animal husbandmen, invented the harp and the organ, and instructed all artificers in brass and iron (Gen. iv 11–12, 17–22). Donne ponders
the paradox of blest things coming from evil, and evil things coming from good.
Cain's race has achieved cultural prominence by having been denied success
with natural things.
517. *Seth:* a son of Adam, born to replace Abel. Astronomy is ill because, like
the Tower of Babel, it seeks to reach and understand heaven itself: it presumes
upon God. Seth's race has brought confusion and distress by trying to dissect
God's gifts of nature.

Divine Poems

Her of your name, whose fair inheritance
  Bethina was, and jointure *Magdalo:*
An active faith so highly did advance,
  That she once knew, more than the Church did know,
The *Resurrection;* so much good there is   5
  Deliver'd of her, that some Fathers be
Loth to believe one Woman could do this;
  But, think these *Magdalens* were two or three.
Increase their number, *Lady,* and their fame:
  To their *Devotion,* add your *Innocence;*   10
Take so much of th'example,'as of the name;
  The latter half; and in some recompence
That they did harbour *Christ* himselfe, a Guest,
  Harbour these *Hymns,* to his dear name addrest.

TO THE LADY MAGDALEN HERBERT, OF ST. MARY MAGDALEN.
  Lady Magdalen Herbert: mother of Edward (Lord Herbert of Cherbury)
and George, she married Sir John Danvers in 1608. Donne preached her funeral
sermon in 1627. Mary Magdalene (Mark xv 40–47) discovered that Jesus had
risen (Mark xvi 1–10), and was identified with a demoniac (Luke vii 37–50)
and Mary of Bethany (John xi). See further, NOTES.
  2. *jointure:* who jointly held Magdala. Bethany was near Jerusalem; Magdala
(Tarichaea) was a northern town on the Sea of Galilee.
  6. *Fathers:* the Church Fathers.
  8. Theologians could not determine the number of Mary Magdalenes; see
note above.
  12. *latter half:* that is, "Magdalen," but not "Mary," and be as she was in
her latter half of life.
  14. *these Hymns:* probably *La Corona* (No. 160).

160 *La Corona.*

1. *Deigne at my hands this crown of prayer and praise,*
Weav'd in my low devout melancholie,
Thou which of good, hast, yea art treasury,
All changing unchang'd Antient of dayes,
But doe not, with a vile crowne of fraile bayes,   5
Reward my muses white sincerity,
But what thy thorny crowne gain'd, that give mee,
A crowne of Glory, which doth flower alwayes;
The ends crowne our workes, but thou crown'st our ends,
For, at our end begins our endlesse rest,   10
The first last end, now zealously possest,
With a strong sober thirst, my soule attends.
'Tis time that heart and voice be lifted high,
Salvation to all that will is nigh.

Annunciation.

2. *Salvation to all that will is nigh,*   15
That All, which alwayes is All every where,
Which cannot sinne, and yet all sinnes must beare,
Which cannot die, yet cannot chuse but die,
Loe, faithfull Virgin, yeelds himselfe to lye
In prison, in thy wombe; and though he there   20
Can take no sinne, nor thou give, yet he'will weare
Taken from thence, flesh, which deaths force may trie.

LA CORONA.

La Corona: "The Crown" identifies the seven sonnets of this sequence, united by repetition of the last line of each poem as the first line of the next. The last line of poem seven is the first line of poem one, thus closing the crown. See further, NOTES.

1. *Deigne:* condescend to accept. *at my hands:* "from my hands" and connoting also his holding of the rosary.

2. *melancholie:* meditation.

3. Thou who has and more than this, who are, a treasury of good.

4. *All changing unchang'd:* referring to God's eternal being and the change (or kenosis) of the Son into Man. The "Antient of dayes" comes from Dan. vii 9.

5. *bayes:* leaves of the laurel.

9. *crown'st:* both by rewarding them and by perfecting them.

12. *sober:* because of the thirst (ardent desire), but meaning paradoxically unaffected by passion or excitement. *attends:* awaits.

14. *to all that will:* to all that (1) choose it, (2) long for it, (3) act to achieve it. *Annunciation:* Gabriel's announcement to Mary that she would bear a son (Luke i 26–35).

22. *trie:* put to the test.

Ere by the spheares time was created, thou
Wast in his minde, who is thy Sonne, and Brother,
Whom thou conceiv'st, conceiv'd; yea thou art now   25
Thy Makers maker, and thy Fathers mother,
Thou'hast light in darke; and shutst in little roome,
Immensity cloysterd in thy deare wombe.

Nativitie.

3.   *Immensitie cloysterd in thy deare wombe,*
Now leaves his welbelov'd imprisonment,   30
There he hath made himselfe to his intent
Weake enough, now into our world to come;
But Oh, for thee, for him, hath th'Inne no roome?
Yet lay him in this stall, and from the'Orient,
Starres, and wisemen will travell to prevent   35
Th'effect of *Herods* jealous generall doome;
Seest thou, my Soule, with thy faiths eyes, how he
Which fils all place, yet none holds him, doth lye?
Was not his pity towards thee wondrous high,
That would have need to be pittied by thee?   40
Kisse him, and with him into Egypt goe,
With his kinde mother, who partakes thy woe.

Temple.

4.   *With his kinde mother who partakes thy woe,*
Joseph turne backe; see where your child doth sit,
Blowing, yea blowing out those sparks of wit,   45

23. Aristotle, *Physics*, IV, 223b: "Time is thought to be the movement of the sphere."

24. *Brother:* since her son is the Father's Son, and all men are sons of God. The unity of the Blessed Trinity lies behind the line.

27. *light in darke:* since God is Light and her womb is dark.

28. *Immensity:* infinite being, greatness.

31. *to his intent:* as was his intention.

35. *prevent:* precede, outrun.

36. *Herods jealous generall doome:* Herod the Great, Roman king of Judaea at Jesus' birth, tried to subvert the prophecy of the coming of a rival "King of the Jews" by slaying the children of Bethlehem (Matt. ii 16).

38. *Which . . . him:* referring to God's omnipresence and infiniteness.

41. The flight into Egypt is told in Matt. ii 13–15. *Temple:* at the temple Jesus first met Simeon, who told Mary that her child was set for a fall, a resurrection, and a sign which would be contradicted. Later (when twelve) he was found in the temple sitting amidst the doctors and answering their questions (Luke ii 27–49). Thus the sonnet evokes the twofold nature of Jesus, his entry into his ministry, and a summary of his life.

Which himselfe on the Doctors did bestow;
The Word but lately could not speake, and loe
It sodenly speakes wonders, whence comes it,
That all which was, and all which should be writ,
A shallow seeming child, should deeply know?   50
His Godhead was not soule to his manhood,
Nor had time mellow'd him to this ripenesse,
But as for one which hath a long taske, 'tis good,
With the Sunne to beginne his businesse,
He in his ages morning thus began   55
By miracles exceeding power of man.

Crucifying.

5.   *By miracles exceeding power of man,*
Hee faith in some, envie in some begat,
For, what weake spirits admire, ambitious, hate:
In both affections many to him ran,   60
But Oh! the worst are most, they will and can,
Alas, and do, unto the'immaculate,
Whose creature Fate is, now prescribe a Fate,
Measuring selfe-lifes infinity to'a span,
Nay to an inch. Loe, where condemned hee   65
Beares his owne crosse, with paine, yet by and by
When it beares him, he must beare more and die;
Now thou art lifted up, draw mee to thee,
And at thy death giving such liberall dole,
Moyst, with one drop of thy blood, my dry soule.   70

Resurrection.

6.   *Moyst with one drop of thy blood, my dry soule*
Shall (though she now be in extreme degree
Too stony hard, and yet too fleshly,) bee
Freed by that drop, from being starv'd, hard, or foule,

47. *The Word:* the Logos, identified with Jesus in John i 14–18.
54. *the Sunne:* consistently identified with the Son.
59. For ambitious spirits (souls) hate what submissive (meek) spirits admire.
63. *prescribe:* also refers to God's prescience and providence.
64. *a span:* a limited space of time (nine inches). Prov. viii 27: "When he prepared the heavens, I was there: when he set a compass upon the face of the depth."
68. "And I, if I be lifted up from the earth, will draw all men unto me" (John xii 32).
69. *dole:* three meanings are involved: distribution, fate, and grief.
70. *dry:* because of its lack of spirituality.
74. *from being starv'd:* from being starved of blood or sustenance and from dying.

And life, by this death abled, shall controule   75
Death, whom thy death slue; nor shall to mee
Feare of first or last death, bring miserie,
If in thy little booke my name thou'enroule,
Flesh in that long sleep is not putrified,
But made that there, of which, and for which 'twas;   80
Nor can by other meanes be glorified.
May then sinnes sleep, and deaths soone from me passe,
That wak't from both, I againe risen may
Salute the last, and everlasting day.

Ascention.

7. *Salute the last and everlasting day,*   85
Joy at the'uprising of this Sunne, and Sonne,
Yee whose just teares, or tribulation
Have purely washt, or burnt your drossie clay;
Behold the Highest, parting hence away,
Lightens the darke clouds, which hee treads upon,   90
Nor doth hee by ascending, show alone,
But first hee, and hee first enters the way.
O strong Ramme, which hast batter'd heaven for mee,
Mild lambe, which with thy blood, hast mark'd the path;
Bright Torch, which shin'st, that I the way may see,   95
Oh, with thy owne blood quench thy owne just wrath,
And if thy holy Spirit, my Muse did raise,
Deigne at my hands this crowne of prayer and praise.

75. *abled:* "empowered," with perhaps a glance at the meaning "given blood."
78. *thy little booke:* the Book of Life in which all men's deeds are recorded (Rev. iii 5).
92. *first enters:* shows the way to enter heaven.
93. *Ramme:* Christ is identified with Aries since under that sign comes the return of spring with the vernal equinox. It is, of course, roughly around the time of Easter. The ascension here is that immediately after the resurrection (see Luke xxiv 6).

161 *To* E. *of* D. *with six holy Sonnets.*

See Sir, how as the Suns hot Masculine flame
   Begets strange creatures on Niles durty slime,
   In me, your fatherly yet lusty Ryme
(For, these songs are their fruits) have wrought the same;
But though the'ingendring force from whence they came   5
   Bee strong enough, and nature doe admit
   Seaven to be borne at once, I send as yet
But six, they say, the seaventh hath still some maime;
I choose your judgement, which the same degree
   Doth with her sister, your invention, hold,   10
As fire these drossie Rymes to purifie,
   Or as Elixar, to change them to gold;
You are that Alchimist which alwaies had
Wit, whose one spark could make good things of bad.

162 *Holy Sonnet.*

As due by many titles I resigne
My selfe to thee, O God, first I was made
By thee, and for thee, and when I was decay'd
Thy blood bought that, the which before was thine,
I am thy sonne, made with thy selfe to shine,   5

TO E. OF D. WITH SIX HOLY SONNETS.
    E. of D.: The Earl of Dorset was Richard Sackville, who became the third
earl on February 27, 1609. The six holy sonnets and the incomplete seventh
(l. 8) were probably Nos. 162–67 and No. 172 or 173; it seems unlikely that
the interrelated sonnets of *La Corona,* written two years earlier, would have
been separated.
    2. *strange creatures:* water-mice ("musculi") are said by Pliny to be so be-
gotten (*Natural History,* IX, lxxxiv).
    3. *lusty:* pleasant.
    7. *at once:* such multiple birth in Egypt was reported by Pliny (*Natural His-
tory,* VII, iii).
    8. *maime:* serious defect; the identity of "they" is uncertain.
    10. *invention:* discovery and solution, as of a problem.
    12. *Elixar:* see *Loves Alchymie* (No. 59), n.
    14. *Wit:* power to conceive, reason, and judge.
HOLY SONNET [NO. 162]. See NOTES.
    4. *bought:* redeemed.

Thy servant, whose paines thou hast still repaid,
Thy sheepe, thine Image, and till I betray'd
My selfe, a temple of thy Spirit divine;
Why doth the devill then usurpe in mee?
Why doth he steale, nay ravish that's thy right? 10
Except thou rise and for thine owne worke fight,
Oh I shall soone despaire, when I doe see
That thou lov'st mankind well, yet wilt not chuse me.
And Satan hates mee, yet is loth to lose mee.

163 *Holy Sonnet.*

Oh my blacke Soule! now thou art summoned
By sicknesse, deaths herald, and champion;
Thou art like a pilgrim, which abroad hath done
Treason, and durst not turne to whence hee'is fled,
Or like a thiefe, which till deaths doome be read, 5
Wisheth himselfe deliverd from prison;
But damn'd and hal'd to execution,
Wisheth that still he might be'imprisoned;
Yet grace, if thou repent, thou canst not lacke;
But who shall give thee that grace to beginne? 10
Oh make thy selfe with holy mourning blacke,
And red with blushing, as thou art with sinne;
Or wash thee in Christs blood, which hath this might
That being red, it dyes red soules to white.

6. *still:* always.
9. *usurpe:* practice his power of seizure.
HOLY SONNET [NO. 163]. See NOTES
5. *deaths doome:* Judgment Day.
11–12. Red was the color of sin and remorse; black indicated its foulness. In alchemy black signified penitential purification; red, the resurrection or immortality. The pilgrim, the prisoner, and the penitent would all be pictured in black. Note the pun on "red/read," l. 5.
13. *Christs blood:* alchemically, blood was thought to act as a tincture. "But if we walk in the light, as he is in the light, we have fellowship one with another, and the blood of Jesus Christ his Son cleanseth us from all sin" (1 John i 7).

164 *Holy Sonnet.*

This is my playes last scene, here heavens appoint
My pilgrimages last mile; and my race
Idly, yet quickly runne, hath this last pace,
My spans last inch, my minutes latest point,
And gluttonous death, will instantly unjoynt   5
My body,'and soule, and I shall sleepe a space,
But my'ever-waking part shall see that face,
Whose feare already shakes my every joynt:
Then, as my soule, to'heaven her first seate, takes flight,
And earth-borne body, in the earth shall dwell,   10
So, fall my sinnes, that all may have their right,
To where they'are bred, and would presse me, to hell.
Impute me righteous, thus purg'd of evill,
For thus I leave the world, the flesh, and devill.

165 *Holy Sonnet.*

At the round earths imagin'd corners, blow
Your trumpets, Angells, and arise, arise
From death, you numberlesse infinities
Of soules, and to your scattred bodies goe,
All whom the flood did, and fire shall o'erthrow,   5
All whom warre, dearth, age, agues, tyrannies,
Despaire, law, chance, hath slaine, and you whose eyes,

HOLY SONNET [NO. 164]. See NOTES.
   4. *spans:* life-span's.
   7. *ever-waking part:* soul. *that face:* the face of God at Judgment Day;
compare *Goodfriday* (No. 185), l. 17.
   9. *seate:* residence.
   11–12. The sense is: So let my sins fall in order that all of them may have
their just claim upon the place where they are bred, the same place to which
they would force me by their weight (that is, hell).
HOLY SONNET [NO. 165]. See NOTES.
   1. "And after these things I saw four angels standing on the four corners of
the earth, holding the four winds of the earth, . . ." (Rev. vii 1). Roundness
was considered perfection; angular things, imperfection.
   5. *fire:* the great conflagration in which the world will be consumed (2 Peter
iii 10).

Shall behold God, and never tast deaths woe,
But let them sleepe, Lord, and mee mourne a space,
For, if above all these, my sinnes abound,   10
'Tis late to aske abundance of thy grace,
When wee are there; here on this lowly ground,
Teach mee how to repent; for that's as good
As if thou'hadst seal'd my pardon, with thy blood.

166 *Holy Sonnet.*

If poysonous mineralls, and if that tree,
Whose fruit threw death on else immortall us,
If lecherous goats, if serpents envious
Cannot be damn'd; Alas; why should I bee?
Why should intent or reason, borne in mee,   5
Make sinnes, else equall, in mee, more heinous?
And mercy being easie, and glorious
To God, in his sterne wrath, why threatens hee?
But who am I, that dare dispute with thee?
O God, Oh! of thine onely worthy blood,   10
And my teares, make a heavenly Lethean flood,
And drowne in it my sinnes blacke memorie.
That thou remember them, some claime as debt,
I thinke it mercy, if thou wilt forget.

8. "But I tell you of a truth, there be some standing here, which shall not taste of death, till they see the kingdom of God" (Luke ix 27).

14. *my pardon:* both my remission of penalty and my indulgence. *thy blood:* compare *Holy Sonnet* (No. 163), ll. 13–14.

HOLY SONNET [NO. 166]. See NOTES.

1. *tree:* the Tree of Knowledge of Good and Evil of whose fruit Adam and Eve ate, breaking their covenant with God.

3. *goats:* see *A nocturnall* (No. 82), n. to l. 39. The goat was identified with Pan and thus with Satan; the serpent was, of course, also identified with Satan.

4. *why should I bee?:* he has covered the mineral, vegetable, and animal kingdoms in ll. 1–3.

6. *else equall:* otherwise (except for intent of reason) the same as the sins of goats (lust) and serpents (envy).

10. *thine onely worthy blood:* only God's blood has merit, moral excellence.

11. *Lethean:* referring to the river of forgetfulness. By "heavenly" he asks heaven to forget and calls such lack of memory comforting and blissful.

13. Some people require as a debt owed to them that you remember their sins and them. See further, NOTES.

167 *Holy Sonnet.*

Death be not proud, though some have called thee
Mighty and dreadfull, for, thou art not soe,
For, those, whom thou think'st, thou dost overthrow,
Die not, poore death, nor yet canst thou kill mee;
From rest and sleepe, which but thy pictures bee,   5
Much pleasure, then from thee, much more must flow,
And soonest our best men with thee doe goe,
Rest of their bones, and soules deliverie.
Thou'art slave to Fate, chance, kings, and desperate men,
And dost with poyson, warre, and sicknesse dwell,   10
And poppie,'or charmes can make us sleepe as well,
And better then thy stroake; why swell'st thou then?
One short sleepe past, wee wake eternally,
And death shall be no more, Death thou shalt die.

168 *Holy Sonnet.*

Spit in my face yee Jewes, and pierce my side,
Buffet, and scoffe, scourge, and crucifie mee,
For I have sinn'd, and sinn'd, and onely hee,
Who could do no iniquitie, hath dyed:
But by my death can not be satisfied   5
My sinnes, which passe the Jewes impiety:
They kill'd once an inglorious man, but I
Crucifie him daily, being now glorified;
Oh let mee then, his strange love still admire:
Kings pardon, but he bore our punishment.   10
And *Jacob* came cloth'd in vile harsh attire

HOLY SONNET [NO. 167]. See NOTES.
HOLY SONNET [NO. 168]. See NOTES.
   3. *hee:* Jesus, who suffered all the cruelties mentioned in ll. 1–2.
   10. *Kings pardon:* kings show a kind of love by pardoning us for our sins.
   11. Jacob wore the raiment of his brother Esau and the skins of goats upon his hands and neck to deceive his father Isaac and thereby receive the blessing intended for Esau (Gen. xxvii 6–29). In Hebrew, Jacob means "one who supplants."

But to supplant, and with gainfull intent:
God cloth'd himselfe in vile mans flesh, that so
Hee might be weake enough to suffer woe.

169 *Holy Sonnet.*

Why are wee by all creatures waited on?
Why doe the prodigall elements supply
Life and food to mee, being more pure then I,
Simple, and further from corruption?
Why brook'st thou, ignorant horse, subjection?   5
Why dost thou bull, and bore so seelily
Dissemble weaknesse, and by'one mans stroke die,
Whose whole kinde, you might swallow'and feed upon?
Weaker I am, woe'is mee, and worse then you,
You have not sinn'd, nor need be timorous,   10
But wonder at a greater wonder, for to us
Created nature doth these things subdue,
But their Creator, whom sin, nor nature tyed,
For us, his Creatures, and his foes, hath dyed.

170 *Holy Sonnet.*

What if this present were the worlds last night?
Marke in my heart, O Soule, where thou dost dwell,
The picture of Christ crucified, and tell
Whether that countenance can thee affright,
Teares in his eyes quench the amasing light,   5
Blood fills his frownes, which from his pierc'd head fell,
And can that tongue adjudge thee unto hell,
Which pray'd forgivenesse for his foes fierce spight?

HOLY SONNET [NO. 169]. See NOTES.
    6. *seelily:* weakly, foolishly.
    7. *Dissemble:* feign.
    13. *whom . . . tyed:* whom neither sin nor nature restricted.
HOLY SONNET [NO. 170]. See NOTES.
    5. *amasing:* fearful.
    7. *tongue:* not only Christ's but that of those who turn the other cheek.

No, no; but as in my idolatrie
I said to all my profane mistresses,   10
Beauty, of pitty, foulnesse onely is
A signe of rigour: so I say to thee,
To wicked spirits are horrid shapes assign'd,
This beauteous forme assures a pitious minde.

171   *Holy Sonnet.*

Batter my heart, three person'd God; for, you
As yet but knocke, breathe, shine, and seeke to mend;
That I may rise, and stand, o'erthrow mee,'and bend
Your force, to breake, blowe, burn and make me new.
I, like an usurpt towne, to'another due,   5
Labour to'admit you, but Oh, to no end,
Reason your viceroy in mee, mee should defend,
But is captiv'd, and proves weake or untrue,
Yet dearely'I love you, and would be lov'd faine,
But am betroth'd unto your enemie,   10
Divorce mee,'untie, or breake that knot againe,
Take mee to you, imprison mee, for I
Except you'enthrall mee, never shall be free,
Nor ever chast, except you ravish mee.

11–12. *Beauty . . . rigour:* Beauty is only a sign of pity; foulness is only a
sign of rigor. That is, beauty arises from tenderness or kindness of love (mercy);
ugliness arises from severity, cruelty, or mercilessness.

14. *forme:* the cross; since he asks that the cross be depicted in his heart, he
seeks a mind given to pity (forgiveness) and piety.

HOLY SONNET [NO. 171]. See NOTES.

1. *three person'd God:* The Trinity: the Father, the Holy Spirit, and the Son.
See further, NOTES.

5. *usurpt towne:* he is usurped by Satan but belongs to God.

7. *mee should defend:* should maintain me against the force that has usurped
me.

8. *untrue:* unfaithful (to God, for whom reason is viceroy).

9. *faine:* with joy.

11. *againe:* the first time occurring with Christ's Incarnation and Passion.

172 *Holy Sonnet.*

Wilt thou love God, as he thee! then digest,
My Soule, this wholsome meditation,
How God the Spirit, by Angels waited on
In heaven, doth make his Temple in thy brest,
The Father having begot a Sonne most blest,   5
And still begetting, (for he ne'r begonne)
Hath deign'd to chuse thee by adoption,
Coheire to'his glory,'and Sabbaths endlesse rest;
And as a robb'd man, which by search doth finde
His stolne stuffe sold, must lose or buy'it againe: 10
The Sonne of glory came downe, and was slaine,
Us whom he'had made, and Satan stolne, to'unbinde.
'Twas much, that man was made like God before,
But, that God should be made like man, much more.

173 *Holy Sonnet.*

Father, part of his double interest
Unto thy kingdome, thy Sonne gives to mee,
His joynture in the knottie Trinitie,
Hee keepes, and gives to me his deaths conquest.
This Lambe, whose death, with life the world hath blest,   5

HOLY SONNET [NO. 172]. See NOTES.
    4. *Temple:* 1 Cor. vi 19: "know ye not that your body is the temple of the Holy Ghost which is in you, which ye have of God, and ye are not your own?"
    6. *he:* the Son. That is, He is eternal; His being did not have a beginning, for He always was.
    8. *Sabbaths:* the word comes from the Hebrew meaning "day of rest."
    12. *unbinde:* (from the ties which man had made with Satan).
HOLY SONNET [NO. 173]. See NOTES.
    1. *double interest:* as part of the Trinity and as blessed man.
    3. *joynture:* joint tenancy of an estate. *knottie:* difficult to comprehend or unravel, alluding to the problem of explaining three persons indivisible.
    5–6. "And all that dwell upon the earth shall worship him, whose names are not written in the book of life of the Lamb slain from the foundation of the world" (Rev. xiii 8).

Was from the worlds beginning slaine, and he
Hath made two Wills, which with the Legacie
Of his and thy kingdome, doe thy Sonnes invest,
Yet such are those laws, that men argue yet
Whether a man those statutes can fulfill;   10
None doth, but thy all-healing grace and Spirit,
Revive againe what law and letter kill.
Thy lawes abridgement, and thy last command
Is all but love; Oh let that last Will stand!

174 *Holy Sonnet.*

Thou hast made me, And shall thy worke decay?
Repaire me now, for now mine end doth haste,
I runne to death, and death meets me as fast,
And all my pleasures are like yesterday,
I dare not move my dimme eyes any way,   5
Despaire behind, and death before doth cast
Such terrour, and my febled flesh doth waste
By sinne in it, which it t'wards hell doth weigh;
Onely thou art above, and when towards thee
By thy leave I can looke, I rise againe;   10
But our old subtle foe so tempteth me,
That not one houre I can my selfe, sustaine;
Thy Grace may wing me to prevent his art
And thou like Adamant draw mine iron heart.

7. *two Wills:* the Old and New Testaments.

8. *doe thy Sonnes invest:* do envelop men; do commit men to a course of action (in order to gain the legacy); do offer men opportunity for moral profit.

14. *last Will:* Jesus' last command: "A new commandment I give unto you, That ye love one another; as I have loved you, that ye also love one another" (John xiii 34).

HOLY SONNET [NO. 174]. See NOTES.

3. *fast:* both "as rapidly" and "as tenaciously."

8. Compare Isa. xxvi 7: "The way of the just is uprightness: thou, most upright, dost weigh the path of the just."

10. *By thy leave:* both "by thy permission" and "by thy releasing me from life."

11. *foe:* Satan, as serpent.

13. *wing:* transport, give me wings (to fly away).

14. *Adamant:* the loadstone (ironically it is supposed to be of impenetrable hardness). *iron:* sinful and obdurate.

175 *Holy Sonnet.*

I am a little world made cunningly
Of Elements, and an Angelike spright,
But black sinne hath betraid to endlesse night
My worlds both parts, and (oh) both parts must die.
You which beyond that heaven which was most high   5
Have found new sphears, and of new lands can write,
Powre new seas in mine eyes, that so I might
Drowne my world with my weeping earnestly,
Or wash it if it must be drown'd no more:
But oh it must be burnt; alas the fire   10
Of lust and envie'have burnt it heretofore,
And made it fouler; Let their flames retire,
And burne me ô Lord, with a fiery zeale
Of thee'and thy house, which doth in eating heale.

176 *Holy Sonnet.*

O Might those sighes and teares returne againe
Into my breast and eyes, which I have spent,
That I might in this holy discontent
Mourne with some fruit, as I have mourn'd in vaine;

HOLY SONNET [NO. 175]. See NOTES.
  2. *spright:* animation, spirit.
  4. *parts:* his soul and his body, which contains his "Angelike spright"; compare 1 Cor. vi 19: "know ye not that your body is the temple of the Holy Ghost which is in you . . . ."
  5. *You:* Christ.
  9. Referring to God's covenant with Noah no more to destroy the earth by flood (Gen. ix 11).
  10. Referring to the fire which will consume the world (2 Peter iii 10).
  14. *which . . . heale:* which by consuming me restores me; which by my partaking of the Eucharist (the body and blood of Christ, constituting His house) nullifies my black sins. In the background may be a phoenix-like resurrection. Compare Psalms lxix 9–10: "For the zeal of thine house hath eaten me up . . . When I wept, and chastened my soul with fasting, that was to my reproach."
HOLY SONNET [NO. 176]. See NOTES.
  2. *spent:* both "sent forth" and "exhausted."
  4. *in vaine:* in emptiness of result and of true feeling; in self-pity.

In mine Idolatry what showres of raine   5
Mine eyes did waste? what griefs my heart did rent?
That sufferance was my sinne, now I repent;
'Cause I did suffer I must suffer paine.
Th'hydroptique drunkard, and night-scouting thiefe,
The itchy Lecher, and selfe tickling proud   10
Have the remembrance of past joyes, for reliefe
Of comming ills. To (poore) me is allow'd
No ease; for, long, yet vehement griefe hath beene
Th'effect and cause, the punishment and sinne.

177 *Holy Sonnet.*

If faithfull soules be alike glorifi'd
As Angels, then my fathers soule doth see,
And adds this even to full felicitie,
That valiantly I hels wide mouth o'rstride:
But if our mindes to these soules be descry'd   5
By circumstances, and by signes that be
Apparent in us not immediately,
How shall my mindes white truth by them be try'd?
They see idolatrous lovers weepe and mourne,
And vile blasphemous Conjurers to call   10
On Jesus name, and Pharisaicall
Dissemblers feigne devotion. Then turne
O pensive soule, to God, for he knowes best
Thy griefe, for he put it into my breast.

   6. *what . . . rent:* both "what griefs did burst from my heart, splitting it asunder" and "what griefs did lease space in my heart."
   9. *hydroptique:* insatiably thirsty.
HOLY SONNET [NO. 177]. See NOTES.
   3. *even:* to the extent of. Compare Rev. xxii 18: "For I testify unto every man that heareth the words of the prophecy of this book, If any man shall add unto these things, God shall add unto him the plagues that are written in this book."
   5. *descry'd:* revealed.
   14. *griefe:* suffering.

178 *Holy Sonnet.*

Since she whome I lovd, hath payd her last debt
To Nature, and to hers, and my good is dead
And her Soule early into heaven ravished,
Wholy in heavenly things my mind is sett.
Here the admyring her my mind did whett   5
To seeke thee God; so streames do shew the head,
But though I have found thee, and thou my thirst hast fed,
A holy thirsty dropsy melts mee yett.
But why should I begg more Love, when as thou
Dost woe my soule, for hers offring all thine: 10
And dost not only feare least I allow
My Love to Saints and Angels, things divine,
But in thy tender jealosy dost doubt
Least the World, fleshe, yea Devill putt thee out.

179 *Holy Sonnet.*

Show me deare Christ, thy spouse, so bright and cleare.
What, is it she, which on the other shore
Goes richly painted? or which rob'd and tore
Laments and mournes in Germany and here?

HOLY SONNET [NO. 178]. See NOTES.
  1. *she:* apparently his wife.
  2. *hers:* her nature as a human being who is subject to death.
  3. *ravished:* transported joyfully.
  4. *Wholy:* with a pun on "holy."
  5. *mind:* object of "whett."
  7. *fed:* both "relieved" and "increased."
  8. *dropsy:* a disease characterized by an accumulation of fluid and unquench-
able thirst.
  13. *jealosy:* requirement of exclusive devotion; zealousness.
  14. *the World, fleshe, . . . Devill:* the triple temptation to avarice, gluttony,
and vainglory.
HOLY SONNET [NO. 179]. See NOTES.
  1. *spouse:* the true Church, with reference to Christ as the Bridegroom (Matt.
XXV 1–13).
  2. *other shore:* the Continent, referring to Rome and the Roman Catholic
Church.
  4. *here:* the Protestant church—such as the Lutheran in Germany and the
Calvinist in England.

Sleepes she a thousand, then peepes up one yeare?　　　5
Is she selfe truth and errs? now new, now'outwore?
Doth she,'and did she, and shall she evermore
On one, on seaven, or on no hill appeare?
Dwells she with us, or like adventuring knights
First travaile we to seeke and then make love?　　　10
Betray kind husband thy spouse to our sights,
And let myne amorous soule court thy mild Dove,
Who is most trew, and pleasing to thee, then
When she'is embrac'd and open to most men.

180　*Holy Sonnet.*

Oh, to vex me, contraryes meete in one:
Inconstancy unnaturally hath begott
A constant habit; that when I would not
I change in vowes, and in devotione.
As humorous is my contritione　　　5
As my prophane Love, and as soone forgott:
As ridlingly distemperd, cold and hott,
As praying, as mute; as infinite, as none.
I durst not view heaven yesterday; and to day
In prayers, and flattering speaches I court God:　　　10
To morrow'I quake with true feare of his rod.

8. *On one, on seaven, or on no hill:* on Mount Moriah, where Solomon built his temple; Rome, on seven hills; or Geneva, by a lake.
11. *Betray:* reveal.
12. *Dove:* symbol of God's mercy and bearer of the olive leaf of peace (as it descended to Noah in Gen. viii 11).
14. *open:* free, accessible.
HOLY SONNET [NO. 180]. See NOTES.
2. *unnaturally:* both "contrary to its nature" and "cruelly."
5. *humorous:* changeable.
7. As cryptically diluted or deranged, whether my contrition comes from melancholy or passion.
8. *As praying, as mute:* as praying is when it is unpronounced. *as infinite, as none:* or it is as infinite as nothing else is.
11. Compare Job ix 34–35: "Let him take his rod away from me, and let not his fear terrify me: Then would I speak, and not fear him; but it is not so with me."

So my devout fitts come and go away
Like a fantastique Ague: save that here
Those are my best dayes, when I shake with feare.

181   *The Crosse.*

Since Christ embrac'd the Crosse it selfe, dare I
His image, th'image of his Crosse deny?
Would I have profit by the sacrifice,
And dare the chosen Altar to despise?
It bore all other sinnes, but is it fit   5
That it should beare the sinne of scorning it?
Who from the picture would avert his eye,
How would he flye his paines, who there did dye?
From mee, no Pulpit, nor misgrounded law,
Nor scandall taken, shall this Crosse withdraw,   10
It shall not, for it cannot; for, the losse
Of this Crosse, were to mee another Crosse.
Better were worse, for, no affliction,
No Crosse is so extreme, as to have none;
Who can blot out the Crosse, which th'instrument   15
Of God, dew'd on mee in the Sacrament?
Who can deny mee power, and liberty
To stretch mine armes, and mine owne Crosse to be?
Swimme, and at every stroake, thou art thy Crosse,
The Mast and yard make one, where seas do tosse.   20
Looke downe, thou spiest out Crosses in small things;
Looke up, thou seest birds rais'd on crossed wings;
All the Globes frame, and spheares, is nothing else
But the Meridians crossing Parallels.

13. *fantastique:* imaginary, fantasy-inducing.
THE CROSSE.
  1. *embrac'd the Crosse:* through the Crucifixion; metaphorically through the Incarnation.
  2. *th'image:* both the trial which man may undergo (a shadow of Christ's cross) and the sign of the cross made, for example, at baptism (l. 16). See further, NOTES.
  10. *Crosse:* object of "withdraw." "Pulpit" means "preaching" or "gospel"; "scandall" indicates a lapse of faith, a collapse to temptation.
  20. *yard:* a long spar, crossing a mast, on which is hung a sail.

Materiall Crosses then, good physicke bee,   25
And yet spirituall have chiefe dignity.
These for extracted chimique medicine serve,
And cure much better, and as well preserve;
Then are you your own physicke, or need none,
When Still'd, or purg'd by tribulation.   30
For when that Crosse ungrudg'd, unto you stickes,
Then are you to your selfe, a Crucifixe.
As perchance, Carvers do not faces make,
But that away, which hid them there, do take.
Let Crosses, soe, take what hid Christ in thee,   35
And be his image, or not his, but hee.
But, as oft Alchimists doe coyners prove,
So may a selfe-dispising, get selfe-love.
And then as worst surfets, of best meates bee,
Soe is pride, issued from humility,   40
For, 'tis no child, but monster; therefore Crosse
Your joy in crosses, else, 'tis double losse,
And crosse thy senses, else, both they, and thou
Must perish soone, and to destruction bowe.
For if the'eye seeke good objects, and will take   45
No crosse from bad, wee cannot scape a snake.
So with harsh, hard, sowre, stinking, crosse the rest,
Make them indifferent; call nothing best.
But most the eye needs crossing, that can rome,
And move; To th'others th'objects must come home.   50
And crosse thy heart: for that in man alone
Points downewards, and hath palpitation.
Crosse those dejections, when it downeward tends,
And when it to forbidden heights pretends.
And as thy braine through bony walls doth vent   55

26. Yet have their greatest worthiness in spiritual matters. See further, NOTES.
30. *Still'd:* both "made inactive" and "distilled" (made pure).
31. *stickes:* "becomes firmly affixed" and "impales."
33. *Carvers:* barbers.
34. But do remove that which hid them there.
37. *prove:* by trying to turn base metal into gold (such as coins).
39. And then as worst bodies be the excessive results of partaking the best food.
41. *'tis:* that is, pride. *Crosse:* cancel; the meaning is used frequently through the rest of the poem.
46. *a snake:* sin (the devil).
50. *To . . . home:* to the other eye (the mind) whatever is to be seen (understood) must come of itself (rather than being sought).

By sutures, which a Crosses forme present,
So when thy braine workes, ere thou utter it,
Crosse and correct concupiscence of witt.
Be covetous of Crosses, let none fall.
Crosse no man else, but crosse thy selfe in all.　　　　60
Then doth the Crosse of Christ worke fruitfully
Within our hearts, when wee love harmlesly
That Crosses pictures much, and with more care
That Crosses children, which our Crosses are.

182　*Resurrection, imperfect.*

Sleep sleep old Sun, thou canst not have repast
As yet, the wound thou took'st on friday last;
Sleepe then, and rest; The world may beare thy stay,
A better Sun rose before thee to day,
Who, not content to'enlighten all that dwell　　　　5
On the earths face, as thou, enlightned hell,
And made the darke fires languish in that vale,
As, at thy presence here, our fires grow pale.
Whose body having walk'd on earth, and now
Hasting to Heaven, would, that he might allow　　　　10
Himselfe unto all stations, and fill all,
For these three daies become a minerall;

56. *sutures:* seams (lines of union) between the bones of the skull. *which . . . present:* man's frontal (metopic) suture crosses the coronal suture.
63. *pictures:* shadows or types of the Cross of Christ. *care:* love; concern; responsibility.

RESURRECTION, IMPERFECT.
The title refers to the fact that the poem is incomplete. (*Desunt cætera*, the remainder is lacking). The crucifixion of Christ (the Son) on Good Friday and His resurrection on Easter Sunday is related in Matt. xxvii 26–xxviii 8.
1. *old Sun:* the planetary sun, but it was identified with the Son. *repast:* recovered from; fed upon; passed beyond. At the Crucifixion the sun was eclipsed (Matt. xxvii 45).
8. *grow pale:* both "grow dim" and "become fearful" (from Latin *palleo*).
10. *allow:* admit and prove (his identity).
11. *fill all:* since His light shines into and fills all places. "Stations" echoes the Stations of the Cross, a series of tablets depicting stages of the Passion.
12. *For:* before (these three days are over). *minerall:* mine. The gold of His body indicates perfection; through dissolution it is refined into a tincture which has power to transmute all base metals to itself.

Hee was all gold when he lay downe, but rose
All tincture, and doth not alone dispose
Leaden and iron wills to good, but is   15
Of power to make even sinfull flesh like his.
Had one of those, whose credulous pietie
Thought, that a Soule one might discerne and see
Goe from a body,'at this sepulcher been,
And, issuing from the sheet, this body seen,   20
He would have justly thought this body'a soule,
If not of any man, yet of the whole.
   Desunt cætera.

183 *The Annuntiation and Passion.*

Tamely fraile body'abstaine to day; to day
My soule eates twice, Christ hither and away.
She sees him man, so like God made in this,
That of them both a circle embleme is,
Whose first and last concurre; this doubtfull day   5
Of feast or fast, Christ came, and went away;
Shee sees him nothing twice at once, who'is all;
Shee sees a Cedar plant it selfe, and fall,
Her Maker put to making, and the head
Of life, at once, not yet alive, and dead;   10
She sees at once the virgin mother stay
Reclus'd at home, Publique at Golgotha.

15. *Leaden and iron wills:* those who are good through lethargy or determination.

22. *whole:* since God is all; see 1 Cor. xv 28: "And when all things shall be subdued unto him, then shall the Son also himself be subject unto him that put all things under him, that God may be all in all."

THE ANNUNTIATION AND PASSION.

The Feast of the Annunciation to Mary (Lady Day) and the Passion both fell on March 25 in 1608.

1. *Tamely:* submissively.

3. *She:* his soul.

4. *embleme:* since the circle was a symbol of perfection.

6. *feast or fast:* Feast of the Annunciation (joyfully celebrated) and the fasting for the Crucifixion of Jesus (sadly mourned).

7. *who'is all:* See *Resurrection, imperfect* (No. 182), note, l. 22.

8. *Cedar:* a symbol of God's presence.

12. *Golgotha:* scene of the Crucifixion.

Sad and rejoyc'd shee's seen at once, and seen
At almost fiftie, and at scarce fifteene.
At once a Sonne is promis'd her, and gone,   15
Gabriell gives Christ to her, He her to John;
Not fully'a mother, Shee's in Orbitie,
At once receiver and the legacie;
All this, and all betweene, this day hath showne,
Th'Abridgement of Christs story, which makes one   20
(As in plaine Maps, the farthest West is East)
Of the'Angels *Ave*,'and *Consummatum est.*
How well the Church, Gods Court of faculties
Deales, in some times, and seldome joyning these;
As by the selfe-fix'd Pole wee never doe   25
Direct our course, but the next starre thereto,
Which showes where the'other is, and which we say
(Because it strayes not farre) doth never stray;
So God by his Church, neerest to him, wee know,
And stand firme, if wee by her motion goe;   30
His Spirit, as his fiery Pillar doth
Leade, and his Church, as cloud; to one end both:
This Church, by letting these daies joyne, hath shown
Death and conception in mankinde is one.
Or 'twas in him the same humility,   35
That he would be a man, and leave to be:
Or as creation he hath made, as God,
With the last judgement, but one period,
His imitating Spouse would joyne in one
Manhoods extremes: He shall come, he is gone: 40
Or as though one blood drop, which thence did fall,
Accepted, would have serv'd, he yet shed all;

16. "When Jesus therefore saw his mother, and the disciple standing by, whom he loved, he saith unto his mother, Woman, behold thy son! Then saith he to the disciple, Behold thy mother! And from that hour that disciple took her unto his own home" (John xix 26–27).

17. *in Orbitie:* in bereavement (for loss of child); raised to the celestial world.

21. Since points at either side of a flat map correspond.

22. *Ave . . . Consummatum est:* "Hail," the greeting of Gabriel at the Annunciation, and "It is finished" (John xix 30), after which Jesus "bowed his head, and gave up the ghost."

31. *fiery Pillar:* "And the Lord went before them by day in a pillar of a cloud, to lead them the way; and by night in a pillar of fire, to give them light; to go by day and night" (Exod. xiii 21).

38. *period:* end, aim; the same point in time.

39. *Spouse:* the Church.

So though the least of his paines, deeds, or words,
Would busie'a life, she all this day affords;
This treasure then, in grosse, my Soule uplay,   45
And in my life retaile it every day.

184   *A Litanie.*

I

The Father.

   Father of Heaven, and him, by whom
It, and us for it, and all else, for us
   Thou madest, and govern'st ever, come
And re-create mee, now growne ruinous:
      My heart is by dejection, clay,   5
      And by selfe-murder, red.
From this red earth, O Father, purge away
All vicious tinctures, that new fashioned
I may rise up from death, before I'am dead.

II.

The Sonne.

   O Sonne of God, who seeing two things,   10
Sinne, and death crept in, which were never made,
   By bearing one, tryed'st with what stings
The other could thine heritage invade;

45. *uplay:* store up in bulk for future distribution. "Lay not up for yourselves treasures upon earth . . . But lay up for yourselves treasures in heaven
. . . For where your treasure is, there will your heart be also" (Matt. vi 19–21).
A LITANIE.
   A Litanie: a series of invocations and supplications such as at a mass. The
structure and persons addressed are those of the litany in the Book of Common
Prayer, 1544.
   4. *ruinous:* full of decay; to almost a fallen condition.
   5. *dejection:* depression, having been cast down.
   6. *red:* bloody, in the last phase of life symbolized by resurrection. Alchemically red tincture was believed to remove sin and thus to achieve God's grace.
Adam was made from clay or red earth ("dust," l. 20), which is the basic
meaning of the name.
   12. *one:* death by the crucifixion. *tryed'st:* proved.

O be thou nail'd unto my heart,
And crucified againe,   15
Part not from it, though it from thee would part,
But let it be by'applying so thy paine,
Drown'd in thy blood, and in thy passion slaine.

III.

The Holy Ghost.

O Holy Ghost, whose temple I
Am, but of mudde walls, and condensed dust,   20
    And being sacrilegiously
Halfe wasted with youths fires, of pride and lust,
     Must with new stormes be weatherbeat;
     Double'in my heart thy flame,
Which let devout sad teares intend; and let   25
(Though this glasse lanthorne, flesh, do suffer maime)
Fire, Sacrifice, Priest, Altar be the same.

IV.

The Trinity.

O Blessed glorious Trinity,
Bones to Philosophy, but milke to faith,
    Which, as wise serpents, diversly   30
Most slipperinesse, yet most entanglings hath,
     As you distinguish'd undistinct
     By power, love, knowledge bee,
Give mee a such selfe different instinct,
     Of these let all mee elemented bee,   35
     Of power, to love, to know, you'unnumbred three.

19. *temple:* "know ye not that your body is the temple of the Holy Ghost which is in you, which ye have of God" (1 Cor. vi 19).

25. *intend:* multiply; direct their course.

26. *glasse lanthorne:* perhaps originally "dark lantern," one with a slide by which the light can be concealed; see Paul Elmen's discussion in *PBSA,* XLIX (1955), 181–86. Thus God's flame in his heart may be obscured by his pride and lust. "Glass" changes the image to the shining of God's light through his flesh even when that flesh is sinful, and emphasizes the brittleness of the flesh.

29. *Bones:* the basic elements of philosophy, on which it is hung and grows. *milke:* sustenance.

32. *undistinct:* referring to the unity of the three separate persons of the Trinity.

34. That is, imbue me with a full sense of the unity of the Trinity and the separate, yet co-ordinated, nature of power, love, and knowledge (attributes of the Trinity respectively).

V.

The Virgin Mary.

For that faire blessed Mother-maid,
　Whose flesh redeem'd us; That she-Cherubin,
　Which unlock'd Paradise, and made
One claime for innocence, and disseiz'd sinne,   40
　　Whose wombe was a strange heav'n, for there
　　God cloath'd himselfe, and grew,
Our zealous thankes wee poure. As her deeds were
Our helpes, so are her prayers; nor can she sue
In vaine, who hath such titles unto you.   45

VI.

The Angels.

And since this life our nonage is,
And wee in Wardship to thine Angels be,
　Native in heavens faire Palaces
Where we shall be but denizen'd by thee,
　　As th'earth conceiving by the Sunne,   50
　　Yeelds faire diversitie,
Yet never knowes which course that light doth run,
So let mee study, that mine actions bee
Worthy their sight, though blinde in how they see.

VII.

The Patriarches.

And let thy Patriarches Desire   55
(Those great Grandfathers of thy Church, which saw
　More in the cloud, then wee in fire,

40. *disseiz'd:* dispossessed, ousted.
45. *such titles:* such titles as "Mother," "Virgin Mary," etc., because of you (the Son); also such just claims upon you.
53. *study:* meditate; be intelligently zealous. *The Patriarches:* the "fathers" of the Apostles, who in turn were the "fathers" of the Church Fathers.
57. *cloud . . . fire:* biblical references to God's appearance in a cloud or in a pillar of fire are numerous. See further, NOTES.

Whom Nature clear'd more, then us grace and law,
    And now in Heaven still pray, that wee
        May use our new helpes right,)   60
Be satisfied, and fructifie in mee;
Let not my minde be blinder by more light
Nor Faith by Reason added, lose her sight.

VIII.

The Prophets.

    Thy Eagle-sighted Prophets too,
Which were thy Churches Organs, and did sound   65
    That harmony, which made of two
One law, and did unite, but not confound;
        Those heavenly Poëts which did see
        Thy will, and it expresse
In rythmique feet, in common pray for mee,   70
That I by them excuse not my excesse
In seeking secrets, or Poëtiquenesse.

IX.

The Apostles.

    And thy illustrious Zodiacke
Of twelve Apostles, which ingirt this All,
    From whom whosoever do not take   75
Their light, to darke deep pits, throw downe, and fall,
        As through their prayers, thou'hast let mee know
        That their bookes are divine;
May they pray still, and be heard, that I goe
Th'old broad way in applying; O decline   80
Mee, when my comment would make thy word mine.

58. *clear'd:* enlightened.
64. *Eagle-sighted:* eagles are noted for keenness of vision.
67. *One law:* Mosaic law and the Word of the Lord.
73. *Zodiacke:* circle.
74. *All:* universe.
76. *throw downe:* cast themselves down.
80. *Th'old broad way:* opposite meanings are involved: so that I shall follow God's path to heaven by devoting myself assiduously to the task; so that I quit the broad way that leads to destruction (Matt. vii 13) by applying their message. *decline:* humble; turn (me) away from my course; inflect (that is, change the first person to the second person).

X.

The Martyrs.

And since thou so desirously
Did'st long to die, that long before thou could'st,
    And long since thou no more couldst dye,
Thou in thy scatter'd mystique body wouldst   85
        In Abel dye, and ever since
        In thine, let their blood come
To begge for us, a discreet patience
Of death, or of worse life: for Oh, to some
Not to be Martyrs, is a martyrdome.   90

XI.

The Confessors.

Therefore with thee triumpheth there
A Virgin Squadron of white Confessors,
    Whose bloods betroth'd, not marryed were;
Tender'd, not taken by those Ravishers:
        They know, and pray, that wee may know,   95
        In every Christian
Hourly tempestuous persecutions grow,
Tentations martyr us alive; A man
Is to himselfe a Dioclesian.

86. *Abel:* the first martyr (Gen. iv 2–8), a type of Christ. *The Confessors:* those who profess evidence of their faith in Christ.

92. *Virgin Squadron:* "And they sung as it were a new song before the throne . . . These are they which were not defiled with women; for they are virgins. These are they which follow the Lamb whithersoever he goeth. These were redeemed from among men, being the firstfruits unto God and to the Lamb" (Rev. xiv 3–4).

94. *Tender'd:* offered in order to avoid forfeiture for nonperformance.

98. *Tentations:* temptations.

99. *Dioclesian:* a Roman emperor (284–305), who persecuted the Christians toward the end of his reign. *The Virgins:* unmarried women devoted to religion, with reference to the wise and foolish virgins of Matt. xxv 1–13.

XII.

The Virgins.

Thy cold white snowie Nunnery, 100
Which, as thy mother, their high Abbesse, sent
   Their bodies backe againe to thee,
As thou hadst lent them, cleane and innocent,
     Though they have not obtain'd of thee,
     That or thy Church, or I, 105
Should keep, as they, our first integrity;
Divorce thou sinne in us, or bid it die,
And call chast widowhead Virginitie.

XIII.

The Doctors.

Thy sacred Academ above
Of Doctors, whose paines have unclasp'd, and taught 110
   Both bookes of life to us (for love
To know thy Scriptures tells us, we are wrought
     In thy other booke) pray for us there
     That what they have misdone
Or mis-said, wee to that may not adhere; 115
Their zeale may be our sinne. Lord let us runne
Meane waies, and call them stars, but not the Sunne.

XIV.

And whil'st this universall Quire,
That Church in triumph, this in warfare here,
   Warm'd with one all-partaking fire 120
Of love, that none be lost, which cost thee deare,
     Pray ceaslesly,'and thou hearken too,
     (Since to be gratious
Our taske is treble, to pray, beare, and doe)

101. *as:* like.
104. *obtain'd of thee:* attained thy example.
105. *That:* the Nunnery. *The Doctors:* the learned exegetes.
111. *Both bookes of life:* the Old and New Testaments.
113. *thy other booke:* the Book of Life (Rev. xiii 8).
124. *pray, beare, and doe:* these are also attributes of the Trinal being: we should pray to the Father, suffer as did the Son, and achieve good works like the Holy Ghost.

Heare this prayer Lord, O Lord deliver us   125
From trusting in those prayers, though powr'd out thus.

XV.

   From being anxious, or secure,
Dead clods of sadnesse, or light squibs of mirth,
   From thinking, that great courts immure
All, or no happinesse, or that this earth   130
      Is only for our prison fram'd,
         Or that thou art covetous
To them whom thou lovest, or that they are maim'd
From reaching this worlds sweet, who seek thee thus,
With all their might, Good Lord deliver us.   135

XVI.

   From needing danger, to bee good,
From owing thee yesterdaies teares to day,
   From trusting so much to thy blood,
That in that hope, wee wound our soule away,
      From bribing thee with Almes, to'excuse   140
         Some sinne more burdenous,
From light affecting, in religion, newes,
From thinking us all soule, neglecting thus
Our mutuall duties, Lord deliver us.

XVII.

   From tempting Satan to tempt us,   145
By our connivence, or slack companie,
   From measuring ill by vitious,
Neglecting to choake sins spawne, Vanitie,
      From indiscreet humilitie,
         Which might be scandalous,   150
And cast reproach on Christianitie,
From being spies, or to spies pervious,
From thirst, or scorne of fame, deliver us.

127. *From . . . secure:* free from anxiety and fear.
133. *maim'd:* disabled by blemish of some agency (such as sadnesse of heart).
142. From conceptions and recent occurrences which alter one's religion.
147. *by vitious:* by vices (rather than by virtues).
152. *spies:* as in Gal. ii 4: "And that because of false brethren unawares brought in, who came in privily to spy out our liberty which we have in Christ Jesus, that they might bring us into bondage."
153. *thirst:* that is, pride in life, but also connoting the first temptation of the Triple Equation, *concupiscentia carnis.*

XVIII.

Deliver us for thy descent
Into the Virgin, whose wombe was a place   155
   Of midle kind; and thou being sent
To'ungratious us, staid'st at her full of grace,
      And through thy poore birth, where first thou
      Glorifiedst Povertie,
And yet soone after riches didst allow,   160
By'accepting Kings gifts in the'Epiphanie,
Deliver, and make us, to both waies free.

XIX.

And through that bitter agonie,
Which is still the'agonie of pious wits,
   Disputing what distorted thee,   165
And interrupted evennesse, with fits,
      And through thy free confession
      Though thereby they were then
Made blind, so that thou might'st from them have gone,
Good Lord deliver us, and teach us when   170
Wee may not, and we may blinde unjust men.

XX.

Through thy submitting all, to blowes
Thy face, thy clothes to spoile; thy fame to scorne,
   All waies, which rage, or Justice knowes,
And by which thou could'st shew, that thou wast born,   175
      And through thy gallant humblenesse
      Which thou in death did'st shew,
Dying before thy soule they could expresse,
Deliver us from death, by dying so,
To this world, ere this world doe bid us goe.   180

XXI.

When senses, which thy souldiers are,
Wee arme against thee, and they fight for sinne,
   When want, sent but to tame, doth warre

165. *distorted:* both in the ecstasy of the passion and by the distortions made of Christ's Incarnation and Word.
178. *expresse:* press out, extract.

And worke despaire a breach to enter in,
    When plenty, Gods image, and seale   185
    Makes us Idolatrous,
And love it, not him, whom it should reveale,
When wee are mov'd to seeme religious
Only to vent wit, Lord deliver us.

XXII.

In Churches, when the'infirmitie   190
Of him which speakes, diminishes the Word,
    When Magistrates doe mis-apply
To us, as we judge, lay or ghostly sword,
        When plague, which is thine Angell, raignes,
        Or wars, thy Champions, swaie,   195
When Heresie, thy second deluge, gaines;
In th'houre of death, the'Eve of last judgement day,
Deliver us from the sinister way.

XXIII.

Heare us, O heare us Lord; to thee
A sinner is more musique, when he prayes,   200
    Then spheares, or Angels praises bee,
In Panegyrique Allelujaes,
        Heare us, for till thou heare us, Lord
        We know not what to say.
Thine eare to'our sighes, teares, thoughts gives voice and word. 205
O Thou who Satan heard'st in Jobs sicke day,
Heare thy selfe now, for thou in us dost pray.

185. *seale:* emblem; guaranty.
189. *vent:* added meanings include such wit's empty windiness, and the opening at the breech of a gun (l. 184) through which ignition reaches powder.
193. *sword:* the sword of government or the sword of Michael (compare Eph. vi 17: "And take the helmet of salvation, and the sword of the Spirit, which is the word of God").
194. *thine Angell:* "So the Lord sent a pestilence upon Israel from the morning even to the time appointed . . . . And when the angel stretched out his hand upon Jerusalem to destroy it, the Lord repented him of the evil, and said to the angel that destroyed the people, It is enough: stay now thine hand" (2 Sam. xxiv 15–16).
196. Compare *LXXX Sermons,* lix, 598 (Potter and Simpson, IX, Sermon 14, p. 329).
198. *sinister:* both the corrupt way and that to the left side of God (where stand all sinners).
206. *Jobs sicke day:* see Job ii 2–7.

XXIV.

That wee may change to evennesse
This intermitting aguish Pietie,
   That snatching cramps of wickednesse 210
And Apoplexies of fast sin, may die;
     That musique of thy promises,
     Not threats in Thunder may
Awaken us to our just offices;
What in thy booke, thou dost, or creatures say, 215
That we may heare, Lord heare us, when wee pray.

XXV.

That our eares sicknesse wee may cure,
And rectifie those Labyrinths aright,
   That wee by harkning, not procure
Our praise, nor others dispraise so invite, 220
     That wee get not a slipperinesse,
     And senslesly decline,
From hearing bold wits jeast at Kings excesse,
To'admit the like of majestie divine,
That we may locke our eares, Lord open thine. 225

XXVI.

That living law, the Magistrate,
Which to give us, and make us physicke, doth
   Our vices often aggravate,
That Preachers taxing sinne, before her growth,
     That Satan, and invenom'd men 230
     Which well, if we starve, dine,
When they doe most accuse us, may see then
Us, to amendment, heare them; thee decline;
That we may open our eares, Lord lock thine.

XXVII.

That learning, thine Ambassador, 235
From thine allegeance wee never tempt,

218. *rectifie:* punning on the meaning "make right."
230. *invenom'd men:* those poisoned by the venom of the serpent Satan.
231. *starve:* die.

That beauty, paradises flower
For physicke made, from poyson be exempt,
   That wit, borne apt, high good to doe,
      By dwelling lazily   240
On Natures nothing, be not nothing too,
That our affections kill us not, nor dye,
Heare us, weake ecchoes, O thou eare, and cry.

XXVIII.

Sonne of God heare us, and since thou
By taking our blood, owest it us againe,   245
   Gaine to thy selfe, or us allow;
And let not both us and thy selfe be slaine;
      O lambe of God, which took'st our sinne
      Which could not stick to thee,
O let it not returne to us againe,   250
But Patient and Physition being free,
As sinne is nothing, let it no where be.

185   *Goodfriday, 1613. Riding Westward.*

Let mans Soule be a Spheare, and then, in this,
The'intelligence that moves, devotion is,
And as the other Spheares, by being growne
Subject to forraigne motions, lose their owne,
And being by others hurried every day,   5
Scarce in a yeare their naturall forme obey:
Pleasure or businesse, so, our Soules admit
For their first mover, and are whirld by it.
Hence is't, that I am carryed towards the West
This day, when my Soules forme bends toward the East.   10

238. *For physicke:* for improvement of health, for purgation (of sin).
GOODFRIDAY, 1613. RIDING WESTWARD.
   Goodfriday, 1613: Donne was riding to visit Sir Edward Herbert in Wales,
according to one manuscript. The date was April 2, 1613.
   2. *intelligence:* the angel supposed to move and direct each of the ten spheres
of the created (Ptolemaic) universe. Motion is imparted to each inner sphere by
the *primum mobile* (the first mover, l. 8).
   8. That is, his *primum mobile* (pleasure or business) forces him to be like a
wandering star moving in reverse of the way he wishes.
   10. *forme:* nature.

There I should see a Sunne, by rising set,
And by that setting endlesse day beget;
But that Christ on this Crosse, did rise and fall,
Sinne had eternally benighted all.
Yet dare I'almost be glad, I do not see   15
That spectacle of too much weight for mee.
Who sees Gods face, that is selfe life, must dye;
What a death were it then to see God dye?
It made his owne Lieutenant Nature shrinke,
It made his footstoole crack, and the Sunne winke.   20
Could I behold those hands which span the Poles,
And turne all spheares at once peirc'd with those holes?
Could I behold that endlesse height which is
Zenith to us, and to'our Antipodes,
Humbled below us? or that blood which is   25
The seat of all our Soules, if not of his,
Make durt of dust, or that flesh which was worne
By God, for his apparell, rag'd, and torne?
If on these things I durst not looke, durst I
Upon his miserable mother cast mine eye,   30
Who was Gods partner here, and furnish'd thus
Halfe of that Sacrifice, which ransom'd us?
Though these things, as I ride, be from mine eye,
They'are present yet unto my memory,

11. *rising:* Christ was referred to as Oriens and identified with the sun. The sphere of the sun is thus considered to direct the motion of all other spheres.
12. *endlesse day:* in the enlightenment which Christ creates for the world.
13. If Christ had not risen and fallen on this Cross.
17. *selfe life:* life itself. See further, NOTES.
19. Richard Hooker, *Ecclesiastical Polity*, I, iii, 4: "Those things which nature is said to do, are by divine art performed, using nature as an instrument . . . ."
20. *footstoole:* "Thus saith the Lord, The heaven is my throne, and the earth is my footstool: where is the house that ye build unto me? and where is the place of my rest?" (Isa. lxvi 1). *Sunne winke:* referring to the eclipse of the sun at Christ's crucifixion.
21. Compare the statement of Wisdom that "When he prepared the heavens, I was there: when he set a compass upon the face of the depth" (Prov. viii 27).
22. *And . . . once:* referring to God as "first mover" (l. 8).
27. *durt:* the dust of which man was created cohered by the blood of God in the Incarnation.
32. *Sacrifice:* as mother, God as Father furnishing the other half.
34. *memory:* the memory was in the back of the mind; thus it faces east and "sees" the Crucifixion.

For that looks towards them; and thou look'st towards mee,   35
O Saviour, as thou hang'st upon the tree;
I turne my backe to thee, but to receive
Corrections, till thy mercies bid thee leave.
O thinke mee worth thine anger, punish mee,
Burne off my rusts, and my deformity,   40
Restore thine Image, so much, by thy grace,
That thou may'st know mee, and I'll turne my face.

186   *To Mr.* George Herbert, *with one of my Seales, of the Anchor and Christ.*

Qui prius assuetus Serpentum fasce Tabellas
  Signare, (hæc nostræ symbola parva Domus)
Adscitus domui Domini, patrióque relicto
  Stemmate, nanciscor stemmata jure nova.
Hinc mihi Crux primo quæ fronte impressa lavacro,   5
  Finibus extensis, anchora facta patet.
Anchoræ in effigiem, Crux tandem desinit ipsam,
  Anchora fit tandem Crux tolerata diu.
Hoc tamen ut fiat, Christo vegetatur ab ipso
  Crux, et ab Affixo, est Anchora facta, Iesu.   10
Nec Natalitiis penitus serpentibus orbor,
  Non ita dat Deus, ut auferat ante data.
Quâ sapiens, Dos est; Quâ terram lambit et ambit,
  Pestis; At in nostra fit Medicina Cruce,
Serpens; fixa Cruci si sit Natura; Crucíque   15
  A fixo, nobis, Gratia tota fluat.
Omnia cum Crux sint, Crux Anchora fixa, sigillum
  Non tam dicendum hoc, quam Catechismus erit.
Mitto, nec exigua, exiguâ sub imagine, dona,
  Pignora amicitiæ, et munera; Vota, preces.   20
Plura tibi accumulet, sanctus cognominis, Ille
  Regia qui flavo Dona sigillat Equo.

38. *leave:* desist.
42. *That . . . mee:* "I am the good shepherd, and know my sheep, and am
known of mine" (John x 14). *I'll turne my face:* since riding westward he
will come to the east; he is following the sun's (God's) course though he had
misunderstood when he started out.

186 (Translation).

A sheafe of Snakes used heretofore to be
My Seal, The Crest of our poore Family.
Adopted in Gods Family, and so
Our old Coat lost, unto new armes I go.
The Crosse (my seal at Baptism) spred below,   5
Does, by that form, into an Anchor grow.
Crosses grow Anchors; Bear, as thou shouldst do
Thy Crosse, and that Crosse grows an Anchor too.
But he that makes our Crosses Anchors thus,
Is Christ, who there is crucifi'd for us.   10
Yet may I, with this, my first Serpents hold,
God gives new blessings, and yet leaves the old;
The Serpent, may, as wise, my pattern be;
My poison, as he feeds on dust, that's me.
And as he rounds the Earth to murder sure,   15
My death he is, but on the Crosse, my cure.
Crucifie nature then, and then implore
All Grace from him, crucified there before;
When all is Crosse, and that Crosse Anchor grown,
This Seal's a Catechism, not a Seal alone.   20
Under that little Seal great gifts I send,
Works, and prayers, pawns, and fruits of a friend.
And may that Saint which rides in our great Seal,
To you, who bear his name, great bounties deal.

TO MR. GEORGE HERBERT, WITH ONE OF MY SEALES. See NOTES.

1–2. Donne used this seal on letters before 1615, although no seal had been officially granted to the family.

5. The new arms depicted Christ upon an anchor; the seal appears on a letter to Sir Edward Herbert, dated January 23, 1615. After he became Dean of St. Paul's, Donne employed three other armorial seals.

11. The serpent was a symbol of sinfulness, but compare Matt. x 16: "be ye therefore wise as serpents."

21. *cognominis* (*surname*): referring to his mother Magdalen Herbert, a close friend of Donne's. The Latin is clearly a cognomen. The anonymous translator misreads these last two lines, producing an allusion to St. George who is shown as a seated figure on the reverse of the Great Seal. (Translation, line 23)

22. "And I saw heaven opened, and behold a white horse; and he that sat upon him was called Faithful and True, and in righteousness he doth judge and make war. His eyes were as a flame of fire and on his head were many crowns . . ." (Rev. xix 11–12). The Greek *leukos* (bright, brilliant, white) was translated in the Vulgate and by Tremellius as *albus* (white), but Donne's *flavo* (glittering, golden) is closer to the original intent. (Translation, line 24)

186A. *To Mr. George Herbert.*

Who was first accustomed to set a mark on letters
with a sheaf of snakes (these little symbols of our family),
admitted to God's family and with our abandoned paternal
crest, I receive new arms justly.
Hence the cross which was impressed on my forehead at baptism,   5
with ends extended, lies open formed into an anchor.
The cross at length closes itself in the likeness of an anchor;
the cross borne a long time becomes finally an anchor.
And since it may be made in this way, the cross is invigorated by
    Christ
himself, and by his crucifixion is the anchor formed by Jesus.   10
Yet I am not deprived of my natal serpents inwardly;
thus God does not give so that he may withdraw those things
    bestowed before.
In this way is my dowry wise; insofar as death bathes the earth
    and
encompasses it; but within my cross the serpent becomes my
    cure;
if nature be fixed on the cross, then from the cross   15
on which He was transfixed, to us may all grace flow.
When all be a cross, the cross an immovable anchor, this seal
will not have to be so affirmed as a catechism.
I send not little gifts, under this little likeness,
pledges of friendship and tributes, prayers, good wishes.   20
May He heap more upon you, sainted of surname,
who seals his princely gifts with a glittering steed.

187 *The Lamentations of* Jeremy,
for the most part according to Tremelius.

Chap. I.

1   How sits this citie, late most populous,
    Thus solitary,'and like a widdow thus!
    Amplest of Nations, Queene of Provinces
    She was, who now thus tributary is!

2   Still in the night shee weepes, and her teares fall   5
    Downe by her cheekes along, and none of all
    Her lovers comfort her; Perfidiously
    Her friends have dealt, and now are enemie.

3   Unto great bondage, and afflictions
    Juda is captive led; Those nations   10
    With whom shee dwells, no place of rest afford,
    In streights shee meets her Persecutors sword.

4   Emptie'are the gates of Sion, and her waies
    Mourne, because none come to her solemne dayes.
    Her Priests doe groane, her maides are comfortlesse,   15
    And shee's unto her selfe a bitternesse.

5   Her foes are growne her head, and live at Peace,
    Because when her transgressions did increase,
    The Lord strooke her with sadnesse: Th'enemie
    Doth drive her children to captivitie.   20

6   From Sions daughter is all beauty gone,
    Like Harts, which seeke for Pasture, and find none,
    Her Princes are, and now before the foe
    Which still pursues them, without strength they go.

THE LAMENTATIONS OF JEREMY.
   Tremelius: Immanuel Tremellius (1510–80), born of Jewish parents, became
a Calvinist around 1530; he held professorships of Hebrew at Cambridge until
1553, and of theology at Heidelberg from 1562 to 1577. His Latin translation
of the Old Testament (with Francis Junius) was published in London in 1580,
1581, and 1585. Donne discussed the interpretation of Lamentations iv 20 in a
sermon of November 5, 1622 (*Fifty Sermons*, xliii; Potter and Simpson, IV,
Sermon 9). The present free translation shows the influence of the Vulgate and
of the Authorized Version.

"How Sits This City"

THOMAS FORD

(From MS 736, f. 21a, with permission of the Library of Christ Church, Oxford.)

7   Now in her daies of Teares, Jerusalem   25
        (Her men slaine by the foe, none succouring them)
     Remembers what of old, shee esteem'd most,
        Whiles her foes laugh at her, for what she'hath lost.

8   Jerusalem hath sinn'd, therefore is shee
     Remov'd, as women in uncleannesse bee: 30
     Who honor'd, scorne her, for her foulnesse they
        Have seene, her selfe doth groane, and turne away.

9   Her foulnesse in her skirts was seene, yet she
     Remembred not her end; Miraculously
     Therefore shee fell, none comforting: Behold   35
        O Lord my'affliction, for the Foe growes bold.

10   Upon all things where her delight hath beene,
        The foe hath stretch'd his hand, for shee hath seene
     Heathen, whom thou command'st, should not doe so,
        Into her holy Sanctuary goe.   40

11   And all her people groane, and seeke for bread;
        And they have given, only to be fed,
     All precious things, wherein their pleasure lay:
        How cheape I'am growne, O Lord, behold, and weigh.

12   All this concernes not you, who passe by mee,   45
        O see, and marke if any sorrow bee
     Like to my sorrow, which Jehova hath
        Done to mee in the day of his fierce wrath?

13   That fire, which by himselfe is governed
        He hath cast from heaven on my bones, and spred   50
     A net before my feet, and mee o'rthrowne,
        And made me languish all the day alone.

14   His hand hath of my sinnes framed a yoake
        Which wreath'd, and cast upon my neck, hath broke
     My strength. The Lord unto those enemies   55
        Hath given mee, from whom I cannot rise.

15   He underfoot hath troden in my sight
        My strong men; He did company invite
     To breake my young men; he the winepresse hath
        Trod upon Juda's daughter in his wrath.   60

16   For these things doe I weepe, mine eye, mine eye
         Casts water out; For he which should be nigh
      To comfort mee, is now departed farre,
         The foe prevailes, forlorne my children are.

17   There's none, though *Sion* do stretch out her hand,   65
         To comfort her, it is the Lords command
      That *Jacobs* foes girt him. *Jerusalem*
         Is as an uncleane woman amongst them.

18   But yet the Lord is just, and righteous still,
         I have rebell'd against his holy will;   70
      O heare all people, and my sorrow see,
         My maides, my young men in captivitie.

19   I called for my *lovers* then, but they
         Deceiv'd mee, and my Priests, and Elders lay
      Dead in the citie; for they sought for meat   75
         Which should refresh their soules, they could not get.

20   Because I am in streights, *Jehova* see
         My heart o'rturn'd, my bowells muddy bee,
      Because I have rebell'd so much, as fast
         The sword without, as death within, doth wast.   80

21   Of all which heare I mourne, none comforts mee,
         My foes have heard my griefe, and glad they be,
      That thou hast done it; But thy promis'd day
         Will come, when, as I suffer, so shall they.

22   Let all their wickednesse appeare to thee,   85
         Doe unto them, as thou hast done to mee,
      For all my sinnes: The sighs which I have had
         Are very many, and my heart is sad.

Chap. II.

1   How over Sions daughter hath God hung
         His wraths thicke cloud! and from heaven hath flung   90
      To earth the beauty'of *Israel,* and hath
         Forgot his foot-stoole in the day of wrath!

2   The Lord unsparingly hath swallowed
         All Jacobs dwellings, and demolished
      To ground the strengths of *Juda,* and prophan'd   95
         The Princes of the Kingdome, and the land.

3   In heat of wrath, the horne of *Israel* hee
Hath cleane cut off, and lest the enemie
Be hindred, his right hand he doth retire,
But is towards *Jacob,* All-devouring fire.   100

4   Like to an enemie he bent his bow,
His right hand was in posture of a foe,
To kill what *Sions* daughter did desire,
'Gainst whom his wrath, he poured forth, like fire.

5   For like an enemie *Jehova* is,   105
Devouring *Israel,* and his Palaces,
Destroying holds, giving additions
To *Juda's* daughters lamentations.

6   Like to a garden hedge he hath cast downe
The place where was his congregation,   110
And *Sions* feasts and sabbaths are forgot;
Her King, her Priest, his wrath regardeth not.

7   The Lord forsake his Altar, and detests
His Sanctuary,'and in the foes hand rests
His Palace, and the walls, in which their cries   115
Are heard, as in the true solemnities.

8   The Lord hath cast a line, so to confound
And levell *Sions* walls unto the ground;
He drawes not back his hand; which doth oreturne
The wall, and Rampart, which together mourne.   120

9   Their gates are sunke into the ground, and hee
Hath broke the barres; their King and Princes bee
Amongst the heathen, without law, nor there
Unto their Prophets doth the Lord appeare.

10   There *Sions Elders* on the ground are plac'd,   125
And silence keepe; Dust on their heads they cast,
In sackcloth have they girt themselves, and low
The Virgins towards ground, their heads do throw.

11   My bowells are growne muddy, and mine eyes
Are faint with weeping: and my liver lies   130
Pour'd out upon the ground, for miserie
That sucking children in the streets doe die.

12   When they had cryed unto their Mothers, where
        Shall we have bread, and drinke? they fainted there,
    And in the streets like wounded persons lay   135
        Till 'twixt their mothers breasts they went away.

13   *Daughter Jerusalem,* Oh what may bee
        A witnesse, or comparison for thee?
    Sion, to'ease thee, what shall I name like thee?
        Thy breach is like the sea, what help can bee?   140

14   For thee vaine foolish things thy Prophets sought,
        Thee, thine iniquities they have not taught,
    Which might disturne thy bondage: but for thee
        False burthens, and false causes they would see.

15   The passengers doe clap their hands, and hisse   145
        And wag their head at thee, and say, Is this
    That citie, which so many men did call
        Joy of the earth, and perfectest of all?

16   Thy foes doe gape upon thee, and they hisse,
        And gnash their teeth, and say, Devoure wee this,   150
    For this is certainly the day which wee
        Expected, and which now we finde, and see.

17   The Lord hath done that which he purposed,
        Fulfill'd his word of old determined;
    He hath throwne downe, and not spar'd, and thy foe   155
        Made glad above thee, and advanc'd him so.

18   But now, their hearts against the Lord do call,
        Therefore, O walle of *Sion,* let teares fall
    Downe like a river, day and night; take thee
        No rest, but let thine eye incessant be.   160

19   Arise, cry in the night, poure, for thy sinnes,
        Thy heart, like water, when the watch begins;
    Lift up thy hands to God, lest children dye,
        Which, faint for hunger, in the streets doe lye.

20   Behold O Lord, consider unto whom   165
        Thou hast done thus; what, shall the women come
    To eate their children of a spanne? shall thy
        Prophet and Priest be slaine in Sanctuary?

    143. *disturne:* revoke.

21   On ground in streets, the yong and old do lye,
        My virgins and yong men by sword do dye;   170
    Them in the day of thy wrath thou hast slaine,
        Nothing did thee from killing them containe.

22   As to a solemne feast, all whom I fear'd
        Thou call'st about mee; when his wrath appear'd,
    None did remaine or scape, for those which I   175
        Brought up, did perish by mine enemie.

Chap. III.

1   I am the man which have affliction seene,
      Under the rod of Gods wrath having beene,
2 He hath led mee to darknesse, not to light,
3 And against mee all day, his hand doth fight.   180

4 Hee hath broke my bones, worne out my flesh and skinne,
5 Built up against mee; and hath girt mee in
    With hemlocke, and with labour; [6]and set mee
      In darke, as they who dead for ever bee.

7 Hee'hath hedg'd me lest I scape, and added more   185
    To my steele fetters, heavier then before,
8 When I crie out, he'out shuts my prayer: [9]And hath
    Stop'd with hewn stone my way, and turn'd my path.

10 And like a Lion hid in secrecie,
     Or Beare which lyes in wait, he was to mee.   190
11 He stops my way, teares me, made desolate,
12 And hee makes mee the marke he shooteth at.

13 Hee made the children of his quiver passe
     Into my reines, [14]I with my people was
    All the day long, a song and mockery.   195
15 Hee hath fill'd mee with bitternesse, and he

    Hath made me drunke with wormewood. [16]He hath burst
    My teeth with stones, and cover'd mee with dust;
17 And thus my Soule farre off from peace was set,
     And my prosperity I did forget.   200

18 My strength, my hope (unto my selfe I said)
     Which from the Lord should come, is perished.
19 But when my mournings I do thinke upon,
     My wormewood, hemlocke, and affliction,

20   My Soule is humbled in remembring this;   205
21   My heart considers, therefore, hope there is.
22   'Tis Gods great mercy we'are not utterly
           Consum'd, for his compassions do not die;

23   For every morning they renewed bee,
           For great, O Lord, is thy fidelity.   210
24   The Lord is, saith my Soule, my portion,
           And therefore in him will I hope alone.

25   The Lord is good to them, who'on him relie,
           And to the Soule that seeks him earnestly.
26   It is both good to trust, and to attend   215
           (The Lords salvation) unto the end:

27   'Tis good for one his yoake in youth to beare;
28   He sits alone, and doth all speech forbeare,
        Because he'hath borne it. [29]And his mouth he layes
           Deepe in the dust, yet there in hope he stayes.   220

30   He gives his cheekes to whosoever will
           Strike him, and so he is reproched still.
31   For, not for ever doth the Lord forsake,
32   But when he'hath strucke with sadnes, hee doth take

           Compassion, as his mercy'is infinite;   225
33   Nor is it with his heart, that he doth smite,
34   That underfoot the prisoners stamped bee,
35   That a mans right the Judge himselfe doth see

           To be wrunge from him, [36]That he subverted is
           In his just cause; the Lord allowes not this: 230
37   Who then will say, that ought doth come to passe,
           But that which by the Lord commanded was?

38   Both good and evill from his mouth proceeds;
39   Why then grieves any man for his misdeeds?
40   Turne wee to God, by trying out our wayes;   235
41   To him in heaven, our hands with hearts upraise.

42   Wee have rebell'd, and falne away from thee,
           Thou pardon'st not. [43]Usest no clemencie;
        Pursuest us, kill'st us, coverest us with wrath,
44   Cover'st thy selfe with clouds, that our prayer hath   240

No power to passe. [45]And thou hast made us fall
As refuse, and off-scouring to them all.
46 All our foes gape at us. [47]Feare and a snare
With ruine, and with waste, upon us are.

48   With watry rivers doth mine eye oreflow
For ruine of my peoples daughter so;
49 Mine eye doth drop downe teares incessantly,
50   Untill the Lord looke downe from heaven to see.

51   And for my city daughters sake, mine eye
Doth breake mine heart. [52]Causles mine enemy,
Like a bird chac'd me. [53]In a dungeon
They'have shut my life, and cast on me a stone.

54   Waters flow'd o'r my head, then thought I, I'am
Destroy'd; [55]I called Lord, upon thy name
Out of the pit. [56]And thou my voice didst heare;
Oh from my sigh, and crye, stop not thine eare.

57   Then when I call'd upon thee, thou drew'st nere
Unto mee,'and said'st unto mee, do not feare.
58 Thou Lord my Soules cause handled hast, and thou
Rescud'st my life. [59]O Lord do thou judge now,

Thou heardst my wrong. [60]Their vengeance all
they'have wrought;
61   How they reproach'd, thou'hast heard, and what they
thought,
62 What their lips utter'd, which against me rose,
And what was ever whisper'd by my foes.

63   I am their song, whether they rise or sit,
64   Give them rewards Lord, for their working fit,
65 Sorrow of heart, thy curse. [66]And with thy might
Follow,'and from under heaven destroy them quite.

Chap. IV.

1   How is the gold become so dimme? How is
Purest and finest gold thus chang'd to this?
The stones which were stones of the Sanctuary,
Scatter'd in corners of each street do lye.

2   The pretious sonnes of Sion, which should bee
       Valued at purest gold, how do wee see
   Low rated now, as earthen Pitchers, stand,   275
      Which are the worke of a poore Potters hand.

3   Even the Sea-calfes draw their brests, and give
       Sucke to their young; my peoples daughters live
   By reason of the foes great cruelnesse,
      As do the Owles in the vast Wildernesse.   280

4   And when the sucking child doth strive to draw,
       His tongue for thirst cleaves to his upper jaw.
   And when for bread the little children crye,
      There is no man that doth them satisfie.

5   They which before were delicately fed,   285
       Now in the streets forlorne have perished,
   And they which ever were in scarlet cloath'd,
      Sit and embrace the dunghills which they loath'd.

6   The daughters of my people have sinn'd more,
       Then did the towne of *Sodome* sinne before;   290
   Which being at once destroy'd, there did remaine
      No hands amongst them, to vexe them againe.

7   But heretofore purer her Nazarite
       Was then the snow, and milke was not so white;
   As carbuncles did their pure bodies shine,   295
      And all their polish'dnesse was Saphirine.

8   They'are darker now then blacknes, none can know
       Them by the face, as through the streetes they goe,
   For now their skin doth cleave unto their bone,
      And withered, is like to dry wood growne.   300

9   Better by sword then famine 'tis to dye;
       And better through pierc'd, then through penury.
10   Women by nature pitifull, have eate
      Their children drest with their owne hands for meat.

11   *Jehova* here fully accomplish'd hath   305
       His indignation, and powr'd forth his wrath,
   Kindled a fire in *Sion*, which hath power
      To eate, and her foundations to devour.

303. *eate:* archaic past form.

12 Nor would the Kings of the'earth, nor all which live
    In the inhabitable world beleeve,   310
That any adversary, any foe
    Into *Jerusalem* should enter so;

13 For the Priests sins, and Prophets, which have shed
    Blood in the streets, and the just murthered:
14 Which when those men, whom they made blinde, did stray   315
    Thorough the streets, defiled by the way

    With blood, the which impossible it was
    Their garments should scape touching, as they passe,
15 Would cry aloud, depart defiled men,
    Depart, depart, and touch us not, and then   320

    They fled, and strayd, and with the *Gentiles* were,
    Yet told their friends, they should not long dwell there;
16 For this they'are scatter'd by Jehovahs face
    Who never will regard them more; No grace

    Unto their old men shall the foe afford,   325
    Nor, that they'are Priests, redeeme them from the sword.
17 And wee as yet, for all these miseries
    Desiring our vaine helpe, consume our eyes:

    And such a nation as cannot save,
    We in desire and speculation have.   330
18 They hunt our steps, that in the streets wee feare
    To goe: our end is now approached neere,

    Our dayes accomplish'd are, this the last day.
19 Eagles of heaven are not so swift as they
    Which follow us, o'r mountaine tops they flye   335
    At us, and for us in the desart lye.

20 The'annointed Lord, breath of our nostrils, hee
    Of whom we said, under his shadow, wee
Shall with more ease under the Heathen dwell,
    Into the pit which these men digged, fell.   340

21 Rejoyce O *Edoms daughter,* joyfull bee
    Thou which inhabitst *Huz,* for unto thee
This cup shall passe, and thou with drunkennesse
    Shalt fill thy selfe, and shew thy nakednesse.

22   And then thy sinnes O *Sion*, shall be spent,   345
      The Lord will not leave thee in banishment.
      Thy sinnes O *Edoms daughter*, hee will see,
      And for them, pay thee with captivitie.

Chap. V.

1   Remember, O Lord, what is fallen on us;
      See, and marke how we are reproached thus,   350
2 For unto strangers our possession
      Is turn'd, our houses unto Aliens gone,

3   Our mothers are become as widowes, wee
      As Orphans all, and without father be;
4 Waters which are our owne, wee drinke, and pay,   355
      And upon our owne wood a price they lay.

5   Our persecutors on our necks do sit,
      They make us travaile, and not intermit,
6 We stretch our hands unto th'*Egyptians*
      To get us bread; and to the'*Assyrians*.   360

7   Our Fathers did these sinnes, and are no more,
      But wee do beare the sinnes they did before.
8 They are but servants, which do rule us thus,
      Yet from their hands none would deliver us.

9   With danger of our life our bread wee gat;   365
      For in the wildernesse, the sword did wait.
10   The tempests of this famine wee liv'd in,
      Black as an Oven colour'd had our skinne:

11   In *Judaes* cities they the maids abus'd
      By force, and so women in *Sion* us'd.   370
12   The Princes with their hands they hung; no grace
      Nor honour gave they to the Elders face.

13   Unto the mill our yong men carried are,
      And children fell under the wood they bare.
14   Elders, the gates; youth did their songs forbeare,   375
15   Gone was our joy; our dancings, mournings were.

16   Now is the crowne falne from our head; and woe
      Be unto us, because we'have sinned so.
17   For this our hearts do languish, and for this
      Over our eyes a cloudy dimnesse is.   380

18   Because mount *Sion* desolate doth lye,
         And foxes there do goe at libertie:
19   But thou O Lord art ever, and thy throne
         From generation, to generation.

20   Why should'st thou forget us eternally?   385
         Or leave us thus long in this misery?
21   Restore us Lord to thee, that so we may
         Returne, and as of old, renew our day.

22   For oughtest thou, O Lord, despise us thus
         And to be utterly enrag'd at us?   390

188   Translated out of *Gazæus,*
Vota Amico facta. fol. 160.

God grant thee thine own wish, and grant thee mine,
Thou, who dost, best friend, in best things outshine;
May thy soul, ever chearfull, nere know cares,
Nor thy life, ever lively, know gray haires.
Nor thy hand, ever open, know base holds,   5
Nor thy purse, ever plump, know pleits, or folds.
Nor thy tongue, ever true, know a false thing,
Nor thy word, ever mild, know quarrelling.
Nor thy works, ever equall, know disguise,
Nor thy fame, ever pure, know contumelies.   10
Nor thy prayers, know low objects, still Divine;
God grant thee thine own wish, and grant thee mine.

TRANSLATED OUT OF GAZÆUS.
   out of Gazæus: from Angelinus Gazaeus, "Prayers composed by a friend" in
Pia Hilaria Variaque Carmina (*Poems and Songs to Saint Hilary*); the Latin
(from the edition of 1623, not the one used by Donne) and a literal translation
are included here for comparison.
   6. *pleits:* folds; that is, be so empty that its cloth will lie in folds.
   9. *equall:* just. *disguise:* falsity.

188A.   From Angelinus Gazaeus,
Pia Hilaria Variaque Carmina, 1623.

Tibi quod optas et quod opto, deut Divi,
(Sol opimorum in optimis Amicorum)
Vt anima semper laeta nesciat curas
Vt vita semper viva nesciat canos,
Vt dextra semper larga nesciat sordes,   5
Vt bursa semper plena nesciat rugas,
Vt lingua semper vera nesciat lapsum,
Vt verba semper blanda nesciant rixas,
Vt facta semper æqua nesciant fucum,
Vt fama semper pura nesciant probrum,   10
Vt vota semper alta nesciant terras,
Tibi quod optas et quod opto, deut Divi.

188A   (Translation).

May God grant you what you desire and what I wish
([May] the sun of fruitful friends [shine] on the best friends),
that your soul, ever cheerful, know no cares,
that your life, ever lively, know no gray hairs,
that your right hand, ever abounding, know no base men,   5
that your purse, ever full, know no wrinkles,
that your tongue, ever true, know no lapse,
that your word, ever mild, know no quarrels,
that your deeds, ever equal, know no deceit,
that your fame, ever pure, know no reproach,   10
that your prayers, ever lofty, know no earthly things,
may God grant you what you desire and what I wish.

Thou, whose diviner soule hath caus'd thee now
To put thy hand unto the holy Plough,
Making Lay-scornings of the Ministry,
Not an impediment, but victory;
What bringst thou home with thee? how is thy mind   5
Affected since the vintage? Dost thou finde
New thoughts and stirrings in thee? and as Steele
Toucht with a Loadstone, dost new motions feele?
Or, as a Ship after much paine and care,
For Iron and Cloth brings home rich Indian ware,   10
Hast thou thus traffiqu'd, but with farre more gaine
Of noble goods, and with lesse time and paine?
Thou art the same materials, as before,
Onely the stampe is changed; but no more.
And as new crowned Kings alter the face,   15
But not the monies substance; so hath grace
Chang'd onely Gods old Image by Creation,
To Christs new stampe, at this thy Coronation;
Or, as we paint Angels with wings, because
They beare Gods message, and proclaime his lawes,   20
Since thou must doe the like, and so must move,
Art thou new feather'd with cœlestiall love?
Deare, tell me where thy purchase lies, and shew
What thy advantage is above, below.
But if thy gainings doe surmount expression,   25
Why doth the foolish world scorne that profession,
Whose joyes passe speech? Why do they think unfit
That Gentry should joyne families with it?

TO MR. TILMAN AFTER HE HAD TAKEN ORDERS.
    Mr. Tilman: Edward Tilman was ordained a deacon on December 20, 1618, and a priest of the Anglican Church on March 12, 1620. However, he did not receive a divinity degree until 1623 (compare l. 3). An alumnus of Pembroke Hall, Cambridge, he died in 1642.
    1–2. "And Jesus said unto him, No man, having put his hand to the plough, and looking back, is fit for the kingdom of God" (Luke ix 62).
    6. *since the vintage:* since reaching the time of harvest of your worth (with your decision to take orders).
    8. *Loadstone:* a magnet which would cause steel to move rapidly toward it.
    23. *purchase:* pursuit (of celestial love).
    24. *above, below:* in understanding heavenly things and in understanding worldly sins.

As if their day were onely to be spent
In dressing, Mistressing and complement;   30
Alas poore joyes, but poorer men, whose trust
Seemes richly placed in refined dust;
(For, such are cloathes and beautyes, which though gay,
Are, at the best, but as sublimed clay)
Let then the world thy calling disrespect,   35
But goe thou on, and pitty their neglect.
What function is so noble, as to bee
Embassadour to God and destinie?
To open life, to give kingdomes to more
Than Kings give dignities; to keepe heavens doore?   40
Maries prerogative was to beare Christ, so
'Tis preachers to convey him, for they doe
As Angels out of clouds, from Pulpits speake;
And blesse the poore beneath, the lame, the weake.
If then th'Astronomers, whereas they spie   45
A new-found Starre, their Opticks magnifie,
How brave are those, who with their Engines, can
Bring man to heaven, and heaven againe to man?
These are thy titles and preheminences,
In whom must meet Gods graces, mens offences,   50
And so the heavens which beget all things here,
And the'earth our mother, which these things doth beare,
Both these in thee, are in thy Calling knit,
And make thee now a blest Hermaphrodite.

30. *Mistressing and complement:* marrying and begetting a family.
32. *refined dust:* man ennobled or elevated.
34. *sublimed:* refined.
36. *neglect:* indifference to or neglect of godly things.
39–40. *to give . . . dignities:* to give kingdoms to more people than those to whom kings give dignities (titles).
46. *Opticks:* telescopes, referring probably to Galileo's optic tube of c. 1609. Brahe had seen a new star in 1572; Kepler reported another in 1604.
47. *brave:* excellent. *Engines:* devices.
54. *Hermaphrodite:* since his calling as cleric encompasses opposites such as "Gods graces" and men's sins.

190 *A Hymne to Christ, at the Authors last going into Germany.*

In what torne ship soever I embarke,
That ship shall be my embleme of thy Arke;
What sea soever swallow mee, that flood
Shall be to mee an embleme of thy blood;
Though thou with clouds of anger do disguise   5
Thy face; yet through that maske I know those eyes,
    Which, though they turne away sometimes, they never will
       despise.

I sacrifice this Iland unto thee,
And all whom I lov'd there, and who lov'd mee;
When I have put our seas twixt them and mee,   10
Put thou thy sea betwixt my sinnes and thee.
As the trees sap doth seeke the root below
In winter, in my winter now I goe,
    Where none but thee, th'Eternall root of true Love I may
       know.

Nor thou nor thy religion dost controule,   15
The amorousnesse of an harmonious Soule,
But thou would'st have that love thy selfe: As thou
Art jealous, Lord, so I am jealous now,

A HYMNE TO CHRIST.
    the Authors . . . Germany: Donne accompanied Lord Doncaster on a con-
ciliatory mission to the German princes on May 12, 1619; he returned in December 1620. Compare the sermon delivered at Lincoln's Inn on April 18, 1619
(*Fifty Sermons,* xi; Potter and Simpson, II, Sermon 2).
    2. *Arke:* a symbol of God's Providence in a time of tribulation (referring to
Noah and the flood, Gen. vi ff.).
    5. *clouds:* the pillar of cloud of Exod. xiii 21 is seen as wrath in Psalms
xcvii 2: "Clouds and darkness are round about him: righteousness and judgment are the habitation of his throne." It is the dimming of the mercy of the
Son (sun).
    10. *seas:* emblem of God's blood (l. 4), signifying that they are not really
separated.
    11. *sea:* such as the flood of Noah which drowned the sinful.
    13. *winter:* apparently since his wife had died two years before.
    16. *harmonious:* such as those who could hear the harmony of the spheres,
the sinless as Pythagoras believed. The lines refer to man's free will.
    18. *jealous:* exacting of exclusive devotion.

Thou lov'st not, till from loving more, thou free
My soule: Who ever gives, takes libertie: 20
  O, if thou car'st not whom I love alas, thou lov'st not mee.

Seale then this bill of my Divorce to All,
On whom those fainter beames of love did fall;
Marry those loves, which in youth scatterd bee
On Fame, Wit, Hopes (false mistresses) to thee.   25
Churches are best for Prayer, that have least light:
To see God only, I goe out of sight:
  And to scape stormy dayes, I chuse an Everlasting night.

191   *Upon the translation of the Psalmes by Sir* Philip Sydney, *and the Countesse of Pembroke his Sister.*

Eternall God, (for whom who ever dare
Seeke new expressions, doe the Circle square,
And thrust into strait corners of poore wit
Thee, who art cornerlesse and infinite)
I would but blesse thy Name, not name thee now;   5
(And thy gifts are as infinite as thou:)
Fixe we our prayses therefore on this one,
That, as thy blessed Spirit fell upon
These Psalmes first Author in a cloven tongue;
(For 'twas a double power by which he sung   10
The highest matter in the noblest forme;)

20. *Who ever gives, takes libertie:* one meaning is, Whoever gives liberty (such as God gives liberty of choice whom one loves) takes away liberty (in not allowing one's soul to be free from the devil).
  24. *Marry:* unite.
UPON THE TRANSLATION OF THE PSALMES.
  the translation . . . : Not published until 1823, the *Psalms* are the joint work of Sir Philip Sidney (1554–86) and his sister Mary, Countess of Pembroke (1561–1621). See further, NOTES.
  1–2. Who dare seek new expressions for God try to make imperfect that which is perfect. Compare quadrature of the circle.
  4. *cornerlesse and infinite:* perfect and boundless.
  9. *first Author:* supposedly David, but Donne was aware of the problem of authorship (see l. 48). *cloven:* divided, split; that is, he sang with both his own tongue and with the tongue of God.

So thou hast cleft that spirit, to performe
That worke againe, and shed it, here, upon
Two, by their bloods, and by thy Spirit one;
A Brother and a Sister, made by thee   15
The Organ, where thou art the Harmony.
Two that make one *John Baptists* holy voyce,
And who that Psalme, *Now let the Iles rejoyce,*
Have both translated, and apply'd it too,
Both told us what, and taught us how to doe.   20
They shew us Ilanders our joy, our King,
They tell us *why,* and teach us *how* to sing.
Make all this All, three Quires, heaven, earth, and sphears;
The first, Heaven, hath a song, but no man heares,
The Spheares have Musick, but they have no tongue,   25
Their harmony is rather danc'd than sung;
But our third Quire, to which the first gives eare,
(For, Angels learne by what the Church does here)
This Quire hath all. The Organist is hee
Who hath tun'd God and Man, the Organ we: 30
The songs are these, which heavens high holy Muse
Whisper'd to *David, David* to the Jewes:
And *Davids* Successors, in holy zeale,
In formes of joy and art doe re-reveale
To us so sweetly and sincerely too,   35
That I must not rejoyce as I would doe
When I behold that these Psalmes are become
So well attyr'd abroad, so ill at home,
So well in Chambers, in thy Church so ill,
As I can scarce call that reform'd, untill   40

16. *Organ:* both musical instrument and medium.
17. *voyce:* which says, "Repent ye: for the kingdom of heaven is at hand" (Matt. iii 2).
18. *Psalme:* Psalm xcvii; the psalms are their application of rejoicing in the Lord and giving thanks at the remembrance of his holiness.
23. *all this All:* "And when all things shall be subdued unto him, then shall the Son also himself be subject unto him that put all things under him, that God may be all in all" (1 Cor. xv 28).
26. *danc'd:* because of the movement of the spheres.
29–30. That is, David (as inspired by the divine muse) has harmonized God and Man in the psalms, and men are now the instrument through which they are played. See further, NOTES.
38. *abroad:* see NOTES.
39. *Chambers:* music rooms.
40. *that:* the Anglican Church.

This be reform'd; Would a whole State present
A lesser gift than some one man hath sent?
And shall our Church, unto our Spouse and King
More hoarse, more harsh than any other, sing?
For *that* we pray, we praise thy name for *this*,   45
Which, by this *Moses* and this *Miriam,* is
Already done; and as those Psalmes we call
(Though some have other Authors) *Davids* all:
So though some have, some may some Psalmes translate,
We thy Sydnean Psalmes shall celebrate,   50
And, till we come th'Extemporall song to sing,
(Learn'd the first hower, that we see the King,
Who hath translated these translators) may
These their sweet learned labours, all the way
Be as our tuning, that, when hence we part   55
We may fall in with them, and sing our part.

192   *Hymne to God my God, in my sicknesse.*

Since I am comming to that Holy roome,
    Where, with thy Quire of Saints for evermore,
I shall be made thy Musique; As I come
    I tune the Instrument here at the dore,
    And what I must doe then, thinke here before.   5

Whilst my Physitians by their love are growne
    Cosmographers, and I their Mapp, who lie

43. *Spouse:* Christ the Bridegroom (Matt. xxv 1–13).
45. We pray for reform of the church; we praise God for the reforming of the psalms by Sidney and his sister.
46. *Moses . . . Miriam:* see Exod. xv 1–19 for Moses' song; "And Miriam answered them, Sing ye to the Lord for he hath triumphed gloriously" (verse 21).
51. *Extemporall song:* "and I heard the voice of harpers harping with their harps: And they sung as it were a new song before the throne" (Rev. xiv 2–3).
53. *translated these translators:* removed Sidney and his sister to heaven.
55. *tuning:* tuning up to be ready to sing before the throne of God.
HYMNE TO GOD MY GOD, IN MY SICKNESSE.
in my sicknesse: according to some, written during his great sickness in December 1623 (so noted by Sir Julius Caesar), although Walton dated it March 23, 1631. See further, NOTES.
3. *thy Musique:* see NOTES.
4. *Instrument:* his soul.

Flat on this bed, that by them may be showne
   That this is my South-west discoverie
   Per fretum febris, by these streights to die,   10

I joy, that in these straits, I see my West;
   For, though theire currants yeeld returne to none,
What shall my West hurt me? As West and East
   In all flatt Maps (and I am one) are one,
   So death doth touch the Resurrection.   15

Is the Pacifique Sea my home? Or are
   The Easterne riches? Is *Jerusalem?*
Anyan, and *Magellan,* and *Gibraltare,*
   All streights, and none but streights are wayes to them,
   Whether where *Japhet* dwelt, or *Cham,* or *Sem.*   20

We thinke that *Paradise* and *Calvarie,*
   Christs Crosse, and *Adams* tree, stood in one place;
Looke Lord, and finde both *Adams* met in me;
   As the first *Adams* sweat surrounds my face,
   May the last *Adams* blood my soule embrace.   25

So, in his purple wrapp'd receive mee Lord,
   By these his thornes give me his other Crowne;

9. *South-west discoverie:* probably referring to the Straits of Magellan.

10. *Per fretum febris:* through the raging of fever. There is a pun in the word "fretum," which also means "strait." Thus Donne's discovery is that he proceeds westward (dies) by going south (by fever).

11. *straits:* probably in the background is Christ's admonition: "Enter ye in at the strait gate: for wide is the gate, and broad is the way, that leadeth to destruction, and many there be which go in thereat: Because strait is the gate, and narrow is the way, which leadeth unto life, and few there be that find it" (Matt. vii 13–14).

14. Since points on the right side (east) correspond exactly to points on the left (west). See further, NOTES.

18. *Anyan:* the Bering Strait.

20. *Japhet, Cham, Sem:* the three sons of Noah who populated the world: Europe, Africa, and Asia, respectively.

22. *Adams tree:* the Tree of Knowledge of Good and Evil in Paradise, supposed to have stood on the place of the Crucifixion on Calvary.

23. *Adams:* that is, Adam and Christ, the sinner and the receiver of punishment for sins.

24–25. "The first man Adam was made a living soul; the last Adam was made a quickening spirit" (1 Cor. xv 45). See also *Holy Sonnet* (No. 163), n. to l. 13.

26–27. "And they clothed him with purple, and plaited a crown of thorns, and put it about his head" (Mark xv 17).

And as to others soules I preach'd thy word,
  Be this my Text, my Sermon to mine owne,
  Therefore that he may raise the Lord throws down.   30

193 *A Hymne to God the Father.*

Wilt thou forgive that sinne where I begunne,
  Which is my sin, though it were done before?
Wilt thou forgive those sinnes through which I runne,
  And do them still: though still I do deplore?
    When thou hast done, thou hast not done,   5
      For, I have more.

Wilt thou forgive that sinne by which I wonne
  Others to sinne? and, made my sinne their doore?
Wilt thou forgive that sinne which I did shunne
  A yeare, or two: but wallowd in, a score?   10
    When thou hast done, thou hast not done,
      For I have more.

I have a sinne of feare, that when I'have spunne
  My last thred, I shall perish on the shore;
Sweare by thy selfe, that at my death thy Sunne   15
  Shall shine as it shines now, and heretofore;
    And, having done that, Thou haste done,
      I have no more.

28–29. Compare 1 Cor. ix 27: "lest that by any means, when I have preached to others, I myself should be a castaway."

30. "Dominus erigit elisos" ("The Lord raises those who are struck down"), from the Vulgate version of Psalms cxlvi 8.

A HYMNE TO GOD THE FATHER.

According to Walton, this poem was written during Donne's illness in winter 1623. It was set to music, by Donne's suggestion says Walton, by John Hilton, organist to St. Margaret's Church, Westminster.

1. *that sinne:* original sin.

5. *done* (second): perhaps a pun is intended on his name.

14. *thred:* referring to the spinning of his life as by the three Fates. *perish on the shore:* rather than be transported to heaven.

15–16. Compare the angel's remark to Abraham: "By myself have I sworne, saith the Lord, for because thou hast done this thing, and hast not withheld thy son, thine only son" (Gen. xxii 16). The Son symbolized mercy.

JOHANN SEBASTIAN BACH

Wilt thou for-give that sin, by man be-gun, Which was my sin though it __ were done be-fore? Wilt thou for-give that sin through which I run, And do run still, though __ still __ I do de-plore When thou hast done thou __ hast not done, For I have more.

(From *The English Hymnal with Words* (1902), No. 515, with permission.)

194   (Epigraph beneath portrait in his shroud,
Deaths Duell, 1632).

Corporis hæc Animæ sit Syndon, Syndon Jesu.
                                        Amen.

194   (Epigraph)

May this shroud of the body be the shroud of the soul of Jesus.
                                        Amen.

EPIGRAPH . . . , DEATHS DUELL.
    The shroud covered his body, which metaphorically is the tabernacle of his
soul while he is man on earth. Shortly before his death, Donne wished to know
how he would look in his coffin, and thus had an etching made in a shroud. He
prays that in death his soul will become one with Jesus, the Bridegroom; see
also No. 192, l. 26. Compare Luke xxiii 52–53, xxiv 3, 6: "This man went unto
Pilate, and begged the body of Jesus. And he took it down, and wrapped it in
linen, and laid it in a sepulchre . . . And they entered in, and found not the
body of the Lord Jesus . . . He is not here, but is risen . . . ." "Jesu" may also
be translated as a vocative, "O Jesus," but less meaningfully.

NOTES, INDEXES
AND
BIBLIOGRAPHY

EXPLANATORY NOTES

1. SATYRE I: The poem is a debate between one's body ("thou") and soul ("I"), seen indoors in ll. 1–12 (they do not leave until l. 52), in the street (ll. 67–105) with the soul's requests of ll. 13–24 being denied in turn, and in his love's chambers (ll. 106–10), from which he returns home (ll. 110–12). The questions debated are, "Shall I leave all this constant company, And follow headlong, wild uncertaine thee?" (ll. 11–12) and "Why should'st thou . . . hate vertue, though shee be naked, and bare?" (ll. 37–41). 43–44. The soul's bliss when divested of the body is contrasted by implication with the body's bliss when naked in intercourse. 58. The Infanta (princess) of Spain had been advanced as the Roman Catholic heir of the English throne since 1587. 68. Compare the proverb, "The weakest goeth to the wall." 77. That is, a fiddler bends over as he fingers high notes. 78. That is, he is the most subservient to the most superior people. 111–12. Indicating exhaustion from his previous activities.

2. SATYRE II: 52. Lucille S. Cobb (*Explicator*, XV [1956], Item 8) interprets this to mean that the rival's suit has been shown to be unjust or frivolous. 72. The coins which are produced (born) are all similar (like). The point is that lawyers, since they are like wedges, must press at the bar of law (extort information and thence payment by twisting testimony), and thus they show themselves to be asses and two-faced. Perhaps Donne was also aware that the as had been extremely devalued (from 12 oz. to ½ oz.). Intended also seems to be the pun "baring posteriors similar" to those of the "carted whores," which emphasizes the meaning of "twist" for "wring." 74–76. "Bastardy" because he is like a strumpet (l. 64), "symonie" because he looks out for money (l. 66), and "sodomy" because of "bearing like asses" (l. 72 and n.). 78. From Scotland (north) to the Isle of Wight in the English Channel (south); from Land's End (St. Michael's Mount) in Cornwall (west) to the shore at Dover (east). 104. The lawyer-owner lets the woods rot; Donne's point is not only that they should be put to use, but that lands should be used as in the past and not owned by so few mere landlords as now, as the succeeding lines show.

3. SATYRE III: 17. The English came to the aid of the Dutch, who repeatedly revolted against Spanish rule during the last quarter of the sixteenth century, in 1582 and later. 62. Wards who refused to marry their guardians' choices paid a sum equal to the value of such a marriage; recusants likewise paid for not attending the church established in their parish. 79. Hesiod's Hill of Virtue (*Works and Days*, 287) is the "holy hill of Zion" (e.g. in Psalms ii 6). 96–97. Probably Philip II of Spain and Pope Gregory XIII (Roman Catholic), Henry VIII of England and Martin Luther (Protestant)—all important in religious affairs of the sixteenth century.

4. SATYRE IV: based on Horace's "Ibam forte via Sacra" (*Satires, I* 9) for form, the poem satirizes the king's court and its courtiers. 22. Perhaps with reference to Ralegh's exploration of Guiana in 1595. 24. William the Conqueror's rout of the Danes from northeastern England. 50. Among the numerous Biblical citations, the following are noteworthy: "I am the man that hath

seen affliction by the rod of his wrath" (Lam. iii 1); "And out of his mouth
goeth a sharp sword, that with it he should smite the nations: and he shall
rule them with a rod of iron: and he treadeth the winepress of the fierceness
and wrath of Almighty God" (Rev. xix 15). 57. The Dobell MS names the
reverend men as Lancelot Andrewes, Master of Pembroke College, Cambridge
(1589–1605), and John Reynolds, president of Corpus Christi College, Oxford
(1598–1607). 132–33. *Giant Statutes:* The lines suggest the erroneous, ob-
solete meaning of "statue" (the reading of 1639), for such pronouncers are but
unthinking semblances of man.

   5. SATYRE V: 8. Those in authority, the officers, create wretchedness by
limiting liberty and those who plead suits, both entreaters for justice of a right
or claim and the needy, evoke charity for their misery. 24. *warre:* referring
secondarily to the war with Spain in 1588 and afterward. 85. A Spanish gal-
leon, the Madre de Dios, was captured by Ralegh and towed to England in
September 1592. 87. Haman sought to exterminate the Jews because "their
laws are diverse from all people; neither keep they the king's laws" (Esther
iii 8). He offered to pay "ten thousand talents of silver to the hands of those
that have the charge of the business, to bring it into the king's treasuries." But
Haman himself was hanged.

   6. UPON MR. THOMAS CORYATS CRUDITIES: 5. "Discover'd" puns on acquiring
first-hand knowledge of, exploring, and unclothing; "well" seems to pun on
the adverb and the noun, as a deep fountain. 28. The book is likened to the
sun in its progress across the skies. 30–34. The gold of the Biblical triad
offered to the Christ child is, of course, here obtained from the West Indies;
the addition of pepper (apparently the "spicy" matter) indicates that the book
is "blessed" with all the offerings it needs for a prosperous life.

   8. ELEGIE: THE BRACELET: No. XI in Grierson. 1–2. Compare *The Relique*
(No. 70), l. 6 and n. to l. 18.   7. The number seven symbolized repentance
and forgiveness of sin (Luke xvii 4), perfect completeness, and man as creature
in distinction from the creator; sevenfold implies the nature of the world and
future glory and regeneration since the resurrection of Christ occurred on the
eighth day (Augustine, *Civ. Dei,* xv 20). Twelve (l. 9) was another form of
seven since both factored into three and four; but "twelve righteous Angels"
recalls the twelve Apostles, those "faithful guides" (l. 14) and "innocents" who
bear man's sin (ll. 17–18). There is a pun throughout on "angel," the English
gold coin which shows the archangel Michael slaying the dragon. The angels
are "righteous" (l. 9), as coins, because their value has not been debased, and,
as ethereal beings, because they have not yet fallen with Satan (compare l. 71).
As the Apostles, they will be debased when Judas Iscariot betrays Jesus for
thirty pieces of *silver.* 42. The seventeen provinces of the Netherlands and
Belgium were Holland, Zeeland, Utrecht, Gelderland, Zutphen, Friesland,
Overyssel, and Groningen; Brabant, Flanders, Hainault, Namur, Artois, Cam-
brai, Limburg, Luxemburg, and the Bishopric of Liege.   43–48. The lines play
on the man-gold coin equation: the alchemists are duped in trying to extract
gold, for they "pull out" only an agent (form, not matter).   78. Again there is
a pun on the coin, the angel; that is, money is more influential than good virtues, abilities, and positions of authority.

9. ELEGIE: THE COMPARISON: No. VIII in Grierson. The poet's mistress is described in ll. 1–6, 15–18, 23–24, 27–28, 35–38, 49–52; another's is compared in ll. 7–14, 19–22, 25–26, 29–34, 39–48.

10. ELEGIE: THE PERFUME: No. IV in Grierson.

11. ELEGIE: JEALOSIE: No. I in Grierson.

12. ELEGIE: "OH, LET MEE NOT SERVE SO": No. VI in Grierson; it is addressed to Love.

13. ELEGIE: "NATURES LAY IDEOT": No. VII in Grierson.

14. ELEGIE: LOVES WARRE: No. XX in Grierson. 16. Allowing Ireland to get rid of its rebellious patriots (who generate the ague of their war, which is conducted in an unusual manner against aliens) and its hotheadedness (which has been a result of the ague it suffers). 25. Like long sieges of a vitiating disease for the crew; long periods of waste and destruction for others. 26. Referring to the custom of transporting those to be hanged from prison to the gallows through the streets in carts.

15. ELEGIE: GOING TO BED: No. XIX in Grierson. The poem is built on sexual meanings appropriate to its title.

16. ELEGIE: CHANGE: No. III in Grierson. 23. *Then . . . doe:* that is, if you change in your affections from him to me, "us" becoming the woman and the poet; but also, if you change in your affections from me to another, "us" becoming the two discarded lovers and "like" meaning "alike." 26. The change in dramatic situation allows the poet to muse on what he will do unbeknown to his love. This will be more successful in keeping her than informing her of his intentions, and thereby teaching her. By his reciprocal change she will become jealous and return to him alone.

17. ELEGIE: THE ANAGRAM: No. II in Grierson. 35–36. Husbandmen say most fertile land has most dirt, rather than stones, trees, etc.

18. ELEGIE: ON HIS MISTRIS: No. XVI in Grierson.

19. ELEGIE: HIS PICTURE: No. V in Grierson.

20. ELEGIE: LOVES PROGRESS: No. XVIII in Grierson.

21. ELEGIE: HIS PARTING FROM HER: No. XII in Grierson.

22. ELEGIE: THE EXPOSTULATION: No. XV in Grierson.

23. ELEGIE: VARIETY: No. XVII in Grierson.

24. SAPHO TO PHILÆNIS: 1–2. Ultimately the thought goes back to the Spirit of God as inspiration (as light and as sun); compare Acts ii 3–4: "And there appeared unto them cloven tongues like as of fire, and it sat upon each of them. And they were all filled with the Holy Ghost, and began to speak with other

tongues, as the Spirit gave them utterance." 3–4. Verse copies the work of nature, according to the law of nature; but Sappho's verse cannot elicit the holy fire (inspiration), which is the greatest achievement of nature, to depict nature (because it is not in accord with the law of nature).

30. LECTURE UPON THE SHADOW: 3–17. Biographical interpretation of these lines by Donne's courtship of Anne More seems unavoidable. 9. Just as shadows appear early in the morning, before the sun is overhead, so our young and rising love is disguised and unclear until now, when we and our love are mature. 15. "Just as shadows appear after noon (when the sun declines) falling in an opposite direction from those of morning, so, if our love abates, new shadows will be created falling opposite in direction to the previous ones. Those early deceive others; those later deceive ourselves." The shadows of their infant loves fall in front of them since those after noon come behind (l. 17). As in the usual image of life as the race of the sun across the sky, they are walking westward.

31. A VALEDICTION FORBIDDING MOURNING: 2. The compass image also appears in *Fifty Sermons*, i, p. 3 (Potter and Simpson, VIII, 3, p. 97), *Devotions* (Expostulation 20, pp. 525–26), and *Obsequies to the Lord Harrington* (No. 153), ll. 105–10. 34. The compass line is curved, of course, and Donne's itinerary was not to be a "straight-line" trip (Drury went first to Amiens, then to Frankfurt) and they were to "circle" back by way of the Lowlands. 35–36. His wife's steadfastness makes him complete his trip as planned, not with erratic movement due to whim, and brings him home to her rather than his remaining elsewhere, perhaps with another woman. Only if the fixed foot of a compass is firm may a perfect circle be drawn, and the moving foot end at the same place that it started. (If the fixed foot moves, the moving foot can obviously not return to the same place.) The circumscribed circle with the compass in its center ⊙ was the symbol for gold, alchemically the only metal that was indestructible. The compass device of the Belgian printer Christopher Plantin may have offered Donne a hint for this conceit; the fixed foot is labeled "Constantia." John Freccero (*ELH*, XXX [1963], 335–76) sees the image in astronomical terms, referring to spiral movement, and with the theme of resurrection in the background.

32. THE GOOD-MORROW: 17. As Robert L. Sharp suggests in *MLN*, LXIX (1954), 493–95, Donne probably thought of cordiform maps where each hemisphere was pictured as a heart.

35. "IMAGE OF HER WHOM I LOVE": Elegie No. X in Grierson.

38. LOVES USURY: The poet pleads to the God of Love not to make him fall truly in love (soulfully): he asks to be allowed to engage in only bodily activity, for the God is a usurer requiring too great a price for true love. Thus he believes a bargain can be struck which will bring Love a twentyfold return (the monetary symbol deriving from the number of shillings in a pound). Stanza one is concerned with bodily love (his "shame," l. 19); stanza two, with mental images of loving (his "paine," l. 19); and stanza three, with the triumph of the God through true love (the God's "inflaming" of his soul). 4. Besides the obvious meaning of growing older, the word means young (brown) and older (gray) women: "when I have lain with as many older women as I have young ones."

39. THE CANONIZATION: Not only does the poem deal with the lovers' becoming saints in the religion of love, but comments upon the nonacceptance of saints on earth for their saintly acts, which when pursued will bring them to be canonized, since they "die" for their belief. John A. Clair (*PMLA*, LXXX [1965], 300–2) sees the poem structured by the procedure for determining the acceptance of a proposed saint in the Roman Catholic Church.   22. The debate between the two daughters of God, righteousness and mercy, in medieval literature, produced Peace; see l. 39. Compare Donne's *Sermons*, VIII, 123: "I shall see God as a Dove with an Olive Branch (peace to my soul) or as an Eagle, a vulture to prey."   25–27. In Platonic terms, as Donald L. Guss makes clear in *JEGP*, LXIII (1964), the "neutrall thing" is their spiritual love which will persist after "death" (bodily love) in their resurrection.

41. LOVES INFINITENESSE: An answer to this poem appears with music for four parts in John Dowland's *A Pilgrim Solace* (London, 1612), "To aske for all thy love, and thy whole heart t'were madnesse," C_1b–C_2a.

47. THE PROHIBITION: An analysis by Thomas O. Sloan (*QJS*, XLVIII [1962], 38–45) indicates that stanzas one and two, by presenting opposite extreme possibilities, constitute discretive axioms, and that stanza three, by uniting the dichotomy, sets forth a disjunctive axiom.

49. A VALEDICTION OF MY NAME, IN THE WINDOW: 3. According to the system of gematria (giving numerical values to letters), "Jo: Donne" equals seven and thirty-six, two of the most powerful numbers. Seven is associated with infinity.

50. THE AUTUMNALL: Elegie No. IX in Grierson; written to Magdalen Herbert according to Walton and some MSS.

51. TWICKNAM GARDEN: Twickenham Park was the residence of the Countess of Bedford from 1608 to 1617.

59. LOVES ALCHYMIE: 24. When acting their best (before marriage), women exhibit sweetness and wit; they are only a body without a mind (or must be put under the influence of mummy) when they are actually possessed (after marriage). This is part of the "imposture" of l. 6, the mummy being parallel to the "odoriferous or medicinall thing" (balm) of l. 10 by which the alchemist glorifies *his* pregnant pot (his alembic, synonymous with the womb).

62. THE EXTASIE: Such extreme mystical awareness seems to be derived from the detachment of the soul from the body, the soul standing outside the body contemplating their unity and relationship. In comparing Saint Teresa's *Vida*, Eleanor McCann, in *HLQ*, XVII (1954), 125–32, sees a "surprising amount of agreement about the position of bodies and the movements of souls during a contorted ecstasy" (p. 125).

69. THE PRIMROSE: 1635 adds, "being at Mountgomery Castle, upon the hill, on which it is situate." Montgomery Castle was the home of Magdalen Herbert, but this addition was probably not Donne's. Line 1 most likely refers to Primrose Hill near London.   25. Man is ten in the symbol, and woman only half

a man. According to Bonaventura, ten indicated the fallen angels who would be replaced as the tenth order by Man in the final perfection; and according to Augustine and Methodius, five, because of the number of senses, was the symbol of flesh. The latter accounts for Donne's saying that primroses represent women: the primrose, being gaily and brilliantly hued, is a synonym for "devoted to sensual pleasures." 30. The specious logic of the last line is: Since man is made up of the factors of two and three, and two and three, women, being five, may take all men completely. Woman as equal to only half a man derives ultimately from the doubled days of purification necessary when a maid child is born to equate the number of days when a man child is born (Lev. xii 2–5).

70. THE RELIQUE: 6. Giraldus Cambrensis referred to such bracelets of hair in *Speculum Ecclesiae* and *De Principis Instruction*. Compare "Thou hast . . . stolen the impression of her fantasy with bracelets of thy hair . . ." (*MND*, I, i, 30–33). However, bracelet (thus placing it past the hand and at varying positions on the bone of the arm) and "bright" hair suggest a phallic joke: though in life they "knew not . . . difference of sex," in death they have become "a loving couple." 33. "Was" does not require that she be dead, and "now alas" in l. 31 may simply mean: "but at this point where my paper should teach the greatest miracle it is too bad" that I can not summon poetry and language enough.

72. THE DISSOLUTION: The poet's world has dissolved with his loved one's death as the "heavens being on fire shall be dissolved, and the elements shall melt with fervent heat" (2 Peter iii 12). The alchemical and Christian relationships of the word indicate that the dissolution (the death of the loved one) was necessary to transform the base material of the poet into a penitent, resurrected being, hopefully now indestructible.

81. "WHEN MY HARTE WAS MINE OWNE": Elegy No. XXI in Bennett.

82. A NOCTURNALL UPON S. LUCIES DAY: December 12 under the Julian calendar, then in use in England, was the date of the winter solstice, the time when the sun enters the zodiacal sign of Capricorn ("the Goat," l. 39) and the day when the sun is visible for the least time ("the shortest day"). December 12 is classified as a ferial day, ecclesiastically neither a festival nor a feast day, but etymologically a festival day (see l. 42). The full title was probably not Donne's.
The "shee" of the poem is apparently his wife Anne, who died on August 15, 1617, the references to weeping (ll. 22–24) and absences (ll. 26–27) thus calling for comparison with the extant valedictions. Similar to Lucy's death for refusal to renounce her faith was Anne's continued pledge of faith in their love by giving birth to their twelfth child. The theme of resurrection perhaps came to Donne's mind because (1) Anne died on the feast of the Assumption of the Virgin Mary (the taking up of Mary into heaven) and (2) St. Lucy's Day was the first day that the sun began to rise earlier and stay risen longer. The "darkness" imagery is ironic: St. Lucy's Day was identified with festivals of light and with invocations against afflictions of sight. One legend says that she was blind. 29. In *Essays in Divinity*, p. 30, Donne wrote: "For to be nothing is so deep a curse, and high degree of punishment, that Hell and the prisoners there, not only have it not, but cannot wish so great a loss to themselves."

93. ANTIQUARY: An alternate title and first-line specification of "Hammon" refers to Haman, a collector of great riches, who, through the advice of his wife, sought to have King Ahasuerus hang Mordecai, but he was hanged himself (Esther v–vii). Donne cites Haman and his "antiquities" in *Satyre V* (No. 5), l. 87.

106. EPITHALAMION MADE AT LINCOLNES INNE: David Novarr, in *RES*, N.S. VII (1956), 250–63, suggested that Donne may have written this marriage song for a mock wedding during the Midsummer Revels of June 1595 (compare l. 55). The relation of marriage to death seems to indicate a lack of seriousness, and there are likenesses to Spenser's *Epithalamion*. If so, a man would have taken the part of the bride, adding another level of humor to such words as "Hermaphrodits," l. 30. There may also be a pun on "Temple," l. 31, as Inner Temple or Middle Temple.

112. TO SR. HENRY WOTTON: 65–66. The poem is thus placed after 1594, the date when Wotton returned from his travels. The German states were disunited, though part of the Holy Roman Empire, and hostile to one another.

113. TO MR. ROWLAND WOODWARD: 11. See Job xxxi 6: "Let me be weighed in an even balance, that God may know mine integrity," and Isa. xl 12: "Who hath measured the waters in the hollow of his hand, and meted out heaven with the span, and comprehended the dust of the earth in a measure, and weighed the mountains in scales, and the hills in a balance?" 33. Compare Rom. ii 5–6: "But after thy hardness and impenitent heart treasurest up unto thyself wrath against the day of wrath and revelation of the righteous judgment of God; Who will render to every man according to his deeds," and Matt. vi 19–21: "Lay not up for yourselves treasures upon earth . . . But lay up for yourselves treasures in heaven . . . For where your treasure is, there will your heart be also."

118. TO MR. R. W.: When Donne wrote, he had apparently not heard recently from Woodward. See also other poems addressed to him: "Like one who'in her third widdowhood doth professe" (No. 113), "Muse not that by thy mind thy body'is led" (No. 119), "If, as mine is, thy life a slumber be" (No. 122), and "Kindly'I envy thy songs perfection" (No. 123).

131. TO THE COUNTESSE OF HUNTINGDON: The poem seems to be fragmentary or a combination of fragments; apparently some lines preceding this are missing. There are breaks after ll. 10, 20, 76. The reference in the first ten lines is the New World and its Indian natives. Donne's authorship is not certain; the verses have also been attributed to Sir Walter Ashton.

134. TO THE COUNTESSE OF BEDFORD: See also "Honour is so sublime" (No. 136), "You have refin'd mee" (No. 137), "T'have written then." (No. 138), "This twilight of two yeares" (No. 139), "Though I be *dead,* and buried" (No. 143), and "That I might make your Cabinet my tombe" (No. 147).

138. TO THE COUNTESSE OF BEDFORD: 26. Compare the status of woman in "Man to Gods image" (No. 141). 35–36. Donne means that no matter how the body strains toward good, it does not rise to God's holy hill but stays earthbound (compare Psalms cxxi 1: "I will lift up mine eyes unto the hills, from

whence cometh my help"). The lightness which should create buoyancy to rise
presses man down, for it is but bodily pleasure and we are happy (filled) with
such uselessness. The state of light which is God, also intended, saddens by
its contrast with our vain and idle lives. 47–48. "And Jesus said unto him,
No man, having put his hand to the plough, and looking back, is fit for the kingdom of God" (Luke ix 62). 54–56. We could remove these bodies, which
are not lastingly impressed as are caskets and which are not in graves though
they are the caskets (and temples and palaces) of our souls; these bodies are
rather dignities which are born to us and they are "worthies" because in them
are borne our souls. But we could not remove foreign tyrants like love which is
engraved (acquired) rather than inborn. 57–58. Compare 2 Cor. v 1 (and
ff.): "For we knew that if our earthly house of this tabernacle were dissolved,
we have a building of God, an house not made with hands, eternal in the
heavens."

140. TO SR. EDWARD HERBERT, AT JULYERS: In 1610 he went with Lord
Chandos to Juliers (a duchy in the Lowlands), held by Archduke Leopold
and besieged by Protestant forces. Out of the siege came the beginning of the
Thirty Years' War. Perhaps written to answer Herbert's *Satire 1: The State
Progress of Ill*. 1. *beasts:* the following lines seem to owe something to the
Republic, IX, 588B-E, which presents an allegory of a many-headed monster
(desires) and a lion (temper). 15–17. Matt. viii 28–34 tells how Jesus expelled devils from two possessed, "And when they were come out, they went
into the herd of swine: and, behold, the whole herd of swine ran violently down
a steep place into the sea, and perished in the waters."

141. TO THE COUNTESSE OF HUNTINGDON: 58. Undoubtedly he met her at the
time of her mother's marriage to his employer, Sir Thomas Egerton, some fifteen
years earlier. From ll. 67, 70 it seems that the poem was written at least close to
Donne's ordination.

142. A LETTER TO THE LADY CAREY, AND MRS. ESSEX RICHE, FROM AMYENS:
Lettice, married to Sir George Carey of Cockington, Devon, and Essex, later
married to Sir Thomas Cheeke of Pirgo, Essex, were the daughters of Penelope
Devereux, wife of Robert, third Lord Rich. Their true father was Charles
Blount, Earl of Devonshire, to whom Lady Rich was married after her divorce
in 1605. The verse letter was sent from Amiens while Donne was there with
the Drurys in 1611.

144. DE LIBRO CUM MUTUARETUR, IMPRESSO . . . : Lines 3–4 have frequently
been separated from the remainder of the poem; but H. W. Garrod argues
for their inclusion in *RES*, XXI (1945), 38–42. The recipient of the book, who
is otherwise unknown, apparently was a medical doctor. 5. Compare Matt. vi
19–21. 17. *ancient of days:* derived from Dan. vii 9 ff.

146. ELEGIE ON THE L.C.: He was the father of George Carey, husband of
Lady Elizabeth, to whom Donne wrote "Here where by All, All Saints invoked
are." Lord Hunsdon's portrait was drawn by Nicholas Hilliard, who is mentioned in *The Storme* (No. 109), l. 4, written c. August 1597. Miss Gardner's
circular argument for rejection of Carey (in her edition of the love elegies) is
insubstantial.

149. ELEGIE ON THE LADY MARCKHAM: 49. "And the cherubims shall stretch forth their wings on high, covering the mercy seat with their wings, and their faces shall look one to another; toward the mercy seat shall the faces of the cherubims be. . . . And there I will meet with thee, and I will commune with thee from above the mercy seat, from between the two cherubims . . ." (Exod. xxv 20, 22).

152. ELEGIE ON THE UNTIMELY DEATH OF THE INCOMPARABLE PRINCE HENRY: According to William Drummond, Ben Jonson quoted Donne as saying that he wrote the epitaph to match Sir Edward Herbert in "obscurenesse" (*Conversations*, ed. R. F. Patterson, London, 1923, p. 12).

153. OBSEQUIES TO THE LORD HARRINGTON: 253. Thomas North's translation of Plutarch's "Life of Alexander" relates that "Alexander unwisely tooke the chaunce of his death, and commanded . . . al the battlements of the walls of cities should be overthrown, and hong up pore Glaucus his Phisitian upon a crosse, ... In the end, to passe over his mourning and sorrow, he went unto the warres, as unto a hunting of men, and there subdued the people of the Cossæians, whom he pluckt up by the rootes, and slue man, woman, and childe. And this was called the sacrifice of Hephæstions funeralls."

154. AN HYMNE TO THE SAINTS, AND TO MARQUESSE HAMYLTON: As High Commissioner to the Parliament, Hamilton opposed the French War policy of Buckingham in 1624; he may have been poisoned at the instigation of Buckingham.

155. THE FIRST ANNIVERSARIE: The poem dwells on the meaning of life and death, and as such has evoked much speculation of its "subject" and its relation to Donne's spiritual biography. Ben Jonson, William Drummond relates, believed "That Done's Anniversarie was profane and full of blasphemies: that he told Mr. Done, if it had been written of the Virgin Marie it had been something; to which he answered that he described the Idea of a Woman, and not as she was." To Marius Bewley (*KR*, XIV [1952], 619–46) Elizabeth is a symbol of the Church; to Marjorie Nicolson she is both Christ and Astraea; to Frank Manley (*SCN*, XVII [1959], 26) she represents "a woman who in her abstract femininity is the imagistic realization of the lost completeness of man's soul. She is wisdom, an eternal woman who in the mind and heart of man is the knowledge, awareness and presence of God." In the tradition of the *stilnovisti* Donne conceives that emotional love, love of woman's beauty, becomes evil in itself; one should love the beauty of God in woman, which is intellectual love. Elizabeth's death thus becomes the vehicle by which Donne is able to symbolize the death (or decay) of the world (a concern of seventeenth-century England explored by Victor Harris in *All Coherence Gone*) and all death within the world. Her death embraces the fall of man, the curse of death put upon nature, and the corruption which pervades the world. Paradoxically, woman has caused man's fall and has brought death into the world, but it is only through the idea of woman (Lady Virtue, Lady Justice, etc.) that man can approach God, that is, only through his fall and through his death. Evil comes from corruption, manifested in the chaos in the world; from sin, manifested in man's loss of memory, understanding, and will; and from the death of the idea of woman, manifested in Elizabeth's death. *The First Anniversarie*

anatomizes the world, as Patrick J. Mahony has remarked in an unpublished dissertation at New York University (1965), in order to stimulate the sin-deadened memory of man into realization of what the world is and of what goodness has departed from it.

Hardison (pp. 176–77) divides the poem into five sections: Introduction (ll. 1–60), Physical Decay (ll. 61–248), Qualitative Decay of the World (ll. 249–376), Spiritual Decay (377–434), and Conclusion (435–74). Seeing it as a "week" of threefold Ignatian meditations, Martz (*Poetry of Meditation,* pp. 219 ff.) distinguishes five sections, each divided into a Meditation, a Eulogy, and a Refrain and Moral, with an Introduction (1–90) and conclusion (435–74): I (91–190) discusses man as a poor trifling thing; II (191–246), the world as a cripple; III (247–338), the world in its ugliness; IV (339–76), the world as a ghost; V (377–434), the world as a dry cinder. The meditations ponder the decay of the world and the effects of original sin; the eulogies praise Elizabeth as a lost pattern of virtue; and the refrains and morals urge us to forget the crippled and dying world and to think of virtue. Martz argues that the poem indicates an intention to take ecclesiastical orders, being concerned with the problem of his election. "Meditation . . . comes to be regarded . . . as an exercise essential for the ordinary conduct of 'good life' and almost indispensable as preparation for the achievement of the highest mystical experiences" (Martz, p. 16).

136. D. C. Allen in *MLN,* LXI (1946), 257–60, refers the following lines to the interpretation of certain fossil evidence as indicating man as a giant.   148. Such as Wisdom's words in the Bible, "Blessed is the man that heareth me, watching daily at my gates, waiting at the posts of my doors. For whoso findeth me findeth life, and shall obtain favour of the Lord. But he that sinneth against me wrongeth his own soul: all they that hate me love death" (Prov. viii 34–36).   161. Compare Gen. i 26: "And God said, Let us make man in our image, after our likeness: and let them have dominion over the fish of the sea, and over the fowl of the air, and over the cattle, and over all the earth, and over every creeping thing that creepeth upon the earth."   204. Compare 2 Esdras v 51–55: "He replied to me, 'Ask a woman who bears children, and she will tell you. Say to her, "Why are those whom you have borne recently not like those whom you bore before, but smaller in stature?" And she herself will answer you, "Those born in the strength of youth are different from those born during the time of old age, when the womb is failing." Therefore you also should consider that you and your contemporaries are smaller in stature than those who were before you, and those who come after you will be smaller than you, as born of a creation which already is dying and passing the strength of youth.'"   450. Compare "We know that we have passed from death unto life, because we love the brethren. He that loveth not his brother abideth in death" (1 John iii 14). 462–64. See Deut. xxxi 19–30, xxxii 1–43, especially "For a fire is kindled in mine anger, and shall burn unto the lowest hell, and shall consume the earth with her increase, and set on fire the foundation of the mountains. . . . Rejoice, O ye nations, with his people: for he will avenge the blood of his servants, and will render vengeance to his adversaries, and will be merciful unto his land, and to his people" (xxxii 22, 43).

157. OF THE PROGRES OF THE SOULE . . . THE SECOND ANNIVERSARY: Whereas the *First Anniversary* is concerned with the *de contemptu mundi* theme and the mutability of the world, the *Second Anniversary* contemplates the glory of heaven and the distinction between the temporary and the permanent.

Hardison (pp. 176–77) divides the poem into nine sections: Introduction (1–44), Disestimation of the World (45–84), Death (85–156), The Soul in the Body and Its Release (157–250), Knowledge and Art of the Body (251–320), Society (321–82), Essential Joy (383–470), Accidental Joys (471–510), and Conclusion (511–28). Martz's meditative analysis (in *The Poetry of Meditation*) yields seven sections under the same divisions plus introduction and conclusion. Only the first two sections include a refrain and moral. As compared with the five sections of *The First Anniversarie*, which indicate finitude, the seven sections of its sequel seem to symbolize infinity and immortality. 23–24. On the first day "God divided the light from the darkness. And God called the light Day, and the darkness he called Night" (Gen. i 4–5); on the fourth day "God said, Let there be lights in the firmament of the heaven to divide the day from the night . . . the greater light to rule the day, and the lesser light to rule the night" (Gen. i 14, 16). 33–44: Christian overtones equate the "Immortal Mayd" with the Father; the Muse, who chastely begets a child, with the Virgin Mary; the poem with Christ leading mankind away from vice. Thus Mankind may continue to produce good men until Judgment Day when man will vanish from the earth, but will not die. 44. "O come, let us sing unto the Lord: let us make a joyful noise to the rock of our salvation" (Psalm xcv); in heaven, the song is that of the palmers, "Salvation to our God which sitteth upon the throne, and unto the Lamb" (Rev. vii 10). 45–48. "They shall hunger no more, neither thirst any more; neither shall the sun light on them, nor any heat. For the Lamb which is in the midst of the throne shall feed them, and shall lead them unto living fountains of waters: and God shall wipe away all tears from their eyes" (Rev. vii 16–17).

158. METEMPSYCHOSIS: How many songs Donne intended is not known. William Drummond reported that Ben Jonson saw this soul as that of Cain and of all heretics, to be left at last in the body of Calvin. Others have seen it finally residing in Queen Elizabeth because of her treatment of the Earl of Essex in February 1601. But Donne wrote of the "sinner putrified in his owne earth, resolv'd in his owne dung, especially that hath passed many transformations, from shape to shape, from sin to sin, (he hath beene a Salamander and lived in the fire, in the fire successively, in the fire of lust in his youth, and in his age, in the fire of Ambition; and then he hath beene a Serpent, a Fish, and lived in the waters, in the water successively, in the troubled water of sedition in his youth, and in his age in the cold waters of indevotion) . . ." (*Sermons,* IV, No. 13, p. 327). Indeed the concept of physical transformation is frequent in the sermons.

We proceed up the chain of being to mankind. The soul which Donne describes is that in thinking but depraved man: the soul has freedom of will, creates change, is practical and inventive like Cain's race, and intellectual like Seth's; but it is impious, heretical, and sinful too. Donne's thesis is that the things of life are ambivalent of good and evil; compare stanza III. 21. Compare "Thou almost makest me waver in my faith, To hold opinion with Pythagoras, That souls of animals infuse themselves Into the trunks of men" (*Merchant of Venice,* IV, i, 130–33). 74. Referring to God's eternity and omnipresence, but also to 1 Cor. xv 28: "And when all things shall be subdued unto him, then shall the Son also himself be subject unto him that put all things under him, that God may be all in all."

The Complete Poetry of John Donne

159. TO THE LADY MAGDALEN HERBERT, OF ST. MARY MAGDALEN: A letter said to enclose holy hymns and sonnets was dated July 11, 1607 (July 22, N.S.), St. Mary Magdalen's Day, by Walton. The present sonnet was written as an introduction to them (see l. 14). See also "Mad paper stay, and grudge not here to burne" (No. 133).

160. LA CORONA: The sequence represents a kind of rosary of seven decades, each preceded by a kind of Pater Noster and followed by a kind of Gloria Patri. The crown represents both the crown of thorns borne by Christ, symbolizing the punishment and atonement which all men must suffer, and the crown of reward given to God's true servants. Titles attached to the last six sonnets are probably not Donne's.

162. HOLY SONNET: No. II in Grierson, No. 1 in Gardner.

163. HOLY SONNET: No. IV in Grierson, No. 2 in Gardner.

164. HOLY SONNET: No. VI in Grierson, No. 3 in Gardner.

165. HOLY SONNET: No. VII in Grierson, No. 4 in Gardner.

166. HOLY SONNET: No. IX in Grierson, No. 5 in Gardner.   13. Compare Psalms xxv 7: "Remember not the sins of my youth, nor my transgressions: according to thy mercy remember thou me for thy goodness' sake, O Lord."

167. HOLY SONNET: No. X in Grierson, No. 6 in Gardner.

168. HOLY SONNET: No. XI in Grierson, No. 7 in Gardner.

169. HOLY SONNET: No. XII in Grierson, No. 8 in Gardner.

170. HOLY SONNET: No. XIII in Grierson, No. 9 in Gardner.

171. HOLY SONNNET: No. XIV in Grierson, No. 10 in Gardner. The first quatrain pleads for the heart to be freed of sin; the second, for the mind; the sestet involves both of the preceding by pleading for the body to be freed. Since Christ is the Bridegroom (see *Holy Sonnet* [No. 179]), the sonnet also presents sexual images symbolizing the author as His consort. The poet asks to be "overthrown" for purposes of ravishment, l. 4 containing references to passionate and productive intercourse. A kind of phoenix symbol also lies in this line with its wish for death and rebirth. The last four lines depict the hoped-for ravishment.
1–4. The Father, who is power, now only knocks (l. 2) but is asked to "breake" (l. 4); the Holy Spirit, who is the infusion of love, now only breathes (l. 2) but is asked to "blowe" (l. 4); the Son, who is light and synonymous with the sun, now only shines (l. 2) but is asked to "burn" (l. 4). The entire Trinity thus only seeks to mend the author's sinfulness by these only partially destructive forces; it is asked to make him new by complete destruction. Thus he rises (to heaven) by being overthrown and stands upright (firm in Faith) by the bending of God's force.

172. HOLY SONNET: No. XV in Grierson, No. 11 in Gardner.

173. HOLY SONNET: No. XVI in Grierson, No. 12 in Gardner.

174. HOLY SONNET: No. I in Grierson, No. 1 of second group in Gardner.

175. HOLY SONNET: No. V in Grierson, No. 2 of second group in Gardner.

176. HOLY SONNET: No. III in Grierson, No. 3 of second group in Gardner.

177. HOLY SONNET: No. VIII in Grierson, No. 4 of second group in Gardner.

178. HOLY SONNET: No. XVII in Grierson, No. 1 of third group in Gardner.

179. HOLY SONNET: No. XVIII in Grierson, No. 2 of third group in Gardner.

180. HOLY SONNET: No. XIX in Grierson, No. 3 of third group in Gardner.

181. THE CROSSE: 2. Christ's death absolved of original sin those who had died before; baptism is a sacrament continuing such absolution for the living. Puritans were, however, averse to using the sign of the cross in baptism. 26. They are physic (as ll. 29–30 indicate) because such "crosses to bear" extract sin from one's polluted being as do drugs opposite in quality to one's excessive humour disease (Galen) or as do purgative remedies (Paracelsus).

184. A LITANIE: 57. Perhaps here Donne is remembering the covenant of the rainbow set in a cloud made with Noah (Gen. ix 12–16) and the burning bush in which Moses did not see the Lord (Exod. iii 2–6). Not only does man not see God in the peaceful heavens; he does not see Him in His lightning and thunderbolts.

185. GOODFRIDAY, 1613. RIDING WESTWARD: 17. Compare *XXVI Sermons*, iv, 168 (Potter and Simpson, III, Sermon 9, p. 210). Delivered February 16, 1621, the sermon shows that Donne refers to those of faith. Perhaps also in his mind was Luke ii 29–30: "Lord, now lettest thou thy servant depart in peace, according to thy word: For mine eyes have seen thy salvation"; see *LXXX Sermons*, iv (Potter and Simpson, VII, Sermon 11), preached on December 25, 1626.

186. TO MR. GEORGE HERBERT, WITH ONE OF MY SEALS, . . . Miss Gardner (*Divine Poems*, pp. 141–42) suggests that Walton, from whom the full title comes, thought that the poem was sent with a gift of the seal c. 1630–31, and thus erroneously added "one of." The translator of the accompanying loose and inaccurate version is unknown.

191. UPON THE TRANSLATION OF THE PSALMES BY SIR PHILIP SYDNEY AND . . . HIS SISTER: Unknown to Donne, Sidney's share ended with Psalm xliii. The poem seems to be dated after the Countess' death (see l. 53). 29–30. Donne is making a plea for acceptance of these new ("reformed" and "re-formed," l. 41) translations of the psalms. There was much discussion at this time of the need for literarily worthy renditions in the vernacular. 38. *abroad:* perhaps with reference to French versions by Clément Marot.

192. HYMNE TO GOD MY GOD, IN MY SICKNESSE: There are similarities of images
to *LXXX Sermons*, xxiv (Potter and Simpson, VIII, Sermon 16), written for
Easter 1629, and lv (Potter and Simpson, VI, Sermon 1), now dated April–
June 1623.   3. "and I heard the voice of harpers harping with their harps: And
they sung as it were a new song before the throne, and before the four beasts,
and the elders: and no man could learn that song but the hundred and forty
and four thousand, which were redeemed from the earth" (Rev. xiv 2–3).   14.
See also *LXXX Sermons*, lv, 558 (Potter and Simpson, VI, Sermon 1, p. 59):
"In a flat Map, there goes no more, to make West East, though they be distant
in an extremity, but to paste that flat Map upon a round body, and then West
and East are all one."

CHRONOLOGICAL SCHEDULE OF THE POEMS

Detailed notes on the dates of epigrams, elegies, songs and sonnets, and satires follow this schedule. Most poems are here identified by number and abbreviated titles or first lines.

No.	Poem	Date	Evidence
	PRIOR TO LINCOLN'S INN		
	Epigrams[1]	1587?–1602?	
86	A burnt ship	1587?–1591?, 1596?	Abroad in armed conflict ?
87	Fall of a wall	1589?–1591?	Noted by George Buc in 1614 in expedition against Spain and Portugal in 1589; Donne probably in army during this period.
88	A lame begger	1590?–1591?, 1596?	Perhaps after acquaintance with Spain.
95	The Lier	1590?–1591?, 1596?	Perhaps after acquaintance with Spain.
	AT LINCOLN'S INN		
115	To Mr. T.W.: "Hast thee harsh verse"	c. 1593?	Reference to plague.
116	To Mr. T.W.: "Pregnant again"	1593?	Conjectural.
117	To Mr. T.W.: "At once, from hence"	1593?	Conjectural.
118	To Mr. R.W.: "Zealously my Muse"	1593?	Conjectural.
119	To Mr. R.W.: "Muse not that by"	1593?	Conjectural.
121	To Mr. E.G.	summer 1593	Closing of theaters, before winter.
123	To Mr. R.W.: "Kindly'I envy thy"	c. mid-1593	Reference to grief over brother's death ?
124	To Mr. S.B.	c. mid-1593	S.B.'s matriculation at Trinity, Harvey-Nashe controversy.
125	To Mr. I.L.: "Of that short Roll"	before end of 1594; autumn 1593?	Date of Wotton's return to England, reference to harvest.
126	To Mr. B.B.	c. May 1594	B.B.'s admission to Lincoln's Inn.

127	To Mr. I.L.: "Blest are your"	August ? 1594	Reference to great rain and summer.
96	Mercurius Gallo-Belgicus	1594 (or after)	Date of first issue.
106	Epithalamion at Lincolnes Inne	June 1595?	For midsummer revels during attendance at Lincoln's Inn.
	Elegies²	1593?–1596?	
	Songs and Sonnets³	1593?–1601?	

BEFORE EMPLOYMENT BY EGERTON

146	Elegy on the L. C.	1596?	Date of Carey's death ?
91	Cales and Guyana	summer 1596	Date of Cadiz Expedition.
92	Sir John Wingefield	summer 1596	Date of Wingfield's death.
109	The Storme	August ? 1597	During Islands expedition.
122	To Mr. R.W.: "If, as mine is"	August ? 1597	During Islands expedition; after *Storme* and apparently before *Calme*.
110	The Calme	August ? 1597	During Island expedition; after *Storme*.

DURING EMPLOYMENT BY EGERTON

24	Sapho to Philænis	1597?–1598?	Conjectural.
1	Satyre I⁴	1597?–1598?	After 1594, reference to Banks' elephant and ape; before *Skialetheia* (1598).
2	Satyre II	1597?–1598?	After 1594 if reference to author of *Zepheria;* after 1597 if Sclavonian (l. 59) refers to contemporary event of July 23, 1597. Before November 1598, not yet Elizabeth's quadragesimus (l. 50).
3	Satyre III	1597?–1598?	See note 4.
112	To Sr. Henry Wotton: "Sir, more then"	before April 1598	Allusion in Thomas Bastard's *Chrestoleros,* entered April 3, 1598.
111	To Sr. Henry Wootton: "Here's no more newes"	July 20, 1598	Date given in various mss.
4	Satyre IV	1598?	After March 1597 (fall of Amiens, l. 114), after *Mercurius Gallo-Belgicus* began (1594, l. 112), probably after Reynolds became president of Corpus Christi (1598, l. 56).
5	Satyre V	1598?	When with Egerton (ll. 31–33).
114	To Mr. T.W.: "All haile"	before 1599	Allusion in John Weever's *Epigrammes in the Oldest Cut and Newest Fashion* (1599); stanzaic form suggests later than others to T.W.

128	H.W.: "Went you to conquer"	1599	When Wotton was in Ireland with Essex.
62	The Extasie	1598?–1601?	Sincere treatment of love (for
63	The undertaking		Anne More?); after 1599 if reference to Pancirollus' *Rerum memorabilium* in No. 63 ?
158	Metempsychosis	August 1601	Date given.
30	Lecture upon the Shadow	c. end of 1601?	Reference to difficulties at time of marriage ?

BETWEEN EMPLOYMENT BY EGERTON AND BY DRURY

113	To Mr. Rowland Woodward: "Like one who'in"	c. 1601–1604?	In retirement, writing little verse, much poetry written in the past; but appearance in mss suggests earlier date.
120	To Mr. C.B.	c. Jan.–Feb. 1602?	Allusion to imprisonment ?; but appearance in mss suggests earlier date.
44	A Feaver	after early 1602?	Reference to wife ?
103	Raderus	1602 (or later)	Date of edition.
129	To Sir H.W.	July 1604	Date Wotton became ambassador to Venice.
130	To Sr. Henry Goodyere	1605–1608	Living at Mitcham.
104	Ad Autorem (Scaliger)	1605?–1609?	Conjectural; book published in 1583.
105	Ad Autorem (Covell)	1605?–1609?	Conjectural; book published in 1603.
43	The Legacie	1605–1610?	Reference to stays in London or at Twickenham ?
49	A Valediction of my name	1605–1611?	Reference to stays in London or at Twickenham, or trip abroad ?
58	A Valediction of weeping	1605–1611?	Reference to stays in London or at Twickenham, or trip abroad ?
131	To Countesse of Huntingdon: "That unripe side"	1605?–1611?	Conjectural; countess married in 1603; perhaps before Donne's ordination.
132	Amicissimo (Jonson)	1607	Date of edition of *Volpone*.
160	La Corona	July 1607	Identification as hymns sent to Mrs. Herbert.
159	To the Lady M.H.	July 1607	On basis of dated letter.
181	The Crosse	1607?–1609?	Conjectural.
133	To Mrs. M.H.	c. 1608	Shortly before M.H.'s marriage to Danvers.
183	The Annuntiation and Passion	March 1608	Date of holy days.
135	A Letter by Sr. H.G. and J.D.	spring, 1608?–1610?	Season from internal evidence, years conjectural.

134	To Countesse of Bedford: "Reason is our Soules"	1608?	Conjectural on basis of probable start of association with Lady Bedford.
147	Epitaph on Himselfe	1608?	Perhaps during serious illness ?; addressed to Lady Bedford.
184	A Litanie	autumn 1608?	Conjectural.
137	To Countesse of Bedford: "You have refin'd"	1608–1609?	Conjectural.
51	Twicknam garden	1608–1610?	Association with Lady Bedford.
162–67	Holy Sonnets	Feb.–August 1609	Probably after Sackville became Earl of Dorset and before death of Mrs. Boulstred.
161	To Earl of Dorset	after Feb. 1609	Date Dorset assumed title.
136	To Countesse of Bedford: "Honour is so sublime"	1609?–1610?	Conjectural.
172–73	Holy Sonnets	1609?	Later than Nos. 162–67, on basis of mss.
168–71	Holy Sonnets	1609?	Later than Nos. 172–73, on basis of mss.
149	Elegie on Lady Marckham	May 1609	Date of Lady Markham's death.
148	Elegie to Lady Bedford	May 1609?	Date of Lady Markham's death ?
150	Elegie on Mris. Boulstred	August 1609	Date of Mrs. Boulstred's death.
151	Elegie: Death	August 1609?	Date of Mrs. Boulstred's death ?
138	To Countesse of Bedford: "T'have written then"	autumn 1609?	Reference to new stars, Virginia, and perhaps deaths of Lady Markham and Mrs. Boulstred.
182	Resurrection, imperfect	Easter, 1609?–1611?	Years conjectural.
174–77	Holy Sonnets	1609–1611?	Conjectural, later than 168–71.
139	To Countesse of Bedford. New-yeares	January 1610?	Conjectural, preceding decision to join Drurys (or others).
140	To Sir Edward Herbert	1610	When E.H. was at Juliers with Lord Chandos.

EMPLOYMENT BY DRURY AND PERIOD PRECEDING ORDINATION

156	A Funerall Elegie	Dec. 1610	Date of Elizabeth Drury's death.
155	The First Anniversarie	early 1611	See l. 39; apparently a few months after Elizabeth's death.
6	Upon Coryats Crudities	1611	Date of edition.
7	In eundem Macaronicon	1611	Date of edition.
69	The Primrose	after 1610?–1613?	Galileo's discovery of Milky Way (1610); terminal date conjectural.

52	Valediction of the booke	July 1611?	Reference to going abroad with Drurys, l. 55 ?
42	Song: "Sweetest love"	July 1611	Connected with trip with Drurys.
31	A Valediction forbidding mourning	July 1611	Written when Donne went abroad with Drurys, according to Walton.
142	Letter to Lady Carey, Mrs. Riche	late 1611	At Amiens with Drurys.
157	The Second Anniversary	Dec. 1611	See ll. 3–6, 511–18 (date of first anniversary and while in France).
143	To Countesse of Bedford	April 1612	Easter in France with Drurys.
144	De libro cum . . .	1612?	When in Paris with Drurys ?
152	Elegie on Prince Henry	Nov. 1612	Date of Prince's death.
107	Epithalamion on Lady Eliz.	Feb. 1613	Date of Elizabeth's marriage.
185	Goodfriday	April 1613	Year date given.
108	Ecclogue . . . Earle of Sommerset	Dec. 1613	Date of Somerset's marriage.
145	To Countesse of Salisbury	August 1614	Date given.
153	Obsequies . . . Lord Harrington	August ? 1614	Harington died Feb. 27, 1614; ll. 257–58 remark delay in writing; l. 258 says Donne will not poetize further; letter to Goodyere (Dec. 20) refers to not writing after this poem; and No. 145 dated in August.

AFTER ORDINATION

141	To Countesse of Huntingdon: "Man to Gods image"	c. 1615?	Reference to ordination, ll. 67, 70 ?
186	To Mr. George Herbert	c. Jan. 1615	Shortly after ordination ?
179–80	Holy Sonnets	after Jan. 1615	After ordination.
72	The Dissolution	c. August 1617?	Date of wife's death ?
178	Holy Sonnet	after August 1617	Date of wife's death.
82	A nocturnall	Dec. 1617	Date of St. Lucy's Day, after wife's death.
187	Lamentations	c. 1617–1618?	Position relative to other poems in mss ?

188	Vota Amico facta	c. 1618?	Date of English edition; however, C. E. Merrill has suggested this as translation mentioned in letter LXXIII, August 10 [1608–9]; see n. in Merrill's edition of *Letters* (London, 1910), p. 304.
189	To Mr. Tilman	December 1618?	Date of Tilman's taking orders.
190	A Hymne to Christ	May 1619	Date of trip with Doncaster.
191	Upon translation of Psalmes	after Sept. 25, 1621	Date of death of Countess of Pembroke.
193	A Hymne to God the Father	c. Dec. 1623	Date of serious illness.
192	Hymne to God my God	c. Dec. 1623 (or March 1631)	Date of serious illness; Walton dated before his death.
154	An hymne to the Saints	March 1625	Date of Hamilton's death.
194	Epigraph	c. March 16, 1631	Shortly before death ?

NOTES TO THE CHRONOLOGICAL SCHEDULE

[1] Dating of the epigrams is particularly uncertain. Some may have been written when Donne was in the army, 1587?–1591?; some during his days at Lincoln's Inn, 1593–95; some during the Cadiz expedition, 1596; some around the time of the writing of the satires, 1597?–1598?. Those perhaps allowing a general early date of 1587?–1595? are printed as Nos. 83–85, 89–90, 93–94, 97–102; those which seem possible of more specific assignment are listed separately. Poems like the former may fall into other additional periods of Donne's life as here divided.

[2] The elegies (Nos. 8–23) were probably written about the same general time and before 1601. Nos. 14, 18, and 19 seem to lie before 1598 because of their apparent use in *Skialetheia*. No. 8 dates before 1598 or 1597 (depending upon what one takes to have been intended as Donne's birth date) according to Jonson's remarks to Drummond. Nos. 18 and 19 seem to make biographical reference to Donne's going abroad as he did in 1596 and 1597 (possible trips before 1592 seem too early for the references). In all, the elegies seem to date from about 1592 to 1598. I should think that they were written during his days at Lincoln's Inn as a part of the schoolboy rivalry for virtuosity in verse and before his employ by Egerton: 1593?–1596? with outside dates of 1592? and 1598?.

Nos. 50, 35, and 81 (Grierson's elegies IX and X, and Bennett's XXI) have been grouped with the Songs and Sonets because of their dissimilarity to the elegies, their stanzaic structure, and, in the latter two, their alternate rhyme. Chambers suggested that No. 81 was an early working of what came to be Nos. 12 and 13.

[3] Most of the songs and sonnets cannot be dated, but generally they are placed

between 1593 and 1601. Perhaps the period of 1593–95 (when Donne was at Lincoln's Inn) is most appropriate for the witty treatments of love, particularly that which is inconstant: Nos. 25–29, 32–41, 45–48, 50, 53–57, 59–68, 70–71, 73–81. However, these might have been written later, from 1596–98, the period of the trips abroad and his early employment by Egerton when the satires seem to have been composed. It has been suggested that No. 36 (*The Sunne Rising*) dates after 1603 because of line 7, which mentions "the King." The context of the line, however, indicates that Donne means "king" generically rather than with any temporal allusion, and so I reject it as evidence of date. (Note for comparison Donne's use of "the Prince" in 1601; *Metempsychosis*, No. 158, l. 137.) It has been suggested also that No. 48 (*The Anniversarie*) dates after 1603 because of line 1, which mentions "Kings and their favorites." But the whole poem and the modifier "All" obviate any temporal meaning. No. 70 has been associated with Magdalen Herbert because of the appearance of her first name in the poem, but the similar reference in No. 154 shows the invalidity of this argument. Walton's connecting No. 50 with Mrs. Herbert has suggested 1607–9 as its date, but there seems no reason to accept such a connection. In contrast with love elegies about younger mistresses, No. 50 examines love for an older woman, but it need not be autobiographical. The greater part of the poem seems inappropriate for Mrs. Herbert. Perhaps the period of 1598–1601 (when Donne was in Egerton's employ and surreptitiously wooing Anne More) is most likely for the more sincere treatments of love: Nos. 62, 63. But biographical interpretation in terms of a dichotomized Donne is most dangerous. Other songs and sonnets seem to be dated by allusions or meaning, and are treated separately. Miss Gardner's attempt (in her recent edition, pp. lvii–lxii) to separate these lyrics into two periods—one before 1598 and one from 1607 to 1614–is most unconvincing, except for a few late pieces as here indicated.

[4] The satires seem to have been written in the order given and around the same time. They would less likely have been composed in 1596–97 when Donne was frequently away from London on expeditions. The satire on the Court parallels remarks in the verse letter to Henry Wotton ("Here's no more newes," No. 111), dated July 20, 1598. Thus they probably were written during his early years of secretaryship for Egerton: 1597?–1598?.

TEXTUAL NOTES

Printed versions and manuscripts in which each poem appears in full or abbreviated form are indicated by dates or short titles; sources are given in the preceding list. Only the few contemporary examples of Donne's direct poetical influence cited by W. Milgate in "Early References" are omitted. The now nonexistent Burley MS, the Monckton-Milnes MS, and a miscellany owned by Mr. John Sparrow of All Souls College, Oxford, are listed from other sources as I have not examined them myself.

The Burley MS, reported by Grierson in 1912, contained the unique No. 128 and thirty-five other poems perhaps by Donne, according to a note in the transcription owned by the Clarendon Press: nineteen epigrams (at least one being doubtful), two epistles, five elegies, two sonnets, and eight shorter poems. However, this does not seem to include at least one satire (No. 4), which is referred to in the transcription, and the list may include the eleven ascribed poems which Grierson printed in the apocrypha. He cites the Burley MS only for Nos. 93, 95, 99, 128, 129, in the canon; a note in the transcription indicates that No. 15 was also included.

The Monckton-Milnes MS, also reported by Grierson in 1912, was once owned by the Marquis of Crewe; it is a miscellaneous collection of poems with Donne's the most numerous. Mr. Sparrow's volume contains copies of three poems according to Miss Gardner's citations; she prints only one verbal variant. Lansdowne MS 777 (BM), Additional MS 11811 (BM), and Rawlinson Poetical MS 61 (Bod), listed by Grierson, contain no poems accepted into the Donne canon; nor does MS HM 116 (Huntington), which has sometimes been cited. The manuscript currently owned by the Long Island Historical Society (Samuel Bowne Duryea catalogue, p. 23) has only the Paradoxes and Problems, no authentic poems. The single reference in Grierson to "R212" for *Elegie XI*, line 6, is to Rawlinson Poetical MS 212; see also Grierson, II, 271–72. The citation of S as including No. 106 is in error. Christian Huygens translated a few poems into Dutch in 1621 and later; these are noted.

All differences from the copy text are noted, and selected verbal variants from selected manuscripts are given. The basis of selection has been an important manuscript from Group I (C57), from Group II (TCD), from Group III (Dob), plus O'F and W, and whatever others seem sig-

nificant because of differences in readings within groups or because of
the paucity of texts for a particular poem. The citation of C57, TCD,
and Dob usually indicates the reading of Group I, II, or III, respectively.
When a significant variant appears within a group, it is recorded also.
The term "and others" means that the reading appears in manuscripts
associated with Group III; this is particularly important when the reading
does not appear in Dob. Variants reported are those which seem to
represent a distinctly alternate reading rather than a scribal error. Variants cited, therefore, represent appearance in more than one significant
manuscript or a wide selection of minor manuscripts. Originally all variants in all texts were prepared for listing, but the overwhelming numbers
—so many of them unimportant and scribal errors—necessitated revision
of this plan. Such older printing practices as "v" for "u," "i" for "j," long
"s," and the ampersand are generally and silently modernized.

An index following records differences from Miss Gardner's texts of
the divine poems, elegies, and songs and sonnets, with reason for such
difference where significant.

TEXTS

PRINTED SOURCES

1633–1669, primary collection; §2, primary separate poems; §3, second-
ary separate poems; §4, musical versions.

1. *Collected Poems*

1633   *Poems,* first edition, 1633 (Univ. of London).
1635   *Poems,* second edition, 1635 (Rutgers).
1639   *Poems,* third edition, 1639 (Yale).
1649   *Poems,* fourth edition, 1649 (Yale).
1650   *Poems,* reissue of fourth edition, augmented, or fifth edition, 1650
            (Yale).
1654   *Poems,* reissue of 1650, but printed as sixth edition, 1654 (Yale).
1669   *Poems,* fifth or sixth edition, but printed as seventh edition, 1669
            (Rutgers).

2. *Separate Poems*

An Anatomie of the World, first edition, 1611 (Huntington).
Anniversaries, second edition of *Anatomie* and *Funerall Elegie,* first edi-
tion of *Progress,* 1612 (Yale).
Anniversaries, third and second editions, respectively, 1621 (NYPL).
Anniversaries, fourth and third editions, respectively, 1625 (Yale).

Deaths Duell, 1632, "Epigraph," frontispiece (Keynes, *Bibliography*).

Ben Jonson, *Volpone,* 1607, "Amicissimo, et meritissimo," f. A$_1$a (Huntington).

Ben Jonson, *Works,* 1616, "Amicissimo, et meritissimo," f. G$_6$a (Huntington).

Ben Jonson, *Under–wood,* 1640, "Elegy XV," pp. 204–6 (NYPL).

Coryat's Crudities, 1611, "Upon Mr. Thomas Coryats Crudities," ff. E$_2$b–E$_3$b; "In eundem Macaronicon," f. E$_4$a (Huntington).

Joshua Sylvester, *Lachrymæ Lachrymarum,* 1613, "Elegie on the Death of Prince Henry," ff. E$_1$a–E$_2$b (BM); cat: G 11296(2).

Isaac Walton, *Life of John Donne,* in *LXXX Sermons,* 1640, "Hymn to God the Father," f. B$_4$a; *Life of George Herbert,* 1670, "Elegy IX," p. 15, and "To the Lady Magdalen Herbert," p. 18; *The Life of John Donne,* second edition, 1658, "To George Herbert," pp. 83–84; *Lives of John Donne, . . . Wotton, . . . Hooker, . . . Herbert,* 1670, "To George Herbert," pp. 58–59; "Hymn to God my God," p. 60; "To H. W. at his going to Venice," pp. 30–31 (all NYPL); *Lives of John Donne, . . . Herbert,* 1675, "Valediction forbidding mourning," pp. 33–34 (Yale).

3. *Corroborative Texts*

Joseph Wybarne, *The New Age of Old Names,* 1609, "Satire IV," ll. 18–23, p. 113 (Huntington).

Helpe to Memory and Discourse, 1630, "The Lovers complaint written by a gentleman of Quality" ("The Broken Heart"), C$_2$, pp. 45–46; "Poem" ("Song: Goe and catch"), G$_3$a, p. 143 (Harvard).

[John Gough], *The Academy of Complements Wherein Ladies . . . ,* 1640, "Breake of day," p. 159 (Huntington).

Isaac Walton, *The Compleat Angler,* 1653, "The Baite," pp. 184–86 (Bod).

[John Cotgrave], *Wits Interpreter,* 1655, "Breake of Day" (two copies), pp. 14, 25–26 (Folger).

Parnassus Biceps, 1656, two elegies, pp. 86–88, 118–19 (Yale).

Wit and Drollery, 1661, "Elegy: Loves Progress," pp. 237–40 (Bod).

Loyal Garland, 1686, "A Love Song" ("Breake of day"), in Percy Society Reprints, *Early English Poetry, Ballads,* 1849, Vol. 29, Song XXXIV, p. 37 (NYPL).

F. G. Waldron, *The Shakespearean Miscellany,* 1802, "Elegy XX," pp. 1–2 (Yale).

4. *Musical Versions*

Alfonso Ferrabosco, *Ayres,* 1609, "The Expiration," VII, f. C$_2$b (Huntington).

William Corkine, *Second Booke of Ayres*, 1612, "Breake of day," IIII,
    f. B$_1$b, with music, and "The Baite," VIII, f. C$_1$b, music only (Hun-
    tington).

Pelham Humfrey (Henry Playford, compiler), *Harmonica Sacra*, 1688,
    pp. 51–52, "Hymne to God the Father" (Harvard).

MANUSCRIPT SOURCES

1–34, primary collections; 35–42, primary short groups or individual
poems; 43–60, corroborative collections; 61–151, other corroborative
texts; 152–59, musical versions. Primary groups: *I*, 1–5; *II*, 6–10; *III*,
11–26 (11–14, 15, 16, 17–19, 20–21, 22–24, 25, 26); and Miscellanies,
27–34.

1. *Primary Collections*

    Group I

1. Harleian MS 4955, ff. 88a–167b (BM); Grierson, Gardner: H49.
2. MS Eng. Poet. e.99, Dowden MS (Bod); Grierson, Gardner: D.
3. MS 49 B 43 (St. Paul's Cathedral); Gardner: SP.
4. Leconfield MS, or Percy MS (Geoffrey Keynes); Grierson, Gard-
    ner: Lec.
5. Additional MS 5778(c), ff. 5b–87a (Cambridge); Gardner: C57.
    (Included here are a few poems in a brief miscellany added to
    the Group I collection; this miscellany and its poems are not
    mentioned by Miss Gardner.)

    Group II

6. MS G.21, first collection (Trinity College, Dublin); Grierson, Gard-
    ner: TCD.
7. Eng. MS 966.3, Norton MS 4503 (Harvard); Grierson, Gardner: N.
8. MS R 3.12 (Trinity College, Cambridge); Grierson, Gardner: TCC.
9. Additional MS 18647 (BM); Grierson, Gardner: A18.
10. Dolaucothi MS (National Library of Wales); Gardner: DC.

    Group III

11. Eng. MS 966.4, Norton MS 4506, Dobell MS (Harvard); Gardner:
    Dob.
12. Stowe MS 961 (BM); Grierson, Gardner: S96.
13. Narcissus Luttrell MS (Geoffrey Keynes); Gardner: Lut.
14. Eng. MS 966.5, Norton MS 4504, O'Flaherty MS (Harvard);
    Grierson, Gardner: O'F.

    MSS Associated with Group III

15. MS HM 198, Book I: pp. 34–44, 64–95, 138, 165–73; Book II:
    pp. 1–5, 12–34, 46–51, 109–26; referred to by Grierson as
    Haslewood-Kingsborough MS (Huntington); Grierson: H-K (in
    notes); Gardner: HK 1, HK 2, HK 2*.

16. Eng. MS 966.7, Norton MS 4620 (Harvard); Gardner: Hd.
17. Eng. MS 966.1, Norton MS 4502, Carnaby MS (Harvard); Grierson, Gardner: Cy.
18. MS of Donne's Poems (James H. Osborn); Gardner: O.
19. MS Eng. Poet. f.9, Phillipps MS (Bod); Grierson, Gardner: P.
20. John Cave MS (Arents Collection, NYPL); Grierson, Gardner: JC.
21. MS D25, F17, ff. 3a–54b, Dyce Collection (Victoria and Albert Museum); Gardner: D17.
22. MS EL 6893, Bridgewater MS (Huntington); Grierson, Gardner: B.
23. Eng. MS 966.6, Norton MS 4500, Stephens MS (Harvard); Grierson, Gardner: S.
24. Raphael King MS (James H. Osborn); Gardner: K.
25. Westmoreland MS (Berg Collection, NYPL); Grierson, Gardner: W.
26. Hawthornden MS XV (Society of Antiquaries of Scotland), on permanent loan to the National Library of Scotland, cat. MS 2067, ff. 10b–37a; Grierson, Gardner: HN.

Miscellanies Related to the Above

27. Lansdowne MS 740, ff. 58a–72a, 82a–86b, 95a–100a, 106a–127a (BM); Grierson, Gardner: L74. (Placed as adjunct to Group II by Miss Gardner.)
28. Harleian MS 4064, ff. 235b–298a (BM); Grierson, Gardner: H40, H40*. (Main collection placed as adjunct to Group I by Miss Gardner.)
29. Stowe 962, ff. 48a–49a, 55b–56b, 65, 80a–106a, 109a–137b, 155a–164a, 167b–168a, 186b–191a, 208a–220b (BM); Gardner: S962.
30. Additional MS 25707, ff. 5b–39a, 48a–57b, 60a–65a (BM); Grierson, Gardner: A25.
31. MS III.493, Laing MS, ff. 88a–109a (Edinburgh Univ.); Gardner: La.
32. MS MA 1057, Holgate MS, pp. 4–5, 61–68, 86–87, 97–104, 125–27, 140 (Morgan); Gardner: Hol.
33. MS G.2.21, second collection, pp. 310–508 *passim* (Trinity College, Dublin); Grierson, Gardner: TCD (II).
34. Rawlinson Poet. MS 117, ff. 26a–28a, 32b, 55a, 82a, 94a–93b (reverse) (Bod); Gardner: RP117(2).

2. Primary Short Groups or Individual Poems

35. Harleian MS 5110, ff. 95–101 (BM); Grierson: H51.
36. MS D25, F16, Dyce Collection (Victoria and Albert Museum).
37. MS 216, separate MS gathering (Queen's College, Oxford); Grierson, Gardner: Q.

38. MS V.a.241, Gosse MS, "Metempsychosis" (Folger); Grierson: G.
39. Harleian MS 3998, "Metempsychosis," ff. 154a–167a (BM); Grierson: H.
40. Burley MS; destroyed; statistics from Grierson and transcription of part of MS, containing one poem on p. 1, owned by the Delegates of the Clarendon Press (Bod); Grierson: Bur.
41. William Covell, *Defence of the five books of Ecclesiastical Policie,* 1603, "Ad Autorem," holograph, opposite title leaf (Harvard).
42. Joseph Scaliger, *A New Work Concerning the Correction of Chronology,* 1583, "Ad Autorem," holograph, opposite title leaf (Geoffrey Keynes; facsimile in Keynes, *Bibliography*).

3. Corroborative Collections

43. MS Ee.4.14, pp. 61–78 (Cambridge).
44. Additional MS 29, ff. 1a–19a, 38b–40b (reverse), Baumgartner Collection (Cambridge); Grierson: C.
45. MS I.3.16, second MS gathering, ff. 3a–6b (Emmanuel College, Cambridge).
46. MS CCC.E.327, Corpus Christi College MS, ff. 2a–8a, 17a, 21b–30a (Bod); Gardner: CCC.
47. MS Eng. Poet. e.14, ff. 29b–45b, 60b–61a (Bod).
48. Rawlinson Poet. MS 31, ff. 10b–12b, 22a–23b, 37a–47a (Bod); Grierson: RP31.
49. Rawlinson Poet. MS 160, ff. 29b–30b, 51a, 103b, 104b, 113a, 163b, 171–72 (Bod).
50. Additional MS 10309, ff. 50b–51a, 53b–54b, 95, 98b, 126a, 127b, 132, 141b–142a (BM); Grierson: A10.
51. Additional MS 23229, ff. 10a–14b, 55a, 76a–77a, 95a–98a, 132, Conway Papers (BM); Grierson, Gardner: A23.
52. Additional MS 30982, ff. 27–28, 31–32, 46–49, 52, 61–63, 81–82, 142, 159 (BM).
53. Egerton MS 2230, ff. 3, 11–23, 33a, 48a, 51b (BM); Grierson: E22.
54. Harleian MS 3511, ff. 19b–54a, 73a (BM).
55. Sloane MS 1792, ff. 11b–12a, 27a–28a, 38b–41b, 47, 58b–59a, 83a–84a (BM).
56. MS 5308 E, ff. 1–9 (National Library of Wales).
57. Grey MS 2.a.II (South African Public Library, Capetown).
58. MS PwV 37, Welbeck MS, unpaged (Duke of Portland Library, Univ. of Nottingham); Gardner: Wel.
59. Edward Hyde MS, ff. 2b–11b, 30a–32b (Geoffrey Keynes).

60. Monckton-Milnes MS (formerly owned by the late Marquis of Crewe); Grierson: M.

4. *Other Corroborative Texts*

61. Additional MS 5956, f. 37a (BM).
62. Additional MS 15226, f. 29a (BM).
63. Additional MS 15227, f. 75a (BM).
64. Additional MS 19268, ff. 10a, 19, 24, 36b (BM).
65. Additional MS 21433, ff. 147b–148a, 161–62 (BM).
66. Additional MS 22118, ff. 7–8 (BM).
67. Additional MS 25303, ff. 164–65 (BM).
68. Additional MS 27407, ff. 125, 154–55 (BM).
69. Additional MS 32463, f. 39b (BM).
70. Additional MS 34324, Sir Julius Caesar's Papers, f. 316 (BM); Gardner: A34.
71. Additional MS 34744, West Papers XVIII, ff. 47a–48b (BM); Grierson: A34.
72. Egerton MS 923, f. 20 (BM).
73. Egerton MS 2421, ff. 25a, 35, 46b (BM).
74. Egerton MS 2725, ff. 63b–64a, 104b–105a (BM).
75. Harleian MS 3910, ff. 22, 50a (BM); Grierson: H39.
76. Harleian MS 3991, ff. 113–115 (BM).
77. Harleian MS 4888, ff. 253, 254 (BM).
78. Harleian MS 6057, ff. 33b–34a (BM).
79. Harleian MS 6918, f. 13 (BM).
80. Harleian MS 6931, ff. 7b–8a (BM).
81. Sloane MS 542, ff. 11, 17b, 53b–54a (BM).
82. Additional MS B.97, ff. 39b, 55b–56a (Bod).
83. Ashmole MS 36, 37 ff. 29b, 61b (Bod).
84. Ashmole MS 38, pp. 14, 40–43, 49, 63, 202 (Bod); Grierson: Ash 38; Gardner: Ash.
85. Ashmole MS 47, ff. 73a, 97b, 100b–101a (Bod).
86. Ashmole MS 51, f. 7a (Bod).
87. MS CCC.F.328, Corpus Christi College MS, pp. 52, 94, 147 (Bod).
88. MS Eng. Poet. c.50, ff. 42b, 43b, 64, 65, 117b, 120b (Bod).
89. MS Eng. Poet. c.53, f. 9a (Bod).
90. MS Eng. Poet. e.37, pp. 31–34, 58–59, 63–66, 69–71 (Bod).
91. MS Eng. Poet. e.97, pp. 101–4, 183 (Bod).
92. MS Eng. Poet. f.25, ff. 11, 17 (Bod).
93. MS Don.b.9, ff. 56a–58b (Bod).
94. MS Don.c.54, ff. 8a–9b[a], 24b–25a (Bod).
95. MS Don.d.58, ff. 27a, 37b, 48 (Bod).
96. Malone MS 16, pp. 30–33 (Bod).

97. Malone MS 19, pp. 57–58, 79–83, 150 (Bod).
98. Malone MS 23, p. 220 (Bod).
99. Rawlinson Poet. MS 26, ff. 91b–92b, 112 (Bod).
100. Rawlinson Poet. MS 84, ff. 59a–58b (reverse) (Bod).
101. Rawlinson Poet. MS 90, f. 107b (Bod).
102. Rawlinson Poet. MS 116, ff. 51–52 (Bod).
103. Rawlinson Poet. MS 142, ff. 16b, 18b, 23 (Bod).
104. Rawlinson Poet. MS 172, f. 74b (Bod).
105. Rawlinson Poet. MS 199, pp. 14–15 (Bod).
106. Rawlinson Poet. MS 212, ff. 152b–151a (reverse) (Bod); Grierson:
     R212 (in notes).
107. Rawlinson Poet. MS 214, f. 81b (reverse) (Bod).
108. Sancroft MS 53, p. 58 (Bod).
109. Tanner MS 465, f. 95a (Bod).
110. Miscellany owned by John Sparrow.
111. MS Ee.5.23, pp. 1, 3 (Cambridge).
112. MS S.32, pp. 29b, 30b, 32b, 37b–38a (St. John's College, Cam-
     bridge).
113. MS U 26, pp. 92–98, 112–15, 126 (St. John's College, Cambridge).
114. MS Eng. 626, ff. 4, 67, 78a–79a (Harvard).
115. MS Eng. 686, ff. 14a, 35b–37b, 52b, 61b, 94b (Harvard).
116. Farmer-Chetham MS 8012, A.4.15, pp. 95–102 (Chetham's Li-
     brary).
117. MS PwV 191, "Satire IV" (Univ. of Nottingham).
118. Commonplace Book (James H. Osborn).
119. MS HM 172, p. 96 (Huntington).
120. MS 401 (Halliwell-Phillips Collection), f. 70b (Edinburgh Univ.).
121. Hawthornden MS VIII, ff. 165a–166b, 246a–247b (Society of An-
     tiquaries of Scotland), on permanent loan to the National Li-
     brary of Scotland, cat. MS 2060.
122. MS FPR 2247, E37, "Elegie XVIII" (Rutgers).
123. State Papers Miscellaneous 9/51, No. 7, "Letter" and "A hymne to
     the Saints" (PRO).
124. Peniarth 500B, pp. 20–24 (National Library of Wales).
125. MS 5390, pp. 6–7, 444–42 (reverse) (National Library of Wales).
126. MS V.b.43, ff. 9b–10 (Folger).
127. MS V.a.96, ff. 39b–40b, 50b (Folger).
128. MS V.a.97, pp. 27, 34–35, 42–43, 63, 68–70, 151 (Folger).
129. MS V.a.103, ff. 31b–40a, 54a–56b, 68b–77a (Folger).
130. MS V.a.124, ff. 24a–25a (Folger).
131. MS V.a.125, ff. 30b–32b, 51b–52b (Folger).
132. MS V.a.162, ff. 11b, 20b–49b, 66a–83a, 90a (Folger).
133. MS V.a.169, f. 3 (Folger).

134. MS V.a.170, pp. 20, 57–59, 89, 200–3, 210–15, 241–42 (Folger).
135. MS V.a.245, ff. 12a–13b, 42a, 47 (Folger).
136. MS V.a.262, pp. 12–26, 73–74, 83, 102 (Folger).
137. MS V.a.276, f. 36b (Folger).
138. MS V.a.319, ff. 24a–25a, 44b–45b (Folger).
139. MS V.a.322, pp. 39–41, 149–53 (Folger).
140. MS V.a.339, ff. 182, 195 (Folger).
141. MS V.a.345, pp. 6, 25, 74–75, 80–82, 88–89, 131–32, 146–47, 237 (Folger).
142. MS W.a.118, f. 6 (Folger).
143. MS 239/18, pp. 78–79 (Rosenbach).
144. MS 239/22, pp. 4b, 7b, 8a, 44a–45b, 51a–52b (Rosenbach).
145. MS 239/23, p. 43 (Rosenbach).
146. MS 239/27, pp. 47–52, 308–9 (Rosenbach).
147. MS 240/7 (MS paged: 75, 76, 77, 76, 77, 78; poem appears on second p. 76) (Rosenbach).
148. MS 243/4, pp. 21, 42–47, 72–73, 130–31 (Rosenbach).
149. MS 1083/15, p. 139 (Rosenbach).
150. MS 1083/16, pp. 51–52, 117, 199–206, 241–42, 303–5 (Rosenbach).
151. MS 1083/17, pp. 103a–104a, 135a–138a (Rosenbach).

5. *Musical Versions*

152. MS 1018, f. 44b, anonymous setting of "Deerest Love . . . ," No. 59 (St. Michael's College, Tenbury Wells).
153. MS 1019, f. 1b, John Coprario's "The Message," No. 3 (St. Michael's College, Tenbury Wells).
154. MS D.C.1.69, pp. 13–14 (reverse), William Lawes's "The Apparition" (Edinburgh Univ.).
155. Fitzwilliam Virginal Book (erroneously known as Queen Elizabeth's virginal book), Martin Peerson's "The Primerose," No. 264, pp. 381–82, music only (Fitzwilliam Museum, Cambridge).
156. MS F.575, f. 8b, Music School MS, anonymous setting of "The Expiration" (Bod).
157. MSS 736–38, three MSS, ff. 21a, 21a, 22a, respectively, Thomas Ford's "Lamentations of Jeremy" for three voices (Christ Church, Oxford).
158. Additional MS 10337 (known as "Elizabeth Rogers hir Virginal Book"), f. 55b (reverse), anonymous setting of "Sweetest Love . . ." (BM).
159. Egerton MS 2013, ff. 13b, John Hilton's "Hymn to God the Father," and 58b, anonymous setting of "Go and catch a falling star . . ." (BM); Grierson, Gardner: E20.

1. SATYRE I.

COPY TEXT: 1633.

TEXTS: 1633–69; H49, D, SP, Lec, C57, TCD, N, Dob, S96, Lut, O'F, Hd, Cy, O, P, JC, D17, B, S, K, W, L74, S962, A25; D16, H5110, Q, Ee.4.14.

COLLATION: 1633–69, C57 (plus SP), TCD, Dob, O'F, W, Q; some readings from H49 and Lec. 1 fondling / changeling *1669, SP, TCD* (*changed from* fondling), *Dob, O'F, W, Q.* 5 conduits, . . . Divines; *Gr.* / ~; . . . ~, *1633.* 6 Natures / Is natures *1669, Dob.* Philosopher; *Gr.* / ~. *1633.* 7 jolly / wily *1635–69, O'F.* 13 sweare / sweare heere *O'F.* love / love here *1635–69.* 14 canst / can *Q.* 16 dost / doe *SP, W, Q.* 19 Not / Nor *SP, TCD, Dob, O'F.* piert / neat *Q.* 20 courtesie / curtesies *O'F, Q.* 23 Wilt / Shalt *SP, Dob, O'F, W, Q.* 24 heire! *Gr.* / ~? *1633.* 25 *first* or / and *Dob, W.* 27 monstrous / Monster *SP, W.* 32 raise / vaile *Dob, O'F, W, Q.* hat *1635* / hate *1633.* 33 none / with none *Dob, O'F.* untill / till *1669, O'F, Q.* have / hast *Dob, O'F, Q.* 36 Jointures / jointers *O'F.* 37 dost not onely / not onely dost *Dob, O'F.* 39 barenesse *O'F* / barrennesse *1633–69, C57, TCD.* 40 Of *Ed.* / of *1633.* or / *omitted 1635–54, O'F.* 42 birth . . . death / births . . . deaths *Dob, O'F.* 45 blest / best *O'F, Q.* 46 yet / *omitted 1635–69, Dob, O'F.* 47 I now / now I *O'F, W, Q.* 50 warn'd *1635* / warm'd *1633.* 52 goe. *Gr.* / ~, *1633.* 53 who / that *C57, TCD, Dob, W, Q.* 54 Worne / Worne out *1649–69.* 55 colour / coloured *1639–69, O'F, Q.* 56 right / *omitted O'F.* 'mongst / amongst *O'F, Q.* 58 an / *omitted Dob.* Infanta *O'F* / infant *1633–54, C57, TCD, Dob, W, Q.* 60 Scheme / Sceanes *1633, C57, TCD.* 61 fashion'd *Ed.* / fashioned *1633.* hats . . . suits / suites . . . hatts *O'F.* 62 subtile-witted / ~ˌ~ *1633.* subtile / supple *O'F, W, Q.* witted *C57* / wittied *1633–54, TCD, Dob.* 63 from / *omitted Dob, O'F, Q.* mee / hence *H49, Dob, O'F, W, Q.* canst *TCD* / can *1633–69, C57.* 64 Wither / Whether *Dob.* 65 my / myne *Lec, O'F, Q.* 66 conscience? *Gr.* / ~. *1633.* 68 Improvidently / Unprovidently *O'F.* 69 Imprison'd *Ed.* / imprisoned *1633.* 70 his *1635* / high *1633.* 71 skip . . . now / now step forth *Dob, O'F.* 72 silken painted / paynted silken *O'F.* 73 them *1635* / then *1633.* 78 most brave / bravest *Q.* stoops *1635* / stoopt *1633, C57, TCD. second* the / *omitted H49, W, Q.* 81–82 *omitted 1633.* 84 favour'd *Ed.* / favoured *1633.* Oh / yea *W, Q.* 87 which / that *Lut.* 88 in / for *Q.* 89 us; *Gr.* / ~, *1633.* whisper'd *Ed.* / whispered *1633.* 90 'T / *omitted SP, O'F, W, Q.* 92 Peacock / peacocks *Dob, O'F.* 94 on / in *W, Q.* 95 all *1635* / s'all *1633, C57.* 96 For / In *Dob.* 97 panes / pane *Dob, O'F.* print, cut / cutt, print *SP, O'F, W, Q.* and / or *SP, O'F, W, Q.* 98 Court / towne *O'F.* 100 stoop'st / stopp'st *1635–54, O'F.* 101 travalyd. Long? *H49* / travailed long? *1633.* 102 Which / Who *Dob, O'F.* 108 lechery. *1635* / liberty; *1633.* 109 were there / there were *1649–69.* 111 the / his *Q.*

2. SATYRE II.

COPY TEXT: 1633.

TEXTS: 1633–69; H49, D, SP, Lec, C57, TCD, N, Dob, S96, Lut, O'F, Hd, Cy, O, P, JC, D17, B, S, K, W, HN, L74, S962, A25; D16, H5110, Q, Ee.4.14.

COLLATION: 1633–69, C57 (plus SP), TCD, Dob, O'F, W, Q; some readings from Lut. 3 ill / *omitted* Q. 4 toward / towards 1669, C57, TCD, Dob, O'F, Q. them / it *Dob;* that *O'F.* towards / toward 1635–54, SP; to O'F, Q. 6 dearths W / dearth 1633–69, SP, Dob, O'F, Q. 7 and / or SP, Dob, O'F, W, Q. 8 Ridlingly it / It ridlingly SP, Dob, O'F, W, Q. 11 One / or SP, Dob. which / that O'F. as / is Q. 12 which / who *Dob;* that *O'F.* cannot / could not SP, Dob, O'F, W, Q. 15 Organ / Organs 1669, SP, Dob, Q. 17 rithmes / rimes SP, Dob, O'F, W. witchcrafts / witchcraft O'F, Q. 18 now / *omitted* Q. 19 now are / are now Q. 20 are / are nowe *Dob;* nowe are Q. the / your O'F. 22 singers at doores / Boyes at doores singing *Dob.* singers / Boyes singing SP, *Lut,* O'F (*as alternate reading*), W, Q. doores / doore O'F, Q. 24 excuse / 'scuse SP, Dob, O'F, W. 27 digested / disgested C57, Dob, O'F. 31 they / those O'F. which / that O'F. 32 doe / swive SP, O'F, W; ly *Dob.* Dildoes, 1635 / ———; 1633. and / to O'F. usure / usury *Dob.* 33 to / *omitted* *Dob,* W, Q. Letanie; TCD / ——— ∧ 1633; *omitted* 1635–39; gallant, he 1649–54. 34 all 1635 / of all 1633, C57 (*and others*). 36 new . . . hell / in Hell newe Tenements *Dob.* tenements / torments O'F (> tenements). 40 just / great SP, Dob, O'F, W, Q. 43 was / *omitted* 1635–69, O'F. 44 a scarse TCD / scarse a 1633–69, C57, O'F. this / his O'F; that Q. 46 *omitted* SP, W. 49 Lady. *Ed.* / ∼, 1633. 50 tricesimo / 37° Q. 51 claimes / clayme Q. 53 Proceed; *Gr.* / ∼, 1633. 54 return'd 1635 / Returne 1633, C57, TCD (*and others*). next / this W, Q. 57 which / that Q. 58 eare, *Gr.* / ∼. 1633. 59 *one* more / *omitted* Dob, Q. Sclavonians / Sclavonian Q. scolding / scoldings Q. 61 Which / When 1654, C57, TCD, O'F, Q; Then *Dob.* 63 meere / more C57. gaine, . . . soule, *Gr.* / ∼; . . . ∼∧ 1633. bold / hold TCD, Dob. 67 which / who O'F. 69–70 *dashes* 1633. 70 Like / Lye like Q. yea / or 1635–69. 73 grave Judge / Judges Q. 74–75 *dashes* 1633. 75 and / nor C57 (*and others*). 77 our TCD / the 1633–69, Q. 78 strand / sandes *Dob.* 79 luxurie / gluttonie SP, Dob, O'F (> luxury), W. 80 will / would Q. 84 Relique-like / Reliquely 1633–69, C57 (*and others*). buyes / gets O'F. 86 Wringing / In wringinge Q. 87 parchments *Dob* / parchment 1633–69, C57, TCD, O'F. 88 bigge / as bigg Q. gloss'd / glossy Q. 89 that / as Dob, Lut. 91 *second* these / those SP, *Dob.* 94 nosters / noster *Dob.* 95 those / his SP (*and others*); theis Q. 97 land / landes Q. 98 writings / writing TCD, O'F. ses / his SP, *Dob;* omitted (*space*) Lut. 99 slily / sly O'F. goes / goeth Q. 104 Those / These TCD, Dob, W. nor / or O'F. 105 Where's / Where 1635–69, SP, Dob, O'F, W, Q. almes? *Gr.* / ∼, 1633. In W / *omitted* 1633, C57, TCD. great / *omitted* 1635–69, O'F. hals∧ *Gr.* / ∼? 1633. 107 blesse / blest 1635–69 (*and others*). 108 no / not SP, Dob, O'F. 111 none drawes / neere draw O'F. 112 huge / *omitted* Q. lawes / Lawe O'F.

3. SATYRE III.

COPY TEXT: 1633.

TEXTS: 1633–69; H49, D, SP, Lec, C57, TCD, N, Dob, Lut, O'F, Hd, Cy, O, P, JC, D17, B, S, K, W, L74, S962, A25; D16, H5110, Q.

COLLATION: 1633–69, C57 (plus SP), TCD, Dob, O'F, W, Q. 1 chokes / checks 1635–54. 2 Those / These SP, Dob, W. 3 not / nor W. sinnes / sinne SP, W. 4 Can / May SP, Dob, O'F, W, Q. 7 to 1635 / in 1633, C57, TCD. first blinded / first blind SP, W; soules first Dob. 9 was / were SP. 14 so . . . wayes / wayes easie SP, Dob, W; wayes so easy O'F (so added); waies waies easy Q. 17 and / omitted SP, Dob, O'F, W, Q. 19 dearth / death O'F (> dearth), Q. 20 dungeons / dangers SP. 22 discoveries? Gr. / ~, 1633. 23 Salamanders, Gr. / ~? 1633. 28 words? Gr. / ~, 1633. 29 coward / cowards O'F. 31 Sentinell / Souldier SP, Dob, O'F, W, Q. his / this 1669, Dob, O'F, Q. 32 forbidden / forbid 1635–69, O'F, W. 33 foes 1635 / foe 1633, C57, TCD. h'is / he 1635–69, O'F; omitted SP, Dob. 35 quit / rid SP, Dob, O'F, W, Q. 38 wayne / vaine Q. 39 wither'd Ed. / withered 1633. 40 selfes TCD / selfe 1633, SP. 42 this / thy Q. 44 here 1635 / her 1633. 47 He / And 1635–54, O'F. her / the 1633–69, TCD. 49 Crants / Morus Dob; Grants O'F. 51 sullen / solemne O'F, Q. 53 that / which SP, O'F, W, Q. 54 drudges. Gr. / ~: 1633. 55 Graius / Grugus SP. 57 bid TCD / bids 1633–69, C57. 70 must . . . but / but . . . must Q. 75 that / which SP, Dob, W. 78 stray / stay Q. 79 huge / high SP, O'F, W, Q. 80 Cragged / Ragged SP, Dob, O'F, W. stands / dwells SP, Dob, O'F, W, Q. 81 her / it Dob, W, Q. second must / omitted C57, Dob, W, Q. 83 that / as O'F. 84 Soule / Mind SP, Dob, O'F, W, Q. that / the 1635–54, SP, O'F, Q. night. Gr. / ~, 1633. 85–88 omitted Lut. 85 doe. Ed. / ~ₐ 1633. 86 too W / to 1633. 88 like / as SP, Dob, W, Q. 89 which / that SP. 90 case / case heere SP, Dob, O'F, W, Q. 93 Soule / selfe O'F. 94 mans / mens SP, Dob, W. she / hee O'F. not / omitted 1635–54. 95 Oh, will W / Will 1633, C57, TCD; Or will 1635–69, O'F. boot / serve SP, Dob, O'F, W, Q. 97 thee / me 1669, Dob, W. 99 strong? Gr. / ~ₐ 1633; true SP; strange W. 101–2 omitted Dob. 101 chang'd; Gr. / ~ₐ 1633. beₐ Gr. / ~, 1633. 103 is; Gr. / ~, 1633. flowers / streames O'F (> flowrs). that / which SP, Dob, W, Q. 104 do / prove SP, Dob, O'F, W, Q. 105 left / lost Dob, Q. 107 first and / omitted 1635–69, SP, O'F, W. rockes, and woods / woods, rocks O'F. at / at the O'F. 108 sea / Seas SP. 109 mens / mans O'F.

4. SATYRE IV.

COPY TEXT: 1633.

TEXTS: 1633–69; Wybarne (ll. 18–23); H49, D, SP, Lec, C57, TCD, N, Dob, S96, Lut, O'F, Hd, Cy, O, P, JC, D17, B, S, K, W, HN, L74, S962, A25; D16, Q; A23 (ll. 203–244); Ash 38, PwV191. An abbreviated prose version, not part of the Group III collection, also appears in Dob.

COLLATION: 1633–69, C57 (plus SP), TCD, Dob, O'F, W, Q; some readings from Lec, Lut, and HN. HN is headed: "This Satyr (though it here have the first place because no more was intended to this booke) was indeed the authors

fourth in nomber & order; he hauing wreten fiue in all to which this caution will
sufficientlie direct in the rest"; and is dated: "anno 1594." 2 but / but yet
1635–69, O'F. 4 and / to and *Q.* scant / scarse *Q, Dob.* 5 neither / nor *SP,
Dob, W, Q;* neithers *C57;* not *O'F.* 7 there / at Court *Dob, Q.* new / no *Lec;*
yet *O'F; omitted Dob, Q.* 8 Glaze / Glare *1635–69, TCD, Dob, O'F, W, Q.*
9 a / *omitted 1635–69, C57, O'F, Q.* catch'd / and *Dob.* 10 The / An *Dob.*
is / was *TCD.* 12 *second* of / in *1635–54, O'F.* 14 *second* as / *omitted
1635–69, SP, O'F;* and *Dob.* 16 at *TCD* / in *1633–69, C57.* 18 slime /
shines *O'F.* 23 strangers / strangest *SP.* 26 'gainst / against *Q.* 28 Justice
/ Justices *Dob.* 33 Become Tufftaffatie / Tuftaffata become *O'F.* 35 This /
The *1635–69, O'F.* 36 knoweth / knowes *O'F, W, Q.* what . . . States / to
all States what *O'F, Q.* belongs. *Gr.* / ~, *1633.* 37 all / *omitted SP, O'F, Q.*
38 no *Q* / one *1633–69, C57, TCD, Dob, O'F, W.* 42 enough preparatives /
preparatives enough *O'F.* 43 yet / but *Dob.* 47 or / and *SP, Dob, O'F, W,
Q.* 48 Surius / Sleydan *Dob (changed from Surius), O'F* (> Surius), *Q.* 51
chuseth / chaseth *Q.* 54 that / *omitted Q.* 56 *Dob has note:* Dr Reinolds and
Dr Andrewes. two / two most *O'F.* 57 nam'd *Ed.* / named *1633.* There / here
1635–69. 59 Good pretty / Pretty good *O'F, Q.* Panurge *1635* / Panirge
1633. 60 Yet / But *Dob, O'F.* 62 prais'd *Ed.* / praised *1633.* words / wonders *1635–69, Dob, O'F, W, Q.* 63 If you'had / Had you *Dob.* 65 the /
that *SP, Dob, W.* 66 adds / answears *Dob.* 67 lonenesse *1635* / lonelinesse
1633, C57, TCD. 68 lonenesse *1635* / lonelinesse *1633, C57, TCD.* 69 last
/ tast *1635–54, O'F, Q.* 73 to'a / an *Dob;* a to' *W.* squeakt / squeakes *O'F.*
74 At / In *O'F.* 76 price / penny *Dob.* with / *omitted Dob.* 77 Harries /
Henryes *Dob.* 79 Your eares / You *Dob.* Kings / King *O'F, W.* 82 all / *omitted O'F.* 83 Mine? *1635* / Fine, *1633.* 84 frenchman / Sir *1635–69, O'F,
Q.* 86 wearing / weare *Q.* your / this *SP, Dob, O'F, W;* his *Q.* Grogaram. *Gr.*
/ ~; *1633.* 88 him / *omitted Dob.* 89 and / or *Dob.* ground *Gr.* / grown'd
1633. 90 (foole) *Gr.* / ᴧ~ᴧ *1633.* 92 addresse, *TCD* / ~. *1633;* dresse
1635–69, SP, Dob, O'F, W, Q. 95 drop / note *Dob.* 96 so tells / tells he
Dob. lie. *Ed.* / ~, *1633.* 97 or . . . or / and . . . and *W.* 98 trashᴧ he *Gr.*
/ ~; He *1633.* 99 frown'd . . . smil'd / smil'd . . . frown'd *SP, Dob, W.* he
knowes / *omitted Dob, Q.* 102 Hasts / Hast *C57;* Hastneth *Q.* 103 hath /
omitted O'F, Q. 104 bootes, shooes / shooes, bootes *SP, O'F, W, Q.* and / or
O'F, W, Q (and others). 106 span-counter . . . blow-point / blow-point . . .
span-counter *SP, O'F, W, Q.* they *TCD* / shall *1633–69 (and others);* they
shall *Dob.* 108 what / which *SP, O'F, W, Q (and others).* 109 tries / cloyes
1635–69, O'F. 111 on / *omitted SP, W, Q (and others);* me *C57, TCD;* in
Dob. And / *omitted Dob, Q.* if / *omitted 1635–69, O'F.* he / hee had *1635–69,
Dob, O'F.* 113 that / which *SP, Dob, O'F, W, Q.* have *1635* / hath *1633,
C57, TCD.* 115 a / to a *W.* 116 sigh / belche *SP, W.* 117 this / his *TCD,
O'F, W.* 122 He / *omitted Dob.* saith / saies *SP, O'F, W;* howe *Dob.* because
/ because th'are *Dob.* 123 *second* that / *omitted 1635–54.* 127 meat . . .
clothes / Clothes . . . meate *O'F.* 128 loves / loveth *O'F.* goats / love goates
O'F. 133 in; *Gr.* / ~, *1633.* 134–35 *dashes 1633.* 134 venome / venom'd
Dob, Q. do / might *Dob; omitted Q.* 135 I / so I *Dob.* 136 Guilty . . . free /
dashes 1633. he / be *TCD.* free / freed *C57, TCD.* 137–39 *combined TCD*

(But . . . farthing *omitted*).   141 mercy / my redemption *Dob;* redempcõn *Q.*   142 pay / *omitted O'F.*   145 *first* as / as a *SP, Dob, O'F;* for *Q.*   146 needs / *omitted Dob.*   153 Ran / Run *W.*   154 doth make / makes *O'F, Q.* make *W* / hast *1633–69, C57, TCD.*   156 precious / piteous *1635–69, Dob, O'F, W, Q.*   159 on / ore *1635–69, SP, Dob, O'F, W, Q.* Such / and such *SP, Dob, O'F, W.*   160 I saw / saw I *Dob.* worse . . . more / more . . . worse *Dob.*   161 Then / why should I then *Dob.*   162 Shall I / being *Dob.* 164 th' *Dob* / omitted *1633–54, C57, TCD.* Nobility? *Gr.* / ~. *1633.*   166 whole / *omitted C57, Dob.*   168 our / the *Dob, Q.*   169 made / *omitted Dob.* your / the *SP, Dob;* yond *O'F, W, Q.* and / brought, and *Dob.*   170 Transported / Transplanted *SP, O'F, W (and others).*   171 Presence / Court heere *SP, W, Q (and others);* Courtiers *1635–69, O'F.*   173 And / and seeme *Dob.* 174 Some / branches *Dob.*   178 made . . . day / that day made ready *Dob.* are / were *1635–54.*   180 their / th' *SP, W (and others).*   182 Those / these *SP (and others).* cry / cries *C57, W, Q.* the / his *1635–54, SP, W, Q;* those *Dob.*   183 weeke to / week unto *C57, TCD;* unto *Dob.*   184 seemes / thinks *SP, Dob, O'F, Q.*   186 For / for they *O'F.* goe / *omitted O'F, Q.* o'r / on *Dob;* in *O'F, Q.*   188 doe / did *SP, Dob, O'F, W.*   193 These / Those *O'F, Q.*   194 scarlets / scarlet *SP, Dob, O'F, W, Q.*   195 call'd / calls *Dob, O'F, Q.* beauty / beauties *Dob, O'F.*   196 loose / ill *Q.*   199 if / *omitted SP, O'F, W, Q (and others).* the / the Queens *SP (and others).*   200 shirts and hose / cloake aloft *Dob.*   203 wherewith / with which *SP, O'F, W;* by which *Dob.* fornicate: *Gr.* / ~. *1633.*   204 survay / survayes *SP, Dob, O'F (> survaye),* W.   205 trye *Gr.* / tries *1633–69, C57, TCD, Dob, O'F, W, Q.* strings / stringe *Dob.*   206 Of / from *Dob.* thighe *Gr.* / thighes *1633–69, C57, TCD, O'F (and others),* W; his thighes *Dob, Q.*   209 his / the *O'F.*   211 he / straight *SP, O'F, W (and others);* he straight *Dob, Q.*   213 serve / have serv'd *O'F (> serve).*   215 whisperd / whispers *1635–69, O'F.* by Jesu, so often / so often, by Jesu *Dob.* 216 Pursevant / Topcliff *Dob (changed from Pursevant), O'F (> pursevant), Q.* him / him quite *O'F, Q.*   217 of / *omitted SP, Dob, O'F, W, Q.* our Ladies / Jesus *O'F.*   220 the / an *Dob.*   222 whom / or whom *1635–69, O'F.*   223 not / not he *1635–69, O'F.*   224 rusheth / rushes *1639–69, SP (and others).* 225 meant / came *Dob, O'F, W.*   226 theirs / those *Dob, O'F.* which / who *Dob, Q.* still *1635* / yet still *1633, C57, TCD.*   229 I / Ile *SP, W.*   230 Which *TCD* / omitted *1633–69.*   231 it / that *Dob.*   232 sinnes? *Gr.* / ~ₐ *1633.*   234 that / which *O'F, W (and others).*   236 Living, *Gr.* / ~ₐ *1633;* swallowing *Dob (> living).* beefe / Beere *Dob.*   238 Seas / great seas *O'F.* Wits / Witt *TCD, Dob, O'F, Q.* Arts / Art *Dob, O'F.*   239 Drowne / To drowne *O'F.*   240 Which / Who *SP, Dob, O'F.* but / *omitted SP, Dob, O'F, W, Q.* scarce / scant *1635–69, Dob, O'F, W, Q;* shallowe *SP.*   241 the / their *SP, Dob, O'F, W, Q;* these *TCD.* though / Although *1635–69, O'F;* And though *Dob.*   242 the / have not the *Dob.* knowne / *omitted SP, Dob, W.* 243 worke / coud *Dob.* man / men *1649–69, TCD, Dob, W, Q.*   244 writs / witt *Dob (> writt), Q;* writt *O'F.*

5. SATYRE V.

COPY TEXT: 1633.

TEXTS: 1633–69; D, SP, Lec, C57, TCD, N, Dob, Lut, O'F, Hd, O, P, JC, D17, B, S, K, W, L74, S962, A25; D16, Q; A23.

COLLATION: 1633–69, C57 (plus SP), TCD, Dob, O'F, W, Q; one reading from Lut. 2 warmes / warnes SP, Q. 6 these / those Dob; the Q. 12 implyes 1635 / employes 1633, C57. represents. Gr. / ~, 1633. 13 Officers∧ Gr. / ~, 1633. 14 ravishing / raveninge Dob; ravenous O'F, Q. 19 excrements / excrement Dob, O'F, W. voyd. All Gr. / ~; all 1633. dust; Gr. / ~, 1633. 20 who / which Dob; that O'F. 22 do / omitted O'F. 23 yet / and Dob, O'F. 26 their / the 1635–69, O'F, Q. 27 th' / and th' TCD. 30 armes / arme O'F. drowne / drownes O'F; drownd Q. 33 authoriz'd Ed. / authorized 1633. 37 that was / omitted O'F; which was Q. 38 farre / omitted 1635–54; deleted O'F. allow / did allowe 1635–54, Dob; I did allow TCD, O'F. 39 demands / claymed 1635–69, Dob, O'F, W, Q. 40 sweat, and sweare / sweare and sweat Dob, O'F, W, Q. 41 other / others Dob, O'F, Q. 42 Scape, like Angelica / Like Angelica, scape W, Q. 46 Flow / Flowes O'F. maine / meane C57. these / those O'F. 47 to / into O'F, Q. 49 complaine, Gr. / ~; 1633. 51 most / omitted O'F. these / those Dob, O'F, Q. 52 the / thy 1635–69, Dob, O'F, Q. 56 like / likes W. only∧ . . . have∧ . . . more. Gr. / ~, . . . ~, . . . ~∧ 1633. only / omitted O'F. 57 said / stil'd Dob (changed from calld), O'F. 58 that / omitted O'F (and others). 59 supplications / supplication 1635–54. 61 Courts / Court 1633, C57, TCD, Dob. 63 'tis. Would Gr. / ~, would 1633. 66 cloathes, Copes / copes, clothes and O'F (corrected). 67 mistake / take Q. 68 aske / lack 1633–54, C57. comming? Gr. / ~; 1633. 72 but / omitted 1633–69, C57, TCD. tells / tell Dob. us O'F / omitted 1633–69, C57, TCD. 73 chaires / chaynes W. 75 In / As in O'F. 76 men, Gr. / ~; 1633. th' TCD / omitted 1633–69. 78 else part / part els Dob. 79 to / omitted Dob. yon / yond O'F. 80 erst 1635 / omitted 1633, C57, TCD. bar'd Gr. / bared 1633. 86 much . . . shalt / shalt much more O'F; shalt more Q. 87 Haman / Hammon 1635–69; Hammond O'F. when / if 1635–54, O'F, Q. 88 fortunes / fortune Q. 90 the / that Dob, W, Q. cosened / ledd O'F. 91 And / Which 1635–69, O'F; Who Dob, Q. div'st / divedst C57; divd Dob, O'F, Q. what / that Lut.

6. UPON MR. THOMAS CORYATS CRUDITIES.

COPY TEXT: Coryat.

TEXTS: Coryat, 1649–69.

COLLATION: Coryat, 1649–69. Title 1649 / Incipit Ioannes Donne. Coryat. 2 indented Coryat. leaven'd Ed. / leavened Coryat; learned 1649–69. 5 discover'd Ed. / discovered Coryat. 19 sometimes 1649 / sometime Coryat. 28 booke, 1649 / ~. Coryat. 39 Tomes / Tons 1649–54; Tuns 1669. 52 Scatter'd Ed. / Scattered Coryat. 70 note omitted 1649–69. 74 beares∧ 1649 / ~, Coryat.

7. IN EUNDEM MACARONICON.

COPY TEXT: *Coryat.*

TEXT: *Coryat.*

COLLATION: Coryat. *signed:* Explicit Ioannes Donne. *Coryat.* 1 dos / *dos Coryat.* 2 fara *Gr.* / fata *Coryat.* 3 a *Gr.* / A Coryat.

8. ELEGIE: THE BRACELET.

COPY TEXT: 1635.

TEXTS: 1635–69; H49, D, SP, Lec, C57, TCD, N, DC, Dob, S96, Lut, O'F, HM198 (twice), Hd, Cy, O, P (twice), JC, D17, B, S, K, W, L74, S962, A25, La, Hol, RP117, Ee.4.14, Add 29, CCC.E.327 (ll. 111–14), EP.e.14, E2230, Hyde, M, RP160, Sloane 1792; Ash 36, Eng 686 (ll. 27–28), H3991 (ll. 27–30), Don.c.54, Malone 19 (ll. 27–28), Malone 23 (ll. 27–28), RP212, V.a.170, V.a.262, U26, Wales 5390D, Rosenbach 239/22. (A number of mss omit various lines.)

COLLATION: 1635–69, C57, TCD, Dob, O'F (and Lut), W (some readings from SP, DC, and Cy). *Title* 1635 / Elegie *C57, TCD, W;* Armilla. To a Lady whose chaine was lost. *Dob;* Elegy. To a lady whose chayne was lost. The Bracelet. Armilla *O'F.* 3 thy / this *C57, TCD.* 6 these / those *C57, TCD, Dob, O'F, W.* are tyed *C57* / were knit 1635–69; are knitt *Cy.* love / loves 1669, DC, Dob; hearts *O'F.* 8 luck / lucks *DC, Dob, O'F, W.* 11 fault *C57* / way 1635–69; taint *Dob, O'F, W.* or / and *C57, TCD.* 14 to / for *Dob.* 19 damn'd / burnt *O'F.* 24 them / these 1635–54, Cy. naturall Countreys *O'F* / Countreys naturall 1635–54. Countreys / countrey 1669, C57, TCD, Dob, W. 26 leane . . . pale . . . lame *C57* / pale . . . lame . . . leane 1635–69, Cy; leane . . . lame . . . pale *TCD.* 35 which *C57* / that 1635–69, Cy. 36 course; *Gr.* / ∼. 1635. 38 streames, *Gr.* / ∼∧ 1635. run / runs *C57, DC.* every / eache *Cy.* 40 ruin'd, . . . decay'd; *Gr.* / ∼: . . . ∼∧ 1635. ruin'd, ragged / ragged ruined *Dob, O'F, W.* 47 are / were *C57, TCD, O'F, W.* 48 are / were *O'F* (> ar). 52 lustyhead *Gr.* / lusty head 1635. 53 vanish; *Gr.* / ∼, 1635. 54 me / *omitted C57.* 55 Oh *C57* / And 1635–69. 58 conscience, *Gr.* / ∼; 1635. they *C57* / hee 1635–54. 60 Which *C57* / That 1635–69, Cy. scheames *C57* / scenes 1635–69, TCD. fils full / fullfill *Dob;* fullfills *C57, TCD, O'F, Cy, W.* 61 hath / have *TCD.* heaven / hell *O'F* (*changed from* heaven). 62 stuft / filld *O'F.* his / her *TCD, Dob* (*changed from* his), *O'F.* 65 indented 1635. And *C57* / But 1635–69. 66 Oh *C57* / yet 1635–69, Cy. 67 from . . . doome / the doome from him *Dob, O'F, W.* that / the 1669, C57, Cy. 71 the / those *Dob, O'F, W.* 73 these / those *SP, TCD.* 76 being, *Gr.* / ∼: 1635. 85 a *C57* / an 1635–69. 87 which *C57* / that 1635–69, Cy. 90 few / *omitted TCD.* few∧ fellowes *Gr.* / ∼-∼ 1635. 91 ô thou / thou O *Dob, O'F.* 92 that / much that *C57, TCD;* much as *Dob, W;* as *O'F.* almost / *omitted C57.* thy / thine *Lut, Cy.* estate / state *C57, DC, Dob, W.* 95–114 *missing O'F.* 95 hang'd / tyed *TCD.* 96 chaind / ty'd *Lut.* to / in *C57, Dob.* 98 that *C57* / it 1635–69. thy / *omitted 1669, Dob.* 104 Itching / Itchy *C57, Dob, TCD, Lut, W.* 105 hurt . . . Gold *C57* / evils that gold ever 1635–69. which / that *TCD.* 106 mischiefes *C57* / mischiefe *1635–69*. which *C57* / that *1635–69, Cy.* 108 love / love, and *1669, C57, TCD, Dob, Lut, W.* 109 last / latest *C57, TCD, Dob* (*changed from* last), *W.* 111 thee / thou *C57, TCD;* then *Dob, W.* 113 Or *C57* / But *1635–69, Cy.*

9. ELEGIE: THE COMPARISON.

COPY TEXT: 1633.

TEXTS: 1633–69; TCD, N, TCC, A18, Dob, S96, O'F, HM198, Hd, Cy, O, P, JC, D17, B, S, K, W, L74, S962, A25, RP117; Ee.4.14, Add 29, CCC.E.327 (ll. 1–32), EP.e.14 (ll. 1–25, 30–54), M, Emmanuel (ll. 1–14, 19–34), Grey; RP142 (ll. 1–22, 33–35, 53–54), V.a.125 (ll. 1–6).

COLLATION: 1633–69, TCD, Dob, O'F, W (some readings from Cy). *Title 1635* / Elegie *1633, TCD, Dob, W; omitted O'F.* 4 sweat / sweet *O'F, Cy.* of / on *TCD, W.* breast, *Gr.* / ~. *1633.* 6 carcanetts *W* / coronets *1633– 69, TCD, Dob, O'F.* 9 the / that *Dob, W.* 13 lying stones *1635* / stones lying *1633, 1669.* 14 they hang *TCD* / it hangs *1633–69, O'F* (*changed from* they hang). 16 the / that *Dob, O'F.* 20 yet scarce / scarsely *Dob, O'F.* 25 Thine's / Thine *Dob, O'F, W.* 26–29 *omitted Dob.* 26 dust / durt *TCD, O'F.* stinke / stench *O'F, Cy.* 27 that / the *W.* 28 hands. *Gr.* / ~, *1633.* 34 The / Thy *Dob.* of / on *Dob.* thy *1635* / her *1633.* hand. *Gr.* / ~; *1633.* 37 durt *1635* / part *1633, TCD, Cy.* 38 heat / heates *Dob, O'F, W.* 39 Thine's / Thine *Dob.* 41 to / *omitted TCD, Cy, W.* 43 kisses / kissings *W.* 45 fearefull / *omitted TCD.* 46 feares / feard *TCD, Dob, O'F, W.* 48 when *1635* / where *1633.* 50 Are / As *Dob.* 51 such / nice *1633–69.*

10. ELEGIE: THE PERFUME.

COPY TEXT: 1633.

TEXTS: 1633–69; H49, D, SP, Lec, C57, TCD, N, TCC, A18, DC, Dob, S96, Lut, O'F, Hd, Cy, O, P, JC, D17, B, S, W, HN, L74, S962, A25, Hol, RP117; Add 29, CCC.E.327, EP.e.14, Sloane 1792, Emmanuel; H3991 (ll. 31–32), Malone 19 (ll. 1–50), Peniarth 500B, Rosenbach 239/22, Rosenbach 1083/16 (ll. 53–62), Rosenbach 1083/17. Miss Gardner also lists E2230 and V.a.125.

COLLATION: 1633–69, C57, TCD, Dob, O'F, W (some readings from SP, TCC, and Cy). *Title 1635* / Elegie IV. *1633* (*similar C57, TCD, Dob, O'F, W*). 2 escapes / scapes *Dob, O'F.* on / to *Cy.* 7–8 *omitted 1633, C57, DC.* 7 glazed / glaciers *Cy.* 9 hath / have *TCD, W.* would / will *Dob.* 15 Takes / Take *TCD, O'F, Cy, W.* 16 all / at *O'F.* 21 To / And to *1635–69, TCD, O'F, W.* meates, *Gr.* / ~. *1633.* 22 blushing / blushings *C57, TCD, Dob, O'F, W.* 23 will to thee / to the will *Cy.* 25 these / those *O'F.* 26 thine / thy *Cy.* 29 ingled / dandled *1669, Dob, O'F;* nigled *TCC, Cy.* 30 next . . . tell / to tell, next day *O'F, Cy.* 31 grim∧ eight . . . high∧ iron *Gr.* / ~-~ . . . ~-~ *1633.* 37 to / for *C57, TCD, Dob, O'F, W.* 40 my / mine *1635–69, SP, TCD, Dob, O'F, W.* 41 my / mine *TCD, O'F.* 42 were wee / we were *SP, TCD, Dob, W.* 43 When / Then *Dob, O'F.* that / which *O'F.* 44 pale / *omitted TCD.* 46 feet . . . breath / breath . . . feet *O'F.* wrought / brought *Cy.* 48 diverse / some *Dob, O'F.* 49 Unicornes / Unicorne *Cy.* 51 whistling / whistlings *C57.* 52 speechlesse / sencelesse *O'F*

(> speechles).   53 whom / which *O'F*.   54 *first* mee / to my heart *O'F*. hast / *omitted Dob*.   55 unsuspected / unexpected *O'F*.   60 breath; *Gr*. / ∼, *1633*. 63 you / thou *TCD*, *O'F*.   64 There / These *C57*, *O'F* (> There), *Cy*.   65 yee / you *C57*, *O'F*, *Cy*.   66 Because / That *Dob*, *O'F*. you / the *Dob*. your / the *O'F*, *Cy*. smell; *Gr*. / ∼, *1633*.   67 You / Yee *TCD*. taken simply / simply t'ane *Dob*, *O'F*.   69 your / that *O'F*. doth / would *Cy*.   70 takes / take *O'F*. the / your *Cy*.

11. ELEGIE: JEALOSIE.

COPY TEXT: *1633*.

TEXTS: *1633–69*; H49, D, SP, Lec, C57, TCD, N, TCC, A18, DC, Dob, S96, Lut, O'F, Hd, Cy, O, P, JC, D17, B, S, K, W, A25, RP117; Add 29 (ll. 1–14), H3511, Grey.

COLLATION: *1633–69*, C57, TCD, Dob, O'F, W. *Title 1635* / Elegie I. *1633* (*similar C57*, *TCD*, *Dob*, *O'F*, *W*).   9 poore / pure *C57*, *W*. howling / *omitted TCD*.   10 few / some few *TCD*.   20 nor / or *O'F*.   21 great / high *1669*, *Dob*, *O'F*.   22 his / a *O'F* (> his).   25 that *C57* / it *1633–69*.   27 which / that *O'F*.   30 We into some third place retired were *Dob*, *O'F*.   31 There / Then *C57*. we will / will wee *O'F*.   34 Mayor *C57* / Major *1633–69*. or / added *O'F*.

12. ELEGIE: "OH, LET MEE NOT SERVE SO."

COPY TEXT: *1633*.

TEXTS: *1633–69*; H49, D, SP, Lec, C57, TCD, N, TCC, A18, DC, Dob, S96, Lut, O'F, Hd, Cy, O, P, JC, D17, B, S, K, W, L74, S962, A25, TCD(II), RP117; Add 29 (ll. 1–20), Hyde, H3511, Grey; H3991 (ll. 37–38), HNVIII (ll. 15–34, 39–40); Huygens (ll. 11–34).

COLLATION: *1633–69*, C57, TCD, Dob, O'F, W (some readings from Cy).   2 fatten / flatter *TCD*, *Cy*.   3 or / and *TCD*, *Cy*.   4 so / to *C57*.   6 stiles / stile *O'F*. with *TCD* / which *1633–69*.   11 her / mine *TCD*, *Cy*.   12 oathes / breathe *Cy*.   24 then / there *1635–69*, *TCD*, *O'F*, *Cy*.   26 to *TCD* / or *1633*, *C57*. upmost / utmost *1635–69*, *O'F* (*and others*).   28 banks / banke *TCD*, *Dob*, *W*.   29 rusheth / rushes *Dob*.   30 native / nature *O'F* (> native).   33 the / her *1635–69*, *TCD*, *O'F*, *Cy*. who / which *1635–69*, *O'F*. is / growes *O'F*.   34 that / this *Dob*.   38 nor / nor soe *TCD*; and *Dob*; or *O'F*.   41 bred / breed *1635–69*, *C57*, *TCD*, *Dob*, *O'F*.

13. ELEGIE: "NATURES LAY IDEOT."

COPY TEXT: *1633*.

TEXTS: *1633–69*; H49, D, SP, Lec, C57, TCD, N, TCC, A18, DC, Dob, Lut, O'F, HM198 (twice), Hd, Cy, O, P, JC, D17, B, S, K, W, S962, A25, RP117; Ee.4.14, Add 29 (ll. 25–30), Hyde, M; Eng 686, H3991 (ll. 3–7), Malone 19, V.a.162, Rosenbach 239/22.

COLLATION: *1633–69*, C57, TCD, Dob, O'F, W (some readings from Cy).   2 thou dost / thou didst *Dob*; dost thou *Cy*.   3 Foole / a foole *Dob*, *O'F* (> Foole). didst / dost *Cy*.   4 nor / or *O'F*; and *Cy*.   6 and / nor *Cy*. sounds / shewes *O'F* (> sounds).   7 call / know *1635–69*, *Dob*, *O'F* (> call).   10 they devisefully / their device in *Cy.*   16 that / which *Dob.*   17 could / would *TCD.*   18 One / An *O'F* (> One).   23 who / which *TCD, Dob, O'F, W.*   25 words / workes *C57, Dob.*   30 then / *omitted TCD.* ready / better *Cy.*

14. ELEGIE: LOVES WARRE.

COPY TEXT: W.

TEXTS: Waldron; H49, D, SP, Lec, C57, TCD, N, TCC, A18, DC (ll. 1–28, 31–32, 41–46), Dob, S96, Lut, O'F, HM198 (twice), Hd, Cy, O, P, JC, D17, B, S, K, W, L74, S962, A25, RP117; Add 29 (*passim*), CCC.E.327, EP.e.14, A30982, Hyde, Grey; EP.e.97 (ll. 1–28, 31–40, 43–46), V.a.103, V.a.345, Rosenbach 239/27 (ll. 29–32, 33–46).

COLLATION: C57, TCD, Dob, O'F, W (some readings from DC and Cy). *Title* Gr. / Elegy *C57, TCD, Dob, O'F, W.*   1 *indented W.* Till∧ *Gr.* / Tell; *W.*   6 presse / peeres *Dob, O'F.*   7 say, *Gr.* / ∼∧ *W.*   8 which / that *TCD, Dob, O'F.*   12 *second* which *TCD* / that *O'F, W.*   18 but / yet *O'F* (*changed from* but). food / meanes *O'F* (*changed from* food).   19 should *TCD* / shall *C57, W.* that / the *C57, TCD, Dob.*   22 fall; *Gr.* / ∼. *W.*   29 ly; *Gr.* / ∼∧ *W.*   31 Thy / Thine *TCD, Dob, O'F.* myne / my *DC, Cy.*   32 for / from *O'F.*   33 their / ther *W.* gayne; *Gr.* / ∼∧ *W.*   35 love, *Gr.* / ∼∧ *W.*   36 wee are / are we *Dob.*   37 off *O'F* / of *W.*   44 To / Unto *O'F.* warrs / warre *TCD, Cy.*

15. ELEGIE: GOING TO BED.

COPY TEXT: 1669.

TEXTS: 1669; H49, D, SP, Lec, C57, TCD, N, TCC, A18, Dob, S96, Lut, O'F, HM198, Cy, O, P, JC, D17, B, S, K, W, L74, S962, A25, Hol, RP117; Ee.4.14 (ll. 1–19), A30982 (*passim*), RP160, Sloane 1792, Grey; A19268, Ash 38, Eng 686, EP.c.50, EP.e.97 (*passim*), EP.f.25, H6931, Don.b.9, Osborn (CPB), RP199, Sloane 542, V.a.97 (*passim*), V.a.124, V.a.125, V.a.170 (ll. 39–48), V.a.262, V.a.319 (*passim*), V.a.345, S32, Rosenbach 239/27 (*passim*). Miss Gardner reports V.a.103. Many MSS present a frequently variant text.

COLLATION: 1669, C57, TCD, Dob, O'F, W (some readings from Lut, Cy, and JC). *Title* B / Elegy. To his Mistress going to bed. *1669;* Elegie *C57, TCD, Dob, O'F, W.*   3 the / his *O'F, Cy.*   4 he / they *C57, TCD, O'F, W.* 5 Zone / Zones *TCD, Dob, W.* glittering / glistering *C57, TCD, O'F, Cy, W.* 10 it is / tis your *C57, TCD, Cy, W;* is your *Dob, O'F.*   11 which / whome *C57, TCD, Dob, W.*   12 stand / bee *O'F.*   13 gown / gowne's *C57, TCD, Dob, W.*   14 when / where *TCD.* from *MSS* / through *1669.* th' / *added O'F;* *omitted Cy.* shadowe *C57* / shadows *1669.*   15 that / your *C57, TCD, O'F, W.*   16 you *MSS* / your head *1669.*   17 Now / *omitted C57, TCD, Dob, O'F.* those / these *C57.* and then / you weare, and *Dob, O'F.* softly / safely *TCD, Dob, O'F, W.*   19 us'd / use *TCD, Cy.*   20 Receavd by *MSS* / Reveal'd to *1669.*   22 Ill / All *O'F, Cy.* spirits / angells *O'F.* white, *Gr.* / ∼; *1669.* we easly / by this we *O'F.*   23 By . . . these / These better *O'F.*   24 Those / They *C57, TCD, Dob, W.* *second* our / the *C57, TCD.*   26 Behind . . . between *C57* / Before, behind, between, above *1669.* below. *Gr.* / ∼, *1669.*   28 kingdome, safeliest∧ *C57* / Kingdom's∧ safest, *1669, O'F, Cy.*   30 blest am I

MSS / am I blest *1669*. this *MSS* / thus *1669*. discovering thee / discovery *O'F*. theel *Gr*. / ∼? *1669*.   31–32 *after l. 46, Cy*.   31 in / into *C57, TCD, O'F, Cy*. these / those *C57*. bonds / Bands *C57, TCD*.   32 Then / There *C57, Cy*.   35 which / that *Cy*.   36 like / as *C57, TCD, W*. balls, *Gr*. / ∼: *1669*.   38 may / might *O'F* (*changed from* may), *Cy*. covet *C57* / court *1669, Lut*. theirs *C57* / that *1669, O'F*.   39 or like / in a *O'F*. made∧ *Gr*. / ∼, *1669*.   40 men, *Gr*. / ∼∧ *1669*.   41 are . . . only wee∧ *MSS* / are only . . . we, *1669*. books / bodies *Dob* (*changed from* bookes).   43 see / be *C57, TCD*. reveal'd *Gr*. / revealed *1669*. since / sweet *Cy*. that / *omitted C57, TCD, Dob, W*.   44 a *C57* / thy *1669, JC*.   45 hence, *Gr*. / ∼∧ *1669*.   46 There / Here *Dob*. due to / much less *C57, TCD, Dob, W*.   47 teach / shewe *O'F*. first; *Gr*. / ∼, *1669*.

16. ELEGIE: CHANGE.

COPY TEXT: 1633.

TEXTS: 1633–69; H49, D, SP, Lec, C57, TCD, N, TCC, A18, DC, Dob, S96, Lut, O'F, HM198, Hd, Cy, O, P, JC, D17, B, S, K, W, L74, S962, A25, RP117; Ee.4.14, Wel; V.a.103, E923, HNVIII (ll. 5–6).

COLLATION: 1633–69, C57, TCD, Dob, O'F, W (some readings from Cy). *Title 1635* / Elegie III *1633* (*similar C57, TCD, Dob, O'F, W*).   5 Women∧ *Gr*. / ∼, *1633*.   8 these / those *1669, TCD, W, Cy*; the *O'F*.   15 not / and *C57, Dob*.   17 plow / plow'd *TCD, Dob*.   23 Then . . . thou *TCD* / and if that thou so *1633–69*; And then . . . thou *O'F*.   24 like / alike *TCD*. like . . . love / love . . . like *O'F*.   30 a / is *Dob*.   32 worse / more *1633–54*.   35 are they / they are *Cy*.   36 joy / joyes *Dob*.

17. ELEGIE: THE ANAGRAM.

COPY TEXT: 1633.

TEXTS: 1633–69; *Parnassus Biceps;* H49, D, SP, Lec, C57, TCD, N, TCC, A18, DC, Dob, S96, Lut, O'F, Hd (twice), Cy, O, P, JC, D17, B, S, W, L74, S962, A25, Hol, RP117; Ee.4.14, Add 29 (*passim*), EP.e.14, A30982, Hyde, M, Wel, RP160, Sloane 1792, Emmanuel (ll. 1–16, 35–36), Grey; A22118, Add B.97, Chetham, E2421, Eng 686 (twice; ll. 35–36), EP.e.37, Don.d.58, Sloane 542, V.b.43, V.a.97, V.a.103, V.a.170, V.a.245, V.a.319, V.a.322, W.a.118, U26, Sparrow, Rosenbach 239/22; Huygens. Various lines are omitted in several texts.

COLLATION: 1633–69, C57, TCD, Dob, O'F, W (some readings from SP, TCC, Lut, and Cy). *Title 1635* / Elegie II. *1633* (*similar C57, TCD, Dob, O'F, W*).   4 *second* be / are *TCD, Dob, O'F, W*.   6 rough / tough *1635–54, Dob, O'F*.   8 Give / And give *Dob*.   15 her / the *O'F*.   16 She'hath yet / Yet shee hath *O'F*.   18 the / that *1635–69, TCD, Dob, W*. words / letters *C57, Cy, W*.   24 she is / she is as *C57*; is she *Cy*.   26 wonderfull / wondrous *O'F*.   30 which / that *O'F* (*and others*). worse / worst *Dob*.   39 needs / neede *O'F*.   40 foes / foe *Dob*.   41 round . . . drowne / foule Country drownes *Dob, O'F*.   42 guards . . . armes / armes . . . guards *Cy*. towne / townes *Dob, O'F*.   44 Which / Who *TCC, Dob, O'F*.   45 like / like to *O'F*. turnes / makes *Dob*. the / *omitted Dob, O'F*.   49 childbeds / childbirths *1669*,

SP (*changed from* childbedd), *TCD, Dob, O'F* (*changed from* childbeds);
child-birth *Lut, Cy.* 50 'twere / 'twas *Dob.* 53–54 *omitted 1635–54.* 53
and her / or a *O'F.*

18. ELEGIE: ON HIS MISTRIS.

COPY TEXT: 1635.

TEXTS: 1635–69; H49, D, SP, Lec, C57, TCD, N, TCC, A18, DC, Dob, S96,
Lut, O'F, HM198, Hd, O, P, JC, D17, B, S, K, W, S962, A25, RP117; Ee.4.14,
Add 29 (ll. 33–44), EP.e.14, M, Wel; V.a.103, V.a.262, Rosenbach 1083/16
(ll. 1–18, 25–26, 47–56).

COLLATION: 1635–69, C57, TCD, Dob, O'F, W (one reading from Lut).
Title / Elegie *C57, TCD, W;* . . . desire to be disguised, and to goe like a Page
with him. *Dob;* . . . desiring . . . and goe . . . *O'F.* 1 interview, *Gr.* / ∼ₐ
1635. 3 starving / starv'ling *C57, TCD.* 7 fathers / parents *C57, TCD,
Dob, W.* 9 the / those *C57, TCD.* 11 overswear / ever sweare *C57, TCD.*
12 wayes / means *1669, C57, TCD, Dob, W.* 18 My . . . thee / From other
lands my soule towards thee *C57, TCD, Dob* (t'ward), *W.* 26 Lovers /
Freinds *Dob.* 28 mindes; *TCD and Gr.* / minde, *1635–69, C57, Dob, O'F.*
35 Loves / Lives *1669, C57, Dob, W.* 37 no lesse / *omitted C57, Dob;*
knowe thee and *TCD, W.* 39 Page, *Gr.* / ∼ₐ*1635.* 40 hunt / haunt *C57,
TCD, W.* 46 greatest / greate *C57, TCD, W.* call / doe call *TCD.* to / into
W. 49 *third* nor / *omitted C57, TCD, W.* 51 midnights / midnight *C57,
Dob, Lut.* startings / starting *C57.*

19. ELEGIE: HIS PICTURE.

COPY TEXT: 1633.

TEXTS: 1633–69; H49, D, SP, Lec, C57, TCD, N, TCC, A18, DC, S96, Lut,
O'F, HM198, Hd, Cy, O, P, JC, D17, B, S, K, W, S962, A25, RP117; Ee.4.14,
E2230, H3511, RP160; V.a.103, Rosenbach 243/4.

COLLATION: 1633–69, C57, TCD, S96, O'F, W (some readings from Lut and
Cy). *Title 1635* / Elegie V *1633* (*similar C57, TCD, S96, O'F, W*). 6 Perhaps / Perchance *W.* 8 rash / harsh *1635–69, O'F.* stormes, being / horinesse
1635–69, O'F, W; stormes *C57, S96.* 10 powders / powder *S96.* on / are
S96, Lut. 16 now / like and *C57, S96, O'F, W.* did love / lov'd *O'F.* 19
nurse / nourish *TCD.* now is / is now *Cy.* strong / tough *Cy.* 20 that, which
/ what *S96, O'F.*

20. ELEGIE: LOVES PROGRESS.

COPY TEXT: 1669.

TEXTS: 1669; *Wit and Drollery;* H49, D, SP, Lec, C57, TCD, N, TCC, A18,
S96, Lut, O'F, Hd, Cy, O, P, JC, D17, B, S, K, A25, RP117; Add 29, Emmanuel
(ll. 41–64), Grey; RP116, V.a.245, V.a.262 (ll. 1–64), V.a.322, Rutgers, Rosenbach 239/27 (ll. 41–74, 79–96), Rosenbach 239/18 (*passim*).

COLLATION: 1669, C57, TCD, S96, O'F (some readings from Cy). *Title Ed.*
/ An Elegie on Loves Progresse *1669, S96* (An *omitted*); Elegie *C57, TCD;*
Loves Progresse *O'F.* 2 that / which *C57, TCD.* 4 Love is / And love is
C57, TCD; And Loves *S96, O'F.* 5 strange *MSS* / strong *1669.* 11 I, *Gr.*

/ ∼ₐ *1669*. 14 ever / forever *S96, O'F*. 18 and / but *C57, TCD, O'F, Cy*.
20 them / *omitted O'F*. 21 woman / women *S96*. 22 be / see *S96*. 24
woman / women *S96*. 25 beauty'is not *MSS* / beauties no *1669*. thusₐ *Gr*.
/ ∼: *1669*. 27 if he / hee that *O'F, Cy*. 30 abound; *Ed*. / ∼, *1669*. 32
in *TCD* / on *1669, S96, O'F, Cy*. 40 erre / stray *C57, TCD, O'F, Cy*. face!
Ed. / ∼? *1669*. 42 springes *O'F* / springs *1669, C57, TCD*. 46 and *O'F* /
but *1669*. our *O'F* / a *1669, S96*. 47 first *MSS* / sweet *1669*. 52 Canaries
/ Canary *C57*. Ambrosiall, *Ed*. / ∼. *1669*. 53 Her . . . lips; To which when
MSS / Unto her . . . lips when *1669*. 55 *first* there / their *C57, Cy*. 57
There *O'F* / Then *1669, Cy*. where / when *C57*. 59 These / That *O'F*. 60
Ore . . . streight *MSS* / Being past the straits of *1669*. 62 but / but of *TCD*.
63 yet / that *C57, TCD, S96, O'F*. 64 scatter'd *Ed*. / scattered *1669*. 65
Sailing *Ed*. / Sailng *1669*. 67 thence *MSS* / there *1669*. thy *MSS* / the *1669*.
68 wouldst *MSS* / should'st *1669*. 70 many / some doe *C57, TCD, S96*.
further / farther *C57, O'F*. 75 thy / as *O'F* (*added*). 79 that / which
C57. 82 Which / That *S96*. began / begun *TCD*. 90 elements *MSS* / enemies *1669*. 95 He which . . . not / Who . . . not so *O'F*. 96 Clyster *S96* /
glister *1669, Cy*; Glysters *C57*. gave *S96* / gives *1669, TCD, O'F, Cy*.

21. ELEGIE: HIS PARTING FROM HER.

COPY TEXT: 1669.

TEXTS: Short (various: e.g. ll. 1–4, 45–56, 67–82, 95–104)–1635–54; B, A25,
RP117; A30982, Emmanuel (ll. 1–4); V.a.97, V.a.103, V.a.125, V.a.170,
V.a.245, V.a.262, V.a.339, V.a.345, Malone 16, Sparrow, Rosenbach 239/27.
Long–1669; S96, Lut, O'F, HM198, O, P, H40, S962, TCD(II) (ll. 1–94);
RP31.

COLLATION: 1635–69, S96, O'F (some readings from H40). *Title 1635* /
Elegie XIII *1669* (*similar S96, O'F*). 1 night, *Gr*. / ∼ₐ *1669*. 4 Love /
soule *1635–54*. 6 Thou and *H40* / And that *1669*. 9 thee *H40* / them
1669, S96, O'F. 11 felt want *H40* / self-want *1669*. sight, *Gr*. / ∼ₐ *1669*.
12 fires *H40* / fire *1669*. 14 Or / Are *S96*. soe *H40* / such *1669*. 17 the
H40 / thy *1669*. 18 Pains / paine *S96, O'F*. 20 That thus with parting thou
seek'st us to spight? *1669*. merits / causes *S96*. 21 was *H40* / is *1669*. to /
omitted O'F. 23 lov'dₐ . . . before) *Gr*. / ∼) . . . ∼ₐ *1669*. forme *H40* /
me *1669*. 25 now, sooner *H40* / sooner now *1669*. 26 golden / gold *S96*,
O'F. rapt *Gr*. / wrapt *1669*. 27 a *H40* / the *1669*. 30 my / mine *S96, O'F*.
31 my *H40* / *omitted 1669*. own *H40* / one *1669*. glad *H40* / sad *1669*. 34
followers *H40* / favourites *1669, S96, O'F*. 36 blouds / harts *S96*; bloud *O'F*.
37 glow / blow *1669*. 38 flame / flames *1669*. 40 dark, so *Gr. and MSS*
/ ∼ₐ and *1669*. 42 towring / towred *S96, O'F*. 43 That . . . oylie *H40* /
Inflam'd with th'ouglie *1669*. 44 with *H40* / in *1669*. 45 not kept our
S96 / for this kept *1669*. on / o'r *1635–54*. 46 whilst / when *S96, O'F*. 49
most *H40* / best *1669*. 52 *second* our / *omitted 1635–54*. 53 these / the
1635–69, O'F. 54 inwards . . . panting / colours inwards as thy *S96, O'F* (inward). 56 Must / Shall *S96, O'F*. 61 rive *H40* / ruine *1669*. 62 her *H40*
/ his *1669, O'F*. yet / it *S96*. 66 thy / thine *S96, O'F*. shame *H40* / name
1669. 67 Do thy great / Fortune doe thy *1635–54*. 69 Rend / Bend *1635–*

54. in sunder / asunder *O'F.* 70 that / still *S96, O'F.* 72 shifts. *Gr.* / ~,
1669. 76 Water / Waters *1635–69, S96, O'F.* 78 How . . . the / Shall tell,
our Love was fresh in the *S96;* . . . how fresh our Love in *O'F.* 79 ripen'd in
H40 / inripened *1639–69.* eare *H40* / yeare *1635–69.* 85 Though *H40* /
The *1669, S96, O'F.* 87 he *H40* / we *1669.* 92 be / by *S96.* constancy
H40 / her inconstancy *1669.* 93 enamour'd *Ed.* / enamoured *1669.* on / of
S96, O'F. 94 my / mine *S96, O'F.* there reflected *H40* / here neglected *1669.*
95 For *H40* / And *1635–69.* th' / *omitted O'F.* 96 words *H40* / deeds *1635–
69, S96, O'F.* 97 Poles / Pole *S96, O'F.* ere / when *S96, O'F.* 102 oft, *Gr.*
/ ~ₐ *1669.* would *H40* / most *1669.*

22. ELEGIE: THE EXPOSTULATION.

COPY TEXT: 1633.

TEXTS: 1633–69; *Underwood;* TCD (ll. 31–70), N, Dob, S96, Lut, O'F,
HM198, Hd, Cy, O, P, B, S, HN, L74, H40, S962; CCC.E.327, RP31, Hyde,
M; V.a.162 (ll. 1–54), Rosenbach 1083/17. I do not find this poem in A25 as
listed by Miss Gardner.

COLLATION: 1633–69, TCD (and N), Dob, O'F (some readings from Cy).
Title 1635 / Elegie. *1633, Dob, O'F.* 2 prove / find *O'F.* 7 *second* or /
and *Dob, O'F.* 8 it / she *Dob, O'F* (> it). 16 sweeter / sweetened *1635–69,
Dob, O'F.* 24 thought / thoughts *1635–69, Dob, O'F.* 25 love / loved *Dob,
O'F* (> love). though / *omitted N, Dob; added O'F.* 26 inconstancie / constancy *Cy.* 30 would / will *1635–69, Dob, O'F.* his / her *O'F.* 33 breast /
beast *O'F* (> brest). 37 he / The *Dob, O'F.* 52 dogges, *Gr.* / ~; *1633.* 53
have I / I have *1669, Dob, O'F.* 58 Delight . . . worke / not in made workes
delight *Dob, O'F.* whiles / whilst *Dob, O'F.* 62 Actors / Actor *Dob, O'F.*

23. ELEGIE: VARIETY.

COPY TEXT: 1650.

TEXTS: 1650–69; [O'F], HM198 (twice), JC, D17; A10; Don.b.9 (ll. 53–82).
COLLATION: 1650–69, HM198 (Bk. II), JC. *Title Gr.* / *omitted 1650–69;*
Elegy *HM198.* 1 motion, why *Gr.* / ~ₐ~, *1650.* 2 much lov'd / belov'd
HM198. 3 love *JC* / lov'd *1650–69.* 4 diversifi'd: *Gr.* / ~ₐ *1650.* 8 beginnes / beginne *HM198.* 12 farr *JC* / cleare *1650–69.* 16 share / inheire
HM198. 19 aver *JC* / ever *1650–69.* 21 would / could *HM198.* 24–36
omitted A10 (with additional line after 23). 29 brown, *Gr.* / ~ₐ *1650.* 31
are *JC* / were *1650–69.* 37 times / time *HM198.* 38 crime! *Gr.* / ~? *1650.*
41 Kindreds / Kindred *HM198, JC.* 43 ask'd *Ed.* / asked *1650.* 45 title *JC*
/ little *1650–69.* 49 liberty / Liberties *HM198.* 52 is / is as *HM198, JC.*
53 it *JC* / its *1650–69.* 71–78 *omitted A10.* 72 same / flame *HM198, JC.*
76 returnes / returne *HM198.* 81 being / havinge *HM198.* one, *Gr.* / ~ₐ
1650. 82 leave / love *HM198.*

24. SAPHO TO PHILÆNIS.

COPY TEXT: 1633.

TEXTS: 1633–69; TCD, N, TCC, A18, DC, Lut, O'F, HM198, Hd (ll. 55–64),
O, P, JC, D17, A25; A10, Grey.

COLLATION: 1633–69, TCD, O'F, HM198, JC. *Title* / Eleg. 18th *JC; omitted HM198.* 1 holy / hott *HM198, JC.* 2 have? *Gr.* / ∼, 1633. 3 workes / worke *1649–69, O'F.* 8 maker, *Gr.* / ∼; 1633. want / wants *JC.* 10 that / it *HM198, JC.* fires environ / fire envyrons *O'F.* 13 Dwells . . . mine / with one still dwels my *HM198;* Within still dwells my *JC.* 15 Thou art / even *HM198, JC.* 16 to . . . doe / I doe to men *HM198;* I doe to thee *JC.* 17 thereby / by thee *HM198, JC.* 18 to / *omitted JC.* 22 Cedars / as Cedars *TCD.* 26 oh / *omitted HM198, JC.* be / thou bee *1635–69, O'F, HM198, JC.* ever / forever *HM198, JC.* 30 of thy / *omitted Lut; deleted O'F.* 31–54 *omitted HM198, JC.* 32 which / that *O'F.* 36 pleasure / pleasures *TCD.* 37 needs / need *TCD.* 40 are∧ *Gr.* / ∼, 1633. 53 mine / my *O'F.* 56 mine / my *O'F, JC.* 58 thee *TCD* / shee *1633.* halfe / hearte *HM198, JC.* 60 *omitted HM198, JC.* 61 mighty, *Gr.* / ∼∧ 1633.

25. THE MESSAGE.

COPY TEXT: 1633.

TEXTS: 1633–69; H49, D, SP, Lec, C57 (twice), TCD, N, TCC, A18, DC, Dob, S96, Lut, O'F, HM198 (twice), Hd, Cy, O, P, JC, D17, B, S, K, S962, A25, La, RP117; Ee.4.14, A10, Hyde, Wel, Emmanuel; A19268, A32463, Ee.5.23, CCC.F.328, E2421, EP.e.37, V.a.103, V.a.339, Rosenbach 243/4; St. Michael's 1019 (ll. 1–8).

COLLATION: 1633–69, C57, TCD, Dob, O'F. Title: Songs which were made to certaine Aires which were made before *TCD* (*Nos. 25, 42, 27*). *Title 1635* / *omitted 1633, TCD;* Songe *C57, Dob, O'F.* 4 forc'd / forg'd *O'F.* 11 Which / But *O'F;* yet *some Gr. III MSS.* if / since *some Gr. III MSS.* be / hath *some Gr. III MSS.* 14 crosse *TCD* / breake *1633–69.* 18 know . . . see / see . . . know *O'F* (*and others*). 19 laugh . . . when / laugh when that *C57, Dob;* joy and laugh when *O'F.*

26. WITCHCRAFT BY A PICTURE.

COPY TEXT: 1633.

TEXTS: 1633–69; Lec (added), TCD, N, TCC, A18, DC, Dob, S96, Lut, O'F, HM198, Cy, O, P, JC, D17, B, H40, S962, Hol; RP31, Grey; HNVIII (ll. 1–4); Huygens.

COLLATION: 1633–69, Lec, TCD, Dob, O'F. *Title* / *omitted Lec;* Picture *Dob, O'F.* 4 espie; *Gr.* / ∼, 1633. 6 kill, *Gr.* / ∼? 1633. 8 sweet salt / sweetest *Dob, O'F.* 10 feares / all feares *1635–54, O'F.* 11 that / thy *Dob* (> that), *O'F.* 14 all / *omitted Dob, O'F.*

27. THE BAITE.

COPY TEXT: 1633.

TEXTS: 1633–69; Walton, *Compleat Angler;* Corkine (music only); H49, D, SP, Lec, C57, TCD, N, TCC, A18, DC, S96, Lut, O'F, HM198 (twice), Cy, O, P, JC, D17, H40, S962, La, TCD(II), RP117; H3511, Grey; A19268, Ash 47, EP.e.97 (*passim*), Eng 626, RP84, Sloane 542, HM172, V.a.96, V.a.162, V.a.169, Rosenbach 243/4.

COLLATION: 1633–69, C57, TCD, S96, O'F (plus Cy). *Title 1635 / missing 1633, C57, TCD;* Songe S96, O'F. 2 will / shall TCD. some new / all the Cy. 5 There / Then TCD. 6 thy / thine 1669, TCD, O'F, Cy. 7 there / then O'F, Cy. *9–12 added O'F.* 9 When / If O'F. 11 to / unto O'F, Cy. 14 darknest / darknes C57; dark'st them Cy. 15 selfe / heart TCD. 17 freeze / fish Cy. 18 with 1635 / which 1633. 20 snare / haire Cy. windowie / winding 1669, Cy; windowe Lec. *21–24 omitted S96.* 21 bold / cold Cy. 23 sleavesilke 1635 / sleavesicke 1633; with silke Cy. 25 thou / there SP, S96; then C57. 26 bait; Gr. / ~, 1633. 27 catch'd / caught TCD, S96.

28. THE APPARITION.

COPY TEXT: 1633.

TEXTS: 1633–69; H49, D, SP, Lec, C57, TCD, N, TCC, A18, DC, Dob, S96, Lut, O'F, HM198, Hd, Cy, O, P, JC, D17, B, S, H40, S962, A25, RP117; H3511, Wel, Sloane 1792, Grey; Ash 36, EP.c.50, Eng 626, V.a.103, HNVIII (ll. 11–12), Rosenbach 239/23, Rosenbach 243/4; Edinburgh D.C.1.69 (*passim*); Huygens.

COLLATION: 1633–69, C57, TCD, Dob, O'F (some readings from Cy). Title: The / An TCD, Dob, O'F. 2 free / farr O'F. 3 solicitation / sollicitations O'F. from / by O'F. 5 thee, . . . vestall, Gr. / ~_∧ . . . ~_∧ 1633. fain'd vestall / fond virgin O'F (> faynd vestall). 8 or . . . to / or . . . or TCD; to . . . or O'F (> or . . . to). 10 in / in a TCD, O'F. will / *omitted 1635–54,* O'F. 11 And then / Thou C57, TCD, Cy; And there Dob. thou / then C57, TCD, Cy. 12 lye / be TCD. 17 rest still / keepe thee O'F, Cy.

29. THE BROKEN HEART.

COPY TEXT: 1633.

TEXTS: 1633–69; *Helpe to Memory* (ll. 1–16); H49, D, SP, Lec, C57 (twice), TCD, N, TCC, A18, DC, Dob, S96, Lut, O'F, HM198, Hd, Cy, O, P, JC, D17, B, S, K, L74, H40, S962, A25, La, RP117; Ee.4.14, Add 29, EP.e.14 (ll. 1–14), A10, A30982, E2230, M, Wales 5308E, Grey; Eng 626, V.a.103, V.a.345 (ll. 9–32), Rosenbach 1083/16; Huygens.

COLLATION: 1633–69, C57, TCD, Dob, O'F (some readings from Cy). *Title / Songe C57, Dob; omitted TCD, O'F.* 8 flaske / flash 1635–69, C57, TCD, Dob (> flask), O'F (> flaske). 10 come! Gr. / ~? 1633. 12 some; Gr. / ~, 1633. 15 chain'd / chaine TCD, Dob, O'F. 17 did / could TCD, Dob, O'F; would Cy. 20 But / And TCD, Cy. 21 thee / thine TCD, O'F, Cy. 22 thine / thy C57, TCD, Dob, O'F. 23 alas, Gr. / ~_∧ 1633. 24 one / the Dob. first / fierce TCD. 30 hundred / thousand TCD, Cy.

30. LECTURE UPON THE SHADOW.

COPY TEXT: 1635.

TEXTS: 1635–69; H49, D, SP, Lec, C57, TCD, N, TCC, A18, DC, Dob, S96, Lut, O'F, HM198 (twice), O, P, JC, D17, B, S, K, L74, H40, S962, A25, La; Add 29 (ll. 1–13), E2230.

COLLATION: 1635–69, C57, TCD, Dob, O'F (some readings from Lec and DC). *Title 1650 / Song 1635; omitted C57;* Shaddow Dob; The Shadow O'F.

3 These / Those C57, DC (*and others*). that / which C57, DC, Dob, O'F. 4 Walking / In walking C57, DC, Dob. here, Gr. / ~; 1635. 7 those / these Dob. 9 whilst / while Lec, Dob; whyles C57. loves / love C57, Dob, O'F. 11 care C57 / cares 1635–69, TCD, O'F (*changed from* eares). but / *omitted* O'F. 12 high'st / last C57; least Lec, Dob, O'F. 13 is still / still is O'F. diligent / vigilant O'F. 14 loves / love C57, DC, Dob, O'F. 17 Others / other O'F. 19 our / once C57, DC, Dob (*as alternate*). loves / love C57, DC, Dob, O'F. 21 mine / my O'F. 26 first MSS / short 1635–69.

31. A VALEDICTION FORBIDDING MOURNING.

COPY TEXT: 1633.

TEXTS: 1633–69; Walton; H49, D, SP, Lec, C57, TCD, N, TCC, A18, DC, Dob, S96, Lut, O'F, HM198, Cy, O, P, JC, D17, B, S, L74, H40, S962, A25, La; Add 29, EP.e.14, A10, E2230, Hyde, H3511, Sloane 1792, Emmanuel, Grey; Ash 51, Chetham, EP.e.37, H4888, RP142 (ll. 1–8), V.a.170, Rosenbach 243/4, Sparrow; Huygens.

COLLATION: 1633–69, C57, TCD, Dob, O'F (some readings from DC, Cy, and JC). *Title* / Upon the parting from his Mistresse Dob, O'F (. . . Valediction 1). A / *omitted* TCD. forbidding mourning / *omitted* C57, Cy. 3 Whilst /And C57, TCD (*and others*). 4 The . . . now / nowe his breath parts Dob (*and others in variant*). 6 No / Nor Dob. 8 our / of our TCD, O'F (*and others*). 9 Moving / Movinges DC, Dob, O'F. brings / cause Dob, O'F. 10 it / they JC. 11 trepidation / trepidations Dob. 12 is / are Dob. 16 which / that Dob. 17 a / *omitted* O'F, Cy. 18 That / as Dob, O'F. 20 Care lesse / Carelesse 1639–54, TCD (*and others*). and O'F / *omitted* 1633. 21 therefore / then Dob, O'F. are / are but Dob, O'F. 22 goe / part Dob, O'F. 24 Like / As DC, Dob, O'F. 28 but / yet Dob, O'F. 30 when / whilst Dob, O'F. 32 that / yt C57, TCD, Dob (> that). 33 wilt thou be / then be thou JC. 35 makes / drawes JC. circle / circles 1639–54.

32. THE GOOD-MORROW.

COPY TEXT: 1633.

TEXTS: 1633–69; H49, D, SP, Lec, C57, TCD, N, TCC, A18, DC, Dob, S96, Lut, O'F, HM198, Hd, O, P, JC, D17, B, S, K, L74, H40, S962, A25, TCD(II); Add 29 (ll. 15–21); E2230, Emmanuel, Wales 5308E, Grey; V.a.103, HNVIII (ll. 4, 15–18), Rosenbach 1083/16.

COLLATION: 1633–69, C57, TCD, Dob, O'F. *Title* / *omitted* C57, Dob (*added in different hand*), O'F. 2 lov'd? Gr. / ~, 1633. 3 countrey . . . childishly / childish . . . sillily C57 (*changed from* countrey . . . childishly), TCD, Dob, O'F. pleasures / pleasure O'F. 4 snorted / slumbered C57 (*changed from* snorted), TCD (*and others*). 10 For / But TCD (*and others*). 11 one / a TCD (*and others*). 13 others MSS / other 1633–69. 14 first one / our TCD, Dob, O'F. 16 true plaine / plaine true TCD (*and others*). 17 better / fitter 1635–69, TCD, Dob, O'F. 18 North / Frost C57. 19 was / is 1669, TCD (*and others*). 20 our two / both our TCD (*and others*). or / both 1635–69, O'F. 21 so / just 1635–69, TCD, Dob, O'F. that / in all 1635–69, TCD, Dob, O'F. doe . . . none / of these loves 1635–69, TCD, Dob, O'F.

33. SONG: "GOE, AND CATCHE A FALLING STARRE."

COPY TEXT: 1633.

TEXTS: 1633–69; *Helpe to Memory* (*passim*); H49, D, SP, Lec, C57, TCD, N, TCC, A18, DC, Dob, S96, Lut, O'F, HM198, Cy, O, P, JC, D17, B, S, L74, H40, S962, A25, Hol, RP117; Ee.4.14, Add 29, Grey; A5956, EP.e.37, Osborn (CPB), V.a.103, V.a.162, Wales 5390D, Rosenbach 240/7 (variant of ll. 1–6), Rosenbach 243/4; E2013; Huygens.

COLLATION: 1633–69, C57, TCD, Dob, O'F. *Title / omitted DC, O'F; A . . . Dob.* 6 *indented 1633.* 7 And / or *Dob* (> and). 11 to / go *1669, Dob; omitted C57, TCD.* 14 Thou / Then *TCD.* when thou / at thy *Dob, O'F.* retorn'st / returne *Dob, O'F.* 15 wonders / things *O'F.* that / that e're *O'F.* 20 were / is *TCD.* 21 I / for I *Dob, O'F (changed from I).* 22 might / should *Dob.*

34. WOMANS CONSTANCY.

COPY TEXT: 1633.

TEXTS: 1633–69; H49, D, SP, Lec, C57, TCD, N, TCC, A18, DC, Dob, Lut, O'F, HM198, O, P, B, S, L74, H40, S962, Hol; CCC.E.327, Grey; H3991 (ll. 8–10); Huygens. (Miss Gardner correctly states in the textual notes that S96 omits, but incorrectly does not except this poem from S96 in the list on p. 166.)

COLLATION: 1633–69, C57, TCD, Dob, O'F. *Title / omitted C57.* 8 Or / For *1635–54, O'F.* 14 these / those *TCD, Dob.*

35. "IMAGE OF HER WHOM I LOVE."

COPY TEXT: 1633.

TEXTS: 1633–69; H49, D, SP, Lec, C57, TCD, N, TCC, A18, DC, Dob, S96, Lut, O'F, HM198 (twice), Hd, O, P, JC, D17, B, S, L74, H40, S962; H3991 (l. 24); HNVIII (ll. 23–26).

COLLATION: 1633–69, C57, TCD, Dob, O'F. *no stanzas, 1633. Title /* Elegie *1633, TCD, O'F;* Elegie X. The Dreame *1635–54; omitted C57, Lut.* 6 great . . . good / good . . . great *O'F.* 7 sense∧ *Gr. / ~, 1633.* 8 dull; *Gr. / ~, 1633.* 17 a such / such a *1669, C57.*

36. THE SUNNE RISING.

COPY TEXT: 1633.

TEXTS: 1633–69; H49, D, SP, Lec, C57, TCD, N, TCC, A18, DC, Dob, S96, Lut, O'F, HM198, Cy, O, P, JC, D17, B, S, K, L74, S962, A25; Add 29, Wel, Grey; V.a.103; Huygens.

COLLATION: 1633–69, C57, TCD, Dob, O'F (some readings from Lut). *Title / Ad Solem SP;* To the Sunne *C57, Cy;* Ad solem. A songe *Dob;* Ad Solem. To the Sunne. Song *O'F.* The / *omitted TCD.* 6 sowre / fowre *O'F.* 7 will / doth *TCD.* 8 offices; *Gr. / ~, 1633.* 12 Why shouldst thou / Dost thou not *1635–69, O'F.* 17 the / *omitted C57, TCD, Dob, O'F.* spice / space *1649–54.* 18 leftst / left *1635–69.* lie / bee *Dob* (> ly). 19 whom / which *Dob, O'F.* 21 States . . . Princes / princes . . . states *Dob.* 23 us; *Gr. / ~, 1633.* to / with *O'F.* 28 world / worlds *C57.* that's / that *TCD.*

37. THE INDIFFERENT.

COPY TEXT: 1633.

TEXTS: 1633–69; H49, D, SP, Lec, C57, TCD, N, TCC, A18, DC, Dob, S96, Lut, O'F, HM198, Hd, O, P, JC, D17, B, S, K, H40, S962; Ee.4.14, A10, Wales 5308E; V.a.162 (ll. 1–9).

COLLATION: 1633–69, C57, TCD, Dob, O'F (some readings from SP, TCC, and Lut). *Title* / Songe *C57, Dob; omitted O'F.* 3 *first* and / *omitted 1649–54.* 11 did / *omitted C57.* mothers / mother *O'F.* 12 Or / *omitted C57, Dob, O'F.* all / *omitted C57, Dob, O'F.* spent / worn *1669, Dob (changed from* spent). others / other *O'F.* 13 feare / shame *Dob* (> feare). 16 Rob / Rack *C57.* 17 who / which *SP, TCD, O'F.* 18 subject / object *O'F* (> subject). 20 Part / sweet *1669, Dob* (> part). 21 and / *omitted 1635–69.* that / *omitted 1635–69, TCD, Dob, O'F.* so / *omitted TCC, O'F.* 23 Some / but *C57, TCD.* 26 you / they *C57.* 27 are / were *C57.*

38. LOVES USURY.

COPY TEXT: 1633.

TEXTS: 1633–69; H49, D, SP, Lec, C57, DC, Dob, S96, Lut, O'F, HM198 (twice), Hd, Cy, O, P, B, S, K, L74, H40, S962.

COLLATION: 1633–69, C57, DC, Dob, O'F. *Title* / *omitted C57, O'F.* 5 raigne / range *1635–69, Dob, O'F.* 6 snatch / match *1635–54, O'F.* 13 sport; *Gr.* / ~∧ *1633.* 15 let / let not *1635–54, Dob, O'F.* 19 *second* or / and *1635–54, O'F, Cy.* 20 covet, most∧ *C57* / ~∧~, *1633.* 21 *second* then / *omitted DC;* the *Dob, O'F* (> then). 22 fruit / fruits *C57, Dob, O'F.* 24 loves / love *1635–54.*

39. THE CANONIZATION.

COPY TEXT: 1633.

TEXTS: 1633–69; H49, D, SP, Lec, C57, TCD, N, TCC, A18, DC, Dob, S96, Lut, O'F, HM198 (twice), Hd, Cy, O, P, JC, D17, B, S, K, H40, S962 (twice), La, TCD(II), RP117; Ee.4.14, Grey; HNVIII (*passim*).

COLLATION: 1633–69, C57, TCD (plus TCC), Dob, O'F (some readings from DC and Cy). Title: The / *omitted 1649–69, Dob.* 3 five / true *1635–54;* fine *Dob, O'F.* 4 your . . . Arts / with Artes your minds *Dob.* improve, *Gr.* / ~∧ *1633.* 7 Or / And *C57, TCD, Dob, O'F.* reall / Royall *C57.* 13 omitted *C57.* colds / cold *TCD, Cy.* 14 the / those *TCD, Dob.* 15 more / man *TCD, Dob, O'F.* 20 mee / and mee *TCD.* 22 dove. *Gr.* / ~, *1633.* 24 two / *omitted Dob, O'F.* 29 tombes / tomb *1669, TCD, O'F, Cy.* and / or *1669, TCD, Dob.* 30 legend *TCD* / legends *1633, C57.* 31 Chronicle / Chronicles *TCD.* 34–45 *missing TCD.* 35 these / those *1635–69, DC, Dob* (*changed from* this), *O'F, Cy.* hymnes / Hymne *Dob* (> Hymnes). 37 reverend / reverenc'd *TCC.* 40 worlds soule / world *TCC.* extract *C57* / contract *1633, O'F* (*changed from* extract). drove / drawe *C57, DC, Cy.* 44 from *Ed.* / frow *1633.* 45 your / our *1633–54, C57, DC, O'F* (*changed from* your).

40. THE TRIPLE FOOLE.

COPY TEXT: 1633.

TEXTS: 1633–69; H49, D, SP, Lec, C57, TCD, N, TCC, A18, DC, Dob, S96, Lut, O'F, HM198, Hd, Cy, O, P, JC, D17, B, S, K, HN, L74, H40, S962; Ee.4.14, Grey; H3991 (ll. 10–11), H4888, V.a.103; Huygens.

COLLATION: 1633–69, C57, TCD, Dob, O'F. *Title* / Song *C57, O'F* (A . . .), *Cy.* 6 narrow crooked / crooked narrow *Dob, O'F.* 9 should / could *C57.* 13 art / act *TCD.* art . . . voice / voyce . . . art *Dob, O'F.* 14 Set / sitt *TCD, Dob, O'F* (> sett). 20 triumphs / trialls *Dob* (*changed from* triumphs), *O'F.*

41. LOVES INFINITENESS.

COPY TEXT: 1633.

TEXTS: 1633–69; H49, D, SP, Lec, C57, DC, Dob, S96, Lut, O'F, HM198, O, P, JC, D17, B, S, K (ll. 1–22), H40, S962, A25, RP117; A23, Add 29, E2230; EP.c.50, Rosenbach 1083/16.

COLLATION: 1633–69, C57, DC, Dob, O'F. *Title Gr.* / Lovers . . . *1633–69; A* Lovers . . . *DC; omitted C57, O'F.* 1 thy / your *C57, Dob.* 5 And / *omitted C57, DC, Dob, O'F* (*added*) (*and others*). 6 *first* and / *omitted C57.* 8 Then / That *1639–54.* 11 Thee / It *1635–69, O'F.* 16 Which / who *Dob, O'F.* 17 and / in *1635–69, Dob.* 20 it *1635* / is *1633.* 21 is / was *1635–54, Dob* (*changed from* is), *O'F.* 32 them / thee *C57; omitted Dob.*

42. SONG: "SWEETEST LOVE, I DO NOT GOE."

COPY TEXT: 1633.

TEXTS: 1633–69; H49, D, SP, Lec, C57, TCD, N, TCC, A18, DC, Dob, S96, Lut, O'F, HM198 (twice), Hd, O, P, JC, D17, B, S, K, H40, S962, A25, La, RP117; Add 29, EP.e.14, Wel; Eng 626, V.a.103, V.a.345, H6918, Rosenbach 1083/16; St. Michael's 1018, A10337.

COLLATION: 1633–69, C57, TCD, Dob, O'F (some readings from TCC, DC, and JC). *Title* / *omitted TCD.* 1–2, 3–4, 6–7 *one line each in each stanza, C57, TCD* (*and others*). 6 Must . . . last / At the last must part *1635–54, O'F.* 7 To / Thus to *1635–69, O'F* (*and others*). 8 Thus / *omitted 1635–69, O'F.* deaths / death *JC.* 9 Yesternight / Yesterday *TCC, O'F* (*and others*). 15 journeyes / returne *Dob.* since I / since I doe *Dob;* and doe *JC.* 19 Cannot / It cannot *JC.* another / one other *C57, JC;* one *DC.* 20 recall! *Gr.* / ~? *1633.* 22 joyne / adde *O'F* (*and others*). 25–32 *omitted TCD* (*l.* 32 *given as l.* 24 *and deleted*). 25 not / no *1635–69.* 28 lifes / life *O'F* (*and others*). 32 Thou / That *1635–54, Dob, O'F.* 36 may / make *1639–54, TCD* (> may).

43. THE LEGACIE.

COPY TEXT: 1633.

TEXTS: 1633–69; H49, D, SP, Lec, C57, TCD, N, TCC, A18, DC, Dob, S96, Lut, O'F, HM198, Hd, Cy, O, P, B, S, K, L74, H40, S962, A25, La, Hol, TCD(II) (ll. 9–24); E2230, Hyde, Emmanuel, Wales 5308E, Grey; RP116 (ll. 9–24), V.a.345, Rosenbach 1083/16; Huygens. Miss Gardner lists RP117 and CCC.E.327.

COLLATION: 1633–69, C57, TCD, Dob, O'F. *Title* / Song *C57, Dob, O'F;* Elegie *TCD. no indentation, 1633.* 3 but / *omitted TCD, O'F, Cy.* 4 be / are *Dob.* 7 sent / meant *1635–54, Dob* (> sent), *O'F* (> sent). 9 mee / thee *C57.* 10 that is *1635* / that's *1633.* is / *omitted C57.* 12 bid / bad *Dob.* 13 I alas / alas I *O'F.* 14 me / *omitted 1635–69, TCD, Dob, O'F.* hearts / heart *C57, Dob.* should *1635* / did *1633, C57, Dob.* lye; *Gr.* / ~, *1633.* 18 But / For *1649–69.* 22 losses / losse be yee *C57 (and others).* 23 meant / thought *TCD, Dob, O'F.* this / that *1635–69, TCD, O'F (and others).*

44. A FEAVER.

COPY TEXT: 1633.

TEXTS: 1633–69; H49, D, SP, Lec, C57, TCD, N, TCC, A18, DC, Dob, S96, Lut, O'F, HM198 (three times), Hd, Cy, O, P, JC, D17, B, S, L74, H40, S962, Hol, TCD(II); Grey.

COLLATION: 1633–69, C57, TCD, Dob, O'F. Title: A / *omitted TCD;* The *O'F.* 5 know; *Gr.* / ~, *1633.* 6 this / the *O'F.* 18 torturing / tormenting *O'F (changed from* torturing). 19 much / more *1635–69, O'F.* 22 is soone / soone is *1669, O'F (and others).*

45. AIRE AND ANGELS.

COPY TEXT: 1633.

TEXTS: 1633–69; H49, D, SP, Lec, C57, TCD, N, TCC, A18, DC, Dob, S96, Lut, O'F, HM198 (twice), Hd, O, P, JC, D17, B, S, K, H40, S962.

COLLATION: 1633–69, C57, TCD, Dob, O'F. 1 indented *1633.* 4 bee; *Gr.* / ~, *1633.* 5 Still / Till *C57.* came, *Gr.* / ~ᴧ *1633.* 13 assume / assumes *C57.* 14 lip / lips *Dob, O'F.* 17 wares / warrs *TCD, Dob, Lut;* waves *O'F.* 19 Ev'ry / Thy Every *1649–69.* 22 inhere / inheritt *TCD.* 24 it / yett *C57.* 28 love / Loves *Dob, O'F.*

46. BREAKE OF DAY.

COPY TEXT: 1633.

TEXTS: 1633–69; Gough (ll. 1–6), Cotgrave (twice; ll. 1–6); *Loyal Garland* (ll. 1–6); Corkine; H49, D, SP, Lec, C57, TCD, N, TCC, A18, DC, Dob, S96, Lut, O'F, HM198 (twice), P, JC, D17, B, S, L74, H40, S962, A25, Hol, A10, RP117; Ee.4.14, Add 29, A30982, E2230, H3511, Wel, Sloane 1792, Grey; A15227 (ll. 1–12), A19268 (ll. 1–6), Ash 47 (ll. 1–6), CCC.F.328 (ll. 1–6), Eng 686 (ll. 1–6), EP.f.25 (ll. 1–12), H4888, Don.d.58, RP214 (ll. 1–6), Sloane 542 (ll. 1–6), V.a.97 (ll. 1–6), V.a.103, V.a.262 (ll. 1–6), V.a.345 (ll. 1–6), Rosenbach 239/27 (ll. 1–6), Rosenbach 243/4, Rosenbach 1083/17; Huygens. Sometimes combined with verses by John Dowland; stanza one appears in a frequent variant as noted.

COLLATION: 1633–69, C57, TCD, Dob, O'F. *Title* / *omitted C57;* Sonnet *Dob, O'F.* 1 though / if *(variant).* 2 O wilt / Wilt *TCD (and others);* And will *O'F.* thou / you *O'F.* therefore / *omitted C57.* rise / arise *(variant).*

3–4 *reversed* (*variant*). 3 Why should / And shall *or* And wilt (*variant*). because 'tis / for feare of (*variant*). 5 which / that *TCD*. spight / despight
1650–54, C57, TCD. variant: No, since in darkness we came hither. 6 in
despight / in spight *1635–39*. keepe / hold *TCD. variant:* In spight of light
wee'l lye together. 7 *omitted Lec.* 7–12 *omitted SP.* 9 were / is *TCD, Dob,
O'F.* 11 lov'd / love *TCD, O'F.* 12 that / which *C57, TCD;* as *O'F.* had /
hath *TCD, Dob, O'F.* 17 which / that *TCD, O'F* (*and others*). 18 when
. . . doth / when . . . should *1635–54;* if . . . should *TCD, O'F* (*and others*).

47. THE PROHIBITION.

COPY TEXT: 1633.

TEXTS: 1633–69; H49, D, SP, TCD, N, TCC, A18, DC, Dob, S96, Lut, O'F,
HM198 (twice), Hd, Cy, O, P, JC, D17, B, H40, S962; CCC.E.327 (ll. 11–24),
RP31.

COLLATION: 1633–69, SP, TCD, Dob, O'F (some readings from Cy). *Title /
omitted SP, O'F, Cy.* 2 forbade / forbid *Dob, O'F.* 5 *omitted SP, TCD.* thee
1635 / mee *1633, Dob, O'F* (> thee). what to me / that which *1633.* 6 our
life at once / at once our life *Dob.* 7 bee / thee *Dob* (*changed from* be).
17–24 *omitted TCD, Dob.* 18 neythers *SP* / ne'r their *1633–69;* neyther *O'F;*
neyther their *Cy.* 22 Stage *TCD* / stay *1633, SP.* 23 Lest / Then least *1635–
54, SP, O'F, Cy.* thou / *omitted SP, O'F, Cy. first* and / *omitted 1635–54, SP,
O'F, Cy.* mee / me thou *1635–69, SP, O'F, Cy.* undoe, *Gr.* / ∼∧ *1633.* 24 To
/ O *1635–69, SP, O'F, Cy.* Oh / yet *1635–69, O'F, Cy.*

48. THE ANNIVERSARIE.

COPY TEXT: 1633.

TEXTS: 1633–69; H49, D, SP, Lec, C57, TCD, N, TCC, A18, DC, Dob, S96,
Lut, O'F, HM198 (twice), Hd, Cy, O, P, JC, D17, B, S, H40, S962; Grey.

COLLATION: 1633–69, C57, TCD, Dob, O'F (some readings from Cy). *Title /
omitted C57, O'F, Cy.* 3 they / these *1635–54, O'F.* 10 his / the *C57, Dob,
O'F.* 12 divorce. *Gr.* / ∼, *1633.* 17 love∧ *Gr.* / ∼; *1633.* 20 *first* graves /
grave *1635–39, Cy.* 22 wee / now *1633–69.* 23 none / *omitted 1669, C57,
Dob; added O'F.* 24 Can be / None are *1669, C57, Dob, O'F* (> Can bee).
nor / and *C57, Cy.*

49. A VALEDICTION OF MY NAME, IN THE WINDOW.

COPY TEXT: 1633.

TEXT: 1633–69; H49, D, SP, Lec, C57, TCD, N, TCC, A18, DC, Dob, S96,
Lut, O'F, HM198 (twice), Cy (ll. 1–38), O, P, JC, D17, B, S (twice), K, H40,
S962; HNVIII.

COLLATION: 1633–69, C57, TCD, Dob, O'F (some readings from SP, TCC,
DC, Cy). *Title /* Valediction 4. of Glasse. Upon the engraving of his name with
a Dyamond in his Mrs. Windowe when hee was to travell *O'F* (Upon . . .
added). A / *omitted TCD.* my / his *Dob.* 3 Which / who *O'F.* 4 was; *Gr.*
/ ∼, *1633.* 5 eye / Eyes *TCD, Dob, O'F.* 6 diamonds / diamond *O'F.* 10
thee / mee *O'F* (thee> mee> thee). 13 nor / or *TCD, Dob, O'F.* 14 accessaries / accessarye *C57, TCD, Cy.* 15 tempests / tempest *1635–54.* 21 as

/ is *TCD*.   23 ragged / rugged *O'F*.   32 scatter'd *Ga*. / scattered *1633*.   34
flow_∧ *Gr*. / ~, *1633*.   36 these / those *1635–69, SP, TCD, Dob, O'F*.   39
'gainst / against *C57, O'F*.   44 ope / out *C57, TCD, Dob*. this / the *DC, Dob,
O'F* (> this).   45 on / *omitted SP;* in *TCC;* at *O'F*.   50 and / or *O'F*.   53
towards / to *O'F*.   55 goe / growe *C57, O'F*.   56 that / *omitted TCD*.   58
pane / Pen *1635–69, O'F*.   60 unaware / unawares *TCD, Dob, O'F*.   64 this
/ thus *1635–69, O'F* (*and others*).

50. THE AUTUMNALL.

COPY TEXT: *1633*.

TEXTS: *1633–69;* Walton (ll. 1–2, 23–34), *Parnassus Biceps;* H49, D, SP,
Lec, C57, TCD, N, TCC, A18, DC, Dob, S96, Lut, O'F, HM198, Hd, O, P, JC,
D17, B, S, K, L74, H40, S962, A25, TCD(II), RP117; EP.e.14, Hyde, M, Wel,
RP160, Emmanuel, Wales 5308E, Grey; H3991 (ll. 9–14), V.a.97, V.a.103,
E2725.

COLLATION: *1633–69,* C57, TCD, Dob, O'F (some readings from Lec and
DC). *Title* / Elegie. The Autumnall *1633,* C57 (The *omitted*), *Dob* (The
omitted); Elegie *TCD;* Elegye 12. On the Lady Herbert afterwards Danvers
O'F.   1 Summer / Summers *1635–69*.   2 one / an *O'F*.   3 our / your *1635–
54, TCD, Dob, O'F*.   6 Affection *TCD* / Affections *1633–69, DC, O'F;* Affliction *C57*. takes *TCD* / take *1633–69, O'F*.   8 shee's *TCD* / they'are *1633,
DC*.   10 tolerable / habitable *1635–69, TCD, O'F*.   14 for / or *1635–69,
DC, Dob, O'F*.   15 *second* here / hee *O'F*.   16 like / like to *O'F* (*and others*).
17 hers / her *TCD*. come / comes *O'F*.   22 Where / Where's *Dob, O'F*.   24
you / you may *C57* (*and others*).   26 enrages / brings *SP;* breeds *C57;* en-
rageth *Dob, O'F*.   27 seasonabliest / seasonablest *1635–69, C57, TCD, Dob*.
28 appetite / appetites *C57*. is / are *Lec*. past. *Gr*. / ~; *1633*.   30 large / old
1635–69, O'F.   38 soules / fooles *1635–54*.   40 made; *Gr*. / ~_∧ *1633*.   42
at / at the *Dob, O'F*.   43 Deaths / Death *1635–69*.   44 Ancient / Ancients
1635–54, O'F. Antique / Antiques *1635–54, TCD, Dob, O'F*.   47 naturall
lation *TCD* / motion natural *1633;* naturall station *1635–69, C57, Dob, O'F*.
50 out / on *1635–69, C57, TCD, Dob, O'F*. home-ward / homewards *C57,
Dob, O'F*.

51. TWICKNAM GARDEN.

COPY TEXT: *1633*.

TEXTS: *1633–69;* H49, D, SP, Lec, C57, TCD, N, TCC, A18, DC, Dob, S96,
Lut, O'F, HM198, Cy, O, P, JC, D17, B, S, K, L74, H40, S962, A25, La, Hol,
TCD(II), RP117; Ee.4.14, Add 29 (ll. 5–7, 22–27), H3511, Wel, Emmanuel
(ll. 18–22), Grey; Ee.5.23, EP.c.50, H3991 (ll. 23–25), V.a.103; Huygens.

COLLATION: *1633–69,* C57, TCD, Dob, O'F (some readings from SP, Lec,
and TCC). *Title* / *omitted C57* (*and others*).   2 come / came *TCD*.   4 balmes
/ balme *1635–69, Lec, TCC, Dob, O'F*. cure / cures *1635–69, TCD, Dob,
O'F*.   5 selfe / false *O'F* (> selfe).   8 may / might *TCD* (*and others*).   12
grave / gray *Dob, O'F*. did / would *TCD* (*and others*).   14–16 But . . . disgrace endure / Love let mee some . . . bee *C57*.   14 that / *omitted TCD*
(*and others*).   15 leave this garden *MSS* / yet leave loving *1633*.   16 peece

/ parte *TCD* (*and others*). 17 groane *SP, TCD* / grow *1633–69, C57, TCC, Dob, O'F*. 18 *not indented 1633*. my / the *1635–54, TCD, Dob, O'F*. 22 that / which *TCD* (*and others*). 24 womans *TCD* / womens *1633–69, Lec, Dob, O'F*; woemen *C57*.

52. VALEDICTION OF THE BOOKE.

COPY TEXT: *1633*.

TEXTS: *1633–69*; H49, D, SP, Lec, C57, TCD, N, TCC, A18, DC, Dob, Lut, O'F, HM198 (twice), Cy, O, P, JC, D17, B, S (twice), K, H40, S962.

COLLATION: *1633–69, C57, TCD, Dob, O'F* (some readings from SP, TCC, and DC). *Title* / A . . . *Dob, O'F; omitted Lec*. of the *TCD* / to his *1633–54*. 7 Pindar could / old *C57*. 8 her / *omitted C57*. 9 booke / looke *C57*. they say / there (*space*) *TCD*. 18 keep / helpe *DC*. these / those *Dob*. 20 tome / to me *1639–54*; Tombe *C57*. 22 only'are / ar onely *O'F*. 25 Goths *TCD* / the Goths *1633–54*. inundate *TCD* / invade *1633–54, Dob, O'F*. 30 abstract / abstracted *1654–69*. 32 loth / doth *TCD*. so / *omitted C57*. amuze∧ *Gr.* / ∼, *1633*. 33 Faiths / ffaithless *TCD*. infirmitie / infirmities *1669, C57*. 35 minde / the mind *Dob*. 37 in / *omitted C57*. 39 these / those *TCD, Dob, O'F*. states / rites *TCD*. 40 from / by *O'F*. womankinde / women-kinde *Dob*. 41 who / for *Dob, O'F* (> who). 43 Forsake / And forsake *Dob, O'F* (And *deleted*). 44 or / and *O'F*. 46 which / that *Dob*. 47 occupation / occupations *O'F*. 52 dares / dare *SP, TCC, O'F*. 53 their nothing *1635* / there something *1633*. 55 vent / went *1635–54*. 56 great heights / shadowes *O'F*. 60 fitliest / fittest *TCD*; fitly *O'F* (> fitly'st).

53. COMMUNITIE.

COPY TEXT: *1633*.

TEXTS: *1633–69*; H49, D, SP, Lec, C57, TCD, N, TCC, A18, DC, Dob, S96, Lut, O'F, HM198 (twice), Hd, Cy, O, P, JC, D17, B, S, K (ll. 1–6, 13–24), L74, H40, S962, TCD(II); E2230.

COLLATION: *1633–69, C57, TCD, Dob, O'F*. *Title 1635* / *omitted 1633, C57, TCD, O'F*. 3 there *1635* / these *1633, C57*. 14 *first* as / *omitted C57*. 15 betrayes: *Gr.* / ∼, *1633*. 21 that / which *C57, TCD, Dob, O'F*. well: *Gr.* / ∼, *1633*.

54. LOVES GROWTH.

COPY TEXT: *1633*.

TEXTS: *1633–69*; H49, D, SP, Lec, C57, TCD, N, TCC, A18, DC, Dob, S96, Lut, O'F, HM198, Hd, Cy, O, P, JC, D17, B, S, K, S962; CCC.E.327, Grey; HNVIII (ll. 11–12).

COLLATION: *1633–69, C57, TCD, Dob, O'F* (some readings from TCC and Cy). *Title* / Springe *C57*; Springe. Loves growth *Dob*; The Springe *O'F*. 6–7 *spaced 1633*. 6 make / makes *TCD*. 9 paining / vexing *1635–69, Dob, O'F*. 10 *omitted TCD*. working / active *1635–69, O'F, Cy*. 11 and / an *1669, Dob, O'F*. 12 which / who *O'F, Cy*. 13 else / these *C57*. 14 sometimes would / would sometimes *O'F, Cy*. 15 no / not *C57, TCD, Dob, O'F*. 19 bough / flower *C57*. 20 awaken'd *Ed.* / awakened *1633*. 21 water / waters *TCC, Dob, O'F*. 23 to *MSS* / so *1633*. 25 doe / doth *Dob*. 26 times / time *C57, Dob, O'F*. action / Actions *C57*. 27 remit / remitts *C57*. 28 the / this *1635–69, O'F, Cy*.

55. LOVES EXCHANGE.

COPY TEXT: 1633.

TEXTS: 1633–69; H49, D, SP, Lec, C57, TCD, N, TCC, A18, DC, Dob, Lut, O'F, HM198 (twice), Hd, O, P, JC, D17, B, H40; HNVIII (ll. 29–35), Rosenbach 1083/16.

COLLATION: 1633–69, C57, TCD, Dob, O'F. *Title* / *omitted C57, O'F*. 4 and *O'F* / or *1633*. 5 who *O'F* / which *1633*. 8 no / not *TCD, Dob, O'F*. 9 teare, or sigh, or / teare, or *C57, TCD, O'F* (*added*); sigh, a teare a *Dob*. 13 thee . . . thine / thine . . . thee *TCD*. 19–20 *combined C57* (That . . . knowes *omitted*). 20 paine *O'F* / paines *1633*. 21 mine / my *O'F*. new / *omitted 1669, Dob*. 24 which stand / withstand *TCD*. 36 For∧ this, *Gr.* / ~, ~∧ *1633*. 37 Yet kills / Itt skills *C57*. 38 future / fortunes *O'F*. 39 learne / become *O'F* (> learne).

56. CONFINED LOVE.

COPY TEXT: 1633.

TEXTS: 1633–69; H49, D, SP, Lec, C57, TCD, N, TCC, A18, DC, Dob, Lut, O'F, HM198 (twice), Cy, P, JC, D17, B, S, L74, S962. Miss Gardner does not except O from the collections.

COLLATION: 1633–69, C57, TCD, Dob, O'F (one reading from Cy). *Title 1635* / *omitted 1633, C57, TCD, O'F*; A Songe. Confined Love *Dob*. 3 lesser / the lesser *Dob*. 6 should *O'F* / might *1633–69*. 9 or / and *O'F*. 12 doe / did *C57, TCD, Dob*. joyntures / Jointers *C57, O'F, Cy*. 13 choose / chose *TCD, Dob*. 14 we / *omitted TCD*. 16 new / *omitted 1639–69*. 17 built / build *1639–69, C57, TCD*. 18 up / them up *O'F*.

57. THE DREAME.

COPY TEXT: 1633.

TEXTS: 1633–69; H49, D, SP, Lec, C57, TCD, N, TCC, A18, DC, Dob, S96, Lut, O'F, HM198 (twice), Cy, O, P, B, S, L74, S962, A25 (ll. 1–20), RP117; Add 29 (ll. 1–20), CCC.E.327 (ll. 1–11), RP31, Grey; Huygens. Miss Gardner lists Wel.

COLLATION: 1633–69, C57, TCD, Dob, O'F (some readings from Cy). Title: The / *omitted Dob*; A *Cy*. 7 truth / true *1635–69, Dob, O'F*. 7–8 that . . . truths / *omitted DC*. 8 truths / Truth *C57, TCD, O'F* (> Truths); true *Dob*. 10 act / doe *C57, Dob, O'F*. 14 For / *omitted C57, TCD*. an / but an *C57, TCD*. 19 doe *O'F* / must *1633*. it / I *Cy*. 20 Prophane / Profanenes *C57, TCD, Dob, O'F* (> Profane). 22 doubt, that / doubt it *C57, Dob* (> thinke that). 24 That / For *Dob* (> that); Yet *O'F*. where / when *C57, O'F*. feare's as / Feare is *C57* (> feare's as), *TCD*; feares are *1669, Dob, O'F*. 28 deal'st / doest *Dob, O'F*. 29 Then / Thus *C57, TCD*. 30 but / or *Dob*. would / will *C57*.

58. A VALEDICTION OF WEEPING.

COPY TEXT: 1633.

TEXTS: 1633–69; H49, D, SP, Lec, C57, TCD, N, TCC, A18, DC, Dob, S96, Lut, O'F, HM198 (twice), Cy, O, P, JC, D17, B, S, L74, H40, S962; A30982, H3511, Wales 5308E; H3991 (ll. 26–27), V.a.170; Huygens.

COLLATION: 1633–69, C57, TCD, Dob, O'F (one reading from Cy). Title: A / *omitted TCD, O'F.* of weeping / *omitted* C57; of Teares *Dob, O'F.* 2 whil'st / while *TCD, Cy.* 3 face / stamp *TCD.* coines / joynes *TCD.* 6 thee; *Gr.* / ∼, *1633.* 8 *second* falls C57 / falst *1633–69;* fall'st *Dob, O'F.* 14 doth / doe *1635–69.* 21 thine / thy *TCD, Dob.* 22 soone; *Gr.* / ∼, *1633.* 25 purposeth; *Gr.* / ∼, *1633.*

59. LOVES ALCHYMIE.

COPY TEXT: 1633.

TEXTS: 1633–69; H49, D, SP, Lec, C57, TCD, N, TCC, A18, DC, Dob, S96, Lut, O'F, HM198 (twice), Cy, O, P, JC, D17, B, S, K, L74, H40, S962, A25; Ee.4.14, E2230, Emmanuel, Grey; V.a.162 (ll. 1–12), Rosenbach 1083/16.

COLLATION: 1633–67, C57, TCD, Dob, O'F (some readings from Cy). *Title* / Mummy C57, *TCD, Dob* (Loves Alchymy *added*), *O'F.* 12 get / yet *TCD.* winter / winters C57, *DC, Cy.* 14 Bubles shadow / shadowes bubble *O'F.* 19 bodies / body *Cy.* marry / marrowe *Dob* (*changed from* marry). 23 women / woman *TCD, O'F.*

60. THE FLEA.

COPY TEXT: 1633.

TEXTS: 1633–69; H49, D, SP, Lec, C57, TCD, N, TCC, A18, DC, Dob, S96, Lut, O'F, HM198, Cy, O, P, B, S, K, L74, H40, S962, A25, RP117; Ee.4.14, Add 29, CCC.E.327, E2230, Grey; Malone 19, RP172, V.a.103, V.a.170, Rosenbach 243/4; Huygens.

COLLATION: 1633–69, C57, TCD, Dob, O'F (one reading from Lec). *Title* / *omitted TCD.* 3 It . . . me / Me it suckt *1669, TCD* (*and others*). 5 Thou know'st that / Confess it *1669, TCD, Dob, O'F.* 6 *first* nor / or *Lec.* nor . . . nor / or . . . or *TCD, Dob, O'F.* shame, *Gr.* / ∼‿ *1633.* 11 yea / nay *TCD, Dob, O'F.* 14 w'are / yet wee are *Dob, O'F.* 16 you / thee *TCD, Dob, O'F.* 17 that / thy *TCD;* this *Dob, O'F.* 21 Wherein / In what *TCD, Dob, O'F.*

61. THE CURSE.

COPY TEXT: 1633.

TEXTS: 1633–69; H49, D, SP, Lec, C57, TCD, N, TCC, A18, DC, Dob, Lut, O'F, HM198 (three times), Hd, O, P, JC, D17, B, S, K, L74, H40, S962, A25, RP117; Q; Ee.4.14, Add 29, E2230, Emmanuel (ll. 14–15, 25–32), Grey; Ash 38, H3991 (ll. 31–32), HNVIII (ll. 20–21).

COLLATION: 1633–69, C57, TCD, Dob, O'F, Q (one reading from TCC). *Title* / Dirce *Q.* 8 feare . . . shame / shame . . . feare *Q.* torne: *Gr.* / ∼; *1633.* 9 cramp / cramps *1669,* C57, *TCD, Dob, Q.* 12 fame / shame *TCC.* 13 shee / hee *Q.*

14–16: Or may he for her vertue reverence
One, that hates him only for impotence
And equall traytors bee, shee and his sence. *1635–69, TCD, O'F (1633 lines in margin)*, *Q.* 15 *(variant)* One / her *Q.* 18 Meant / Went *TCD.* performe / enact *O'F* (> performe). 24 last / length *Q.* 27 Mynes *TCD* / Myne *1633–69, C57.* 28 ill_∧ *Gr.* / ~, *1633.* 29 spake / spoke *TCD, Dob;* speake *O'F.* 32 before hand / already *O'F* (> before hand).

62. THE EXTASIE.

COPY TEXT: 1633.

TEXTS: 1633–69; H49, D, SP, Lec, C57, TCD, N, TCC, A18, DC, Dob, S96, Lut, O'F, HM198, O, P, JC, D17, B, S, H40, A25, RP117; HNVIII (ll. 1–4, 7–8); Huygens.

COLLATION: 1633–69, C57, TCD, Dob, O'F (one reading from DC). Title: The / *omitted TCD. no stanzas 1633.* 4 best / brest *Dob.* 6 *not indented 1633.* With / By *1635–69, O'F.* 9 entergraft / engraft *1635–69, Dob, O'F.* 10 the / our *TCD, Dob, O'F.* 11 in / on *C57, TCD, Dob, O'F.* 14 uncertaine / unequall *O'F* (> uncertayne). 15 their / our *1635–69, O'F.* 16 hung / hangs *C57.* her / thee *Dob, O'F* (> her). 17 whil'st / while *Dob, OF.* 18 lay; *Gr.* / ~, *1633.* 19 postures / pictures *Dob, O'F* (> postures). 23 were / was *O'F* (> were). 25 knew *1635* / knowes *1633, C57.* 31 sexe, *Gr.* / ~_∧ *1633.* 42 Interinanimates *O'F* / Interanimates *1633–69, C57.* 44 lonelinesse / loveliness *1669, TCD.* 48 soules / soule *1635–54.* 51 they'are *MSS* / *omitted 1633–69.* 52 spheares / spheare *C57, TCD, O'F.* 55 forces, sense, *TCD* / senses_∧ force_∧ *1633–69;* forces, senses, *C57.* 59 Soe *TCD* / For *1633–69, C57, O'F.* 64 makes / make *1635–39.* 72 his / the *1669, Dob.* 75 marke / mocke *Dob, O'F.* 76 to / two *DC, O'F* (> to). gone / growne *1635–69, Dob* (> gone), *O'F.*

63. THE UNDERTAKING.

COPY TEXT: 1633.

TEXTS: 1633–69; H49, D, SP, Lec, C57, TCD, N, TCC, A18, DC, Dob, Lut, O'F, HM198 (twice), Hd, O, P, JC, D17, B, S, K, H40.

COLLATION: 1633–69, C57, TCD, Dob, O'F (one reading from TCC). *Title 1635* / *omitted 1633, C57, Dob, O'F;* Platonique Love *TCD.* 2 Worthies *Gr.* / worthies *1633.* 3 And / *omitted C57, TCD, Dob, O'F.* 7 art_∧ *Gr.* / ~, *1633.* 14 outward / other *O'F* (> outward). 18 attir'd / *omitted 1635–69, O'F.* woman / women *Dob, O'F.* 25 you have / have you *TCC, Dob, O'F.*

64. LOVES DEITIE.

COPY TEXT: 1633.

TEXTS: 1633–69; H49, D, SP, Lec, C57, TCD, N, TCC (ll. 1–13, 21–28), A18, DC, Dob, S96, Lut, O'F, HM198, Hd, Cy, O, P, JC, D17, B, S, K, L74, H40, S962, A25, TCD(II); Add 29, Wales 5308E; V.a.103, V.a.345, Rosenbach 1083/16; Huygens.

COLLATION: 1633–69, C57, TCD, Dob, O'F (some readings from Cy). 4 which / who *Cy.* 8 which / that *Dob, O'F.* 10 flame / desire *Cy.* 14 till . . . her, that loves / if . . . who loves not *1635–54, O'F* (her *deleted*). 21

That I should love *TCD* / I should love her *1633–69;* that I should love her *Dob, O'F* (> I should love). 24 *first* might / may *1635–69, C57.* 28 *first* love / loved *Cy.*

65. LOVES DIET.

COPY TEXT: 1633.

TEXTS: 1633–69; H49, D, SP, Lec, C57, [TCD], N, TCC, A18, DC, Dob, S96, Lut, O'F, HM198 (twice), Hd, Cy, O, P, B, S, L74, H40, S962, A25 (twice), La, RP117; Ee.4.14, Add 29, CCC.E.327 (ll. 23–30), Emmanuel (ll. 25–30), Wales 5308E, Grey; EP.c.50 (ll. 1–12, 21–30), EP.c.53 (ll. 1–18), H3991 (l. 18), Eng 626 (ll. 1–12), HM172, V.a.96 (ll. 1–12), V.a.125, V.a.345, HNVIII (ll. 28–30), Rosenbach 1083/16. Pages in TCD which would contain this poem are missing. Miss Gardner does not except this poem from K.

COLLATION: 1633–69, C57, TCC, Dob, O'F (some readings from Cy). *Title* / The Dyet *DC;* Amoris Dieta *Dob.* 2 had / was *O'F* (> had). 6 worst / least *Dob.* endures / endues *C57, DC.* 8 fortune / fortunes *Dob, O'F.* 11 feast / feede *Dob, O'F.* 12 neither / never *TCC.* 13 wroung / wrought *Cy.* so / too *C57.* 16 which / that *Dob, O'F.* 18 which / that *TCC, Dob, O'F.* 19 what ever / Whatsoever *TCC.* he . . . I / might him distast I still *1649– 54.* dictate / distast *TCC, O'F* (*changed from* dictate). writ / wrote *Dob, O'F.* 20 But / And *TCC.* my / her *1635–54.* When / If *Dob, O'F.* writ / wrote *Dob, O'F.* 21 *first* that / if *1635–69, O'F* (*changed from* that), *Cy.* 24 name / man *1669, C57.* 25 reclaim'd *1635* / redeem'd *1633, C57.* 27 sport *1635* / sports *1633.* 29 sweare . . . sigh / sigh, sweare, write *Dob, O'F.* 30 and / or *1635–69, Dob, O'F.*

66. THE WILL.

COPY TEXT: 1633.

TEXTS: 1633–69; H49, D, SP, Lec, C57, [TCD], N, TCC, A18, DC, Dob, S96, Lut, O'F, HM198 (twice), Hd, Cy, O, P, JC, D17, B, S, K, L74, H40, S962, A25, La, RP117; Ee.4.14, Add 29, CCC.E.327, A10, E2230, M, Grey; A27407, Malone 19 (ll. 1–18, 28–29), V.a.125 (ll. 1–18, 28–35), HNVIII, U26, E2725. Pages in TCD which would contain this poem are missing.

COLLATION: 1633–69, C57, TCC, Dob, O'F (some readings from DC, Lut, and Cy). *Title* / Testamentum *Dob;* Loves Legacies *TCC.* 5 mine / my *Cy.* 6 teares. *Gr.* / ~; *1633.* 8 serve / love *1669, Dob.* 9 That . . . as / Only to give to those that *Dob;* Only . . . those which *O'F.* 12 Mine / My *Cy.* 16 appointing / making *Dob, O'F.* 17 can / could *TCC, Dob* (> can). 18 such as / those which *Dob, O'F.* 19–27 *omitted Group I, Group II* (*and others*). 28 I . . . reputation / My reputation I give *Dob, O'F.* 29 Which / That *Dob.* Mine / my *TCC, Lut* (*and others*). 33 wit. *Gr.* / ~; *1633.* 35 who / that *Dob, O'F.* 36 did / do *1635–69, Dob, O'F.* 39 counsels / counsell *Cy.* 40 which / that *Dob, O'F.* 41 which / that *Dob.* 42 mine / my *O'F* (*and others*). 45 gifts / gift *1639–54.* 49 where / when *Dob.* doth / do *Dob.* forth; *Gr.* / ~. *1633.* 50 shall / will *Dob.* 51 grave. *Gr.* / ~, *1633.* 52 making / appointing *Dob.* 53 Love / To love *Dob.* doth neglect / neglects *Dob.* mee . . . thee / thee . . . me *DC, Dob, O'F.*

67. THE FUNERALL.

COPY TEXT: 1633.

TEXTS: 1633–69; H49, D, SP, Lec, C57, TCD, N, TCC, A18, DC, Dob, S96, Lut, O'F, Hd, Cy, O, P, B, S, L74, S962; Grey; U26.

COLLATION: 1633–69, C57, TCD, Dob, O'F (some readings from SP and DC). 1 not / noe *C57, Dob.* 3 my / mine *TCD, Dob, O'F.* 6 then to *TCD* / unto *1633–69.* 8 these / those *DC, Dob.* 12 These *TCD* / Those *1633–69, C57, O'F.* grew / grow *1650–69.* 16 condemn'd *Ed.* / condem'nd *1633.* 17 with *1635* / by *1633.* 22 to / *omitted C57.* that / which *SP, TCD, Dob, O'F.* 24 save *TCD* / have *1633–69, C57, Dob, O'F.*

68. THE BLOSSOME.

COPY TEXT: 1633.

TEXTS: 1633–69; H49, D, SP, Lec, C57, TCD, N, TCC, A18, DC, Dob, S96, Lut, O'F, Hd, JC, D17, B, S, S962, A25; Grey; Huygens.

COLLATION: 1633–69, C57, TCD, Dob, O'F. 10 labour'st *TCD* / labours *1633, C57.* 15 that / the *1635–69, Dob, O'F.* 21 love / loves *TCD, Dob.* 23 tongue *MSS* / tast *1633–69.* 24 you'a *TCD* / your *1633–69.* 38 would *TCD* / will *1633–69, C57, O'F* (*changed from* would).

69. THE PRIMROSE.

COPY TEXT: 1633.

TEXTS: 1633–69; H49, D, SP, Lec, C57, TCD, N, TCC, A18, DC, Dob, S96, Lut, O'F, Hd, B, S, S962; Grey; Peerson (music only).

COLLATION: 1633–69, C57, TCD, Dob, O'F. *Title* / . . . being at Montgomery Castle upon the hill, on which it is situate *1635–69.* 11 know I / I knowe *TCD.* 17 and / *omitted 1635–39, C57, TCD, Dob, O'F.* 25 number; *Gr.* / ~, *1633.* 26 Belonge *TCD* / Belongs *1633–69, C57.* 28 their / the *1649–69.* 29 and / since *1635–69.* 30 this / *omitted 1635–69, O'F.*

70. THE RELIQUE.

COPY TEXT: 1633.

TEXTS: 1633–69; H49, D, SP, Lec, C57, TCD, N, TCC, A18, DC, Dob, S96, Lut, O'F, Hd, JC, D17, B, S, S962, A25; Grey.

COLLATION: 1633–69, C57, TCD, Dob, O'F. 7 he not / not hee *O'F.* 9 thought / hop'd *C57, Dob, O'F.* some / a *C57, Dob, O'F.* 14 Then / *omitted C57, Dob, O'F.* digges us / doth digge yt *C57, Dob, O'F.* 17 Thou . . . be / You shalbe *C57, Dob, O'F.* 20 time / tymes *TCD, Dob, O'F.* 21 have / *omitted TCD.* age / age were *TCD.* 25 no more wee / we never *1635–69, C57, Dob, O'F.* 26 Then our / No more then *1635–69, O'F;* More then our *C57* (*and others*); No more then our *Dob.* doe; *Gr.* / ~, *1633.* 27 wee∧ *Gr.* / ~, *1633.* 28 between / betwixt *C57, Dob, O'F.* meales; *Gr.* / ~∧ *1633.* 29 the / those *TCD.* 30 free: *Gr.* / ~, *1633.* 32 measure / measures *TCD.*

71. THE DAMPE.

COPY TEXT: 1633.

TEXTS: 1633–69; H49, D, SP, Lec, C57, TCD, N, TCC, A18, DC, Dob, S96,

Lut, O'F, HM198, Hd, O, P, JC, D17, B, S, S962, TCD(II); Grey; EP.f.25 (ll. 1–4, 7–8), H3991 (ll. 22–24).

COLLATION: 1633–69, C57, TCD, Dob, O'F. 4 my / mine *1649–69.* 15 arts / Acts *TCD (changed from* Arts). 20 professe; *Gr. /* ∼, *1633.* 24 In that / Naked *1635–69, C57, Dob, O'F.*

72. THE DISSOLUTION.

COPY TEXT: 1633.

TEXTS: 1633–69; TCD, N, TCC, A18, DC, Lut, O'F, S962.

COLLATION: 1633–69, TCD, O'F, S962. 10 earthly / earthy *1635–69, O'F.*

73. A JEAT RING SENT.

COPY TEXT: 1633.

TEXTS: 1633–69; TCD, N, TCC, A18, DC, Lut, O'F, W, S962; A21433, A25303, E2421, Eng 686 (ll. 1–4).

COLLATION: 1633–69, TCD, O'F, W, S962. 6 Oh / or *TCD, S962.* 7 loves / love *O'F.*

74. NEGATIVE LOVE.

COPY TEXT: 1633.

TEXTS: 1633–69; TCD, N, TCC, A18, DC, Lut, O'F, Hd, A25; Add 29; Wales 5308E.

COLLATION: 1633–69, TCD, O'F, Hd (one reading from Lut). *Title* / . . . or The Nothinge *O'F;* The Nothing *Hd.* 5 For / Both *Hd.* 8 may I / I may *TCD, O'F* (> may I). 11 way / means *1669, O'F.* 15 know not, ourselves can / our selves know not doth *Hd.* 16 teach mee that / tell what *O'F, Hd.* This / 'tis *Lut, Hd.* 17 my / mine *O'F, Hd.*

75. THE EXPIRATION.

COPY TEXT: 1633.

TEXTS: 1633–69; Ferrabosco; TCD, N, TCC, A18, DC, Dob, S96, Lut, O'F, HM198, Hd, O, P, JC, D17, B, S, K, S962, A25, Hol; Add 29, CCC.E.327, Wales 5308E; EP.c.50; F575 (ll. 1–6).

COLLATION: 1633–69, TCD, Dob, O'F. *Title* / Valedictio *Dob, O'F.* 1 breake / leave *Dob, O'F.* 4 selves / soules *Dob, O'F.* happiest / happy *Dob, O'F.* 5 ask'd *TCD* / aske *1633 (and others).* 9 Oh / Or *1635–69, Dob, O'F.* let / may *TCD.* word / words *TCD.*

76. THE COMPUTATION.

COPY TEXT: 1633.

TEXTS: 1633–69; TCD, N, TCC, A18, DC, Dob, Lut, O'F, HM198, O, P, B, S, K, S962; Wales 5308E.

COLLATION: 1633–69, TCD, Dob, O'F (some readings from TCC and Lut). *Title* / omitted *O'F.* 1 the / my *1635–69, Dob, O'F.* 2 thou / you *Dob, O'F.* could'st / wouldst *TCC;* could *Dob, O'F.* 3 For / And *1669, Dob, O'F.* 4 thou / you *Dob, O'F.* would'st / wish *Dob, O'F.* might / may *Dob.* 5 drown'd . . . and . . . blew / have . . . drownd . . . blowne *Dob, O'F.* 6 A / One

Dob, O'F. neither / nothing *Dob, O'F.* nor / or *O'F.* doe, *Gr. / ∼.* 1633.   7
omitted *TCD.* divide / deem'd 1635–54, *Dob, Lut;* deni'd *O'F.*   8 a / one
Dob, O'F. forgot / forget 1669, *TCC.*   9 call / thinke *Dob, O'F* (> call).

77. THE PARADOX.

COPY TEXT: 1633.

TEXTS: 1633–69; TCD, N, TCC, A18, S96, Lut, O'F, HM198, Hd, S, L74,
H40, S962; RP31.

COLLATION: 1633–69, TCD, S96, O'F (plus L74 and H40). *Title* 1635 /
omitted 1633, *TCD, S96, O'F.*   3 can, *Gr. / ∼∧* 1633. nor *O'F* / or 1633–69.
6 yesterday? *Gr. / ∼.* 1633.   14 lights life *L74, H40* / lifes light 1633–69, *TCD,
S96, O'F.*   15 which *Gr. / ∼,* 1633.   17 lov'd *O'F* / love 1633–69.   20 lye
O'F / dye 1633–69, *TCD.*

78. SONNET. THE TOKEN.

COPY TEXT: 1649.

TEXTS: 1649–69; S96, O'F, HM198, Hd, Cy, O, P, B, S962; Wales 5308E.

COLLATION: 1649–69, S96, O'F (plus Cy). *Title* / Ad Lesbiam S96; Sonnet
O'F; omitted Cy.   1 token *O'F* / Tokens 1649–69, *Cy.*   2 Or / And *O'F.*   4
passion *S96* / passions 1649–69, *O'F, Cy.*   5 noe *O'F* / nor 1649–69.   6 loves
/ love *S96, O'F.*   9 loves / love *S96, O'F.*   10 Coralls / Corrall *O'F, Cy.* infold
/ infolds *S96, O'F.*   11 in / with *S96, O'F.*   12 hold / holds *S96, O'F.*   14
most / more *S96, O'F.* because best like the *O'F* / 'cause 'tis like thee 1649–
69 (the), *Cy* (because . . . the).   17–18 *not separated from text,* 1649.   17
store *O'F* / score 1649–69.

79. FAREWELL TO LOVE.

COPY TEXT: 1635.

TEXTS: 1635–69; S96, O'F, Hd, S962; Rosenbach 1083 /16 (ll. 35–40).

COLLATION: 1635–69, S96, O'F, Hd.   10 sise / rise *S96.*   12 highnesse *Ed.*
/ hignesse 1635.   21 Ah / Oh *S96.*   25 Diminisheth / Diminishes *S96.*   34
indammag'd / indamage *S96.*   36 summers *O'F* / summer 1649–69.

80. SELFE LOVE.

COPY TEXT: 1650.

TEXTS: 1650–69; Lut, O'F, JC, D17.

COLLATION: 1650–69, O'F, JC (two readings from Lut). *no stanzas,* 1650.
Title Gr. / omitted 1650–69, JC; Elegy *O'F.*   4 'gaynst *O'F* / against 1650–
69.   6 cannot / can att *Lut, JC;* can all *O'F.*   11. foul ones / fouleness *O'F.*
12 then / *omitted O'F.*   14 slave; *Gr. / ∼∧* 1650.   15 fool, *Gr. / ∼∧* 1650.
others, . . . / *omitted O'F.*   16 want nor crave *O'F* / . . . . 1650.   17 payes
O'F / prays 1650–69.   19 payes∧ *Gr. / ∼,* 1650.   24 In / E're in *Lut.*

81. "WHEN MY HARTE WAS MINE OWNE."

COPY TEXT: HM198.

TEXTS: HM198, Hol; Huygens.

COLLATION: HM198, Hol. *Most words at the beginning of lines capitalized by editor; all punctuation added. Title Ed. / omitted HM;* Dr: D: *Hol.* 2 Betrothd / by thee oth'd *Hol.* sighes / sigh'ts *Hol.* 3 teares . . . showes / what tears, what passions, what shows *Hol.* 4 mutely / humbly *Hol.* 5 could / might *Hol.* 9 all *Hol* / ill *HM.* ere *Hol* / before *HM.* 11 piety / prettie *Hol.* 12 sow . . . seedes / show . . . deeds *Hol.* 24 deliver'd *Ed.* / delivered *HM.* 25 thee *Ed.* / the *HM.* 28 They *Ed.* / they *HM.* 29 *first* bene / *omitted Hol.* 30 How *Ed.* / how *HM.* 39 mayst / might *Hol.* 40 may / might *Hol.* 41 thought / thoughts *Hol.* 43 That *Ed.* / that *HM.* 45 will / would *Hol.* 46 *first* on / upon *Hol.* raine on / rainy *Hol.* 49 and *Hol* / is *HM.* 50 in / *omitted Hol.* 51 Doe *Ed.* / doe *HM.*

82. A NOCTURNALL UPON S. LUCIES DAY, BEING THE SHORTEST DAY.

COPY TEXT: 1633.

TEXTS: 1633–69; TCD, N, TCC, A18, DC, Lut, O'F.

COLLATION: 1633–69, TCD, O'F (one reading from Lut). 4 no / not *O'F.* 7 feet, *Gr.* / ~ₐ 1633. 12 every / a very 1635–69, *O'F* (*changed from* every). 16 emptinesse: *Gr.* / ~ₐ 1633. 20 have; *Gr.* / ~, 1633. 31 know; *Gr.* / ~, 1633. 34 love; *Gr.* / ~, 1633. *second* all / *omitted Lut; added O'F.* invest; *Gr.* / ~, 1633. 41 all; *Gr.* / ~, 1633. 44 Eve *Gr.* / eve 1633.

83. HERO AND LEANDER.

COPY TEXT: 1633.

TEXTS: 1633–69; TCD, N, TCC, A18, DC, O'F, W, HN, S962, Grey; E22 (twice); H3991.

84. PYRAMUS AND THISBE.

COPY TEXT: 1633.

TEXTS: 1633–69; TCD, N, TCC, A18, DC, O'F, Cy, O, P, W, HN, S962, Grey; H3991, Malone 19.

85. NIOBE.

COPY TEXT: 1633.

TEXTS: 1633–69; TCD, N, TCC, A18, DC, O'F, W, HN, S962.

COLLATION: 1633–69, TCD, O'F, W (one reading from DC). 1 birth *O'F* / births 1633–69, *DC, W.* 2 mine owne sad / mine owne *TCD;* made myne owne *O'F, W.*

86. A BURNT SHIP.

COPY TEXT: 1633.

TEXTS: 1633–69; TCD, N, TCC, A18, DC, O'F, W, S962, Grey; H3991.

COLLATION: 1633–69, TCD, O'F, W. *Title* / De Nave arsa *O'F;* Nave arsa *W.* 6 being / *omitted O'F.*

87. FALL OF A WALL.

COPY TEXT: 1633.

TEXTS: 1633–69; TCD, N, TCC, A18, DC, Dob, O'F, B, W, HN, S962, Grey.

COLLATION: 1633–69, TCD, Dob, O'F, W (some readings from HN). *Title* / *missing Dob;* Caso d'un muro *O'F, W;* Caso di muro *HN.* 4 bones / corps *Dob, O'F, W;* corse *HN.*

88. A LAME BEGGER.

COPY TEXT: 1633.

TEXTS: 1633–69; TCD, N, TCC, A18, DC, O'F, O, P, W, S962, Grey; Ash 47, H3991, Sancroft, S.32, Rosenbach 239/22. Variant text: Dob, HN; Ee.4.14, H3511; E2421, CCC.F.328, Don.d.58, Tanner, V.a.97, V.a.170 (twice), V.a.262, Rosenbach 1083/15, Rosenbach 1083/16.

COLLATION: 1633–69, TCD, O'F, W. *Title* / Zoppo *O'F, W.*

VARIANT TEXT FROM CCC.F.328:

On a Cripple.
I cannot goe sit, stand, the cripple cries
What doth he then? if he say true he lyes.

COLLATION: Dob. *Title* / *missing Dob.* 1 I . . . stand / I can not goe, nor sitt, nor stand *Dob.* cripple / begger *Dob.* 2 yf that be true the beggar sayes, he lyes. *Dob.*

89. A SELFE ACCUSER.

COPY TEXT: 1633.

TEXTS: 1633–69; DC, Dob, O'F, B, W, HN; H3991, S.32.

COLLATION: 1633–69, DC, Dob, O'F, W. *Title* / *missing Dob, O'F, W.* 1 still taxeth / oft taxes *Dob;* doth taxe *O'F.* 2 that / *omitted Dob, O'F, W.* thus / *omitted Dob, O'F, W.* it / *omitted Dob, O'F.*

90. A LICENTIOUS PERSON.

COPY TEXT: 1633.

TEXTS: 1633–69; TCD, N, TCC, A18, DC, Dob, O'F, W, HN; RP31, Grey; Add.B.97, CCC.F.328, H3991, E2230, Don.d.58, Osborn (CPB), Sancroft, V.a.97, V.a.162, S.32, Rosenbach 239/22.

COLLATION: 1633–69, TCD, Dob, O'F, W. *Title* / *missing Dob, O'F.* 1 haires / hayre *TCD.*

91. CALES AND GUYANA.

COPY TEXT: W.

TEXTS: O'F, W.

92. SIR JOHN WINGEFIELD.

COPY TEXT: W.

TEXTS: O'F, W.

COLLATION: O'F, W. *Title Ed.* / On Cavallero Wingfeild *O'F;* Il Cavalliere Gio: Wingef: *W.* 2 throne / grave *O'F.* 4 late / Lady *O'F.*

93. ANTIQUARY.

COPY TEXT: 1633.

TEXTS: 1633–69; TCD, N, TCC, A18, DC, Dob, S96, O'F, Hd, Cy, O, P, B, W, HN, S962, Grey; Bur; H3991, Malone 19, V.a.162.

COLLATION: 1633–69, TCD, Dob, O'F, W, HN. *Title / missing Dob, O'F;
Hammon HN.* 1 he / Hammon *Dob, O'F, W, HN.* hath / have *TCD.* so
much / such *Dob, O'F, W.* 2 strange / *omitted Dob, O'F.*

94. DISINHERITED.

COPY TEXT: 1633.
TEXTS: 1633–69; DC, Dob, O'F, Hd, Cy, O, P, B, W, HN; RP160; H3991,
Malone 19, Sancroft.
COLLATION: 1633–69, DC, Dob, O'F, W. *Title / missing Dob, O'F, W.*

95. THE LIER.

COPY TEXT: W.
TEXTS: Dob, O'F, Hd, Cy, O, P, B, W, HN; Bur; Malone 19, V.a.162.
COLLATION: Dob, O'F, W, HN. *Title HN / missing Dob, O'F, W.* 2 swearst
/ saist *Dob, O'F.* 4 dyeting / dyettings *Dob.*

96. MERCURIUS GALLO-BELGICUS.

COPY TEXT: 1633.
TEXTS: 1633–69; TCD, N, TCC, A18, DC, Dob, O'F, HM198, Hd, B, S, K,
W, S962; Rosenbach 1083/16.
COLLATION: 1633–69, TCD, Dob, O'F, W. 8 but / and *O'F (Dob has
margin notation of* and).

97. PHRYNE.

COPY TEXT: 1633.
TEXTS: 1633–69; TCD, N, TCC, A18, DC, Dob, O'F, Hd, B, W, HN, S962,
Grey; CCC.F.328, H3991.
COLLATION: 1633–69, TCD, Dob, O'F, W. *Title / missing Dob, O'F, W.* 1
like / like to *1649–69.* 2 you / wee *TCD.*

98. AN OBSCURE WRITER.

COPY TEXT: 1633.
TEXTS: 1633–69; TCD, N, TCC, A18, DC, Dob, O'F, Hd, B, W, Grey;
H3991.
COLLATION: 1633–69, TCD, Dob, O'F, W. *Title / missing Dob, O'F, W.* 2
beleev'd? *Gr. / ~. 1633.*

99. KLOCKIUS.

COPY TEXT: 1633.
TEXTS: 1633–69; TCD, N, TCC, A18, DC, Dob, O'F, Hd, B, W, HN; Bur;
H3991, Sancroft.
COLLATION: 1633–69, TCD, Dob, O'F, W, HN. *Title HN / missing 1633–69,
TCD, Dob, O'F, W.* 1 sworne / vowd *Dob, O'F, W.* more / *omitted Dob, O'F.*

100. RALPHIUS.

COPY TEXT: 1633.
TEXTS: 1633–69; DC, Dob, O'F, B, W, HN; H3991.

COLLATION: 1633–69, DC, Dob, O'F, W, HN. *Title HN / missing 1633–69, Dob, O'F, W.*

101. THE JUGHLER.

COPY TEXT: W.
TEXTS: W, HN.
COLLATION: W, HN. *Title HN / missing W.* 1 for / that *HN.* joyes; *Ed. / ~*ₐ W; toyes*ₐ HN.*

102. FAUSTUS.

COPY TEXT: HN.
TEXT: HN.
COLLATION: HN. *Title Ed. / missing HN.* 2 more. *Ed. / ~, HN.*

103. RADERUS.

COPY TEXT: 1633.
TEXTS: 1633–69; TCD, N, TCC, A18, DC, O'F, W, S962.
COLLATION: 1633–69, TCD, O'F, W. *Title / Randerus TCD;* Martial: castrat^d W.

104. AD AUTOREM.

COPY TEXT: Scaliger.
TEXT: Scaliger.

105. AD AUTOREM.

COPY TEXT: Covell.
TEXT: Covell.
COLLATION: Covell. 2 Auxilio. *Ed. / ~*ₐ *Covell.*

106. EPITHALAMION MADE AT LINCOLNES INNE.

COPY TEXT: 1633.
TEXTS: 1633–69; TCD, N, TCC, A18, DC, Dob, S96, Lut, O'F, O, P, B, W, Grey; Hyde; A34744.
COLLATION: 1633–69, TCD, Dob, O'F, W (one reading from TCC). *Title /* Epithalamion: one yᵉ Marriage of yᵉ La: Elizabeth *O;* Epithalamion on a Citizen *Dob, O'F;* Epithalamiun *W.* 8 these / those *Dob, O'F.* 10 must be, oft / oft must be *Dob, O'F.* 12 day / night *Dob.* 23 and rich / rich, glad, and *TCD, W.* 24 To day / *omitted Dob; added O'F.* 26 Sonnes *1635 /* Some *1633, TCD.* these / those *1635–69, TCD, Dob, O'F.* 28 who / which *Dob, O'F.* 29 those / these *W.* 31 bring. *Gr. / ~*ₐ *1633.* 32 Loe / So *Dob, O'F* (> Lo). straw'd / *omitted Dob, O'F.* 35 shame / blame *Dob.* 38 these / those *Dob.* 39 mystically / mistually *TCD.* but / both in *Dob, O'F* (> but). 42 fatten thee / satten there *TCD.* 45 Which / Never *TCD.* 46 all th' / th'each *Dob, O'F.* each / th'each *Dob, O'F.* 47 praise / prayer *TCD, W;* prayers *TCC.* 49 Oh *W /* omitted *1633–69, TCD;* our *Dob.* winter *W /* Winter *1633;* winters *O'F.* 51 these / those *Dob, O'F.* 54 that / if *Dob, O'F* (> that). 55 he now / nowe he *Dob, O'F, W.* 57 will / nill *W.* 58 West-

erne / Easterne *O'F*. 59 runne *W* / come *1633, TCD*. worlds / heavens *1635–69, O'F;* world *TCD*. 60 To night / *omitted Dob; added O'F*. put *1635* / but *1633*. 62 should not then *W* / then should not *1633–69*. 63 your / the *Dob, O'F*. 65 these / those *Dob, O'F*. 73–96 *missing DC*. 73 Thy / The *O'F*. 76 these / those *TCD, Dob, O'F*. 82 thee / shee *TCD*. 95 maime / name *1635–69, TCD, Dob, O'F* (> maime).

107. AN EPITHALAMION, OR MARIAGE SONG ON THE LADY ELIZABETH . . .

    COPY TEXT: 1633.

    TEXTS: 1633–69; H49, D, SP, Lec, C57, TCD, N, Dob, S96, Lut, O'F, HM198, Hd, O, P, JC, D17, B, A25, RP117; Add 29 (ll. 1, 15–28), H3511, RP160; EP.e.37 (ll. 1–70, 85–112), RP142 (*passim*).

    COLLATION: 1633–69, C57, TCD, Dob, O'F (some readings from H49 and Lec). *Slightly different indentations at times in 1633. Title* / Upon the marriage of the Prince Palatine and the Lady Elizabeth on St. Valentines day. *Dob;* Uppon ffrederick Count Palatine & the Lady Elizabeth marryed on St. Valentines day *O'F;* Epithalamium *TCD*. 11 straight / soone *Dob, O'F*. 18 Phœnixes; *Gr.* / ∼, *1633*. 21 foules / fowle *1635–69*. 25 Where / Whose *Dob, O'F* (> Where). motion / motions *Dob*. 27 Whose / Where *O'F*. 29 Bride / bird *JC*. 33 Bride / bird *O'F* (> Bride), *JC*. 35 forth / out *TCD*. 37 their / this *H49, TCD, Dob, O'F* (> theyr). 40 ends. *Gr.* / ∼, *1633*. 46 unseparable / inseparable *TCD*. growe *TCD* / goe *1633–69, C57*. 54 *omitted O'F* (*added*). hearts / heart *Dob*. 55 left / more *TCD*. 56 or *C57* / O *1633–54*. 59 new . . . these / from the new light *Dob*. these / thee *TCD*. 60 store / starres *1635–69, O'F*. 64 be to / to be *TCD, Dob*. 65 gluttonous / glorious *Dob*. 67 too / *omitted 1635–69, TCD, O'F*. thinke / feare *TCD*. 81 passes / passeth *1649–69*. 82 where. *Gr.* / ∼, *1633*. 83 Let / Oh let *O'F*. this day, then / then this day *C57, TCD* (*and others*). then / *omitted O'F*. 84 the / thy *C57*. 85 here / there *1649–69, O'F*. 91 *second* nor / or *Dob, O'F*. 94 acquittances / acquittance *1633, C57*. 95 give . . . lend / lend . . . give *TCD*. 97 more / and *TCD*. do / doth *Dob*. 99 And / Now *O'F*. 105 open'd *Ed.* / opened *1633*. day, *Gr.* / ∼. *1633*. 109 win . . . then / wiselie observing then *Lec;* then observing wiselye *C57*. then / *omitted O'F* (*added*). 112 wee / all *Dob*.

108. ECCLOGUE . . . AT THE MARIAGE OF THE EARLE OF SOMMERSET.

    COPY TEXT: 1633.

    TEXTS: 1633–69; H49, D, SP, Lec, C57, TCD, N, TCC, A18, Dob, S96, Lut, O'F, HM198, Hd, B, Grey; A23; Rosenbach 1083/16 (*passim*).

    COLLATION: 1633–69, C57, TCD, Dob, O'F (some readings from H49, Lec, TCC, and Hd). Title: 1613. December 26. / Induceing an Epithalamion at the Marriage of the E. of S. *TCD;* omitted *Dob*. time / *omitted TCD, Dob, O'F*. Of . . . Sommerset / *omitted TCD*. absence thence / Actions there *1635–69, H49, TCD, Dob, O'F* (*changed from* Absence). 2 countries / countrey *TCD*. 5 small / smaller *1635–69*. 8 freeze / buff *O'F*. 12 Have / Having *1635–69*.

murmure *TCD* / murmures *1633–69, C57, Hd.* 27 sowes / lowes *TCD.* 29 kindle *1635* / kindles *1633, C57.* 34 plotts *1635* / places *1633, 1669, C57.* 37 disgest / digest *1649–69, Lec, TCD, O'F.* 38 our / one *C57.* 52 farther / further *Lec, TCD, Dob.* 54 one / own *1635–69, C57, Dob, O'F* (> one). 55 I am not / And am I *1635–69, O'F.* art. *Gr.* / ~, *1633.* 57 East *TCD* / omitted *1633–69.* 61 inward *TCD* / inner *1633–69.* 76 where / when *TCD.* 77 second that / the *TCC, Dob, O'F.* 78 trust? *Gr.* / ~. *1633.* 84 to the / unto *O'F.* pretend? *Gr.* / ~. *1633.* 92 onely therefore / therefore only *TCD.* withdrew. *Gr.* / ~ₐ *1633.* 98 joy, . . . some; *Gr.* / ~; . . . ~, *1633.* after *104:* Epithalamion *C57* / omitted *1633–69, TCD.* 107 expire, *Gr.* / ~ₐ *1633.* 108 by / from *1635–69.* 121 man. *Gr.* / ~, *1633.* 126 *second* both *TCD* / omitted *1633–69.* eyes *TCD* / eye *1633–69, O'F* (*changed from* eyes). 128 Singly *TCD* / Single *1633–69, C57.* 129 Yet let *O'F* / Let *1633–69, C57, TCD, Dob.* 140 tis fit / omitted *TCD.* 141 it. *Gr.* / ~, *1633.* 143 would'st / shouldst *SP, O'F* (*changed from* wouldst). 144 *second* which / that *Dob, O'F.* come / comes *TCD.* 145 Art *TCC, Dob* / Are *1633, C57, TCD;* Wert *1635–69, O'F.* forₐ . . . Phaëton. *Gr.* / ~, . . . ~, *1633.* 157 thou / those *TCD.* 167 more. *Ed.* / ~, *1633.* 168 who / whose *TCD.* 170 *second* or *Gr.* / Or *1633.* 177 to / omitted *TCD.* 178 from / for *C57, O'F* (> from). you / yours *Dob, O'F* (> you). 179 Art. *Gr.* / ~, *1633.* 183 causeth / causes *C57, Dob, O'F.* 184 groane / grow *TCD.* 189 where / when *TCD.* 194 wouldst / would *1669, C57.* 200 too *1635* / to *1633.* 201 faire . . . bed / to bed, faire bride *O'F.* 210 they / there *TCD.* 214 eye / hand *1649–69.* 222 these / them *C57, Dob, O'F.* 223 where / when *TCD, Dob.* 226–35 omitted *Dob.* 230 all; *Gr.* / ~. *1633.* 231 Festivall / nuptiall *O'F.*

109. THE STORME.

COPY TEXT: 1633.

TEXTS: 1633–69; H49, D, SP, Lec, C57, TCD, N, DC, Dob, Lut, O'F, HM198, Hd, Cy, O, P (twice), JC, D17, B, S, K, W, HN, L74, S962, A25, La, Hol, RP117; D16, Q; Ee.4.14, EP.e.14, H3511 (*passim*), Wales 5308E.

COLLATION: 1633–69, C57, TCD, Dob, O'F, W, Q; one reading from Lut. Title / To Mr Christopher Brooke from the Iland voyage with the Earle of Essex. The Storme *1635–69, Dob, O'F.* 2 these / this *1635–69, O'F.* 9 to . . . and / mother of us and what we *Dob.* 11 soothsay *1649* / Southsay *1633.* 12 *second* and / one *1635–54, Dob, O'F;* on *Q.* 16 Downeward / downewards *Q.* 18 Withering / Waiting *Dob.* 21 swole / swell'd *Dob, O'F, Q.* 23 as / as are *Q.* 24 leave / leaves *C57, Q.* 25 which / whoe *Q.* 29 you . . . the / these lines read, the boisterous *Dob.* 38 I / yea *Q* (*Hayward's emendation to* Aye *is not found in any text; the alteration is unjustified for meaning*). should teach / taught *Dob.* 39 and / yet then *Dob* (yet> and). onely / omitted *C57;* but *TCD, Dob, W, Q;* then but *O'F.* 40 now / yet *1635–54, O'F.* 47 sin-burd'ned / Sun-burnt *Q.* graves *TCD* / grave *1633–54.* 49 tremblingly / trembling *1635–69, Dob, O'F, Q.* 50 Like / As *1635–69, O'F* (*and others*). 52 feare away / affright Pale *Dob.* 53 Then / There *1669, TCD, Dob, O'F* (> Then). 54 this / an *1635–69, Dob, O'F.* 56 like too / like too-too *1635–54;* like to too *1669, O'F;* like to *C57, TCD;* in two

like *Dob*. 57 totterd / tattred *TCD, O'F (and others)*. 58 hang'd / hung
O'F. 59 Even / Yea even *1635–69, Dob, O'F*. 60 Strive / Strives *1635–69,
O'F*. 62 into / to *Q*. 64 knowes / knew *TCD, W*. 65 to *TCD* / in *1633–
69, Q;* with *Dob, O'F*. 66 and / *omitted 1635–69; added O'F*. Bermuda / Bermudas *1635–69, Dob, O'F, Q*. 67 elder *TCD* / eldest *1633–69,
C57*. 68 Claims *1635* / Claim'd *1633*. this / the *1635–69, Dob, O'F, Q*. 71
wee / *omitted C57*. 72 shall / we shall *C57*. 73 violent, yet long / long but
vyolent *O'F* (but>yet), *Q*. 74 thine / thy *Lut (and others)*; this *O'F*.

110. THE CALME.

COPY TEXT: 1633.

TEXTS: 1633–69; H49, D, SP, Lec, C57, TCD, N, DC, Dob, Lut, O'F,
HM198, Hd, Cy, O, P, JC, D17, B, S, K, HN, L74, S962, A25, RP117; D16, Q;
Ee.4.14, H3511 *(passim)*; Wales 5308E (ll. 1–18), Don.c.54.

COLLATION: 1633–69, C57, TCD, Dob, O'F, Q; some readings from SP, DC,
and Lut. *Title* / The Calme in the same voyage *DC;* A Calme *Q*. 4 now /
us now *Dob*. 5 and / and rage *Q*. 6 Heaven / heavens *O'F*. 7 can / could
1635–69, Dob, O'F. that / *omitted 1635–69, TCD, Dob, O'F*. 8 thy / my
Dob. 9 the / this *SP;* those *TCD, Dob, O'F, Q*. 12 one / a *O'F*. 15 now /
the *O'F, Q*. ragges / rage *1669, Dob;* place *Q*. 20 aire / th'ayre *Dob*. 21
lost / left *C57, TCD (and others)*. 24 great / *omitted Q*. jawes / mawes
1635–69, O'F. 25 the / *omitted Q*. 29 these / this *TCD, Dob, O'F, Q*. 30
our / a *1635–69, Dob, O'F*. 31 But from / Out of *O'F*. ship / sea *Q*. 34 Or
/ And *Dob*. 37 gaoles *Ed.* / goales *1633;* gulls *1635–54, O'F*. 38 Pinnaces
1635 / Venices *1633, C57, TCD, Dob, Q*. 41 and / or *O'F*. 43 my / myne
Q. 44 may / man may *Dob*. and / *omitted Dob*. a / *omitted 1635–69, O'F*.
45 all / each *Dob, O'F, Q*. flies / us flyes *O'F* (us *deleted*). 46 *second* or / or
with *Q*. 47 grudges / grudgeth *Q*. all / all these *Dob, O'F* (these *deleted*).
subtly / soe *TCD; omitted Dob*. 48 all forget / all forgot *1669, TCD, Dob,
Q;* had forgott *O'F*. 49 winde / winds *TCD, Dob*. 50 poles / pole *O'F, Q*.
55 *first* no / nor *Dob, Q*. power / will *TCD, Dob, O'F, Q*. *second* no / nor
Dob, O'F, Q. will / power *TCD, Dob, O'F, Q*. *third* no / nor *Dob, Lut*.

111. TO SR. HENRY WOOTTON.

COPY TEXT: 1633.

TEXTS: 1633–69; H49, D, SP, Lec, C57, TCD, N, TCC, A18, DC, Dob, S96,
Lut, O'F, HM198, Cy, O, P, JC, D17, B, S, K, W, HN, L74, S962; Ee.4.14;
Don.c.54.

COLLATION: 1633–69, C57, TCD, Dob, O'F, W. Title: Sʳ / Mʳ *TCD, W*.
dated 20 July 1609> 1598 *W*. 2 tale / tales *1635–54, Dob, O'F*. for newes
/ *omitted 1635–54, O'F*. 9 still, is / is still *TCD;* s'still *Dob, O'F*. 12 Courts
/ Court *Dob*. state: *Gr.* / ~ₐ *1633*. 14 wishing / wishes *1635–54, O'F (and
others)*. 16–18 *omitted K*. 20 playes / players *1639–69, O'F* (> plays)
(and others). 21 are / *omitted 1635–69, O'F (and others)*. 22 antiques /
antique *TCD*. jeast / jeasts *C57, TCD*. 27 From Court *W (italics)* / from
Court *1633 (no italics)*.

112. TO SR. HENRY WOTTON.

COPY TEXT: 1633.

TEXTS: 1633–69; H49, D, SP, Lec, C57, TCD, N, TCC, A18, DC, Dob, S96, Lut, O'F, HM198, Hd, Cy, O, P, JC, D17, B, S, K, W, HN, S962, A25, La; Don.c.54.

COLLATION: 1633–69, C57, TCD, Dob, O'F, W; some readings from Lec, SP, DC, and Cy. *Title* / To Mr H.W. *W.* 1 more . . . letters / letters more than kisses *C57.* 5 I / *omitted Dob, O'F.* wither . . . day / in one day (*space*) *Dob;* in one day whither away *O'F.* 6 that / which *Dob, O'F.* 10 then . . . worse / they stayne worse then pitch *O'F.* 11 even *TCD* / raging *1633–54, DC.* 12 poles *W* / pole *1633–69, TCD.* 17 and *TCD* / or *1633–69, O'F* (*and others*). a / *omitted 1635–54, O'F.* 18 and / or *1633–69, C57, Dob, O'F.* 20 each / all *O'F.* is / are *O'F.* 21 who / which *Dob, O'F.* 22 no / none *1635–69, Dob, O'F.* there *W* / they *1633;* then *TCD.* 23 where / wherin *O'F.* men / *omitted O'F* (*and others*). 24 and / *omitted 1635–54, O'F.* clay / day *1649–69.* 25 no / the *1635–54, Dob, O'F.* 26 as habits / inhabits *1635–54, O'F, W.* is / is not *1635–54, Dob, O'F.* 27 more / meere *Lec* (*and others*); men *TCC, Dob;* all *1635–69, Dob, O'F.* 28 a / *omitted TCD.* court / Courts *TCD.* 32 these / those *Dob, O'F.* all are / are all *SP, Dob, O'F.* 33 issue / issue is *1635–69, Dob, O'F.* 34 denizon'd / denisons *C57;* Denizen *TCD;* Denized *Dob, O'F.* 35 there / then *C57.* 44 for *TCD* / in *1633–69;* into *Dob, O'F.* 47 thou / then *1635–69, TCD, Dob, W.* 50 his / her *O'F.* 51 easie / easily *O'F* (> easy). 52 gaile. *1635* / goale; *1633.* 59 one thing / *omitted 1635–69, Dob, O'F.* 61 Countries / Countrey *TCD.* 62 chymiques / drinkes to *Dob.* 63 not you / you not *O'F.* 64 you: / ∼. *1633.* 65 German / Germanies *1635–69, O'F* (> Germans); Germanes *Cy.* 70 have / had *TCD.*

113. TO MR. ROWLAND WOODWARD.

COPY TEXT: 1633.

TEXTS: 1633–69; H49, D, SP, Lec, C57, TCD, N, TCC, A18, DC, Dob, S96, Lut, O'F, Hd, Cy, O, P, JC, D17, B, S, K, W, L74, H40; V.a.103.

COLLATION: 1633–69, C57, TCD, Dob, O'F, W; one reading from TCC. *Title* / *omitted TCD;* A letter to Rowland Woodward *O'F.* 2 tyed to / tired to a *TCD, W.* 3 fallownesse / holines *Dob* (> fallownes), *O'F* (> fallownes). 4 *second* to / *added O'F.* showne / flowne *1635–54, O'F* (> shewne). 5 lovesong / long loves *1635–54, O'F.* 9 good / good as *O'F* (as *deleted*) (*and others*). 10 and be / but *1635–69, O'F* (*and others*). 13 white / whites *O'F* (*and others*). 14 honestie / Integrity *Dob, O'F* (> Honesty). 15 native / naked *O'F* (> native). 16–18 *missing DC.* 16 Religion: *Gr.* / ∼, *1633.* 23 our / the *TCD.* 26 any / an *TCC, O'F.* Soule *C57* / Soules *1633–69.* 27 lie still / still lye *O'F.* 31 farmers *1635* / termers *1633.* 32 and thrive / and there *C57* (*and others*); *omitted TCD; changed to* even heere *Dob.* 33 deare / good *1635–69, Dob, O'F.* 35 things / shewes *O'F.* 36 to / *omitted Dob.* lov'd / beloved *TCD* (*and others*).

114. TO MR. T. W.: "ALL HAILE SWEET POËT."

COPY TEXT: 1633.

TEXTS: 1633–69; TCD, N, TCC, A18, DC, Dob, S96, Lut, O'F, HM198, Hd, Cy, O, P, B, S, K, W; E2230; Chetham, Don.c.54.

COLLATION: 1633–69, TCD, Dob, O'F, W; some readings from DC and Lut. *Title* / A letter incog. *Dob*. Mr. / M. *1633–69, TCD.* T. / I. *1633–69, DC, O'F.* 11–12a, 15a *deleted* W. 1 strong / strange *O'F* (> strong). 2 any / my dull *1635–69, Dob, O'F.* 3 lov'd / love *Dob, O'F.* this / thy *1635–69, Dob, O'F.* 5 have / hath *Dob, O'F.* 7–8 *not indented 1633.* 8 and / or *Dob, O'F* (> and). twilights / twilight *Dob, Lut.* 13 mee: *Gr.* / ~, *1633.* ever / never *Dob, O'F* (> ever). 14–16 ∧alas, (Before . . . Schoole∧ . . . begger,) *Gr.* / (~, ∧~ . . . ~) . . . ~,∧ *1633.* 14 Natures, and in fortunes / Fortunes or in Natures *Dob, O'F.* 15 Before / But for *1635–69;* but by *Dob, O'F* (> But for). Before . . . the Muses *TCD* / Before by . . . th'Muses *1633.* 16 am / am now *Dob, O'F, W.* 18 easie / all soft *Dob, O'F* (> easy). 21 For, but / But for *Dob, O'F* (> for but). 22 nor / or *Dob, O'F.* 23 worth *O'F* / worke *1633–54, TCD.* 28 passe. *Gr.* / ~, *1633.* 29 that *O'F* / then *1633–54, TCD.* 30 *second, third, and fourth* thy / th' . . . the . . . the *TCD.* eccho . . . foyle / foyle . . . eccho *Dob, O'F.*

115. TO MR. T. W.: "HAST THEE HARSH VERSE."

COPY TEXT: 1633.

TEXTS: 1633–69; TCD, N, TCC, A18, DC, Lut, O'F, W.

COLLATION: 1633–69, TCD, O'F, W; one reading from Lut. *Title:* Mr. *W* / M. *1633–69, TCD, Lut.* 2b, 5, 6, 8, 9, 10 *deleted* W. 5–6 W / *omitted 1633–69, TCD, O'F.* 14 And / *omitted 1635–69, O'F.*

116. TO MR. T. W.: "PREGNANT AGAIN."

COPY TEXT: 1633.

TEXTS: 1633–69; TCD, N, TCC, A18, DC, Lut, O'F, W; A23.

COLLATION: 1633–69, TCD, O'F, W, A23; one reading from DC. *Title:* Mr. *W* / M. *1633–69, TCD, A23.* T. / F. *DC.* 5 Watch / Marke *W, A23.* and *W* / or *1633–69.* 7 thy / thine *TCD, O'F, W, A23.* 8 body / bodye's *O'F.*

117. TO MR. T. W.: "AT ONCE, FROM HENCE."

COPY TEXT: 1633.

TEXTS: 1633–69; H49, D, SP, TCD, N, TCC, A18, DC, Dob, S96, Lut, O'F, HM198, O, B, W, S962; A23; A34744, RP116.

COLLATION: 1633–69, H49, TCD, Dob, O'F, W. *No break with preceding poem (No. 116), 1633, TCD. Title* W / Incerto *1635–69;* An old Letter *H49;* A letter incog. *Dob;* Letter. Incerto *Lut;* Letter *O'F.* 2b, 9, 14 *deleted* W. 6 Lyes / Is *O'F.* his / the *Dob, O'F.* 7 Melancholy *1635* / Malancholy *1633.* 14 love, *Gr.* / ~∧ *1633.*

118. TO MR. R. W.: "ZEALOUSLY MY MUSE."

COPY TEXT: W.

TEXTS: W, A23.

COLLATION: W, A23. *Title* / omitted A23.   1 thee, *Ed.* / ~∧ W.   11 myne,
Ed. / ~∧ W.

119. TO MR. R. W.: "MUSE NOT THAT BY THY MIND."

COPY TEXT: W.

TEXTS: W, A23.

COLLATION: W, A23. *Title* / omitted A23.   8 Body *Ed.* / body W.   11 my
/ thy A23 (> my). thyne / myne A23 (> thyne).

120. TO MR. C. B.

COPY TEXT: 1633.

TEXTS: 1633–69; TCD, N, TCC, A18, DC, Lut, O'F, W; A23.

COLLATION: 1633–69, TCD, O'F, W, A23; one reading from DC. Title: Mr.
W / M *1633–69, TCD, O'F.*   2 unexcusable / inexcusable *DC, O'F, W.*   6
nor / or *O'F.* this / omitted W; their A23 (*deleted*).   9 But / And W, A23.
10 earths / the *1635–54;* the earths *O'F.* fairer W / faire *1633–69, TCD, O'F.*
11 sterne / serv'd *1635–69, O'F.*

121. TO MR. E. G.

COPY TEXT: W.

TEXT: W.

COLLATION: W.   3 hart, *Gr.* / ~∧ W.   6 staying *Gr.* / staing W.   7 posses,
Gr. / ~∧ W.   15 too *Gr.* / to W.

122. TO MR. R. W.: "IF, AS MINE IS, THY LIFE."

COPY TEXT: 1633.

TEXTS: 1633–69; TCD, N, TCC, A18, DC, Lut, O'F, W; A21433, A25303.
(Grierson cited A23, but apparently meant to cite that MS for No. 117.)

COLLATION: 1633–69, TCD, O'F, W. Title: Mr. *TCD* / M. *1633–69.*   2 of /
on *O'F.*   6 hand / hands *TCD, O'F.*   8 my / thy *O'F* (> my).   13 enamor'd
Ed. / enamored *1633.*   18 *not indented 1633.*   22 Oh, *TCD* / Our∧ *1633–69;*
Ah, *W.*   23 businesse / businesses *1635–69, O'F, W.*   24 betweene / betwixt
O'F.   27 all *Gr.* / All *1633.*

123. TO MR. R. W.: "KINDLY'I ENVY THY SONGS."

COPY TEXT: W.

TEXT: W.

COLLATION: W.   10 emptines, *Gr.* / ~∧ W.

124. TO MR. S. B.

COPY TEXT: 1633.

TEXTS: 1633–69; TCD, N, TCC, A18, DC, Lut, O'F, W; Eng 686.

COLLATION: 1633–69, TCD, O'F, W; one reading from Eng 686. Title: Mr.

O'F / M. *1633–69, TCD, W.* Epigramme of Dr Donnes makinge to Mr S.B. *Eng 686.* 10 nor / not *TCD.* 12 seeing *1635* / seing *1633;* seene *TCD, O'F, W.* 13 though / thought *1649–54.* had / but *1649–54.*

125. TO MR. I. L.: "OF THAT SHORT ROLL."

COPY TEXT: 1633.
TEXTS: 1633–69; TCD, N, TCC, A18, DC, Lut, O'F, W.
COLLATION: 1633–69, TCD, O'F, W. Title: Mr. *W* / M. *1633–69, TCD.* I. / T. *O'F.* 5 sometimes / sometime *1635–39.* 6 Lethe'; *Gr.* / ~', *1633.* forget. *Gr.* / ~, *1633.* 9 stretch'd / wretched *O'F.* 10 joyes / Joy *O'F.* 14 *second* that / *omitted O'F.*

126. TO MR. B. B.

COPY TEXT: 1633.
TEXTS: 1633–69; TCD, N, TCC, A18, DC, Lut, O'F, HM198, W.
COLLATION: 1633–69, TCD, O'F, HM198, W; one reading from DC. Title: Mr. *W* / M. *1633–69, TCD.* 7 digest / disgest *DC, O'F, HM198.* 16 ever, ever / still: encrease and *HM198, W.* 18 widowhed *W* / widdowhood *1633–69, TCD.* 19 Muse *W* / nurse *1633–69.*

127. TO MR. I. L.: "BLEST ARE YOUR NORTH PARTS."

COPY TEXT: 1633.
TEXTS: 1633–69; TCD, N, TCC, A18, DC, Lut, O'F, W.
COLLATION: 1633–69, TCD, O'F, W; one reading from DC. Title: Mr. *O'F* / M. *1633–69, TCD, W.* I. / P. *1633–69, DC;* T. *O'F.* 6 rages, *Gr.* / ~∧ *1633.* chafes / burnes *W.* 8 *second* no / nor *O'F.* 11–12 *W* / *omitted 1633–69, TCD, O'F.* 16 thee / shee *1635–69, O'F.* list / wilt *W.* 20 lov'd / young *O'F;* fair *W.*

128. H. W. IN HIBER. BELLIGERANTI.

COPY TEXT: Bur.
TEXT: Bur.
COLLATION: Bur. *First words of lines consistently capitalized.* 2 most, *Gr.* / ~∧ *Bur.* 3 frendship, *Gr.* / ~∧ *Bur.* 9 shotts / > shott *Bur (later hand).* 10 restreynes; *Gr.* / ~∧ *Bur.* 11 attack *Ed.* / attach *Bur.* best, *Gr.* / ~∧ *Bur.* 12 arrest *Gr.* / crest *Bur.* 13 first∧ *Gr.* / ~) *Bur.* 17 labor'd *Ed.* / labored *Bur.* 19 Art: *Gr.* / ~∧ *Bur.*

129. TO SIR H. W. AT HIS GOING AMBASSADOR TO VENICE.

COPY TEXT: 1633.
TEXTS: 1633–69; Walton; TCD, N, TCC, A18, DC, Lut, O'F, HM198, La; Bur.
COLLATION: 1633–69, TCD, O'F, HM198. Title: H.W. / Henry Wootton *1669, TCD, O'F.* 2 fear'd / serv'd *HM198.* 9 After / Amongst *HM198.* 10 pleasures / pleasure *1633–69, O'F, HM198.* 11 rich / safe *HM198.* 13 After / Amongst *HM198.* where / which *1635–69, O'F, HM198.* 14 to / for *O'F (> to).* 19 must / would *HM198.* 24 honour / noble *1635–69,*

TCD, O'F, HM198. it / wit *1635–69, O'F*. 25 load / boate *O'F* (> load). 35 I . . . well / well I beare *HM198*. 38 mee here / my heare *TCD;* my hart *O'F* (> mee heere).

130. TO SR. HENRY GOODYERE.

    COPY TEXT: 1633.

    TEXTS: 1633–69; H49, D, SP, Lec, C57, TCD, N, TCC, A18, DC, Dob, Lut, O'F, HM198, Hd, Cy, B, A25; Add 29; Wales 5308E.

    COLLATION: 1633–69, C57, TCD, Dob, O'F; some readings from H49 and Lut. *Title* / To Sr. H.G. moving him to travell *TCD, O'F*. 2 leafe / leaves *TCD*. things / still *TCD;* thinge *Dob, O'F*. reads / read *1649–54*. 4 like / as *O'F*. 7 But / *omitted C57*. 8 upward / upwards *TCD*. fortune / fortunes *TCD, O'F* (*and others*). 16 unto / untill *Lut* (*changed from* unto), *O'F*. the / her *TCD, Dob, O'F*. 20 harvests / harvest *1669, O'F* (*and others*). 23 no / not *TCD*. 27 Goe; *Gr.* / ~, *1633*. 28 in / to *1635–69, Dob, O'F*. 29–32 *omitted Lut*. 37 However / Howsoever *C57, TCD, Dob, O'F*. 38 as / *omitted 1639–69*. 40 morning / Mornings *TCD*. 44 Tables / Fables *1669, H49, TCD, Dob, O'F*. 45 make / made *TCD*. 48 with / to *TCD*. to / att *TCD*.

131. TO THE COUNTESSE OF HUNTINGDON: "THAT UNRIPE SIDE OF EARTH."

    COPY TEXT: 1635.

    TEXTS: 1635–69; O, P, TCD(II).

    COLLATION: 1635–69, O, P, TCD(II). *Title* / Sr: Walter Ashton to the Countess of Huntington *O, P, TCD*. 3 ate / eat *1649–69, O, P, TCD*. that / what *O, P*. 4 it / yett *O, P*. 11 downward / inward *TCD*. 13 your / the *O, P*. 17 who / that *O, P, TCD*. 21 neither / never *TCD*. 26 faithfully / finally *O, P*. you smil'd / your smile *1669, O, P, TCD*. 30 whispers / whispered *P;* vapours *TCD*. 31 love is / love's a *O, P*. 32 ague / ffeaver *P*. 35 paine, *Gr.* / ~. *1635*. 38 disorder'd *Ed.* / disordered *1635*. heape / shape *O, P*. 41 but / once *O, P*. 48 by / with *O, P*. 49 sigh'd / fight *O, P*. 50 both / butt *O, P, TCD*. 52 consider'd *Gr.* / considered *1635*. 55 passion / passions *O, P*. 57 sueth / sues *O, P*. 65 know, *Gr.* / ~. *1635*. 67 must bee / is meer *1669*. one / once *O, P*. 69 sigh *TCD* / sinne *1635–69*. 74 and *P* / I *1635–69, O, TCD*. 83 a / all *O, P, TCD*. perfectnesse / perfections *O, P*. 84 youngest / the quaintest *TCD*. flatteries / flatterers *O, P, TCD*. doe / *omitted TCD*. 86 though / whats *O, P*. 89 you's / God's *O, P*. 92 Zani's / fames *O, P*. 98 but / *omitted 1649–69;* is *O*. nearer / never *O;* ever *P*. 99 thoughts / through *O, P*. 103 us / *omitted O, P*. 105 wholy / holy *O, P, TCD*. 107 dares *TCD* / dare *1635–69*. 108 waight / waights *O, TCD;* wights *P*. 113 *indented 1635*. eye / eyes *P, TCD*. hand / hands *P, TCD*. 114 *second* they / *omitted O, P, TCD*. break. *Gr.* / ~ᴧ *1635*. 115 *not indented 1635*. removed / remotenesse *O, P*. 116 Sunnes / Sun's sweet *1669*. comfort; *Gr.* / ~? *1635*. others / yet some *1669*. 119 as / as the *O, P*. takes / take *O*. the / all *O, P*. 120 first Rayes / rayes first *1669, O, TCD;* rise first *P*. 121 men *P* / man *1635–69, O, TCD*. 123 Their *P* / there *1635*. 125 violent *TCD* / valiant *1635–69*. 127 imparts / imports *1669, TCD*. 128 fain'd *P* / fancied *1635–69;* thought *TCD*. which . . . appetite *P* / *omitted 1635–39;* in the soule, not appetite *1649–54;* by the Soul, not appetite *1669;* the Mansion of sweet appetite *TCD*. 130 contract in *P* / contracted *1635–39, TCD*.

132. AMICISSIMO, ET MERITISSIMO BEN. JONSON. IN VULPONEM.

COPY TEXT: *Volpone*.

TEXTS: 1650–69; *Volpone, Works*.

COLLATION: All texts. Title: In Vulponem. *Works / missing Volpone*.

133. TO MRS. M. H.

COPY TEXT: *1633*.

TEXTS: 1633–69; TCD, N, TCC, A18, DC, Dob, S96, Lut, O'F, HM198, Hd, O, P, B, A25; Add 29; Wales 5308E.

COLLATION: 1633–69, TCD, Dob, O'F; some readings from DC and O. Title: Mrs. *O'F* / M. *1633–69, TCD. Title / omitted Dob.* 2 my / thy *1635–69*. 3 returne *Gr.* / ~. *1633*. 4 is / was *Dob, O'F*. 7 much; / ~, *1633*. embold-ens / it unboldens *Dob*. 8 'tis / that's *Dob, O'F*. all; Thou *Gr.* / ~, thou *1633*. 10 goe? *Gr.* / ~, *1633*. 12 not / to *Dob, O'F* (> not). 14 reverence, *Gr.* / ~. *1633*. 16 have then / wilt have *O'F* (> have then). 19 saples / shape-less *Dob, O'F* (> sapp-lesse). 22 mis-speake *Gr.* / mispeake *1633*. utter'd *Ed.* / uttered *1633*. 27 For / From *1635–69, TCD, Dob, O'F*. ill, and her / her, and ill *O'F*. 32 first and / *omitted Dob, O'F*. 33 Who knowes / We knowe *Dob, O'F*. 39 his / her *Dob, O'F*. 41 get / get to *Dob*. o'r skip / doe skip *TCD;* skip *DC, O;* skips *Dob;* skipps o're *O'F*. 42–45 *omitted Dob*. 42 kisse / teare *O'F* (> kisse). 44 whether / whither *1635–69*. 47 grieves / grieve *1635–69*.

134. TO THE COUNTESSE OF BEDFORD: "REASON IS OUR SOULES LEFT HAND."

COPY TEXT: *1633*.

TEXTS: 1633–69; H49, D, SP, Lec, C57, TCD, N, DC, Dob, S96, Lut, O'F, HM198, Hd, Cy, B, S, L74, La; RP31, M.

COLLATION: 1633–69, C57, TCD, Dob, O'F. Title: Bedford / B. *TCD*. Mad-ame / *omitted O'F*. 3 Their / those *TCD*. blessings / blessing *1635–69, TCD, Dob, O'F*. light / sight *C57, TCD, Dob, O'F*. 4 faire / farr *C57* (*and others*). faire faith grew / Fayth doth grow *O'F* (> fayre fayth grew). 16 voice *1635* / faith *1633*. 19 top'd and / to sense *1635–54, O'F;* to some and *C57;* to seeme *Dob*. 24 are / is *O'F*. 33 then / thus *O'F*. 36 This *1635* / Thy *1633*. 38 which / that *O'F*.

135. A LETTER WRITTEN BY SR. H. G. AND J. D. ALTERNIS VICIBUS.

COPY TEXT: A25.

TEXT: A25.

COLLATION: A25. *Italics added; first words of lines consistently capitalized.* 29 traine, *Ed.* / ~ₐ A25.

136. TO THE COUNTESSE OF BEDFORD: "HONOR IS SO SUBLIME."

COPY TEXT: 1633.

TEXTS: 1633–69; TCD, N, DC, Dob, S96, Lut, O'F, HM198, B.

COLLATION: 1633–69, TCD, Dob, O'F; one reading from DC. Title: Bedford / B. *TCD. Addressed* Madame *O'F.* 4 these / those *O'F* (> these). 8 honour'd *Ed.* / honoured *1633.* 10 part / parts *TCD, Dob, O'F.* 12 of / or *1633, TCD, O'F.* 13 Madame / Lady *Dob, O'F.* praysers / prayses *1633–69;* praiers *DC;* prayer *Dob.* lye / bee *O'F.* 26 quicke / grosse *TCD.* 27 front / face *Dob, O'F. second* your / our *1633–69.* 40–42 *placed after l. 33, 1635–69, TCD, Dob, O'F.* 42 one; *Gr.* / ~, *1633.* 45 but / *omitted Dob, O'F.* 48 all wayes *Gr.* / always *1633–69, TCD, O'F.* 53 so / ere *Dob, O'F.*

137. TO THE COUNTESSE OF BEDFORD: "YOU HAVE REFIN'D MEE."

COPY TEXT: 1633.

TEXTS: 1633–69; H49, D, SP, Lec, C57, TCD, N, DC, Dob, Lut, O'F, HM198, Cy, B, H40; HNVIII (ll. 37–42).

COLLATION: 1633–69, C57, TCD, Dob, O'F; one reading from Lut. Title: Bedford / B. *TCD.* Madame / *omitted TCD.* 6 and / or *1669, Dob.* 8 ^Where *Ed.* / (~ *1633.* 11 need / needes *C57.* there some / some there *1669, O'F.* 16 Exhale / Awake *TCD.* 21 light / sight *O'F* (> light). 42 thinke / *changed to* make *Dob.* 45 enfold / unfold *TCD.* 52 and / all *C57, TCD, Dob, O'F.* 55 lovely / learned *O'F.* 56 and / you th' *O'F.* 58 both / worth *1635–69, O'F;* but *Dob.* 60 thinge / things *1635–69, C57.* 66 As / A *O'F.* aliens / alters *1635–54, O'F.* 68 sense / Sences *C57, Dob, O'F.* 71 had / hath *1639–69, Lut.*

138. TO THE COUNTESSE OF BEDFORD: "T'HAVE WRITTEN THEN."

COPY TEXT: 1633.

TEXTS: 1633–69; TCD, N, DC, Lut, O'F.

COLLATION: 1633–69, TCD, O'F. Title: Bedford / B. *TCD, O'F.* 1 writ / wrote *O'F.* 3 seemes / is *O'F.* 5 debt / doubt *1633–54.* 7 nothings *1635* / nothing *1633, 1669, TCD.* may^ *Gr.* / ~, *1633.* 14 hath / *added TCD.* 20 part / parts *O'F.* all^ it, *Ed.* / ~, in^ *1633.* 25 Your (or you) vertue^ *Gr.* / ~, ~~^~, *1633.* 30 is *1635* / it *1633.* 31 praises / Phrases *TCD.* 32 Stoop, others ills^ *Gr.* / Stop^ ~~, *1633.* 35 Lightnesse / Lightens *TCD.* depresseth / depresses *TCD.* 46 Who / Whose *TCD.* prayes / praise *TCD.* 51 be but / but be *O'F.* 55 dignities, *Gr.* / ~^ *1633.* 58 not / borne *1635–69, O'F.* 59 new / now *1635–69, TCD, O'F.* 60 vice *1635* / it *1633, TCD.* 66 That^ *Gr.* / ~, *1633.* grow? *Gr.* / ~. *1633.* 72 true / truth *O'F.* 74 ill. *Gr.* / ~, *1633.* 75 you, *Gr.* / your^ *1633.* 79 makes / make *1635–39.* 85 tame / thrall *O'F* (> tame). 88 or / nor *TCD, O'F.*

139. TO THE COUNTESSE OF BEDFORD. ON NEW-YEARES DAY.

COPY TEXT: 1633.

TEXTS: 1633–69; TCD, N, DC, Lut, O'F.

COLLATION: 1633–69, TCD, O'F. Title: Bedford / B. *TCD, O'F.* On / At

TCD, O'F. day / tide *TCD, O'F.* 7 th'new / new *TCD, O'F* (> th'new). 10 times *1635* / time *1633.* 12 towards / toward *TCD.* such. *Gr.* / ∼, *1633.* 14 Preserve / preserves *TCD.* 16 short-liv'd *Gr.* / ∼∧∼ *1633.* 18 spirits *1635* / spirit *1633.* 20 bodies last / Bodie lastes *TCD.* 27 I, *Gr.* / ∼∧ *1633.* 29 name, know, *Gr.* / ∼∧∼∧ *1633.* 35 praiser *1635* / prayer *1633, TCD.* prayes / praise *TCD.* 37 His / your *O'F.* blood; *Gr.* / ∼, *1633.* 39 doubts; *Gr.* / ∼, *1633.* 42 Court; *Gr.* / ∼, *1633.* 43 got; *Gr.* / ∼, *1633.* 45 sinne∧ *Ed.* / ∼; *1633.* may / doth *O'F* (> may). 46 he, *Gr.* / ∼∧ *1633.* 47 Which *1635* / With *1633.* 57 discreet / Direct *TCD.*

140. TO SR. EDWARD HERBERT. AT JULYERS.

COPY TEXT: 1633.

TEXTS: 1633–69; H49, D, SP, Lec, C57, TCD, N, TCC, A18, DC, Dob, S96, Lut, O'F, HM198 (twice), Cy, O, P, B, S, K.

COLLATION: 1633–69, C57 (plus H49), TCD, Dob, O'F. *Title* / . . . Herbert, now Lord Herbert of Cherbury, being at the siege of Julyers. *1635–69;* To Sr. E. H. *TCD.* at Julyers / *omitted Dob; added O'F.* 3 these / those *Dob.* 10 minde! *Gr.* / ∼? *1633.* 14 is / *omitted TCD.* 15 the / a *Dob.* 17 a / an *1635–54; omitted 1669.* 28 we / men *1635–69, Dob, O'F.* 30 our / *omitted C57.* 35 show; *Gr.* / ∼, *1633.* 41–50 *omitted Lec, C57.* 41 it is / is all *TCD.* 44 icy *Ed.* / jcy *1633.* 48 an / a *TCD, Dob, O'F.* 49 those / these *Dob.*

141. TO THE COUNTESSE OF HUNTINGDON: "MAN TO GODS IMAGE."

COPY TEXT: 1633.

TEXTS: 1633–69; TCD, N, DC, Lut, O'F.

COLLATION: 1633–69, TCD, O'F; one reading from DC. *Title* / To the C. of H. *TCD.* Madame / *omitted O'F.* 1 mans / man *1649–69.* 13 the *1635* / which *1633;* thy *TCD.* Magi / mages *TCD, O'F.* 16 and the / and *TCD;* have, and *DC.* 17 argu'd *Ed.* / argued *1633.* 22 you; *Gr.* / ∼, *1633.* 23 in / on *O'F.* 24 amass'd / a masse *1635–69, TCD, O'F* (> amassd). 25 Shee; *Gr.* / ∼, *1633.* 26 Us she inform'd / Informed us *1635–69, O'F;* Us informed *TCD.* you; *Gr.* / ∼, *1633.* 43 ye / you *1635–69, O'F.* 47 doe so, *1635* / to you∧ *1633.* so / *omitted (space) TCD.* 48 due. / ∼, *1633.* 55 But / And *1635–69.* 56 flattery / flatteryes *O'F* (> flatterye). 58 my / mine *TCD, O'F.* 59 these / those *O'F.* praises / prayers *TCD.* 63 these / those *TCD, O'F.* 64 that *1635* / thar *1633.* 66 or / and *1635–69, TCD, O'F.*

142. A LETTER TO THE LADY CAREY AND MRS. ESSEX RICHE, FROM AMYENS.

COPY TEXT: 1633.

TEXTS: 1633–69; H49, D, SP, Lec, C57, TCD, N, DC, Dob, S96, Lut, O'F, HM198, Cy, O, P, B; M; V.a.170.

COLLATION: 1633–69, C57, TCD, Dob, O'F; one reading from SP. *Title* / To the La. Co. of C. *TCD;* To the Lady Cary *Dob;* To the Lady Cary and her sister Mrs Essex Rich. From Amiens *O'F.*   7 would / could *Dob, O'F.*   8 it / you *TCD.*   10 too / some *Dob.*   13 are *1635* / is *1633.*   21 flegme_∧ *Gr.* / ~, *1633.*   26 contributions / contribution *SP, TCD, Dob, O'F.*   28 which / who *Dob, O'F.*   30 this *1635* / their *1633, C57.*   34 aguish / anguish *1649–54, C57.*   40 Shee / Shee'hath *TCD.*   49 that / your *O'F.*   57 twice / t'will *TCD.* our / your *C57, Dob.*

143. TO THE COUNTESSE OF BEDFORD. BEGUN IN FRANCE BUT NEVER PERFECTED.

COPY TEXT: 1633.

TEXTS: 1633–69; DC, O'F.

COLLATION: 1633–69, DC, O'F. Title: Bedford / B. *DC.*   5 begot *1635* / forgot *1633.*   6 *second* mee, *Ed.* / ~; *1633.*   14 or / and *1649–69.*   18 upon_∧ *Gr.* / ~, *1633.* Desunt cætera / The rest wants. *O'F.*

144. DE LIBRO CUM MUTUARETUR, IMPRESSO . . .

COPY TEXT: 1635.

TEXTS: 1635–69.

COLLATION: 1635–69. Title: frustatim *Gr.* / frustratim *1635.*   6 abit; *Gr.* / ~, *1635.*

145. TO THE COUNTESSE OF SALISBURY.

COPY TEXT: 1633.

TEXTS: 1633–69; H49, D, SP, Lec, C57, TCD, N, DC, Lut, O'F.

COLLATION: 1633–69, C57 (plus H49), TCD, O'F; one reading from DC. Title: Salisbury / S. *TCD. date omitted, TCD, O'F.*   2 and / *omitted 1635–54, TCD, O'F.*   5 disshevel'd / discover'd *C57.* scatter'd *Ed.* / scattered *1633.*   8 booke / barke *O'F.*   9 wither'd *Ed.* / withered *1633.*   10 Vertues / Vertue *C57, O'F.*   11 sand / Land *TCD.*   12 by / *omitted TCD.*   16 Citie / Citties *TCD.*   27 those / these *DC, O'F.*   29 Where / When *TCD, O'F.*   36 sparke / sparks *TCD.* it / them *TCD.*   38 Idolatrie / Adulterie *TCD.*   40 greene, *Gr.* / ~_∧ *1633.*   43–46 *omitted C57.*   50 spoke / spake *O'F.*   53 When / Where *C57.*   54 swallow'd *Ed.* / swallowed *1633.*   57 I / if I *1635–69, O'F.*   60 the / a *O'F.*   61–84 *omitted Lut.*   64 home / hrme *1633.*   69 new great / great new *TCD.*   77–78 *omitted C57.*   79 borne_∧ *Gr.* / ~, *1633.*

146. ELEGIE ON THE L. C.

COPY TEXT: 1633.

TEXTS: 1633–69; H49, D, SP, Lec, C57, S96, Lut, O'F, HM198, Cy, O, P, JC, D17, B, S, K, W, HN; HNVIII.

COLLATION: 1633–69, C57, S96, O'F. *Title 1635* / Elegie VI. *1633;* Elegye *C57;* Funerall Elegie *S96;* Elegy funer. *O'F.*   1 who / that *1649–69;* which *S96, O'F.*   6 serve / sterve *C57.*   11 fell'd / pilld *C57.*   16 share. *Gr.* / ~_∧ *1633.*   17 friends / things *S96, O'F* (> frinds). him; *Gr.* / ~, *1633.*   20 names / name *1635–69.*   21 that / *omitted S96, O'F.*   24 he. *Gr.* / ~, *1633.*   25 Tombe / ston *C57.*

147. EPITAPH ON HIMSELFE.

COPY TEXT: 1635.

TEXTS: 1635–69 (two versions: ll. 1–16, 7–24); H49, D, SP, Dob, S96, Lut, O'F, HM198 (ll. 1–6), P (ll. 7–24), B (ll. 1–6, 7–24, separated), H40, S962 (ll. 1–6), A25 (ll. 1–6); Add 29 (ll. 1–6), RP31, A10309, Hyde (ll. 1–6), H3511 (ll. 1–16); U26 (ll. 1–6). Others give ll. 1–24.

COLLATION: 1635–69, H49, Dob, O'F; one reading from P. *Title /* Elegie. *1635–69 (I)*; On himselfe *1635–69 (II)*; Epitaph *H49 (ll. 1–6)*; Omnibus *H49 (ll. 7–24)*; To . . . Bedford *Dob, O'F;* Another on the Same *P (referring to Mrs. Boulstred).* 5 Others / O then *H49.* Wills / testament *H49, Dob, O'F* (> Wills). 7 choice / will *1635–69 (I), O'F.* 8 speechlesse / sencelesse *1635–69 (I), O'F.* 10 seest / see *1635–69 (I), H49, Dob, O'F.* 11 death us / us death *1635–69 (I), H49, Dob, O'F.* 12 here / there *1635 (I), 1669 (I), Dob, O'F;* thee *1639–54 (I).* 22 to / for *1635–69.*

148. ELEGIE TO THE LADY BEDFORD.

COPY TEXT: 1633.

TEXTS: 1633–69; TCD, N, Lut, O'F, HM198, Hd, Cy, O, P, S, L74, H40; RP31, A30982; H3910, Don.b.9.

COLLATION: 1633–69, TCD, O'F, Hd. Title: Elegie / *omitted 1635–69, O'F.* 1 she_∧ . . . you, *Gr. /* ~, . . . ~_∧ *1633.* 13 you here / heere you *O'F.* 14 th'other *Gr. /* thother *1633.* 17 honour_∧ . . . due_∧ *Gr. /* ~: . . . ~; *1633.* due / show *O'F.* 20 were *1635 /* was *1633, TCD.* 22 as / that *TCD, Hd.* all in you / in you All *TCD, O'F, Hd.* 28 *second* the / a *TCD, O'F, Hd.* 32 their / the *O'F* (> their). 35 or / nor *O'F.* 42 can / *repeated 1633.*

149. ELEGIE ON THE LADY MARCKHAM.

COPY TEXT: 1633.

TEXTS: 1633–69; H49, D, SP, Lec, C57, TCD, N, TCC, A18, DC, Dob, S96, Lut, O'F, Hd, Cy, O, P, JC, D17, B, K, L74, H40, S962, A25, La, Hol, TCD (II); Add 29, A30982, Wel, Grey; A19268 (ll. 43–46), HP401 (ll. 41–44, 17–20, 53–62), HNVIII (ll. 15–16, 59–60).

COLLATION: 1633–69, C57, TCD, Dob, O'F; some readings from SP, Lec, and DC. Two sections, ll. 41–44, with title *Epitaphe;* ll. 17–20, 53–62, with given title *HP401. Title /* An Elegie upon the death of the Ladie Marckham *TCD;* A funerall Elegy . . . *Dob, O'F (with slight differences).* 1–44 *missing DC.* 1 the Ocean *Ed. /* th'Ocean *1633.* 2 parts / part *Lec.* 3 This / The *O'F* (> This). 5 rore / weare *SP (and others).* 6 bankes *C57 /* banke *1633–69, TCD.* 8 firmament, *Gr. /* ~. *1633.* 9 sins / synne *C57, TCD, Dob, O'F.* 10 Funerall, *Gr. /* ~. *1633.* 11 these *C57 /* those *1633–69, TCD, Dob, O'F.* 12 Noe / No *1635–54, Dob, O'F.* our *C57 /* the *1633–54, Dob.* 16 mist / mists *TCD.* wee / they *C57.* or / nor *TCD.* shee / wee *C57.* 19 workes / worke *Dob.* 22 Porcelane / *spelled variously in the MSS.* 24 Mines / myne *C57.* 28 then / them *1649–69.* 29 the sea, when / when the sea *TCD.* it gaines / gaines it *TCD.* loseth / looses *O'F.* 33 when / who *C57.* they / *omitted C57.* 34 both_∧ *Gr. /* ~, *1633.* deaths / dead *C57, Dob.* 36 that / which

TCD (*and others*). sinne / death C57. is / are *TCD* (*and others*).   37 doe /
did C57.   38 hath she / shee hath *TCD* (*and others*).   42 breakes C57 / cracks
1633–69. glasse! *Gr.* / ~? 1633.   44–45 *omitted* 1633.   45 rarefie / rectifye
C57, *Dob, O'F* (> rarify); ratifie *DC*.   47 acts / artes *DC*. the / that *Dob*.
48 that / which *TCD, O'F* (*and others*). sometimes / sometime 1635–69.   57
this / that *O'F*. forward / froward *Dob* (> forward).   58 women 1635 /
woman 1633.   60 vertues / vertue 1639–54. old: *Gr.* / ~. 1633.   62 try-
umph / triumphs C57, *TCD, Dob, O'F*.

150. ELEGIE ON MRIS. BOULSTRED.

COPY TEXT: 1633.

TEXTS: 1633–69; H49, D, SP, Lec, C57, TCD, N, TCC, A18, DC, Dob, S96,
Lut, O'F, Cy, O, P, B, S, K, HN, L74, H40, S962, A25, La; Add 29 (*passim*),
A30982, Wel; A19268 (ll. 5–6, 46–52, 73–74), HNVIII (ll. 35–40, 46–48).

COLLATION: 1633–69, C57, TCD, Dob, O'F; some readings from SP, Lec, and
Lut. *Title* / An Elegie upon the death of Mrs Boulstred *TCD*; Upon . . .
Boulstred *O'F*.   5 there / where *O'F*. there are set / and the meate *TCD*.   6
dishes / dished 1635–39, *TCD, O'F*.   8 *first* or / *omitted O'F*.   10 first / fruite
TCD.   15 Who / Which *O'F*. by / the 1635–69. Roes / rowes 1669, *TCD,
Dob, O'F*.   25 thee / *omitted Dob*.   26 else is / is else *Dob*.   27 lives 1635 /
life 1633, C57, *TCD*. vices . . . vertues / vertues . . . vices *Lec, Dob, O'F*.
34 leaves / leave *SP, Lut*. to / for 1635–69, *O'F*.   35 now thou / thou nowe
TCD.   36 blow‸ *Gr.* / ~, 1633. nor / not *TCD*.   37–38 *omitted DC*.   41 As
/ All *TCD*. King / Kings 1635–69.   45 worke / makes C57; workes *TCD,
Dob*.   56 ambitious; *Gr.* / ~, 1633.   61 bin / growne *TCD*.   62 mis-thinking
/ mistaking *O'F* (> misthinking).   64 profane, *Ed.* / ~. 1633.   65 sinne /
some *O'F*.   68 thine / thy *Dob, O'F*. army / Armor C57; Armies *Dob*.   69
lost / lefte *O'F*.   71 that / the *O'F* (> that).   74 though 1635 / but 1633,
C57, DC.

151. ELEGIE: DEATH.

COPY TEXT: 1633.

TEXTS: 1633–69; TCD, N, TCC, A18, S96, Lut, O'F, HM198, Cy, O, P, B,
S, K, HN, L74, H40, S962; RP31, Grey; A19268 (*passim*), V.a.162 (*passim*),
HNVIII.

COLLATION: 1633–69, TCD, S96, O'F. *Title* 1635 / Elegie 1633; Elegie upon
the death of Mistress Boulstred *TCD*; A Funerall Elegie upon the Death of
Mrs Boulstred *S96*; Another upon the same Mrs Boulstred *O'F*.   2 sorrow /
sorrows 1635–69, *S96, O'F*.   10 fift / first *S96*.   21 for 1635 / to 1633.   22
dwellings / dwelling *S96*.   26 for in her / in her we 1635–69, *O'F*.   28 They
/ That 1635–69, *S96, O'F*. that / who 1635–69, *O'F*.   29 *first* and / or *TCD,
S96, O'F*. *second* and / or *O'F*.   30 shee / the *TCD*. not / no *S96*; in *O'F*.   34
The / That 1635–69, *S96, O'F*.   44 have / *omitted TCD, S96; added O'F*.
46 but‸ inspire *Ed.* / ~'~ 1633.   48 what / which *S96*. turne / turnd *S96*.
feast / feasts *TCD, O'F*.   53 body / bodie's 1635–69, *S96, O'F*.   54 except /
unlesse *S96, O'F*.   57 be‸ *Gr.* / ~, 1633.   58 a / *omitted TCD, S96; added*

O'F. 61 And / While *O'F.* sad glad / glad sad *S96, O'F.* all / each *S96, O'F.* beare / beares *O'F* (*changed from* all beare). 62 waste / breake *1635–69, S96, O'F.*

152. ELEGIE ON THE UNTIMELY DEATH OF THE INCOMPARABLE PRINCE, HENRY.

COPY TEXT: Sylvester.

TEXTS: 1633–69; Sylvester; TCD, N, DC, Lut, O'F, Cy; A27407, RP26. Title and space in D.

COLLATION: 1633–69, Sylvester, TCD, O'F, Cy. *Title* / Elegie on Prince Henry *1633–54, TCD, Cy; . . .* since in print but out of print *O'F.* 8 Men / Man *1633–69, TCD, O'F, Cy.* 12 How, When / when, how *O'F, Cy.* 18 that *1633* / the *Sylvester.* 19 *first* could / might *1635–69, TCD, O'F, Cy.* 21 Movings / Moving *1633–69, Cy.* 22 World to shake / earth to quake *O'F.* 29 From / for *O'F.* 32 Was / Were *O'F.* 34 through / to *1635–69.* 39 For / And *Cy.* 42 Warrs / war *1633.* should / did *1633, TCD, Cy.* 47 ease / eate *TCD.* us / as *TCD, O'F.* 48 will / *omitted TCD, O'F.* not lett's / lets us not *O'F.* 66 With / Of *1633–69, TCD, O'F, Cy.* 71 Faith / Fate *1633–69, TCD, O'F, Cy.* 73 ioine / come *1633–69, TCD, O'F, Cy.* to / so *1633–69, TCD, O'F, Cy.* 77 Proofs / proofe *1633–69, TCD, O'F, Cy.* 82 Wee / and we *1633–54, TCD, O'F, Cy.* 83 I would not *1633* / would not I *Sylvester, 1669.* 87 can / may *TCD, O'F.* 88–98 *missing DC.* 90 which / that *Cy.* 92 Which / That *O'F.* 95 yee / you *TCD, O'F.*

153. OBSEQUIES TO THE LORD HARRINGTON.

COPY TEXT: 1633.

TEXTS: 1633–69; H49, D, SP, Lec, C57, TCD, N, DC, Dob, S96, Lut, O'F, HM198, JC, D17, B, S, K, A25; Add 29, EP.e.14.

COLLATION: 1633–69, C57, TCD, Dob, O'F; some readings from SP, DC, and Lut. *Title Dob* / . . . Harringtons brother. To the Countesse . . . *1633;* Elegie Lo: Harrington *TCD.* Lady Lucy / *omitted C57.* brother . . . Bedford / the last that dyed. *O'F.* 1–108 *missing DC.* 1 wast / was *C57.* 2 wast / wert *O'F.* 5 God / heaven *O'F.* 6 finde / findst *O'F.* 7 mans / mens *1635–69, TCD, Dob, O'F.* 11 these / those *SP, TCD, O'F* (*and others*). 26 that / this *TCD.* Sunne / Sunnes *C57.* 29 this / that *O'F* (> this). 34 these / those *TCD, Dob, O'F.* wayes / way *TCD, Dob, O'F.* 35 our true / truly our *C57, TCD, Dob, O'F.* 39 living / beeing *1635–69, Dob, O'F.* 48 which . . . on / on which . . . *TCD, Dob, O'F.* 50–51 *combined C57* (can . . . vertues *omitted*). 51 on; *Gr.* / ~, *1633.* vertues / virtue *TCD.* 53 feed *1635* / feeds *1633, C57.* 60 and / *omitted Dob; deleted O'F.* 63 would / should *1635–69, O'F.* 66 Which / Who *O'F.* parts / spirits *TCD.* 69 have / have had *1635–69, O'F.* vertues / virtue *Dob.* 76 exercise / encrease *C57;* exercisd *Dob.* lacke / want *O'F.* time / room *TCD, Dob, O'F.* 78 lack / want *O'F.* 84 he / *omitted 1669, O'F* (*and others*). 87 instant∧ *Gr.* / ~, *1633.* 89 formes / shapes *O'F.* 102 this *TCD* / the *1633–69, C57.* tempests *TCD* / tempest *1633–69, C57, O'F.* 103 by / thy *TCD.* 106 and / thy *O'F* (*and others*). death, *Gr.* / ~∧ *1633.* 108 might securely / securelye might *C57.*

110 Which / That *O'F.* 117 When . . . when / Where . . . where *TCD, Dob, O'F.* 118 can∧ *Ed.* / ∼, *1633.* 120 thy / their *SP, DC.* 121 it / that *C57, TCD.* 125 ambitious / ambition *1669, TCD.* 126 agues, *Gr.* / ∼; *1633.* 127 need / needs *C57.* 128 well∧ *Gr.* / ∼, *1633.* 129 these / those *C57.* medicines / medicine *Dob, Lut.* 130 tell / set *1635–54, Dob, O'F.* 133 hand gets *TCD* / hands get *1633–54, O'F.* 135 flye / flee *1635–69.* 138 men / mens *O'F.* which / who *Dob, O'F.* houres / hour *1669, O'F (and others).* 139 these / theyre *C57.* 146 wearer / wearers *O'F.* 151 who / that *Dob.* 152 Instructions / Instruction *TCD.* it could never / never yet could *Dob, O'F.* 155 any / an *1639–69, C57.* 158 when / where *TCD, Dob, O'F.* 159–61 *combined C57* (did . . . flood *omitted*). 161 was / were *1635–69, SP, TCD.* 163 word / now *TCD.* 164 growne / is *C57, DC.* 165 grow / am *1635–69, Dob, O'F.* 169 children, house, Provision / house, provision, children *O'F.* 170 and / or *TCD, Dob, O'F.* 172 that / who *TCD, Dob;* which *O'F.* 176 Which / Who *Dob.* utmost / walles and *Dob.* 183 Triumphs / Triumph *TCD, Dob, O'F.* 186 that / the *TCD.* 187 destin'd / defend *C57.* 188 counsailes / counsayle *C57.* 191 could'st / shouldst *Dob* (*changed from* could'st), *O'F.* this / thy *O'F* (> thys). 192 usurp'dst *TCD* / usurp'st *1633, C57;* usurpe *1635–69, O'F.* 193 Then *1635* / That *1633, C57;* When *Dob* (> Then). as yet / *omitted TCD.* 194 thine / thy *C57.* heate / heates *TCD, Dob.* 196 successefully / successively *TCD, Dob, O'F* (> successfully). 198 acclamations *TCD* / acclamation *1633–54.* 200 which / that *Dob, O'F.* 216 then't had *Gr.* / then t'had *1633–39.* 217–18 *omitted TCD.* 224 then / but *SP, TCD, Dob, O'F.* 229 this / their *Dob, O'F.* 232 this / the *Dob, O'F.* 239 I am / am I *Dob, O'F.* 241 with / for *C57, TCD.* 243 early / earthly *Dob, O'F* (> early). 247 time / times *1669, TCD, Dob, O'F.* be / that be *C57.* 254 which / that *Dob, O'F.* 257 Who / Which *1639–69, O'F.*

154. AN HYMNE TO THE SAINTS, AND TO MARQUESSE HAMYLTON.

COPY TEXT: *1633.*

TEXTS: *1633–69*; TCD, TCC, A18, Lut, O'F; Grey, A30982; Ash 38, RP26, PRO 9/51. Copy in TCD is not part of Group II collection.

COLLATION: *1633–69,* TCD, TCC, O'F. Letter: To . . . Carr *1635* / *omitted 1633.* verse; *1635* / ∼, *1633.* subjects. *1635* / ∼, *1633.* Title: An / A *TCD, O'F.* 1 Whether *1635* / Whither *1633.* that / the *O'F.* which / that *O'F.* 3 Whether / Whither *1633.* 6–7 so, . . . alone? *Gr.* / ∼? . . . ∼; *1633.* 8 Greater / Great *TCC.* 12 are / is *1635–69, O'F.* 15 wants / lacks *TCC.* 16 lacks / wants *O'F.* 17 losse / lacke *TCD.* 18 Gangreend *1635* / Gangred *1633.* 20 former / *omitted TCC.* 23 an *1635* / one *1633.* 25 this / his *1635–69, O'F.* 27 soule shall / body *O'F.* 29 in / it *1649–54;* it is *1669.* 36 eyes / th'eyes *TCD, TCC, O'F.*

155. THE FIRST ANNIVERSARIE.

COPY TEXT: *1611.*

TEXTS: *1611, 1612,* errata for *1612, 1621, 1625, 1633–69.*

COLLATION: All texts. FIRST TITLE: The First Anniversarie. / *omitted 1611.*

An / *omitted 1635–69.* POEM: *Title 1612* / *omitted 1611.* 12 maid, *1633* / ∼; *1611–25.* FIRST ANNIVERSARY: *marginal notes 1612* / *omitted 1611, 1635–69. Title 1612* / *omitted 1611. marginal note* (1–2) / *omitted 1625–33.* 2 Whom / Who *1633.* do *1621* / they *1611.* 6 In-mate / immate *1633.* 14 then / them *1649–69.* 40 times / time *1635–69.* 50 glue / give *1649–69.* 57 Thy'intrinsique *errata* / Thy'ntrinsique *1611. marginal note* (67–68) / *omitted 1625–33.* 79 though / thought *1621–33. marginal note* (88–89): sicknesses / sicknesse *1621–33.* world / Word *1625.* 89 then / them *1649–69.* 129 trie∧ *1633* / ∼: *1611.* 130 new *1611, errata* / true *1612–69.* 144 scarse *errata* / scarsc *1611;* searse *1612–21.* 153 weaving *1633* / weaning *1611–25.* 161 Thus / This *1635–69.* 164 there / thers *1621–25.* 181 thoughts / thought *1621–33.* 186 no / no no *1621.* 195 Angels, *1612* / ∼. *1611.* 217 there *errata* / then *1611–69.* 244 contrould, *1633* / ∼. *1611.* 259 those / these *1612–69.* there *errata* / then *1611–69.* 262 Townes *errata* / Towres *1611–69.* 273 with / of *1635–69.* reeling *1621* / recling *1611.* 275 Starres *1612* / Stares *1611.* 284 pace / peace *1612–33.* 286 Tenarif / Tenarus *1633–69.* 302 disfigur'd *Ed.* / disfigured *1611.* 318 proportions / proportion *1621–69.* 325 shee is *1612* / shee's *1611.* 333 fitly'and *errata* / fitly'nd *1611. margin* (377): *earth. 1612* / ∼∧ *1611.* 394 an / a *1635–69.* 415 Impressions / Impression *1612–69.* 449 widow'd *Ed.* / widowed *1611.* 474 fame *errata* / same *1611–25.*

156. A FUNERALL ELEGIE.

COPY TEXT: 1611.

TEXTS: 1611, 1612, 1621, 1625, 1633–69; EP.e.37, H3991 (ll. 1–8, 75–76).

COLLATION: All texts. *Italics 1612–25; no indentation 1633–69. Title* / The Funerall Elegie uppon yᵉ death of Mʳˢ Elizabeth Drury. *EP.e.37.* 1 lost / losse *1635–69.* 13 aborted / Abortive *1635–69.* 18 a / an *1635–69.* 33 as / *omitted 1625;* was *1633–69.* 64 worth / worke *1633.* 76 doe / doth *1633–69.* 83 sad / said *1612–33.* Finis. / *omitted 1633–69;* J.D. *EP.e.37.*

157. OF THE PROGRES OF THE SOULE . . . THE SECOND ANNIVERSARY.

COPY TEXT: 1612.

TEXTS: 1612, *errata* for 1612, 1621, 1625, 1633–69; H3991 (ll. 463–64).

COLLATION: All texts. HARBINGER: 8 are: *1633* / ∼∧ *1612.* 15 relate *1621* / re-relate *1612.* 27 soules Hy *errata* / soules by *1612.* 28 owne, *1635* / ∼. *1612.* SECOND ANNNIVERSARY: *marginal notes* / *omitted 1635–69. margin* (1) / *omitted 1625–33.* 1 confesse∧ *1633* / ∼. *1612.* 10 though *errata* / through∧ *1612–25.* 12 be / he *1621–33.* 16 meet∧ *1621* / ∼. *1612.* 17 soule; *1621* / ∼, *1612.* 28 drown'd / drown' *1612.* 29 all; *1635* / ∼, *1612.* 41 For *1621* / for *1612.* 42 vanish / banish *1625.* 43 thy / they *1621–25. margin* (45–46): disestimation / estimation *1625–33.* 46 sealing *1649* / fealing *1612–39.* 47 till∧ *errata* / ∼, *1612.* 48 'Tis *errata* / T'o *1612.* Hydropique *errata* / Hydrodoptique *1612.* 50 be, *1639* / ∼∧ *1612.* 51 nor / or *1669.* 67 was *errata* / twas *1612–25.* 82 is∧ *1633* / ∼. *1612.*

86 roome *1621* / romme *1612*. 96 parch'd / pach'd *1625;* patch'd *1633–35*. 103 thrust / trust *1669*. 116 goe, *1625* / ∼. *1612*. 117 thee *1621* / the *1612*. 119 rite *errata* / right *1612–69*. 129 on *1621* / no *1612*. 137 wonne *errata* / worne *1612–25*. 146 Accident_∧ *Ed.* / ∼, *1612*. linke; *Ed.* / ∼, *1612*. 153 a long *1621* / along *1612*. 154 who / whose *1669*. margin (157–58) / *omitted 1625–33*. 157 thinke_∧ *Ed.* / ∼; *1612*. 161 and *1621* / And *1612*. 171 Bedded *1621* / Beddded *1612*. 173 didst / dost *1669*. 176 skinne, *1633* / ∼. *1612*. 177 usurp'd / usurped *1612*. the / a *1633–69*. 180 expansion *errata* / expausion *1612*. 197 retards *errata* / recards *1612–25*. 198 bee; *1633* / ∼, *1612*. 204 barrd *Ed.* / bard *1612*. 209 the / those *1669*. 214 this / *omitted 1649–69*. 216 as / *omitted 1669*. 220 shee, *Ed.* / ∼_∧ *1612*. 224 others / other *1633–69*. 232 there *errata* / then *1612–69*. 234 make / wake *1635–69*. 236 assign'd *Gr.* / assigned *1612*. 243 _∧we *1635* / (∼ *1632*. understood / unstood *1621–25*. margin (251–52) / *omitted 1633*. 253 so. *1625* / ∼, *1612*. 261 too *Ed.* / to *1612*. 266 new / knew *1635–39*. 268 'tis *1625* / ty's *1612*. lay. *1621* / ∼_∧ *1612*. 281 recant, *1633* / ∼. *1612*. 292 taught *errata* / thought *1612–25*. 300 shall / shalt *1633–50*. 304 and *1621* / And *1612*. 308 aie / are *1625;* all *1633–69*. 314 print *errata* / point *1612–33*. 315 not / nor *1669*. 323 earthly / early *1625*. 326 choose / chose *1633–39*. 327 first nor / not *1625–69*. 338 will *errata* / wise *1612–25;* lyes *1633–69*. 339 Up, *Ed.* / ∼_∧ *1612*. 349 runne_∧ *Ed.* / ∼, *1612*. 353 thought *errata* / thoughts *1612–25*. 359 herselfe_∧ . . . state, *1633* / ∼, . . . ∼_∧ *1612*. 361 triumph'd; *1633* / ∼, *1612*. 362 o'rthrow *1633* / overthrow *1612*. 366 rebellious / rebellions *1635–69*. 369 impressions / impression *1633–69*. 378 ill,) *1635* / ∼, _∧ *1612*. 380 whither *errata* / whether *1612–33*. 398 vow *errata* / row *1612–25*. 404 to *1621* / to to *1612*. 413 assign'd / assigned *1612*. 416 Thinks *1633* / Thinke *1612–25*. 417 t'erect *errata* / to'rect *1612*. 421 this / his *1621–69*. 422 too *1621* / to *1612*. 423 world *1633* / worlds *1612–25*. 429 that / the *1625*. 435 up *1633* / upon *1612–25*. 449 joye, *1633* / ∼. *1612*. 462 Betroth'd *Ed.* / Betrothed *1612*. 475 swell / smell *1669*. 476 a / *omitted 1625–69*. Man. *1633* / ∼, *1612*. 477 Redresse *errata* / Reders *1612–25*. 482 eie / eye *1621–25*, e'r *1633–69*. 501 even / ever *1625*. 506 within. *1649* / ∼, *1612*. 515 religion_∧ *Ed.* / ∼, *1612*. 516 invoque *errata* / ivoque *1612*, inroque *1621*. 522 doe, *errata* / ∼_∧ *1612*. Finis / *omitted 1633–69*.

158. METEMPSYCHOSIS.

COPY TEXT: *1633*.

TEXTS: *1633–69*; C57, TCD, N, TCC, A18, O'F; G, H3998 (part of letter, stanza LII missing); H3991 (ll. 507–9).

COLLATION: *1633–69*, C57, TCD, O'F, G (some readings from TCC and H3998). *Heading and letter given before Songs and Sonets, 1635. Heading /* Dr Donnes Metempsychosis G. EPISTLE: 4 say quickly / quicklie say TCD, O'F, G. 8 others / others as O'F, G. 14 debt; *Gr.* / ∼, *1633*. 20 *second* will / would C57, TCD, O'F, G. 25 Mucheron / Maceron *1635–69,* O'F;

Mushrome *G.* 30 now / can now *1635–69, O'F.* 32 ever been / bene ever
TCD, O'F. 34 apple *Gr.* / aple *1633.* 35 hee / shee *1635–69, O'F.* POEM:
Title / omitted *C57, TCD, O'F, G.* 7 gold / cold *1635–54.* 10 writt *1635* /
writs *1633, TCD.* 13 beginst / begins *1633, C57.* 16 Danow *MSS* / Danon
1633. dine, *Gr.* / ∼. *1633.* 36 vouch thou safe *MSS* / vouch-safe thou *1633–*
69. 47 others / other *TCD, O'F.* 54 shall / hold *1635–69, O'F* (> shall).
lone *1635* / love *1633, TCD, G.* 61 the / this *TCD, G;* that *O'F.* 69 when
/ where *TCD, O'F, G.* 74 where, *Ed.* / ∼ₐ *1633.* 83 enlive, *Gr.* / ∼ₐ *1633;*
omitted *C57, TCD.* 93 poison'd *Ed.* / poisoned *1633.* 94 Rivolets; *1635*
/ omitted *1633, C57, TCC;* nothing letts *O'F* (> rivooletts). 95 nets; *Gr.*
/ ∼, *1633.* 99 beare; *1635* / here, *1633, C57;* heare *TCD.* 108 is't *Gr.*
/ i'st *1633.* 112 vanities / vanitie *1635–69.* 117 doe / and doe *1635–69,*
O'F. spill: *Gr.* / ∼, *1633.* 125 day. *Gr.* / ∼, *1633.* 130 anew *Gr.* / a
new *1633.* 134 throng'd *Ed.* / thronged *1633.* 137 have *G* / omitted
1633–69, C57, TCD, O'F, H. fill'd / fill up *1635–69;* filld up *O'F.* 144 bed,
Gr. / ∼; *1633.* 147 middle / Mid *TCD.* parts / part *1635–69.* 150 kindle
1635 / kinde *1633, TCD, O'F.* 159 guest, *Gr.* / ∼ₐ *1633.* 166 light; *Gr.*
/ ∼, *1633.* 167 might, *Gr.* / ∼; *1633.* 177 free, *Gr.* / ∼; *1633.* 180 inclos'd *1635, G, H* / uncloath'd *1633, C57;* encloath'd *TCD, O'F* (> unclothd>
inclos'd). pick'd / peck'd *C57, TCD;* prickt *G.* 185 a new downy mantle
1635 / downy a new mantle *1633;* a new Mantle downy *C57.* 187 howre
/ hows *C57, TCD, O'F.* 192 ripen'd *Ed.* / ripened *1633.* 193 tree, *Gr.* /
∼ₐ *1633.* 194 hen; *Gr.* / ∼, *1633.* 199 use; *Gr.* / ∼, *1633.* 203 ill, *Gr.*
/ ∼; *1633.* not. *Gr.* / ∼ₐ *1633.* 204 souleₐ is, *Gr.* / ∼, ∼ₐ *1633.* 206 selfe-
preserving *Gr.* / ∼ₐ∼ *1633.* 212 grow, *Gr.* / ∼ₐ *1633.* 214 hid *G* / his
1633–69, TCD, O'F. 220 his race *1635* / omitted *1633, C57.* 225 had
1635, G / omitted *1633, C57, TCD, O'F.* intertouch'd *Gr.* / intertouched
1633. 227 row *1635* / roe *1633.* 238 swallow'd *Ed.* / swallowed *1633.*
240 armed *1635* / arm'd *1633.* 251 her *MSS* / the *1633–69.* 267 water
1635 / wether *1633, TCD.* 270 two. *Gr.* / ∼ₐ *1633.* 273 Thus / Thus her
1635–69. 277 away: *Gr.* / ∼, *1633.* 280 It's *1635* / It *1633, TCD, G.*
287 industrious *1635* / industruous *1633.* 296 many leagues *G, H* / leagues
o'er-past *1633–69;* leagues *C57, TCD, O'F* (or'e past *added*). 297 dies: *Gr.*
/ ∼, *1633.* 303 vastnesseₐ as, *Gr.* / ∼, ∼ₐ *1633.* 311 take, *Gr.* / ∼ₐ *1633.*
316 swallow'd *Gr.* / swallowed *1633.* 322 at / as *C57, TCC, G;* in *TCD.*
337 this / his *1635–69.* 351 finnd *1635* / find *1633.* 358 well *1635* / were
1633, C57, G. 383 no more had gone / none had *1635–69, O'F.* more /
omitted *C57, TCD.* one / him *1635–69, O'F.* 389 dreames; *Gr.* / ∼, *1633.*
395 downe; *Gr.* / ∼, *1633.* 397 ment / went *C57, TCD.* 403 goe: *Ed.*
/ ∼, *1633.* 413 foes. *Gr.* / ∼, *1633.* 419 Nor / Now *TCD, G.* Nor much resist / Resistance much *O'F.* 420 *first* nor / not *1649–69, C57, TCD, O'F*
(> nor). 422 hides. *Gr.* / ∼, *1633.* 427 ends all / End and *C57;* ending
TCD; end, both *TCC;* ends both *O'F;* ended *G, H.* 435 dead; *Gr.* / ∼, *1633.*
443 field. Being *Gr.* / ∼, being *1633.* thus *1635* / omitted *1633, C57, TCD, G.*
446 cosen'd *Ed.* / cosened *1633.* 453 play. *Gr.* / ∼, *1633.* 470 find. *Gr.*
/ ∼, *1633.* 480 *second* hath / have *TCD, G;* was *O'F* (> hath). 481 ment.
Gr. / ∼, *1633.* 483 quite; *Gr.* / ∼, *1633.* 484 now / nor *1635–69, O'F;*

then *TCC.* 485 loth, *H* and *Gr.* / Tooth *1633, G;* wroth *1635–69, O'F;*
omitted C57, TCD. 487 Tethlemite *TCD* / Tethelemite *1633.* 489 flew. *Gr.*
/ ∼, *1633.* 492 in. *Gr.* / ∼, *1633.* 498 Life-keeping *Gr.* / ∼ʌ∼ *1633.*
508 enow / enough *TCD, G.* 515 those / these *TCD.* 517 Astronomie. *Gr.* /
∼, *1633.*

159. TO THE LADY MAGDALEN HERBERT, OF ST. MARY MAGDALEN.

COPY TEXT: Walton.
TEXT: Walton.
COLLATION: Walton. *Reverse italics throughout. Signed:* "J.D." 4 know,
Walton (1675) / ∼ʌ Walton (1670).

160. LA CORONA.

COPY TEXT: 1633.
TEXTS: 1633–69; H49, D, SP, C57, TCD, N, TCC, A18, DC, Dob, S96, Lut,
O'F, Hd, B, S, K, W.
COLLATION: 1633–69, C57, TCD, Dob, O'F, W (some readings from H49,
TCC, DC, and S96). *Title* / Holy Sonnetts written 20 yeares since *H49;* The
Crowne *Dob, O'F. No other titles C57, Dob, W.* 1 prayer . . . praise / praise
. . . prayer *Dob.* 2 low / love *1635–69, C57, O'F;* Loves *Dob.* 3 art / arte
a *Dob, O'F.* 5–7 *combined TCC.* 5 of . . . bayes / *omitted TCC.* 6 *omitted*
TCC. 7 But . . . crowne / *omitted TCC.* 9 *first* ends / end *Dob, O'F.* crowne
/ crownes *Dob, O'F. second* ends / dayes *Dob, O'F* (> ends). 10 For / So
Dob, O'F, W. end / ends *1635–69, Dob.* begins / begin *Dob.* begins . . .
rest / *omitted H49.* 11 The / This *TCD, Dob, O'F, W.* The . . . end / *omit-*
ted H49. 13 heart . . . voice / voice . . . heart *Dob, O'F, W.* 14 nigh. *Gr.*
/ ∼, *1633.* 23 created / begotten *Dob, O'F* (> created), *W.* 24 who / wᶜʰ
Dob, W. 25 conceiv'd / conceiv'dst *Dob, O'F, W.* 31 There / Therefore *C57.*
he hath / hath he *Dob, O'F.* 32 our / the *Dob, O'F.* 33 thee / there *TCD.*
hath th'Inne / th'inn hath *Dob.* 34 this / his *1669, TCD.* 35 will / shall
Dob, O'F, W. prevent / present *Dob, O'F* (> prevent). 36 effect *TCD* /
effects *1633–54, H49.* jealous / zealous *TCD;* dire & *Dob, O'F* (> iealous),
W. 37 Soule . . . faiths / faythelesse *O'F* (> Soule with thy fayths). faiths /
faithless *Dob.* eyes / eye *1635–69, TCD.* 38 Which / That *Dob;* Who *O'F.*
40 by / of *Dob, O'F.* 43 his / this *TCC, 1669.* 44 your / thy *Dob, O'F.* 46
the / those *H49, TCD, Dob, O'F, W.* 52 had / hath *C57.* mellow'd *Ed.* /
mellowed *1633.* to / in *TCD; omitted Dob, O'F, W.* 53 for / *omitted Dob;*
some *O'F;* to *S96, W.* which / who *O'F.* a / *omitted TCD, Dob, O'F, W.* taske
/ taskes *TCD, Dob, O'F, W.* 'tis *Ed.* / 'Tis *1633;* thinkes it *Dob;* thinkes *O'F,*
W. 64 infinity / infinite *1669, TCD;* infirmitie *Dob, O'F* (> Infinity). to'a
TCD / to *1633–69, C57.* 65 inch. Loe *Gr.* / inch, loe *1633.* 71 soule *Gr.*
/ ∼, *1633.* 72 now be / be now *TCD, Dob, O'F.* 75 this / thy *Dob, O'F, W.*
death / *omitted TCD.* 76 shall / shall now *TCD, O'F.* 78 little / life *1635–*
69, Dob, O'F, W. 79 long / *omitted C57;* last long *Dob, O'F, W.* 81 glorified / purified *Dob, O'F* (> glorified), *W.* 82 deaths *TCD* / death *1633–69,*
C57, Dob, O'F. soone . . . me / from mee soone *TCD.* 86 Sonne / sinn *C57;*
Summe *Dob.* 87 Yee / Yea *C57, DC* (*and others*); You *O'F* (> Yee). just /

true *1635–69, Dob, O'F, W.* 88 Have / Hath *Dob, O'F, W.* 92 way. *Gr.* / ~, *1633*. 94 lambe, *Gr.* / ~ₐ *1633*. 95 the way / thee *TCC;* thy wayes *Dob, O'F* (> the waye), *W.* may / *omitted TCD;* might *O'F.* 96 thy . . . thy / thine . . . thine *TCD, Dob, O'F, W.*

161. TO E. OF D. WITH SIX HOLY SONNETS.

COPY TEXT: 1633.
TEXTS: 1633–69; DC, O'F, W; A23.
COLLATION: 1633–69, DC, O'F, W, A23. *Title* / To L. of D. *W;* E: of D: *A23.* 4 their fruits / the fruite *W, A23.* 6 doe / doth *1635–69.* 9 *indented 1633–69.* choose / chose *W, A23.* 11 drossie / drosse *1649–54.* 13–14 *indented O'F, A23.*

162. HOLY SONNET: "AS DUE BY MANY TITLES."

COPY TEXT: 1633.
TEXTS: 1633–69; H49, D, SP, C57, TCD, N, TCC, A18, DC, Dob, S96, Lut, O'F, B, W.
COLLATION: 1633–69, C57, TCD, Dob, O'F, W (for all Holy Sonnets where texts appear). 2 I was / was I *Dob, O'F.* 5 sonne / sun *TCD.* 7 thine / thy *Dob, O'F.* 9 then / thus *Dob, O'F.* in *W* / on *1633–69, C57, DC.* 10 steale, *Gr.* / ~ₐ *1633.* 12 doe / shall *1635–69, Dob, O'F.* 13 wilt not *Ed.* / ~'~ *1633.*

163. HOLY SONNET: "O MY BLACKE SOULE!"

COPY TEXT: 1633.
TEXTS: 1633–69; H49, D, SP, C57, TCD, N, TCC, A18, DC, Dob, S96, Lut, O'F, B, W.
COLLATION: 3 art / *omitted Dob, O'F (inserted).* hath / had *TCD, O'F* (> hath), *W.* 4 to / from *Dob, O'F* (> to). 5 like / as *Dob, O'F, W.* 6 deliverd *D* / delivered *1633.* 13 this / his *TCD.*

164. HOLY SONNET: "THIS IS MY PLAYES LAST SCENE."

COPY TEXT: 1633.
TEXTS: 1633–69; H49, D, SP, C57, TCD, N, TCC, A18, DC, Dob, S96, Lut, O'F, B, W.
COLLATION: 2 pilgrimages / pilgrimage *C57.* 4 latest / last *C57, TCD, W.* 6 soule *W* / my soule *1633, Dob.* a space / a pace *C57, O'F* (> a space). 7 But . . . shall / Or presently (I knowe not) *C57, Dob, O'F, W.* 8 my / mee *C57, Dob, O'F.* 10 earth-borne *1635* / earth borne *1633.* 11 fall / falls *C57.* 13 thus purg'd / purged thus *O'F.* 14 thus / so *O'F.* flesh, *Gr.* / ~ₐ *1633.* and devill *W* / the devill *1633–69.*

165. HOLY SONNET: "AT THE ROUND EARTHS."

COPY TEXT: 1633.
TEXTS: 1633–69; H49, D, SP, C57, TCD, N, TCC, A18, DC, Dob, S96, Lut, O'F, B, W.
COLLATION: 6 dearth *W* / death *1633–69, C57, TCD, Dob, O'F.* 9 space / pace *C57.*

166. HOLY SONNET: "IF POYSONOUS MINERALLS."

COPY TEXT: 1633.

TEXTS: 1633–69; H49, D, SP, C57, TCD, N, TCC, A18, DC, Dob, S96, Lut, O'F, B, W.

COLLATION: 1 and / or *Dob, O'F.* that / the *Dob, O'F.* 5 or / and *Dob, O'F.* 9 dare / dates *TCD.* 10 thine / thy *Dob, O'F.* 12 memorie. *Gardner* / ~, *1633.* 13 thou / you *TCD.* some claime / no more *Dob, O'F.* 14 forget. *1635* / ~, *1633.*

167. HOLY SONNET: "DEATH BE NOT PROUD."

COPY TEXT: 1633.

TEXTS: 1633–69; H49, D, SP, C57, TCD, N, TCC, A18, DC, Dob, S96, Lut, O'F, B, W.

COLLATION: 1 have / hath *TCD.* 5 pictures / picture *1635–69.* 7 doe / doth *C57.* 8 bones / bodyes *Dob, O'F* (> bones). deliverie. *Gr.* / ~∧ *1633.* 10 dost *W* / doth *1633.* dwell, *1635* / ~. *1633.* 12 better / easyer *Dob, O'F, W.* 13 wake / live *Dob, O'F* (> wake), *W.* 14 Death *W* / death *1633.*

168. HOLY SONNET: "SPIT IN MY FACE."

COPY TEXT: 1633.

TEXTS: 1633–69; H49, D, SP, C57, TCD, N, TCC, A18, DC, Lut, O'F, W.

COLLATION: 1 yee *TCD* / you *1633–69, C57.* 3 onely / humbly *W.* 4 Who / W^{ch} *W.* no / none *C57, TCD.* 6 impiety / Iniquitye *H49;* Iniquityes *C57.* 7 man / *omitted W.*

169. HOLY SONNET: "WHY ARE WEE BY ALL CREATURES."

COPY TEXT: 1633.

TEXTS: 1633–69; H49, D, SP, C57, TCD, N, TCC, A18, DC, Lut, O'F, W.

COLLATION: 1 are wee / ame I *W.* 4 Simple / Simpler *1635–69, TCD, O'F.* further / farder *C57;* farther *TCD, O'F.* 6 bore / Beare *O'F.* 9 Weaker I am / Alas I'ame weaker *W.* 11 *second* wonder / *omitted 1635–69.*

170. HOLY SONNET: "WHAT IF THIS PRESENT."

COPY TEXT: 1633.

TEXTS: 1633–69; H49, D, SP, C57, TCD, N, TCC, A18, Lut, O'F, W.

COLLATION: 2 Marke / Looke *W.* 4 that *TCD* / his *1633–69, C57.* 6 fell, *Gardner* / ~∧ *1633.* 7 unto / to *C57.* 8 fierce / ranck *W.* 9 my / mine *W.* 14 assures *W* / assumes *1633–69.*

171. HOLY SONNET: "BATTER MY HEART."

COPY TEXT: 1633.

TEXTS: 1633–69; H49, D, SP, C57, TCD, N, TCC, A18, Lut, O'F, W.

COLLATION: 9 you, and *Gardner* / you,'and *1633.*

172. HOLY SONNET: "WILT THOU LOVE GOD."

COPY TEXT: 1633.
TEXTS: 1633–69; H49, D, SP, C57, TCD, N, TCC, A18, Dob, S96, Lut, O'F, B, W.
COLLATION: 5 begot / begotten *Dob.* 10 stuffe / steede *Dob, O'F* (> stuff). 11 Sonne / Sun *1635–69, C57.* 12 stolne / stole *1635–69, O'F.*

173. HOLY SONNET: "FATHER, PART OF HIS DOUBLE INTEREST."

COPY TEXT: 1633.
TEXTS: 1633–69; H49, D, SP, C57, TCD, N, TCC, A18, Dob, S96, Lut, O'F, B, W.
COLLATION: 4 to / *omitted C57, TCD, Dob, W.* 7 which / he *Dob, O'F* (> which). 8 doe / *omitted 1635–69;* doth *C57, TCD, Dob, O'F* (> doe), W. 9 those *TCD* / these *1633–69, C57;* thy *Dob, O'F, W.* 11 thy / *omitted C57, TCD, W.* 12 againe / and quicken *Dob, O'F, W.* kill. *1635* / ~, *1633.* 14 that *W* / this *1633–69;* thy *Dob, O'F.*

174. HOLY SONNET: "THOU HAST MADE ME."

COPY TEXT: 1635.
TEXTS: 1635–69; Dob, S96, Lut, O'F, B, W.
COLLATION: 1 decay? *Gr.* / ~, *1635.* 7 febled *W* / feeble *1635–69.* 8 it t'wards / towards *W.* 12 I can my selfe *W* / myselfe I can *1635–69, O'F.* sustaine; *Gr.* / ~, *1635.*

175. HOLY SONNET: "I AM A LITTLE WORLD."

COPY TEXT: 1635.
TEXTS: 1635–69; Dob, S96, Lut, O'F, B, W.
COLLATION: 6 lands *W* / land *1635–69, O'F.* 10 burnt; *Gardner* / ~, *1635.* 11 envie'have *W, apostrophe Ed.* / envie *1635–69;* envie hath *O'F.* 12 fouler; *Gr.* / ~, *1635.* their / those *W.* 13 Lord / God *W.*

176. HOLY SONNET: "O MIGHT THOSE SIGHES."

COPY TEXT: 1635.
TEXTS: 1635–69; Dob, S96, Lut, O'F, B, W.
COLLATION: 5 mine / my *Dob, W.* 6 griefs / greefe *O'F.* 7 sinne, now I repent; *W* / sinne I now repent, *1635–69, Dob, O'F.* 8 'Cause / Because *Dob, W.*

177. HOLY SONNET: "IF FAITHFULL SOULES."

COPY TEXT: 1635.
TEXTS: 1635–69; Dob, S96, Lut, O'F, B, W.
COLLATION: 8 by / to *Dob, W.* 10 vile *W* / stile *1635–69.* 14 griefe / true griefe *W.*

178. HOLY SONNET: "SINCE SHE WHOME I LOVD."

COPY TEXT: W.

TEXT: W.

COLLATION: 2, 3, 6, 7, 10, 12 *indented* W.   10 soule, . . . hers∧ *Bennett* / ∼∧ . . . ∼; W.   12 Angels, . . . divine, *Gardner* / ∼∧ . . . ∼∧ W.

179. HOLY SONNET: "SHOW ME DEARE CHRIST."

COPY TEXT: W.

TEXT: W.

COLLATION: 2, 3, 6, 7, 10, 12 *indented* W.   2 What, *Gardner* / ∼∧ W.

180. HOLY SONNET: "OH, TO VEX ME, CONTRARYES MEET."

COPY TEXT: W.

TEXT: W.

COLLATION: 2, 3, 6, 7, 10, 11, 13, 14 *indented* W.

181. THE CROSSE.

COPY TEXT: 1633.

TEXTS: 1633–69; H49, D, SP, Lec, C57, TCD, N, TCC, A18, DC, Dob, Lut, O'F, HM198, Hd, O, P, JC, D17, B, S, S962, A25, La, Hol, RP117, Grey; CCC.E.327, H3511 (ll. 19–24), Hyde (ll. 31–48, 51–54, 57–58, 61–62).

COLLATION: 1633–69, C57, TCD, Dob, O'F (some readings from various MSS). *Title* / On the Crosse *TCD;* Of the Crosse *TCC, DC, Dob, O'F.*   2 his / yᵉ C57 (*and others*).   6 sinne / sinns *TCD.*   8 who / that *O'F* (*and others*).   13 affliction, *Gr.* / ∼∧ 1633.   15 which / wᵗʰ *TCD.*   20 make / makes *C57.* where / when *C57, Dob, O'F.*   23 spheares / spheare *O'F* (*and others*).   25 good / and *TCD.*   26 And *C57* / But *1633–69, Dob, O'F.*   27–28 *omitted* HM198, La.   27–29 *omitted* Hol.   33 make, *Gr.* / ∼: 1633.   34 there / thence *Dob.*   36 And / Or *Dob, O'F.*   37 oft∧ *Gr.* / ∼, 1633.   44 destruction / corruption *Dob, O'F.*   45–48 *omitted* A25.   45 seeke / see *1649–69;* seekes *Dob.*   46 crosse / crosses *Dob.* scape a snake / scarce awake *O'F.*   47 harsh, hard / hard, harsh *TCD* (*reversed by numbers*), *Dob, O'F.*   48 call / all *1635–69, O'F* (> call *in margin*).   50 others *1635* / other *1633,* O, P, RP117, *Hyde.* second th' / *omitted 1635–69, Dob, O'F.*   52 Points *TCD* / Pants *1633–69, C57* (*and others*).   53 dejections / detorsions *1635–69, O'F;* defections *Dob.* tends / bends *Dob* (> tends).   54 heights / height *Dob.*   55 thy *TCD* / the *1633–69, C57, N* (> thy), *TCC, DC* (*and others*). braine / braynes *O'F* (> brayne). doth / do *Dob, O'F* (> doth).   57 braine / braines *Dob, O'F.* workes / worke *Dob, O'F.*   60 but / and *Dob, O'F.*   61 fruitfully *TCD* / faithfully *1633–69,* S (> fruitfully), *A25, Hyde.*   63 That *TCD* / The *1633–69.*

182. RESURRECTION, IMPERFECT.

COPY TEXT: 1633.

TEXTS: 1633–69; TCD, N, TCC, A18, DC, Lut, O'F, Grey.

COLLATION: 1633–69, TCD, O'F. 8 fires grow / fire growes *O'F*. 13 lay / layd *TCD*. Desunt cætera / *omitted TCD, O'F*.

183. THE ANNUNTIATION AND PASSION.

COPY TEXT: 1633.

TEXTS: 1633–69; H49, D, SP, Lec, C57, TCD, N, DC, Dob, S96, Lut, O'F, HM198, O, P, B, S, K, La.

COLLATION: 1633–69, C57, TCD, Dob, O'F (some readings from SP and Lec). *Title* / . . . and Passion *omitted C57;* Upon the Annunciation: when Good friday fell upon the Same daie. *TCD;* Upon the Annunciaĉon and Passion fallinge upon one day 1608 *Dob, O'F* (. . . on one day Anno: Do: 1618). 1 body / flesh *Dob, O'F. second* to day / *omitted 1649–69.* 2 twice, Christ / Christ twice *O'F.* 10 at once / *omitted Dob.* and *TCD* / yet *1633, Lec* (*and others*). 13 Sad and rejoyc'd / Rejoyc't and sadd *Dob, O'F.* 15 At once a Sonne / A Sonne at once *Dob, O'F.* 19 hath / is *Dob, O'F.* 21 farthest *TCD* / furthest *1633–69, SP* (*and others*). West is East / East is West *Dob, O'F.* 31 as / and *1635–69.* 33 these *TCD* / those *1633–69.* daies / feastes *1635–69, Dob, O'F.* 34 is / are *1635–69, O'F* (*and others*). 35 Or / & *Dob.* 'twas / that *Dob, O'F.* the same / 'twas one *Dob, O'F.* 37 hath / had *TCD, Dob, O'F.* 38 the / his *Dob, O'F.* 44 busie / buy *Dob, O'F* (> busye). she / he *Dob.* 46 my / thy *Dob, O'F* (> my).

184. A LITANIE.

COPY TEXT: 1633.

TEXTS: 1633–69; H49, D, SP, Lec, C57, TCD, N, TCC, A18, DC, Dob, S96, Lut, O'F, HM198, Hd, O, JC, D17, B, S, K, S962; A30982 (ll. 1–72, 82–90), H3910 (ll. 87–90).

COLLATION: 1633–69, C57, TCD, Dob, O'F (some readings from various MSS). *Titles and stanza nos. may have variations or be omitted.* Title: A *TCD* / The *1633–69, C57, DC, O.* 6 selfe-murder, red / myselfe murdered *Dob, Lut;* selfe murdered *HM198.* red / red, red *TCD.* 9 before / ere *Dob, O'F.* 13 could / did *Dob;* would *O'F.* thine / thy *Dob, O'F.* 23 stormes / stones *TCD.* 24 thy / the *TCD* (*and others*). 26 glasse / dark *Dob.* 34 a such / such *1635–69;* such a *C57, TCD.* instinct, *1635* / ~ʌ *1633.* 35 Of these / Of thee *TCD;* Of all these *Dob, O'F* (*corrected*). (36–37) *Title for V:* Our Lady *Dob.* 40 disseiz'd / diseas'd *HM198* (*and others*). 47 thine / thy *Dob, O'F.* 48 faire / *omitted 1649–69.* 52 which / what *1635–69, O'F.* 53 mee / us *O'F* (> mee). mine / our *Dob, O'F* (> mine). 54 how / what *Dob, O'F* (> how). 56 of / in *O'F.* 57 cloud / clouds *TCD, Dob. second* in / in the *TCD* (*and others*); doe in the *O'F.* 58 then / that *1635–69.* and / or *Dob, O'F.* 61 satisfied / sanctified *1633, C57.* 65 Organs / Organ *Dob.* 72 In / Of *Dob, O'F.* or / in *Dob.* 73 thy / the *Dob.* 74 this / thy *O'F* (*and others*). 75 whosoever / whoever *C57, Dob, O'F.* do / doth *TCC, Dob, O'F.* 76 throw / thrown *1635–69, Dob, O'F.* and / do *1635–69, Dob, O'F* (> doth> do); doth *Lut.* 78 bookes / workes *Dob,*

O'F.   83 *second* long / love *Dob, O'F;* live *Hd* (*and others*). thou / thy *TCD.*
93 were / bee *Dob.*   100 Thy *TCD* / The *1633, C57, N.*   107 or / & *O'F*
(> or) (*and others*).   109 Thy / The *1635–69.* Academ *TCD* / Academie
1633, C57, B; Academs *S962.*   111 to / for *Dob, O'F.*   112 thy / the *1649–*
69. wrought / wrote *1635–69, O'F.*   113 thy / the *Dob, O'F.*   115 adhere;
Gr. / ~, *1633.*   118 this / that *O'F* (*and others*).   122 Pray ceaslesly *TCD*
/ Prayes ceaslesly *1633;* Ceaselesly prayes *Dob, O'F.* too, *Gr.* / ~ʌ *1633.*
128 clods / clouds *1635–69, Dob, O'F* (> clods).   134 sweet / sweets *1635–*
69, *TCD, O'F.*   139 soule / souls *1669, Dob, O'F.*   148 sins spawne / sinne
spunne *Dob.*   153 fame *1635* / flame *1633;* fame good Lord *Dob, O'F.*   154
for / through *1635–69, Dob, O'F.*   163 through *1635* / though *1633.* that
/ thy *Dob, O'F.*   164 is still / still is *1635–69, C57.* pious / *omitted Dob.*
168 thereby they were / they were thereby *Dob, O'F.*   173 clothes / robes
1635–69, Dob, O'F.   175 And / Or *Dob, O'F.*   181 senses *C57* / sense *1633,*
SP (*and others*).   182 sinne / him *TCD.*   190 when / where *C57, TCD.*
191 which / that *C57, TCD, Dob, O'F.* diminishes / diminisheth *Dob, O'F.*
195 Or / When *Dob, O'F.*   196–97 *reversed Dob, O'F* (*corrected*).   196
When / With *TCD.*   205 gives / give *N, O'F.*   206 O / And *Dob.* who /
which *TCD, Dob, O'F.*   208 evennesse / enemies *Dob, O'F* (> evennesse).
209 aguish / anguish *A18* (*and others*).   213 in / of *Dob.*   214 offices; *Gr.*
/ ~, *1633.*   217 wee / me *1635–69.*   220 nor / or *Dob.* so / to *TCD, Dob,*
O'F (> so).   226–34 *omitted S96.*   227 give us / us give *TCD.*   231 Which
/ That *Dob, O'F.* well / will *1635–69, C57, Dob, O'F.*   233 heare them /
hearken *Dob, O'F.*   234 lock / stop *Dob, O'F.*   236 thine / his *Dob.*   239 doe,
Gr. / ~ʌ *1633.*   243 ecchoes / wretches *Dob.* cry / eye *Dob, O'F.*   245
againe, *Gr.* / ~ʌ *1633.*   246 or / and *1635–69, Dob, O'F.*   252 As / A *O'F.*

185. GOODFRIDAY, 1613. RIDING WESTWARD.

COPY TEXT: *1633.*

TEXTS: *1633–69; H49, D, SP, Lec, C57, TCD, N, TCC, A18, DC, Dob, S96,*
Lut, O'F, Hd, Cy, B, S, A25, Grey; A23; Huygens. Lines 1–2, without title, are
found in Cambridge MS Add 29.

COLLATION: *1633–69, C57, TCD, Dob, O'F* (some readings from various
MSS). *Title* / Goodfriday, 1613. Riding to Sr Edward Harbert in Wales. *H49;*
Goodfriday, 1613. Riding towards Wales. *C57, O'F;* Goodfriday Made as I was
rideing westward that daye. *TCD;* A Meditation upon Good ffriday. 1613. *Dob;*
Mr. J: Duñ goeing from Sr H: G: on good fryday sent him back this Meditacõn,
on the Waye *A25.*   4 motions *O'F* / motion *1633–69.*   5 by others hurried /
hurryed by others *C57.*   6 forme / course *Dob.*   10 toward / to *1635–69,*
O'F; towards *C57, TCD, Dob.*   11 I should / should I *SP, O'F.*   13 this / his
1635–69, TCD.   22–25 *omitted Lec, C57.*   22 turne *TCD* / tune *1633–69,*
H49, D, S96, Lut, O'F, Hd, A25, A23.   24–25 *omitted D, SP, Cy.*   24 to'our
TCD / our *1633–69, TCC, O'F.*   25 which / that *Dob.*   27 Make *TCD* /
Made *1633–69, Dob.*   30 Upon his miserable / On his distressed *1635–69.*
31–33 *omitted Lec.*   31 partner / patterne *C57.*   36–38 *omitted A25.*   40
rusts / rust *1635–69, TCC.*

186. TO MR. GEORGE HERBERT, WITH ONE OF MY SEALES . . .

COPY TEXT: 1650.

TEXTS: 1650–69; Walton (ll. 1–3a).

COLLATION: All texts. *Title / see note.* Seales *Walton* (*1650*) / Seal *1650–69.* Christ / Crest *Walton 1658*). . . . sent him with one of my Seals . . . *Walton* (*1670*). 1 fasce / falce *Walton.*

186. (TRANSLATION).

COPY TEXT: 1650.

TEXTS: 1650–69; Walton.

COLLATION: All texts. *Lines 1–2 given as title, 1650–69* (*l. 2 in italics and lower case* my), *Walton.* 2 The Crest / which is the Crest *Walton.* 4 unto / into *Walton.* 11 may . . . this / with this I may *Walton.* 16 My . . . is / He is my death *Walton.* 22 Works / Both works *Walton.* 23 And / Oh *Walton.* which / that *Walton.* in / on *Walton.* 24 who / that *Walton.* great bounties / large bounty *Walton.*

187. THE LAMENTATIONS OF JEREMY.

COPY TEXT: 1633.

TEXTS: 1633–69; TCD, N, DC, O'F, O, B, CCC736–738 (ll. 1–8).

COLLATION: 1633–69, TCD, O'F (some readings from DC). *Some verse nos. misplaced, 1633–69.* 2 thus! *Gr.* / ~? *1633.* 4 is! *Gr.* / ~? *1633.* tributary / solitarie *DC, O'F.* 16 unto / to *DC, O'F.* 25 her *O'F* / their *1633–69, TCD;* the *B.* 27 esteem'd *Ed.* / esteemed *1633.* 28 Whiles / Whilst *O'F.* 50 and / & hath *TCD, O'F.* 53 hand / hands *1649–69.* 56 whom *1635* / whence *1633.* 58 invite / accite *1635–69, O'F.* 59 men; *Gr.* / ~, *1633.* 65 hand, *Gr.* / ~ₐ *1633.* 68 as / *omitted TCD.* 76 they . . . not / and none could *1635–69, O'F;* they none could *B.* 78 o'rturn'd *1635* / return'd *1633, TCD.* 81 heare / here *1639–69.* 90 cloud! *Gr.* / ~? *1633.* flungₐ *Gr.* / ~. *1633.* 92 wrath! *Gr.* / ~? *1633.* 95 strengths / strength *1635–69, N, O'F.* 113 forsake / forsakes *TCD, O'F.* 114 hand *O'F* / hands *1633–69.* 118 ground; *Gr.* / ~. *1633.* 121 Their / The *1635–69.* 122 barres *O'F* / barre *1633–69, TCD.* 135 streets *O'F* / street *1633–69, TCD.* 141 Forₐ *Gr.* / ~, *1633.* thee *1635* / the *1633, 1669, TCD.* 155 not / *omitted TCD.* 157 against / unto *1635–69, O'F.* 158 walle *DC* / walls *1633–69, TCD, O'F* (> walle). 161 for / out *1635–69;* forth *DC.* 166 thus *TCD* / this *1633–69, O'F.* 174 his / thy *1635–69, O'F.* 176 mine / the *O'F.* 177 have / hath *TCD, O'F.* 182 girt / hemd *O'F.* 198 cover'd *Ed.* / covered *1633.* 220 there *O'F* / then *1633–69; omitted TCD.* 229 wrunge *1635* / wrong *1633.* him, *Gr.* / ~. *1633.* 231 doth / will *O'F.* 245 watry *1635* / water *1633, TCD.* 246 daughter *O'F* / daughters *1633–69.* 249 city / Cittyes *O'F.* 250 *second* mine / my *O'F.* 252 on me *TCD* / me on *1633–69, O'F.* 256 sigh / sight *1649–69.* 260 Rescud'st *O'F* / Rescuest *1633–69, TCD.* 263 utter'd *Ed.* / uttered *1633.* (268–69) Chap. *Gr.* / CAP. *1633.* 272 Scatter'd *Ed.* / Scattered *1633.* 273 sonnes / stones *O'F.* 274 at / as *1649–69, TCD, O'F.* 284 doth them / them doth *DC, O'F.* 289 sinn'd *Ed.* / sinned *1633.* 296 Saphirine *1635* /

Seraphine *1633*. 298 streetes *O'F* / street *1633–69, TCD*. 299 *second* their
/ the *O'F*. 302 *second* through *1635* / by *1633, TCD*. penury. *Gr.* / ∼, *1633*.
304 hands *B* / hand *1633–69, TCD, O'F*. 318 garments / garment *1635–69*.
322 dwell∧ there; *Gr.* / ∼; ∼. *1633 (two lines)*. 323 scatter'd *Ed.* / scattered
1633. 325 their / the *1649–69*. the / their *1649–69*. 333 day. *Gr.* / ∼,
1633. 335 mountaine / mountaines *1649–69*. 340 fell. *Gr.* / ∼∧ *1633*.
342 which / that *1635–69*. Huz *B* / her *1633;* Uz *1635–69, O'F;* Hus *TCD*.
(348–49) Chap. *Gr.* / CAP. *1633*. 349 us; *Gr.* / ∼∧ *1633*. 354 father *O'F*
/ fathers *1633–69, TCD (and others)*. 355 drinke *1635* / drunke *1633, TCD*.
356 lay. *Gr.* / ∼, *1633*. 368 Oven *1635* / Ocean *1633*.

188. TRANSLATED OUT OF GAZÆUS, VOTA AMICO FATA.
COPY TEXT: 1650.

TEXTS: 1650–69.

189. TO MR. TILMAN AFTER HE HAD TAKEN ORDERS.
COPY TEXT: 1635.

TEXTS: 1635–69; Dob, O'F; Wel, V.a.276 (ll. 1–14, rest missing).

COLLATION: 1635–69, Dob, O'F, Wel, V.a.276. *Title* / Dr Dunne to Mr Til-
man after his taking of Order *Wel, V.a.276 (without* of). 2 thy / thine
V.a.276. 4 but / but a *Dob*. 6 since / in *Dob, O'F*. the / thy *V.a.276*.
vintage / voyage *Dob*. 7 stirrings / stirring *V.a.276*. 10 brings / bringst
Dob, Wel, V.a.276. 11 more gaine / againe *V.a.276*. 12 noble / nobler
V.a.276. and / or *V.a.276*. 13 Thou art / Art thou *Dob, O'F, Wel, V.a.276*.
14 Onely . . . is changed / Only is . . . changed *Wel, V.a.276*. 18 Christs
O'F / Chists *1635*. stampe / birth *Dob*. 20 message / image *Wel*. 25 thy /
they *O'F*. gainings / gaininge *Dob, O'F*. 27 think / thinkt' *Dob;* think'd *Wel*.
29 Would they thinke it well if the day were spent *Dob, O'F;* Would they
thinke you that the whole day were spent *Wel*. 30 Mistressing / undressinge
Dob; mis-dressing *O'F*. 32 refined *O'F* / sublimed *1635–69*. 33 beautyes
O'F / beauty *1635–69, Wel*. 34 as *O'F* / of *1635–69*. 44 the . . . beneath / beneath the poore *Wel. third* the / and *Wel*. 47 Engines *O'F* / Engine
1635–69. 48 againe / omitted *Dob, O'F, Wel*. 52 these things doth / doth
those things *Dob, O'F*. beare, *Gr.* / ∼∧ *1635*. 53 Both these / Are both *Wel*.
are / and *Wel*.

190. A HYMNE TO CHRIST, AT THE AUTHORS LAST GOING INTO GERMANY.
COPY TEXT: 1633.

TEXTS: 1633–69; C57 (not in Gr. I collection), TCD, N, TCC, A18, Dob,
S96, Lut, O'F, O, P, B, Hol; RP160, H6057.

COLLATION: 1633–69, C57, TCD, Dob, O'F. *Line 7 in each stanza given as
two lines with first word capitalized, 1633–69, S96. Title* / Doctor Dunn's going into Bohemia. Himn to Christ. *C57;* A Hymne to Christ *TCD;* At his de-
parture wᵗʰ my L: of Doncaster. *1619 Dob;* At the Sea-side going over wᵗʰ the
Ld Doncaster. *1619 O'F*. 3 swallow / swallowes *Dob, O'F*. mee / mee up
Dob, O'F. 5 with / in *Dob, O'F*. do / dost *O'F*. 9 lov'd . . . lov'd / love

. . . love *1635–69, Dob, O'F*. there / here *1635–69*. 10 our / this *1635–69;* those *Dob, O'F*. seas / flood *1635–69*. 11 sea *O'F* / seas *1633;* blood *1635–* *69*. 14 thee, th' / thy *Dob, O'F* (> thee th'). root / worke *Dob, O'F* (> roote). 15–28 omitted *C57*. 15 dost / doth *Dob, O'F*. 16 an / a *TCD*. 18 I am / am I *Dob, O'F*. 20 Who / which *Dob, O'F* (> who). 21 alas / *omitted Dob, O'F*. 24 scatterd *O'F* / scattered *1633*. 25 Fame / face *1635–69, Dob, O'F*. 26 Prayer / Prayers *Dob, O'F*.

191. UPON THE TRANSLATION OF THE PSALMES BY SIR PHILIP SYDNEY, AND . . . HIS SISTER.

COPY TEXT: 1635.

TEXTS: *1635–69;* O'F.

COLLATION: All texts. 28 here *Gr.* / heare *1635*. 46 *first* this *O'F* / thy *1635–69*. 53 these *O'F* / those *1635–69*. 56 part. *Gr.* / $\sim_\wedge$ *1635*.

192. HYMNE TO GOD MY GOD, IN MY SICKNESSE.

COPY TEXT: 1635.

TEXTS: *1635–69;* Walton (ll. 1–8a, 26–30); S96, A34324, RP142 (ll. 1–5, 21–30).

COLLATION: All texts. *Title* / . . . March 23. 1630 *Walton, old style;* A Hym̃e in sicknes *RP142*. 4 *second* the / any *Walton*. 5 here / now *S96, A34324*. 6 Whilst / Since *Walton*. love / loves *Walton*. 12 theire *S96* / those *1635–69;* theis *A34324*. 19 none / we *Walton*. 22 Christs / X[t] *RP142*. 30 Therefore . . . raise / That, he may rise; therefore *Walton*.

193. A HYMNE TO GOD THE FATHER.

COPY TEXT: 1633.

TEXTS: *1633–69;* Walton, Humfrey; TCD, N, TCC, A18, Dob, S96, Lut, O'F, S962; Ash 38, H3910, RP90, A15226, E2013. Apparently taken from the printed editions are the texts of Tanner MS 466, f. 4 (Bod), and the English Hymnal With Words (1902), No. 515, with music by Johann Sebastian Bach.

COLLATION: *1633–69,* TCD, Dob, O'F. *Musical erratum given on f. A₂r, Humfrey. Stanza numbers included, 1633–69. Title* / To Christ *TCD, Dob;* Christo Salvatori *O'F*. 2 Which *1635* / which *1633*. is *O'F* / was *1633–69*. were / was *Dob, O'F*. 3 those sinnes *O'F* / that sinne *1633–69*. 4 them *O'F* / run *1633–69*. 5 *second* thou hast / I have *Dob, O'F*. 7 by which I *O'F* / which I have *1633–69;* by w[ch] I have *TCD*. 8 sinne / sins *1639–69*. 10 wallowd *O'F* / wallowed *1633*. 15 Sweare *O'F* / But sweare *1633–69*. thy / this *TCD*. Sunne *O'F* / sonne *1633–69*. 16 it *O'F* / he *1633–69*. 18 have *O'F* / feare *1633–69*.

194. EPIGRAPH . . . , DEATHS DUEL.

COPY TEXT: *Deaths Duell*.

TEXT: *Deaths Duell*.

INDEX OF TEXTUAL DIFFERENCES FROM GARDNER'S TEXT

Present text generally derives from copy text. Miss Gardner's text here usually derives from certain MSS (in opposition to the editions and other MSS) or modernization. Discussion is included only when the lack of agreement does not result from this difference of approach (or from difference in MS reading) or is crucial. *Gr.* indicates that the same difference occurs in Grierson.

Poem	Lines	Text / Gardner
8		(Note: different copy text; no accidentals noted.)
	6	these / those
	24	Countreys / country
	47	are / were
	60	fils full / fullfills
	67	that / the
	92	So / So much
	108	love / love and
	109	last / latest
	111	thee / thou
9	19	*italics / removed*
	26	dust / durt
	46	feares / fear'd
10	9	hath / have
	15	Takes / Take
	21	To / And to
	22	blushing / blushings
	29	And∧ / ~,
		kist, / ~∧
	30	see. / ~:
	38	kisse; / ~.
	40	my / mine
	42	were wee / wee were
	44	shivered; / ~.
	64	substantiall. / ~;
	67	alone, / ~:
11	1	woman∧ / ~,
	12	free, / ~;
	21	fare∧ / ~,
	34	Mayor, / ~;
12	28	banks / banke
	40	eye; / ~.
13	14	agree. / ~;
	25	bee, / ~;
	28	glasse / Glasse

Poem	Lines	Text / Gardner
14		(Note: different copy text.)
	31	Thy / Thine
15		(Note: different copy text.)
	Title	Elegie: Going to Bed / To his Mistris Going to Bed.
	11	which / whom
	15	that / your
	17	Now off / Off
	24	Those / They
		our / the
	36	like / as
	43	that / *omitted*
	46	There / Here
		due to / much lesse
16	15	not / and
17	7	yellow, her haire's / yellow,'her haire is
	22	unfit; / ~.
	28	deformities; / ~.
	37	bee∧ / ~,
	44	businesse / business
	49	childbeds / childbirths
18		(Note: different copy text.)
	7	fathers / parents
	9	the / those
	12	wayes / meanes
	18	My . . . to / From other lands my soule towards
	37	and no lesse / 'and knowe thee; and
	40	hunt / haunt
	46	greatest / greate
		to / into
	49	*third* nor / *omitted*

Poem	Lines	Text / Gardner
19	6	Perhaps / Perchance
	8	stormes, being / hoari-nesse
	16	now / like'and
20	(Note:	different copy text.)
	2	that / which
	4	Love is / And love's
		we o're lick / wee'over-licke
	40	erre / stray
	63	yet / that
	70	many / some doe
		further / farther
	82	began / begun
21	1	night / Night
	6	great / greate
	13	*not indented / indented*
	23	Which (. . . before) /
		~, . . . ~,
	25	say, / ~∧
	30	my / mine
	42	all∧ / ~,
		husbands towring / towred husbands
	43	jealousie, / ~:
	53	our / thy
	54	inwards, and thy panting / colours, inward as thy
	61	fortune / Fortune
		us∧ / ~,
	62	yet / it
		bleed. / ~:
	65	*not indented / indented*
		fortune / Fortune
	66	thy / thine
		own / owne
	70	that / still
	76	sure; / ~.
	78	How / Shall tell how
		the / *omitted*
	83	*not indented / indented*
	87	Portion / portions
	88	Mass / mass
	89	self / selfe
	92	be / by
	94	my / mine
	97	Poles / Pole
22		*not indented / indented*
	12	cold) at once∧ / ~∧ ~ ~)
	32	yours; / ~.

Poem	Lines	Text / Gardner
	36	*second* me / mee
	38	third; / ~.
	52	beast; / ~.
23	6	else so ever doth / ever else
		seem / seemes
	13	bark / bank
	37	times / time
	41	Kindreds / Kindred
	60	hearts; / ~.
	72	same: / flame.
	74	deny. / ~,
	78	dispos'd∧ / ~,
	79	obeying, / ~;
	82	leave / love
24		*italics / removed*
	2	have? / ~,
	26	be / Thou be
27	3	brookes: / ~,
	6	thy / thine
	23	sleavesilke / sleave-silke
	26	bait; / ~,
29		*indentation / reversed*
	15	chain'd shot / chain-shot,
	22	thine / thy
30		*indentation / different*
	4	Two / two
	8	clearnesse / clearenesse
31	*Title*	Valediction∧ / ~:
	4	no. / ~:
	7	T'were / 'Twere
	32	that / it
	34	runne. / ~;
32		*indentation / different*
	4	in the'seaven / i'the seaven
	5	T'was / 'Twas
	7	t'was / 'twas
	14	*first* one / our
		(Reason: Readings of Group I seem preferable for this poem; "one" puts emphasis on the lovers' unity.)
35		*some italics / removed*
36	2	(in each stanza) / *further indented*
	10	moneths / months
	24	alchimie; / ~.
	26	thus. / ~;

Poem	Lines	Text / Gardner
54	8–9	not indented / indented
	18	showne, / ~.
	24	thee, / ~;
55		indentation / different
	4	play / Play
	8	no / not
	28	love / Love
	36	love / Love
	37	not; if / ~. If
56	17	arbors / arbours
57		indentation / different
	10	act / do
	14	lovest / lov'st
	15	sawest / saw'st
	26	have; / ~.
58	Title	Valediction_∧ / ~:
	9	(in each stanza) / on margin
59	10	medicinall / med'cinall
	11–12	(in each stanza) / not indented
	23	best, / ~_∧
	24	Sweetnesse, / ~_∧
		wit_∧ / ~,
		are, / ~_∧
		but, / ~_∧
60		indentation / different
	3	It suck'd me / Mee it suck'd
	5	Thou . . . that / Confesse it,
	6	nor . . . nor / or . . . or
	11	yea / nay
		are. / ~:
	16	you / thee
	17	that / this
	21	Wherein / In what
61	8	getting_∧ / ~,
62	8	string, / ~;
	13	equall / equal
	23	growen / grown
	52	spheares / spheare
	67	Which / That
63	3	And / omitted
	8	it_∧ / ~,
	27	spring_∧ / ~,
64	7	(in each stanza) / further indented
	26	Which_∧ / ~,
65	12	mee; / ~.

Poem	Lines	Text / Gardner
66	7	(in each stanza) / aligned with l. 6
	10	give, / ~;
67	3	my / mine
	8	(in each stanza) / on margin
68	2	(in each stanza) / not aligned with l. 1
69	22	number_∧ / ~,
	27	men, / ~;
	30	this_∧ / ~,
70	21	have . . . age / that age were
71	2	(in each stanza) / aligned with ll. 5–6
	6	through / thorough
	9	victories; / ~!
	24	In that / Naked
72	12	ne'r / neere
75	2	Both / both
	6	(in each stanza) / not indented
76		indentation / removed
77	3	can, / ~_∧
78	4	passion / passions
	9	simplicity. / ~;
	17–18	/ on margin and not separated from preceding lines
79	2	love_∧ / ~,
	9	indented / not indented
	23	pleasures, unlesse / ~? Unlesse
	29	minute_∧ / ~,
	34	had_∧ / ~,
		indammag'd / indammage
80		not indented / alternate indentation
	11	foul ones / fouleness
	20	Within_∧ / ~,
	24	own / owne
82	1	Tis / 'Tis
	5	worlds / world's
146	Title	Elegie on the L. C. / To L. C. (The reasons advanced to reject the early published title also reject Gardner's substituted title.)

Poem	Lines	Text / Gardner
		moving one way but bending the other. Agreement of many MSS.)
		once∧ / ∼, *Gr.*
186	5	fronte / fronti *Gr.*
	7	effigiem, / ∼∧ *Gr.*
	17	fixa / facta *Gr.*
	19	Mitto, / ∼∧ *Gr.*
186	22	Works / <Wishes> *Gr.* (trans.)
187	27	esteem'd / esteemed *Gr.* (Metrical considerations.)
	32	seene, / ∼; *Gr.*
	50	spred / hath spred (1633 reading and metrical considerations.)
	76	they could not / and none could
	119	hand; / ∼, *Gr.*
	145	hisse∧ / ∼, *Gr.*
	198	cover'd / covered *Gr.* (Metrical considerations.)
	238	not. / ∼; *Gr.*
	263	utter'd / uttered *Gr.* (Metrical considerations.)
	272	Scatter'd / Scattered *Gr.* (Metrical considerations.)
	278	live∧ / ∼, *Gr.*
	289	sinn'd / sinned *Gr.* (Metrical considerations.)
	312	so; / ∼. *Gr.*
	320	not, / ∼; *Gr.*
	323	scatter'd / scattered *Gr.* (Metrical considerations.)
	374	fell . . . bare / fall . . . beare (Evidence is divided.)
	389	thus∧ / ∼, *Gr.*
189	6	since / in (Either reading may be defended. The vintage has come to pass with

Tilman's decision to become a cleric. *In* suggests "through" or "as a result of"; *since* allows time for Tilman to be aware of personal changes [which, if they exist, Donne says are only superficial]. The MSS are not decisive, being divided between the two readings. Gardner's comment that the phrase with "in" is Biblical is unclear: the phrase does not appear in the Bible, and the usage of "vintage" closest to Donne is preteritive; see Isaiah xxiv 13, "as the gleaning grapes when the vintage is done.")

13	Thou art / Art thou (Donne is making a statement as "Onely the stampe is changed" [l. 14] indicates. Donne is trying to convince Tilman that he is not a different person now that he has taken orders. It was his diviner soul which had caused him to become a cleric. Lines 19–22 also make a statement: "as we paint Angels with wings . . . Art thou new feather'd." The poem alternates throughout between questions and statements.)
14	more. / ∼?
18	Coronation; / ∼?
25	gainings / gayning (If Tilman has gained advantage both above and below [l. 24], the word should be plural.)
29	As if their day were

Poem	Lines	Text / Gardner
		onely to be spent / Would they thinke it well if the day were spent
	30	complement; / ~?
	33	beautyes / beauties
	34	clay∧) / ~.) *Gr.*
190	7	*one line in each stanza / two lines Gr.* (Agreement of MSS, the lack of rhyme for 7 when two lines, the septenary created as the seventh line in each stanza when one line [with mystic overtones].)

Poem	Lines	Text / Gardner
	24	scatterd / scattered *Gr.* (Metrical requirements.)
191	22	sing. / ~; *Gr.*
	40	reform'd, / ~∧ *Gr.*
192	19	streights∧ / ~, *Gr.*
193		*stanza nos. omitted / given Gr.* (Agreement of MSS.)
	4	do . . . do / doe . . . doe
	10	wallowd / wallowed *Gr.* (Metrical requirements.)
	12	For∧ / ~,
	17	haste / hast

TABLE FOR USE WITH COMBS
AND SULLENS' *CONCORDANCE*

Lov inf	Loves infiniteness, 41
Lov U	Loves Usury, 38
Luc	A nocturnall upon St. Lucies day Being the shortest day, 82
Mag	To the Lady Magdalen Herbert, of St. Mary Magdalen, 159
Marc	Elegie on the Lady Marckham, 149
Merc	Mercurius Gallo-Belgicus, 96
Mess	The Message, 25
MH	To Mrs. M. H., 133
Neg	Negative love, 74
Niobe	Niobe, 85
Obsc	An obscure writer, 98
Para	The Paradox, 77
Pass	Upon the Annuntiation and Passion, 183
Phryne	Phryne, 97
Prim	The Primrose, 69
Pro	The Prohibition, 47
Prog	Metempsychosis, 158
Pyramus	Pyramus and Thisbe, 84
Rad	Raderus, 103
Ralph	Ralphius, 100
Rel	The Relique, 70
Res	Resurrection, imperfect, 182
RWI	To Mr. R. W. ("Zealously my Muse"), 118
RWII	To Mr. R. W. ("Muse not that by thy mind"), 119
RWIII	To Mr. R. W. ("If, as mine is, thy life"), 122
RWIV	To Mr. R. W. ("Kindly'I envy thy songs"), 123
Sal	To the Countesse of Salisbury, 145
Sapho	Sapho to Philænis, 24
Sat I–V	Satyre I (1); II (2); III (3); IV (4); V (5)
SB	To Mr. S. B., 124
Sec An	Of the Progres of the Soule . . . The Second Anniversary, 157
Self ac	A selfe accuser, 89
Self l	Selfe Love, 80
S Goe	Song: "Goe, and catche a falling starre," 33
Sir HW	To Sir H. W. at his going Ambassador to Venice, 129
S Sweet	Song: "Sweetest love, I do not goe," 42
Storm	The Storme, 109
Sun R	The Sunne Rising, 36
Syd	Upon the translation of the Psalmes by Sir Philip Sydney and . . . his Sister, 191
Til	To Mr. Tilman after he had taken orders, 189
Token	Sonnet. The Token, 78
Triple	The triple Foole, 40
TWI	To Mr. T. W. ("All haile sweet Poët"), 114
TWII	To Mr. T. W. ("Hast thee harsh verse"), 115
TWIII	To Mr. T. W. ("Pregnant again"), 116
TWIV	To Mr. T. W. ("At once, from hence"), 117
Twick	Twicknam garden, 51
Under	The undertaking, 63
Val book	Valediction of the booke, 52
Val mourn	A Valediction forbidding mourning, 31
Val name	A Valediction of my name, in the window, 49

Changes from Concordance

Not included in Concordance

APPENDIX: AN ADDITIONAL ATTRIBUTION

P. G. Stanwood of the University of British Columbia has discovered a Latin epigram attributed to Donne, not previously noted. Through his kindness I am able to include here the text of the poem, a slightly revised translation, and notes based on his remarks. The poem is found in the Hunter MSS, Vol. 27, section 4, Durham Cathedral Library, in the hand of Thomas Carre (died 1641). Carre was rector of Huggate, Yorks, during the period when the poem may have been written (1622–31). Although authorship is not certain, the subject matter of the epigram and the possible connections between Donne and Carre, Professor Stanwood believes, make the attribution plausible.

Apotheosis Ignatij Loyolae

Qui sacer antefuit, sanctus nunc incipit esse
  Lolyola et in divis annumeratus ovat.

Sed queritur plenis a tergo et margine fastis
  in minio, quo stet non superesse locum.

Repperit: expuncto multum Librarius audax   5
  Germano, haud veritu'st substituisse nothum.

Lis hinc orta ferox, neque enim novus hospes abire,
  cedere nec primus, nec simul esse volunt.

Quid pater hic sanctus? qui vincit et omnia solvit
  Solvit et hunc nodum dexteritate novâ,   10

Apotheosis: Ignatius' canonization in 1622.
1. sacer (venerable): a pun on "accursed" may be intended.
2. nunc (now): Ignatius had been beatified earlier in 1609.
4. in minio (in red): in rubrics; that is, in red letters.
6. Germano (Germanus): St. Germanus of Auxerre was dropped from the Calendar and his feast day, July 31, was assigned to St. Ignatius.
9–10. Referring to Matthew xvi.19: "and whatsoever thou shalt bind on earth shall be bound in heaven; and whatsoever thou shalt loose on earth shall

State simul dixit, stabuloque quiescite vestro,
  Ut Simon et Judas, quos tenet una dies;

Sin minus expectet quartani Ignatius anni
  Februa, conflatum possideatque diem.

Dr Dun. Deane of Paules.

The Apotheosis of Ignatius of Loyola

Loyola, who previously was venerable, now begins to be holy,
  and, numbered among the divine, he rejoices.

But he complains that the calendar is filled on the back and margin
  in red, and a place does not remain [for him] to be present.

He finds one: the most audacious copyist blots out   5
  Germanus, by no means afraid to substitute a counterfeit.

A fierce dispute arises from this, for the new arrival will not go away,
  the first will not budge, and they will not share.

What says the Holy Father to this? He who binds and looses all things
  unloosens this knot with singular cleverness.   10

'Stand together,' he says, 'and be quiet in your stable,
  like Simon and Jude who share one day.

If not, let Ignatius wait for the fifteenth of February
  in every fourth year and take possession of the conflated day.

---

be loosed in heaven." The text was used by the Roman Catholic Church to prove the powers of the Papacy.

12. The feast day of both St. Simon and St. Jude is October 28.

14. *Februa (fifteenth of February)*: this was the feast of purification and expiation. But the lines involve "conflated" dates. The fifteenth under the Julian Calendar would be the twenty-fifth under the Gregorian Calendar (since there was a ten-day difference between them in the seventeenth century). But the twenty-fifth in the Julian Calendar was Leap Year, and thus the poet is assigning only the one day of Leap Year to Ignatius.

BIBLIOGRAPHY

Texts and Textual Studies

Allen, Don Cameron, "Dean Donne Sets His Text," *ELH*, X (1943), 208–29.
Bennett, Roger E., ed., *The Complete Poems of John Donne* (Chicago, 1942).
Bryan, Robert A., "John Donne's Poems in Seventeenth-Century Commonplace
Books," *ES*, XLIII (1962), 170–74.
Chambers, E. K., "An Elegy by John Donne," *RES*, VII (1931), 69–71.
Gardner, Helen, ed., *John Donne: The Divine Poems* (Oxford, 1952).
——, *John Donne: The Elegies and the Songs and Sonnets* (Oxford, 1965).
Grierson, Herbert J. C., ed., *The Poems of John Donne* (Oxford, 1912), two
volumes. New editions in 1929, 1952.
Hayward, John, ed., *Complete Poetry and Selected Prose* (London, 1936).
Manley, Frank, ed., *John Donne: The Anniversaries* (Johns Hopkins Press,
1963).
Potter, George R., and Evelyn M. Simpson, eds., *The Sermons of John Donne*
(University of California Press, 1953–62), ten volumes.
Redpath, Theodore, ed., *The Songs and Sonets of John Donne* (London, 1956).
Ricks, Don M., "The Westmoreland Manuscript and the Order of Donne's 'Holy
Sonnets'," *SP*, LXIII (1966), 187–95.
Simpson, Evelyn M., "A Note on Donne's Punctuation," *RES*, IV (1928),
295–300.
——, "Jonson and Donne," *RES*, XV (1939), 274–82.
——, "The Text of Donne's 'Divine Poems'," *Essays and Studies*, XXVI (1940),
88–105.
Whitlock, Baird, "A Note on Two Donne Manuscripts," *RN*, XVIII (1965),
9–11.
Williamson, George, "Textual Difficulties in the Interpretation of Donne's Po-
etry," *MP*, XXXVIII (1940), 37–72.

Biography

Bald, R. C., *Donne and the Drurys* (Cambridge, 1959).
——, "Dr. Donne and the Booksellers," *SB*, XVIII (1965), 69–80.
——, *John Donne A Life* (Oxford, 1970), ed. Wesley Milgate.
Fausset, Hugh I'anson, *John Donne: A Study in Discord* (New York, 1925).
Garrod, H. W., "Donne and Mrs. Herbert," *RES*, XXI (1945), 161–73.
Gosse, Edmund, *The Life and Letters of John Donne* (New York, 1899), two
volumes.
Hardy, Evelyn, *Donne: A Spirit in Conflict* (London, 1942).
LeComte, Edward S., *Grace to a Witty Sinner: A Life of Donne* (New York,
1965).
Milgate, W., "The Date of Donne's Birth," *NQ*, CXCI (1946), 206–8.
——, "The Early References to John Donne," *NQ*, CXCV (1950), 229–31,
246–47, 290–92, 381–83.
Novarr, David, *The Making of Walton's Lives* (Cornell University Press, 1958),
especially Part I, 19–126.
Shapiro, I. A., "Donne's Birthdate," *NQ*, CXCVII (1952), 310–13.

508 *The Complete Poetry of John Donne*

——, "Walton and the Occasion of Donne's *Devotions*," *RES*, N.S. IX (1958), 18–22.

Sprott, S. Ernest, "The Legend of Jack Donne the Libertine," *UTQ*, XIX (1950), 335–53.

Walton, Isaac, *Lives of John Donne, etc.* (London, 1675; frequently reprinted).

Whitlock, Baird W., "The Heredity and Childhood of John Donne," *NQ*, VI (1959), 257–62, 348–53.

——, "The Family of John Donne, 1588–91," *NQ*, VII (1960), 380–86.

——, "Donne's University Years," *ES*, XLIII (1962), 1–20.

Wilson, F. P., "Notes on the Early Life of John Donne," *RES*, III (1927), 272–79.

General

Bewley, Marius, "Religious Cynicism in Donne's Poetry," *KR*, XIV (1952), 619–46.

Bryan, Robert A., "John Donne's Use of the Anathema," *JEGP*, LXI (1962), 305–12.

Combs, Homer C., and Z. R. Sullens, *A Concordance to the English Poems of John Donne* (Chicago, 1940).

Duncan, Edgar Hill, "Donne's Alchemical Figures," *ELH*, IX (1942), 257–85.

Ellrodt, Robert, *Les Poètes Métaphysiques Anglais* (Paris, 1960), three volumes.

Gransden, K. W., *John Donne* (London, 1954).

Hagopian, John V., "The Morphology of John Donne Including a Pun Index, Rhyme Index, and Studies in the Relations Between Linguistics and Literature," unpublished dissertation, Western Reserve University, 1955.

Harding, D. W., "Coherence of Theme in Donne's Poetry," *KR*, XIII (1951), 427–44.

Kermode, Frank, *John Donne* (London, 1957).

Keynes, Geoffrey, *A Bibliography of Dr. John Donne* (Cambridge, 1958), third edition.

Lederer, Joseph, "The Manifestations of the Baroque in the Works of John Donne," unpublished dissertation, University of London, 1951.

Leishman, J. B., *The Monarch of Wit* (London, 1951).

Mahood, M. M., *Poetry and Humanism* (London, 1950). "Donne: The Progress of the Soul," pp. 87–130; "Donne: The Baroque Preacher," pp. 131–68.

Martz, Louis L., "John Donne: the Meditative Voice," *Massachusetts Review*, I (1960), 326–42.

——, *The Poetry of Meditation* (Yale University Press, 1954; second edition, 1962).

Matsuura, Kaichi, *A Study of Donne's Imagery* (Tokyo, 1953).

Moloney, Michael F., "John Donne and the Jesuits," *MLQ*, VIII (1947), 426–29.

Mueller, William R., *John Donne: Preacher* (Princeton University Press, 1962).

Nicolson, Marjorie Hope, *The Breaking of the Circle* (Columbia University Press, 1960), revised edition.

Quinn, Dennis B., "John Donne's Principle of Biblical Exegesis," *JEGP*, LXI (1962), 313–29.

Roberts, Donald R., "The Death Wish of John Donne," *PMLA*, LXII (1947), 958–76.

Rugoff, Milton A., *Donne's Imagery* (New York, 1962), reprint.

Simon, Irene, "Some Problems of Donne Criticism," *Langues Vivantes*, No. 40 (Brussels, [1952?]).

Simpson, Evelyn M., *A Study of the Prose Works of John Donne* (Oxford, 1924).
Sparrow, John, "John Donne and Contemporary Preachers," *Essays and Studies,* XVI (1930), 144–78.
Spencer, Theodore, ed., *A Garland for John Donne, 1631–1931* (Harvard University Press, 1931).
Webber, Joan, *Contrary Music: The Prose Style of John Donne* (University of Wisconsin Press, 1963).
White, William, "Sir Geoffrey Keynes's Bibliography of John Donne: A Review with Addenda," *Bulletin of Bibliography,* XXII (1959), 186–89.

Poetry

Andreasen, N. J. C., "Theme and Structure in Donne's *Satyres,*" *SEL,* III (1963), 59–75.
Archer, Stanley, "Meditation and the Structure of Donne's 'Holy Sonnets'," *ELH,* XXVIII (1961), 137–47.
Bald, R. C., "Donne's Early Verse Letters," *HLQ,* XV (1952), 283–89.
Chambers, A. B., "The Meaning of the 'Temple' in Donne's *La Corona,*" *JEGP,* LIX (1960), 212–17.
——, "Goodfriday, 1613. Riding Westward: The Poem and the Tradition," *ELH,* XXVIII (1961), 31–53.
——, "The Fly in Donne's 'Canonization'," *JEGP,* LXV (1966), 252–59.
Dunlap, Rhodes, "The Date of Donne's 'The Annunciation and Passion'," *MLN,* LXIII (1948), 258–59.
Ellrodt, Robert, "Chronologie des Poèmes de Donne," *EA,* XIII (1960), 452–63.
Emerson, Katherine T., "Two Problems in Donne's 'Farewell to Love'," *MLN,* LXXI (1957), 93–95.
Freccero, John, "Donne's 'Valediction: Forbidding Mourning'," *ELH,* XXX (1963), 335–76.
Gardner, Helen, "The Argument about 'The Ecstasy'," *Elizabethan and Jacobean Studies* (Oxford, 1959), pp. 279–306.
——, "The Titles of Donne's Poems," *Friendship's Garland* (Rome, 1966), I, 189–207.
Garrod, H. W., "The Latin Poem Addressed by Donne to Dr. Andrews," *RES,* XXI (1945), 38–42.
Guss, Donald L., "Donne's Conceit and Petrarchan Wit," *PMLA,* LXXVIII (1963), 308–14.
——, *John Donne: Petrarchist* (Wayne State University Press, 1967).
Hardison, O. B., Jr., *The Enduring Monument: A Study of the Idea of Praise in Renaissance Literary Theory and Practice* (University of North Carolina Press, 1962). Chapter VII: The Idea of Elizabeth Drury, pp. 163–86.
Hughes, Merritt Y., "Some of Donne's 'Ecstasies'," *PMLA,* LXXV (1960), 509–18.
Hunt, Clay, *Donne's Poetry* (Yale University Press, 1954).
Jordan, John, "The Early Verse-Letters of John Donne," *University Review* (Dublin), II, x (1962), 3–24.
Levine, Jay Arnold, " 'The Dissolution': Donne's Twofold Elegy," *ELH,* XXVIII (1961), 301–15.
Louthan, Doniphan, *The Poetry of John Donne: A Study in Explication* (New York, 1951).
Moloney, Michael F., "Donne's Metrical Practice," *PMLA,* LXV (1950), 232–39.

Morillo, Marvin, "Donne's 'Farewell to Love': The Force of Shutting Up," *TSE*, XIII (1963), 33–40.

Moses, W. R., "The Metaphysical Conceit in the Poems of John Donne," Summary of a Thesis at Vanderbilt University, 1941.

Novarr, David, "Donne's 'Epithalamion Made at Lincoln's Inn': Context and Date," *RES*, N.S. VII (1956), 250–63.

——, "The Dating of Donne's *La Corona*," *PQ*, XXXVI (1957), 259–65.

Peterson, Douglas L., "John Donne's *Holy Sonnets* and the Anglican Doctrine of Contrition," *SP*, LVI (1959), 504–18.

Sloan, Thomas O., "A Rhetorical Analysis of John Donne's 'The Prohibition'," *QJS*, XLVIII (1962), 38–45.

Smith, A. J., "Donne in His Time: A Reading of 'The Extasie'," *Rivista di Letterature Moderne e Comparate* (1957), 260–75.

Sparrow, John, "Donne's 'Anniversaries'," *TLS*, June 29, 1946, p. 312.

Stein, Arnold, "Donne and the Couplet," *PMLA*, LVII (1942), 676–96.

——, "Donne's Prosody," *PMLA*, LIX (1944), 373–97.

——, "Structures of Sound in Donne's Verse," *KR*, XIII (1951), 20–36, 256–78.

——, *John Donne's Lyrics* (University of Minnesota Press, 1962).

Zyfers, Dorothea, "John Donne's Use of Numbers in 'Songs and Sonets'," unpublished Master's Thesis, New York University, 1954.

Concepts

Bredvold, Louis I., "The Naturalism of Donne in Relation to Some Renaissance Traditions," *JEGP*, XXII (1923), 471–502.

——, "The Religious Thought of Donne in Relation to Medieval and Later Traditions," *Studies in Shakespeare, Milton and Donne* (New York, 1925), pp. 193–232.

Coffin, Charles M., *John Donne and the New Philosophy* (New York, 1958).

Doggett, Frank A., "Donne's Platonism," *Sewanee Review*, XLII (1934), 274–92.

Husain, Itrat, *The Dogmatic and Mystical Theology of Donne* (London, 1938).

——, *The Mystical Element in the Metaphysical Poets of the Seventeenth Century* (London, 1948). "The Sceptical, Scholastic and Mystical Elements in John Donne's Thought," pp. 37–119.

Mazzeo, Joseph A., "Notes on John Donne's Alchemical Imagery," *Isis*, XLVIII (1957), 103–23.

Moloney, Michael F., *John Donne: His Flight From Medievalism* (University of Illinois Press, 1944).

Murray, W. A., "Donne and Paracelsus: An Essay in Interpretation," *RES*, XXV (1949), 115–23.

Ornstein, Robert, "Donne, Montaigne, and Natural Law," *JEGP*, LV (1956), 213–29.

Ramsay, Mary Paton, *Les Doctrines Médiévales chez Donne, Le Poète Métaphysicien de l'Angleterre* (Oxford, 1917).

Scott, Robert I., "Donne and Kepler," *NQ*, VI (1959), 208–9.

Influence

Alvarez, Alfred, *The School of Donne* (London, 1961).

Bald, R. C., *Donne's Influence in English Literature* (Morpeth, New South Wales, 1932).

Bennett, Joan, *Four Metaphysical Poets* (Cambridge, 1957).

Duncan, Joseph E., *The Revival of Metaphysical Poetry* (University of Minnesota Press, 1959).

Hughes, Merritt Y., "Kidnapping Donne," *Essays in Criticism,* Second Series (University of California Press, 1934), pp. 61–89.

Leishman, J. B., *The Metaphysical Poets* (Oxford, 1934).

Miles, Josephine, "The Language of the Donne Tradition," *KR,* XIII (1951), 37–49.

Unger, Leonard, *Donne's Poetry and Modern Criticism* (Chicago, 1950).

White, Helen C., *The Metaphysical Poets* (New York, 1936).

Williamson, George, *The Donne Tradition* (Harvard University Press, 1930).

INDEX OF TITLES

(For ease of reference, these titles have been modernized. They do not therefore correspond exactly with the titles in the rest of the book, where the original titles have been used. The numbers following the titles are the poem numbers.)

INDEX OF FIRST LINES